McGraw-Hill
networks™
A Social Studies Learning System

Discovering Our Past:
A History of the United States

READING
ESSENTIALS
& STUDY GUIDE

Student Workbook

Mc Graw Hill **Education**

Bothell, WA • Chicago, IL • Columbus, OH • New York, NY

Discovering Our Past: United States 2013 National Survey
Cover Credits:
Abraham Lincoln, The Huntington Library, Art Collections &
Botanical Gardens/Bridgeman Art Library

Send all inquiries to:
McGraw-Hill Education
8787 Orion Place
Columbus, OH 43240

ISBN: 978-0-07-659695-9
MHID: 0-07-659695-8

Printed in the United States of America.

7 8 9 10 DOH 16 15 14 13

Table of Contents

To the Student

Dear Student,

We know that taking notes, using graphic organizers, and developing critical thinking skills are vital to achieve academic success. Organizing solid study materials can be an overwhelming task. McGraw-Hill has developed this workbook to help you master content and develop the skills necessary for success.

This workbook includes all core content found in the *Discovering Our Past: History of the United States* program. The note-taking, graphic organizer, and Foldables® activities will help you learn to organize content for improved comprehension and testing.

Note-Taking System

You will notice that the pages in the *Reading Essentials and Study Guide* are arranged in two columns. The large column on the page contains running text and graphics that summarize each lesson of the chapter. The smaller column will help you use information in various ways and develop note-taking skills.

Graphic Organizers

Many graphic organizers appear in this workbook. Graphic organizers allow you to see the lesson's important information in a visual format. In addition, they help you summarize information and remember the content.

Notebook FOLDABLES®

Notebook Foldables®, invented by Dinah Zike, M.Ed., show you how to make interactive graphic organizers based upon skills. Foldables® are easy to create. Every Notebook Foldable® is placed directly within the content pages to help you with your note-taking skills. Making a Foldable® gives you a fast way to organize and retain information. Each Notebook Foldable® is designed as a study guide for the main ideas and key points presented in lessons of the chapter.

The *Reading Essentials and Study Guide* is a thoroughly interactive workbook that will help you learn social studies content. You will master the content while learning important critical-thinking and note-taking skills that you will use throughout your life.

Notebook Foldable® Basics

Notebook Foldables® are an easy-to-use, unique way to enhance learning. Instructions are located where the Foldable® is used and every template is provided at the back of this workbook. You will cut out the appropriate Foldable® template and place it into the workbook as instructed. This quickly turns a workbook into a study guide.

Using Notebook Foldables®

You will write information such as titles, vocabulary words, concepts, questions, main ideas, summaries, definitions, and dates on the tabs of the Foldables®. This will help you easily recognize main ideas and important concepts as you read the content.

In the back of this workbook are several pages with four different Foldable® templates—one-tab, two-tab, three-tab, and Venn diagram styles. Each style has an instruction page followed by the templates. Cutting and using the different templates is very simple to master.

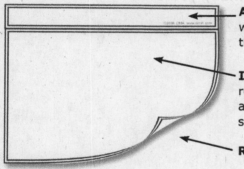

Anchor Tab—Glue the back of the Foldable® to the workbook with the anchor tab. A dotted line is provided on the workbook page to guide you to proper placement.

Information Tab—Write information on the front and reverse of the information tab. This tab may be cut again after gluing if it is a two-tab, three-tab, or Venn diagram style.

Reverse Tab

Folding Instructions

1. **Cut** out the appropriate Foldable® template.
2. **Fold** the anchor tab over the information tab.
3. **Glue** the anchor tab to the workbook page according to the instructions. *(Just a dab is needed!)*

   Multiple Foldables® can be placed together by gluing anchor tabs on top of anchor tabs. This creates a small book on the page.

Supplies

The only supplies needed to utilize Notebook Foldables® are scissors and glue. All paper templates are in the back of the workbook. Consider using crayons and colored pencils, a stapler, clear tape, and anything else you like to make your Foldables® more interesting.

Who is Dinah Zike?

Dinah Zike, M.Ed., is an award-winning author, educator, and inventor known for designing three-dimensional hands-on manipulatives and graphic organizers known as Foldables®. Foldables® are used nationally and internationally by teachers, parents, and educational publishing companies. Dinah has developed more than 150 supplemental educational books and materials. Her two latest books, *Notebook Foldables®* and *Foldables®*, *Notebook Foldables®*, *& VKV®s for Spelling and Vocabulary 4th–12th* were both awarded *Learning®* magazine's Teachers' Choice℠ Award for 2011. In 2004, Dinah was honored with the Council for Elementary Science International (CESI) Science Advocacy Award. Dinah received her M.Ed. from Texas A&M, College Station, Texas. Dinah has been a valued contributing editor to the McGraw-Hill K–12 education programs for many years.

networks

The First Americans

Lesson 1 Migration to the Americas

ESSENTIAL QUESTION
What are characteristics that make up a culture?

GUIDING QUESTIONS
1. *Who were the first Americans and how did they live?*
2. *How did agriculture change the way of life for early Americans?*

Terms to Know
archaeology the study of ancient peoples
artifact a tool, weapon, or object left behind by early peoples
strait narrow strip of water connecting two larger bodies of water
migration the movement of a large number of people into a new area
nomad a person who moves from place to place
maize a type of corn
carbon dating a scientific way to find out the age of an artifact
culture a people's shared values, beliefs, traditions, and behaviors

Where in the world?

When did it happen?

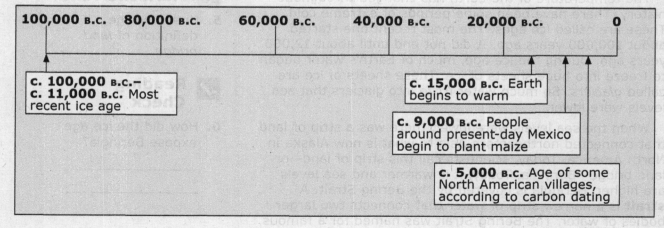

| 100,000 B.C. | 80,000 B.C. | 60,000 B.C. | 40,000 B.C. | 20,000 B.C. | 0 |

c. 100,000 B.C.– c. 11,000 B.C. Most recent ice age

c. 15,000 B.C. Earth begins to warm

c. 9,000 B.C. People around present-day Mexico begin to plant maize

c. 5,000 B.C. Age of some North American villages, according to carbon dating

1

netw⊕rks

The First Americans

Lesson 1 Migration to the Americas, *Continued*

The Migration Begins

People lived in the Americas for thousands of years before Christopher Columbus arrived. Where did they come from? How did they get there? When did they arrive?

Scientists want to answer these questions. Some are experts in the study of ancient peoples, which is called **archaeology.** To discover clues, they study **artifacts,** or things that ancient peoples left behind. These things can be tools, weapons, or other objects. Artifacts are one of the tools archaeologists use to put together the pieces of the puzzle.

Some archaeologists think they understand how the first people arrived in North America. They believe that many thousands of years ago, a strip of land connected Asia and the Americas. This gave people a way to travel from one continent to the other. These scientists think that people used this strip of land to cross from Asia to the Americas 20,000 or more years ago.

Learning About Ancient Peoples	
archaeology	the study of ancient peoples
archaeologist	a scientist who studies ancient peoples
artifacts	objects left behind by ancient peoples, such as tools and weapons

The temperature of the Earth has changed throughout history. There have been some periods of extreme cold. These are called ice ages. The most recent one started about 100,000 years ago. It did not end until about 12,000 years ago. During the ice age, much of Earth's water began to freeze into huge sheets of ice. These sheets of ice are called *glaciers*. So much water froze into glaciers that sea levels were lower.

When the sea levels were lower, there was a strip of land that connected northeastern Asia to what is now Alaska in North America. Today, scientists call this strip of land—or land bridge—Beringia. Today, it is warmer and sea levels are higher. Beringia is covered by the Bering Strait. A **strait** is a narrow strip of water that connects two larger bodies of water. The Bering Strait was named for a famous explorer, Vitus Bering.

Identifying

1. What scientists study ancient peoples? What do they use for clues?

_____

Assessing

2. When do some scientists think people first arrived in North America?

Defining

3. What is an *ice age*?

_____

Calculating

4. How long did the last ice age last?

_____

Mark the Text

5. Underline the definition of *land bridge*.

Reading Check

6. How did the ice age expose Beringia?

_____

_____

_____

Lesson 1 Migration to the Americas, *Continued*

Identifying

7. What are two ways scientists think people may have traveled from Asia to the Americas?

_____

_____

Mark the Text

8. Underline the definition of *migration*.

Identifying

9. What did nomads eat?

_____

_____

Mark the Text

10. What did mammoths and mastodons look like? Circle the answer in the text.

? Understanding Cause and Effect

11. How did farming change the lives of early Americans?

_____

_____

_____

Many scientists think that people traveled from Asia to North America over this land bridge, but some scientists disagree. They think people may have come from Asia in boats. Coming by boat would have made it easier for people to spread throughout North and South America faster.

Ice age

↓

Ocean water freezes into glaciers and lowers sea levels

↓

Ancient peoples from Asia use land bridge to cross into North America

No matter how they came, people eventually spread east all the way to the Atlantic Ocean. They also spread south to the southern tip of South America.

When a lot of people move from one area to another like this, it is called **migration.** People probably traveled in search of food. Early peoples were **nomads.** Nomads are people who move from place to place, looking for good hunting grounds. Even though these people also ate wild grains and fruits, much of their food came from hunting.

When the first peoples arrived from Asia, they found many animals to hunt. For example, they hunted bison and two animals that looked like elephants—mammoths and mastodons. These people hunted with spears.

Around 15,000 years ago, Earth began to warm. As temperatures rose, glaciers began to melt. The oceans rose, and water covered the Beringia land bridge. This cut Asia off from North America once again. The large animals began to disappear, too. Early Americans had to find other sources of food, which included fish and small animals.

Settlement

Around 10,000 years ago, there was a major change in how people got food: farming. People in what is now Mexico began planting a type of corn called **maize.** They also grew pumpkins, beans, and squash. These crops gave them a good supply of food. Because they could grow their own food, they did not have to move around anymore. This meant they could spend more time doing other things. Their quality of life got better.

The First Americans

Lesson 1 Migration to the Americas, *Continued*

After the early people learned to farm, some remained nomads. Others lived in permanent settlements, or villages. They built houses from clay, stone, or wood. They made pottery, tools, and cloth. Today, we sometimes find such artifacts where their villages once stood.

Carbon dating is a scientific process that measures how much radioactive carbon an artifact contains. Scientists use this measurement to decide how old the artifact is. They have used this process on artifacts from North American villages and found that some villages existed about 5,000 years ago.

Scientists can tell that farming changed people's lives. As early Americans settled down, they began to share beliefs and ways of doing things. These shared traditions and behaviors are called **cultures.**

//////////////////// Glue Foldable here ///////////////

Check for Understanding

List two ways that changes in the climate affected the migration of prehistoric peoples.

1. _____

2. _____

How did farming change the lives of early people?

_____

_____

☑ **Reading Check**

12. What changes affected the nomadic way of life?

_____

_____

_____

❓ **Analyzing**

13. How can scientists tell how old a village is?

_____

_____

_____

🔤 **Defining**

14. What is a *culture*?

_____

_____

FOLDABLES

15. Place a two-tab Foldable along the dotted line to cover Check for Understanding. Label the tabs *Nomadic Culture* and *Farming Culture*. Use both sides of the tabs to list the characteristics that you remember about each kind of lifestyle.

The First Americans

Lesson 2 Cities and Empires

ESSENTIAL QUESTION
How do civilizations rise and fall?

GUIDING QUESTIONS
1. **What civilizations in Mexico, Central America, and South America predated the arrival of Europeans?**
2. **Why were the Inca considered a highly developed culture?**

Terms to Know
civilization highly developed society
theocracy a society ruled by religious leaders
hieroglyphic a form of writing that uses symbols or pictures to represent things, ideas, and sounds
terrace broad platform of land cut into a slope

Where in the world?

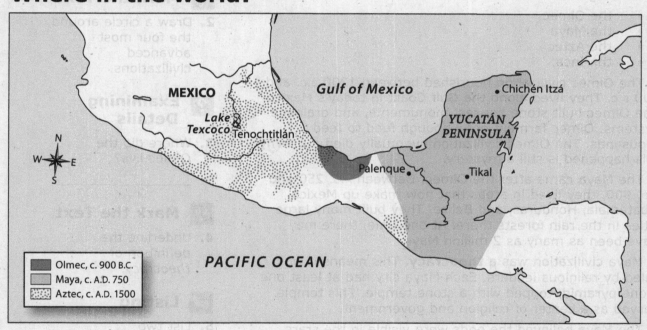

MEXICO
Gulf of Mexico
Chichén Itzá
Lake Texcoco
Tenochtitlán
YUCATÁN PENINSULA
Palenque
Tikal
N W E S
PACIFIC OCEAN

Olmec, c. 900 B.C.
Maya, c. A.D. 750
Aztec, c. A.D. 1500

When did it happen?

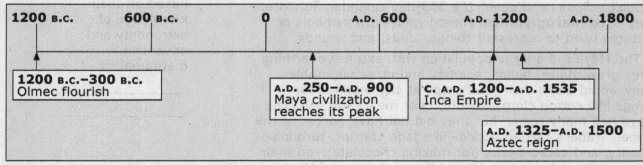

1200 B.C.   600 B.C.   0   A.D. 600   A.D. 1200   A.D. 1800

1200 B.C.–300 B.C.
Olmec flourish

A.D. 250–A.D. 900
Maya civilization reaches its peak

C. A.D. 1200–A.D. 1535
Inca Empire

A.D. 1325–A.D. 1500
Aztec reign

networks

The First Americans

Lesson 2 Cities and Empires, *Continued*

Great Civilizations of Mexico, Central America, and South America

Hundreds of years before European explorers arrived, there were great **civilizations** in Mexico, Central America, and South America. Each civilization controlled large areas and had millions of people. They built cities in forests and on mountains. They created great art and advanced tools. This included complex, or very detailed, ways to track time, count, and write.

The largest and most advanced civilizations were:

- the Olmec
- the Maya
- the Aztec
- the Inca.

The Olmec civilization flourished between 1200 B.C. and 300 B.C. They lived along the Gulf Coast in today's Mexico. The Olmec built stone houses, monuments, and drainage systems. Olmec farmers grew enough food to feed thousands. The Olmec civilization eventually died out. Why this happened is still a mystery.

The Maya came after the Olmec. Between A.D. 250 and A.D. 900, they lived in areas that now make up Mexico, Guatemala, Honduras, and Belize. They built many large cities in the rain forests there. At one time, there may have been as many as 2 million Maya.

Maya civilization was a **theocracy.** This means it was ruled by religious leaders. Each Maya city had at least one stone pyramid, topped with a stone temple. This temple served as a center of religion and government.

The Maya believed the gods were visible in the stars, sun, and moon. Maya priests studied astronomy and advanced mathematics. They used their knowledge to predict eclipses and develop a 365-day calendar. To write, they used **hieroglyphics.** Hieroglyphics are symbols or pictures used to represent things, ideas, and sounds.

The Maya fed a large population with extensive farming. They grew maize, beans, squash, and other vegetables. They would trade their food crops at city markets for things like cotton cloth, pottery, deer meat, and salt. The Maya had many roads, but they did not have horses or the wheel. Traders carried goods—like jade statues, turquoise jewelry, and cacao beans (for making chocolate)—on their backs or by canoe up and down the east coast of Mexico.

📝 Identifying

1. List two facts about the great civilizations before the Europeans arrived.

_____

_____

🔤 Mark the Text

2. Draw a circle around the four most advanced civilizations.

❓ Examining Details

3. Where did the Olmec live?

_____

🔤 Mark the Text

4. Underline the definition of *theocracy*.

📝 Listing

5. List two accomplishments of the Maya that were based on their knowledge of astronomy and advanced mathematics.

_____

_____

6

The First Americans

Lesson 2 Cities and Empires, *Continued*

📝 Describing

6. How did the Aztec know where to settle down?

_____

_____

_____

✓ Reading Check

7. Name the capital city of the Aztec Empire, and describe its location.

_____

_____

_____

📝 Explaining

8. How did the Aztec treat the people they conquered?

_____

_____

_____

✓ Making Connections

9. How were the Inca like the Aztec?

_____

_____

_____

Eventually the Maya civilization declined. No one knows why. One idea is that the soil grew weak and could not produce enough food for the population. Its once-great cities were nearly empty by 1200. The descendants of the Maya still live in Mexico and Central America.

Many centuries later, another great civilization arose in central Mexico—the Aztec. An Aztec legend said that a god would send them a sign to tell them where to build their permanent home. In 1325, a group of Aztec hunters saw that sign on an island in the middle of Lake Texcoco: an eagle with a snake in its beak sitting on a cactus.

The Aztec built their capital city on the island and called it Tenochtitlán. It was a wonder of construction. Workers dug soil from the bottom of the lake to build bridges between the city and the shore and to make fields for crops in the lake. Tenochtitlán became an important trade center. It was the largest city in the Americas and one of the largest in the world.

In the 1400s, the Aztec used their military to conquer many other groups. They forced conquered people to give them food and goods and to work as slaves. They also sacrificed prisoners of war to their gods to ensure rich harvests. Their empire was still strong when the Europeans came.

	Location	Accomplishments
Olmec	Gulf Coast of Mexico	Built stone houses, monuments, and drainage systems
		Grew crops to feed thousands
Maya	Mexico, Guatemala, Honduras, and Belize	Could predict eclipses
		Developed 365-day calendar
		Wrote with hieroglyphics
		Grew crops to feed millions
Aztec	Central Mexico	Built Tenochtitlán
		Conquered large empire

The Great Inca Civilization

The largest early American empire developed in western South America—the Inca. Like the Aztec, the Inca had a powerful military and conquered many neighboring groups.

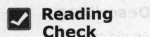

The First Americans

Lesson 2 Cities and Empires, *Continued*

All Inca men between 25 and 50 might have to serve in the army. They were skilled warriors and used weapons like clubs, spears, and slings. At its peak, the Inca empire stretched from Columbia to northern Argentina and Chile.

The Inca founded their capital city of Cuzco around 1200. Another important city was Machu Picchu, which may have been a place for religious ceremonies. Religion was a central part of Inca life. The Inca believed their emperor was a descendant of the sun god. They made beautiful jewelry and tributes for this god.

Farming was important to Inca life. In order to farm in their mountainous land, the Inca cut broad platforms called **terraces** into the slopes. They grew:

- maize
- squash
- tomatoes
- peanuts
- chili peppers
- cotton
- potatoes

To connect the large empire, the Inca built more than 10,000 miles (16,093 km) of roads. These were built over mountains, across deserts, and through rain forests. The Inca, who spoke Quechua, used quipus for keeping records. Quipus were different colors of string knotted in special patterns.

/ / / / / / / / / / / / / Glue Foldable here / / / / / / / / / / / /

Check for Understanding

List four great early cultures of Mexico, Central America, and South America.

1. _____

2. _____

3. _____

4. _____

How were the Aztec and Inca civilizations similar? How were they different?

_____

_____

_____

✓ Reading Check

10. How did the Inca Empire grow so large?

_____

_____

_____

👁 Visualize It

11. In the box, draw a diagram of the terraces the Inca built for their crops.

✍ Mark the Text

12. Circle the name of the Inca language.

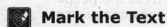

13. Place a three-tab Foldable along the dotted line to cover Check for Understanding. On the anchor tab write *Accomplishments*. Label the tabs *Olmec*, *Maya*, and *Aztec*. List two accomplishments for each group.

The First Americans

Lesson 3 North American Peoples

ESSENTIAL QUESTION
What makes a culture unique?

GUIDING QUESTIONS

1. **What did the Adena, Hopewell, Mississippian, Hohokam, and Ancient Puebloan cultures have in common?**
2. **How did early Native Americans adapt to their environment?**

> **Terms to Know**
> **irrigate** to supply water to crops by artificial means
> **federation** government that links different groups

Where in the world?

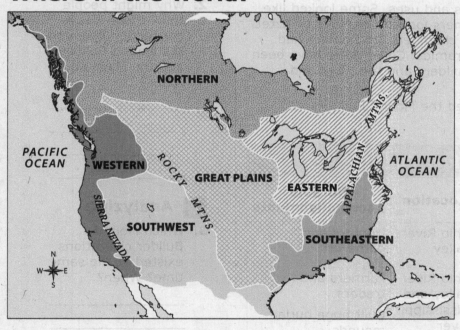

When did it happen?

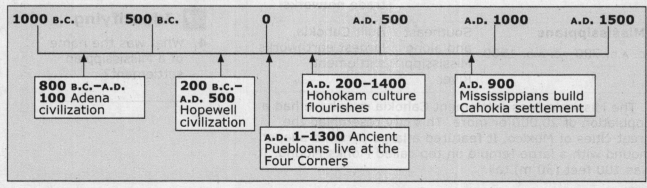

| 1000 B.C. | 500 B.C. | 0 | A.D. 500 | A.D. 1000 | A.D. 1500 |

800 B.C.–A.D. 100 Adena civilization

200 B.C.–A.D. 500 Hopewell civilization

A.D. 1–1300 Ancient Puebloans live at the Four Corners

A.D. 200–1400 Hohokam culture flourishes

A.D. 900 Mississippians build Cahokia settlement

The First Americans

Lesson 3 North American Peoples, Continued

Early North American Cultures

North America produced advanced cultures in the centuries before Europeans arrived. Among them were:

- the Adena
- the Hopewell
- the Mississippians
- the Hohokam
- the Ancient Puebloans.

In Central and Eastern North America lived the Mound Builders. Scientists call them the Mound Builders because they built thousands of mounds out of earth. These mounds had different shapes and uses. Some looked like animals, such as snakes. Others looked like Maya or Aztec pyramids. Some were burial chambers, and others had temples on top like Maya pyramids. Could there have been a link between the Mound Builders and the Maya and Aztec?

Archaeologists have divided the Mound Builders into three different groups.

Mound Builder Cultures		
Culture	**Location**	**Notable Accomplishments**
Adena c. 800 B.C.—A.D. 100	Ohio River valley	Hunters and gatherers
Hopewell c. 200 B.C.—A.D. 500	Ohio River valley and Mississippi River valley	Farmers and traders Built huge burial mounds Indications of wide trade networks
Mississippians c. A.D. 700—c. A.D. 1500	Southeast and along Mississippi River	Built Cahokia, largest earthworks settlement

The Mississippians settlement Cahokia may have had a population of 20,000 or more. This city resembled the great cities of Mexico. It featured a large pyramid-shaped mound with a large temple on top called Monks Mound. It was 100 feet (30 m) tall.

Listing

1. List two shapes the Mound Builders used in their earthworks.

_____

_____

Making Inferences

2. Why might people think there was a connection between the Mound Builders and the Maya and Aztec?

_____

_____

_____

_____

Analyzing

3. Which Mound Builder civilzations existed at the same time? When?

_____

_____

_____

Identifying

4. What was the name of a Mississippian settlement?

_____

networks

The First Americans

Lesson 3 North American Peoples, *Continued*

Abc Mark the Text

5. Underline the definition of *irrigate*.

Describing

6. Describe the area called the Four Corners.

_____

_____

_____

☑ Reading Check

7. Name two types of dwellings the Ancient Puebloans built.

_____

_____

Abc Defining

8. What is an *igloo*?

_____

☑ Reading Check

9. Give two examples of how Western peoples adapted to their environment.

_____

_____

_____

_____

The Hohokam lived in the hot desert of what is now Arizona from about A.D. 200 to 1400. In order to farm in that climate, the Hohokam built hundreds of miles of channels to **irrigate,** or bring water to, their fields. They grew corn, cotton, and other crops. They also made pottery, carved stone, and used acid to make patterns in shells, which they got from coastal peoples.

From about A.D. 1 to 1300, the Ancient Puebloans lived in the Four Corners region. This is the area where the modern states of Utah, Colorado, Arizona, and New Mexico meet. The Ancient Puebloans are known for their huge stone dwellings, later called *pueblos* by Spanish explorers. One pueblo—Pueblo Bonito—has four stories and hundreds of rooms.

The Ancient Puebloans also built shelters into the walls of steep cliffs. These cliff dwellings were good protection from winter weather and enemy attacks. One of the largest was Mesa Verde in Colorado, where thousands lived.

The Native Americans Circa 1492

The Inuit settled the cold region of North America near the Arctic Ocean. Scientists think they originally came from Siberia, which is also very cold, and brought cold-weather survival skills with them. They built shelters called *igloos* out of snow blocks. They hunted whales, seals, and walruses from small boats and caribou on land. They used animal skins to make clothes and burned seal oil in lamps.

The western coast of North America provided a milder climate and dependable food sources. Western peoples included:

- The Tlingit, Haida, and Chinook of the northwestern coast (present-day Canada, Washington, and Oregon). These cultures relied on the woods and the waters. They built houses and canoes from wood. Their main food was salmon.

- The Nez Perce and Yakima of the plateau region between the Cascade Mountains and the Rocky Mountains. These groups lived in earthen houses. They fished, hunted deer, and gathered roots and berries.

- Today's California was home to many groups. Along the northern coast, people fished for food. In the central valley, the Pomo pounded acorns into flour. In the southern deserts, nomads gathered roots and seeds.

The First Americans

Lesson 3 North American Peoples, Continued

- In the Great Basin of the Southwest between the Sierra Nevada and the Rocky Mountains, the Ute and Shoshone hunted small game and gathered pine nuts, juniper berries, roots, and even some insects.

The Hopi, Acoma, and Zuni of the Southwest descended from the Ancient Puebloans. They built houses from bricks made of dried mud called *adobe*. They irrigated their fields and farmed maize, beans, squash, melons, pumpkins, and fruit. In the 1500s, the nomadic Apache and Navajo came to this region. The Navajo later formed villages, living in square houses called *hogans*.

The nomadic Plains peoples lived in hide tents called *tepees*. The women planted maize, squash, and beans. The men hunted antelope, deer, and buffalo. Buffalo provided more than food. Their skin was used for clothes and shelter, and their bones were used to make weapons.

In the woodlands of eastern North America lived many Algonquian peoples, who all spoke a similar language. The Cherokee and Iroquois had formal laws and alliances called **federations.** There were five Iroquois nations—the Onondaga, Seneca, Mohawk, Oneida, and Cayuga. They were often at war until, in the 1500s, they formed the Iroquois League, which was organized by clans, or groups of people related. Under the League's constitution, the Grand Council settled disputes.

Southeastern peoples were farmers. The Creek grew corn, squash, and tobacco. The Chickasaw farmed the fertile area where the Mississippi River connects to the sea.

Check for Understanding

What evidence might connect the Mound Builders with the Maya and Aztec?

_____

_____

Name one way each of these Native American groups adapted to their environment:

Hohokam _____

Ancient Puebloans _____

Inuit _____

Plains People _____

🖉 Describing

10. How did the Southwest people grow crops in such a dry region?

_____

🖉 Listing

11. List three things buffalo provided for the Plains peoples.

_____

_____

_____

❓ Analyzing

12. How did the five Iroquois nations come together?

_____

FOLDABLES®

13. Place a one-tab Foldable along the dotted line to cover Check for Understanding. Create a memory map by writing *Dwellings* in the middle of the tab. Draw arrows to words or phrases you remember about the kinds of shelter Native Americans built. Write additional information on the back.

Exploring the Americas

Lesson 1 A Changing World

ESSENTIAL QUESTION
How do new ideas change the way people live?

GUIDING QUESTIONS
1. *Where did the Renaissance take place?*
2. *What technological advancements paved the way for European voyages of exploration?*
3. *What were the most powerful empires in Africa?*

Terms to Know

Crusade one of a series of expeditions Europeans made to regain control of Christian holy sites in the Middle East from the A.D. 1000s to the 1200s

classical related to the culture of ancient Greece and Rome

Renaissance a reawakening of culture and intellectual curiosity in Europe from the 1300s to the 1600s

technology the use of scientific knowledge for practical purposes

astrolabe an instrument used to plan a course, using the stars

compass an instrument that shows the direction of magnetic north

pilgrimage a journey to a holy place

mosque a Muslim house of worship

When did it happen?

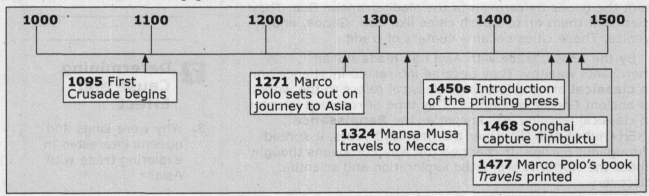

1000	1100	1200	1300	1400	1500

1095 First Crusade begins

1271 Marco Polo sets out on journey to Asia

1324 Mansa Musa travels to Mecca

1450s Introduction of the printing press

1468 Songhai capture Timbuktu

1477 Marco Polo's book *Travels* printed

What do you know?

In the first column, answer the questions based on what you know before you study. After this lesson, complete the last column.

Now...		Later...
	What church dominated Europe after the fall of the Roman Empire?	
	What countries in Europe became strong by the 1400s?	
	Which country developed the fastest ships during this period?	

networks

Exploring the Americas

Lesson 1 A Changing World, *Continued*

New Ideas, New Nations

The people of Western Europe were isolated for centuries after the Roman empire fell in A.D. 476. The area was dominated by the Catholic Church. In the early 600s, Islam began to spread across the Middle East and Africa. The rise of Islam led to the end of Europe's isolation.

In 1095 Europeans started the **Crusades**. These were expeditions to gain control of the Christian holy sites from Muslims in the Middle East. There, Europeans came in contact with Arab merchants. These merchants sold them spices, silks, and other goods from faraway China and India. Europeans became interested in Asia.

Interest in Asia grew after an explorer named Marco Polo returned from China. He wrote about his trip in a book called *Travels*. Many Europeans read the book.

Wealthy Europeans wanted silks and spices from Asia. Merchants bought these goods from Arab traders. They sent the goods by caravan to the Mediterranean Sea. They then sent them on to Italian cities like Pisa, Genoa, and Venice. These cities became centers of trade.

By the 1300s, trade with Asia had made Italian merchants wealthy. They became interested in science and in **classical** art and learning. Classical refers to the works of ancient Greece and Rome. This time of renewed interest in classical learning was known as the **Renaissance** (REH•nuh•SAHNTS). Over the next 200 years, it spread throughout Europe. It changed the way Europeans thought about the world. It promoted exploration and scientific discovery.

European merchants were interested in exploration. They wanted to find a way to buy goods directly from Asia. This would be less expensive than buying them from Arab merchants.

By the 1400s, strong kings and queens had come to power in several nations. They set up laws and national armies. They wanted to find ways to increase trade to make their countries richer. Soon, Spain, Portugal, England, and France were competing with the Italian cities which had become rich through trade. This competition encouraged a period of exploration.

? Making Inferences

1. How did the rise of Islam affect Western Europe during this period?

_____
_____

✓ Reading Check

2. What was the Renaissance?

_____
_____

? Determining Cause and Effect

3. Why were kings and queens interested in exploring trade with Asia?

_____
_____

14

Exploring the Americas

Lesson 1 A Changing World, *Continued*

✔️ **Reading Check**

4. What three things helped sailors figure out their location?

_____

_____

_____

📝 **Marking the Text**

5. Underline the sentences that describe the advantages of the Portuguese caravel.

✔️ **Reading Check**

6. How did Islamic religion and culture come to West Africa?

_____

_____

The Effects of New Technology

Advances in **technology** helped pave the way for exploration. Technology is the use of scientific knowledge for practical purposes. The invention of the printing press in the 1450s made it possible for more people to read books and get information.

Mapmakers started to make better maps. They mapped the direction of the ocean currents. They also showed lines of latitude that measured the distance north and south of the Equator. The invention of new instruments helped sailors travel. The **astrolabe** measured the positions of stars. This helped sailors figure out their latitude while at sea. Europeans also began to use the magnetic **compass**, a Chinese invention. The compass helped sailors find their direction when they were far from land.

The design of ships also improved. Sailors were now able to make long ocean voyages. In the late 1400s, the Portuguese created the caravel. It had three masts and could sail into the wind. This ship sailed faster than other ships. It could carry more goods. All of these inventions helped start a new time of exploration. Countries like Portugal began searching for sea routes to Asia. Portugal started by sending ships south along the west coast of Africa.

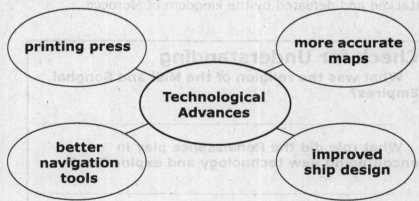

Kingdoms and Empires in Africa

Between A.D. 400 and 1600, several powerful kingdoms prospered in Africa. They became powerful through mining and trade. Arab traders traveled along Africa's east coast. West Africans traded with societies in North Africa. This trade brought wealth and Islamic religion and culture to West Africa. The Portuguese set up trading posts along the west coast of Africa in the mid-1400s.

Lesson 1 A Changing World, *Continued*

Ghana was a trading empire in West Africa. Caravans with gold and other goods from Ghana crossed the Sahara to North Africa. There, Muslim traders loaded the caravans with salt, cloth, and other goods to take back to Ghana. Ghana grew wealthy from the taxes it collected on this trade.

In 1076 people from North Africa attacked Ghana. Trade slowed down. New trade routes were set up that did not go through Ghana. Ghana then began to lose power.

Another powerful kingdom, called Mali, developed in the same region. Like Ghana, it developed trade routes across the desert to North Africa. Mali's greatest king was Mansa Musa. He made Mali famous. In 1324 Musa made a grand **pilgrimage** to the Muslim holy city of Mecca. A pilgrimage is a journey to a holy place. Musa returned to Mali with an Arab architect who built great **mosques** in Timbuktu, the Mali capital. Mosques are Muslim houses of worship. Timbuktu became an important center of Islamic learning.

In 1468 the Songhai (sawng•GEYE) people rose up against Mali rule and captured Timbuktu. Under Askiya Muhammad, the Songhai Empire became strong. Askiya divided Songhai into provinces. Each province had its own officials. He also set up laws for Songhai. These laws were based on Islamic teaching. In the late 1500s, Songhai was attacked and defeated by the kingdom of Morocco.

/ / / / / / / / / / /Glue Foldable here/ / / / / / / / / / / /

Check for Understanding
What was the religion of the Mali and Songhai Empires?

_____

What role did the Renaissance play in encouraging new technology and exploration?

_____

_____

FOLDABLES

7. Place a one-tab Foldable along the dotted line to cover Check for Understanding. Draw a large circle on the tab and label it *A Changing World*. Draw two smaller circles inside the large circle. Label the small circles *Marco Polo* and *African Empires*. Use the space inside the circles to list words or short phrases that explain why both were important to the changing world. Use the reverse side to write additional information. Use the Foldable to help answer Check for Understanding.

netw⊙rks

Exploring the Americas

Lesson 2 Early Exploration

ESSENTIAL QUESTION
Why do people trade?

GUIDING QUESTIONS
1. **Which country took the lead in finding a trade route to India?**
2. **How did Spain and Portugal protect their claims in the Americas?**

> **Terms to Know**
> **cape** a point of land that sticks out into water, much like a peninsula
> **circumnavigate** to travel completely around something, usually by water

Where in the world?

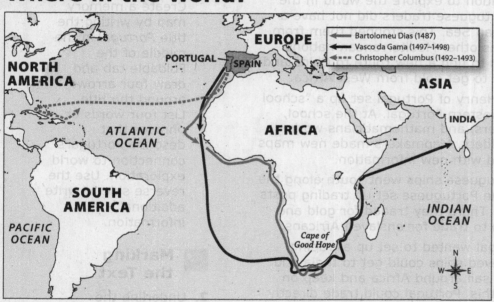

Bartolomeu Dias (1487)
Vasco da Gama (1497–1498)
Christopher Columbus (1492–1493)

EUROPE
PORTUGAL SPAIN
NORTH AMERICA
ATLANTIC OCEAN
ASIA
INDIA
AFRICA
SOUTH AMERICA
PACIFIC OCEAN
INDIAN OCEAN
Cape of Good Hope
N W E S

When did it happen?

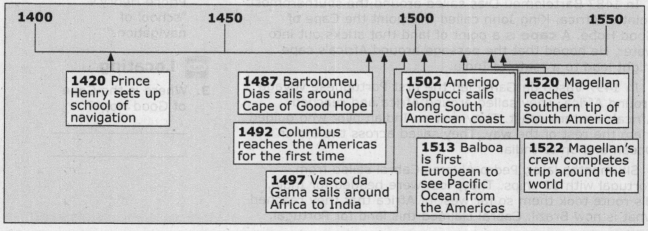

1400   1450   1500   1550

1420 Prince Henry sets up school of navigation

1487 Bartolomeu Dias sails around Cape of Good Hope

1492 Columbus reaches the Americas for the first time

1497 Vasco da Gama sails around Africa to India

1502 Amerigo Vespucci sails along South American coast

1513 Balboa is first European to see Pacific Ocean from the Americas

1520 Magellan reaches southern tip of South America

1522 Magellan's crew completes trip around the world

17

Exploring the Americas

Lesson 2 Early Exploration, *Continued*

The Search for New Trade Routes

When Columbus began his voyage to America in 1492, he did not know North America existed. The maps that sailors used showed just three continents joined together—Europe, Asia, and Africa. Columbus believed that by sailing west, he would reach the Indies islands near China. Explorers believed that the Atlantic and Pacific Oceans were a single large body of water they called the Ocean Sea.

/ / / / / / / / / / ,Glue Foldable here / / / / / / / / / / /

The first European nation to explore the world in the 1400s was Portugal. Portuguese traders did not have a port on the Mediterranean Sea. This stopped them from using the same routes as other Mediterranean nations. Portugal's rulers wanted to find a new route to China and India. They also wanted to get gold from West Africa.

Around 1420, Prince Henry of Portugal set up a "school of navigation" in southwestern Portugal. At the school, astronomers, geographers, and mathematicians worked with sailors and shipbuilders. Mapmakers made new maps when explorers returned with new information.

The route of the Portuguese ships went south along the coast of West Africa. The Portuguese set up trading posts along the African coast. There they traded for gold and ivory. Later, they began to trade for enslaved Africans.

King John II of Portugal wanted to set up a trading empire in Asia. He believed ships could get to India and China. They just had to sail around Africa and keep on going. If they could do this, Portugal could trade directly with Asia. They would not have to rely on caravans to bring goods across Asia and North Africa.

In 1487 Bartolomeu Dias sailed around the southernmost point of Africa. King John called this point the Cape of Good Hope. A **cape** is a point of land that sticks out into water. He hoped that the passage around Africa's cape might lead to a route to India.

In 1497 Vasco da Gama led the first Portuguese voyage around Africa. They sailed around Africa and reached Africa's eastern coast. They met an Indian pilot who guided them the rest of the way. They sailed across the Indian Ocean and on to India.

Six months later, Pedro Álvares Cabral sailed from Portugal with 13 ships. They, too, were headed for India. His route took them so far west of Africa that they reached what is now Brazil. Cabral claimed this land for Portugal.

FOLDABLES

📖 Describing

1. Place a one-tab Foldable along the dotted line to cover the text beginning with "The first European nation ..." Create a memory map by writing the title *Portugal* in the middle of the Foldable tab and draw four arrows around the title. List four words or phrases that describe Portugal's connection to world exploration. Use the reverse side to write additional information.

📖 Marking the Text

2. Underline the groups of people that contributed to Prince Henry's "school of navigation."

👁 Locating

3. Where is the Cape of Good Hope?

_____

_____

netw⊚rks

Exploring the Americas

Lesson 2 Early Exploration, *Continued*

He went on to India and returned with spices and other goods. The Portuguese continued their voyages to India. Soon, Lisbon, the Portuguese capital, became an important marketplace in Europe.

Columbus Crosses the Atlantic

Columbus was born in Genoa, Italy, in 1451. He became a sailor for Portugal. After many voyages north and south, he came up with a new idea. He planned to reach Asia by sailing west, not east.

Columbus had studied the works of Ptolemy (TAHL•uh•mee). Ptolemy was an ancient Greek astronomer. Based on his works, Columbus thought Asia was 2,760 miles (4,441.8 km) from Europe. However, Ptolemy was incorrect, so Columbus believed Asia was much closer than it is.

Columbus was not the first European to sail to the Americas. Hundreds of years earlier, people from northern Europe, called Vikings, had already sailed there. Norse sagas, or traditional stories, tell of a Viking sailor named Leif Eriksson who explored a land west of Greenland around A.D. 1000. Some ruins in eastern Canada suggest this may be true. But Europeans did not know about Viking voyages.

Spain saw the success of Portugal's sailing voyages. They wanted to trade with Asia as well. Spain's queen, Isabella, agreed to pay for Columbus's voyage. She had two reasons for doing this:

- Columbus promised to bring Christianity to any lands he found.

- If Columbus found a sea route to the Indies, Spain would become very wealthy. Trade would increase.

On August 3, 1492, Columbus set out from Spain. He had a crew of about 90 sailors. They had three ships, the *Niña*, the *Pinta*, and the larger *Santa María*. Columbus was captain of the *Santa María*. They sailed with a six-month supply of food and water. A little over two months later, on October 12, 1492, the ship's lookout saw land. The land he saw was in an island chain now called the Bahamas. When Columbus went ashore, he claimed the island for Spain. He named it San Salvador. Columbus believed he had reached the East Indies near China because of the earliest maps. He named the people he saw "Indians."

✎ Identifying

4. Who was the first European to reach the Americas? What date did he do it?

_____

_____

❓ Comparing

5. How were the missions of Spanish and Portuguese explorers similar in the 1400s?

_____

_____

❓ Drawing Conclusions

6. Why did Christopher Columbus name the native people "Indians"?

_____

_____

_____

_____

Exploring the Americas

Lesson 2 Early Exploration, *Continued*

He returned to Spain. Spain's king and queen, Ferdinand and Isabella, received him with great honor. They agreed to pay for more voyages. He made three more trips: in 1493, 1498, and 1502. He explored the Caribbean islands. These included what are now Haiti, the Dominican Republic, Cuba, and Jamaica. He sailed along the coasts of Central America and part of South America. He made maps of the coastline of Central America.

Spain and Portugal wanted to protect their claims in the new world. With the help of the Pope, they chose a line down the center of the Atlantic Ocean. Portugal would control all new lands east of the line. Spain would control everything to the west. They divided the entire unexplored world between them.

Others followed Columbus. As a result of their voyages, the Spanish built an empire in the Americas. In 1502 Amerigo Vespucci (veh•SPOO•chee) sailed along the coast of South America. He discovered that South America was a continent. "America" is named for him.

In 1513, Vasco Núñez de Balboa (bal•BOH•uh) landed in Panama in Central America. He hiked through the jungle and saw the Pacific Ocean. He was the first European to see it from the Americas.

Ferdinand Magellan was a Portuguese seaman. He wanted to **circumnavigate**, or sail around, the world. In 1520 he reached the southern tip of South America. He sailed through a narrow sea passage to another ocean. He noticed that the waters were very calm. *Pacifico* means "peaceful" in Spanish. Magellan named the ocean the Pacific. Magellan died on the journey, but his crew kept on going. In 1522 they returned to Spain.

/ / / / / / / / / / / / Glue Foldable here / / / / / / / / / / / /

Check for Understanding

List two reasons Spain chose to pay for Columbus's voyage.

1. _____

2. _____

What effect did the Portuguese school of navigation have on future explorations?

_____

_____

? Evaluating

7. Which voyage of exploration do you think was the most important? Why?

_____

_____

_____

FOLDABLES®

8. Place a one-tab Foldable along the dotted line to cover Check for Understanding. Create a memory map by writing the title *Columbus* in the middle of the tab and drawing four or more arrows. List words or phrases describing Christopher Columbus's first voyage. Use the reverse side to write additional information. Use your Foldable to help answer Check for Understanding.

Exploring the Americas

Lesson 3 Spain in America

ESSENTIAL QUESTION

What are the consequences when cultures interact?

GUIDING QUESTIONS

1. *What were the goals of early Spanish explorers?*

2. *What did Spain hope to find in the Americas?*

3. *What effect did Spanish rule have on society?*

Terms to Know

conquistador Spanish explorer
immunity resistance, such as to a disease
pueblo a town in the Spanish-ruled lands
mission a religious community where farming was carried out and Native Americans were converted to Christianity
presidio a fort
plantation a large farm

Where in the world?

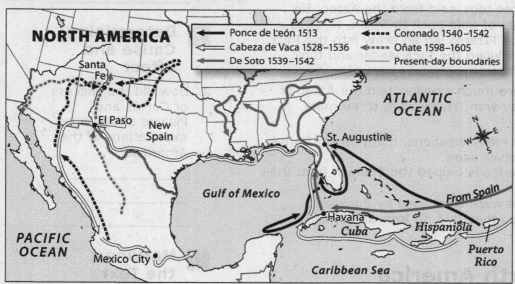

When did it happen?

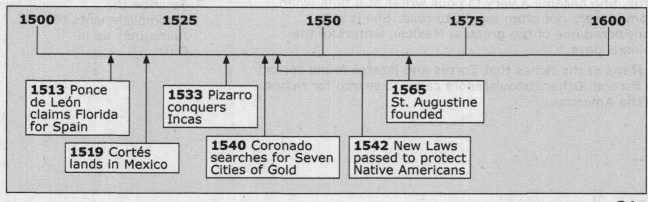

1513 Ponce de León claims Florida for Spain

1519 Cortés lands in Mexico

1533 Pizarro conquers Incas

1540 Coronado searches for Seven Cities of Gold

1542 New Laws passed to protect Native Americans

1565 St. Augustine founded

21

Lesson 3 Spain in America, *Continued*

European Explorers and Conquerors

Early Spanish explorers were known as **conquistadors**, or conquerors. Their main goal was to find riches. Spanish rulers gave them the right to explore and settle in the Americas. The conquistadors would give the rulers part of the wealth they found.

The Aztec Empire was in the area that is present-day Mexico and Central America. The Inca Empire was in present-day Peru. Both of these empires were very wealthy.

Hernán Cortés was a conquistador. He landed on the east coast of Mexico in 1519. He conquered the Aztec Empire by 1521. Cortés took gold from the Aztec. He shipped great amounts of gold back to Spain. In 1533 conquistador Francisco Pizarro led an army into the Inca capital city, Cuzco. He killed the Inca leader and took control of the Inca Empire.

Spanish armies were much smaller than the Aztec or Inca armies. Still, they won. There were three main reasons for this:

- The Spanish had many weapons, many which Native Americans had never seen
- Many Native Americans helped the Spanish fight their Aztec rulers
- Native Americans were weakened by European diseases for which they had no **immunity**, or resistance.

Spain in North America

Not everyone in the Spanish Empire was a conquistador. One important figure of the time was Juana Inés de la Cruz. She became a very famous writer at a time when women were not often taught to read. She is still considered one of the greatest Mexican writers of the colonial days.

News of the riches that Cortés and Pizarro found spread in Europe. Other conquistadors came to search for riches in the Americas.

☑ **Reading Check**

1. How were the Spanish able to conquer the Aztec Empire and the Inca Empire?

_____

_____

? **Determining Cause and Effect**

2. How did the success of Cortés and Pizarro affect later explorations of the Americas?

_____

_____

_____

✎ **Marking the Text**

3. Underline the sentences that describe the accomplishments of Juana Inés de la Cruz

Exploring the Americas

Lesson 3 Spain in America, *Continued*

✓ Reading Check

4. What can you conclude about the Seven Cities of Gold?

_____

_____

_____

? Contrasting

5. How was a pueblo different from a mission?

_____

_____

_____

Explorer	Year	Achievement
Juan Ponce de León	1513	• landed on Florida coast • established first Spanish settlement in modern United States • searched for the "Fountain of Youth"
Álvar Núñez Cabeza de Vaca	1528	• sailed south toward Mexico • spent time in present-day Texas • told his eager audience a legend about "Seven Cities of Gold"
Hernando de Soto	1541	• searched for "Seven Cities of Gold" • crossed Mississippi River • got as far west as Oklahoma
Francisco Vásquez de Coronado		• searched for "Seven Cities of Gold" • wound up in present-day Kansas

Life Under Spanish Rule

In 1598 Juan de Oñate (day ohn•YAH•tay) traveled north from Mexico. He started the province of New Mexico. He established Santa Fe in 1607. Santa Fe was the first Spanish city there. It became the province capital in 1610.

Spanish law called for three kinds of settlements in their colonies: **pueblos**, **missions**, or **presidios**.

pueblo	town, trading center
mission	religious community, including a small town, surrounding farmland, a church; goal of the mission was to spread the Catholic religion and the Spanish way of life among the Native Americans
presidio	fort, usually built near a mission

There were different classes, or levels, in Spanish American society:

Exploring the Americas

Lesson 3 Spain in America, *Continued*

- People who were born in Spain were the top class of society. They were called *peninsulares*. Peninsulares owned land and ran the government. They served in the Catholic Church.
- People who were born in America to Spanish parents were next. They were called *creoles*.
- People with one Spanish parent and one Native American parent were called *mestizos*.
- Native Americans and enslaved Africans were at the bottom level of society. The conquistadors could demand taxes or labor from the Native Americans. Therefore, they also became slaves to the Spanish. For example, Native Americans were forced to work in silver mines owned by the Spanish.

A Spanish priest, Bartolomé de Las Casas, helped to convince the Spanish government to pass the New Laws in 1542 to protect Native Americans.

Some Spanish settlers had **plantations**, or large farms. They shipped crops and raw materials to Spain. At first, they made Native Americans do the hard labor. Later, they were replaced by enslaved Africans.

In the 1600s and the 1700s, the Spanish settled the Southwest, including modern California, Texas, and New Mexico. California was the northern border of Spain's empire. Spain wanted more colonists to live there.

The Spanish, with the help of the Native Americans, built missions along the southern coast of California. After the missions were built, Native Americans were made to live and work on the missions. They were forced to become Christians.

Check for Understanding

What were the goals of the Spanish conquistadores?

_____

_____

How did Native Americans contribute to the success of the Spanish American colonies?

_____

_____

? Explaining

6. What was the purpose of the New Laws in 1542?

_____

_____

FOLDABLES®

7. Place a two-tab Foldable along the dotted line to cover Check for Understanding. Write the title *Searching for Riches* on the anchor tab. Label the tabs *Fountain of Youth*, and *Seven Cities of Gold*. Use both sides of the tabs to write two or more facts that you remember about each. Use your Foldable to help answer Check for Understanding.

Glue Foldable here

24

Exploring the Americas

Lesson 4 Competing for Colonies

ESSENTIAL QUESTION
What are the consequences when cultures interact?

GUIDING QUESTIONS
1. **What were the religious motives behind the Age of Exploration?**
2. **How did French and Dutch settlements compare to the Spanish colonies?**

Terms to Know
Reformation a sixteenth-century religious movement rejecting or changing some Roman Catholic teachings and practices and establishing the Protestant churches

Protestantism a form of Christianity that was in opposition to the Catholic Church

armada a fleet of warships

Northwest Passage a sea passage between the Atlantic and the Pacific along the north coast of North America

tenant farmer settler who pays rent or provides work to a landowner in exchange for the right to use the landowner's land

Where in the world?

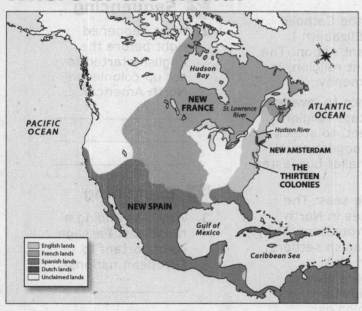

When did it happen?

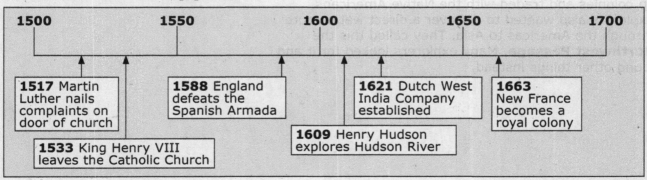

1500	1550	1600	1650	1700

1517 Martin Luther nails complaints on door of church

1588 England defeats the Spanish Armada

1621 Dutch West India Company established

1663 New France becomes a royal colony

1533 King Henry VIII leaves the Catholic Church

1609 Henry Hudson explores Hudson River

25

netw⊛rks

Exploring the Americas

Lesson 4 Competing for Colonies, *Continued*

Religious Rivalries

Part of the purpose of exploring the Americas was to spread the Christian religion there. The first explorers were Roman Catholics. In 1517, a new form of Christianity began. It opposed the Catholic Church. It was called **Protestantism**.

Protestantism started with Martin Luther, a German priest. He did not agree with many Catholic Church practices. In 1517, he nailed a list of complaints on the door of the local Catholic Church. He questioned the power and authority of Catholic leaders. His actions led to the **Reformation**. This was a religious movement that took hold in many parts of Europe. It led to widespread conflict within and between the nations of Europe.

In 1533, King Henry VIII of England left the Catholic Church. His daughter ruled later as Queen Elizabeth I. During her rule, England became a Protestant nation. The people were required to follow the Protestant religion. If they didn't, they might lose their land and money.

The king of Spain, a Catholic, saw a chance to invade England. He wanted to wipe out the Protestant religion there. The king sent an **armada**, or war fleet, to attack England. The fleet was huge. It was the strongest naval force in the world. The English fleet was smaller but faster. The British defeated the Spanish.

This meant that Spain no longer ruled the seas. The English decided it was time to set up colonies in North America. English and Dutch settlers were Protestant. They set up colonies along the Atlantic coast. Spanish settlers were Catholic. They settled in southwestern and southeastern North America. The French were also Catholic. They settled in the northeast. Religious differences caused conflicts between the colonies.

Explorers mapped the coast of North America. They set up colonies and traded with the Native Americans. Explorers also wanted to discover a direct water route through the Americas to Asia. They called this the **Northwest Passage**. Many explorers looked for it and found other things instead.

? ### Determining Cause and Effect

1. What was a major cause of conflict between England and Spain in the 1500s?

_____

_____

? ### Sequencing

2. What happened right before the English started to set up colonies in North America?

_____

_____

_____

? ### Explaining

3. Why was finding a Northwest Passage so important to European nations?

_____

_____

Exploring the Americas

Lesson 4 Competing for Colonies, *Continued*

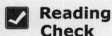

Listing

4. Which countries sent explorers to find a Northwest Passage to Asia?

_____

_____

_____

✔ Reading Check

5. What were France's main interests in North America?

_____

_____

_____

Marking the Text

6. Underline the sentences which describe *tenant farmers.*

Searching for the Northwest Passage			
Explorer	**Sailed For**	**Year**	**Found Instead**
John Cabot	England	1497	Probably present-day Newfoundland
Giovanni de Verrazano	France	1524	Explored coast of North America from Nova Scotia to the Carolinas
Jacques Cartier	France	1535	Sailed up St. Lawrence River, named the mountain at the site of modern Montreal
Henry Hudson	Netherlands	1609	Discovered Hudson River, sailed as far north as Albany; later discovered Hudson Bay

French and Dutch Settlements

At first, the French were mainly interested in the rich natural resources of North America. They fished and trapped animals for their fur. French trappers and missionaries went far inland into North America. They traded with Native Americans. They built forts and trading posts. They treated the Native Americans with respect. Native Americans did not see them as a threat to their way of life.

In 1663 New France became a colony. New France was made up of estates along the St. Lawrence River. Those who owned estates received land in exchange for bringing settlers. The settlers were known as **tenant farmers**. They paid rent to the estate owner. They also worked for him a certain number of days each year.

The French explored the Mississippi River. In the 1670s, fur trader Louis Joliet and priest Jacques Marquette explored the Mississippi River by canoe. They turned back when they realized the river flowed south, not west to Asia. A few years later, Robert Cavelier de La Salle also traveled the Mississippi. He went all the way to the Gulf of Mexico and claimed the whole area for France. He called it

27

Exploring the Americas

Lesson 4 Competing for Colonies, *Continued*

Louisiana, after France's king, Louis XIV. In 1718, the French established a port city where the Mississippi River meets the Gulf of Mexico. It was named New Orleans.

French explorers had traveled west to the Rocky Mountains and southwest to the Rio Grande. This led to New France claiming that entire territory.

The Netherlands was a small country in Europe. It had few natural resources and a limited amount of farmland. The people of the Netherlands were called the Dutch. They were attracted by the vast lands and natural resources of North America. They already had a large fleet of trading ships. They sailed all over the world. In 1621 the Netherlands set up the Dutch West India Company. Its purpose was to ship goods for the Netherlands between the Americas and Africa. In 1623 this company took control of the country's North American colony, New Netherland.

The center of New Netherland was New Amsterdam. New Amsterdam was located on the tip of Manhattan Island, where the Hudson River enters New York Harbor. Governor Peter Minuit purchased the land from the Manhattoes people in 1626 for about $24 worth of trade goods.

/ / / / / / / / / / / Glue Foldable here / / / / / / / / / / / /

Check for Understanding

What started the Protestant Reformation? What was the result of that action?

_____

_____

What were the French hoping to find as they explored the Mississippi River?

_____

_____

? Describing

7. How did the Dutch acquire the land for New Amsterdam?

_____

_____

_____

FOLDABLES®

8. Place a one-tab Foldable along the dotted line to cover Check for Understanding. Draw a large circle on the tab and label it *Religion in North America*. Next, draw two smaller circles inside the large circle. Label the small circles *Catholic* and *Protestant.* Use the space inside the circles to list the countries of each religion that established colonies in North America. Use your Foldable to help answer Check for Understanding.

networks

Colonial America

Lesson 1 Roanoke and Jamestown

ESSENTIAL QUESTION

How does geography influence the way people live?

GUIDING QUESTIONS

1. **What problems did the Roanoke settlers encounter?**

2. **Why did the Jamestown settlement succeed?**

Terms to Know

charter a document granting the recipient the right to settle a colony

joint-stock company a company in which investors buy stock in return for a share of the company's future profits

headright a 50-acre grant of land given to settlers who came to the colony

burgess an elected representative to an assembly

When did it happen?

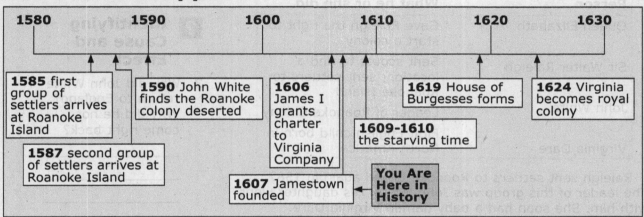

| 1580 | 1590 | 1600 | 1610 | 1620 | 1630 |

1585 first group of settlers arrives at Roanoke Island

1587 second group of settlers arrives at Roanoke Island

1590 John White finds the Roanoke colony deserted

1606 James I grants charter to Virginia Company

1607 Jamestown founded

1609-1610 the starving time

1619 House of Burgesses forms

1624 Virginia becomes royal colony

You Are Here in History

What do you know?

In the first column, answer the questions based on what you know before you study. After this lesson, complete the last column.

Now...		Later...
	Who were the Powhatan?	
	Where was Jamestown located?	

29

The Mystery of Roanoke

England wanted to settle some people on land it claimed in North America. England's Queen Elizabeth gave Sir Walter Raleigh the right to start a colony there. Raleigh sent scouts to find a good place for the colony. They said Roanoke Island would be a good place. Roanoke Island is just off the coast of what is now North Carolina. The first settlers arrived in 1585. They had a rough winter and gave up and returned to England.

People Involved with Roanoke Colony	
Person	**What he or she did**
Queen Elizabeth	Gave Raleigh the right to start a colony
Sir Walter Raleigh	Sent scouts to find a location; sent settlers to Roanoke Island
John White	Leader of Roanoke Colony
Virginia Dare	First English child born in North America

Raleigh sent settlers to Roanoke Island again in 1587. The leader of this group was John White. His daughter went with him. She soon had a baby named Virginia Dare. Virginia Dare was the first English child born in North America.

The colony needed supplies, so White returned to England to get them. He did not come right back, though. England was fighting a war with Spain. All of England's ships were being used in the war. It took three years for White to get back to Roanoke Island.

When White arrived back at Roanoke Island all the settlers were gone. What happened to them? The only clue was a word carved on a tree trunk. That word was *Croatoan*. Maybe the word meant the settlers went to Croatoan Island. No one knows for sure. They were never seen again.

Success at Jamestown

The Roanoke Colony failed. However, England still wanted a colony in North America. The English decided to try again.

England had a new king, James I. He gave a business a "charter" to start a colony. A **charter** is a document

Identifying

1. Who sent settlers to Virginia?

Mark the Text

2. Circle the date the second group of settlers went to Roanoke Island.

Identifying Cause and Effect

3. Why did John White return to England? Why did he not come right back?

_____

_____

Speculating

4. What do you think happened to the Roanoke colonists?

_____

_____

Reading Check

5. Why did the English decide to settle on Roanoke Island?

_____

_____

30

Lesson 1 Roanoke and Jamestown, *Continued*

FOLDABLES®

Listing

6. Place a one-tab Foldable along the dotted line to cover the text that begins with "The Virginia Company was a joint-stock company." Label the anchor tab *Virginia Company*. Write *Making Money* in the middle of the tab. Draw three arrows around the title. List words or phrases that explain how investors felt they would make money by investing in the Virginia Company.

Abc Mark the Text

7. Circle the date the settlers built Jamestown.

Identifying

8. Who forced the settlers to work? Who helped the colonists?

_____

_____

that gives someone the right to start a colony. The name of the business that received the charter was the Virginia Company.

/ / / / / / / / / / / , Glue Foldable here / / / / / / / / / / / /

The Virginia Company was a **joint-stock company**. This meant that many people each owned a small part of the company. If the company made money, each owner would get part of the money the company made.

> **Why is it called a joint-stock company?**
>
> *Joint* means "together." All of the owners owned the Virginia Company together. *Stock* is the word for the part of the company each person owned.

The people who each owned stock, or small parts, of the Virginia Company, wanted to make money. They hoped that a colony in North America would make money for the company. How? They thought the colonists would find gold, or collect and sell furs and fish.

The Virginia Company sent 144 settlers to North America. They sailed from England, across the Atlantic Ocean, and to the coast of North America. They sailed up a river and on its bank built a tiny town in 1607. They named the river the James River. They named their town Jamestown. Both names were to honor King James.

Life was difficult in Jamestown. The colonists suffered from disease and hunger. Captain John Smith forced the settlers to work. He also made friends with the local people. They were Native Americans called the Powhatan. Their chief was also named Powhatan. He gave the colonists food and helped them survive.

Then, things got worse. The colonists and the Powhatan stopped getting along. Powhatan stopped giving the colonists food. The winter of 1609–1610 was called "the starving time." Many colonists died.

Soon after that, new colonists arrived. The colony started to do well. The colonists started growing and selling tobacco. This made money for the owners of the Virginia Company. Then, things got even better. A colonist named John Rolfe married a Powhatan woman. Her name was Pocahontas, and she was the chief's daughter.

Colonial America

Lesson 1 Roanoke and Jamestown, *Continued*

Jamestown Succeeded For Many Reasons

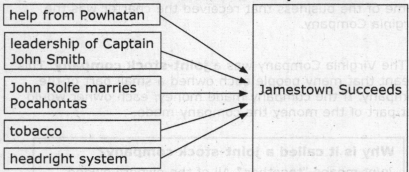

help from Powhatan

leadership of Captain John Smith

John Rolfe marries Pocahontas

tobacco

headright system

→ Jamestown Succeeds

The Virginia Company wanted even more settlers to go to Virginia. They gave 50 acres of land free to each new settler who would go there. This land grant is called a **headright.** The headright system brought many new settlers to the colony.

At first, the Virginia Company and the leaders it appointed made the rules for the colonists. In 1619, the company began letting the colonists make some of the rules themselves. It allowed them to choose representatives called **burgesses** to make the rules for them. These representatives met in a group called the House of Burgesses. The House of Burgesses was the first legislature in North America to be elected by the people.

///////////// Glue Foldable here ///////////////

Check for Understanding

What happened to the colony at Roanoke?

_____

_____

How did the colony at Jamestown survive?

_____

_____

Identifying

9. What was the purpose of the House of Burgesses?

_____

10. Who did the burgesses represent?

_____

Reading Check

11. Why was the House of Burgesses important?

_____

_____

FOLDABLES®

12. Use a three-tab Venn diagram Foldable and write the title *English Colonies* on the anchor tab. Place it along the dotted line to cover the Check for Understanding. Label the tabs— *Roanoke*, *Both*, and *Jamestown*. On both sides of the tabs, list words and short phrases that you remember about each to compare the colonies. Use the Foldable to help do the activity below the tabs.

networks

Colonial America

Lesson 2 The New England Colonies

ESSENTIAL QUESTION

How do new ideas change the way people live?

GUIDING QUESTIONS

1. **Why did the Puritans settle in North America?**
2. **What role did religion play in founding the various colonies?**

Terms to Know

dissent to disagree with an opinion
persecute to mistreat a person or group on the basis of their beliefs
tolerance the ability to accept or put up with different views or behaviors

Where in the world?

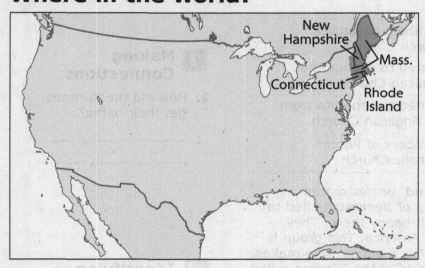

When did it happen?

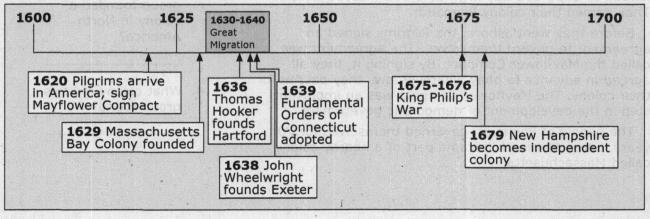

33

Colonial America

Lesson 2 The New England Colonies, *Continued*

Seeking Religious Freedom

Many English settlers came to North America to have religious freedom. In England, the main church was the official Anglican Church. The Anglican Church was a Protestant church. Many people who were Catholic did not want to practice the Anglican religion. Even many Protestants were unhappy with the Anglican Church. They **dissented,** or disagreed with, what the church was doing. Members of the Anglican Church who wanted to change or "purify" it were called Puritans. Persons who wanted to leave the Anglican Church, or separate from it, were called Separatists.

English religious groups in 1600s	Anglicans	members of Anglican Church
	Puritans	wanted to change the Anglican Church
	Separatists	wanted to separate from the Anglican Church
	Catholics	members of Roman Catholic Church

   The Separatists were **persecuted**, or mistreated because of their beliefs. One group of Separatists fled to the Netherlands, but they were not happy there. They decided to start a colony in North America. This group is known as the Pilgrims. (A "pilgrim" is a person who makes a journey for religious reasons.) In 1620 the Pilgrims sailed to North America aboard a ship called the *Mayflower*. They landed at Cape Cod Bay in what is now Massachusetts. They named their colony Plymouth.

   Before they went ashore, the Pilgrims signed an agreement to govern themselves. The agreement was called the Mayflower Compact. By signing it, they all agreed in advance to obey whatever laws they passed for their colony. The Mayflower Compact was an important step in the development of democratic government.

   The people of Plymouth governed themselves for 70 years. Later, Plymouth became part of a nearby colony called Massachusetts.

Ꭺᵇᴄ Defining

1. Write the definition of *dissent* here.
   _____
   _____

❓ Making Connections

2. How did the Puritans get their name?
   _____
   _____

🖌 Identifying

3. Which Separatist group founded a colony in North America?
   _____

4. What colony did this group found?
   _____

Colonial America

Lesson 2 The New England Colonies, *Continued*

Ac Defining

5. What is another word that has the same meaning as *compact?*

_____

Identifying

6. Name three ways that Squanto and Samoset helped the Pilgrims survive.

_____

_____

_____

Reading Check

7. Why is the Mayflower Compact an important document in American history?

_____

_____

_____

Ac Defining

8. What is another word for *tolerance?*

_____

Why was it called the Mayflower Compact?

The Pilgrims named their document the Mayflower Compact because they were on their ship the *Mayflower* when they signed it. *Compact* means "an agreement." So the Mayflower Compact was an *agreement* signed on board the *Mayflower*.

At first life was very difficult in the Plymouth colony. Nearly half of the colonists died during the first winter. Then, in the spring, two Native Americans befriended the Pilgrims: Squanto and Samoset. They showed the Pilgrims how to grow corn and other crops and where to hunt and fish. The Pilgrims might not have survived without their help. Squanto and Samoset also helped the Pilgrims be accepted by other Native Americans nearby. In the fall of 1621, they all celebrated together in a great feast of thanksgiving.

New Colonies

In 1629 another colony was established nearby. This was the Massachusetts Bay Colony. It was founded by Puritans. The leader of the colony was John Winthrop.

In the 1630s, more than 15,000 Puritans left England to settle in Massachusetts. They were escaping persecution and bad economic times. This movement of people is known as the Great Migration (*migration* means "movement").

The Puritans in Massachusetts had no **tolerance**, or acceptance, of different beliefs. This resulted in people leaving Massachusetts to start their own colonies.

New Colonies from Massachusetts			
	Connecticut	**New Hampshire**	**Rhode Island**
Founded in year ...	1636	1638	1644
by founder ...	Thomas Hooker	John Wheelwright	Roger Williams
who left ...	Massachusetts	Massachusetts	Massachusetts
in search of ...	democracy	religious freedom	religious freedom

35

netw⦿rks

Colonial America

Lesson 2 The New England Colonies, *Continued*

One man who helped start a new colony was a minister named Thomas Hooker. He and his followers left Massachusetts to form a new colony in what is now Connecticut. In 1639, they wrote out a plan for government. It was called the Fundamental Orders of Connecticut. The Fundamental Orders of Connecticut was the first written constitution, or written plan of government, in America.

In 1638, John Wheelwright also left Massachusetts with a group of religious dissenters. He led them north and founded the town of Exeter in New Hampshire. New Hampshire became an independent colony in 1679.

Another man who helped start a new colony was a minister named Roger Williams. He believed in religious freedom. He also believed in treating Native Americans fairly. When the Puritans expelled him from Massachusetts, he started the colony of Rhode Island in 1644. Rhode Island was the first place in America where people of all faiths could worship freely.

Gradually the colonists created settlements throughout New England. The settlers and Native American peoples traded with each other. Sometimes there was conflict. Usually, it was because settlers moved onto Native American lands without permission.

In 1675, the Wampanoag leader Metacomet fought a war against settlers in Massachusetts, Connecticut, and Rhode Island. He got other Indian groups to help. The settlers called Metacomet "King Philip," so the war became known as King Philip's war. Hundreds of Native Americans and colonists died. In the end, the colonists won the war. They were now free to expand their colonies and take even more land.

//////////////////// Glue Foldable here /////////////////////

Check for Understanding

Why did the Pilgrims start a colony in North America?

_____

_____

Why did people form the colonies of Connecticut, Rhode Island, and New Hampshire?

_____

_____

Identifying

9. What was America's first written constitution?

_____

Identifying Cause and Effect

10. What was the cause of King Philip's War?

_____

Reading Check

11. Which colony let people of all faiths worship freely?

_____

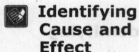

12. Use a two-tab Foldable and place it along the dotted line to cover Check for Understanding. Write the title *New Colonies* on the anchor tab. Label the two tabs— *Pilgrims*, and *Puritans*. Write key words and phrases that you remember about each group. Use the Foldable to help answer Check for Understanding.

netw⊙rks

Colonial America

Lesson 3 The Middle Colonies

ESSENTIAL QUESTION

How does geography influence the way people live?

GUIDING QUESTIONS

1. **Why did the Middle Colonies grow?**
2. **How did Pennsylvania differ from the other English colonies?**

Terms to Know

patroon landowner in the Dutch colonies who ruled over large areas of land

pacifist a person who refuses to use force or fight in wars

Where in the world?

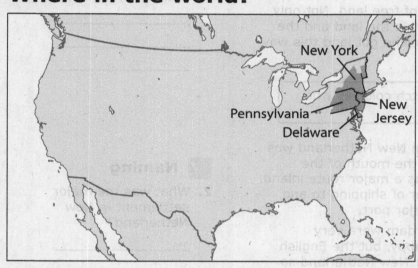

New York

Pennsylvania

New Jersey

Delaware

When did it happen?

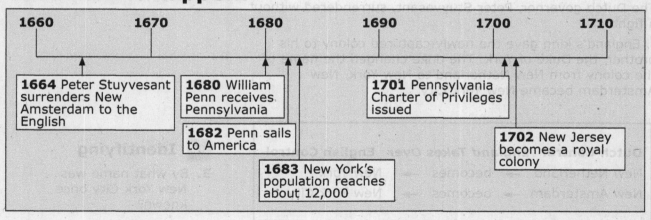

1660   1670   1680   1690   1700   1710

1664 Peter Stuyvesant surrenders New Amsterdam to the English

1680 William Penn receives Pennsylvania

1682 Penn sails to America

1683 New York's population reaches about 12,000

1701 Pennsylvania Charter of Privileges issued

1702 New Jersey becomes a royal colony

37

Colonial America

Lesson 3 The Middle Colonies, Continued

New York and New Jersey

The Middle Colonies were the colonies in the middle of the east coast of North America. Some of these colonies were at first controlled by the European country called the Netherlands. This colony was called New Netherland. People from the Netherlands are called "Dutch." New Netherland was under Dutch control.

The Dutch wanted more people to move to their colony of New Netherland. To get people to move there, they gave away land. The land giveaway worked like this: If someone could bring at least 50 new settlers to New Netherland, the Dutch would give that person a lot of free land. Not only that, but that person would get to rule the land and the settlers like a king. The landowners who got land this way were called **patroons**.

> **patroon** landowner in the Dutch colonies who ruled over large areas of land

The most important settlement in New Netherland was New Amsterdam. It was located at the mouth of the Hudson River. The Hudson River was a major route inland. This made New Amsterdam a center of shipping to and from the Americas. It became a major port.

New Netherland and New Amsterdam were very successful. The Dutch were very happy, but the English were not. They wanted to take over New Netherland so they could have this valuable colony for themselves. In 1664, the English sent warships to attack New Amsterdam. The Dutch governor, Peter Stuyvesant, surrendered without a fight.

England's king gave the newly captured colony to his brother, the Duke of York. The duke changed the name of the colony from New Netherland to New York. New Amsterdam became New York City.

Dutch Control	*England Takes Over*	English Control
New Netherland →	becomes →	New York
New Amsterdam →	becomes →	New York City

? Analyzing

1. What was the purpose of the patroon system?

_____

_____

_____

✍ Naming

2. What was the major settlement in New Netherland?

_____

✍ Identifying

3. By what name was New York City once known?

_____

38

Colonial America

Lesson 3 The Middle Colonies, *Continued*

ABC Defining

4. What is another word for *owner*?

_____

✓ Reading Check

5. Why did no major city develop in New Jersey?

_____

_____

ABC Mark the Text

6. Underline the definition of *pacifist*. What religious group practiced pacifism?

_____

7. Underline the last sentence in the last paragraph on this page. What caused this result?

_____

_____

New York continued to grow and prosper under English rule. When England took over in 1664, the colony was home to about 8,000 people. This included 300 enslaved Africans. By 1683, its population had grown to about 12,000. The residents included many Dutch, Germans, Swedes, and Native Americans. New York was also home to the first Jews to settle in North America.

Before long, the Duke of York decided to divide his colony. He gave part of the land to two other nobles. This land became the colony of New Jersey. The two proprietors, or owners, named their colony after an island off the coast of England called Jersey.

Unlike New York, New Jersey had no natural harbors that could become a good port. So New Jersey did not develop a major city. However, like New York, people of many different racial, religious, and national backgrounds lived in New Jersey. To attract settlers, the proprietors offered large amounts of land. They also promised settlers freedom of religion, trial by jury, and a representative assembly.

Pennsylvania and Delaware

The colony of Pennsylvania was founded by Quakers. The Quakers were a Protestant religious group who had been mistreated in England. They believed that everyone was equal. They were also **pacifists**. Pacifists are people who refuse to use force or fight in wars. Welsh, Irish, Dutch, and German settlers also came to Pennsylvania.

The owner of the colony was named William Penn. (In fact, the name *Pennsylvania* means "Penn's Woods.") Penn founded his colony to put his Quaker ideas into practice.

He designed the colony's main city of Philadelphia. The name means "city of brotherly love." Penn came to America in 1682 to supervise the building of the city. Philadelphia quickly became the most popular port in the colonies.

What really makes Pennsylvania stand out, however, is the way Penn treated Native Americans. He believed that the land belonged to the Native Americans. Instead of just taking their land, he paid them for it. As a result, Pennsylvania had better relations with Native Americans than many other colonies.

networks

Colonial America

Lesson 3 The Middle Colonies, *Continued*

Penn wrote Pennsylvania's constitution and he took an active role in governing his colony. In 1701, Penn issued the Charter of Privileges. This document gave the colonists the right to elect representatives to a legislature, or lawmaking body. The Charter of Privileges was important because it was another step in setting up democracy in America.

When the colonists got the right to elect people to make their laws, some colonists in southern Pennsylvania wanted to have their own legislature. Many of these colonists were from Sweden. Sweden had started a colony there years before the Dutch and then the English took over the region. Penn let these colonists have their own legislature. Eventually this region became a separate colony called Delaware.

////////////////// Glue Foldable here //////////////////

Check for Understanding
Name two colonies that were formed from parts of other colonies and the colony from which each was formed.

_____

_____

Name two groups of people, besides the English, who lived in the Middle Colonies.

_____

Defining

8. What does a legislature do?

_____

Reading Check

9. What was William Penn's main reason for founding Pennsylvania?

_____

_____

FOLDABLES

10. Use a one-tab Foldable and place it along the dotted line to cover *Check for Understanding.* Write *Middle Colonies* in the center of the Foldable tab. Create a memory map by drawing arrows around the title and writing five or more short phrases that you remember about each of the Middle Colonies and the people that lived there. Use the reverse side to list additional information you recall.

networks

Colonial America

Lesson 4 The Southern Colonies

ESSENTIAL QUESTION
How does geography influence the way people live?

GUIDING QUESTIONS
1. **What problems faced Maryland and Virginia?**
2. **What factors contributed to the growth of the Carolinas?**

Terms to Know
indentured servant person who agrees to work without pay for a certain period of time in exchange for passage to America
constitution written plan of government; a set of fundamental laws to support a government
debtor person who owes money to another

Where in the world?

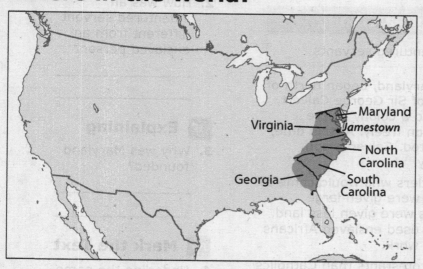

When did it happen?

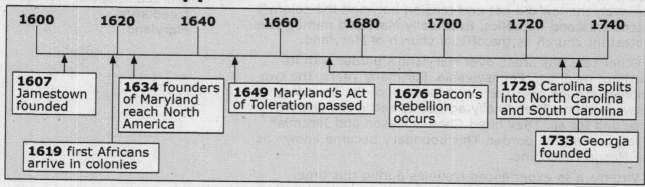

41

networks

Colonial America

Lesson 4 The Southern Colonies, *Continued*

Virginia and Maryland

Jamestown was settled in 1607. Over the years, it grew into a larger colony: the Virginia Colony. The Virginia colonists made their living by growing tobacco. It took a lot of workers to plant, take care of, and harvest this crop. Landowners forced enslaved Africans to do much of this work. The first Africans arrived in Virginia in 1619.

Not all workers were slaves. Many were **indentured servants**. These were people who agreed to work for a certain number of years for no pay. In exchange, their employers paid for their voyage to the colony.

Workers in the Virginia Colony	
enslaved Africans	indentured servants

In 1634, a new colony, called Maryland, began north of Virginia. Maryland was the dream of Sir George Calvert, Lord Baltimore. He wanted to found a colony where Catholics could practice their religion freely. At this time, Catholics in England were persecuted. Calvert's son, Cecilius, worked to start the colony.

Cecilius offered free land to settlers who would come to Maryland. Upper class Englishmen were given large amounts of land. Average colonists were given less land. As in Virginia, wealthy landowners used enslaved Africans and indentured servants to do the work.

Before long, there were more Protestants than Catholics living in Maryland. To protect the Catholics' religious freedom, the colony passed the Act of Toleration in 1649. However, the law did not end tension between the colony's Protestants and Catholics. Eventually Maryland named one Protestant church as the official church of Maryland.

Other tensions arose over Maryland's border with its northern neighbor, Pennsylvania. For many years, the two colonies argued over the exact location of the boundary between them. They finally agreed to settle the dispute once and for all. They hired Charles Mason and Jeremiah Dixon to map the border. This boundary became known as the Mason-Dixon line.

Virginia also experienced troubles during this time. James Berkeley, the governor of Virginia, promised Native Americans that settlers would not go farther west into their lands. Nathaniel Bacon was a farmer in western Virginia. He did not like the promise Governor Berkeley had made.

? Analyzing

1. Why might a person agree to become an indentured servant and work for no pay?

_____

_____

? Contrasting

2. How was an indentured servant different from an enslaved person?

_____

_____

✍ Explaining

3. Why was Maryland founded?

_____

_____

A♭c Mark the Text

4. Underline the name of the law that granted religious freedom in Maryland.

42

Colonial America

Lesson 4 The Southern Colonies, *Continued*

📝 Explaining

5. Why was Bacon's Rebellion important?

_____

_____

_____

✅ Reading Check

6. Why did Nathaniel Bacon oppose the colonial government?

_____

_____

_____

_____

🔤 Defining

7. What is a constitution?

_____

_____

_____

📝 Listing

8. List three products that were important in North Carolina.

_____

_____

_____

In fact, many people in western Virginia did not like it. They wanted to be able to move farther west. They felt that the government of the colony was controlled by people from eastern Virginia who did not care about the problems of western Virginia.

In 1676, Bacon led attacks on Native American villages. His army even marched to Jamestown and drove out Berkeley. They burned Jamestown down. Bacon was about to take over the colony when he died. Today, we remember this event as Bacon's Rebellion. Bacon's Rebellion was important in history because it showed that people wanted a government that would listen to their demands.

Bacon's Rebellion

Cause	Effect
• unhappy with promise not to move into Native Americans' land • felt the government was controlled by people in the east	• showed that government must listen to the demands of the people

The Carolinas and Georgia

In 1663, King Charles II created a new colony. It was called Carolina, which is Latin for "Charles's Land." The new colony needed a constitution. A **constitution** is a written plan of government. An English political thinker named John Locke wrote the constitution for Carolina.

Farmers from Virginia settled in the northern part of Carolina. They grew tobacco and sold timber and tar. There was no good harbor in northern Carolina, so the farmers used Virginia's ports. However, southern Carolina did have a good port at Charles Town (later Charleston).

Other crops were more important in southern Carolina. One of these was indigo. Indigo is a blue flowering plant. It was used to dye cloth. The other important crop was rice. Growing rice requires much labor, so the demand for slave labor increased.

Lesson 4 The Southern Colonies, *Continued*

In 1729, Carolina split into two separate colonies: North Carolina and South Carolina.

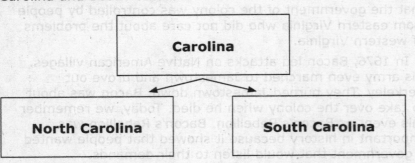

The colony of Georgia was founded in 1733. It was the last colony set up by the English in North America. The founder of Georgia was James Oglethorpe. Georgia was to be a place where poor people and debtors (DEH • tuhrs) could get a fresh start. **Debtors** are people who owe other people money. England also hoped Georgia would protect the colonies from Spain. Spain had a colony in Florida, and Georgia stood between Spain and the other English colonies.

///////////// Glue Foldable here // / / / / / / / / / / /

Check for Understanding

What two things caused Bacon's Rebellion?

_____

_____

List two problems that Maryland faced.

_____

_____

Copyright by The McGraw-Hill Companies.

Mark the Text

9. Underline the definition of *debtors*.

✓ **Reading Check**

10. Why was Georgia founded?

_____

_____

_____

FOLDABLES

11. Use a one-tab Foldable and place it along the dotted line to cover *Check for Understanding*. Write the title *Southern Colonies* on the anchor tab. Label the top of the Foldable tab *Problems in Maryland and Virginia*. Recall and record the problems that Southern colonies had to face.

Life in the American Colonies

Lesson 1 Colonial Economy

ESSENTIAL QUESTION
How does geography influence the way people live?

GUIDING QUESTIONS
1. *How did the economic activity of the three regions reflect their geography?*
2. *Why were enslaved Africans brought to the colonies?*

Terms to Know
subsistence farming producing just enough to meet immediate needs

cash crop a crop that can be sold easily in markets

diversity variety, such as of ethnic or national groups

triangular trade trade route between three destinations, such as Britain, Africa, and America

slave code rules focusing on the behavior and punishment of enslaved people

Where in the world?

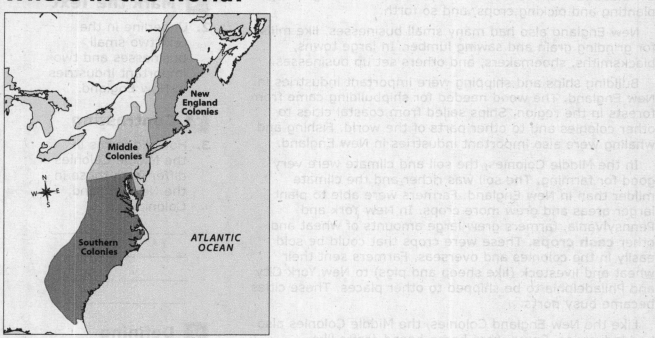

When did it happen?

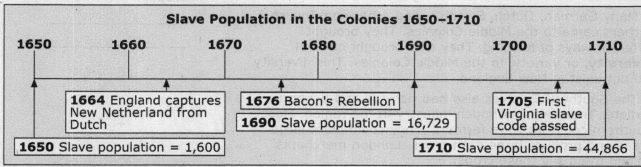

Slave Population in the Colonies 1650–1710

1650   1660   1670   1680   1690   1700   1710

1664 England captures New Netherland from Dutch

1676 Bacon's Rebellion

1690 Slave population = 16,729

1705 First Virginia slave code passed

1650 Slave population = 1,600

1710 Slave population = 44,866

45

Life in the American Colonies

Lesson 1 Colonial Economy, *Continued*

Making a Living in the Colonies

In Colonial America, most colonists were farmers or had a business linked to farming. For example, a farmer who grew wheat would need someone to mill (grind) the wheat into flour. In each region, the colonists learned how to best use the climate and land.

In New England, winters were long. The soil was poor and rocky. This made large-scale farming difficult for the colonists. Instead, farmers practiced **subsistence farming.** This means that they grew only enough crops to feed their families. They did not have crops to sell or trade. On these farms, the whole family worked—milking cows, planting and picking crops, and so forth.

New England also had many small businesses, like mills for grinding grain and sawing lumber. In large towns, blacksmiths, shoemakers, and others set up businesses.

Building ships and shipping were important industries in New England. The wood needed for shipbuilding came from forests in the region. Ships sailed from coastal cities to other colonies and to other parts of the world. Fishing and whaling were also important industries in New England.

In the Middle Colonies, the soil and climate were very good for farming. The soil was richer and the climate milder than in New England. Farmers were able to plant larger areas and grew more crops. In New York and Pennsylvania, farmers grew large amounts of wheat and other **cash crops.** These were crops that could be sold easily in the colonies and overseas. Farmers sent their wheat and livestock (like sheep and pigs) to New York City and Philadelphia to be shipped to other places. These cities became busy ports.

Like the New England Colonies, the Middle Colonies also had industries. Some were home-based crafts like carpentry and flour making. Others were larger businesses like lumber (wood) mills and mining.

Many German, Dutch, Swedish, and other non-English settlers came to the Middle Colonies. They brought different ways of farming. They also brought cultural **diversity,** or variety, to the Middle Colonies. This diversity did not exist in New England.

The Southern Colonies also had rich soil and a warm climate. There was not much industry in the region. Most Southern colonists were farmers. They could plant large areas and produce large cash crops. London merchants helped them sell these crops.

Explaining

1. Why did New England farmers practice subsistence farming?

Mark the Text

2. Underline in the text two small businesses and two important industries in New England.

Contrasting

3. How did farms in the Middle Colonies differ from those in the New England Colonies?

Defining

4. What are *cash crops*?

46

Life in the American Colonies

Lesson 1 Colonial Economy, *Continued*

? Contrasting

5. How were plantations in the Southern Colonies different from small farms?

_____

_____

_____

_____

✓ Reading Check

6. Why was agriculture so important to the economy of the Southern Colonies?

_____

_____

_____

_____

A♭c Mark the Text

7. Circle in the text two examples of important cash crops grown in the Southern Colonies.

A♭c Defining

8. What was the Middle Passage?

_____

_____

_____

Large farms, called plantations, were often located along rivers. This made it easier to ship crops to market by boat. Most large plantations were near the coast. Each plantation was like a small village. It could provide almost everything a person needed to live and work. Some plantations even had a school and a church.

In the hills and forests of the Southern Colonies, smaller farms grew corn and tobacco. There were many more small farms than there were plantations. Even so, the plantation owners had more money and more power. They controlled the economy and politics in the Southern Colonies.

Tobacco was the main crop in Maryland and Virginia. Many workers were needed for growing tobacco and preparing it for sale. It cost a lot of money to hire workers, so Southern farmers began using enslaved Africans.

The main cash crop in South Carolina and Georgia was rice. Growing and harvesting rice was hard work. Many workers were needed, so rice growers also used slave labor. Rice was very popular in Europe. Its price kept rising. Farmers made more money from growing rice than from growing tobacco.

The Growth of Slavery

There was slavery in West Africa before the Europeans came to the Americas.

In the colonies, plantation owners needed workers. West African slave traders had workers to sell and began shipping enslaved people to America. Here, they were traded for goods. Slavery and the slave trade became important parts of the colonial economy.

Enslaved Africans were sent by ship to the Americas. Slave ships traveled from Europe to West Africa to buy or trade for slaves. Next, the ships went to the Americas. Here the slavers sold or traded the enslaved Africans. Finally, the ships returned to Europe, now filled with trade goods. This three-sided route (shaped like a triangle) was called the **triangular trade**. The second, or middle, part across the ocean from West Africa was called the "Middle Passage."

Many Africans died during the Middle Passage. Conditions on the ships were terrible. The slavers chained the enslaved Africans together. They could hardly sit or stand. They had little food or water. If they became sick or died, the slavers threw them into the sea. If they refused to eat, the slavers whipped them.

Life in the American Colonies

Lesson 1 Colonial Economy, *Continued*

When the slave ships reached American ports, plantation owners bought the survivors. Slave owners often split up families by selling a husband, wife, or child to another slave owner. Many colonies had **slave codes.** These were rules about the behavior and punishment of enslaved people.

On the plantations, some enslaved Africans worked in the houses, but most worked in the fields. A few learned trades, like weaving. Sometimes they set up shops and shared the money they made with the slaveholders. In this way, some earned enough money to buy their freedom.

In the colonies, there were also people who did not like slavery. They believed no human had the right to own another. Puritans, Quakers, and Mennonites were among those with this point of view.

/ / / / / / / / / / / / /Glue Foldable here/ / / / / / / / / / / / /

Check for Understanding

Why were New England farmers unable to grow cash crops?

_____

_____

Why were enslaved Africans brought to the colonies?

_____

_____

_____

Copyright by The McGraw-Hill Companies.

Vocabulary

9. What is a set of rules that says how enslaved people should behave and be punished?

_____

Reading Check

10. What role did enslaved Africans play in the economy of the Southern Colonies?

_____

_____

FOLDABLES®

11. Use a two-tab Foldable and place it along the dotted line to cover Check for Understanding. Write the title *Farming in the Colonies* on the anchor tab. Label the two tabs *Geography* and *Labor Force*. Recall and describe how the land and the work force affected farming in the colonies. Use the Foldable to help answer Check for Understanding.

netw⊙rks

Life in the American Colonies

Lesson 2 Colonial Government

ESSENTIAL QUESTION
How do new ideas change the way people live?

GUIDING QUESTIONS
1. **Why are protected rights and representative government important principles?**
2. **How did the colonists react to England's economic policies?**

Terms to Know
representative government a system by which people elect delegates to make laws and conduct government
mercantilism an economic theory whose goal is building a state's wealth and power by increasing exports and accumulating precious metals in return
export to sell to other countries
import to bring in from foreign markets

When did it happen?

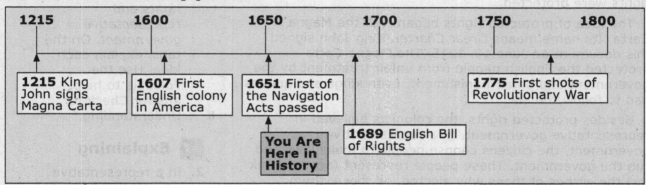

| 1215 | 1600 | 1650 | 1700 | 1750 | 1800 |

1215 King John signs Magna Carta

1607 First English colony in America

1651 First of the Navigation Acts passed

You Are Here in History

1689 English Bill of Rights

1775 First shots of Revolutionary War

What do you know?

Before you read, decide whether the following statements are true or false. Write a T or an F before each one. After you read, look at your answers again. Were they right or wrong?

_____ 1. English colonists in America believed the government should respect their rights.

_____ 2. English colonists in America believed the king should make all the laws.

_____ 3. The king of England controlled all the English colonies in America.

_____ 4. Everyone in the colonies could vote.

_____ 5. England forced the colonists to sell their raw materials to England.

netw⊙rks

Life in the American Colonies

Lesson 2 Colonial Government, *Continued*

English Principles of Government

/ / / / / / / / / Glue Foldable here / / / / / / / / / /

English colonists brought their ideas about government with them. Two beliefs were especially important to the English system of government. The first was in protected rights (rights that are protected by law), such as the right to a trial by jury. The second belief was in **representative government.** This is a system where voters elect people to make laws and run the government. Colonists believed that their lawmakers should represent the common people. Later, these two beliefs became important parts of the U.S. Constitution.

The colonists believed that government must respect the rights of the people it governs. Laws made sure these rights were protected.

The idea of protected rights began with the Magna Carta. Its name means *Great Charter*. King John signed this document on June 15, 1215. The Magna Carta protected the English people from unfair treatment by the government and unfair punishment. Even kings and queens had to follow the law.

Besides protected rights, the colonists believed in representative government. In a representative government, the citizens choose people to make laws and run the government. These people represent (act or speak for) the wishes of those who elected, or chose, them.

In England, these representatives gathered in the Parliament. It was made up of two parts, or houses: the House of Lords and the House of Commons. The House of Commons included commoners (everyday people). Most of these were property owners and merchants. The people in the House of Lords were members of the aristocracy— dukes, earls, barons, and so forth. Together, as Parliament, these two houses had the power to make laws.

Parliament was a model for the lawmaking branches of government in America. Like Parliament, the U.S. Congress has two houses: the House of Representatives and the Senate.

In the mid-1600s, King James II and Parliament struggled for control of the government. At last, in 1688, Parliament removed King James II from power. William and Mary became king and queen. The English call this peaceful change the Glorious Revolution. William and Mary promised to rule by the laws agreed upon in Parliament. From then on, no king or queen had more power than Parliament.

FOLDABLES®

Aᵇc Defining

1. Place a two-tab Foldable along the dotted line under the title "English Principles of Government." Write *Colonists Brought Ideas* on the anchor tab. Label the two tabs *protected rights* and *representative government*. On the tabs, explain each idea. Use the Foldable to help answer Check for Understanding.

Explaining

2. In a representative government, whom do the lawmakers represent?

_____

_____

☑ Reading Check

3. How did the Magna Carta influence government in the colonies?

_____

_____

_____

Life in the American Colonies

Lesson 2 Colonial Government, *Continued*

Identifying

4. In the colonies, whose wishes did the upper house usually represent?

_____

Drawing Conclusions

5. Why might a decision by the upper house upset the lower house?

_____

_____

Finding Examples

6. Name two exports from the colonies.

_____

_____

Explaining

7. If a colonist bought cloth from France, what happened to it under the rules of the Navigation Acts?

_____

_____

_____

In 1689, an important document set clear limits on a ruler's power. This was the English Bill of Rights. It limited the ruler's ability to set aside Parliament's laws. Rulers could no longer require taxes without Parliament's say-so. The bill said that members of Parliament would be freely elected. It gave citizens the right to a fair trial by jury. It banned cruel and unusual punishment.

How did these ideas of government work in the colonies? Some of the thirteen colonies were owned by an individual or group. They were called proprietary colonies. These colonies set up most of their own rules. Pennsylvania was a proprietary colony. Other colonies, like Massachusetts, had been started by a company with permission of the English king. They were called charter colonies.

In time, some colonies in America became royal colonies. This put them under direct English control. Virginia was a royal colony. In every royal colony, Parliament appointed (chose) a governor and a council. This was called the upper house. The colonists chose an assembly, called the lower house. The upper house usually did what the king and Parliament told them to do. Often this went against the wishes of the lower house.

Not everyone in the colonies had a voice in government. Only white men who owned property could vote. Even so, a large share of the population did take part in government in some way. In towns, people often met to talk about local issues. In time, town meetings turned into local governments. What they learned was useful when the colonies became independent.

English Economic Policies

In the early 1600s, many European nations followed an idea called **mercantilism.** Mercantilism is a system for building wealth and power by building supplies of gold and silver. To do this, a country must **export,** or sell, to other countries more than it **imports,** or buys, from them. A country must also set up colonies. Colonies have two purposes. They provide raw materials and are a market for exports.

The English followed this system of mercantilism. The American colonies provided raw materials. These raw materials might be crops such as tobacco and rice. They might be natural resources, too, like lumber and fur. The colonies also bought English-made goods such as tools, clothing, and furniture.

Life in the American Colonies

Lesson 2 Colonial Government, *Continued*

In the 1650s, the English passed laws to control Colonial trade. These were the Navigation Acts. They forced colonists to sell their raw materials to England. Also, if a colonist bought goods from a country in Europe, those goods went to England first. Here they were taxed, then shipped to the colony. In addition, all ships carrying trade goods had to be built in England or the colonies. The crews on these ships had to be English.

The colonists welcomed the trade laws at first. The laws made sure that the colonists had a place to sell their raw materials. Later, the colonists felt the laws limited their rights. They wanted to make their own products to sell. Also, they wanted to sell their products to countries other than England. Many colonial merchants began smuggling—shipping goods without paying taxes or getting permission from the English government. Later, controls on trade would cause problems between the colonies and England.

/////////////// Glue Foldable here ///////////////

Check for Understanding

How do people benefit from a limited government?

_____

_____

_____

Why did colonists begin smuggling goods into and out of the colonies?

_____

_____

_____

Copyright by The McGraw-Hill Companies.

Explaining

8. How did the trade laws help the colonists?

_____

_____

_____

Reading Check

9. What was the purpose of the Navigation Acts?

_____

_____

_____

FOLDABLES

10. Use a two-tab Foldable and place it along the dotted line to cover Check for Understanding. Write the title *Colonial Government* on the anchor tab. Label the two tabs— *British Actions* and *Colonial Reactions.* Write one thing that you remember about each. Use the Foldable to help answer Check for Understanding.

Life in the American Colonies

Lesson 3 Culture and Society

ESSENTIAL QUESTION
How do new ideas change the way people live?

GUIDING QUESTIONS
1. **What was life like for people living in the thirteen colonies?**
2. **What values and beliefs were important to the American colonists?**

Terms to Know
immigration the permanent movement of people into one country from other countries

epidemic an illness that affects a large number of people

apprentice a young person who learns a trade from a skilled craftsperson

civic virtue the democratic ideas, practices, and values that are at the heart of citizenship in a free society

Where in the world?

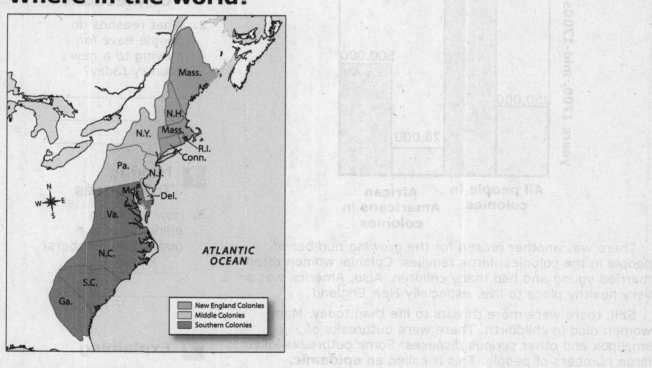

New England Colonies
Middle Colonies
Southern Colonies

ATLANTIC OCEAN

When did it happen?

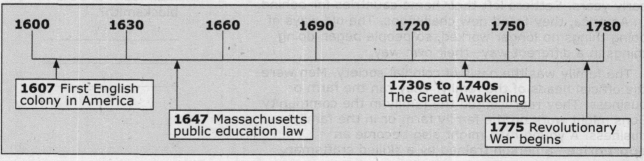

1600   1630   1660   1690   1720   1750   1780

1607 First English colony in America

1647 Massachusetts public education law

1730s to 1740s The Great Awakening

1775 Revolutionary War begins

53

networks

Life in the American Colonies

Lesson 3 Culture and Society, *Continued*

Life in the Colonies

In 1700, there were about 250,000 people living in the colonies. By the mid-1770s, there were about 2.5 million colonists. The number of African Americans grew from 28,000 to more than 500,000. **Immigration** was important to this growth. Immigration occurs when people move permanently to one country from another.

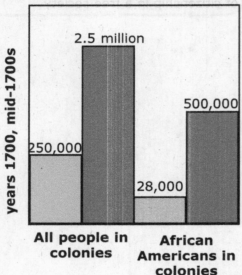

Colonial population growth

There was another reason for the growing number of people in the colonies: large families. Colonial women often married young and had many children. Also, America was a very healthy place to live, especially New England.

Still, there were more threats to life than today. Many women died in childbirth. There were outbreaks of smallpox and other serious diseases. Some outbreaks killed large numbers of people. This is called an **epidemic.**

The American spirit of independence began in these early years. Settlers left their home countries far behind. In America, they faced new challenges. The old ways of doing things no longer worked, so people began doing things in a different way—their own way.

The family was the basis of colonial society. Men were the official heads of the family. They ran the farm or business. They represented the family in the community. Sons might work on the family farm or in the family business. A young man might also become an **apprentice**—a person trained by a skilled craftsman.

54

Identifying

1. List two reasons why the population of the colonies was growing.

1. _____

2. _____

Making Connections

2. What reasons do people have for moving to a new country today?

_____

_____

_____

Making Inferences

3. How would an epidemic affect population numbers?

_____

_____

Explaining

4. How could a young man learn to be a blacksmith?

_____

_____

_____

Life in the American Colonies

Lesson 3 Culture and Society, *Continued*

✓ Reading Check

5. What was the role of the family in colonial life?

_____

_____

❓ Determining Cause and Effect

6. Why was there such a high level of literacy in New England?

_____

_____

_____

📝 Listing

7. List three different groups that might run a school.

_____

_____

✓ Reading Check

8. In what ways did the Great Awakening influence religion in the colonies?

_____

_____

_____

Women ran their homes and cared for the children. On farms, many worked in the fields with their husbands. A young, unmarried woman might work as a maid or cook for a wealthy family. A widow (a woman whose husband has died) might sew, teach, or nurse for a living. Widows and unmarried women also could run businesses and own property.

Even children worked. By the time they were four or five years old, they often had jobs. Even so, they did have time to play. Their games and toys were simple.

American Beliefs

Life in the colonies was built upon a strong, two-part foundation: the spirit of independence and the family.

Americans valued education. Parents often taught their children to read and write at home.

In New England and Pennsylvania, people set up schools. In 1647, Massachusetts passed a public education law. It said that communities with 50 or more homes must have a school. The result of this was a high level of literacy (the ability to read and write) in New England. By 1750, about 85 percent of the men and half of the women could read.

In the Middle Colonies, most schools were private. Widows and unmarried women ran many of them. Religious groups, such as Quakers, ran others.

Another kind of school was run by craftspeople. In these schools, apprentices learned a skill. Colleges in the colonies had a special purpose: to train ministers (people who lead religious worship).

Religion shaped much of colonial life. In the 1730s and 1740s, ministers were asking people to renew their faith— to return to the strong faith of earlier days. This renewal of religious faith was called the Great Awakening.

The Great Awakening inspired many new types of churches. These churches stressed personal faith rather than church ceremonies. The most important effect of the Great Awakening was greater religious freedom. More colonists began to choose their own faith. The older, more established churches lost power within the colonies.

The Great Awakening also broke down walls between the colonies. From north to south, the colonists were united by this revival of faith. This helped to spread other ideas— political ideas. In time, the colonies would also share the ideas of revolution and independence.

netw⊕rks

Life in the American Colonies

Lesson 3 Culture and Society, *Continued*

By the mid-1700s, another movement spread from Europe to the colonies—the Enlightenment. With it came the idea that knowledge, reason, and science could improve society. In the colonies, interest in science grew. People, like Benjamin Franklin, began to study nature, do experiments, and write about their findings. The Enlightenment also brought ideas about freedom of thought and expression, equality, and popular government.

Freedom of the press became important. Newspapers carried news about politics. Often the government did not like what the newspapers wrote and told them not to publish the information. The publishers fought this censorship. Their battle helped a free press to grow in the United States.

How should a citizen think, feel, and act in a free society? This is a question that colonists were beginning to think about. They began to wonder what **civic** (public or community) **virtues** (values) would be important to a free and democratic society.

////////////////Glue Foldable here ////////////////

Check for Understanding

How did respect for education influence colonial life in New England?

_____

_____

Which of the following values and beliefs were important to the colonists?

_____ **a.** free press

_____ **b.** religious freedom

_____ **c.** immigration

_____ **d.** education

_____ **e.** workers' rights

? Contrasting

9. How was the Enlightenment different from the Great Awakening?

_____

_____

_____

? Critical Thinking

10. Why is censorship an important issue in a free society?

_____

_____

_____

FOLDABLES®

11. Use a one-tab Foldable and place it along the dotted line to cover Check for Understanding. Write the title *Beliefs That Shaped America* on the anchor tab. Create a memory map by drawing five small arrows from the title to the tab and writing five words or phrases that you remember about the values and beliefs that influenced the colonies. Use the back to list other information.

net**w**orks

Life in the American Colonies

Lesson 4 Rivalry in North America

ESSENTIAL QUESTION
Why does conflict develop?

GUIDING QUESTIONS

1. **How did competition for land in North America lead to the French and Indian War?**
2. **What was the turning point in the French and Indian War?**
3. **How did the American colonists react to new British policies?**

Where in the world?

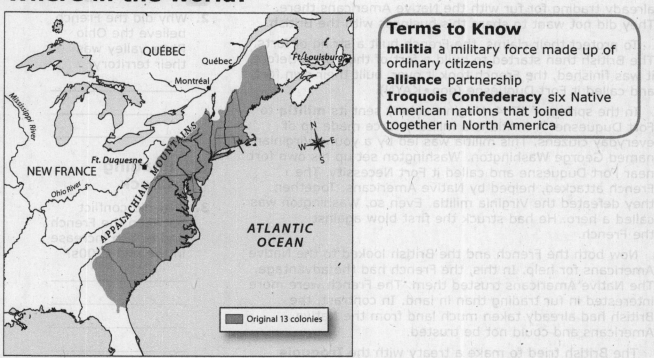

QUÉBEC

Québec

Ft. Louisburg

Montréal

Mississippi River

Ft. Duquesne

NEW FRANCE

Ohio River

APPALACHIAN MOUNTAINS

ATLANTIC OCEAN

Original 13 colonies

Terms to Know
militia a military force made up of ordinary citizens
alliance partnership
Iroquois Confederacy six Native American nations that joined together in North America

When did it happen?

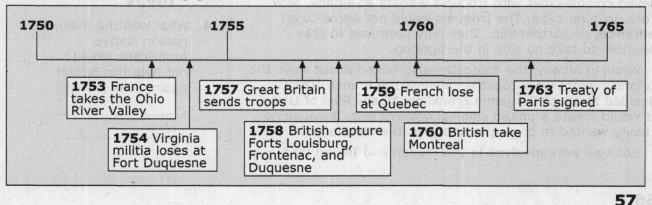

| 1750 | 1755 | 1760 | 1765 |

1753 France takes the Ohio River Valley

1754 Virginia militia loses at Fort Duquesne

1757 Great Britain sends troops

1758 British capture Forts Louisburg, Frontenac, and Duquesne

1759 French lose at Quebec

1760 British take Montreal

1763 Treaty of Paris signed

57

Lesson 4 Rivalry in North America, *Continued*

Rivalry Between the French and the British

In the 1700s, Britain and France were top world powers. They competed for colonies all over the world, including North America.

West of the thirteen English colonies were the Appalachian mountains. Beyond them was the Ohio River valley. This large area had many natural resources. Both the British and French wanted the region. The French were already trading for fur with the Native Americans there. They did not want to share this business with the British.

To protect their claims, the French built a string of forts. The British then started to build a fort of their own. Before it was finished, the French took it over, built their own fort, and called it Fort Duquesne (doo•KAYN).

In the spring of 1754, Virginia colony sent its **militia** to Fort Duquesne. A militia is a military force made up of everyday citizens. This militia was led by a young Virginian named George Washington. Washington set up his own fort near Fort Duquesne and called it Fort Necessity. The French attacked, helped by Native Americans. Together, they defeated the Virginia militia. Even so, Washington was called a hero. He had struck the first blow against the French.

Now both the French and the British looked to the Native Americans for help. In this, the French had the advantage. The Native Americans trusted them. The French were more interested in fur trading than in land. In contrast, the British had already taken much land from the Native Americans and could not be trusted.

The British tried to make a treaty with the **Iroquois Confederacy,** the most powerful group of Native Americans in eastern North America. Representatives from seven colonies met with Iroquois leaders at Albany, New York, in June 1754. The Iroquois would not agree to an **alliance,** or partnership. They only promised to stay neutral—to take no side in the fighting.

While in Albany, the delegates also talked about ways the colonies might work together against the French. They decided to adopt Benjamin Franklin's Albany Plan of Union. It would create a united colonial government. Because no colony wanted to give up any power, the plan failed.

Soon all were involved in the French and Indian War.

📝 Describing

1. What geographical area separated the colonies from the Ohio River valley?

_____

📝 Explaining

2. Why did the French believe the Ohio River valley was their territory?

_____

_____

_____

✅ Reading Check

3. Why did conflict between the French and British increase in the mid-1700s?

_____

_____

_____

_____

❓ Finding Main Ideas

4. What was the main reason Native Americans would not help the British against the French?

_____

_____

Life in the American Colonies

Lesson 4 Rivalry in North America, *Continued*

☑ **Reading Check**

5. Why was William Pitt successful at managing the war for Britain?

_____

_____

_____

✍ **Mark the Text**

6. Underline William Pitt's goals in the war with the French.

✍ **Explaining**

7. What event marked the turning point in the war?

_____

_____

? **Drawing Conclusions**

8. How could the Proclamation of 1763 calm the fighting between colonists and Native Americans?

_____

_____

_____

The French and Indian War

Early in the war, the French were winning. They captured several British forts. Their Native American allies were attacking colonists along the frontier, or edges, of the colonies.

In 1757, William Pitt became the leader of the British government. He was a great military planner. He decided to send more trained British soldiers to fight in North America. He also decided that Great Britain would pay the high cost of fighting the war—for now. Higher taxes on the colonies would pay for it later.

In North America, Pitt had two goals. The first was to open the Ohio River valley to the British. The second was to take over French Canada.

The British had a number of victories in 1758. The first was at Fort Louisburg, in present-day Nova Scotia. They also took Fort Frontenac at Lake Ontario and Fort Duquesne. This they renamed Fort Pitt.

In September 1759, the British won a major victory. They captured Quebec—the capital of New France. The following year, the British took Montreal. This ended the war in North America. The war continued in Europe until it finally ended with the Treaty of Paris in 1763.

In the treaty, Great Britain received Canada, Florida, and French lands east of the Mississippi. French lands west of the Mississippi—the Louisiana Territory—went to Spain.

New British Policies

The British now controlled the Ohio River valley. They would not pay for the use of Native American land and raised the price of their trade goods. Worst of all, British settlers began moving west.

In 1763, Pontiac, chief of an Ottawa village near Detroit, decided to fight back. His forces attacked British forts and killed settlers along the Pennsylvania and Virginia frontiers. This was called Pontiac's War.

Then something surprising happened in Britain. King George III ruled that colonists could not settle west of the Appalachian Mountains. This Proclamation of 1763 was useful to the British. It calmed the fighting between colonists and Native Americans. It also stopped colonists from leaving their colonies on the coast, where the important markets and businesses were. Britain sent ten thousand British troops to America to enforce the new rule.

Life in the American Colonies

Lesson 4 Rivalry in North America, *Continued*

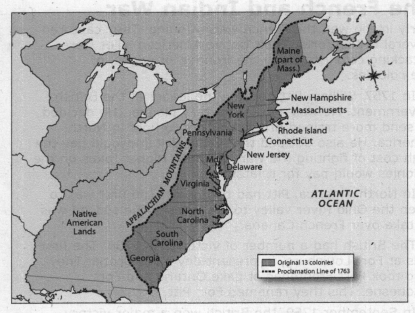

Map labels: Maine (part of Mass.), New Hampshire, New York, Massachusetts, Rhode Island, Connecticut, Pennsylvania, New Jersey, Delaware, Md., Virginia, North Carolina, South Carolina, Georgia, Native American Lands, APPALACHIAN MOUNTAINS, ATLANTIC OCEAN

Legend: Original 13 colonies — Proclamation Line of 1763

Colonists were alarmed. The proclamation limited their freedom of movement. British troops might take away their liberties. They began to distrust their British government.

//////////// Glue Foldable here ////////////////

Check for Understanding

Number these events in the French and Indian War in the order in which they happened.

_____ British capture Quebec

_____ Treaty of Paris signed

_____ Prime Minister Pitt sends British troops to North America

_____ French defeated at Montreal

How might William Pitt defend the decision to tax the colonies to pay for the war?

_____

_____

_____

_____

☑ Reading Check

9. Why were some colonists angered by the Proclamation of 1763?

_____

_____

❓ Critical Thinking

10. Why did the Proclamation of 1763 cause colonists to distrust Britain?

_____

FOLDABLES®

11. Use a three-tab Foldable and place it along the dotted line to cover Check for Understanding. Write the title *French and Indian War* on the anchor tab. Write the following questions on the three tabs: *What led to the war? What was the turning point? What was the reaction of Americans to the war?* Use both sides to record your answers. Use the Foldable to help complete Check for Understanding.

The Spirit of Independence

Lesson 1 No Taxation Without Representation

ESSENTIAL QUESTION
Why does conflict develop?

GUIDING QUESTIONS
1. **Why did the British government establish new policies?**
2. **How did the American colonists react to British policies?**

Terms to Know
revenue money raised from taxes or other sources
writ of assistance legal paper that allows officers to enter a place to search for smuggled goods
resolution a group's official expression of opinion
effigy a doll-like figure that is meant to stand for an unpopular individual
boycott protest by refusing to buy items
repeal cancel

Where in the world?

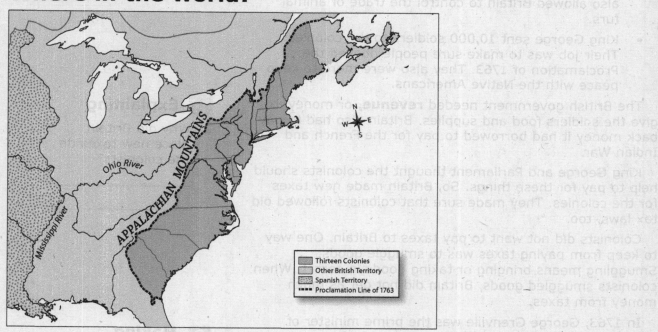

Ohio River
APPALACHIAN MOUNTAINS
Mississippi River

Thirteen Colonies
Other British Territory
Spanish Territory
Proclamation Line of 1763

When did it happen?

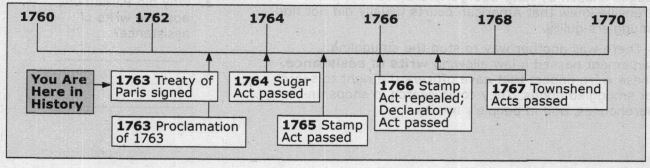

1760   1762   1764   1766   1768   1770

You Are Here in History

1763 Treaty of Paris signed

1763 Proclamation of 1763

1764 Sugar Act passed

1765 Stamp Act passed

1766 Stamp Act repealed; Declaratory Act passed

1767 Townshend Acts passed

netw⊚rks

The Spirit of Independence

Lesson 1 No Taxation Without Representation, *Continued*

Dealing With Great Britain

The French and Indian War was over. Now, the British controlled a lot of land in North America. They had to protect this land. To pay the costs of protecting the land, King George III made the Proclamation of 1763. A proclamation is an important announcement. These are the rules of the Proclamation of 1763.

- Colonists could not live on Native American lands that were west of the Appalachian Mountains. This would keep peace between settlers and Native Americans.

- This also made the colonists live close to the coast. It was easier for the British to control them that way. It also allowed Britain to control the trade of animal furs.

- King George sent 10,000 soldiers to the colonies. Their job was to make sure people obeyed the Proclamation of 1763. They also were there to keep peace with the Native Americans.

The British government needed **revenue,** or money, to give the soldiers food and supplies. Britain also had to pay back money it had borrowed to pay for the French and Indian War.

King George and Parliament thought the colonists should help to pay for these things. So, Britain made new taxes for the colonies. They made sure that colonists followed old tax laws, too.

Colonists did not want to pay taxes to Britain. One way to keep from paying taxes was to smuggle goods. Smuggling means bringing or taking goods in secret. When colonists smuggled goods, Britain did not get as much money from taxes.

In 1763, George Grenville was the prime minister of Britain. He wanted to stop the smuggling. Parliament passed a new law. The law said if a smuggler was caught, judges chosen by King George would hear the case. Grenville knew that American courts usually did not find smugglers guilty.

There was another way to stop the smuggling. Parliament passed a law allowing **writs of assistance.** These were papers that gave officers the right to search for smuggled goods. They could search in shops, in warehouses, and in people's homes.

Listing

1. State three reasons that Britain issued the Proclamation of 1763.

_____

_____

_____

Explaining

2. Why did Britain place new taxes on the colonists?

_____

_____

Making Inferences

3. Why did Parliament approve writs of assistance?

_____

_____

_____

The Spirit of Independence

Lesson 1 No Taxation Without Representation, *Continued*

✓ Reading Check

4. Why did Parliament pass the Sugar Act?

_____

_____

? Making Generalizations

5. Why didn't the colonists like the laws Parliament passed?

_____

_____

In 1764, Parliament passed a law called the Sugar Act. This law lowered the tax on molasses, a kind of sweetener. The British government hoped that colonists would pay a lower tax instead of smuggling. The law also allowed officers to take smuggled goods without getting permission.

Colonists were angry about the Sugar Act. They knew that they were British citizens. They knew that British citizens had certain rights:

- They had the right to a jury trial.

- According to law, they were innocent until proven guilty.

- They had the right to feel safe in their homes without soldiers coming in to search for smuggled goods.

New Taxes on the Colonies

In 1765 Parliament passed the Stamp Act. This law taxed printed items, such as newspapers. Colonists did not like the Stamp Act at all.

In Virginia, a representative named Patrick Henry did not like the law. He convinced the House of Burgesses to act against the law. They passed a **resolution** against the Stamp Act. A resolution is an official statement.

The resolution said that only the Virginia assembly had the power to tax Virginia citizens.

In Boston, Samuel Adams worked against the Stamp Act. He helped to start a protest group called the Sons of Liberty. The Sons of Liberty burned **effigies** (EH•fuh•jeez), or large, stuffed dolls. The dolls were made to look like tax collectors.

In October 1765, delegates from nine colonies met in New York. The meeting was called the Stamp Act Congress. The delegates wrote a resolution. They sent it to the British Parliament and to King George. Colonial businessmen decided to **boycott,** or refuse to buy, British goods. Many businessmen promised not to buy or use goods that came from Britain.

People followed the boycott. Not enough people were buying British goods. As a result, British merchants lost a lot of money. British merchants asked Parliament to **repeal,** or cancel, the Stamp Act.

networks

The Spirit of Independence

Lesson 1 No Taxation Without Representation, *Continued*

In 1766, Parliament canceled the law. It passed another law instead. This law was the Declaratory Act. It said that Parliament had the right to tax the colonists.

In 1767 Parliament passed the Townshend Acts. The Townshend Acts taxed goods that were imported, or brought into, the colonies. By now, any British taxes made colonists angry. Groups of women protested. They told colonists to make cloth at home and wear it. This way, they would not have to buy cloth from Britain. Some of these groups called themselves the Daughters of Liberty.

//////////////////Glue Foldable here/////////////////////

Check for Understanding
List two laws that taxed colonists.

_____

_____

Name three ways that colonists protested the tax laws passed by Parliament.

_____

_____

Mark the Text

6. Circle the words that explain what the Daughters of Liberty encouraged people to do to protest the taxes.

✔ **Reading Check**

7. How did the Townshend Acts differ from the Stamp Act?

_____

_____

FOLDABLES®

8. Use a three-tab Foldable and place it along the dotted line to cover Check for Understanding. Write the title *Taxes* on the anchor tab. Label the tabs *Sugar Act*, *Stamp Act*, and *Townshend Acts*. Use both sides of the tabs to list facts you remember about taxes placed on the colonists. Use the Foldable to help answer Check for Understanding.

64

netw⊗rks

The Spirit of Independence

Lesson 2 Uniting the Colonists

ESSENTIAL QUESTION
Why does conflict develop?

GUIDING QUESTIONS
1. **How did the American colonists react to the Boston Massacre?**
2. **How did the British government react to the actions of the colonists?**

Terms to Know

rebellion open defiance of authority

propaganda ideas or information spread to harm or help a cause

committee of correspondence an organization that spread political ideas and information through the colonies

When did it happen?

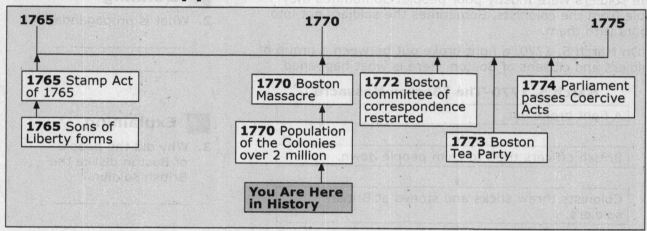

1765   1770   1775

1765 Stamp Act of 1765

1765 Sons of Liberty forms

1770 Boston Massacre

1770 Population of the Colonies over 2 million

You Are Here in History

1772 Boston committee of correspondence restarted

1773 Boston Tea Party

1774 Parliament passes Coercive Acts

What do you know?

In the first column, answer the questions based on what you know before you study. After this lesson, complete the last column.

Now...		Later...
	Who was Crispus Attucks?	
	How did the colonists use propaganda?	

65

The Spirit of Independence

Lesson 2 Uniting the Colonists, *Continued*

Trouble in Massachusetts

Colonists kept on protesting. This made British officials nervous. In 1768 they sent a message to Britain. The message said the colonies were close to **rebellion.** Rebellion means to reject the rules and authority of Britain.

Parliament sent soldiers, called "redcoats," to the city of Boston, Massachusetts. These redcoats set up camp in the center of Boston.

Now, the colonists decided the British had gone too far. Besides, British soldiers were rude to the people of Boston. The soldiers were mostly poor people. Sometimes they stole from the colonists. Sometimes the soldiers got into fights with them.

On March 5, 1770, a fight broke out between a group of soldiers and citizens of Boston. Here is what happened.

March 5, 1770–The "Boston Massacre"

A fight broke out.

↓

British officers tried to calm people down.

↓

Colonists threw sticks and stones at British soldiers.

↓

The soldiers became afraid. They fired their guns into the crowd.

↓

Five colonists were killed.

One of the colonists was Crispus Attucks. He was a worker on the docks. He was part African and part Native American.

The colonists called the event the "Boston Massacre." A massacre is when a large number of people are killed. Colonists used the killings as **propaganda.** Propaganda is using information to make people think or feel a certain way. Samuel Adams put up posters to make people angry at the British. The posters showed soldiers killing the citizens of Boston.

Many colonists called for stronger boycotts. Parliament repealed, or took away, most of the Townshend Acts, but they kept the tax on tea. As a result, colonists ended most of their boycotts. They still kept the boycott on tea.

Mark the Text

1. Locate and underline the definition of *rebellion.*

Defining

2. What is propaganda?

_____

_____

Explaining

3. Why did the people of Boston dislike the British soldiers?

_____

_____

Reading Check

4. What changed after the Boston Massacre?

_____

_____

_____

The Spirit of Independence

Lesson 2 Uniting the Colonists, *Continued*

? Understanding Cause and Effect

5. Why did Parliament pass the Tea Act?

_____

_____

6. Why did Parliament pass the Coercive Acts?

_____

_____

In 1772 Samuel Adams restarted a group called the **committee of correspondence.** The group wrote their complaints about Britain and the British. They sent these writings around to many places. More committees of correspondence started in other colonies. These groups brought protesters together and made them stronger against the British.

Crisis in Boston

There was a British company called the British East India Company. It was not doing well. The reason was that colonists were not importing their tea. They were nearly out of business.

Parliament passed a law to help save the company. The law was the Tea Act. The Tea Act gave the company almost total control of the tea market in the colonies. The Tea Act also took away some, but not all, of the taxes on tea. Colonists did not want to pay any taxes on tea. They also did not want Parliament telling them what tea to buy.

Colonists called for a new boycott. They decided to stop ships from the British East India Company from unloading their tea. The Daughters of Liberty put out a booklet. It said that rather than part with freedom, "We'll part with our tea."

Still, the British East India Company kept on shipping tea to the colonies. Colonists in New York and Philadelphia made the ships turn back.

In 1773, three tea ships arrived in Boston Harbor. The royal governor ordered the ships to be unloaded. On the night of December 16, 1773, the Sons of Liberty in Boston took action. They dressed up as Native Americans and boarded the ships. They threw 342 large boxes of tea overboard. This event became known as the "Boston Tea Party." King George III heard about the Boston Tea Party. He saw that Britain was losing control of the colonies.

In 1774, Britain passed the Coercive (co • UHR • sihv) Acts. *Coercive* means "for the purpose of forcing someone." These laws were passed to punish the colonies. One of the laws forced colonists to let British soldiers live among them.

Massachusetts was punished the hardest. There could be no more town meetings there. Boston Harbor was closed until colonists paid for the tea they had thrown overboard.

The Spirit of Independence

Lesson 2 Uniting the Colonists, *Continued*

With the harbor closed, no other food or supplies could get into Boston. The Coercive Acts united the colonists. They sent food and clothing to Boston.

Parliament then passed the Quebec Act. This law created a government for Canada. Canada's border was the Ohio River, much further south than present-day Canada.

Colonists said all these laws violated their rights as English citizens. Colonists called these laws the Intolerable Acts. *Intolerable* means "unbearable."

/ / / / / / / / / / / / / / Glue Foldable here / / / / / / / / / /

Check for Understanding

What kinds of propaganda were used in reporting about the "Boston Massacre"?

_____

_____

_____

How are the Boston Tea Party and the Intolerable Acts connected?

_____

_____

_____

Copyright by The McGraw-Hill Companies.

☑ **Reading Check**

7. List the effects of the Coercive Acts on the citizens of Boston.

_____

_____

FOLDABLES®

8. Use a one-tab Foldable and place it along the dotted line to cover Check for Understanding. Write the title *Memory Map* on the anchor tab. Write *Colonists React* in the middle of the Foldable tab and draw arrows from the title. Write terms you remember that explain the actions of the colonists. Define the terms on the back of the tab. Use the Foldable to help answer Check for Understanding.

networks

The Spirit of Independence

Lesson 3 A Call to Arms

ESSENTIAL QUESTION
What motivates people to act?

GUIDING QUESTIONS
1. **What role did key individuals play in the movement toward independence?**
2. **Why were the battles at Lexington and Concord important?**
3. **What were the beliefs of the Loyalists and Patriots?**

Terms to Know
minutemen people who could be ready to fight as soldiers with one minute's notice
Loyalists American colonists who remained loyal to Britain and were against the war for independence
Patriots American colonists who wanted American independence

When did it happen?

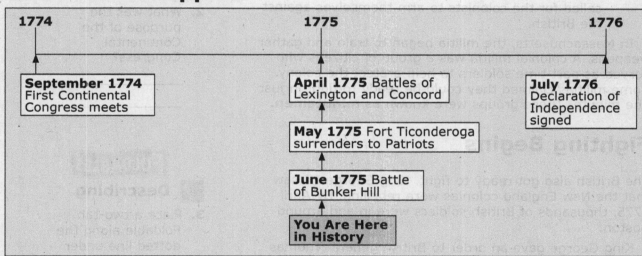

| 1774 | 1775 | 1776 |

September 1774 First Continental Congress meets

April 1775 Battles of Lexington and Concord

May 1775 Fort Ticonderoga surrenders to Patriots

June 1775 Battle of Bunker Hill

You Are Here in History

July 1776 Declaration of Independence signed

What do you know?

In the first column, answer the questions based on what you know before you study. After this lesson, complete the last column.

Now...		Later...
	Who was Thomas Gage?	
	Where is Breed's Hill? What happened there?	

69

The Spirit of Independence

Lesson 3 A Call to Arms, *Continued*

A Meeting in Philadelphia

Fifty-five delegates met in Philadelphia. They came from every colony except Georgia. They met to discuss how the colonies could challenge British control. The meeting was called the Continental Congress. John Adams, Samuel Adams, and Patrick Henry were delegates. John Jay, Richard Henry Lee, and George Washington were also delegates.

The delegates to the Continental Congress:

- **issued** a statement asking Parliament to repeal several laws that violated colonists' rights.

- **voted** to boycott trade with Britain. This included all goods coming into and going out of the colonies.

- **decided** to approve the Suffolk Resolves. This called for the colonists to arm themselves against the British.

In Massachusetts, the militia began to train and gather weapons. A colonial militia was a group of citizens who served as part-time soldiers to help protect the colony. Some militias claimed they could be ready to fight in just one minute. These groups were known as **minutemen.**

Fighting Begins

/ / / / / / / / / / / / Glue Foldable here / / / / / / / / / / / /

The British also got ready to fight. King George III saw that the New England colonies were rebelling. By April 1775, thousands of British soldiers were in and around Boston.

King George gave an order to British general Thomas Gage. He told General Gage to get rid of the militia's weapons. He ordered General Gage to arrest the militia's leaders. General Gage heard that the militia kept its weapons in a town near Boston. The name of the town was Concord. On April 18, 1775, Gage sent 700 soldiers to Concord to destroy the weapons.

Colonists in Boston saw the soldiers march out of town. Paul Revere and William Dawes, members of the Sons of Liberty, rode to Lexington. Lexington was a town near Concord. They warned colonists that the British were coming.

About 70 minutemen met the British at Lexington. Someone fired a shot, and then both sides began firing.

Listing

1. List three things the Continental Congress did.

Reading Check

2. What was the purpose of the Continental Congress?

_____

_____

FOLDABLES®

Describing

3. Place a two-tab Foldable along the dotted line under the heading "Fighting Begins." Write the title *Fighting Begins* on the anchor tab. Label the two tabs *Lexington* and *Concord*. On both sides of the tabs, list words and phrases to describe each encounter.

The Spirit of Independence

Lesson 3 A Call to Arms, *Continued*

? Sequencing

4. Number the events in the order in which they happened.

_____ Revere and Dawes warn that the British are coming.

_____ Battle of Concord

_____ British soldiers ordered to destroy the Massachusetts militia's weapons.

_____ Battle of Lexington

✓ Reading Check

5. Why did British troops march to Concord?

_____

_____

✓ Reading Check

6. What did the British learn from the Battle of Bunker Hill?

_____

_____

Eight minutemen were killed. The British moved on to Concord. They found that most of the militia's gunpowder had been taken away. They destroyed all the supplies that were left. Then the minutemen fought with the British soldiers. They forced the soldiers to turn back.

Word quickly spread that the British were on the move. Along the road from Concord to Boston, colonists hid behind trees and fences. As British troops marched back to Boston, the colonists fired. By the time the British reached Boston, 73 of their soldiers had been killed. At least 174 soldiers had been wounded.

More Military Action

After what happened at Lexington and Concord, many colonists joined militias. Benedict Arnold was an officer in the Connecticut militia. He got 400 men to join his militia.

Benedict Arnold and his army set out to capture Fort Ticonderoga on Lake Champlain. He joined forces with Ethan Allen and the Vermont militia. The Vermont militia were called the Green Mountain Boys.

Together, the two groups attacked the British soldiers. It was a surprise attack. The British surrendered Fort Ticonderoga on May 10, 1775.

Later, Benedict Arnold turned against the Patriot cause. He sold military information to the British. When he was found out, he fled to New York City. New York City was controlled by the British. Arnold commanded British soldiers. He led attacks against the Americans.

More American soldiers began joining colonial militias. Before long, there were about 20,000 militiamen around Boston. On June 16, 1775, Colonel William Prescott had his militia set themselves up on Bunker Hill and Breed's Hill. These places were across the harbor from Boston. The British decided to force the colonists from the hills.

The next day, British soldiers charged up Breed's Hill. (However, this battle is called the Battle of Bunker Hill.) The Americans were running out of ammunition, and Prescott is said to have shouted, "Don't fire until you see the whites of their eyes."

The militia fired. They stopped the British attack. Twice more the British attacked, but were stopped. Finally, the Americans ran out of gunpowder. They had to retreat. The British won this battle, but more than 1,000 of their soldiers were killed or wounded. The British were learning that it was going to be a hard fight against the Americans.

The Spirit of Independence

Lesson 3 A Call to Arms, *Continued*

News about the battles spread. Colonists had to decide whether to join the rebels or stay loyal to Britain. Colonists on the British side were called **Loyalists.** They did not think that unfair taxes and unfair laws were good reasons to fight. Many believed the British would win and did not want to be on the losing side. Colonists who supported the war for independence were called **Patriots.** They felt they could no longer live under British rule. The American Revolution was not just a war between the British and the Americans. It was also a war between American Patriots and American Loyalists.

//////////////// Glue Foldable here ////////////////

Check for Understanding

Identify each battle.

The first shot of the American Revolution is fired.

_____

The Green Mountain Boys catch the British by surprise.

_____

The British attack uphill.

_____

What is the difference between a Loyalist and a Patriot?

_____

_____

_____

FOLDABLES®

7. Place a three-tab Foldable along the dotted line to cover Check for Understanding. Write *Loyalist or Patriot* on the anchor tab. Label the tabs *Paul Revere, Both,* and *Benedict Arnold.* On the reverse sides, write words and phrases that you remember about each to compare and contrast the men. Use the Foldable to help answer Check for Understanding.

networks

The Spirit of Independence

Lesson 4 Declaring Independence

ESSENTIAL QUESTION
What motivates people to act?

GUIDING QUESTIONS
1. **How did individuals and events impact efforts for independence?**
2. **Why did the American colonies declare independence?**

When did it happen?

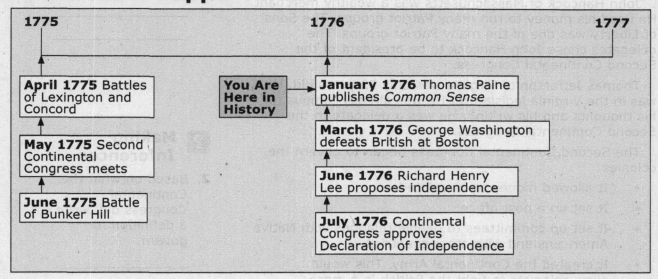

1775

1776

1777

April 1775 Battles of Lexington and Concord

May 1775 Second Continental Congress meets

June 1775 Battle of Bunker Hill

You Are Here in History

January 1776 Thomas Paine publishes *Common Sense*

March 1776 George Washington defeats British at Boston

June 1776 Richard Henry Lee proposes independence

July 1776 Continental Congress approves Declaration of Independence

What do you know?

In the first column, answer the questions based on what you know before you study. After this lesson, complete the last column.

Now...		Later...
	What was the Second Continental Congress?	
	What was the booklet, *Common Sense*?	
	What did Jefferson have to do with the Declaration of Independence?	

The Spirit of Independence

Lesson 4 Declaring Independence, *Continued*

The Second Continental Congress

On May 10, 1775, the Second Continental Congress met. The delegates included some of the greatest leaders in America. Among them were John and Samuel Adams, Patrick Henry, Richard Henry Lee, and George Washington. Several new delegates came as well.

Benjamin Franklin of Pennsylvania was well respected. He had been a leader in the Pennsylvania legislature. In 1765 he had gone to London and worked to have the Stamp Act repealed.

John Hancock of Massachusetts was a wealthy merchant. He used his money to run many Patriot groups. The Sons of Liberty was one of the many Patriot groups. The delegates chose John Hancock to be president of the Second Continental Congress.

Thomas Jefferson of Virginia was only 32 years old. He was in the Virginia legislature. He was already famous for his thoughts and his writing. He was a delegate to the Second Continental Congress.

The Second Continental Congress began to govern the colonies.

- It allowed money to be printed.
- It set up a post office.
- It set up committees to handle relations with Native Americans and with other countries.
- It created the Continental Army. This would allow colonists to fight the British in a more organized way.
- It chose George Washington to command the army.

The Congress gave Britain one more chance to avoid war. It sent a **petition,** a formal request, to King George III. The request was called the Olive Branch Petition. It said that the colonists wanted peace. It asked King George to protect their rights. King George would not accept the petition. Instead, he got ready for war.

The Americans found out that British soldiers were planning to attack New York from Canada. The Americans decided to attack first. They sent soldiers northward from Fort Ticonderoga and captured Montreal.

In July 1775, George Washington arrived in Boston. He found the militia was not well organized, so he trained them. He brought many cannons from far away.

Listing

1. Name five delegates to the Second Continental Congress.

_____

_____

_____

_____

Making Inferences

2. Based on what the Continental Congress did, write a definition for *govern*.

_____

_____

Reading Check

3. What was the purpose of the Olive Branch Petition?

_____

_____

The Spirit of Independence

Lesson 4 Declaring Independence, *Continued*

Mark the Text

4. Underline the name of the booklet and the author who encouraged independence from Britain.

Specifying

5. Who was chosen to write the Declaration of Independence?

_____

_____

✓ Reading Check

6. According to John Locke, what is the purpose of government?

_____

_____

In March 1776, Washington decided the soldiers were ready to fight. He moved the soldiers and the cannons to the hills overlooking Boston while the British soldiers slept.

The British were surprised. British General William Howe commanded his soldiers to sail away from Boston. On March 17, Washington led his soldiers into the city.

Colonist Thomas Paine wrote a booklet called *Common Sense*. It explained why complete independence from Britain would be a good thing. Paine's words had a great effect on colonists and how they felt.

Declaring Independence

The delegates at the Second Continental Congress argued back and forth. Some wanted the colonies to declare independence. Others did not. In June 1776, Richard Henry Lee of Virginia came up with a resolution. The resolution stated that the United Colonies should be free and independent states, a new nation.

Congress chose a committee to write a Declaration of Independence. John Adams, Benjamin Franklin, Thomas Jefferson, Robert Livingston, and Roger Sherman were on the committee. Adams asked Jefferson to write it.

Jefferson was inspired by the ideas of an English philosopher named John Locke.

John Locke's Ideas
People have the right to life, liberty and property.
• People are born with these rights.
• People form a government to protect their rights.
• If the government does not protect their rights, people can get rid of the government.

The delegates discussed Jefferson's Declaration of Independence. They made some changes. Then they approved it on July 4, 1776. John Hancock signed first. He said he wrote his name large enough for King George to read without his glasses. Eventually 56 delegates signed the document announcing the birth of the United States.

Copies were made and sent to the states. George Washington had the Declaration read to his soldiers.

The Spirit of Independence

Lesson 4 Declaring Independence, *Continued*

The Declaration of Independence has four main parts.

1. First is a **preamble,** or introduction. It says that people who wish to form a new country should explain their reasons.

2. and **3.** The next two parts list the rights that the colonists believed they should have and their complaints against Britain.

4. The last section announces that they have formed a new nation.

John Adams thought July 2, 1776, should be the holiday that celebrated independence. This was the day that the Congress voted for independence. Instead, July 4 is celebrated today as Independence Day. This is the day the Declaration was approved.

////////////////Glue Foldable here/////////////////

Check for Understanding

Explain the connection between John Locke, Thomas Jefferson, and the Declaration of Independence.

_____

_____

_____

What was the most important result of the Declaration of Independence??

_____

_____

FOLDABLES®

7. Use a one-tab Foldable and place it along the dotted line to cover Check for Understanding. Write *Declaration of Independence* in the middle of the Foldable tab and draw arrows from the title to words and short phrases that you recall about the Declaration of Independence. Use the Foldable to help answer Check for Understanding.

networks

The American Revolution

Lesson 1 The War for Independence

ESSENTIAL QUESTION
Why does conflict develop?

GUIDING QUESTIONS

1. **Who were the opposing sides in the American Revolution?**

2. **What were significant battles in the early years of the American Revolution?**

3. **Was the British plan for victory successful?**

Terms to Know
mercenary hired soldier
recruit to enlist in the military

Where in the world?

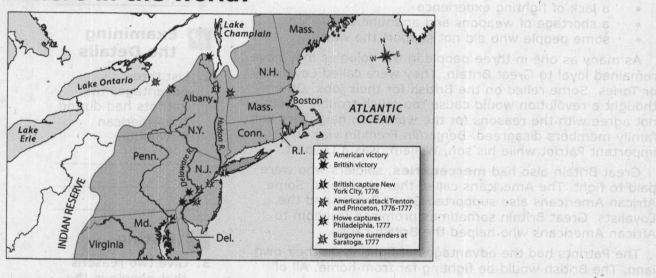

When did it happen?

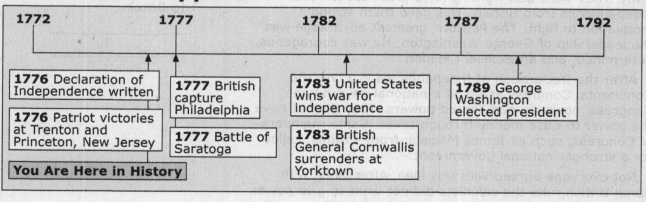

1772   1777   1782   1787   1792

1776 Declaration of Independence written

1776 Patriot victories at Trenton and Princeton, New Jersey

You Are Here in History

1777 British capture Philadelphia

1777 Battle of Saratoga

1783 United States wins war for independence

1783 British General Cornwallis surrenders at Yorktown

1789 George Washington elected president

77

The American Revolution

Lesson 1 The War for Independence, *Continued*

The Two Armies Face Off

The British felt they would crush the colonists. The colonists thought Great Britain would give up quickly after losing a few battles.

The British were confident because they had:
- the strongest navy in the world
- a well-trained army
- great wealth from their worldwide empire
- a large population (over 8 million people)

In comparison, the colonists had
- a weak navy
- no regular army, just local militia groups
- a lack of fighting experience
- a shortage of weapons and ammunition
- some people who did not support the war.

As many as one in three people in the colonies may have remained loyal to Great Britain. They were called Loyalists, or Tories. Some relied on the British for their jobs. Others thought a revolution would cause too much trouble or did not agree with the reasons for the war. Even neighbors and family members disagreed. Benjamin Franklin was an important Patriot while his son, William, was a Loyalist.

Great Britain also had **mercenaries**, soldiers who were paid to fight. The Americans called them Hessians. Some African Americans also supported Great Britain and the Loyalists. Great Britain sometimes promised freedom to African Americans who helped the British cause.

The Patriots had the advantages of fighting on their own land. The British would be fighting far from home. All of the British supplies and soldiers had to come from far away. They were also fighting for a great cause—their independence from Britain. This gave them strong motivation to fight. The Patriots' greatest advantage was the leadership of George Washington. He was courageous, determined, and an excellent leader.

After the Declaration of Independence in 1776, the Continental Congress acted as a national government. Congress, however, had limited powers. They did not have the power to raise money through taxes. Some members of Congress, such as James Madison from Virginia, called for a stronger national government.

Not everyone agreed with this idea. After living with harsh British rule, the colonists did not want to give power to the new government. This made it hard for Congress to raise money and **recruit**, or enlist, soldiers.

☑ Reading Check

1. What disadvantages did the Patriots face in fighting the British?

_____

_____

_____

🖌 Examining the Details

2. List three advantages the Patriots had during the American Revolution.

_____

_____

_____

🖌 Listing

3. Give two reasons that people in the colonies stayed loyal to Britain.

_____

_____

networks

The American Revolution

Lesson 1 The War for Independence, *Continued*

? Critical Thinking

4. Why did Congress need to establish the Continental Army?

_____

_____

📝 Identifying

5. Name three women who were involved in the fighting.

_____

_____

_____

📝 Comparing

6. How did the number of British troops compare with the number of American troops?

_____

_____

✓ Reading Check

7. About how many African Americans fought in the war?

_____

_____

Many of the troops were members of a local militia, or people who are called to fight when needed. Many needed to tend to their farms to support their families. Congress established the Continental Army so that soldiers could be trained and paid. At first, soldiers signed up for a year at a time. General Washington, however, felt soldiers should agree to stay until the war was over. It was also difficult to find good leaders. Some were capable young men from the army. Others had experience in earlier wars.

A few women were involved in the fighting. Margaret Corbin went with her husband, then took his place when he died in battle. A legend says that a woman called "Molly Pitcher" fought in the war and brought pitchers of water to the soldiers. Deborah Sampson disguised herself as a man so she could join the fight, too.

Early Campaigns

Early battles of the American Revolution were fought by smaller numbers of soldiers. At Bunker Hill, in Massachusetts, about 2,200 British soldiers fought about 1,200 Americans. The British outnumbered the Americans and won the battle, but lost many more troops. They quickly realized more troops were needed to fight the war.

In 1776, Great Britain sent 32,000 more troops to help fight the war. The Patriots did not have a large army, about 20,000 soldiers, but they were very determined. In August 1776, the two armies met in the Battle of Long Island in New York. The British caught a Patriot spy, Nathan Hale. Before he was hanged, Hale supposedly said, "I only regret that I have but one life to lose for my country."

The British had more men and more supplies. Many Patriot soldiers had no shoes, socks, or jackets. The Battle of Long Island was a serious defeat for the Continental Army. The British leader chased the Continental Army across New Jersey into Pennsylvania. He could have probably captured all of the Patriot troops, but he was satisfied that Washington was defeated, and he let him go.

This was a difficult time for the Continental Army. Even General Washington worried. They needed more men and more supplies. Many African Americans wanted to join the Army but were not allowed to. Washington asked Congress to reconsider. Historians estimate that around 5,000 African Americans eventually fought.

General Washington did not give up. On Christmas night, he and his troops crossed the icy Delaware River. He

79

The American Revolution

Lesson 1 The War for Independence, *Continued*

surprised a Hessian force camped in Trenton, New Jersey. After this victory, they marched on to Princeton, New Jersey. Washington pushed back the British troops they met there. The battles encouraged the troops to believe they could win.

British Strategy

The British had a plan to win in 1777. They wanted to cut off New England from the Middle Colonies. They needed to take Albany, New York, and control the Hudson River. The British plan involved coming in to Albany from three directions at the same time. General Burgoyne would move south from Canada, Lieutenant Colonel St. Leger would move east from Lake Ontario, and General Howe would move north up the Hudson River.

General Howe changed his plans, capturing Philadelphia instead. The Continental Congress was forced to escape. Howe stayed in Philadelphia for the winter. St. Leger also lost a battle to the Americans and did not reach Albany.

General Burgoyne captured Fort Ticonderoga in July 1777, but needed supplies. He sent troops to Vermont, but the local militia, called the Green Mountain Boys, attacked. Burgoyne's troops retreated to Saratoga, New York. There, American general Horatio Gates surrounded them and Burgoyne surrendered on October 17, 1777.

The British plan to take Albany and the Hudson River had failed. The Americans had won a huge victory at Saratoga. The American win at the Battle of Saratoga changed the course of the war.

/ / / / / / / / / / / / / Glue Foldable here / / / / / / / / / / / /

Check for Understanding

List two important American wins in the early days of the American Revolution.

1. _____

2. _____

Give two reasons that the British plan to take Albany failed.

1. _____

2. _____

? Critical Thinking

8. What was the British plan in 1777?

_____

_____

✓ Reading Check

9. How did Howe's victory in Philadelphia lead to Burgoyne's defeat at Saratoga?

_____

_____

FOLDABLES

10. Place a one-tab Foldable along the dotted line to cover Check for Understanding. Write the title *Factors that led to Independence* on the anchor tab. Create a memory map by drawing five small arrows from the title to the tab and writing what you remember about the advantages the Patriots had that helped them win their independence. Use the Foldable to help answer Check for Understanding.

The American Revolution

Lesson 2 The War Continues

ESSENTIAL QUESTION
Why does conflict develop?

GUIDING QUESTIONS
1. **How did America gain allies?**
2. **What was life like on the home front during the American Revolution?**

Terms to Know
desert to leave without permission or intent to come back
inflation when it takes more and more money to buy the same amount of goods

Where in the world?

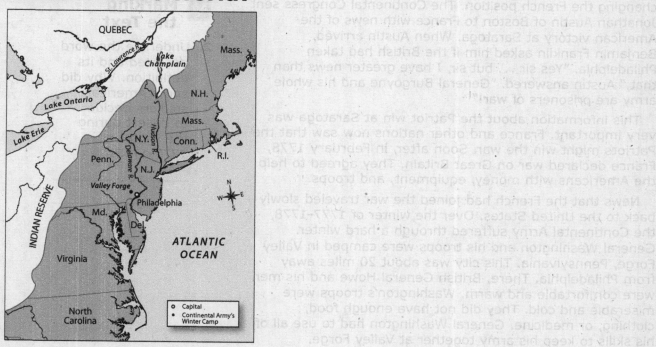

When did it happen?

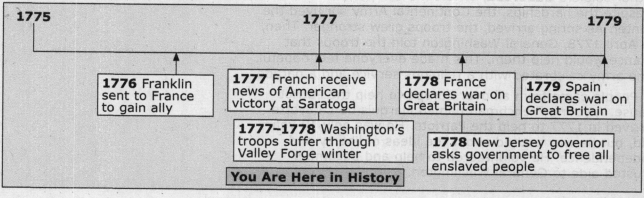

| 1775 | | 1777 | | 1779 |

1776 Franklin sent to France to gain ally

1777 French receive news of American victory at Saratoga

1778 France declares war on Great Britain

1779 Spain declares war on Great Britain

1777–1778 Washington's troops suffer through Valley Forge winter

1778 New Jersey governor asks government to free all enslaved people

You Are Here in History

The American Revolution

Lesson 2 The War Continues, *Continued*

Gaining Allies

The United States needed help to win the American Revolution. The Continental Congress sent Benjamin Franklin to France in 1776. Franklin was a charming, skilled statesman and was very popular in France. The Continental Congress hoped he would be able to win French support for the American war. Early on, the French secretly gave the Americans money for their cause. They did not want to openly take sides against Great Britain.

Some news arrived in 1777, however, that ended up changing the French position. The Continental Congress sent Jonathan Austin of Boston to France with news of the American victory at Saratoga. When Austin arrived, Benjamin Franklin asked him if the British had taken Philadelphia. "Yes sir ... but sir, I have greater news than that," Austin answered. "General Burgoyne and his whole army are prisoners of war!"

This information about the Patriot win at Saratoga was very important. France and other nations now saw that the Patriots might win the war. Soon after, in February 1778, France declared war on Great Britain. They agreed to help the Americans with money, equipment, and troops.

News that the French had joined the war traveled slowly back to the United States. Over the winter of 1777–1778, the Continental Army suffered through a hard winter. General Washington and his troops were camped in Valley Forge, Pennsylvania. This city was about 20 miles away from Philadelphia. There, British General Howe and his men were comfortable and warm. Washington's troops were miserable and cold. They did not have enough food, clothing, or medicine. General Washington had to use all of his skills to keep his army together at Valley Forge.

Many soldiers got sick. Many died. Some soldiers quit. Other soldiers **deserted**, or left without permission. Despite the hardships, the Continental Army survived the winter. As spring arrived, the troops grew stronger. Then, in April 1778, General Washington told the troops that France would help them. This made everyone feel hopeful. The army celebrated with a religious service and a parade.

People came from all over Europe to help the Patriot cause. A young Frenchman named Marquis de Lafayette arrived in 1777 to help the Patriots. He was only 19 years old, but he was excited about the ideas of liberty and independence. He volunteered to help and became a trusted aide to General Washington.

🖊 Explaining

1. Why was the Battle of Saratoga an important victory for the Patriots?

_____

_____

🔤 Marking the Text

2. Underline the word *deserted* and its definition. Why did some American soldiers decide to desert during the winter of 1777–1778?

_____

_____

The American Revolution

Lesson 2 The War Continues, *Continued*

? Critical Thinking

3. Why would foreign-born people come to help the Patriots in their fight for freedom?

_____

_____

☑ Reading Check

4. How did Lafayette help the Patriot cause?

_____

_____

☑ Reading Check

5. What help did the Patriots receive from Spain?

_____

_____

Two Polish men were also important in the war effort: Thaddeus Kosciuszko and Casimir Pulaski. Kosciuszko helped build important defenses for the Americans. Pulaski was promoted to general. He was wounded in battle, and later died in 1779.

Friedrich von Steuben from Prussia was another foreign-born person who helped the Patriots. Through the harsh winter at Valley Forge, von Steuben trained the Continental Army. This made them a better fighting force.

Some people did important work off the battlefield as well. Juan de Miralles came from Spain. He helped persuade Spain, Cuba, and Mexico to help the United States by sending money to support the war.

Marquis de Lafayette	French nobleman and Patriot volunteer; became trusted aide to General Washington
Thaddeus Kosciuszko	Polish nobleman who helped build important defenses for the Americans
Casimir Pulaski	Polish man who rose to rank of general in Continental Army, died fighting for the Patriot cause
Friedrich von Steuben	Former army officer from Prussia who helped train the Continental Army
Juan de Miralles	Spanish supporter who persuaded Spain, Cuba, and Mexico to send money to help the Patriots

Even with help from many countries and individuals, the fight for independence was still not over. More battles and challenges were yet to come.

Life on the Home Front

The war affected the lives of everyone in the United States. Getting money to pay for the war was a challenge for the government. It printed millions of dollars of paper money. But the paper money lost value. The economy suffered from **inflation**. It took more and more money to buy the same amount of goods.

Women raised their children and took care of their homes on their own. They also ran businesses and farms while their fathers, husbands, and brothers were away at war. Children lived without their fathers present.

The American Revolution

Lesson 2 The War Continues, *Continued*

This caused some people to think differently about women's roles. Abigail Adams, the wife of Congressman John Adams, wrote to ask him to think about the rights of women as he helped form the new nation.

For others, the fight for freedom made them change their thoughts about slavery. In 1778, the governor of New Jersey, William Livingston, asked his state government to free all enslaved people. He felt that slavery went against the ideas of Christianity. African Americans also spoke up for their freedom. The conflict over slavery would continue for many years to come.

The war also affected another group of people in the United States. These people were Loyalists, or American settlers who supported Great Britain. Some Loyalists joined the British troops and fought against the Patriots in the war. Some were spies for Great Britain. Others fled to Canada or went back to Great Britain.

The people who stayed faced trouble. Many were treated badly by their neighbors. Some were attacked or hurt. Those caught spying could be arrested or even put to death.

/ / / / / / / / / / / / / Glue Foldable here / / / / / / / / / / / / /

Check for Understanding

Name two people from other nations who helped the United States gain freedom. Describe what each contributed.

1. _____

_____

2. _____

_____

Name two groups of people who sought greater freedom as a result of the Revolution and how people's thinking changed.

1. _____

_____

2. _____

_____

✓ **Reading Check**

6. How were Loyalists treated by the Patriots during the war?

_____

_____

FOLDABLES

7. Place a two-tab Foldable along the dotted line to cover Check for Understanding. Write the title *Foreign Allies* on the anchor tab. Label the two tabs *France* and *Spain*. Recall and list ways that each helped the Patriots during their fight for independence. Use the Foldable to help answer Check for Understanding.

networks

The American Revolution

Lesson 3 Battlegrounds Shift

ESSENTIAL QUESTION

Why does conflict develop?

GUIDING QUESTIONS

1. **How did the war in the West develop?**

2. **What was the result of the war at sea?**

3. **What was the result of the war in the South?**

Terms to Know

blockade measure that keeps a country from communicating and trading with other nations

privateer privately owned ship outfitted with weapons

When did it happen?

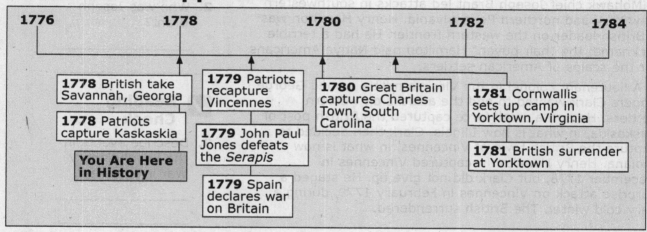

| 1776 | 1778 | 1780 | 1782 | 1784 |

1778 British take Savannah, Georgia

1778 Patriots capture Kaskaskia

You Are Here in History

1779 Patriots recapture Vincennes

1779 John Paul Jones defeats the *Serapis*

1779 Spain declares war on Britain

1780 Great Britain captures Charles Town, South Carolina

1781 Cornwallis sets up camp in Yorktown, Virginia

1781 British surrender at Yorktown

What do you know?

In the first column, answer the questions based on what you know before you study. After this lesson, complete the last column.

Now ...		Later ...
	On which side did most Native Americans fight during the Revolution?	
	How did Americans fight back against the British naval blockade?	
	What area of the United States did the British focus on winning?	

networks

The American Revolution

Lesson 3 Battlegrounds Shift, *Continued*

Fighting in the West

There were many Native American nations in the different colonies. Some of these nations took sides in the war between the Patriots and the British. Some helped the Patriots. More Native Americans decided to help the British. The Patriots had fought against them, taken land that belonged to them, and changed their way of life. To Native Americans, the British seemed like less of a threat.

The American Revolution was fought in many areas. One important area was along the western frontier, or land west of the Appalachian Mountains. The British and some Native Americans raided American settlements.

Mohawk chief Joseph Brant led attacks in southwestern New York and northern Pennsylvania. Henry Hamilton was a British leader on the western frontier. He had a terrible nickname: the "hair buyer." Hamilton paid Native Americans for the scalps of American settlers.

A lieutenant colonel in the Virginia militia named George Rogers Clark wanted to end the attacks on western settlers. He and a small force captured the British post of Kaskaskia, in what is now Illinois. Clark then decided to capture the British town of Vincennes, in what is now Indiana. Henry Hamilton recaptured Vincennes in December 1778, but Clark did not give up. He staged a surprise attack on Vincennes in February 1779, during a very cold winter. The British surrendered.

The War at Sea

The war was also fought at sea. The United States did not have a strong navy. Congress called for building 13 warships, but only two ever sailed. Great Britain had a very powerful navy. Its many ships blocked American ports and harbors. This stopped ships from coming or going with people or supplies. This is known as a **blockade**.

Something had to be done to break the blockade. So Congress gave special permission to about 2,000 privately owned merchant ships to have weapons attached. The ships could then capture enemy ships and take their cargo. These ships were called **privateers**. They played an important role in the American Revolution because they captured more British ships than the American navy.

A very famous battle at sea took place in 1779 off the coast of Great Britain. It was between a British ship called the *Serapis* and an American ship called the *Bonhomme*

Explaining

1. Why did more Native Americans side with the British than with the Patriots?

Identifying

2. Who was Joseph Brant?

_____

_____

✓ Reading Check

3. Describe events in the Revolutionary War in the West.

_____

_____

_____

_____

Marking the Text

4. Underline the word *blockade* and its definition. What did Americans do to combat the blockade?

_____

_____

86

The American Revolution

Lesson 3 Battlegrounds Shift, *Continued*

Identifying

5. Who was John Paul Jones?

_____

6. What did he do?

_____

Explaining

7. What special method of fighting did Francis Marion use in his attacks on the British?

_____

Identifying

8. Who was Bernardo de Gálvez and how did he help the Americans?

_____

_____

Richard. The American captain was John Paul Jones. The ships fought for hours. Eventually, the British captain asked Jones if he wanted to surrender. Jones refused and said, "I have not yet begun to fight." John Paul Jones and his crew captured the *Serapis.* The victory was the first time an American ship had captured a British ship in British waters. John Paul Jones became a Patriot hero.

Fighting in the South

The British had more troops and supplies during the American Revolution, but they realized that they would not be able to win quickly. They came up with a new strategy. They wanted to win the South.

The Americans won some important early battles in the South. The Patriots beat Loyalist forces at Wilmington, North Carolina. They also kept the British from capturing Charles Town, now called Charleston, South Carolina. They were small battles, but had a big impact on the war.

The British also had some successes in the South. They took the city of Savannah, Georgia. In 1780, they finally captured Charles Town. Thousands of troops were taken prisoner by the British. This was the worst American defeat of the war. The British success would not last, however.

The British believed they could use strong Loyalist support and their naval power to help them win the South. The British did not get the Loyalist support they hoped for. They also had to deal with American hit-and-run tactics. Patriot forces would attack the British by surprise, and then disappear again. Francis Marion, called the "Swamp Fox," was a successful Patriot leader in the South. He was quick and smart, and he hid from the British easily in the eastern South Carolina swamps.

Other countries were also keeping Great Britain distracted in the South. In 1779, Spain declared war on Great Britain. At that time, Louisiana had a Spanish governor named Bernardo de Gálvez. He helped the Patriots a great deal. He did this by giving them money and allowing them to use the Port of New Orleans. He also shipped tons of supplies and ammunition up the Mississippi River. Gálvez also fought the British in the South. This fighting with Spain weakened the British.

The British gained a big victory at Camden, South Carolina. General Cornwallis led the British troops, and General Horatio Gates led the Patriot forces. The British

netwrks

The American Revolution

Lesson 3 Battlegrounds Shift, *Continued*

won the battle but could not control the area. British forces under Cornwallis moved north.

Some settlers in the South were neutral, meaning they did not take sides. The British told these local people that they must support them. The British said if the locals did not help them, they would hang their leaders and destroy their land. This angered the Americans who lived in the mountains of the South. They formed a militia.

They clashed with a Loyalist force at Kings Mountain. The Patriots surrounded the Loyalist forces. They killed or captured nearly all of the 1,000 Loyalist troops. This victory won more support from Southern settlers.

More victories followed. Nathaniel Greene took command of the Continental Army in the South. He decided to split his troops into two sections. One part had success against the British at Cowpens, South Carolina. The other part of the army helped in raids with Francis Marion.

Later in 1781, the two sections met Cornwallis' army at what is now Greensboro, North Carolina. The Patriots did not win, but the British suffered great losses. General Cornwallis decided to give up the fight in the Carolinas.

Cornwallis and his troops went north into Virginia. Cornwallis set up camp with his men at Yorktown on the Virginia coast. Both Marquis de Lafayette and Anthony Wayne went south into Virginia to push Cornwallis back. The battle for the South was entering its final phase.

////////////// Glue Foldable here ///////////////

Check for Understanding

Identify each of these people.

1. John Paul Jones _____

2. Francis Marion _____

3. General Charles Cornwallis _____

How did the treatment of neutral settlers in the South hurt British chances for success?

_____

_____

? Critical Thinking

9. Why do you think neutral Americans decided to fight against the British?

_____

_____

_____

✓ Reading Check

10. What effect did the Patriot victory at Kings Mountain have?

_____

_____

FOLDABLES®

11. Place a three-tab Foldable along the dotted line to cover Check for Understanding. Label the three tabs *War in the West*, *War at Sea*, and *War in the South*. List the key words, dates, names, and events that you remember about each. Use the Foldable to help answer Check for Understanding.

The American Revolution

Lesson 4 The Final Years

ESSENTIAL QUESTION
Why does conflict develop?

GUIDING QUESTIONS
1. What events occurred in the victory at Yorktown?
2. What helped the Patriots win independence?

> **Terms to Know**
> **siege** an attempt to force surrender by blocking the movement of people or goods into or out of a place
> **ratify** to approve officially
> **ambush** an attack in which the attacker hides and surprises the enemy

Where in the world?

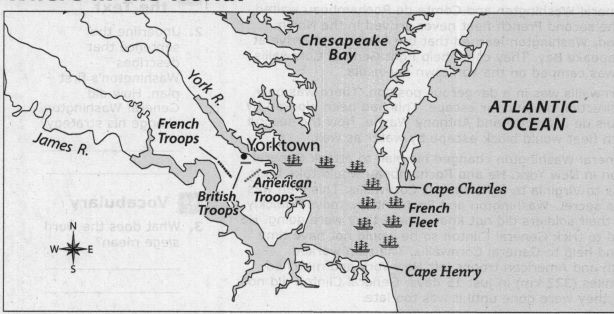

When did it happen?

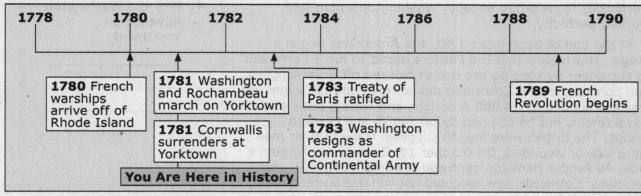

1780 French warships arrive off of Rhode Island

1781 Washington and Rochambeau march on Yorktown

1781 Cornwallis surrenders at Yorktown

1783 Treaty of Paris ratified

1783 Washington resigns as commander of Continental Army

1789 French Revolution begins

You Are Here in History

89

netw⊙rks

The American Revolution

Lesson 4 The Final Years, *Continued*

Victory at Yorktown

While battles were going on in the South, General Washington and his troops were in New York. In July 1780, French warships arrived off of Rhode Island to help the Americans. They carried thousands of French troops led by Comte de Rochambeau. They joined General Washington and waited for a second French fleet to arrive.

General Washington had a plan. He wanted to attack an army base in New York commanded by British general Clinton. A second fleet of French ships was expected. The attack would happen when that force arrived.

General Washington and Comte de Rochambeau waited, but the second French fleet never arrived in the North. Instead, Washington learned that the fleet would arrive at Chesapeake Bay. They could help fight General Cornwallis, who was camped on the Yorktown Peninsula.

Cornwallis was in a dangerous position. There was only one direction on land for escape. This had been blocked by Marquis de Lafayette and Anthony Wayne. Now the second French fleet would block escape by water as well.

General Washington changed his plan to attack General Clinton in New York. He and Rochambeau would take their troops to Virginia to fight against Cornwallis. This plan was kept a secret. Washington and Rochambeau moved quickly. Even their soldiers did not know where they were going. He hoped to trick General Clinton so he would not have time to send help to General Cornwallis. The plan worked. French and American troops left New York and marched 200 miles (322 km) in just 15 days. General Clinton did not know they were gone until it was too late.

The Continental forces at Yorktown were ready. Washington, Rochambeau, Lafayette, and the French fleet had Cornwallis cornered. British ships could not reach Cornwallis to help him escape. Washington's plan had worked perfectly.

At the end of September 1781, the Americans began a **siege**. This means that the Patriots hoped to force Cornwallis to surrender by keeping the British blocked off from supplies and communication. Cornwallis did not give up right away. He was surrounded by 14,000 American and French army and naval forces, but he still had 8,000 British and Hessian troops. The British were low on supplies. Many of their men were sick or wounded. On October 14, General Washington's aide, Alexander Hamilton captured important British defenses. Cornwallis saw he could not win. He surrendered.

🖎 Describing

1. Explain how General Cornwallis was trapped on the Yorktown Peninsula.

_____

_____

Aᵇᴄ Marking the Text

2. Underline the sentence that describes Washington's first plan. How did General Washington change his strategy?

_____

_____

Aᵇᴄ Vocabulary

3. What does the word *siege* mean?

_____

_____

✔ Reading Check

4. Why did Washington advance on Yorktown?

_____

_____

_____

90

The American Revolution

Lesson 4 The Final Years, Continued

? Critical Thinking

5. Why was the Treaty of Paris important?

_____

_____

✓ Reading Check

6. Why did Washington take action to end the soldier's threat in Newburgh?

_____

_____

The Patriots won the Battle of Yorktown. The French band played the song "Yankee Doodle" which the British had used to make fun of the Americans. In response, the British band played a children's tune called "The World Turned Upside Down."

Independence Achieved

Yorktown was not the last battle of the American Revolution. The British still held cities such as Savannah, Charles Town, and New York. Yet the British realized that the fight was finished. The war was too costly to continue.

Both sides sent representatives to France to work out a peace agreement. Benjamin Franklin, John Adams, and John Jay represented the United States. The first draft of the Treaty of Paris was **ratified**, or approved, by Congress. The final agreement was signed in September 1783.

The treaty was a success for the Patriots. Great Britain agreed to recognize the United States as an independent nation along with other agreements.

United States	Great Britain
Recognized as independent nation	British merchants could collect debts from Americans
Promised that Congress would advise state governments to return Loyalist property	British agree to withdraw troops
	Americans granted permission to fish off of Canada

Some time passed between the end of the war and the signing of the treaty. The Continental Army was kept active during this time in Newburgh, New York. The soldiers wanted to get paid. They were angry because they were owed money. Some thought they should use force against Congress if they were not paid. General Washington stepped in to settle the dispute. He understood the threat was very serious for the new nation. He asked the soldiers to be patient. He also asked Congress to meet the soldiers' demands. Congress agreed. General Washington showed his superior leadership once again.

networks

The American Revolution

Lesson 4 The Final Years, *Continued*

When the last of the British troops left New York City in November 1783, Washington decided to resign. He wanted to retire to Virginia and live a quiet life with his family.

Even though the British were strong, the Americans won the war because they had certain advantages. They fought on their own land for a cause they believed in. They knew the land and how to use it, often using **ambushes** to surprise the enemy. The British, on the other hand, fought a war far from home. Their troops and supplies had to be shipped in. They also had a hard time controlling the Americans even when they captured major cities.

The Americans also had help from many others. The French supplied soldiers and naval support as well as money. The Spanish gave aid when they attacked Britain. Individuals from other countries came to help the Americans fight and build their defenses.

Most of all, the British could not fight against the power of independence. Americans fought hard because they believed in what they were fighting for. They wanted to protect their land, their families, and their freedom.

This spirit spread to other places in the world as well. Shortly after the American Revolution, French rebels fought for freedom. They fought for the ideals of "Liberty, Equality, and Fraternity." These ideas also took root in the French colony of Saint Domingue, which is now Haiti. Led by a man named Toussaint L'Ouverture, enslaved Africans fought for their freedom. In 1804, Saint Domingue became the second nation in the Americas to win its freedom.

/ / / / / / / / / / / /Glue Foldable here/ / / / / / / / / / / /

Check for Understanding

Give two reasons that General Cornwallis was defeated at Yorktown.

1. _____

2. _____

List two elements that helped the Patriots win the war.

1. _____

2 _____

Explaining

7. How did France and Spain help the Americans win the war?

_____

_____

FOLDABLES

8. Use a two-tab Foldable and place it along the dotted line to cover Check for Understanding. Write *American Independence* on the anchor tab. Label the two tabs *Patriots Win* and *British Defeated*. Recall and list reasons for the Patriots' victory and the defeat of the Loyalists. Use the Foldable to help answer Check for Understanding.

net w⊛rks

A More Perfect Union

Lesson 1 The Articles of Confederation

ESSENTIAL QUESTION

Why do people form governments?

GUIDING QUESTIONS

1. **What kind of government was created by the Articles of Confederation?**

2. **What process allowed new states to join the union?**

3. **In what ways was the Confederation government weak?**

> **Terms to Know**
>
> **bicameral** having two separate lawmaking organizations
> **republic** a government in which citizens rule through elected representatives
> **ordinance** law
> **depreciate** lose value

Where in the world?

Northwest Territory
Present-day state boundaries

SPANISH LOUISIANA
Lake Superior
Mississippi River
Wisconsin
Lake Michigan
Lake Huron
Michigan
Lake Ontario
Illinois
Indiana
Ohio
Lake Erie
Ohio River

When did it happen?

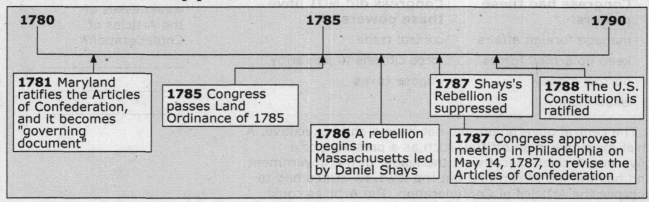

1780 — 1785 — 1790

1781 Maryland ratifies the Articles of Confederation, and it becomes "governing document"

1785 Congress passes Land Ordinance of 1785

1786 A rebellion begins in Massachusetts led by Daniel Shays

1787 Shays's Rebellion is suppressed

1787 Congress approves meeting in Philadelphia on May 14, 1787, to revise the Articles of Confederation

1788 The U.S. Constitution is ratified

93

networks

A More Perfect Union

Lesson 1 The Articles of Confederation, *Continued*

The Making of a Republic

In May 1776, the Continental Congress asked each state to set up its government. Each state wrote a constitution. A constitution is a plan of government.

Americans did not want to give too much power to one ruler or one branch of government. State constitutions solved that problem. They split the power between the governor and legislature. The governor had less power than the legislature. Most states set up two-house, or **bicameral,** legislatures. This divided the power even more.

Americans had to set up a national government, too. Americans wanted their country to be a **republic.** In a republic, citizens elect people to represent them and make decisions based on what they want.

People could not agree on what powers the national government should have. Americans felt the central government should have only the power to fight wars and to deal with other countries.

In 1776 the Second Continental Congress had a group of people make a plan for a central government. This group created the Articles of Confederation. The Articles called for a weak central government. They also let states keep most of their powers. Congress accepted the Articles of Confederation in November, 1777.

The Articles of Confederation gave Congress certain powers, but there were important powers that Congress did not have. For example, if Congress needed to raise money or an army, it had to ask the states. The states did not have to say yes.

Powers of Congress Under The Articles of Confederation	
Congress had these powers:	**Congress did NOT have these powers:**
manage foreign affairs	control trade
keep up armed forces	force citizens to join army
borrow money	impose taxes
issue money	

The central government did not have a chief executive. A chief executive is an official, such as a president or a governor. A chief executive is the leader of the government and has the job of carrying out the laws. All states had to approve the Articles of Confederation. The Articles could

 Mark the Text

1. Underline the meaning of a *constitution*.

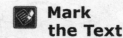 **Analyzing**

2. What might be one result of state constitutions that limited the power of the governor?

_____

_____

 Mark the Text

3. Circle the meaning of *republic*.

 Listing

4. What were three weaknesses of the Articles of Confederation?

_____

_____

94

A More Perfect Union

Lesson 1 The Articles of Confederation, *Continued*

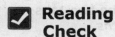

Reading Check

5. How many votes did each state have in the new Congress?

_____

_____

Mark the Text

6. Underline how a western district could apply to become a state.

Reading Check

7. What did the Northwest Ordinance say about slavery?

_____

_____

not be changed unless all states agreed to change it. Each state had one vote.

The states also did not agree on what to do with land in the West. Some states believed land west of the Appalachian Mountains belonged to them. Maryland did not want to approve the Articles until other states gave up claims to this land. The states finally agreed and approved the Articles. On March 1, 1781, the Articles of Confederation became the government of the United States of America.

The new national government was weak. This made it difficult for the government to handle the nation's problems. Congress could not pass a law unless 9 states voted for it. Congress also did not have the power to change the Articles of Confederation. Any plan to change the Articles needed to be approved by all 13 states.

Even so, America's government did some important things. America made a peace treaty with Britain. It expanded foreign trade. It set up plans for people to settle lands to the west.

Policies for Western Lands

The Articles of Confederation did not tell how to add new states. Settlers were already living west of the Appalachian Mountains. This was outside the United States. Western settlers wanted to form new states and join the Union. Congress needed to give people a way to settle the Western lands and form new states.

In 1785, the Confederation Congress passed an **ordinance,** or law, about western lands. This law set up a way to divide and then sell the western lands. Land was divided into townships. Land in the township was divided into smaller sections. These sections were sold to settlers.

In 1787, the Northwest Ordinance created the Northwest Territory. This territory included lands north of the Ohio River and east of the Mississippi River. The lands were divided into three to five smaller territories. A territory could apply to become a state when 60,000 people lived there. New states would have the same rights as the original 13 states. Settlers had a bill of rights. They had freedom of religion and trial by jury. The bill of rights said there could be no slavery in the Northwest Territory.

The Land Act of 1800 was passed to make it easier for people to buy land in the Northwest Territory. Some settlers did not have all of the money needed to buy land.

95

netw🔾rks

A More Perfect Union

Lesson 1 The Articles of Confederation, *Continued*

The Act made it possible for people to pay for the land over a period of four years.

Problems at Home and Abroad

The national government had problems paying its bills. By 1781, American dollars, called Continentals, had **depreciated,** or lost value. They were worth almost nothing. The War for Independence left the Continental Congress with a large debt. Congress did not have the power to raise taxes to pay these debts.

In 1781, Congress created a department of finance, led by Robert Morris. Morris made a plan to charge a 5 percent tax on goods brought in from other countries to help pay the debts. All 13 states had to approve Morris' plan for it to pass, but Rhode Island voted no. The plan did not pass.

The new government faced other problems. The British did not let Americans trade in the West Indies and other British areas. British soldiers were still in several important forts in the Great Lakes region.

The American government had problems with Spain, too. Spain controlled Florida and lands west of the Mississippi River. Spain wanted to stop America's growth in Spanish territory. In 1784, Spain closed the lower Mississippi River to American shipping. Western settlers could no longer use the river for trade.

It became clear that the Confederation was not able to deal with major problems. Americans came to agree that their new country needed a stronger government.

/////////////// Glue Foldable here ///////////////

Check for Understanding

What kind of government was created by the Articles of Confederation?

_____

List three problems the Confederation government faced in its relations with other countries.

_____

_____

_____

? Analyzing

8. Why did Robert Morris's plan to pay the country's war debts fail?

_____

✓ Reading Check

9. Why did Spain close the lower Mississippi River to American shipping in 1784?

_____

FOLDABLES

10. Glue a three-tab Foldable behind a two-tab Foldable along the anchor tabs to cover *Check for Understanding*. Write *Articles of Confederation* on the anchor tab. Label the two-tabs— *Strengths*, *Weaknesses*. Label the three-tabs— *Problems at Home*, *Problems with Britain*, and *Problems with Spain*. Write two words or phrases you remember about each.

networks

A More Perfect Union

Lesson 2 Forging a New Constitution

ESSENTIAL QUESTION

How do new ideas change the way people live?

GUIDING QUESTIONS

1. **What problems did the government face under the Articles of Confederation?**

2. **How did leaders reshape the government?**

3. **What compromises were reached in the new Constitution?**

Terms to Know

depression a period when economic activity slows and unemployment increases

manumission when a slaveholder frees an enslaved person

proportional having the proper size in relation to other objects or items

compromise an agreement between two or more sides in which each side gives up some of what it wants

When did it happen?

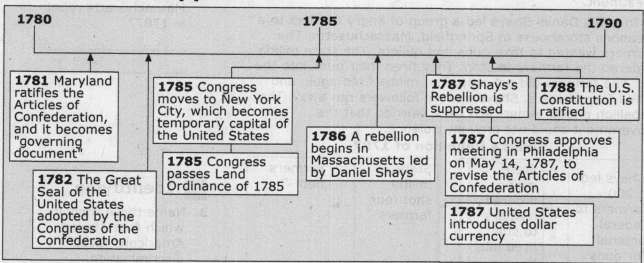

1780

1781 Maryland ratifies the Articles of Confederation, and it becomes "governing document"

1782 The Great Seal of the United States adopted by the Congress of the Confederation

1785 Congress moves to New York City, which becomes temporary capital of the United States

1785 Congress passes Land Ordinance of 1785

1785

1786 A rebellion begins in Massachusetts led by Daniel Shays

1787 Shays's Rebellion is suppressed

1787 Congress approves meeting in Philadelphia on May 14, 1787, to revise the Articles of Confederation

1787 United States introduces dollar currency

1790

1788 The U.S. Constitution is ratified

What do you know?

In the first column, answer the questions based on what you know before you study. After this lesson, complete the last column.

Now...		Later...
	What was Shays's Rebellion?	
	What was the Constitutional Convention?	
	What was the Great Compromise?	

97

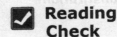

Lesson 2 Forging a New Constitution, *Continued*

The Need for Change

The Articles of Confederation created a weak national government. This made it difficult for the government to deal with the nation's problems. The United States went through a **depression** after the American Revolution. A depression is a period of time when business slows down and many people lose their jobs.

The government had little money. The money it had was used to pay debts, or money owed, to foreign countries. There was not enough money in the United States.

The slow economy meant farmers sold less of their goods. Some farmers could not pay taxes and other debts. As a result, state officials took over their land and put many of them in jail. Farmers grew angry over this treatment.

In 1787, Daniel Shays led a group of angry farmers to a weapons storehouse in Springfield, Massachusetts. The farmers wanted to take guns and bullets. The state militia ordered the farmers to stop. They fired their guns into the air. The farmers did not stop. The militia fired again and killed four farmers. Shays and his followers ran away. The rebellion ended. Americans were worried that the government could not prevent violence.

Shays's Rebellion of 1787

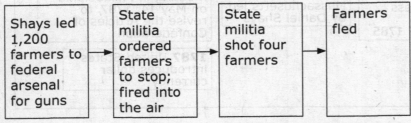

Shays led 1,200 farmers to federal arsenal for guns → State militia ordered farmers to stop; fired into the air → State militia shot four farmers → Farmers fled

The American Revolution was based on freedom. This caused some Americans to believe that slavery should be outlawed. Several northern states began passing laws to end slavery. Free African Americans faced discrimination even in states that did not have slavery. They were not allowed to go to many public places. Few states gave them the right to vote. The children of most free African Americans could not go to school with white children.

Some slaveholders freed their slaves after the American Revolution. Virginia passed a law that encouraged **manumission**, the freeing of individual enslaved persons. The number of free African Americans grew in that state. Even with these efforts, slavery was still a key part of life in Southern states. Southern plantations depended on

Mark the Text

1. Underline the meaning of *depression*.

Reading Check

2. Why did farmers in Massachusetts rebel in 1787?

_____

_____

Identifying

3. Name three ways in which free African Americans faced discrimination.

_____

_____

Defining

4. What was *manumission*?

_____

_____

_____

98

A More Perfect Union

Lesson 2 Forging a New Constitution, *Continued*

slave labor. Many white Southerners were afraid that their economic system would die without slavery. The issue of slavery began to divide Northerners and Southerners.

The American Revolution and Slavery

North		South
American Revolution led to gradual end of slavery in the North.	←→	Economy in South continued to depend heavily on slave labor.

The Constitutional Convention

The American Revolution had not created a united country. Some leaders liked strong, independent state governments. Other leaders wanted a strong national government. They wanted to change the Articles of Confederation. Two of these leaders were James Madison and Alexander Hamilton.

In September 1786, Hamilton called for a convention in Philadelphia to talk about trade issues. He also suggested that people at the convention should talk about how to change the Articles of Confederation.

The convention began in May 1787. George Washington and Benjamin Franklin were among those who attended. This helped people trust the convention's work. Trust was important because the convention's purpose was to create an entirely new constitution. The delegates chose George Washington to lead the meetings.

Edmund Randolph of Virginia surprised the delegates at the convention. He proposed a plan created by James Madison, called the Virginia Plan. The Virginia plan would set up a strong national government. It would create a government with three branches. There would be a two-house legislature, a chief executive chosen by the legislature, and a court system.

The plan also called for the number of members in both houses of the legislature to be **proportional**. The number of members would be based on each state's population. States with more people would have more representatives than states with fewer people.

Delegates from small states were against the Virginia Plan. They wanted all states to have equal representation. They supported the New Jersey Plan. Under the New Jersey plan, the legislature would be a one-house legislature. Each state would have one vote in the legislature.

Analyzing

5. Why was it important for the American people to trust the work of the Constitutional Convention?

_____

_____

Identifying

6. How many representatives would each state have under the Virginia Plan?

_____

_____

Reading Check

7. Why did New Jersey's delegates object to the Virginia Plan?

_____

_____

99

A More Perfect Union

Lesson 2 Forging a New Constitution, *Continued*

Agreeing to Compromise

The delegates agreed to create a new constitution based on the Virginia Plan. The delegates still needed to deal with the issue of representation.

Roger Sherman came up with an agreement called the Great Compromise. A **compromise** is an agreement between two or more sides. Each side gives up some of what it wants. The Great Compromise called for a two-house legislature. Each state would have two members in the Senate. The number of members in the House of Representatives would be based on the size of each state's population.

Southern states wanted to count enslaved people as part of their population. This would raise their population. It would give them more seats in Congress, and it would raise their taxes. Northern states did not want the South to count its enslaved people. The delegates agreed to the Three-Fifths Compromise. Each enslaved person would count as three-fifths of a free person. Northerners also agreed not to block the slave trade until 1808.

George Mason wanted more protection for citizens' rights. He asked for a bill of rights to part of the Constitution. Many delegates felt that the Constitution already protected people's rights.

On September 17, 1787, the delegates gathered to sign the new Constitution. The Constitution was then sent to the states for approval. The new Constitution would take effect when 9 of the 13 states approved it.

/ / / / / / / / / / / / / / / Glue Foldable here / / / / / / / / / / / / /

Check for Understanding

List the three branches of government created by the new Constitution.

_____   _____

_____

What two things did the delegates disagree about that forced them to make compromises?

_____

_____

☑ Reading Check

8. What compromises were made on the issue of slavery?

_____

_____

FOLDABLES®

9. Place a two-tab Foldable along the dotted line to cover *Check for Understanding*. Write the title *Constitutional Convention* on the anchor tab. Label the two tabs— *Agreed* and *Disagreed*. Recall and write about issues of agreement and disagreement. Use your notes to help answer the *Check for Understanding*.

A More Perfect Union

Lesson 3 A New Plan of Government

ESSENTIAL QUESTION
How do governments change?

GUIDING QUESTIONS
1. **From where did the Framers of the Constitution borrow their ideas about government?**
2. **How does the Constitution limit the power of the government?**
3. **How was the Constitution ratified?**

Terms to Know
federalism sharing power between the federal and state governments
legislative branch lawmaking branch of government
executive branch branch of government headed by the president
Electoral College group chosen by each state to vote for president and vice president
judicial branch branch of government made up of courts that settle questions of law and disagreements
amendment a change, correction, or improvement added to a document
checks and balances system in which the branches of government can limit each others' powers

When did it happen?

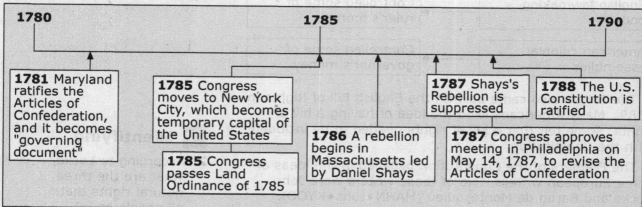

1780

1781 Maryland ratifies the Articles of Confederation, and it becomes "governing document"

1785 Congress moves to New York City, which becomes temporary capital of the United States

1785 Congress passes Land Ordinance of 1785

1785

1786 A rebellion begins in Massachusetts led by Daniel Shays

1787 Shays's Rebellion is suppressed

1787 Congress approves meeting in Philadelphia on May 14, 1787, to revise the Articles of Confederation

1788 The U.S. Constitution is ratified

1790

What do you know?

In the first column, answer the questions based on what you know before you study. After this lesson, complete the last column.

Now...		Later...
	What gave American delegates some of their ideas for the Constitution?	
	What are the three branches of government?	
	What does it mean to ratify the Constitution?	

101

netw⊕rks

Lesson 3 A New Plan of Government, *Continued*

The Constitution's Sources

The delegates in Philadelphia created a new constitution. The delegates liked ideas from European political groups and writers. Some of these ideas are in the Constitution.

Even though Americans broke away from Britain, they still respected many British traditions. Traditions are cultural ideas and practices. Individual rights are part of the British system. The Framers of the Constitution felt it was important to have individual rights.

An English law, the Magna Carta, limited the power of the king or queen. He or she had to accept the laws of the lawmaking body. The lawmaking body paid for wars and the royal government. American colonies worked the same way. American lawmaking bodies controlled their colonies' funds. They also had some control over colonial governors.

Magna Carta as a Model

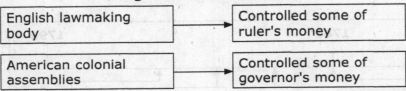

| English lawmaking body | → | Controlled some of ruler's money |
| American colonial assemblies | → | Controlled some of governor's money |

The British also came up with the English Bill of Rights in 1689. Many Americans liked the idea of having a bill of rights. Some felt that a bill of rights needed to be included with the Constitution.

The Framers of the Constitution believed in the ideas of some European writers. Two of these writers were John Locke and Baron de Montesquieu (MAHN•tuhs•KYOO).

The English writer, Locke, believed that all people have natural rights. These rights include the rights to life, liberty, and property. Locke wrote that government is based on an agreement, or contract. This agreement is between the people and the ruler. The Constitution would also be a contract. It would limit the government's power. This would help protect people's natural rights.

Montesquieu was a French writer. He believed that the government's power should be divided and balanced. This would make it difficult for one person or group to have too much power. The Framers of the American Constitution carefully described and divided the powers of government.

The Articles of Confederation had given most power to the states. The Constitution changed this. States had to

---

 Marking the Text

1. Underline the sources, or starting places, of many ideas in the Constitution.

 Identifying

2. According to Locke, what are the three natural rights that all people have?

_____
_____
_____

Lesson 3 A New Plan of Government, *Continued*

📝 Identifying

3. List three powers the U.S. Constitution gives to the states.

_____

_____

✅ Reading Check

4. What is federalism?

_____

_____

_____

📝 Marking the Text

5. Circle the three branches of government.

🔤 Defining

6. What is the Electoral College?

_____

_____

_____

give up some of their powers to the federal, or national, government. The Constitution was set up so federal and state governments share power. This is called **Federalism.**

The Constitution gave new powers to the federal government. It could tax, manage trade, control the supply of money, form an army, and declare war. The federal government could pass laws it decided were "necessary and proper."

The Constitution let states keep some important powers. The states could still control trade inside their borders. They had the power to set up local governments and schools. States also made laws about marriage and divorce.

The Constitution allows some powers to be shared by the federal and state governments. Both the federal and state governments may tax their citizens. Both governments may arrest and punish criminals.

The Constitution is the supreme, or highest, law of the land. Any disagreement between the federal government and the states was to be settled by the federal courts. They make decisions based on what the Constitution says.

Government Structure

The Framers of the Constitution divided the federal government into three branches. These are the legislative, executive, and judicial branches. The first three articles, or sections, of the Constitution explain the powers and tasks of these branches of the federal government.

Article I says the **legislative** (LEH•juhs•lay•tiv) **branch,** or lawmaking branch of the federal government is Congress. Congress has two parts: the Senate and the House of Representatives. Congress's powers include such tasks as deciding how much taxes will be, minting coins, and controlling trade.

Article II describes the **executive branch.** The president is in charge of this branch. The president's job is to carry out the nation's laws. A group called the **Electoral** (ee•lehk•TAWR•uhl) **College** elects the president and vice president. Its members are called electors. Electors are chosen by the voters of each state.

Article III describes the **judicial** (joo•DIH•shuhl) **branch**, or the court system. The Supreme Court is the top court in the nation. Congress sets up federal courts under the Supreme Court. Federal courts make decisions

netw⦿rks

A More Perfect Union

Lesson 3 A New Plan of Government, *Continued*

on cases that have to do with the Constitution, with federal laws, and with problems between states.

The Framers built in a system of **checks and balances.** Each branch of government has ways to check, or limit, the power of the others. This way, no branch can have too much control in the government.

Debate and Adoption

The Constitution could take effect after nine states ratified, or approved, it. People who supported the Constitution were called Federalists. James Madison, Alexander Hamilton, and John Jay were among the Federalists. They wrote a set of essays, called the Federalist Papers. The Federalist Papers explained and defended the Constitution.

People who did not like the new Constitution were called Anti-Federalists. They were afraid that a strong national government would take away freedoms. Anti-Federalists wanted local governments to have more power.

By June 21, 1788, the ninth state ratified the Constitution. That meant the new government could go into effect. New York and Virginia, the two largest states, still had not approved the Constitution.

People worried that the new government would not succeed if those states did not ratify the Constitution. Virginia ratified after it was promised that there would be a bill of rights **amendment.** The Bill of Rights was added in 1791. New York, North Carolina, and Rhode Island also ratified the Consitution.

☑ Reading Check

7. How is power divided among the branches of government?

_____

_____

☑ Reading Check

8. Why was it important that the largest states ratify the constitution?

_____

_____

FOLDABLES®

9. Place a three-tab Venn diagram Foldable along the line to cover Check for Understanding. Write *A New Plan for Government* on the anchor tab. Label the tabs—*Federal Government, Shared Powers,* and *State Government*. On both sides of the tabs, list facts about each to compare the federal and state governments. Use your notes to help answer the questions below the tabs.

Check for Understanding

Explain the principle of Federalism.

_____

_____

Why is the system of checks and balances important?

_____

_____

104

The Constitution

Lesson 1 Principles of the Constitution

ESSENTIAL QUESTION

Why do people form governments?

GUIDING QUESTIONS

1. **What basic principles of government are set forth by the Constitution?**

2. **How is the Constitution able to change over time?**

Terms to Know

popular sovereignty belief that the government is subject to the people's will

limited government a government with limited powers strictly defined by law

enumerated power power belonging only to the federal government

reserved power power belonging only to the states

concurrent power power shared by the federal and state governments

separation of powers division of powers among the branches of government to make sure no branch has too much power

implied power power not specifically stated in the Constitution, but suggested in its language

Where in the world?

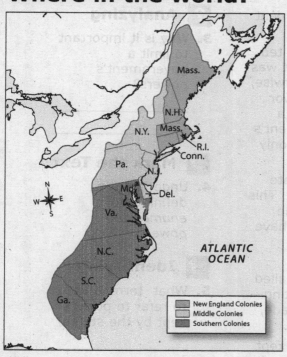

Mass.

N.H.
Mass.
N.Y.
R.I.
Conn.
Pa.
N.J.
Md.
Del.
Va.

N.C.

S.C.

Ga.

ATLANTIC OCEAN

New England Colonies
Middle Colonies
Southern Colonies

When did it happen?

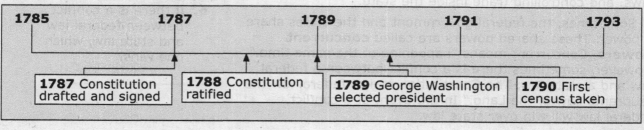

| 1785 | 1787 | 1789 | 1791 | 1793 |

1787 Constitution drafted and signed

1788 Constitution ratified

1789 George Washington elected president

1790 First census taken

105

The Constitution

Lesson 1 Principles of the Constitution, *Continued*

Our Constitution

The United States Constitution sets up our country's government. It is based on seven main ideas: (1) popular sovereignty, (2) a republican form of government, (3) limited government, (4) federalism, (5) separation of powers, (6) checks and balances, and (7) individual rights.

The Constitution begins with the words "We the People." Those words, "We the People," are the basic idea of our government—that the people have the right to govern themselves. The idea that the people control the powers of government is known as **popular sovereignty.**

The Constitution sets up a system of government in which the people rule by electing, or choosing, representatives. This is called a republic. The elected representatives make laws and carry out other government functions for all the people.

The people who wrote the Constitution knew the United States needed a strong government. They also knew it was important to limit the power of the government. Otherwise, the government might take away people's rights or favor certain groups. To avoid this, the Constitution sets up a **limited government,** which means that the government's powers are clearly defined. A limited government has only the powers that the people give it.

The Constitution also divides power between the state governments and the national, or federal, government. This system is called federalism. Under the Constitution, the federal government has some powers, and the states have other powers. Certain powers are shared by both the federal and the state governments.

Powers that belong to the federal government are called **enumerated powers.** These include coining—or printing—money, regulating interstate commerce and foreign trade, maintaining armed forces, and creating federal courts.

All powers not given to the federal government are kept by the states. These are called **reserved powers.** These include setting up schools, creating marriage and divorce laws, and controlling trade inside the state.

Sometimes, the federal government and the states share a power. These shared powers are called **concurrent powers.** Concurrent means "happening at the same time." However, sometimes there is a conflict between a federal law and a state law. The Constitution makes federal law the "supreme Law of the Land." In the event of a conflict, federal law will win over state law.

Explaining

1. What is the purpose of the U.S. Constitution?

_____

_____

Defining

2. What is a *republic*?

_____

Analyzing

3. Why is it important to limit a government's powers?

_____

_____

Mark the Text

4. Underline the definition of *enumerated powers*.

Identifying

5. What term is used to refer to powers kept by the states?

_____

Analyzing

6. If there is a conflict between federal law and state law, which one wins?

_____

106

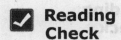

networks

Lesson 1 Principles of the Constitution, *Continued*

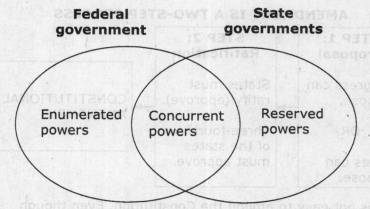

Federal government   **State governments**

Enumerated powers   Concurrent powers   Reserved powers

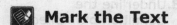
Identifying

7. List the three branches of government.

_____

_____

_____

Reading Check

8. What is the purpose of the system of checks and balances?

_____

_____

Mark the Text

9. What is the Bill of Rights? Underline the answer in the text.

Listing

10. List three important rights mentioned in the Bill of Rights.

_____

_____

_____

The Constitution also includes rules to make sure that no person or group gets too much power. One rule is called the **separation of powers.** This refers to the way the Constitution divides powers among three branches of government: legislative, executive, and judicial. Each branch has a different role.

Another constitutional protection comes from a system of **checks and balances.** This means each branch can prevent the other branches from becoming too powerful. Each branch is given certain powers that can limit the other branches.

The Constitution also protects **individual rights.** These rights are the basic freedoms that Americans enjoy every day. The Bill of Rights, which is the first 10 amendments to the Constitution, lists many of these important freedoms. These include freedom of religion, freedom of speech, the right to a speedy and public trial, and freedom from "cruel and unusual" punishment.

Amending the Constitution

The Constitution can be amended, or changed. One part of the Constitution describes the process for amending the document. As a result, the Constitution can be updated as time passes and society changes.

It takes two steps to amend the Constitution. In the first step, Congress or the states—either one—can propose, or suggest, an amendment. In the second step, the states ratify, or approve, the amendment. Three-fourths of the states must approve the amendment in order for it to become part of the Constitution.

107

netwrks

The Constitution

Lesson 1 Principles of the Constitution, *Continued*

AMENDMENT IS A TWO-STEP PROCESS

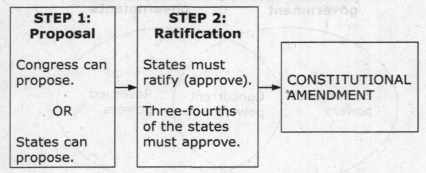

STEP 1: Proposal	STEP 2: Ratification	
Congress can propose. OR States can propose.	States must ratify (approve). Three-fourths of the states must approve.	CONSTITUTIONAL AMENDMENT

It is not easy to amend the Constitution. Even though people have proposed hundreds of amendments, only 27 have been ratified.

Among those 27, there have been many important amendments. Some of them have given more people the right to vote. For example, the Fifteenth Amendment said that African American men can vote. The Nineteenth Amendment gave women the right to vote. The Twenty-Sixth Amendment changed the voting age to 18.

The Constitution can also change in another way. Its words can be interpreted, or understood, in different ways. For example, one section says that Congress may "make all Laws which shall be necessary and proper" to carry out its duties. Another allows Congress to "regulate Commerce with foreign Nations, and among the several States." These clauses give Congress **implied powers**—powers that are suggested even though they are not stated clearly.

//////////////// Glue Foldable here ////////////////

Check for Understanding

What words would you use to describe the main ideas, or principles, of the Constitution?

_____

_____

List the two ways that the Constitution can be changed. How many changes have been added to the Constitution?

_____

_____

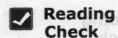 **Identifying**

11. What are the two steps it takes to amend the Constitution?

_____

_____

✓ **Reading Check**

12. How many amendments to the Constitution have actually been ratified?

_____

Mark the Text

13. Underline the definition of *implied powers*.

FOLDABLES®

14. Place a three-tab Foldable along the dotted line to cover Check for Understanding. Write the title *The Constitution* on the anchor tab. Label the three tabs *Main Ideas*, *Making Changes*, and *Bill of Rights*. Write key words or phrases that you remember about each.

The Constitution

Lesson 2 Government and the People

ESSENTIAL QUESTION

How do new ideas change the way people live?

GUIDING QUESTIONS

1. **What are the three branches of government?**
2. **What are the rights and elements of participation of American citizens?**

Terms to Know

judicial review allows the Supreme Court to look at the actions of the other two branches and decide if the Constitution allows those actions

due process rules and processes the government must follow before it takes a person's life, liberty, or property

equal protection the right of all people to be treated equally under the law

naturalization the process of becoming a citizen of another country

Where in the world?

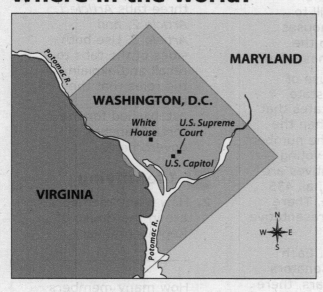

When did it happen?

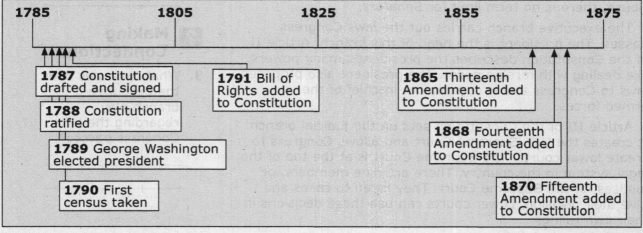

1785	1805	1825	1855	1875

1787 Constitution drafted and signed

1788 Constitution ratified

1789 George Washington elected president

1790 First census taken

1791 Bill of Rights added to Constitution

1865 Thirteenth Amendment added to Constitution

1868 Fourteenth Amendment added to Constitution

1870 Fifteenth Amendment added to Constitution

109

The Constitution

Lesson 2 Government and the People, *Continued*

The Federal Government

The federal government is divided into three branches: legislative, executive, and judicial. This ensures a separation of powers.

////////////////// Glue Foldable here ////////////////

The legislative branch is called Congress. Article I of the Constitution describes what Congress does. Congress makes laws for the nation. These laws can create taxes, permit government spending, and set up government programs. Congress can also declare war.

Congress is made up of two houses: the House of Representatives and the Senate. In order for a bill to become a law, most of the members from both houses must agree on the bill. After that, the bill goes to the president. If the president signs it, the bill becomes a law.

The House of Representatives is the larger house of Congress. The number of representatives that a state sends to the House is based on its population. States that have more people have more representatives. When the population of a state goes up or down, so does the number of its representatives. Today, the House has 435 voting members and 6 nonvoting delegates. Representatives are elected for a term of two years. Every two years, all 435 House seats are up for election at the same time. There are no limits on how many two-year terms a representative can serve.

The Senate has fewer members—100 senators. Each state is represented equally with two senators. Senators are elected for a term of six years. Every two years, there are elections for the Senate. Only one-third of the senators are up for election at a time. As with members of the House, there is no term limit for Senators.

The executive branch carries out the laws Congress passes. The president is the head of this branch. Article II of the Constitution describes the president's many powers, like dealing with foreign policy. The president also proposes laws to Congress and is commander-in-chief of the armed forces.

Article III of the Constitution sets up the judicial branch. It creates the U.S. Supreme Court and allows Congress to create lower courts. The Supreme Court is at the top of the legal system in the country. There are nine members, or justices, of the Supreme Court. They listen to cases and give their decision. Lower courts can use these decisions in their own rulings.

FOLDABLES

Explaining

1. Place a three-tab Foldable along the dotted line to cover the text that begins with "The legislative branch is called Congress." Label the three tabs *Article I*, *Article 2*, and *Article 3*. Use both sides of the tabs to recall and explain the roles that the three Articles established for the three branches of government.

Identifying

2. How many members are in the House of Representatives?

_____

How many members are in the Senate?

_____

Making Connections

3. What two roles does the executive branch play regarding the laws Congress passes?

_____

_____

The Constitution

Lesson 2 Government and the People, *Continued*

 Mark the Text

4. Underline the definition of *judicial review*.

✓ **Reading Check**

5. What parts of the Constitution establish the three branches of our federal government?

_____

_____

_____

A♭c **Defining**

6. What is *due process*?

_____

_____

_____

Identifying

7. What right guarantees that we must be treated the same as everyone else under the law?

_____

The Supreme Court has an important power called **judicial review.** Judicial review allows the Supreme Court to look at the actions of the other two branches and decide if those actions follow the rules of the Constitution. The justices are chosen by the president and approved by Congress.

Constitution, Article I	Constitution, Article II	Constitution, Article III
Defines: Legislative branch	**Defines:** Executive branch	**Defines:** Judicial branch
Headed by: Congress	**Headed by:** The president	**Headed by:** The Supreme Court
Made up of: * House of Representatives * The Senate	**Made up of:** * Vice president and cabinet *Government departments	**Made up of:** * The federal court system * Other lower courts

What It Means to Be a Citizen

As U.S. citizens, our rights fall into three main categories:

- The right to be protected from unfair government actions
- The right to be treated equally under the law
- The right to enjoy basic freedoms

Due process is a right guaranteed by the Fifth Amendment. The amendment states that no one shall "be deprived of life, liberty, or property, without due process of law." This means that the government must follow certain rules before it takes a right or freedom away from a citizen. For example, a person accused of a crime has the right to a trial before his freedom is taken away.

Equal protection is a right guaranteed by the Fourteenth Amendment. Equal protection means that the law must treat all people in the same way—no matter what race, religion, or political group they belong to.

The First Amendment describes many of our basic freedoms. These include freedom of speech, freedom of the press, and freedom of assembly. These freedoms allow us to share ideas, which is necessary in a free society.

111

netw🅞rks

The Constitution

Lesson 2 Government and the People, *Continued*

Our rights and freedoms also have some limits. For example, we cannot exercise our rights or freedoms if it hurts others or takes away their rights or freedoms.

A citizen is a person who owes loyalty to a country and receives its protection. There are several ways to become an American citizen. One way is to be born on American soil. Another is to have a parent who is a citizen. People born in other countries can become citizens by following a process called **naturalization.**

Citizenship comes with duties and responsibilities. A duty is something you must do. U.S. citizens must pay taxes, follow laws, and sit on a jury when called. A responsibility is something you should do even though you do not have to. If citizens do not take care of their responsibilities, it lowers the quality of their government. Voting is a citizen's most important responsibility.

A CITIZEN'S	
DUTIES	**RESPONSIBILITIES**
• Obey the law • Pay taxes • Sit on a jury when called	• Vote • Take part in government • Respect the rights of others

///////////// Glue Foldable here ///////////

Check for Understanding

List three duties and responsibilities of a citizen.

1. _____

2. _____

3. _____

What do you not have the right to do?

_____

_____

📑 Examining Details

8. List three ways a person can become a U.S. citizen.

_____

_____

_____

✓ Reading Check

9. What is the difference between a duty and a responsibility? Why is it important for a citizen to do both?

_____

_____

_____

_____

_____

FOLDABLES®

10. Place a two-tab Foldable along the dotted line to cover Check for Understanding. Label the anchor tab *Citizens*, and label the two tabs *must* and *should*. List words and phrases about the duties and responsibilities of citizens.

The Federalist Era

Lesson 1 The First President

ESSENTIAL QUESTION
What are the characteristics of a leader?

GUIDING QUESTIONS
1. **What decisions did Washington and the new Congress have to make about the new government?**
2. **How did the economy develop under the guidance of Alexander Hamilton?**

Terms to Know
precedent something done or said that becomes an example for others to follow
cabinet a group of advisers to a president
bond certificate that promises to repay borrowed money in the future—plus an additional amount of money, called interest

Where in the world?

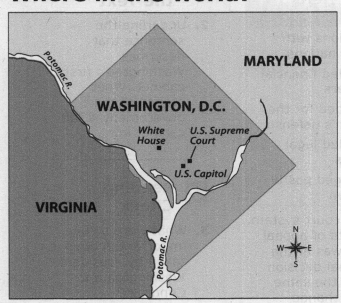

When did it happen?

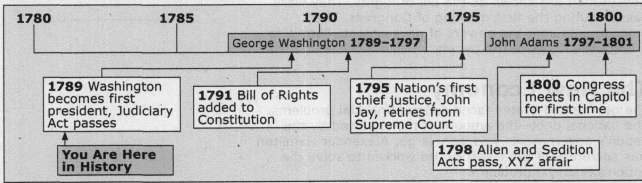

1780   1785   1790   1795   1800

George Washington 1789–1797

John Adams 1797–1801

1789 Washington becomes first president, Judiciary Act passes

1791 Bill of Rights added to Constitution

1795 Nation's first chief justice, John Jay, retires from Supreme Court

1800 Congress meets in Capitol for first time

You Are Here in History

1798 Alien and Sedition Acts pass, XYZ affair

The Federalist Era

Lesson 1 The First President, *Continued*

Washington Takes Office

George Washington was the first president of the United States. He knew that the **precedents**, or traditions, he started would be important. They would shape the future of the country and the government. With Congress, Washington set up departments within the executive branch. Washington and Congress also set up the court system. Congress added the Bill of Rights to the Constitution.

The executive branch began with three departments and two offices. These advisors were called the **cabinet**:

Department or Office	Head	Function
State Department	Thomas Jefferson	Relations with other nations
Department of the Treasury	Alexander Hamilton	Handled financial matters
Department of War	Henry Knox	Provided for the nation's defense
Attorney General	Edmund Randolph	Handled legal affairs
Postmaster General	Benjamin Franklin	Managed postal system

The Judiciary Act of 1789 created a federal court system. It had district courts at the lowest level. Courts of appeal were at the middle level. The Supreme Court was at the top of the court system. It would make the final decision on many issues. State courts and laws stayed the same. However, the federal courts had the power to change state decisions.

The first ten amendments, or changes, to the Constitution are known as the Bill of Rights. They were passed during the first meeting of Congress. The amendments limit the powers of government. They also protect the rights of the people.

The New Economy

The new United States faced serious financial problems. The national debt—the amount of money owed by the nation's government—was very large. Alexander Hamilton was secretary of the treasury. He worked to solve the nation's financial problems.

Critical Thinking

1. Why do you think it was important to set up a federal court system?

Marking the Text

2. Underline the sentence that describes Washington's first cabinet. What branch of the government is the cabinet in?

_____

Reading Check

3. What were three important actions taken by President Washington and Congress?

_____

_____

The Federalist Era

Lesson 1 The First President, *Continued*

? Analyzing

4. Why do you think Alexander Hamilton wanted to pay back the bonds from the confederation government?

_____

_____

_____

Describing

5. Why did some people oppose Hamilton's plan to pay off government bonds?

_____

_____

_____

✓ Reading Check

6. Why did Hamilton support locating the United States capital in the South?

_____

_____

_____

During the Revolutionary War, the confederation government had borrowed a large amount of money. It had issued **bonds**. These are certificates promising to pay back money in a certain length of time. Hamilton argued that the United States should pay back money borrowed from other countries and from American citizens. Hamilton believed that the national government should also pay the war debts of the states.

Some people did not like Hamilton's plan. Many people who bought bonds were worried that they would never be paid back. To get some money for their bonds, many people sold their bonds to speculators for less than the bonds were worth. Speculators hoped to make money later if the government finally paid back the bonds. The original bondholders saw that speculators would get rich and the bondholders would get nothing. Southern states also complained about the plan to pay state war debts. They had built up much less debt than the Northern states. They argued that the plan would make them pay more than their share.

Hamilton worked out a deal with Southern leaders. If they voted for his plan, he would support putting the new capital in the South. A new district called Washington, D.C., would be created between Virginia and Maryland.

To help build a strong national economy, Hamilton asked Congress to start a national bank. It would issue a single type of money for use in all states. Some people were against the idea, but Washington agreed with Hamilton. A national bank called the Bank of the United States was started.

Hamilton also proposed a tariff that would help protect American products. A tariff is a tax on goods bought from foreign countries. It makes products from other nations more expensive than those made at home. This tariff would help American companies compete against foreign companies.

Hamilton's Actions

- Paid back bonds
- Created Bank of the United States
- Introduced a protective tariff to help U.S. companies
- Supported putting the nation's capital in the South

115

The Federalist Era

Lesson 1 The First President, *Continued*

Check for Understanding

List the 3 departments that were part of Washington's executive branch.

1. _____

2. _____

3. _____

List 4 important actions taken by Alexander Hamilton.

1. _____

2. _____

3. _____

4. _____

FOLDABLES®

7. Place a two-tab Foldable along the dotted line to cover Check for Understanding. Write the title *George Washington* on the top tab and *Alexander Hamilton* on the bottom. On both sides of the tabs, list three things you remember about *both* as they helped form the new nation. Use the Foldable to help answer Check for Understanding.

The Federalist Era

Lesson 2 Early Challenges

Copyright by The McGraw-Hill Companies.

ESSENTIAL QUESTION
Why does conflict develop?

GUIDING QUESTIONS
1. **What challenges on the frontier did the new government face?**
2. **Why did Washington want to remain neutral in foreign conflicts?**

Term to Know

impressment seizing people against their will and forcing them to serve in the military or other public service

Where in the world?

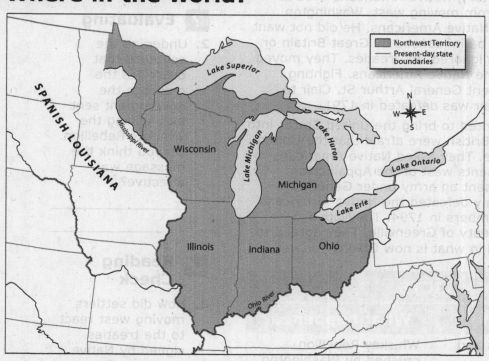

When did it happen?

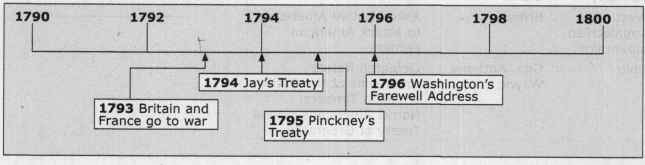

117

The Federalist Era

Lesson 2 Early Challenges, *Continued*

Trouble in the New Nation

The new government faced many problems. In western Pennsylvania farmers opposed a tax on whiskey. In 1794, an armed mob attacked tax collectors. They burned down buildings. This armed protest was called the Whiskey Rebellion. It worried government leaders. President Washington and his advisers decided to crush the protest using the army. This sent a message to people: the government would use force when necessary to maintain, or keep, order.

In the Northwest Territory, Native Americans tried to stop American settlers from moving west. Washington signed treaties with the Native Americans. He did not want the Native Americans to be influenced by Great Britain or Spain. American settlers ignored the treaties. They moved into lands promised to the Native Americans. Fighting broke out. Washington sent General Arthur St. Clair to restore order, but St. Clair was defeated in 1791.

Britain and France wanted to bring the United States into their own conflicts. The British were afraid that the United States would help France. They asked Native Americans to attack American settlements west of the Appalachian Mountains. Washington sent an army under General Anthony Wayne. The army defeated the Native Americans at the Battle of Fallen Timbers in 1794. The Native Americans signed the Treaty of Greenville. They agreed to give up most of the land in what is now Ohio.

CONFLICTS		
Where?	**Who?**	**What happened?**
Western Pennsylvania	Farmers and others	Whiskey Rebellion crushed by Washington
Northwest Territory	Gen. Arthur St. Clair	U.S. troops defeated by Native Americans
West of Appalachian mountains	British	Asked Native Americans to attack American settlers
Ohio	Gen. Anthony Wayne	Defeated Native Americans at the Battle of Fallen Timbers; Native Americans signed Treaty of Greenville

Identifying

1. What three European countries were involved in American affairs?

_____

_____

Evaluating

2. Underline the sentence that describes the message the government sent by crushing the Whiskey Rebellion. Do you think the message was effective?

_____

_____

Reading Check

3. How did settlers moving west react to the treaties signed by Native Americans?

_____

_____

The Federalist Era

Lesson 2 Early Challenges, *Continued*

📖 Vocabulary

4. What was *impressment*?

_____

_____

✊ Determining Cause and Effect

5. What was the result of Pinckney's Treaty?

_____

_____

✔️ Reading Check

6. What did the Proclamation of Neutrality do?

_____

_____

Problems with Europe

Britain and France went to war in 1793. Some Americans sided with France and others supported Britain. Washington hoped that the United States could stay neutral. Neutral means not taking sides in a conflict.

The French tried to get American volunteers to attack British ships. In response, President Washington issued a Proclamation of Neutrality. It declared that American citizens could not fight in the war. It also stopped French and British warships from using American ports. The British captured American ships that traded with the French. They forced the American crews into the British navy. This practice was called **impressment**. It angered the Americans.

Washington sent John Jay to work out a peaceful solution with Britain. Jay proposed a treaty. In Jay's Treaty, the British would agree to leave American soil. But the treaty did not deal with the problems of impressment. It also did not deal with the British interfering with American trade. Jay's Treaty was unpopular, but the Senate approved it.

Spanish leaders feared that the United States and Great Britain would work together against them in North America. Thomas Pinckney went to Spain to settle the differences between the United States and Spain. In 1795 he proposed a treaty that said Americans could travel on the Mississippi River. Pinckney's Treaty also gave Americans the right to trade at New Orleans.

Jay's Treaty	Pinckney's Treaty
• British agreed to leave American soil	• Between Spain and the U.S.
• Did not deal with impressment	• Gave Americans right to travel the Mississippi River
• Did not deal with British interfering with American trade	• Gave Americans right to trade at New Orleans
• Unpopular	

Washington decided to retire and not run for a third term as president. In his last speech, he warned the country not to get involved in foreign problems. He also warned against creating political parties.

119

/ / / / / / / / / / / / Glue Foldable here / / / / / / / / / / / /

Check for Understanding

List four challenges faced by the new government within the United States.

1. _____

2. _____

3. _____

4 _____

List the two treaties that the United States signed with foreign countries to resolve conflicts.

1. _____

2. _____

FOLDABLES

7. Place a two-tab Foldable along the dotted line to cover Check for Understanding. Write the title *Challenges* on the anchor tab. Label the tabs—*Conflicts in U.S.* and *Foreign Conflicts*. Use both sides of the tabs to record what you recall about each and write facts about who was involved and what happened. Use the Foldable to help answer Check for Understanding.

The Federalist Era

Lesson 3 The First Political Parties

ESSENTIAL QUESTION
How do governments change?

GUIDING QUESTIONS
1. **How did different opinions lead to the first political parties?**
2. **What important events occurred during the presidency of John Adams?**

Terms to Know
partisan firmly favoring one party or faction
caucus a meeting of members of a political party to choose candidates for upcoming elections
alien a person living in a country who is not a citizen of that country
sedition activities aimed at weakening the established government by inciting resistance or rebellion to authority
nullify to legally overturn
states' rights the idea that states should have all powers that the Constitution does not give to the federal government or forbid to the states

When did it happen?

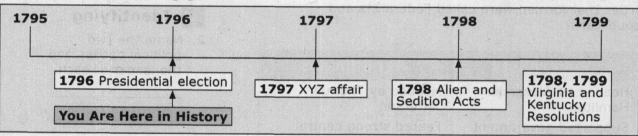

1795	1796	1797	1798	1799

1796 Presidential election

You Are Here in History

1797 XYZ affair

1798 Alien and Sedition Acts

1798, 1799 Virginia and Kentucky Resolutions

What do you know?

In the first column, answer the questions based on what you know before you study. After this lesson, complete the last column.

Now...		Later...
	How did people feel about political parties when Washington was president?	
	What were the first two political parties in America?	
	Did President John Adams and Vice President Thomas Jefferson have similar views about government?	
	Why were Americans suspicious of aliens during this period?	
	Why did some states believe they had the power to overturn federal laws?	

121

The Federalist Era

Lesson 3 The First Political Parties, Continued

Opposing Parties

President Washington warned against political parties. He was afraid that political parties would divide the nation. Others thought that it was natural for people to disagree about issues. By 1796, Americans were beginning to split into two different groups.

In Washington's cabinet, Alexander Hamilton and Thomas Jefferson often disagreed. They disagreed about economic policy and foreign relations. They disagreed about how much power the federal government should have. They also disagreed on the rules of the Constitution. Even Washington was **partisan**—favoring one side of an issue. Washington usually supported Hamilton's positions. These disagreements caused both Hamilton and Jefferson to resign from, or leave, the cabinet. The two political parties that formed were called Federalists and Republicans.

Federalists	Republicans
Headed by Alexander Hamilton	Headed by Thomas Jefferson
Supported government by representatives	Feared strong central government controlled by only a few people
Believed government had broad powers implied by the Constitution	Believed government only had powers specifically stated in the Constitution

In 1796, there was a presidential election. Before the election, the two parties held meetings called **caucuses.** At the caucuses, members of Congress and other leaders chose their parties' candidates for office.

The Federalists chose John Adams for president. The Republicans chose Thomas Jefferson. This was the first time candidates identified themselves as members of political parties.

Adams received 71 electoral votes to win the election. Jefferson finished second with 68 votes. Under the Constitution at that time, the person with the second-highest number of electoral votes became vice president. Jefferson became the new vice president. The new government in 1797 had a Federalist president and a Republican vice president.

? Defending

1. Underline the sentences that describe two opinions about political parties. Which opinion do you agree with? Why?

_____

_____

_____

Identifying

2. Name the two political parties and the leader of each.

_____

_____

✓ Reading Check

3. What was different about the election of 1796?

_____

_____

The Federalist Era

Lesson 3 The First Political Parties, *Continued*

FOLDABLES®

📝 Describing

4. Place a four-tab Foldable along the dotted line to cover the text beneath the title *John Adams as President*. Write the title *John Adams* on the anchor tab. Label the four tabs—*Who*, *What*, *When*, and *Where*. On both sides of the tabs, write what you recall about President John Adams and how he handled the capture of American ships by the French.

📝 Identifying

5. Who were the people that President Adams referred to as X, Y, and Z?

_____

_____

✔️ Reading Check

6. What was important about the Virginia and Kentucky Resolutions of 1798 and 1799?

_____

_____

John Adams as President

/ / / / / / / / / / / Glue Foldable here / / / / / / / / / /

When Adams became president, France and the United States could still not agree. The French thought that Jay's Treaty allowed Americans to help the British. The French captured American ships that carried goods to Britain.

In 1797, Adams sent a team to Paris to try to end the disagreement. The French officials refused to meet with the Americans. Instead, they sent three agents. They demanded a bribe from America and a loan for France. Adams was angry at the French actions. He called the French agents "X, Y, and Z." Adams urged Congress to prepare for war. This was called the XYZ affair.

XYZ Affair

- French captured American ships carrying goods to Britain

- Adams sent a team to France

- Three French agents, known as X, Y, and Z, tried to get a bribe and a loan from Americans

---

People were angry with France. Americans became more suspicious of aliens. **Aliens** are immigrants living in a country who are not citizens of that country. Federalists passed laws to protect the nation's security. In 1798, they passed a group of laws known as the Alien and Sedition Acts. **Sedition** means activities that weaken the government. The Alien Act allowed the president to put aliens in prison. He could also send them out of the country if he thought they were dangerous. Later, France and the United States signed a treaty which stopped French attacks on American ships.

The Virginia and Kentucky Resolutions were passed in 1798 and 1799. They claimed that the Alien and Sedition Acts did not follow the rules of the Constitution. They also said the states should not put them into action. The Kentucky Resolutions said that states might **nullify**, or legally overturn, federal laws if they thought the laws went against the Constitution.

The resolutions supported the idea of **states' rights**. This idea says that the powers of the federal government should be limited. Its powers should be only those clearly given to it in the Constitution. The states should have all other powers. The issue of states' rights would be important in the future.

Lesson 3 The First Political Parties, *Continued*

Alien and Sedition Acts

↓

Inspired

↓

Virginia and Kentucky Resolutions

/ / / / / / / / / / / Glue Foldable here / / / / / / / / / /

Check for Understanding

List the president and vice president elected in 1796 and the political parties they belonged to.

1. _____

2. _____

List the two states that passed resolutions opposing the Alien and Sedition Acts.

1. _____

2. _____

Copyright by The McGraw-Hill Companies.

FOLDABLES®

7. Place a one-tab Foldable along the dotted line to cover Check for Understanding. Write the title *Alien and Sedition Acts* in the middle of the Foldable tab. Create a memory map by drawing arrows from the title. List three words or phrases that you recall about the Alien and Sedition Acts. Use the Foldable to help answer Check for Understanding.

The Jefferson Era

Lesson 1 A New Party in Power

ESSENTIAL QUESTION

How do governments change?

GUIDING QUESTIONS

1. **What did the election of 1800 show about the nature of politics?**
2. **What did Jefferson want to accomplish during his presidency?**

Terms to Know

customs duty tax collected on imported goods

jurisdiction the power or right to interpret and apply a law

Where in the world?

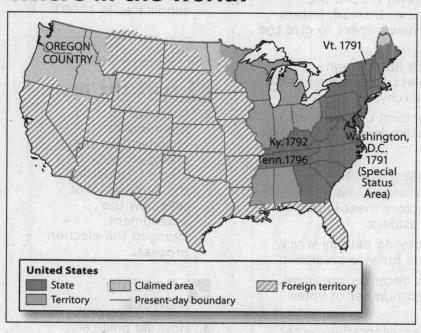

OREGON COUNTRY

Vt. 1791

Washington, D.C. 1791 (Special Status Area)

Ky. 1792

Tenn.1796

United States
- State
- Territory
- Claimed area
- Present-day boundary
- Foreign territory

When did it happen?

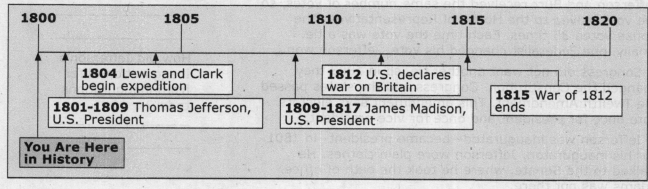

1800   1805   1810   1815   1820

1804 Lewis and Clark begin expedition

1801-1809 Thomas Jefferson, U.S. President

1812 U.S. declares war on Britain

1809-1817 James Madison, U.S. President

1815 War of 1812 ends

You Are Here in History

125

netw✺rks

The Jefferson Era

Lesson 1 A New Party in Power, Continued

The Election of 1800

These were the choices in the election of 1800:

Party	President	Vice President
Federalists	John Adams	Charles Pinckney
Republicans	Thomas Jefferson	Aaron Burr

In 1800, presidential campaigns were not like they are today. The candidates did not travel around the country to ask people to vote for them. Instead, letters were sent to important people and newspapers to give the candidates' views.

Still, in 1800, the two sides fought hard to win. Federalists said Jefferson was "godless." Republicans said Federalists would bring back a monarchy.

In the United States, it is the Electoral College that elects the president. Today, the system is much like it was in 1800.

The Election Process in 1800
1. People choose electors. The electors meet in the Electoral College to elect the president.
2. Electors vote for two people. They do not say which vote is for president and which is for vice president.
3. The person with the most votes becomes president. The person with the next highest number of votes becomes vice president.
4. If there is a tie, the House of Representatives votes.

When the electors voted in 1800, there was a tie. Jefferson and Burr received the same number of votes, so the vote moved to the House of Representatives. The House voted 35 times. Each time the vote was a tie. Finally, one Federalist changed his vote. Jefferson won.

Congress did not want another tie, so in 1803 they changed the Constitution. Congress and the states passed the Twelfth Amendment. This amendment says electors vote once for president and once for vice president.

Jefferson was inaugurated—became president—in 1801. For his inauguraton, Jefferson wore plain clothes. He walked to the Senate, where he took the oath of office. Adams was not there.

126

✍ **Listing**

1. Who were the presidential candidates in 1800?

_____

_____

Who were the vice presidential candidates in 1800?

_____

_____

✍ **Mark the Text**

2. The Twelfth Amendment changed how the president was elected. Underline the sentence that tells how the amendment changed the election process.

☑ **Reading Check**

3. How did political campaigns in 1800 differ from today?

_____

_____

How did Jefferson's inauguration differ from inaugurations today?

_____

_____

The Jefferson Era

Lesson 1 A New Party in Power, *Continued*

 **Mark the Text**

4. Circle four changes Jefferson made to the federal government.

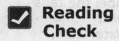 **Identifying**

5. Name two ways the government collected money when Jefferson was president.

_____

_____

? **Critical Thinking**

6. Who controlled the courts during Jefferson's presidency?

_____

How did they gain control?

_____

_____

✓ **Reading Check**

7. Why was the *Marbury* v. *Madison* ruling important?

_____

_____

_____

_____

Jefferson also made a speech called an inaugural address. In his speech, Jefferson said that he wanted to limit the power and size of the federal government. He thought states should have more power. He thought states could protect freedom better than a large federal government. He also wanted to cut government spending.

Jefferson as President

Jefferson chose to work with people who agreed with his ideas. Together, they made many changes to the federal government. These included:

- lowering the national debt.
- cutting military spending.
- cutting the number of government workers to only a few hundred.
- getting rid of most federal taxes.

The government still needed money, though. Jefferson's government got money from two sources:

- **customs duties** (taxes on imported goods).
- selling land in the West.

Before Jefferson became President, Congress passed a law called the Judiciary Act of 1801. This act set up a system of courts. President Adams moved fast. He appointed, or chose, hundreds of people to be judges in these new courts. Adams used these appointments to keep Jefferson from choosing judges. In this way, Adams made sure the Federalists controlled the courts.

There was a problem, though. These people could not become judges until they got special papers. Some of the judges Adams appointed did not receive their papers before Jefferson became president. Jefferson told Secretary of State James Madison not to deliver them.

One judge who did not receive his papers was William Marbury. Marbury wanted to get his papers. He took his case to the Supreme Court. The court decided it did not have the **jurisdiction**—the legal power—to force Madison to deliver the papers. This case was called *Marbury* v. *Madison*.

Marbury v. *Madison* was a very important case. It set up the three principles of judicial review. Principles are basic ideas.

netw⊗rks

The Jefferson Era

Lesson 1 A New Party in Power, *Continued*

The head of the Supreme Court was Chief Justice John Marshall. Marshall wrote the court's opinion. In it he said:

1. The Constitution is the supreme, or highest, law in the country.
2. If the Constitution says one thing and another law says something else, people have to follow the Constitution.
3. The judicial branch (courts) can say laws are unconstitutional.

Marbury v. *Madison* made the Supreme Court more powerful. Chief Justice Marshall made the Supreme Court stronger in other cases, too. This chart shows three of these cases. It also shows the effect of each case.

Case	Effect
McCulloch v. *Maryland*	Congress can do more than the Constitution specifically says it can do. States cannot tax the federal government.
Gibbons v. *Ogden*	Federal law takes priority over state law when more than one state is involved.
Worcester v. *Georgia*	States cannot make rules about Native Americans. Only the federal government can.

With these decisions, Chief Justice Marshall also strengthened the federal government and weakened the states.

////////////////// Glue Foldable here //////////////////

Check for Understanding

State two facts about the election of 1800.

1. _____

2. _____

List two changes Jefferson made to the federal government during his presidency.

1. _____

2. _____

✎ Identifying

8. What three powers did states lose in the three cases listed in the chart?

_____

_____

_____

❓ Drawing Conclusions

9. Do you think Jefferson was pleased with the decisions in these three cases? Why?

_____

_____

FOLDABLES®

10. Place a three-tab Venn diagram Foldable along the dotted line to cover the Check for Understanding. Write *Election of 1800* on the anchor tab. Label the tabs *Federalist Candidate*, *Both*, and *Republican Candidate*. List facts about each to compare the candidates and the election's outcome. Use the Foldable to help answer Check for Understanding.

netw⊛rks

The Jefferson Era

Lesson 2 The Louisiana Purchase

ESSENTIAL QUESTION

How does geography influence the way people live?

GUIDING QUESTIONS

1. **How did Spain and France play a role in Americans moving west?**

2. **How did the Louisiana Purchase open an area of settlement?**

> **Term to Know**
> **secede** break away from a country or group

Where in the world?

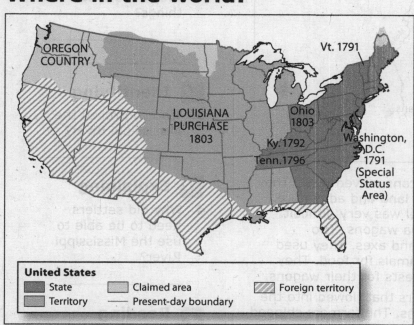

OREGON COUNTRY

Vt. 1791

LOUISIANA PURCHASE 1803

Ohio 1803

Ky. 1792

Tenn. 1796

Washington, D.C. 1791 (Special Status Area)

United States
- State
- Territory
- Claimed area
- —— Present-day boundary
- Foreign territory

When did it happen?

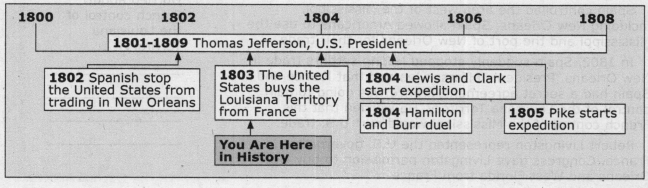

| 1800 | 1802 | 1804 | 1806 | 1808 |

1801–1809 Thomas Jefferson, U.S. President

1802 Spanish stop the United States from trading in New Orleans

1803 The United States buys the Louisiana Territory from France

1804 Lewis and Clark start expedition

1804 Hamilton and Burr duel

1805 Pike starts expedition

You Are Here in History

129

networks

Lesson 2 The Louisiana Purchase, *Continued*

Westward, Ho!

The Mississippi River was the western boundary of the United States in 1800. The area west of the river was called the Louisiana Territory. The Louisiana Territory went west to the Rocky Mountains. It went south to New Orleans. It did not have a clear border to the north.

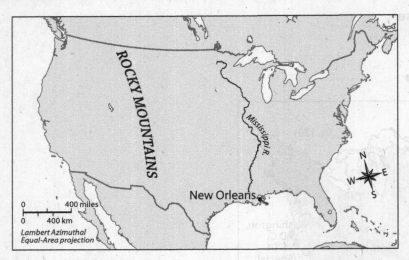

In the early 1800s, many Americans moved west. They were called pioneers. They wanted land and adventure. Many pioneers were farmers. Travel was very difficult. Settlers often traveled in Conestoga wagons. Two important possessions were rifles and axes. They used rifles for protection and to hunt animals for food. They used axes to cut paths through forests for their wagons.

Many pioneers settled along rivers that flowed into the Mississippi River. They started farms. The farmers shipped their crops along the rivers to markets. They shipped many goods down the Mississippi River to New Orleans. From New Orleans, the goods traveled to East Coast markets.

Spain controlled the area west of the Mississippi, including New Orleans. Spain allowed Americans to use the Mississippi and the port of New Orleans for their trade.

In 1802, Spain suddenly stopped letting settlers trade in New Orleans. President Jefferson learned that France and Spain had a secret agreement. France was going to gain control of the Louisiana Territory. He worried that this French control of the Mississippi would hurt U.S. trade.

Robert Livingston represented the U.S. government in France. Congress gave Livingston permission to buy New Orleans and West Florida from France.

130

Visualize It

1. On the map, color and label the Louisiana Territory.

Mark the Text

2. Underline two things that settlers needed. Why did they need these things?

_____

_____

Identifying

3. Who controlled the Mississippi River?

_____

Explaining

4. Why did settlers need to be able to use the Mississippi River?

_____

Reading Check

5. Why was Jefferson worried about French control of the Louisiana Territory?

_____

_____

_____

Lesson 2 The Louisiana Purchase, *Continued*

FOLDABLES

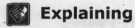

Analyzing

6. Place a three-tab Foldable along the dotted line under the title "An Expanding Nation." Write the title *Louisiana Purchase* on the anchor tab. Label the three tabs *What?*, *What Cost?*, and *What Result?* On the tabs, describe how the United States acquired the Louisiana Territory from France.

Explaining

7. Why was Napoleon willing to sell Louisiana?

_____

Reading Check

8. List two reasons the Louisiana Purchase was important for the United States.

_____

_____

Mark the Text

9. Circle the goals of the Lewis and Clark Expedition.

Napoleon Bonaparte, the French leader, wanted to rule much of Europe and North America. Napoleon wanted to use the Caribbean island of Santo Domingo as a naval base. It was important to his plan to rule in North America.

Napoleon's plan did not work. Enslaved Africans and other workers in Santo Domingo revolted and claimed independence. By 1804, the French had been forced out of Santo Domingo.

An Expanding Nation

/ / / / / / / / / / / Glue Foldable here / / / / / / / / / /

Without Santo Domingo, Napoleon did not want Louisiana. Also, he needed money to pay for his war against Britain. To get money, he decided to sell the Louisiana Territory.

Robert Livingston and James Monroe wanted to buy New Orleans and West Florida. A French official said they could buy all of the Louisiana Territory. They worried they did not have the power to make that decision. In spite of their worry, Livingston and Monroe decided it was too good a chance to miss. They agreed to pay $15 million for the land.

Even Jefferson was not sure he had the authority to buy the Louisiana Territory. The Constitution did not say anything about buying new land. Jefferson decided his right to make treaties allowed him to buy the land. The Senate okayed the purchase in October 1803. The new land doubled the size of the United States.

Having this new territory was good because
- it provided a large amount of new land for farmers.
- it protected shipping on the Mississippi River.

Americans did not know much about the new territory. Jefferson wanted to learn more about it. Congress agreed to send a group to explore the new land.

The group had several goals. They were supposed to
- collect information about the land.
- learn about plants and animals.
- suggest sites for forts.
- find a Northwest Passage, or a water route across North America to Asia.

Jefferson chose Meriwether Lewis to lead the expedition. Lewis's co-leader was William Clark. Both men were interested in science and had done business with Native Americans.

The Jefferson Era

Lesson 2 The Louisiana Purchase, *Continued*

Other Members of the Lewis and Clark Expedition	
sailors	cook
gun makers	Native American–French interpreters
carpenters	York, an African American
scouts	Sacagawea, a Shoshone guide

The group left St. Louis in spring 1804. They traveled about 4,000 miles to the Pacific, and returned in 1806. They brought back a lot of information about the people, plants, animals, and geography of the West. What they found encouraged people to want to move westward.

Zebulon Pike led two expeditions. He brought back information about the Great Plains and the Rocky Mountains. He also mapped part of the Rio Grande and explored what is now northern Mexico and southern Texas.

Federalists in the northeast worried about the country growing in the west. They were afraid they would lose power. One group of Federalists planned to **secede,** or leave, the nation. They decided they needed New York in order to be successful. They asked Aaron Burr to help them, and he agreed.

Alexander Hamilton heard Burr had agreed to help the Federalists secede. He accused Burr of treason. Burr said Hamilton's accusation hurt Burr's political career. To get even, he challenged Hamilton to a duel. Burr shot Hamilton, and Hamilton died the next day. Burr ran away so he would not be arrested.

/////////////// Glue Foldable here ///////////////

Check for Understanding

How did Spain play a role in Americans moving west? How did France play a role?

1. _____

2. _____

List two reasons people moved westward after the Louisiana Purchase.

1. _____

2. _____

❓ Making Connections

10. Why do you think it was important that Lewis and Clark were interested in science and had done business with Native Americans?

_____

_____

👁 Visualize It

11. Make a chart that shows how the Federalists' plan to secede led to Hamilton's death.

FOLDABLES®

12. Place a one-tab Foldable along the dotted line to cover Check for Understanding. Write *Moving West* on the anchor tab. Create a memory map by writing *Exploring New Land* in the middle of the tab and drawing four arrows around the title. List four things you recall about exploration during this time. Use the Foldable to help answer Check for Understanding.

networks

Lesson 3 A Time of Conflict

ESSENTIAL QUESTION
Why does conflict develop?

GUIDING QUESTIONS
1. **How did the United States become involved in a conflict with Tripoli?**
2. **What issues challenged James Madison during his presidency?**

Terms to Know
tribute money paid to a leader or state for protection
neutral rights privileges or freedoms given to countries that don't take sides in a war
embargo blocking of trade with another country
nationalism loyalty or dedication to one's country

Where in the world?

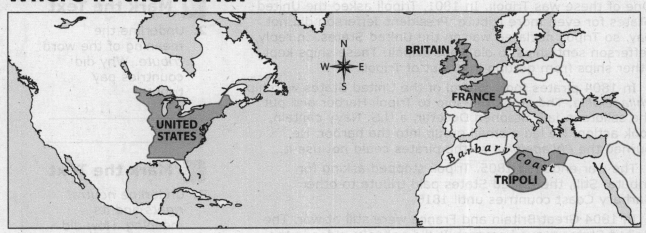

When did it happen?

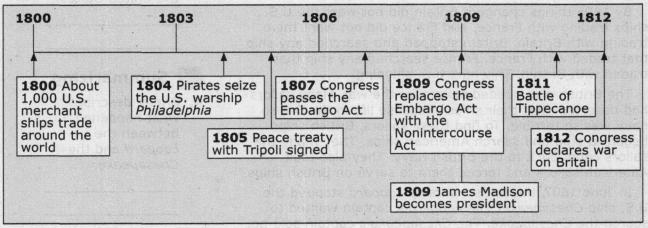

1800 About 1,000 U.S. merchant ships trade around the world

1804 Pirates seize the U.S. warship *Philadelphia*

1805 Peace treaty with Tripoli signed

1807 Congress passes the Embargo Act

1809 Congress replaces the Embargo Act with the Nonintercourse Act

1809 James Madison becomes president

1811 Battle of Tippecanoe

1812 Congress declares war on Britain

133

The Jefferson Era

Lesson 3 A Time of Conflict, *Continued*

American Ships on the High Seas

U.S. shipping grew in the late 1700s. People sailed to China and other parts of the world, hoping to make money. At the same time, France and Britain were at war. Their merchant ships stayed home so they would not be captured. This gave American merchants less competition.

Along the North African coast, there were pirates. The countries along this coast—the Barbary States—demanded **tribute**—money paid for protection. Many countries paid tribute, because it cost less than war with the pirates.

The United States paid tribute to the Barbary States. One of these was Tripoli. In 1801, Tripoli asked the United States for even more tribute. President Jefferson did not pay, so Tripoli declared war on the United States. In reply, Jefferson sent ships to blockade Tripoli. These ships kept other ships from getting in or out of Tripoli.

In 1804 pirates took control of the United States warship *Philadelphia*. They took the ship to Tripoli Harbor and put the sailors in jail. Stephen Decatur, a U.S. Navy captain, took action. He led a small group into the harbor. He burned the *Philadelphia* so the pirates could not use it.

The war ended in 1805. Tripoli stopped asking for tribute. Still, the United States paid tribute to other Barbary Coast countries until 1816.

In 1804 Great Britain and France were still at war. The United States stayed neutral. It did not take sides in the war. American ships had **neutral rights.** They could sail the seas freely and trade with both Britain and France.

By 1805 things changed. Britain did not want the U.S. ships trading with France, and France did not want them trading with Britain. Britain stopped and searched any ship that traded with France. France searched any ship that traded with Britain. This hurt U.S. shipping.

The British also needed sailors for the war. Many sailors had deserted—left their ships—because life in the British navy was so terrible. To find these sailors, British ships began to stop and search American ships. They made the sailors come back to the British Navy. They also took American sailors and forced them to serve on British ships.

In June 1807, the British warship *Leopard* stopped the U.S. ship *Chesapeake*. The *Leopard*'s captain wanted to search the *Chesapeake*. The *Chesapeake*'s captain said no. The British ship shot at the U.S. ship, killing three sailors.

Americans were very angry. Even though many Americans wanted war with Britain, Jefferson did not.

134

? **Critical Thinking**

1. Why did many British and French ships stay home in the mid-1790s?

_____

_____

Mark the Text

2. Underline the meaning of the word *tribute*. Why did countries pay tribute?

_____

_____

Mark the Text

3. Underline *neutral rights* and its meaning. How did Britain go against the neutral rights of the United States?

_____

_____

Summarizing

4. Briefly describe what happened between the *Leopard* and the *Chesapeake*.

_____

_____

_____

The Jefferson Era

Lesson 3 A Time of Conflict, *Continued*

❓ Contrasting

5. What was the difference between the Embargo Act and the Nonintercourse Act?

_____

_____

✔️ Reading Check

6. Did the Embargo Act work? Why?

_____

_____

✏️ Identifying

7. List three problems Madison faced when he became president.

_____

_____

_____

✏️ Mark the Text

8. Underline the reason tensions grew with Native Americans in the West.

❓ Analyzing

9. Did Madison think France or Britain was the bigger enemy?

_____

After the attack on the *Chesapeake*, Jefferson asked Congress to pass the Embargo Act. Congress passed this law in December 1807. The **embargo** stopped U.S. ships from trading with any other countries.

The Embargo Act failed. People who worked in shipping lost their jobs, and farmers lost markets for their crops. Congress ended the Embargo Act in 1809 and replaced it with the Nonintercourse Act. The new law only stopped trade with Britain and France. It also failed.

Like Washington before him, Jefferson did not run for a third term. In 1808, the candidates were:

Party	Candidate
Republicans	James Madison
Federalists	Charles Pinckney

People were angry about the embargo. Federalists hoped this anger would make people vote for Pinckney. Still, Madison easily won the election.

War at Home and Abroad

When James Madison became president, he faced three big problems:

- The embargo hurt the economy, so people were angry.
- Britain kept stopping American ships.
- In the West, tension with Native Americans grew.

In 1810, Congress said it would stop the embargo with the country that lifted its trade ban. Napoleon said France would allow open trade with the United States.

Even though trade started again, the French kept taking American ships. The French sold the ships and kept the money. The United States was about to go to war. Was the enemy Britain or France? Madison thought Britain was more dangerous to the United States.

Madison also had problems in the western United States. White settlers wanted more land. The land they wanted had been given to Native Americans. Tensions grew.

Native Americans tried two things:

- They talked to the British in Canada about working together.
- They joined with other Native American groups.

135

The Jefferson Era

Lesson 3 A Time of Conflict, *Continued*

Tecumseh was a Shawnee chief who got several Native American groups to work together to protect their land rights. He also wanted Native Americans to work with the British. He thought that together they could stop settlers from moving into Native American lands.

Tecumseh's brother, the Prophet, told Native Americans to go back to their old ways. He founded Prophetstown in Indiana near the Tippecanoe and Wabash Rivers.

William Henry Harrison was governor of the Indiana Territory. He worried about the power of Tecumseh and the Prophet. He was afraid they would join forces with the British. Harrison attacked Prophetstown and won. This was called the Battle of Tippecanoe

Americans claimed the Battle of Tippecanoe as a great victory. It was also bad news for the Americans, though. It convinced Tecumseh to join forces with the British.

A group of young Republicans called the War Hawks wanted war with Britain. They wanted the United States to be more powerful. Many Americans liked the War Hawks' **nationalism,** or loyalty to their country. There were two groups in the War Hawks:

- Southern Republicans who wanted Florida
- Western Republicans who wanted lands in Canada

Federalists in the Northeast were against war.

On June 1, 1812, Madison asked Congress to declare war on Britain. In the meantime, the British had decided to stop searching American ships. By the time American leaders learned of the change, it was too late. The United States had already declared war on Britain.

////////////////// Glue Foldable here ///////////////

Check for Understanding

Why did Tripoli declare war on the United States?

_____

_____

Madison faced several challenges as president. List one challenge inside the country and one challenge from outside the country.

1. _____

2. _____

📋 Listing

10. List two things Tecumseh thought Native Americans should do to protect their land.

_____

_____

📋 Mark the Text

11. Underline a negative result of the victory at Tippecanoe.

✔ Reading Check

12. List the three things that led to war with Britain.

_____

_____

FOLDABLES®

13. Place a two-tab Foldable along the dotted line to cover Check for Understanding. Write *Challenges of the Madison Presidency* on the anchor tab. Label the tabs *Shipping* and *Tippecanoe*. List two facts that you remember about each challenge. Use the Foldable to help answer Check for Understanding.

The Jefferson Era

Lesson 4 The War of 1812

ESSENTIAL QUESTION
Why does conflict develop?

GUIDING QUESTIONS

1. **In what ways was the United States unprepared for war with Britain?**
2. **Why were Americans instilled with national pride after the battle of New Orleans?**

> **Term to Know**
> **frigate** fast, medium-sized warship

Where in the world?

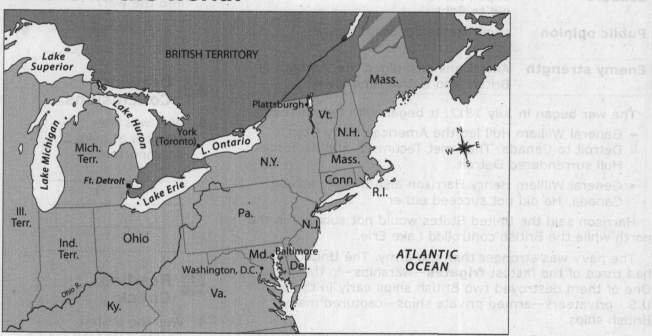

When did it happen?

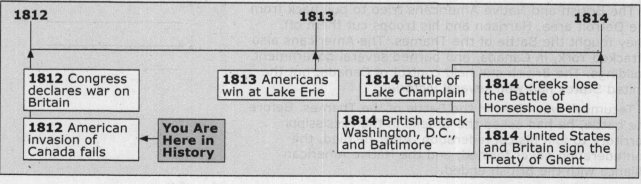

137

networks

The Jefferson Era

Lesson 4 The War of 1812, *Continued*

Defeats and Victories

The War Hawks thought the United States would defeat Britain quickly, but America was not ready for war.

Reasons the United States Was Unprepared for War	
Troops	• fewer than 12,000 soldiers • 50,000–100,000 poorly trained state militia soldiers
Leaders	experienced leaders were too old to fight
Public opinion	some states opposed the war
Enemy strength	Americans misjudged the strength of Britain and Native Americans.

The war began in July 1812. It began with two failures:

• General William Hull led the American army from Detroit to Canada. They met Tecumseh and his forces. Hull surrendered Detroit.

• General William Henry Harrison also tried to invade Canada. He did not succeed either.

Harrison said the United States would not succeed in the north while the British controlled Lake Erie.

The navy was stronger than the army. The United States had three of the fastest **frigates**—warships—in the world. One of them destroyed two British ships early in the war. U.S. privateers—armed private ships—captured many British ships.

Oliver Hazard Perry led a fleet of American ships to get control of Lake Erie. On September 10, 1813, his ships destroyed the British fleet. Americans controlled Lake Erie.

The British and Native Americans tried to pull back from the Detroit area. Harrison and his troops cut them off. They fought the Battle of the Thames. The Americans also attacked York, in Canada, and burned several government buildings. The British still held control of Canada, but the United States had won several victories.

Tecumseh was killed in the Battle of the Thames. Before the battle, he had asked the Creeks in the Mississippi Territory to join his confederation. After he died, the confederation never formed, and the Native American alliance with the British ended.

Mark the Text

1. Underline the definition of *frigate*.

Identifying

2. What was one strength of the United States going into the war?

_____

_____

Drawing Conclusions

3. Why was the success at Lake Erie so important?

_____

_____

_____

_____

Reading Check

4. Was the United States prepared for war? Why?

_____

_____

_____

_____

The Jefferson Era

Lesson 4 The War of 1812, *Continued*

✍ Explaining

5. Why were the British able to send more troops to fight the United States in 1814?

_____

_____

❓ Contrasting

6. What happened when the British attacked Washington, D.C.?

_____

How was the battle in Baltimore different?

_____

❓ Sequencing

7. Number these events to show the order in which they happened:

Americans win Battle of New Orleans.

British defeat France.

British lose Battle of Lake Champlain.

U.S. and Britain sign Treaty of Ghent.

British attack Washington, D. C.

In March 1814, Andrew Jackson attacked the Creeks. He and his forces killed more than 550 Creek people in the Battle of Horseshoe Bend. After this defeat, the Creeks gave up most of their land.

The British Offensive

When the War of 1812 started, the British were still at war with France. In 1814, they won that war. This made it possible for them to send more troops to fight in America.

In August 1814, the British arrived in Washington, D.C. They quickly defeated the American militia. They burned and wrecked much of the city. Americans were surprised when the British did not try to hold the city.

Instead they left Washington, D.C., and headed to Baltimore. They attacked Baltimore in September 1814. Baltimore was ready. Fort McHenry in Baltimore harbor helped defend the city and kept the British out.

Francis Scott Key watched the bombs exploding over Fort McHenry on September 13. The next morning he saw the American flag still flying over the fort. It inspired him to write the poem "The Star-Spangled Banner." In 1931, this became the national anthem.

In the meantime, General Prevost was leading 10,000 British troops from Canada into New York. He wanted to capture Plattsburgh, an important city on Lake Champlain. In September 1814, an American naval force defeated the British fleet on Lake Champlain. Afraid the Americans would surround his troops, Prevost turned them around and went back to Canada.

After the Battle of Lake Champlain, the British decided to stop fighting. The war cost too much, and there was little to gain from it.

In December 1814, representatives from the United States and Britain signed a peace treaty in Ghent, Belgium. The Treaty of Ghent ended the war, but it did not:

- change borders.
- end impressment of sailors.
- mention neutral rights.

On January 8, 1815, before people in the United States knew about the treaty, British troops moved to attack New Orleans. Andrew Jackson and his troops were ready for them. The Americans hid behind cotton bales. The bales protected them from bullets. The unprotected redcoats were easy targets. Hundreds of British soldiers died.

The Jefferson Era

Lesson 4 The War of 1812, *Continued*

The Battle of New Orleans was a clear victory for the Americans. Andrew Jackson became a famous hero. His fame helped him become president in the election of 1828.

Federalists in New England were against the war from the start. They met in Hartford in December 1814. A few wanted to secede. Most wanted to stay in the United States. They made a list of changes they wanted made to the Constitution.

Pride in America grew with the success in the war. After the war, many people thought the Federalist complaints were unpatriotic. They lost respect for the Federalists, and the party grew weaker.

As the Federalists grew weaker, the War Hawks grew stronger. The War Hawks took control of the Republican Party. They wanted five things:

- trade
- more settlement in the West
- fast growth of the economy
- a strong national government
- a strong army and navy

After the war of 1812, Americans had great pride in their country. Other countries had more respect for the United States, too.

////////////////// Glue Foldable here //////////////////

Check for Understanding

List four ways the United States was unprepared for war in 1812.

1. _____

2. _____

3. _____

4. _____

What happened to the Federalists and the Republicans after the War of 1812?

_____

_____

Explaining

8. What were the results of the Battle of New Orleans?

_____

_____

_____

Reading Check

9. List three things that happened as a result of the War of 1812.

_____

_____

_____

FOLDABLES

10. Place a two-tab Foldable along the dotted line to cover Check for Understanding. Write the title *War of 1812* on the anchor tab. Label the tabs *Federalists* and *Republicans*. Recall and list ways the War of 1812 affected each group. Use the Foldable to help answer Check for Understanding.

networks

networks

Growth and Expansion

Lesson 1 A Growing Economy

ESSENTIAL QUESTION
How does geography influence the way people live?

GUIDING QUESTIONS

1. **How did new technology affect the way things were made?**

2. **Why did agriculture remain the leading occupation of Americans in the 1800s?**

3. **How did the growth of factories and trade affect cities?**

Terms to Know

cotton gin a machine that removes the seeds from cotton fiber

interchangeable part a part of a machine or device that can be replaced by another part just like it

patent legal rights to an invention and its profits

capitalism economic system in which people and companies control production

capital money or other resources used to create wealth

free enterprise a type of economy in which people are free to buy, sell, and produce whatever they want

Where in the world?

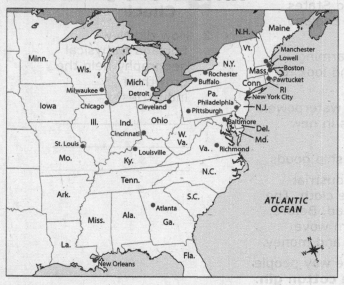

When did it happen?

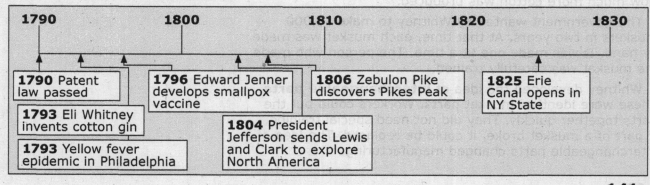

141

networks

Growth and Expansion

Lesson 1 A Growing Economy, *Continued*

Industrial Growth

Most Americans lived and worked on farms in colonial times. People used simple tools to make goods by hand. They made household items, furniture, and farm equipment.

In the mid-1700s, the way goods were made began to change. The changes began in Great Britain. The British began using machines. For example, they used a machine to make cloth. They built textile mills along rivers. The water from the river powered their machines.

People stopped working only in their homes or on their farms. They moved to cities to work in the mills and earn money. This big change in how people worked and how things were made is known as the Industrial Revolution.

The Industrial Revolution came to the United States around 1800. The changes began first in New England. There were three main reasons.

1. New England did not have good soil for farming. People were willing to give up farming and look for other kinds of work.

2. New England had rivers and streams for waterpower. People used waterpower to run machines in new factories.

3. New England had many ports that could ship goods.

Technology was an important part of the Industrial Revolution. There were new machines to make cloth. The water frame and the spinning jenny spun thread. Before, people had to do this by hand. The power loom wove thread into cloth. These machines saved time and money.

The invention of new machines changed the way people made goods. In 1793 Eli Whitney invented the **cotton gin**. The word *gin* is from the word "engine." The cotton gin made it easy and fast to remove the seeds from cotton. Now much more cotton was produced.

The government wanted Eli Whitney to make 10,000 muskets in two years. At that time, each musket was made by hand. It was made one at a time. The person who made the musket was carefully trained.

Whitney developed the idea of **interchangeable parts**. These were identical musket parts. Workers could put the parts together quickly. They did not need special training. If part of a musket broke, it could be replaced. The idea of interchangeable parts changed manufacturing.

⇄ Mark the Text

1. Underline the text that describes interchangeable parts. How did they help the economy?

_____
_____

✓ Reading Check

2. How did New England's physical geography help the growth of industries?

_____
_____
_____

Growth and Expansion

Lesson 1 A Growing Economy, *Continued*

Defining

3. What is a patent?

_____

_____

Reading Check

4. Why did the number of enslaved people grow quickly between 1790 and 1810?

_____

_____

In 1790, the U.S. Congress passed a **patent** law. A patent gives the inventor the sole right to make money from his or her invention for a certain period of time.

The British, too, tried to protect their inventions. Textile workers could not leave the country. They could not tell others about British machines. Still, some people in Britan brought the information to the United States.

Samuel Slater was one of these people. In Britain, he memorized how to make the machines that made cotton thread. In the 1790s Slater built copies of those machines in the United States. Francis Cabot Lowell made Slater's idea even better. All the steps of making cloth, or textiles, were done in one factory. When all the manufacturing steps are done in one place, it is called a factory system.

The economic system of the United States encourages industrial growth. It is called **capitalism.** People put their **capital,** or money, into a business. They hope the business will make a profit.

The American economy is a **free enterprise** economy.

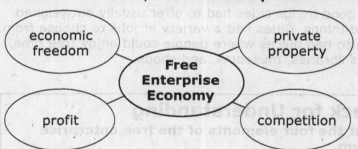

Agriculture Grows

Many people went to work in factories. Still, agriculture (farming) was the main economic activity in the United States in the 1800s. In the Northeast, farms were small. Families did all the work. They sold their products locally.

There were many farmers in the West. They raised such crops as corn and wheat. They produced pork.

The growth of textile industries increased the demand for cotton. Cotton was grown in the South. The cotton gin made it faster to process cotton. Southern farmers moved west to find new land to grow cotton. To grow more cotton, Southern farmers needed more enslaved workers. In 1790 there were 700,000 enslaved Africans in the United States. By 1810, there were 1.2 million.

143

Growth and Expansion

Lesson 1 A Growing Economy, *Continued*

Economic Independence

Small investors began to invest money in new businesses. They hoped to make money in return. Large businesses called corporations were formed. Corporations are companies owned by many people. The corporations sold stock, or shares of ownership in a company. This helped to pay for industrialization.

The growth of factories and trade led to the growth of cities. Many cities grew up near rivers because factories could use water to power their machines. People could ship their goods to markets more easily. Older cities, such as New York and Boston, grew as centers of shipping and trade. In the West, towns such as Cincinnati and Pittsburgh were located on major rivers. These towns grew rapidly as farmers shipped their products by river.

Cities at that time had no sewers to carry away waste. Diseases such as cholera and yellow fever sometimes killed many people. Many buildings were made of wood, and few cities had fire departments. Fires spread quickly.

The good things cities had to offer usually outweighed the bad things. Cities had a variety of jobs to choose from. They also had places where people could enjoy free time, such as libraries, museums, and shops.

////////////////// Glue Foldable here ////////////////

Check for Understanding

List the four elements of the free enterprise system.

_____

_____

_____

_____

List two examples of new technology that helped drive the industrial revolution.

_____

_____

? Analyzing

5. Why did many cities grow along major rivers?

_____

_____

✓ Reading Check

6. Why were cities attractive to people?

_____

_____

FOLDABLES®

7. Place a three-tab Venn diagram Foldable along the dotted line to cover Check for Understanding. Write the title *Capitalism* on the anchor tab. Label the tabs *Industrial Revolution*, *Both*, and *Free Enterprise System*. Recall information about each and list facts to determine what they have in common. Use the Foldable to help answer Check for Understanding.

networks

Lesson 2 Moving West

ESSENTIAL QUESTION

How does geography influence the way people live?

GUIDING QUESTIONS

1. ***What helped increase the movement of people and goods?***

2. ***Why did Americans tend to settle near rivers?***

Terms to Know

census the official count of the population

turnpike a road on which tolls are collected

canal waterway made by people

lock a separate compartment in which water levels rise and fall in order to raise or lower boats on a canal

Where in the world?

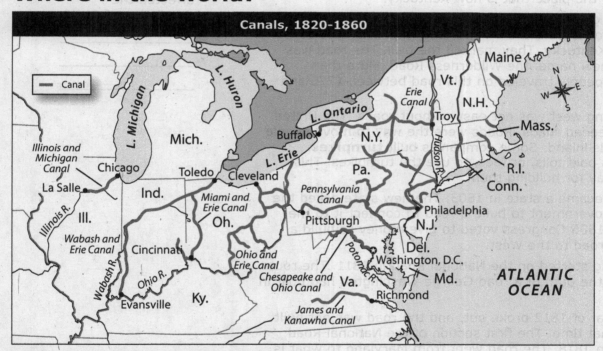

Canals, 1820-1860

When did it happen?

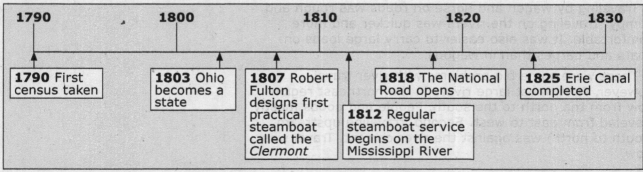

1790	1800	1810	1820	1830

1790 First census taken

1803 Ohio becomes a state

1807 Robert Fulton designs first practical steamboat called the *Clermont*

1812 Regular steamboat service begins on the Mississippi River

1818 The National Road opens

1825 Erie Canal completed

networks

Growth and Expansion

Lesson 2 Moving West, *Continued*

Headed West

In 1790 the first **census** was taken. A census is an official count of the population. The census found that nearly 4 million people lived in the United States. Most Americans lived east of the Appalachian Mountains. That pattern soon changed. More settlers headed west.

Daniel Boone was an explorer. He was one of the early pioneers who went west. In 1769 he explored a Native American trail that crossed the Appalachian Mountains. It was called Warriors' Path. The path went through a break in the mountains called the Cumberland Gap. Beyond the path was the place that is now Kentucky.

Boone got 30 workers. They widened Warrior's Path and cleared rocks from the Cumberland Gap. They cut down trees in Kentucky. They marked the trail. The road was given a new name, the Wilderness Road. More than 100,000 people traveled on this road between 1775 and 1790.

Traveling west was not easy without roads. The United States needed roads. Roads were the way to move people and goods inland. Some companies built **turnpikes.** Travelers paid tolls, or fees, to use the turnpikes. This helped pay for building them.

Ohio became a state in 1803. The new state asked the federal government to build a road to connect it to the East. In 1806 Congress voted to give money to build a national road to the West.

Building started on the National Road in 1811. The route followed the path of a road George Washington had built in 1754.

The War of 1812 broke out, and the road was not built during that time. The first section of the National Road opened in 1818. The road went from Maryland to what is now West Virginia.

Traveling by wagon and horse on roads was rough and bumpy. Traveling on the rivers was quicker and more comfortable. It was also easier to carry large loads on boats and barges than in wagons.

There were some big problems with river travel, however. First, most large rivers in the northeast region flow from the north to the south. People and goods mostly traveled from east to west. Second, traveling upstream (south to north) was against the river current. Travel was slow.

⇄ Locating

1. Where did most people in the United States live in 1790?

_____

❓ Predicting

2. How do you think the National Road affected the population of Ohio?

_____

_____

_____

146

Growth and Expansion

Lesson 2 Moving West, *Continued*

FOLDABLES®

🖌 Describing

3. Place a one-tab Foldable along the dotted line to cover the text that begins with "Thousands of workers built the Erie Canal." Write the title *Locks and Canals* on the anchor tab. Define *lock* and define *canal*. Use the back of the tab to describe how the building of locks and canals affected the growth and economy of the United States.

✓ Reading Check

4. Which regions were connected by the Erie Canal?

_____

_____

Travel by land	Travel by river
• Roads were rough and bumpy • It was hard to carry large loads	• Travel was more comfortable • More goods could be carried on a boat • Rivers could not move people east to west • Traveling against the river current was hard and slow

Robert Fulton developed a steamship with a powerful engine. He called it the *Clermont*. It could travel upstream. In 1807 the *Clermont* traveled north on the Hudson River. It traveled from New York City to the city of Albany in 32 hours. That was a 150-mile trip (241 km). A ship using only sails would have taken four days to make the trip.

The use of steamboats changed river travel. Steamboats made transportation easier and more comfortable. Shipping goods by steamboat became cheaper and faster. Steamboats also helped river cities, such as St. Louis and Cincinnati, grow. By 1850 there were 700 steamboats carrying goods and passengers.

Steamboats improved river transportation. However, steamboats could not link the eastern and western parts of the country. De Witt Clinton and other officials made a plan to link New York City with the Great Lakes region. They would build a **canal** across the state of New York. A canal is a waterway built by people.

/ / / / / / / / / / / Glue Foldable here / / / / / / / / / / /

Thousands of workers built the Erie Canal. Many were Irish immigrants. They built a series of **locks** along the canal. Locks are a way to raise or lower water levels.

The Erie Canal opened in 1825. The governor of New York boarded a barge in Buffalo, New York. He traveled eastward on the canal to Albany. Then he sailed down the Hudson River to New York City. Crowds cheered as officials poured water from Lake Erie into the Atlantic Ocean.

At first, there were no steamboats allowed on the Erie Canal. Their powerful engines could damage the canal. In the 1840s, canals were made stronger to allow steamboats to travel on them. Many other canals were built. By 1850, the United States had more than 3,600 miles (5,794 km) of canals. Canals lowered the cost of shipping goods. They

networks

Growth and Expansion

Lesson 2 Moving West, *Continued*

linked parts of the United States. They helped towns and cities along their routes grow larger.

The Move West Continues

The United States added four new states between 1791 and 1803. The states were Vermont, Kentucky, Tennessee and Ohio.

Between 1816 and 1821, Indiana, Illinois, Mississippi, Alabama, and Missouri became states. By 1820 there were 2.4 million people west of the Appalachian Mountains.

Pioneers moved west to find a better life. Most pioneer families settled along the big rivers and canals. They could more easily ship their crops and goods to markets. People usually settled with others from their original home state.

////////////////////Glue Foldable here.////////////////////

Check for Understanding

List three people who helped make travel to the West easier. Explain what they did.

_____

_____

_____

Explain how America in 1790 was different from America in 1820.

_____

_____

_____

✓ Reading Check

5. How did improved transportation affect the economy and the growth of cities?

_____

✓ Reading Check

6. How did rivers and canals affect where settlers lived?

_____

FOLDABLES®

7. Place a two-tab Foldable to cover Check for Understanding. Write *Moving West* on the anchor tab. Label the right tab *East* and the left tab *West*. Draw an arrow across the tabs from right to left. List why people might have wanted to leave the East and list ways they traveled to the West. Use the Foldable to help answer Check for Understanding.

networks

Growth and Expansion

Lesson 3 Unity and Sectionalism

ESSENTIAL QUESTION
Why does conflict develop?

GUIDING QUESTIONS
1. **How did the country change after the War of 1812?**
2. **How did the United States define its role in the Americas?**

Terms to Know
sectionalism rivalry based on the special interests of different areas
interstate commerce economic activity taking place between two or more states
monopoly a market where there is only one seller
cede to transfer control of something

Where in the world?

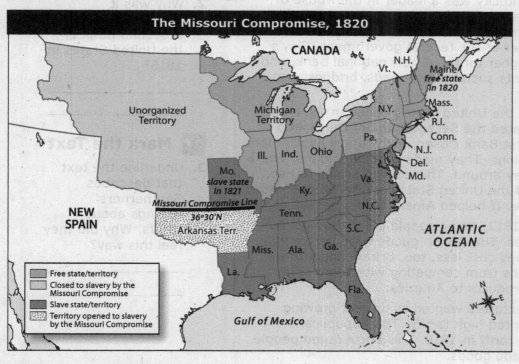

The Missouri Compromise, 1820

CANADA

N.H.
Vt.
Maine *free state in 1820*

Unorganized Territory

Michigan Territory

Mass.
N.Y.
R.I.
Conn.
Pa.
N.J.
Del.
Md.

Ill. Ind. Ohio

Mo. *slave state in 1821*

Va.

Ky.

Missouri Compromise Line
36°30'N
Arkansas Terr.

NEW SPAIN

Tenn.

N.C.

S.C.

ATLANTIC OCEAN

Miss. Ala. Ga.

La.

Fla.

Gulf of Mexico

- Free state/territory
- Closed to slavery by the Missouri Compromise
- Slave state/territory
- Territory opened to slavery by the Missouri Compromise

When did it happen?

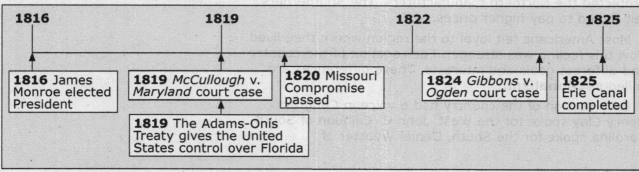

1816	1819	1822	1825

1816 James Monroe elected President

1819 *McCullough* v. *Maryland* court case

1820 Missouri Compromise passed

1824 *Gibbons* v. *Ogden* court case

1825 Erie Canal completed

1819 The Adams-Onís Treaty gives the United States control over Florida

149

Growth and Expansion

Lesson 3 Unity and Sectionalism, *Continued*

National Unity

A feeling of national unity grew in the United States after the War of 1812. James Monroe, a Republican, easily won the election of 1816 because the Federalist Party had become weak.

A Boston newspaper called these years the Era of Good Feelings. President Monroe was a symbol of these good feelings. Other feelings at the time were those of loyalty to the nation, or nationalism. The Republicans wanted a strong federal government.

Henry Clay of Kentucky was a leader in the House of Representatives. Clay proposed the American System to help the economy in each section of the country, and also to increase the power of the federal government. Clay's system called for higher tariffs, a new national bank, and internal improvements such as new roads, bridges, and canals.

The First Bank of the United States ended in 1811. In 1816, Congress created the Second Bank of the United States. After the First Bank closed, many state banks made poor business decisions. They made too many loans. There was too much money around. This caused prices to rise. The Second Bank of the United States controlled how much money was available. It helped American businesses grow.

After the War of 1812, many people purchased goods from British factories. The British goods were better than American goods. They cost less, too. Britain hoped they could keep Americans from competing with them. They sent a lot of their products to America.

American manufacturers wanted to protect growing industries. They wanted high tariffs. The Republicans passed a protective tariff in 1816. This encouraged people to buy American-made goods.

Southerners did not like the tariffs. They felt the tariffs protected the Northern manufacturers. The Southerners felt forced to pay higher prices.

Most Americans felt loyal to the region where they lived. Now this feeling was stronger. Each section of the country had different goals and interests. These differences are called **sectionalism.**

Each section of the country had a voice in Congress. Henry Clay spoke for the West. John C. Calhoun of South Carolina spoke for the South. Daniel Webster of

Describing

1. What was the mood of the country after the War of 1812?

_____

_____

Explaining

2. Why was it necessary to create a Second Bank of the United States in 1816?

_____

_____

_____

Mark the Text

3. Underline the text that describes Southerners' feelings about tariffs. Why did they feel this way?

_____

_____

Growth and Expansion

Lesson 3 Unity and Sectionalism, *Continued*

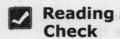

Defining

4. Underline the text that defines *monopoly*. What did the Supreme Court decide about interstate commerce?

_____

_____

✓ Reading Check

5. What problem did the Missouri Compromise try to resolve?

_____

_____

_____

Massachusetts spoke for the North. Each leader tried to protect the interests of his own section of the country.

The Supreme Court made decisions that backed the power of the national government. In *Fletcher* v. *Peck* (1810), the Court decided that courts could overrule decisions of a state's government if the decisions went against the Constitution. In *McCulloch* v. *Maryland* (1819), the Court ruled that a state could not tax property of the national government. In *Gibbons* v. *Ogden*, the Court ruled that only Congress could make laws governing **interstate commerce**, or trade between states. In this case, the state of New York had granted a **monopoly** to a steamship operator. He was running ships between New Jersey and New York. A monopoly is sole control over an industry. People who supported states' rights did not agree with the Court's rulings.

In 1819 there was a clash between the North and the South. Missouri wanted to enter the Union as a slave state. Congress disagreed. Henry Clay came up with a plan to solve this disagreement over slavery. The Missouri Compromise called for Missouri to be admitted as a slave state. Another new state, Maine, would be a free state. This meant that there would still be an equal number of slave and free states. This kept a balance of power in the Senate. Neither side could change the laws governing slavery.

The Missouri Compromise also dealt with slavery in the rest of the Louisiana Territory. The land south of Missouri could allow slavery, and the land north of it could not.

Foreign Affairs

Americans had a lot of pride in their country following the War of 1812.

In 1817, Britain and the United States made an agreement called the Rush-Bagot Agreement. It called for each country to limit the number of war ships on the Great Lakes.

The Convention of 1818 was an agreement between the United States and Britain. It set the boundary of the Louisiana Purchase between the United States and Canada at the 49th parallel. It made a secure border without armed forces. Americans got the right to settle in the Oregon Country

The United States had a dispute with Spain over parts of Florida. Spain controlled Florida. The United States claimed

151

networks

Growth and Expansion

Lesson 3 Unity and Sectionalism, *Continued*

that West Florida was part of the Louisiana Purchase. They argued that it belonged to the United States.

In 1810 and 1812, Americans took control of West Florida to Louisiana and Mississippi. Spain took no action. In 1818 General Andrew Jackson was ordered to stop Native American raids from East Florida. He invaded West Florida and continued into East Florida. He captured several Spanish forts. The Spanish realized they were not strong enough to hold on to Florida. The Adams-Onís Treaty was signed in 1819. In the treaty, Spain **ceded,** or gave up, Florida. At the same time, Spain was losing power in Mexico. In 1821 Mexico finally gained its independence.

Simón Bolívar won independence from Spain for the present-day countries of Venezuela, Colombia, Panama, Bolivia, and Ecuador. José de San Martín won freedom from Spain for Chile and Peru. By 1824, Spain had lost control of most of South America.

In 1822 several European countries talked about a plan to help Spain take back its American colonies. President Monroe did not want more European involvement in North America. In 1823 he issued the Monroe Doctrine. It said that European powers could no longer set up colonies in North America and South America.

////////////// Glue Foldable here //////////////

Check for Understanding

List the three parts of Henry Clay's American system.

_____

_____

What helped bring about feelings of sectionalism in the United States?

_____

_____

📝 Describing

6. What was the result of the Adams-Onís Treaty?

_____

_____

_____

✅ Reading Check

7. Why did President Monroe issue the Monroe Doctrine?

_____

_____

FOLDABLES®

8. Place a two-tab Foldable to cover Check for Understanding. Write the title *After the War* on the anchor tab. Label the two tabs *American System* and *Foreign Affairs*. List two things you recall about each. Use the Foldable to help answer Check for Understanding.

networks

Lesson 1 Jacksonian Democracy

ESSENTIAL QUESTION
What are the characteristics of a leader?

GUIDING QUESTIONS

1. **What new ways of campaigning appeared during the elections of 1824 and 1828?**

2. **How did Andrew Jackson make the American political system more democratic?**

3. **How did a fight over tariffs become a debate about states' rights versus federal rights?**

Terms to Know

favorite son a candidate for national office who has support mostly from his home state

plurality the largest number of something, but less than a majority

majority greater than half of a total number of something

mudslinging a method in election campaigns that uses gossip and lies to make an opponent look bad

bureaucracy a system of government in which specialized tasks are carried out by appointed officials rather than by elected ones

spoils system practice of handing out government jobs to supporters; replacing government employees with the winning candidate's supporters

nominating convention a meeting in which representative members of a political party choose candidates to run for important elected offices

When did it happen?

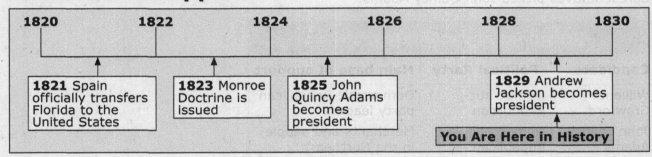

| 1820 | 1822 | 1824 | 1826 | 1828 | 1830 |

1821 Spain officially transfers Florida to the United States

1823 Monroe Doctrine is issued

1825 John Quincy Adams becomes president

1829 Andrew Jackson becomes president

You Are Here in History

What do you know?

In the first column, answer the questions based on what you know before you study. After this lesson, complete the last column.

Now...		Later...
	How many strong political parties were there in the 1824 presidential election?	
	What area of the country favored higher tariffs and what area opposed them?	

The Jackson Era

Lesson 1 Jacksonian Democracy, Continued

New Parties Emerge

Early political groups became political parties. The parties and their views changed over time. From 1816 to 1824, the Democratic-Republican party was the only major political party.

The four candidates for president in the election of 1824 were all members of the same party. Party leaders supported William Crawford. The other three were **favorite sons** who got most of their support from their home states. Each favored the interests of his state.

Support for John Quincy Adams of Massachusetts came from merchants and business owners in the Northeast. Henry Clay of Kentucky was supported by his state on the frontier. Andrew Jackson of Tennessee was a war hero. He was well-known and popular. He came from a poor family and wanted ordinary people to have a voice in politics.

The vote was split among the four candidates. Jackson won a **plurality**, or more votes than any of the other candidates. No candidate had a **majority**, or more than half, of the electoral votes. The Constitution stated that if a candidate does not win a majority of the electoral votes, the House of Representatives must decide the winner. The representatives picked John Quincy Adams.

Presidential candidates, 1824		
Candidate	**Political Party**	**Main base of support**
William Crawford	Democratic-Republican	Democratic-Republican party leaders
John Quincy Adams	Democratic-Republican	Merchants and people in the Northeast
Henry Clay	Democratic-Republican	People in Kentucky and on the frontier
Andrew Jackson	Democratic-Republican	People in Tennessee and the West; people who felt left out of politics

Like many in the Northeast, Adams wanted a strong federal government. Others did not agree, especially those on the frontier. The Democratic-Republicans split into two parties before the election in 1828. The Republicans backed Adams and a strong central government. The Democrats supported Jackson and states' rights.

🖎 Identifying

1. Who won the election of 1824, and how was the winner determined?

_____

_____

❓ Assessing

2. What did Crawford's failure to win the 1824 election say about the strength of the party leaders?

_____

_____

_____

The Jackson Era

Lesson 1 Jacksonian Democracy, Continued

☑ **Contrasting**

3. What were two major differences between the Democrats and the National Republicans in 1828?

_____

_____

❓ **Drawing Inferences**

4. What changes taking place in the country contributed to Jackson's victory?

_____

_____

_____

_____

☑ **Reading Check**

5. What campaign practices of the 1828 election are still used today?

_____

_____

_____

_____

	Democrats	National Republicans
Idea of government	favored states' rights	wanted strong federal government
National bank	opposed national bank	supported national bank
Base of support	workers, farmers, immigrants	wealthy voters, merchants
Candidate	Andrew Jackson	John Quincy Adams

In the election of 1828, Jackson faced Adams. Their ideas and supporters were very different. Adams and the National Republicans wanted a strong federal government and a national bank to help the economy. Many National Republicans were wealthy business owners. Many of the Democrats were workers, farmers, or immigrants.

The campaign grew ugly. Both parties used **mudslinging,** or insults meant to make candidates look bad. The candidates also came up with slogans, handed out printed flyers, and held rallies and barbecues to try to win voters' support. Jackson's popularity gave him an easy victory in the 1828 election.

Jackson as President

Jackson thought more people should be involved in government. By 1828, most people no longer had to own property to be able to vote. Many states had changed their constitutions so that voters selected the presidential electors in their states. Jackson also thought that the federal **bureaucracy** was not democratic. Many workers were not elected officials. He used the **spoils system** to fire many workers and replace them with people who had supported his election.

The caucus system was replaced by special state meetings called **nominating conventions**. At these meetings, elected representatives voted for party candidates.

The Tariff Debate

Americans were also split on their views about **tariffs,** or taxes, on goods from other countries. Merchants in the

The Jackson Era

Lesson 1 Jacksonian Democracy, *Continued*

Northeast wanted higher tariffs so that European goods would cost more than American goods. Southerners, however, liked buying cheaper goods from Europe. They also worried that Europeans might tax the U.S. cotton sold in Europe, meaning Southerners would lose business.

Jackson's vice president, John C. Calhoun of South Carolina, was a strong supporter of states' rights. However, his views were different from those of Jackson. When Congress raised tariffs, Calhoun did not think it was good for his state. He felt that a state could and should nullify, or cancel, federal laws that were not good for that state.

When Congress again raised tariffs in 1832, South Carolina passed a law saying that the state would not pay them. It also threatened to secede from, or leave, the United States if the federal government tried to enforce the tariff law. Jackson did not agree with his vice president. He did not believe the states had the right to nullify federal laws or to secede from the Union.

Jackson did not think the federal government should support projects that helped only one state. He thought the federal government should support projects that helped the entire nation. These included tariff laws which involved international trade.

Jackson tried to calm angry Southerners by working to lower the tariffs. But to keep the union together and strong, he also supported the Force Act. This act would allow him to enforce federal laws by using the military if necessary. South Carolina was happy to have the tariffs lowered. Still, the state nullified the Force Act.

/ / / / / / / / / / / Glue Foldable here / / / / / / / / / /

Check for Understanding

List two ways in which the country became more democratic in the 1820s.

1. _____

2. _____

What was Jackson's opinion when it came to states nullifying a federal law and seceding from the United States?

_____

_____

Reading Check

6. How would Northeastern factory owners react to a high tariff?

_____

_____

_____

FOLDABLES®

7. Place a two-tab Foldable along the dotted line to cover the Check for Understanding. Write the title *Jackson Presidency* on the anchor tab. Label the two tabs *Federal Government* and *States' Rights*. Recall information about each and list facts to compare the candidates and the outcome of the election. Use the Foldable to help answer Check for Understanding.

The Jackson Era

Lesson 2 Conflicts over Land

ESSENTIAL QUESTION
What are the consequences when cultures interact?

GUIDING QUESTIONS

1. **Why were Native Americans forced to abandon their land and move west?**

2. **Why did some Native Americans resist resettlement?**

> **Term to Know**
> **relocate** to move to another place

Where in the world?

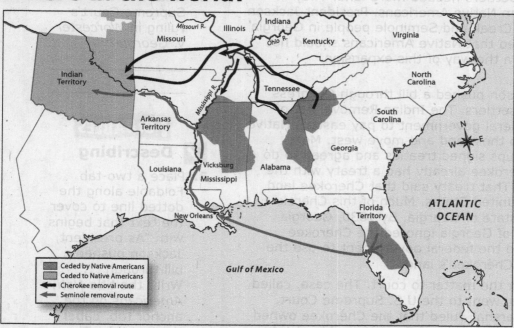

Legend:
- Ceded by Native Americans
- Ceded to Native Americans
- ← Cherokee removal route
- ← Seminole removal route

When did it happen?

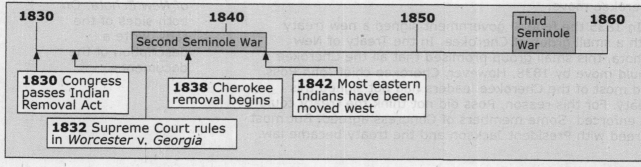

1830	1840	1850	1860

Second Seminole War

Third Seminole War

1830 Congress passes Indian Removal Act

1832 Supreme Court rules in *Worcester* v. *Georgia*

1838 Cherokee removal begins

1842 Most eastern Indians have been moved west

157

The Jackson Era

Lesson 2 Conflicts over Land, *Continued*

Removing Native Americans

In the early 1800s, American settlers were moving both west and south. The country had to decide what to do about Native Americans who lived on this land. The Cherokee, Creek, Seminole, Chickasaw, and Choctaw peoples lived in Georgia, Alabama, Mississippi, and Florida. These Native American groups were farmers. Their communities were much like many other American communities. As a result, other Americans called these groups the "Five Civilized Tribes."

As settlers moved farther south and west, many people wanted the federal government to force the Five Civilized Tribes to **relocate**. Settlers needed more land. They wanted to take it from Native Americans. President Jackson had once fought the Creek and Seminole people in Georgia and Florida. He agreed that Native Americans should not be allowed to stand in the way of this expansion.

/ / / / / / / / / / / Glue Foldable here / / / / / / / / / /

As president, Jackson pushed a bill through Congress that would help the settlers. The Indian Removal Act of 1830 allowed the federal government to pay eastern Native Americans to give up their land and move west. Most Native American groups signed treaties and agreed to do so. However, the Cherokee already had a treaty with the federal government. That treaty said that Cherokee land was not part of the United States. Much of this Cherokee land was inside the state of Georgia. By 1830, Georgia wanted it. The state of Georgia ignored the Cherokee treaty. Georgia asked the federal government to use the new law to take the Cherokee's land.

The Cherokee took the matter to court. The case, called *Worcester* v. *Georgia*, went to the U.S. Supreme Court. Chief Justice John Marshall ruled that the Cherokee owned the land. He said that the state of Georgia could not take control of it. President Jackson disagreed with the Court's ruling. He refused to prevent Georgia from making the Cherokee move.

In 1835 the federal government signed a new treaty with a small group of Cherokee. In the Treaty of New Echota, this small group promised that all the Cherokee would move by 1838. However, Cherokee chief John Ross and most of the Cherokee leaders had not signed this treaty. For this reason, Ross did not think the treaty could be enforced. Some members of Congress agreed. But most agreed with President Jackson and the treaty became law.

Copyright by The McGraw-Hill Companies.

🖐 Locating

1. In which states did most of the "Five Civilized Tribes" live?

_____

_____

🖐 Explaining

2. What was the Supreme Court's ruling in *Worcester* v. *Georgia*?

_____

_____

FOLDABLES

✓ Describing

3. Place a two-tab Foldable along the dotted line to cover the text that begins with "As president, Jackson pushed a bill through ..." Write the title *Native Americans* on the anchor tab. Label the two tabs *The Indian Removal Act of 1830* and *Treaty of New Echota*. On both sides of the tabs, write a description of the documents.

The Jackson Era

Lesson 2 Conflicts over Land, *Continued*

Marking the Text

4. Underline the sentence that explains the meaning of *guerrilla tactics*.

Identifying

5. Who were the Black Seminoles?

_____

_____

Making Connections

6. Why were Black Seminoles willing to support the Seminole fight to stay in Florida?

_____

_____

Summarizing

7. What finally happened to the Seminoles?

_____

_____

Most Cherokee did not want to relocate. In 1838 President Van Buren sent the army to enforce the treaty. The army forced the Cherokee off their land and into a new territory west of the Mississippi River. It was called the Indian Territory because Congress had created it to be the new home of many eastern Native Americans. Most of this territory is the present-day state of Oklahoma. The other Five Civilized Tribes and other Native Americans were also forced to move to the Indian Territory.

The Cherokee had to travel from their homes in Georgia to the Indian Territory. Losing their homes and taking this long and difficult journey greatly saddened the Native Americans. Many died waiting for the journey to begin. Many more died along the way. Their journey was later called the Trail of Tears.

Resistance and Removal

Most of the Five Civilized Tribes did not want to sell their lands. Osceola, a leader of the Seminoles in Florida, refused to move. Instead, he and his followers decided to stay and fight. This began a long and bloody fight called the Seminole Wars. The Seminoles were skilled at fighting in Florida's swamps and marshlands. Small groups surprised and attacked army troops and then ran away into the swamps. This method of fighting is called guerilla tactics. It was successful, at least for a while. The Seminoles were greatly outnumbered, but they kept the army from a quick victory.

In their fight, Seminoles were joined by Black Seminoles. Black Seminoles were escaped slaves who ran away to Florida. Because Florida was not a state yet, they thought they would be safe there. Some of the runaway slaves built their own homes. Others lived with the Seminole people. When war broke out, Black Seminoles fought alongside the Native Americans. They were afraid that the army might return them to slavery.

The fighting continued, on and off, for more than 20 years, from 1832 to 1858. Neither side was able to defeat the other. Eventually, most of the Seminoles either died or moved to the Indian Territory. Some, however, stayed in Florida, where their descendants still live today.

By the end of the Seminole Wars, very few Native American groups were still living in the eastern United States. Most had been removed to the Indian Territory. They shared the land with other Native American groups

159

The Jackson Era

Lesson 2 Conflicts over Land, *Continued*

already living there. In later years, American settlers would look to expand into the Indian Territory, too. Many of the same problems would be repeated years later.

////////// Glue Foldable here ///////////

Check for Understanding

Besides the Cherokee, name three other Native American groups who were forced to relocate.

1. _____

2. _____

3. _____

Identify two ways that Native Americans resisted being relocated.

1. _____

2. _____

FOLDABLES®

8. Place a one-tab Foldable along the dotted line to cover Check for Understanding. Write the title *Trail of Tears* on the anchor tab. Label the right side of the tab *Northeast* and the left side *Oklahoma*. List two things you remember about why Native Americans were forced to leave their land and go west. Use the Foldable to help answer Check for Understanding.

The Jackson Era

Lesson 3 Jackson and the Bank

ESSENTIAL QUESTION

How do governments change?

GUIDING QUESTIONS

1. **What events occurred when President Jackson forced the National Bank to close?**

2. **What events occurred during the 1840s that led to the weakening of the Whig Party?**

Term to Know

veto to reject a bill and prevent it from becoming law

When did it happen?

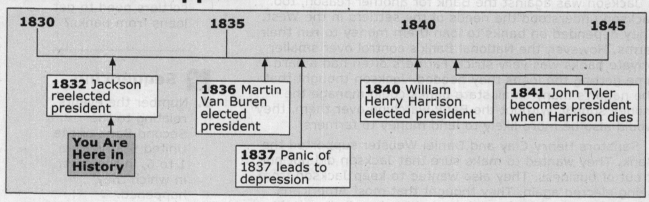

| 1830 | | 1835 | | 1840 | | 1845 |

1832 Jackson reelected president

You Are Here in History

1836 Martin Van Buren elected president

1837 Panic of 1837 leads to depression

1840 William Henry Harrison elected president

1841 John Tyler becomes president when Harrison dies

What do you know?

In the first column, answer the questions based on what you know before you study. After this lesson, complete the last column.

Now...		Later...
	Why was the Second Bank of the United States important to the economy?	
	Why did President Jackson oppose the National Bank?	
	Why did the Whigs think they could win the presidential election in 1840?	
	How did President Harrison's death affect the Whigs' plans for the country?	

161

The Jackson Era

Lesson 3 Jackson and the Bank, Continued

Jackson's War Against the Bank

Congress created the Second Bank of the United States to hold the federal government's money. Its job was to control the nation's money supply. However, the Bank was not run by government officials. Instead it was run by Eastern bankers. Most of these bankers had wealth and a good education.

President Andrew Jackson had neither of these. He was a pioneer from the West. He had worked hard and became president. He did not like the wealthy bankers who ran the Bank.

Jackson was against the Bank for another reason, too. Jackson understood the needs of the settlers in the West. They depended on banks to loan them money to run their farms. However, the National Bank's control over smaller private banks was very strict. Farmers often had a hard time getting the loans they needed. Jackson thought that the nation's many small state banks could manage the money supply. Without the Bank watching over them, they would also be more likely to lend money to farmers.

Senators Henry Clay and Daniel Webster supported the Bank. They wanted to make sure that Jackson did not put it out of business. They also wanted to keep Jackson from being elected again. They thought that most Americans liked the Bank, and if Jackson tried to close it, he would lose votes in the next election.

Years earlier, Congress had given the Bank a charter for 20 years. A charter is a legal document that gives an organization permission to do its work. Clay and Webster helped the Bank get a new charter from Congress before the old charter ran out. They thought Jackson would not dare to **veto** the new charter, or prevent it from becoming a law. They thought he would not veto it because it was an election year and he might lose votes. Jackson vetoed it anyway. This meant that the Bank would be forced to go out of business in a few years. Most people supported Jackson's veto. It actually helped him get reelected.

After the election, Jackson took the federal government's money out of the Bank and put it into smaller state banks. When the Bank's charter ended, the Second Bank of the United States closed.

Martin Van Buren, Jackson's vice president, ran for president in 1836. Jackson was still very popular. Jackson's support helped Van Buren win. Soon after the election,

---

📝 Marking the Text

1. Underline the text that describes the role of the Second Bank of the United States.

✓ Explaining

2. Why did Western settlers need to get loans from banks?

_____

📝 Sequencing

3. Number the events relating to the Second Bank of the United States from 1 to 6, in the order in which they happened.

____ government's money put in state banks

____ Congress passes new charter for Bank

____ Second Bank of United States closes

____ Jackson vetoes new charter

____ Bank's charter expires

____ Jackson removes government's money from Bank

The Jackson Era

Lesson 3 Jackson and the Bank, Continued

✓ **Reading Check**

4. After the Bank closed, what kind of payment did the government require from people who wanted to buy public land?

_____

✎ **Explaining**

5. What was President Van Buren's response to the Panic of 1837?

_____

✓ **Reading Check**

6. What was the purpose of the new treasury system?

_____

✎ **Explaining**

7. Why did the Whigs think they had a chance to win the presidency in 1840?

_____

_____

though, the country was in trouble. Jackson's actions toward the Bank had led to an economic panic.

When the Bank's charter expired and it closed, there was no national bank to control the state banks. They began printing more banknotes. Federal officials became concerned that these notes had little value. As a result, the federal government decided to require gold and silver as payment for public land. It would not accept the banknotes.

People who had banknotes feared their notes might become worthless. This fear set off an economic panic, called the Panic of 1837. Many people lost their jobs and their land. Thousands of businesses had to close.

President Van Buren believed that the government should not do anything to help the nation during the depression. He did, however, work with Congress to create a federal treasury where the federal government would keep its money. The government, not private bankers, would own and run the treasury. Leaders hoped that this new treasury would prevent future panics.

The Whigs in Power

Van Buren ran for reelection in 1840. With the country still in the depths of a depression, the Whigs thought they had a chance to win the presidency. The Whigs ran William Henry Harrison against Van Buren.

Like Andrew Jackson, Harrison became a hero during the War of 1812. He fought at the Battle of Tippecanoe. His running mate was John Tyler, a planter from Virginia. Their campaign slogan was "Tippecanoe and Tyler Too."

Harrison had to gain the support of the workers and farmers who had voted for Jackson. He was wealthy and from Ohio, but his campaign painted him as a simple frontiersman like Jackson. The Democrats responded to this false picture. They said all Harrison was good for was sitting in front of a log cabin and collecting his military pension. The Whigs turned the attack around. They adopted the simple frontier log cabin as the symbol of their campaign.

At the same time, the Whigs painted Van Buren as a wealthy snob with perfume-scented whiskers. They blamed him for the depression. They accused him of spending money on fancy furniture for the White House. The Whigs' plan worked. A record number of voters elected Harrison by a wide margin.

163

The Jackson Era

Lesson 3 Jackson and the Bank, *Continued*

Harrison gave his long inaugural speech in the bitter cold without a hat or coat. He died of pneumonia 32 days later. He served the shortest term of any president. John Tyler became the first vice president to become president because the elected president died in office.

Tyler had been elected as a Whig. He had once been a Democrat and did not support many Whig policies. Whig Party leaders thought he would attract voters in the South. Webster and Clay believed that they would be able to get Harrison to agree to their plans for the country. Harrison's death spoiled their plan.

Tyler vetoed several Whig bills. His lack of party loyalty angered many Whigs. Finally, they threw him out of the party. He became a president without a party. Tyler's biggest success was the Webster-Ashburton Treaty, which was signed by the United States and Great Britain. The treaty ended the disagreement over the border between Maine and Canada. It also settled the location of the long U.S.-Canadian border from Maine to Minnesota.

Unfortunately, the Whigs could not agree on goals for their party. They did agree on their dislike for President Tyler, however. The Whigs continued to vote more and more according to sectional ties—North, South, and West— and not party ties. It is likely that Whig presidential candidate Henry Clay lost the election of 1844 because of this division. James Polk, a Democrat, became the new president.

///////////////////Glue Foldable here//////////////////////

Check for Understanding

List two reasons that President Jackson shut down the Second Bank of the United States.

1. _____

2. _____

Why was John Tyler not an effective president?

_____

_____

✓ Reading Check

8. How did the Whigs lose power in the election of 1844?

_____

_____

FOLDABLES®

9. Place a two-tab Foldable along the dotted line to cover Check for Understanding. Cut the tabs in half to form four tabs. Write the title *Changes* on the anchor tab. Label the four tabs *Andrew Jackson*, *Martin Van Buren*, *William Henry Harrison*, and *John Tyler*. List two things you remember about each president. Use the Foldable to help answer Check for Understanding.

netw**rks**

Manifest Destiny

Lesson 1 The Oregon Country

ESSENTIAL QUESTION
How does geography influence the way people live?

GUIDING QUESTIONS
1. *Why did Americans want to control the Oregon Country?*
2. *What is Manifest Destiny?*

Terms to Know
joint occupation people from two countries living in the same region
mountain man person who lived in the Rocky Mountains and made his living by trapping animals for their fur
emigrants people who leave their country
prairie schooner cloth-covered wagon that was used by pioneers to travel West in the mid-1800s
Manifest Destiny the idea that the United States was meant to spread freedom from the Atlantic Ocean to the Pacific Ocean

Where in the world?

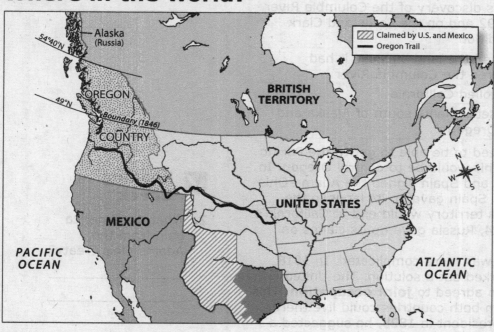

When did it happen?

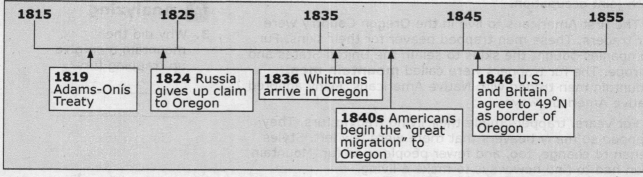

1815		1825		1835		1845		1855

1819 Adams-Onís Treaty

1824 Russia gives up claim to Oregon

1836 Whitmans arrive in Oregon

1840s Americans begin the "great migration" to Oregon

1846 U.S. and Britain agree to 49°N as border of Oregon

networks

Manifest Destiny

Lesson 1 The Oregon Country, Continued

Rivalry in the Northwest

The Oregon Country covered much more land than today's state of Oregon. Oregon, Washington, Idaho and parts of Montana and Wyoming were all a part of it.

In the early 1800s, four countries claimed the Oregon Country. They were the United States, Great Britain, Spain and Russia.

Claims in the Oregon Country	
Country	**Reason for Claim**
United States	Claimed the land based on Robert Gray's discovery of the Columbia River in 1792 and on the Lewis and Clark expedition
Great Britain	Claimed the land because it had explored the Columbia River
Spain	Controlled California
Russia	Had settlements south of Alaska and into Oregon

Many Americans wanted to be able to get to the Pacific Ocean. One way to do this would be to control Oregon. In 1819, the United States and Spain signed the Adams-Onís Treaty. With this treaty, Spain gave up its lands in the Oregon Country. Spain's territory would end at California's northern border. In 1824, Russia gave up its claims on lands south of Alaska.

The deal with Britain was more complicated. In 1818, John Quincy Adams worked out a solution. The United States and Great Britain agreed to **joint occupation.** This meant that settlers from both countries could live there. When Adams became president in 1825, he suggested a plan for Britain and the United States to divide the land. Britain said no to the plan, so both countries continued on with joint occupation.

The first Americans to live in the Oregon Country were fur traders. These men trapped beaver for their skins. Fur companies bought the skins to sell in the United States and Europe. The fur trappers were called **mountain men.** Mountain men traded with Native Americans. Many adopted Native American ways.

For years, trappers made their living trading furs. They trapped so many beavers that there were few left. Styles began to change, too, and fewer people used fur. Mountain men had to find new ways to make a living.

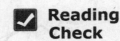

Mark the Text

1. Underline the definition of *joint occupation*. Which two countries agreed to joint occupation of Oregon?

_____

Reading Check

2. What did America gain from the Adams-Onís Treaty?

_____

_____

Analyzing

3. Why did the mountain men give up trapping furs?

_____

_____

_____

166

Manifest Destiny

Lesson 1 The Oregon Country, *Continued*

✏ Making Inferences

4. Why were the Whitmans killed?

_____

_____

_____

A b c Defining

5. What is an *emigrant*?

_____

_____

_____

Some became farmers. Others used their knowledge of the region and became guides. Jim Bridger and Kit Carson were two mountain men who became guides.

Guides helped settlers who were moving west to the Oregon Country. They created new routes that led from the east to the west. The best-known route was the Oregon Trail. Guides created other important routes. One was the California Trail and another was the Santa Fe trail.

Oregon and Manifest Destiny

Americans began to settle all over the Oregon country in the 1830s.

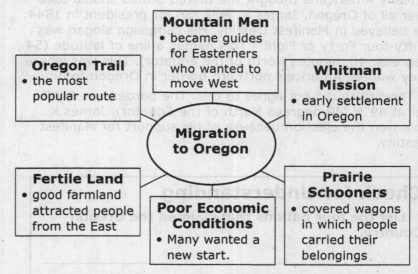

Migration to Oregon

- **Mountain Men**
  - became guides for Easterners who wanted to move West
- **Oregon Trail**
  - the most popular route
- **Whitman Mission**
  - early settlement in Oregon
- **Fertile Land**
  - good farmland attracted people from the East
- **Poor Economic Conditions**
  - Many wanted a new start.
- **Prairie Schooners**
  - covered wagons in which people carried their belongings

Dr. Marcus Whitman and his wife Narcissa were among the first settlers. They built a mission among the Cayuse people in 1836. The Cayuse are Native Americans who lived near what is now Walla Walla, Washington. The Whitmans wanted to convert the Cayuse to Christianity. They also wanted to provide medical care.

New settlers came to the mission. They did not know it, but they carried the disease, measles. The Cayuse had no defenses against measles, and the disease spread. Many children died of measles. The Cayuse blamed the Whitmans for the deaths. In November 1847, the Cayuse attacked the mission. They killed the Whitmans and 11 others.

Settlers kept coming to Oregon. Reports of fertile land attracted many of them. Others faced economic hard times and wanted a fresh start. These pioneers were called **emigrants.** Emigrants are people who leave their home

167

networks

Manifest Destiny

Lesson 1 The Oregon Country, *Continued*

country for another place. To reach Oregon, they had to travel about 2,000 difficult miles. They packed everything they owned in covered wagons. These wagons were called **prairie schooners.** From a distance, they looked like a ship called a schooner. Even though it was a very hard trip, thousands of people started for Oregon.

In the early 1800s, many Americans thought the nation had a special role to play in the world. Many Americans thought they should spread freedom by settling the whole country, all the way to the Pacific Ocean. In the 1840s, newspaper editor John O'Sullivan called this mission **"Manifest Destiny."**

Many Americans thought the United States should take over all of Oregon. James K. Polk ran for president in 1844. He believed in Manifest Destiny. His campaign slogan was "Fifty-four Forty or Fight!" This names a line of latitude (54 degrees, 40 minutes North of the equator). This was where they wanted America's northern border in Oregon to be.

The British did not agree to this. The border was finally set at 49°N (49 degrees North of the Equator). James K. Polk won the election because of his support for Manifest Destiny.

/ / / / / / / / / / / / Glue Foldable here / / / / / / / / / / / /

Check for Understanding

List the four nations that claimed the Oregon Country.

_____

_____

_____

_____

List three reasons Americans moved to Oregon.

_____

_____

_____

📋 Describing

6. "Manifest Destiny" was America's special mission. Describe it.

_____

_____

✔️ Reading Check

7. What views did Polk present in the 1844 election campaign?

_____

_____

FOLDABLES®

8. Place a two-tab Foldable along the dotted line to cover Check for Understanding. Write *Migration to Oregon* on the anchor tab. Label the left tab *West: Oregon Country* and the right tab *East: Manifest Destiny.* Draw an arrow from east to west across both tabs. Write what you remember about each and the migration to Oregon. Use the Foldable to help answer Check for Understanding.

Manifest Destiny

Lesson 2 Statehood for Florida and Texas

ESSENTIAL QUESTION

Why does conflict develop?

GUIDING QUESTIONS

1. **How did Florida become a state?**
2. **How did Texas become a state?**

Terms to Know

Tejano a Texan of Hispanic, and often Mexican, descent
decree official order
barricade block off
annex take control of

Where in the world?

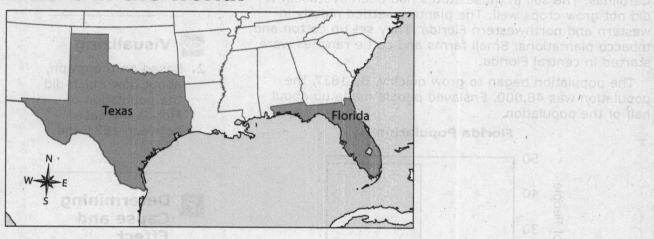

When did it happen?

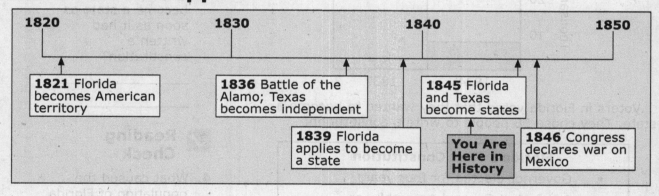

1820   1830   1840   1850

1821 Florida becomes American territory

1836 Battle of the Alamo; Texas becomes independent

1845 Florida and Texas become states

1839 Florida applies to become a state

You Are Here in History

1846 Congress declares war on Mexico

169

Manifest Destiny

Lesson 2 Statehood for Florida and Texas, *Continued*

Florida

Florida belonged to Spain until 1821. In that year, Spain transferred Florida to the United States. Tallahassee was made the capital of the territory in 1824. It was located between two major cities, St. Augustine and Pensacola.

Thousands of new settlers came to Florida from the United States. Many came because of the fertile soil. Among these were planters from Virginia, Georgia, and the Carolinas. The soil in those states had been overused. It did not grow crops well. The planters settled mostly in western and northwestern Florida. They set up cotton and tobacco plantations. Small farms and cattle ranches were started in central Florida.

The population began to grow quickly. By 1837, the population was 48,000. Enslaved people made up about half of the population.

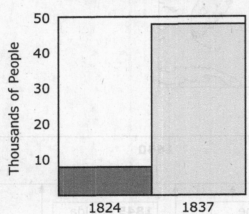

Florida Population

Voters in Florida voted that they wanted to become a state. They chose 56 people to write a constitution.

Florida's First Constitution

- Governor elected for four years
- An elected General Assembly, or legislature
- Public schools to be set up
- Slavery allowed

In 1839, the constitution was submitted to the U.S. Congress for approval. The question of allowing slavery created a problem. Congress wanted to keep the number

170

Copyright by The McGraw-Hill Companies.

Explaining

1. Why did planters move to Florida from Virginia, Georgia, and the Carolinas?

_____

_____

Visualizing

2. Based on the graph, about how much did the population of Florida increase between 1824 and 1837?

_____

Determining Cause and Effect

3. Why didn't Florida become a state as soon as it had written a constitution?

_____

_____

Reading Check

4. What caused the population of Florida to grow?

_____

_____

Manifest Destiny

Lesson 2 Statehood for Florida and Texas, Continued

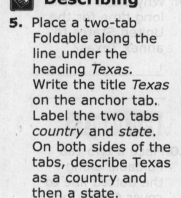

FOLDABLES

🖎 Describing

5. Place a two-tab Foldable along the line under the heading *Texas.* Write the title *Texas* on the anchor tab. Label the two tabs *country* and *state.* On both sides of the tabs, describe Texas as a country and then a state.

🖎 Mark the Text

6. Circle the definition of *decree.* Then underline what the Mexicans decreed.

🖎 Identifying

7. Who was Santa Anna?

_____

_____

❓ Analyzing

8. What happened to Texas after the battle of San Jacinto?

_____

_____

of slave states and the number of free states equal. Admitting Florida as a slave state would make the number uneven. Six years later, in 1845, Iowa joined the Union as a free state and Florida joined as a slave state.

Texas

///////////// Glue Foldable here ///////////

In 1821, Mexico won its freedom from Spain. Mexico owned Texas. Mexican citizens who lived there were called **Tejanos** (teh • HAH • nohs). Mexico wanted more people to settle in Texas. They encouraged Americans to come and live there. Stephen F. Austin brought 300 American families to Texas and became their leader.

Americans did not want to follow the rules that Mexico made for those living in Texas. The rules included learning Spanish and becoming Catholic. Mexico made a **decree,** or official order, that no more Americans could come to Texas. American leaders Stephen Austin and Sam Houston tried to reach an agreement with Mexico, but could not. They decided to break away from Mexico so that they could form their own government.

In 1835, Mexican general Santa Anna led an army into Texas to stop the Americans. The Mexicans had many more soldiers. Still, the Texans captured the city of San Antonio.

Santa Anna did not give up. In 1835, his army marched to San Antonio. It found a group of American soldiers **barricaded,** or blocked off, in a mission building called the Alamo. Santa Anna attacked. The defenders of the Alamo fought long and hard for 13 days. In the end Santa Anna killed all the American soldiers. The general was sure the Texans were beaten. The bravery of the defenders inspired other Texans. "Remember the Alamo!," Texans would cry.

In 1836 while fighting was going on at the Alamo, Texan leaders met. They announced that they were independent of Mexico. Sam Houston gathered an army and supplies. The Texan army made a surprise attack near San Jacinto (san hah • SIHN • toh). They beat the Mexican army and captured General Santa Anna. Santa Anna signed a treaty agreeing that Texas was independent of Mexico.

Texas was now a country. It was named the Lone Star Republic. In September 1836, voters elected Sam Houston president. He asked the United States to annex, or take control of, Texas. Again the problem of balancing slave and free states came up. Adding Texas as a slave state would upset the balance in Congress.

Manifest Destiny

Lesson 2 Statehood for Florida and Texas, *Continued*

Southerners wanted to annex Texas. Northerners were against adding another slave state. By 1844, the mood of the country had changed. Manifest Destiny had become a very popular idea. James K. Polk was elected president. He strongly supported expanding the country in Oregon and in Texas. In 1845 Texas entered the Union.

//////////// Glue Foldable here ////////////

Check for Understanding

Where in Florida did each of the following develop?

cattle ranches _____

cotton plantations _____

tobacco plantations _____

small farms _____

Write one thing each of the following men did in Texas:

Sam Houston _____

Santa Anna _____

Stephen Austin _____

✓ Reading Check

9. Why did it take a long time for the United States to annex Texas?

_____

_____

FOLDABLES®

10. Place a two-tab Foldable along the dotted line to cover Check for Understanding. Write the title *New States* on the anchor tab. Label the two tabs *Texas* and *Florida*. List two things you recall about each. Use the Foldable to help answer Check for Understanding.

_____

_____

_____

_____

networks

Lesson 3 War With Mexico

ESSENTIAL QUESTION
Why does conflict develop?

GUIDING QUESTIONS
1. **How did the Santa Fe Trail benefit the New Mexico Territory?**
2. **How did the culture of California develop?**
3. **Why did war break out between the United States and Mexico?**

Terms to Know
rancho ranch, especially the large estates set up by Mexicans in the American West
ranchero rancher, owner of a rancho

Where in the world?

When did it happen?

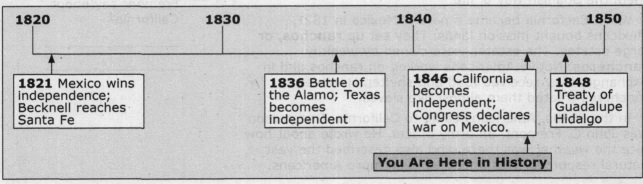

1821 Mexico wins independence; Becknell reaches Santa Fe

1836 Battle of the Alamo; Texas becomes independent

1846 California becomes independent; Congress declares war on Mexico.

1848 Treaty of Guadalupe Hidalgo

You Are Here in History

Lesson 3 War With Mexico, *Continued*

The New Mexico Territory

The New Mexico Territory included all of present-day New Mexico, Arizona, Nevada, Utah, and parts of Colorado and Wyoming. Mexico and the United States fought a war over this land.

Native Americans had lived in the area for thousands of years. Then Spanish explorers claimed it for Spain. They started a settlement at Santa Fe. In 1821, Mexico won its independence. New Mexico then became part of Mexico.

The Spanish did not want Americans to live in Santa Fe. They were afraid the Americans would take the land away from them. However, the new government of Mexico welcomed Americans. They hoped more trade would help the economy.

William Becknell was the first American trader to reach Santa Fe in New Mexico. He arrived in 1821. He brought many goods to sell. The route he took became known as the Santa Fe Trail. It began near Independence, Missouri. That was the western edge of the United States. The trail was mostly flat, so Becknell could use wagons to transport his goods.

Other American traders began to use the trail. It became a busy route. Settlers followed. Many people thought New Mexico was part of the country's Manifest Destiny.

California's Spanish Culture

The Spanish were the first Europeans to reach California. In the 1700s, Spanish explorers and Mexican missionaries settled there. Captain Gaspar de Portolá and Father Junipero Serra (hoo•NIP•uh•roh SEHR•uh) began building missions. Over time, there were many missions built between San Diego and Sonoma. Missions were built to convert Native Americans to Christianity and to teach them the Spanish way of life.

When California became a part of Mexico in 1821, Mexicans bought mission lands. They set up **ranchos,** or large estates. The estates were owned by wealthy **rancheros**. Native Americans worked on ranchos and in exchange, they received food and shelter. However, rancheros treated them almost like slaves.

In the 1840s, Americans came to California. One person was John C. Frémont, an army officer. He wrote about how nice the weather was there, and also described the vast natural resources. This attracted even more Americans.

Identifying

1. Who claimed New Mexico before 1821?

2. Who claimed it after 1821?

Reading Check

3. How did William Becknell affect American settlement in New Mexico?

_____

_____

Defining

4. Circle the definition of *rancho*. Who were *rancheros*?

_____

_____

Summarizing

5. What did John C. Frémont say about California?

_____

_____

174

Manifest Destiny

Lesson 3 War With Mexico, *Continued*

✔ Reading Check

6. Why did Americans want to add California to the United States?

_____

_____

⇄ Identifying

7. Where did the United States say the border between Texas and Mexico was? What did Mexico say?

_____

_____

Americans began to talk about adding California to the United States. If California became a state, the nation's western border would be the Pacific Ocean. Americans would not have to worry about sharing a western border with any other country. Shippers also wanted to build seaports on the coast. From there, they could trade with countries in Asia.

Conflict Begins

President Polk wanted to get both New Mexico and California from Mexico. He offered to buy the land, but Mexico would not sell it. Polk planned to get the land by going to war with Mexico. He hoped to get Mexico to start the fighting.

Mexico and the United States disagreed about where the border was between Texas and Mexico. The United States said it was the Rio Grande, the river to the south. Mexico said the border was the Nueces (nu•AY•sehs) River. It was 150 miles (241 km) farther north. Polk sent General Zachary Taylor to march his army into the area between the two rivers. He hoped that Mexican soldiers would fire first. On April 25, 1846, they did. On May 13, Congress voted to go to war with Mexico.

Polk had three goals to win the war.

U.S. Goals for War With Mexico
1. Push Mexican forces out of Texas
2. Take control of New Mexico and California
3. Capture Mexico City

General Taylor accomplished the first goal in Texas by 1847. General Stephen Kearney led American troops down the Santa Fe trail and captured Santa Fe, New Mexico's capital. Then Kearney headed toward California.

Meanwhile, General John C. Frémont was leading a revolt against Mexico in California. Frémont won. The rebels declared California independent of Mexico.

They named California the Bear Flag Republic. However, the Bear Flag Republic did not stay independent for long. American navy ships sailed into the ports of both San Francisco and San Diego. The Navy claimed California for the United States.

Mexico did not give up, however. Since Mexico had not given up yet, American soldiers were sent to Mexico.

175

Manifest Destiny

Lesson 3 War With Mexico, *Continued*

Finally, General Winfield Scott and his troops captured Mexico City.

In 1848, the Mexicans stopped fighting. The treaty, or agreement, that ended the war was called the Treaty of Guadalupe Hidalgo (GWAH•duh•loop he•DAHL•goh). Mexico gave up California and the New Mexico Territory. It also agreed that the Rio Grande was the border between Mexico and Texas. Mexico gave more than 500,000 square miles (1,295,000 sq. km) of land to the United States. The United States paid Mexico $15 million dollars for the land. They also took on $3.25 million in debts that Mexico owed to American citizens. The dream of Manifest Destiny had become a reality.

//////////////// Glue Foldable here ////////////////

Check for Understanding

What did the Mexican War have to do with the idea of Manifest Destiny?

_____

_____

List three results of the Mexican War.

_____

_____

_____

☑ **Reading Check**

8. What did America gain from the Mexican War?

_____

_____

FOLDABLES®

9. Place a three-tab Venn diagram Foldable along the dotted line to cover Check for Understanding. Write *Compare* on the anchor tab. Label the three tabs *New Mexico Territory*, *Both*, and *California*. List two things you recall about each and what they had in common. Use the Foldable to help answer Check for Understanding.

netw⦿rks

netw⦿rks

Manifest Destiny

Lesson 4 California and Utah

ESSENTIAL QUESTION

How do new ideas change the way people live?

GUIDING QUESTIONS

1. How did the discovery of gold help California?
2. Why did the Mormons settle in Utah?

Terms to Know

forty-niner person who came to California to find gold in 1849
boomtown a fast-growing community
vigilante person who takes it on himself to bring law and order to a place

Where in the world?

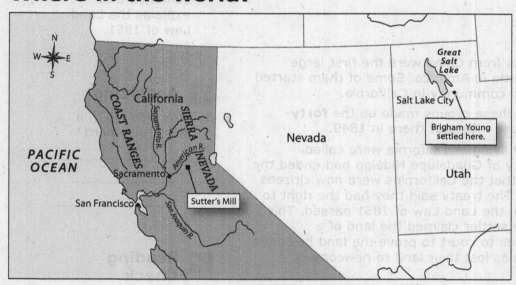

When did it happen?

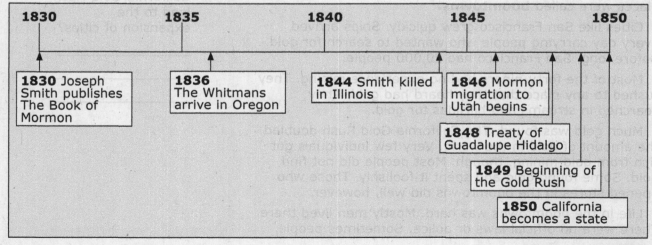

1830 Joseph Smith publishes The Book of Mormon

1836 The Whitmans arrive in Oregon

1844 Smith killed in Illinois

1846 Mormon migration to Utah begins

1848 Treaty of Guadalupe Hidalgo

1849 Beginning of the Gold Rush

1850 California becomes a state

Manifest Destiny

Lesson 4 California and Utah, *Continued*

California Gold Rush

Gold was discovered at Sutter's Mill in California in 1848. The news traveled fast. Soon many people came to California to see if they could get rich.

Where did they come from?

- About 80 percent of these people were American.

Others were from:

- Mexico
- South America
- Europe
- Australia
- China

The 300 immigrants from China were the first large group of Asians to settle in America. Some of them started the Chinese American community in California.

Taken together, all these groups made up the **forty-niners.** That is because most got there in 1849.

The people already living in California were called Californios. The Treaty of Guadalupe Hidalgo had ended the Mexican War. It said that the Californios were now citizens of the United States. The treaty said they had the right to keep their land. Then, the Land Law of 1851 passed. This law said that if a new settler claimed the land of a Californio, he had to go to court to prove the land belonged to him. Many Californios lost their land to newcomers because of this law.

When miners rushed to new areas to look for gold, they built new villages. These grew quickly into cities. Such places were called **boomtowns.**

Cities like San Francisco grew quickly. Ships arrived every day carrying people who wanted to search for gold. Before long, San Francisco had 20,000 people.

Most of the forty-niners had no experience mining. They rushed to any place that they heard had gold. They searched in streams and hillsides for gold.

Much gold was found. The California Gold Rush doubled the amount of gold in the world. Very few individuals got rich from gold mining, though. Most people did not find gold. Some found gold and spent it foolishly. Those who opened stores in the boomtowns did well, however.

Life in the boomtowns was hard. Mostly men lived there. There were no official laws or police. Sometimes people

178

Defining

1. Why were miners called *forty-niners*?

_____

_____

Mark the Text

2. Underline the sentence that explains the Land Law of 1851.

Analyzing

3. Why was life in a boomtown hard?

_____

_____

_____

Reading Check

4. How did the California Gold Rush lead to the expansion of cities?

_____

_____

_____

Manifest Destiny

Lesson 4 California and Utah, *Continued*

📝 Identifying

5. Who was Joseph Smith?

_____

6. What happened to him in Illinois?

_____

❓ Reading Check

7. Why did the Mormons have to keep moving from one place to another?

_____

_____

formed groups of **vigilantes** to protect themselves. Vigilantes took the law into their own hands. They acted as police, judge, and jury.

The Gold Rush had many lasting effects:

- Agriculture, shipping, and trade grew
- Many people who came to look for gold stayed
- Those who stayed went into farming or business
- In 1849 California asked to become a state

Californians wrote a new constitution. The new constitution banned slavery. Southern states did not want California to join the Union. Congress wanted an equal number of slave states and free states. In 1850 a compromise was reached. California became a state.

A Religious Refuge in Utah

While the Gold Rush was taking place in California, change was also taking place in Utah. Mormons were building a new community there.

Joseph Smith founded the Mormon religion. He founded it during the religious awakenings that took place during the 1830s and 1840s.

Smith said he had visions that led him to build a church. He called it the Church of Jesus Christ of Latter-day Saints. The religion is also known as the Mormon religion.

Smith began to preach his ideas in 1830. He published *The Book of Mormon* that year as well.

Smith wanted to build an ideal community. Mormons believed in hard work. They also believed that a man could have more than one wife. This belief made them unpopular wherever they went. They created a prosperous community named Nauvoo in Illinois. Then, in 1844, Joseph Smith was killed by an angry mob.

Brigham Young took over as leader of the Mormons. He decided that the Mormons should move again to find religious freedom. He led them westward to the Great Salt Lake. The territory was in present-day Utah. It was part of Mexico at the time. However, no Mexicans lived there. The land was dry and harsh.

The Mormons built a successful community through hard work. They:

- planned their towns,
- built irrigation canals,

Manifest Destiny

Lesson 4 California and Utah, *Continued*

- taxed property,
- regulated natural resources,
- founded industries, and
- sold supplies to forty-niners who were on their way to California.

In 1850 Congress set up the Utah Territory. Brigham Young was named governor.

The Mormons often had conflicts with the U.S. government. Utah did not become a state until 1896.

//////////////////// Glue Foldable here ////////////////////

Check for Understanding

Read each statement. Write *T* if it is true. If it is false, write *F*.

_____ Mormons worked hard to grow crops in Utah.

_____ Utah became a state soon after it was settled.

In what ways did the Gold Rush affect California?

_____

_____

_____

FOLDABLES®

8. Place a two-tab Foldable along the dotted line to cover Check for Understanding. Write the title *Go West* on the anchor tab. Label the left tab *Gold Rush: California* and the right tab *Religious Refuge: Utah*. List what you remember about each and the movement west. Use the Foldable to help answer Check for Understanding.

North and South

Lesson 1 The Industrial North

ESSENTIAL QUESTION
How does technology change the way people live?

GUIDING QUESTIONS
1. **How did technology and industry change during the 1800s?**
2. **What changes made agriculture more profitable in the 1830s?**

Terms to Know

clipper ship ship with sleek hulls and tall sails that "clipped" time from long journeys

Morse code a system of dots and dashes that represent the alphabet

telegraph a device that used electric signals to send messages

When did it happen?

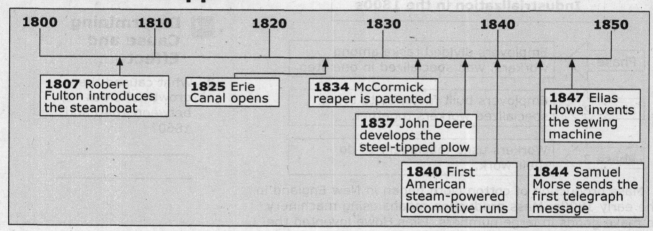

1800	1810	1820	1830	1840	1850

1807 Robert Fulton introduces the steamboat

1825 Erie Canal opens

1834 McCormick reaper is patented

1837 John Deere develops the steel-tipped plow

1840 First American steam-powered locomotive runs

1844 Samuel Morse sends the first telegraph message

1847 Elias Howe invents the sewing machine

What do you know?

In the first column, answer the questions based on what you know before you study. After this lesson, complete the last column.

Now...		Later...
	What was one change as a result of the Erie Canal?	
	In which part of the country was there more industry?	
	What was the telegraph?	

181

networks

North and South

Lesson 1 The Industrial North, *Continued*

Technology and Industry

The early 1800s saw many **innovations** in industry, or the production of goods. Innovations are improved ways of doing things. There were new machines and new ways to use them. The ways in which Americans worked, traveled, and communicated with each other changed as well. Much of this took place in the North.

At the start of the 1800s, most products were made one at a time. A worker would make a product from start to finish. Innovations in industry changed that way of working.

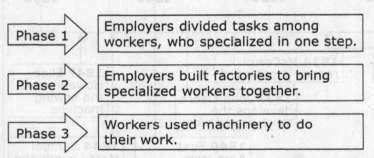

Industrialization in the 1800s

Phase 1 → Employers divided tasks among workers, who specialized in one step.

Phase 2 → Employers built factories to bring specialized workers together.

Phase 3 → Workers used machinery to do their work.

Mass production of cotton cloth began in New England in the early 1800s. Mass production means using machinery to make goods in large numbers. Elias Howe invented the sewing machine in 1846. These changes **transformed,** or changed, the clothing industry. Workers could now make more clothing faster. Other changes transformed other industries. By 1860, the Northeast's factories made at least two-thirds of the country's manufactured goods.

Transportation improved. Between 1800 and 1850, crews built thousands of miles of roads and canals. The canals connected lakes and rivers to make new shipping routes. In 1807, Robert Fulton introduced the steamboat. Steamboats carried goods and people cheaply and quickly.

By 1860 about 3,000 steamboats traveled major rivers and canals, as well as the Great Lakes. Cincinnati, Buffalo, and Chicago grew because they were on major shipping routes.

Sailing was still an important way to travel. A new, faster ship was developed in the 1840s. Called **clipper ships,** they could sail as fast as most steamships at that time.

The railroad was developed. The first steam-powered railroad engine began running in Britain in 1829.

182

Explaining

1. List three changes in the way goods were made during the early 1800s.

_____

_____

_____

Determining Cause and Effect

2. What caused the growth of cities between 1840 and 1860?

_____

_____

networks

North and South

Lesson 1 The Industrial North, *Continued*

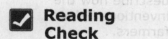

Determining Cause and Effect

3. What were some effects of the railroad on the country?

_____

_____

Reading Check

4. What effect did canals and railways have on transportation from the East to the Midwest?

_____

_____

Peter Cooper built the first American steam-powered railroad engine in 1830. By 1860, there were about 31,000 miles (19,220 km) of track. These tracks were mostly in the North and Midwest. Rail lines connected many cities. They united the Midwest and the East.

Growth of Railroads in 1800s

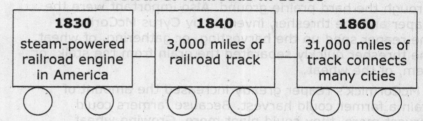

1830	1840	1860
steam-powered railroad engine in America	3,000 miles of railroad track	31,000 miles of track connects many cities

The Erie Canal opened in 1825. With the railroads and the canal, farm products could be moved directly from the Midwest to the East. Farmers and manufacturers could move goods faster and more cheaply. As a result, people could buy them at lower prices than in the past.

The railroads also played an important role in the settlement of the Midwest and the growth of business there. People moved to Ohio, Indiana, and Illinois. New cities and industries developed in the area.

The growth of industry and the speed of travel created a need for faster ways to send messages great distances. Samuel Morse invented the **telegraph**—a machine that uses electric signals to send messages. In 1844 Morse sent his first message.

Telegraph companies formed. Their operators used **Morse code** to send messages. Telegraph lines were put up across the country. By 1852, there were about 23,000 miles (37,015 km) of telegraph lines in the United States.

Farming Innovations

In the early 1800s, few farmers were willing to settle in the West. They were worried that they would not be able to plow on the Great Plains or the prairie. They worried that the soil would not be good enough to grow crops.

North and South

Lesson 1 The Industrial North, *Continued*

//////////// Glue Foldable here ///////////

Three inventions of the 1830s helped farmers overcome these difficulties in farming the land. Because of this, more people moved to the Midwest.

One of these inventions was the steel-tipped plow developed by John Deere in 1837. This plow easily cut through the hard prairie ground. Also important were the reaper and the thresher, invented by Cyrus McCormick. The reaper sped up the harvesting, or gathering, of wheat. The thresher quickly separated the grain from the stalk, or stem, of the wheat.

McCormick's reaper greatly increased the amount of grain a farmer could harvest. Because farmers could harvest more, they could plant more. Growing wheat brought more money than before. Raising wheat became the main economic activity on the Midwestern prairie.

Because of the new machines and the railroads, farmers could plant more crops. Midwestern farmers grew wheat and shipped it east by train and canal barge. Northeast and Middle Atlantic farmers grew more fruits and vegetables.

Despite improvements in farming, the North turned away from farming and toward industry. The number of people working in factories continued to rise.

//////////// Glue Foldable here ///////////

Check for Understanding

List two inventions that transformed the way goods and people were moved in the 1800s.

_____

_____

What are two reasons that farmers were able to make more money growing wheat?

_____

_____

FOLDABLES

Describing

5. Place a three-tab Foldable along the dotted line. Title the anchor tab *Three Inventions*. Label tabs: *Steel-tipped Plow, Mechanical Reaper, Thresher*. On the tabs, describe how the inventions helped farmers.

✓ **Reading Check**

6. What sped up the harvest of wheat?

_____

_____

FOLDABLES

7. Place a one-tab Foldable along the dotted line. Create a memory map. Write *Technology Changed Lives in the 1800s* in the middle. Draw four arrows around the titles. Write words or phrases about the changes industrialization brought. Use this Foldable to help you complete the Check for Understanding.

North and South

Lesson 2 People of the North

ESSENTIAL QUESTION
Why do people adapt to their environment?

GUIDING QUESTIONS
1. **Why did many Americans push for reform in the workplace during this era?**
2. **What challenges did European immigrants face in Northern cities?**

Terms to Know
trade union group of workers with the same trade, or skill

strike a refusal to work in order to force an employer to make changes

prejudice an unfair opinion not based on facts

discrimination unfair treatment

emigrant person who leaves his or her homeland to move elsewhere

famine an extreme shortage of food

nativist person opposed to immigration

Where in the world?

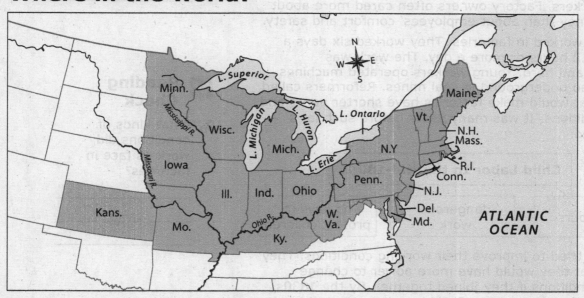

When did it happen?

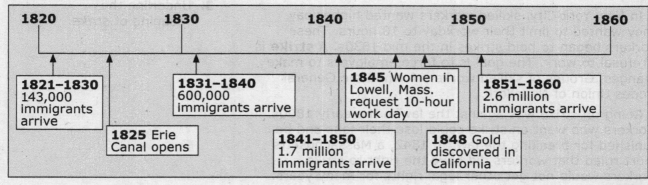

| 1820 | 1830 | 1840 | 1850 | 1860 |

1821–1830 143,000 immigrants arrive

1825 Erie Canal opens

1831–1840 600,000 immigrants arrive

1841–1850 1.7 million immigrants arrive

1845 Women in Lowell, Mass. request 10-hour work day

1848 Gold discovered in California

1851–1860 2.6 million immigrants arrive

networks

North and South

Lesson 2 People of the North, *Continued*

The Factories of the North

By the mid-1800s, more and more things were made by machine. Clothing, shoes, watches, guns, and farming machines were made by machine. Conditions for factory workers were bad. By 1840, the average workday was 11.4 hours. Workers became very tired and more likely to have work accidents. Many factory machines had rapidly moving parts. Workers, especially children, were often hurt by the machines.

Factories had no cooling or heating systems. In the summer, they were very hot. In the winter, workers were often cold.

There were no laws to control working conditions or protect workers. Factory owners often cared more about making money than about employees' comfort and safety.

Children worked in factories. They worked six days a week and 12 hours or more a day. The work was dangerous and hard. Young workers operated machines. They worked underground in coal mines. Reformers called for laws that would make factories have shorter hours and better conditions. It was many years before such laws were passed.

```
        ┌─────────────────────────────────────┐
        │   Child Labor In the Mid-1800s      │
        └─────────────────────────────────────┘
           │              │              │
    ┌────────────┐  ┌────────────┐  ┌────────────────┐
    │ long hours │  │ dangerous  │  │   no laws to   │
    │            │  │   work     │  │ protect children│
    └────────────┘  └────────────┘  └────────────────┘
```

Workers tried to improve their working conditions. They thought that they would have more power to change working conditions if they joined together. By the 1830s, they began forming unions. Skilled workers started **trade unions**. All the workers in these groups had the same trade, or skill.

In New York City, skilled workers wanted higher pay. They wanted to limit their workday to 10 hours. These workers began to hold strikes in the mid-1830s. A **strike** is a refusal to work. The goal is to force employers to make changes. Groups of skilled workers formed the General Trades Union of New York.

Going on strike was against the law in the early 1800s. Workers who went on strike could lose their jobs and be punished for breaking the law. In 1842, a Massachusetts court ruled that workers did have the right to strike. Workers would not get other legal rights for many years.

186

Determining Cause and Effect

1. What were three changes that workers hoped to make by forming trade unions?

   _____

   _____

Reading Check

2. What kinds of conditions did workers face in factories?

   _____

   _____

   _____

Mark the Text

3. Underline the meaning of *strike*.

North and South

Lesson 2 People of the North, Continued

Mark the Text

4. Underline the meanings of *prejudice* and *discrimination*.

Explaining

5. What change was the Female Labor Reform Organization trying to make?

_____

_____

6. How successful were they?

_____

_____

In the North, slavery was mostly ended by the 1830s. However, racial **prejudice**—an unfair opinion of a group— and **discrimination**—unfair treatment of a group— continued. For example, white men in New York could vote even if they did not own property. Few African Americans had the right to vote, however. Rhode Island and Pennsylvania even passed laws to keep them from voting.

Most **communities** in the North did not allow African Americans to go to public schools. African Americans often had to go to lower-quality schools. They had to go to hospitals that were just for them.

A few African Americans did well in business. In 1845, Macon B. Allen became the first African American **licensed**, or given the official right, to practice law in the United States. Most African Americans were poor in the mid-1800s.

```
            Discrimination against
               African Americans
        ┌───────────────┴───────────────┐
  not allowed              not allowed to go to good
   to vote                 public schools or hospitals
```

Women also faced discrimination. They were paid less than men. Men stopped women from joining unions. Men wanted to keep women out of the workplace.

In the 1830s and 1840s, some female workers tried to organize for better working conditions. Sarah G. Bagley was a weaver from Massachusetts. She started the Lowell Female Labor Reform Organization. In 1845, her group asked the state legislature for a 10-hour workday. Because most of the workers were women, the legislature ignored the request.

The Growth of Cities

Industrialization caused big changes in cities. Factories were usually in cities. Because factories attracted workers, Northern cities became much bigger in the early 1800s. Industrialization caused small Western cities to grow.

Between 1820 and 1840, some Midwestern towns grew into major cities. These towns were located along rivers. St. Louis was one. It is located on the Mississippi River, just south of the Illinois and Missouri rivers. By the mid-1800s, many steamboats stopped at St. Louis. Pittsburgh, Cincinnati, and Louisville also were located on waterways.

North and South

Lesson 2 People of the North, *Continued*

These cities became centers of trade. They linked farmers in the Midwest with cities in the Northeast.

Between 1840 and 1860, immigration to the United States increased greatly. Immigration means to enter a new country in order to live there. The greatest number of immigrants came from Ireland. About 1.5 million people came. They left because there was **famine,** or an extreme shortage of food. Over a million people had died in Ireland.

The second-largest group of immigrants came from Germany. Some wanted work and opportunity. Others left to escape political problems.

European immigrants brought their languages, customs, religions, and traditions to the United States.

In the 1830s and 1840s, some Americans were against immigration. These Americans were called **nativists.** They believed that immigrants would make life hard for "native," or American-born, citizens. They said immigrants would take jobs from "real" Americans. They said immigrants brought crime and disease.

In 1849, nativists formed a new political party. Their members often answered questions about their group by saying, "I know nothing." That is why they were known as the Know-Nothing Party. The Know-Nothings wanted laws that would make it harder to become a citizen. In 1854 the Know-Nothings became known as the American Party.

//////////////// Glue Foldable here ////////////////

Check for Understanding

Give three reasons that many Americans wanted reform in the workplace.

_____

_____

_____

How did Americans feel about immigrants?

_____

_____

Mark the Text

7. Circle what nativists believed.

✔ Reading Check

8. Which two nations did most immigrants come from in the mid-1800s?

_____

_____

FOLDABLES

9. Place a Venn-diagram Foldable along the dotted line to cover Check for Understanding. Label the anchor tab *Dealing with Difficulties.* Label the left tab *Workers,* the middle tab *Both,* and the right tab *Immigrants.* Write what you remember about difficulties faced by each group and determine what they had in common. Use the Foldable to answer Check for Understanding.

net**w**rks

North and South

Lesson 3 Southern Cotton Kingdom

ESSENTIAL QUESTION

Why do people make economic choices?

GUIDING QUESTIONS

1. **How were the economies of the South and North different?**
2. **Why did industry develop slowly in the South?**

Where in the world?

Missouri · Kentucky · Virginia · Tennessee · North Carolina · Arkansas Territory · South Carolina · Miss. · Georgia · Texas (Spain) · Alabama · Louisiana · Fla. · **ATLANTIC OCEAN** · *Gulf of Mexico*

Major cotton-producing areas 1820

When did it happen?

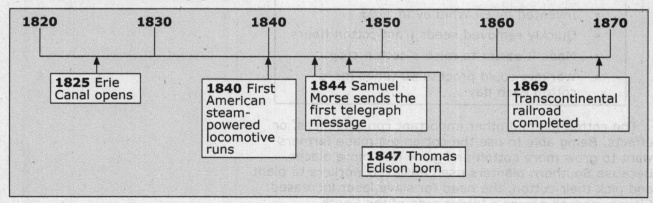

1820	1830	1840	1850	1860	1870

1825 Erie Canal opens

1840 First American steam-powered locomotive runs

1844 Samuel Morse sends the first telegraph message

1847 Thomas Edison born

1869 Transcontinental railroad completed

North and South

Lesson 3 Southern Cotton Kingdom, *Continued*

Rise of the Cotton Kingdom

In the early years of the United States, the South's economy was based mostly on farming. Most Southerners lived in an area called the Upper South. The Upper South was the Atlantic coast of Maryland, Virginia, and North Carolina. Fewer people settled in Georgia and South Carolina.

By 1850, the South had changed. People had moved away from the coast. They now lived in the Deep South. The Deep South included Georgia, South Carolina, Alabama, Mississippi, Louisiana, and Texas.

The economy of the South was very strong. That economy depended, however, on enslaved workers. Slavery was growing in the South, even though it had almost ended in the North.

In colonial times, Southern planters grew mostly rice and tobacco. After the American Revolution, there was less demand for these crops. There was more demand for cotton. Factories in Europe wanted Southern cotton.

It took a lot of time and work to grow and process cotton. After the cotton was picked, workers had to carefully remove the plant's sticky seeds.

Eli Whitney solved this problem. In 1793, he invented a machine called the cotton gin. Whitney's machine quickly removed seeds from cotton fibers. Using the cotton gin, **productivity** went up. Productivity is the amount of anything that a worker can make, or produce, in a given time. Workers could **process** 50 times more cotton using the cotton gin than they used to process by hand.

Explaining

1. On what two things did the economy of the South depend in the early years of the United States?

_____

_____

Mark the Text

2. Underline the definition of the word *productivity*.

Making Connections

3. Why did the need for slave labor increase in the South?

_____

_____

> ### Fact Sheet: The Cotton Gin
> - Invented by Eli Whitney in 1793
> - Quickly removed seeds from cotton fibers
> - Made it easier to raise a cotton crop
> - Workers could process 50 times more cotton each day

The cotton gin had other important consequences, or effects. Being able to use the cotton gin made farmers want to grow more cotton and grow it in more places. Because Southern planters used enslaved workers to plant and pick their cotton, the need for slave labor increased. Slavery spread across a larger area of the South.

Lesson 3 Southern Cotton Kingdom, *Continued*

✏ Explaining

4. What was the domestic slave trade?

_____

_____

_____

✓ Reading Check

5. List three effects that the cotton gin had on the South's economy.

_____

_____

_____

Effects of Cotton Gin on Slavery

| Cotton gin invented | → | Cotton processed faster | → | Farmers want more cotton | → | More slaves needed to plant and pick cotton |

By 1860, the Deep South and Upper South grew different crops. The Upper South produced:

- tobacco
- hemp
- wheat
- vegetables

The Deep South produced:

- rice
- sugarcane
- cotton

Many enslaved workers were needed to produce the cotton and sugar crops. As a result, the sale of enslaved Africans was a big business. The Upper South became the place where most of the sales took place. This kind of slave trade took place within the United States, so it was known as the **domestic slave trade.** *Domestic* means "local."

Southern Industry

Industry did not grow as quickly in the South as it did in the North. One reason was cotton. Cotton brought great profits. Another reason was the cost of building new industries. To raise the money to build factories, planters would have had to sell enslaved people or land. White Southerners made plenty of money growing cotton, rice, sugar, and tobacco. They also made money selling slaves. They did not feel the need to earn money from industry.

There was not much market, or demand, for factory-made products in the South. Many people in the South were enslaved people. They had no money to buy goods. No market for goods stopped industries from growing.

For these reasons, it is not surprising that some white Southerners just did not want industry.

Lesson 3 Southern Cotton Kingdom, *Continued*

```
          ┌─────────────────────────────────┐
          │   Reasons for Slow Growth of    │
          │       Industry in the South     │
          └─────────────────────────────────┘
     ┌──────────────┐  ┌──────────────┐  ┌──────────────┐
     │ Growing cotton│  │ Building new │  │Limited market│
     │   was very    │  │industry is very│ │ for factory │
     │   profitable  │  │  expensive   │  │    goods     │
     └──────────────┘  └──────────────┘  └──────────────┘
```

Some Southern leaders did want industry in the region. They thought the South depended too much on the North for factory goods. These leaders also thought that factories would improve the economy of the Upper South. A few men opened factories.

Transportation systems in the South were different from those in the North. In the South, farmers and the few factory owners moved their goods on natural waterways. Most towns were located on coasts or along rivers. There were few canals, and roads were poor.

The South had fewer railroads than the North. Southern rail lines were not long, and they were not linked together. Poor railroad systems are another reason Southern cities grew more slowly. By 1860, only about one-third of the nation's rail lines lay within the South. This rail shortage would hurt the South in the years to come.

```
          ┌─────────────────────────────────┐
          │        Problems with            │
          │   Transportation in the South   │
          └─────────────────────────────────┘
     ┌──────────────┐  ┌──────────────┐  ┌──────────────┐
     │  few canals  │  │  poor roads  │  │few rail lines│
     └──────────────┘  └──────────────┘  └──────────────┘
```

//////////////// Glue Foldable here ////////////////

Check for Understanding

List two ways that the South's economy was different from the North's economy.

_____

_____

Why did industry develop so slowly in the South?

_____

_____

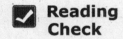

Contrasting

6. How were Southern railroads different from Northern railroads?

_____

_____

✓ Reading Check

7. How did slavery affect the growth of the South's economy?

_____

_____

FOLDABLES

8. Place a Venn-diagram Foldable along the dotted line to cover Check for Understanding. Label the left tab *Northern Economy*, the middle tab *Both*, and the right tab *Southern Economy*. Write what you remember about each region and determine what they had in common. Use the Foldable to help answer Check for Understanding.

netw⭐rks

North and South

Lesson 4 People of the South

ESSENTIAL QUESTION
How do people adapt to their environment?

GUIDING QUESTIONS
1. **How were Southern farms different from Southern plantations?**
2. **How did enslaved African Americans try to cope with their lack of freedom?**
3. **What changes did urbanization introduce in the South by the mid-1800s?**

Terms to Know
yeomen farmers who owned small farms
overseer plantation manager
spiritual African American religious song
slave codes laws in Southern states that controlled enslaved people
Underground Railroad a system to aid the escape of enslaved people
literacy the ability to read and write

When did it happen?

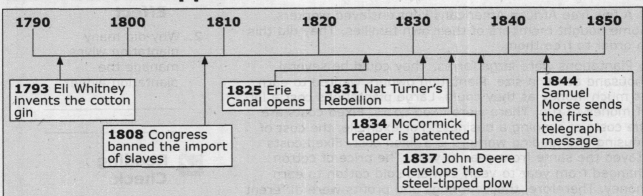

| 1790 | 1800 | 1810 | 1820 | 1830 | 1840 | 1850 |

1793 Eli Whitney invents the cotton gin

1808 Congress banned the import of slaves

1825 Erie Canal opens

1831 Nat Turner's Rebellion

1834 McCormick reaper is patented

1837 John Deere develops the steel-tipped plow

1844 Samuel Morse sends the first telegraph message

What do you know?
In the first column, answer the questions based on what you know before you study. After this lesson, complete the last column.

Now...		Later...
	What were Southern farms like in the 1800s?	
	What kind of family life did enslaved African Americans have?	

193

Southern Agriculture

Slavery was at the center of the Southern economy. That does not mean that every white person owned large numbers of enslaved people. There were four main groups of white society. There were yeomen, tenant farmers, the rural poor, and plantation owners.

Most white people in the South were **yeomen** farmers. Yeomen farmers owned small farms. These farms were in the Upper South and in hilly parts of the Deep South. Yeomen farmers owned only a few slaves. Some owned no slaves. They grew crops for themselves and to trade for things they needed.

Tenant farmers did not own their land. They rented the land that they farmed. Yeomen farmers and tenant farmers were most of the white farmers in the south.

A few free African Americans kept enslaved workers. Some bought members of their own families. They did this in order to free them.

Plantations were large farms. They could be several thousand acres in size. Plantation owners wanted to earn as much money as they could. Large plantations cost a lot of money to run. There were fixed costs. Fixed costs are the costs of running a business. For example, the cost of housing and feeding workers is a fixed cost. Fixed costs stayed the same from year to year. The price of cotton changed from year to year. Owners sold cotton to earn money. Therefore, their earnings and profits were different from year to year.

The owners were usually men. Owners traveled often on business. Their wives ran the households. They managed the enslaved workers. They kept the financial records.

Enslaved people did many different jobs on the plantation. They cleaned the house, cooked, did laundry and sewing, and served meals. They were blacksmiths, carpenters, shoemakers, or weavers. They took care of the or animals. Most enslaved African Americans worked in the fields. They worked from sunrise to sunset. An **overseer**, or plantation manager, was their boss in the fields.

The Lives of Enslaved People

Life was hard for most enslaved African Americans. They worked hard, earned no money, and had little hope of ever being free. They feared that an owner could sell them or members of their family. Even with all this, enslaved

Listing

1. List the four groups of white society in the South in the 1800s.

_____

Determining Cause and Effect

2. Why did many plantation wives manage the plantation alone?

_____
_____

Reading Check

3. Which group made up the largest number of whites in the South?

_____

North and South

Lesson 4 People of the South, *Continued*

Specifying

4. What kind of work did most enslaved African Americans do?

_____

_____

_____

Explaining

5. Why did enslaved people need extended families?

_____

_____

Reading Check

6. How did African American spirituals develop?

_____

_____

African Americans kept up their family lives as best they could. They developed a culture, or way of life. It blended African and American elements.

Enslaved people married and raised families. Still, there were no laws that could stop a slave owner from selling a family member. This broke the family apart.

If an owner sold an enslaved father or mother, then a relative or a close friend took care of the children left behind. Large, close-knit families became an important part of African American culture.

In 1808, Congress stopped new slaves from being brought into the United States. Slavery was still legal, however. By 1860, almost all the enslaved people in the South had been born there.

Enslaved people kept old African customs. They told traditional African folk stories to their children. They performed African music and dance.

Enslaved people created their own kind of music. They used their African music styles for the music. The beat of the music set the pace for their work in the fields.

Many enslaved African Americans followed traditional African religious practices. Others accepted Christianity. Enslaved people expressed their beliefs through **spirituals.** These are African American religious folk songs.

The **slave codes** were laws in the Southern states. Slaves codes controlled enslaved people. One purpose of the slave codes was to prevent slaves from rebelling. Slave codes prevented enslaved people from meeting in large groups. They needed a written pass to leave the slaveowner's property. It was a crime to teach enslaved people to read or write.

White people had reasons to fear slave rebellion. Enslaved African Americans did sometimes openly rebel.

Nat Turner was a popular religious leader among enslaved people. Turner had taught himself to read and write. In 1831, he led a group of followers on a brief, violent rebellion in Virginia.

Effects of Nat Turner's Rebellion

Turner's group kills at least 55 whites.	→	White mobs kill more than 100 African Americans.	→	Whites pass even stricter slave codes.

Enslaved people also resisted by running away. They ran away to find family members on other plantations. They ran away to escape punishment. Sometimes, enslaved

North and South

Lesson 4 People of the South, *Continued*

African Americans ran North to freedom. Harriet Tubman and Frederick Douglass were two such people. They became important African American leaders.

A runaway might receive aid from the **Underground Railroad.** This was a network of "safe houses" owned by people who were against slavery. The Underground Railroad helped enslaved people escape slavery.

Southern Cities

By the mid-1800s, the South had several large cities. Two cities were Baltimore and New Orleans. The ten largest Southern cities were seaports or river ports. Chattanooga, Montgomery, and Atlanta were cities that formed near railroads.

Free African Americans formed communities. They worked. They set up churches and other institutions. They were not equal to whites in economic and political ways, though. They could not move freely from state to state.

In the early 1800s, there were no statewide public school systems in the South. There was less **literacy,** or the ability to read and write, in the South than in other parts of the country. People who had enough money sent their children to private schools. By the mid-1800s, North Carolina and Kentucky set up and ran public schools.

Reasons for Low Literacy in the South

People were spread out over a wide area.	People could not send their children so far away.	Many in the South did not believe in public education.

Check for Understanding

List two differences between Southern farms and plantations.

_____

_____

List two things enslaved African Americans did to help themselves cope with a lack of freedom.

_____

_____

✓ Reading Check

7. What led to the growth of Southern cities?

_____

_____

FOLDABLES®

8. Place a one-tab Foldable along the dotted line to cover Check for Understanding. Create a memory map. Write: *How did enslaved people cope with their lack of freedom?* in the middle of the tab, and draw four arrows around the title. Use both sides of the tab to write words or phrases you remember about ways enslaved people adjusted their lives to survive. Use the Foldable to help answer Check for Understanding.

networks

The Spirit of Reform

Lesson 1 Social Reform

Lesson 1 Social Reform, continued

ESSENTIAL QUESTION
Why do societies change?

GUIDING QUESTIONS
1. **What was the effect of the Second Great Awakening?**
2. **What type of American literature emerged in the 1820s?**

Terms to Know
revival religious meeting
utopia community based on a vision of the perfect society
temperance drinking little or no alcohol
normal school state-supported school for training high-school graduates to become teachers
civil disobedience refusing to obey laws considered unjust

Where in the world?

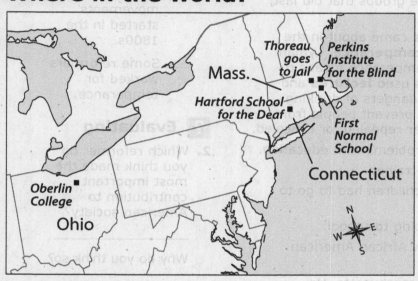

When did it happen?

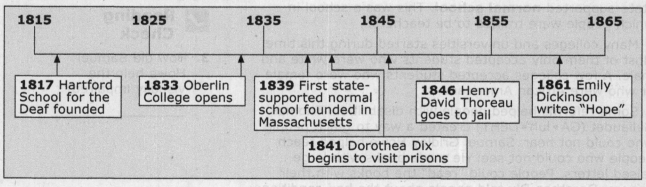

1815	1825	1835	1845	1855	1865

1817 Hartford School for the Deaf founded

1833 Oberlin College opens

1839 First state-supported normal school founded in Massachusetts

1841 Dorothea Dix begins to visit prisons

1846 Henry David Thoreau goes to jail

1861 Emily Dickinson writes "Hope"

197

The Spirit of Reform

Lesson 1 Social Reform, *Continued*

Religion and Reform

Religious meetings, called **revivals**, were popular in the early 1800s. People traveled far to hear certain preachers. It was a time of great interest in religion. It was known as the Second Great Awakening. The first Great Awakening had been in the mid-1700s.

People thought of ways to reform, or improve, society as a result of attending revival meetings. Some thought that they should set up **utopias** (yu•TOH•pee•uhs). These were communities based on their idea of a perfect society. Most utopias did not last. One of the groups that did last, however, was the Mormons.

Several social reform movements came about in the 1800s. Some reformers called for **temperance**. Lyman Beecher was one such reformer. Temperance means to drink little or no alcohol. Reformers used **lectures** and booklets to warn people about the dangers of drinking alcohol. Some laws were passed to prevent people from drinking. Most of the laws were later repealed, or canceled.

Reformers wanted to fix some problems with education.

- Many teachers were not well-trained.
- Many people did not believe children had to go to school.
- Girls were often kept from going to school.
- Many schools refused to allow African American students to attend.

Horace Mann was a lawyer in Massachusetts. He believed education was the key to getting ahead. Thanks to his work, in 1839, Massachusetts founded the nation's first state-supported **normal school**. This was a school in which people were trained to be teachers.

Many colleges and universities started during this time. Most of them only accepted students who were white and male. A few colleges accepted students who were female or who were African American.

Some reforms helped people with disabilities. Thomas Gallaudet (GA•luh•DEHT) created a way to teach people who could not hear. Samuel Gridley Howe helped teach people who could not see. He made books with large raised letters. People could "read" the books with their fingers. Dorothea Dix told people about the bad conditions in prisons.

Finding the Main Idea

1. Place a checkmark next to the best statement of the main idea of this passage.

____ Several social reform movements started in the 1800s.

____ Some reformers worked for temperance.

Evaluating

2. Which reformer do you think made the most important contribution to American society?

_____

Why do you think so?

_____

_____

Reading Check

3. How did Samuel Howe help the visually impaired?

_____

The Spirit of Reform

Lesson 1 Social Reform, *Continued*

Person	Contributions
Lyman Beecher	tried to prevent drinking of alcohol
Horace Mann	started first state-supported teacher's college
Thomas Gallaudet	developed a way to teach the deaf
Dorothea Dix	made people aware of bad conditions in prisons

🖎 **Identifying**

4. Identify the person described in each of the following:

A transcendentalist who supported women's rights in her writings

_____

An American poet who wrote story poems

_____

❓ **Drawing Conclusions**

5. How did art in the United States change in the 1800s?

_____

_____

☑ **Reading Check**

6. How did the spirit of reform influence American authors?

_____

_____

_____

Culture Changes

The changes that were taking place in American society affected art and literature. American artists developed their own style. Their art showed American places and ways of life.

Reform also had an effect on literature. A movement began called Transcendentalism. Its members were called transcendentalists. These thinkers and writers showed more of a connection between people and nature. They wrote that a person's conscience, or sense of right and wrong, was important.

Margaret Fuller wrote about women's rights. Ralph Waldo Emerson was also a writer in that movement. He wanted people to think about right and wrong. He wanted people to treat others fairly.

Henry David Thoreau practiced a form of protest called **civil disobedience** (dihs•uh•BEE•dee•uhns). He would not obey laws he thought were unjust. He went to jail because of this belief. In 1846, he would not pay a tax that supported the Mexican War.

American poets created great works. Henry Wadsworth Longfellow wrote poems that told a story. One of his well-known poems is the *Song of Hiawatha*. In *Leaves of Grass*, a poet named Walt Whitman tried to show the feelings and spirit of America. The poet Emily Dickinson wrote hundreds of poems. They were mostly about her personal feelings. Many of her poems are about nature.

American artists were developing a purely American style. They showed American life and landscapes. One group of painters was called the Hudson River School. They painted scenes of the Hudson River Valley in New York. Two well-known artists were Currier and Ives. They made prints of Americans celebrating holidays or enjoying themselves in other ways.

199

The Spirit of Reform

Lesson 1 Social Reform, *Continued*

| Fuller: supported women's rights | Thoreau: practiced civil disobedience | Longfellow: wrote story poems |

Transcendentalist Thinkers
- humans and nature
- importance of individual conscience

| Emerson: wrote about the importance of conscience | Dickinson: wrote personal poems | Whitman: wrote about the new American spirit |

/ / / / / / / / / / / / / Glue Foldable here / / / / / / / / / / / /

Check for Understanding

List four areas of reform in the 1800s.

_____

_____

List three transcendentalists.

_____

_____

FOLDABLES®

7. Place a one-tab Foldable along the dotted line to cover Check for Understanding. Write *Reform and Change* on the anchor tab. Create a memory map by writing the title *American Society* in the middle of the Foldable tab. Draw five arrows around the title and write words or phrases that explain how society changed due to reforms during the 1800s. Use the Foldable to help complete Check for Understanding.

The Spirit of Reform

Lesson 2 The Abolitionists

ESSENTIAL QUESTION
What motivates people to act?

GUIDING QUESTIONS

1. **How did Americans' attitudes toward slavery change?**
2. **Why did the reform movement gain momentum?**
3. **Who opposed the abolition of slavery?**

Term to Know
abolitionists reformers who worked to abolish, or end, slavery in the early 1800s in the United States

When did it happen?

1785	1795	1805	1815	1825	1835

1787 States given authority to decide whether to allow slavery

1816 American Colonization Society founded

1831 William Lloyd Garrison began publishing *The Liberator*

1832 New England Anti-Slavery Society founded

1833 American Anti-Slavery Society founded

What do you know?

In the first column, write what you know about each person before you study. After the lesson, fill in the last column.

Now...	Who was...	Later...
	William Lloyd Garrison	
	Frederick Douglass	
	Harriet Tubman	

201

The Spirit of Reform

Lesson 2 The Abolitionists, *Continued*

The Start of the Abolition Movement

The early 1800s was a time of reform. One type of reform was the work of abolitionists. **Abolitionists** were people who worked to abolish, or end, slavery. By the early 1800s, Northern states had ended slavery. Slavery was still an important part of the South's economy, however. By the mid-1800s, more and more Americans came to believe that slavery was wrong. The conflict over slavery grew.

Different Attitudes	
North	**South**
Slavery ends throughout the North.	Our economy depends on slavery.
Slavery is wrong.	

The first antislavery work was not to end slavery. It was to resettle African Americans outside of the United States. A group of white people from Virginia started the American Colonization Society. They freed enslaved people and sent them to other places to start new lives. The Society had gotten land to start a colony in West Africa. The colony was called Liberia. In 1847 Liberia became independent.

The American Colonization Society did not stop the growth of slavery. The number of enslaved people kept growing. The society could send only a small number of people to Africa. Besides, most African Americans did not want to go to Africa. Their families had lived in America for many years. They just wanted to be free.

The Movement Builds Strength

Around 1830, slavery became the most important issue for reformers. William Lloyd Garrison had a great effect on the antislavery movement. He started a newspaper called *The Liberator.* He also started the American Anti-Slavery Society. He was one of the first to call for an immediate end to slavery.

Two sisters, Sarah and Angelina Grimké, spoke and wrote against slavery. They used their money to free several of the family's enslaved workers. Their book, *American Slavery As It Is,* was one of the strongest works against slavery at that time.

A♭c Defining

1. Who were the abolitionists?

_____

_____

✓ Reading Check

2. What was the purpose of the American Colonization Society?

_____

_____

? Drawing Conclusions

3. How did William Lloyd Garrison influence the abolition movement?

_____

_____

networks

The Spirit of Reform

Lesson 2 The Abolitionists, *Continued*

Copyright by The McGraw-Hill Companies.

Mark the Text

4. Underline the ways that Samuel Cornish, John Russwurm, and David Walker worked for abolition.

Reading Check

5. What were Underground Railroad "stations"?

_____

_____

FOLDABLES

Describing

6. Place a two-tab Foldable along the dotted line to cover the graphic organizer. Label the two tabs *Free African American Abolitionists* and *Underground Railroad.* On both sides of the tabs, record information about key free African American abolitionists and describe the network of escape routes.

Free African Americans also played an important role in the abolitionist movement. They helped set up and run the American Anti-Slavery Society. Samuel Cornish and John Russwurm began the first African American newspaper. It was called *Freedom's Journal.* David Walker was a writer who urged African Americans to rise up against slavery. In 1830, free African American leaders held an important meeting in Philadelphia.

Frederick Douglass was the best-known African American abolitionist. Douglass escaped from slavery in Maryland in 1838. He settled in Massachusetts. Later he moved to New York. He was a powerful speaker. He spoke at many meetings in the United States and abroad. Douglass was the editor of an antislavery newspaper called *North Star.*

Sojourner Truth escaped from slavery in 1826. She worked with Frederick Douglass and William Lloyd Garrison to end slavery. She traveled throughout the North. She spoke about her life as an enslaved person. She also worked in the women's rights movement.

Some abolitionists helped African Americans escape from slavery. There was a network of escape routes from the South to the North. It was called the Underground Railroad. Along the routes, whites and African Americans guided the runaway "passengers" to freedom in Northern states or in Canada. They traveled at night. By day they rested at "stations." These were barns, basements, and attics in safe houses. Harriet Tubman became the most famous "conductor" on the Underground Railroad.

/ / / / / / / / / / / ,Glue Foldable here / / / / / / / / / / /

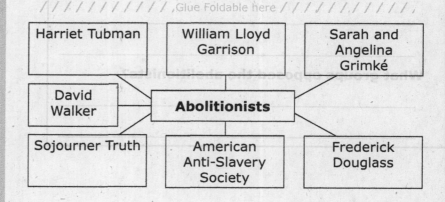

Harriet Tubman	William Lloyd Garrison	Sarah and Angelina Grimké
David Walker	**Abolitionists**	
Sojourner Truth	American Anti-Slavery Society	Frederick Douglass

Lesson 2 The Abolitionists, *Continued*

Reaction to the Abolitionists

Only a small number of Northerners were abolitionists. Many Northerners believed that freed African Americans could never fully be a part of American society.

Some Northerners were afraid that the abolitionists would start a war between the North and South. Other Northerners feared that freed African Americans would take their jobs.

Opposition toward abolitionists was cruel at times. An angry white mob destroyed Elijah Lovejoy's antislavery newspaper offices three times. The fourth time, the mob set fire to the building and killed Lovejoy.

Many Southerners said abolition threatened their way of life. Southerners defended slavery. They thought it was a necessary part of the Southern economy. Southerners said they treated enslaved people well. They said they gave enslaved people food and medical care. Some of their beliefs were based on racism. Many whites believed African Americans could not take care of themselves and were better off under the care of white people.

/ / / / / / / / / / / / / / Glue Foldable here / / / / / / / / / / / / / / / / / /

Check for Understanding

List three ways that abolitionists tried to end slavery in America.

_____

_____

_____

What groups opposed the abolitionists?

_____

_____

Listing

7. List two reasons Northerners opposed abolition.

_____

_____

Reading Check

8. How did Southerners defend the idea of slavery?

_____

_____

FOLDABLES®

9. Place a two-tab Foldable along the dotted line to cover Check for Understanding. Label the tabs: *What motivated the abolitionists?* and *What motivated those who were against the abolitionists?* Recall why each group felt strongly about slavery. Write the reasons for their beliefs. Use the Foldable to help answer Check for Understanding.

The Spirit of Reform

Lesson 3 The Women's Movement

ESSENTIAL QUESTION

How do new ideas change the way people live?

GUIDING QUESTIONS

1. **What did women do to win equal rights?**
2. **In what areas did women make progress in achieving equality?**

Terms to Know
suffrage the right to vote
coeducation the teaching of males and females together

Where in the world?

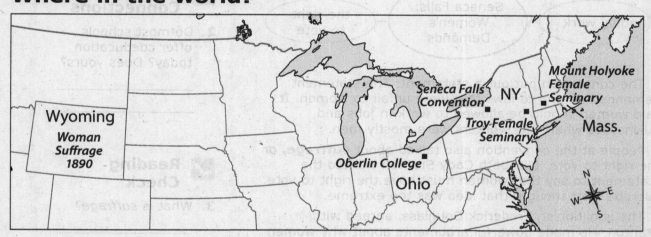

When did it happen?

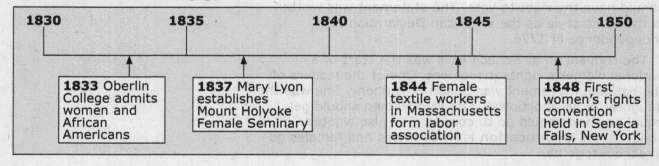

The Spirit of Reform

Lesson 3 The Women's Movement, *Continued*

Reform for Women

Many women abolitionists also worked for women's rights. In July 1848, Lucretia Mott and Elizabeth Cady Stanton held the first women's rights convention. It was in Seneca Falls, New York. The Seneca Falls Convention laid the foundation for the women's rights movement.

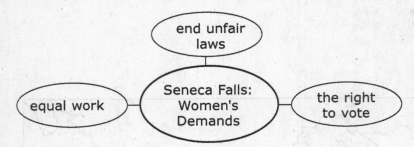

The convention put out a statement. The statement demanded an end to laws that were unfair to women. It said women should be allowed to work in jobs and businesses where the workers were mostly men.

People at the convention also talked about **suffrage,** or the right to vote. Elizabeth Cady Stanton wanted the statement to say that women must have the right to vote. Lucretia Mott thought that idea was too extreme.

The abolitionist, Frederick Douglass, agreed with Stanton. He made powerful arguments about why women should be able to vote.

In the end, the convention did demand that women should have the right to vote. The statement was written in the same style as the American Declaration of Independence of 1776.

The convention at Seneca Falls was the start of a national women's rights movement. One of the leaders of the national movement was Susan B. Anthony. She was the daughter of an abolitionist. She said women should get equal pay and should go to college. She also wanted coeducation. **Coeducation** is when males and females go to school together.

Anthony also started the country's first women's temperance organization. Anthony and Stanton met at a temperance meeting in 1851. They became friends, and they joined together to work for women's rights.

Opportunities for women increased. Women got the right to vote in Wyoming in 1890. Other states followed.

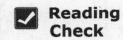

Mark the Text

1. Underline the text that explains the debate at the Seneca Falls Convention over women voting.

? **Making Connections**

2. Do most schools offer coeducation today? Does yours?

_____

_____

✓ **Reading Check**

3. What is *suffrage*?

_____

_____

The Spirit of Reform

Lesson 3 The Women's Movement, *Continued*

Categorizing

4. Match the education reformer with her school.

____ Catherine Beecher

____ Emma Willard

____ Mary Lyon

a. Troy Female Seminary

b. Milwaukee College for Women

c. Mount Holyoke Female Seminary

Mark the Text

5. Underline the text to show the progress of women in the middle to late 1800s in marriage and property laws.

Reading Check

6. What gains did women make in education?

_____

_____

Individual	Contribution
Lucretia Mott	at Seneca Convention
Elizabeth Cady Stanton	at Seneca Convention; worked with Anthony on suffrage and temperance.
Susan B. Anthony	national leader, worked with Stanton on temperance and suffrage.

Women Make Gains

Some people wanted better education for women. Catherine Beecher thought that women should be trained for traditional roles. The Milwaukee College for Women used Beecher's ideas. At that college, women learned to be successful wives, mothers, and homemakers.

Other people thought that women would make good teachers. Still others thought women should be trained to be leaders and have a career.

Emma Willard was one of these women. She taught herself science and mathematics. In 1821, she set up the Troy Female Seminary in New York State. There, young women learned math, history, geography, and physics. They also learned homemaking subjects.

Mary Lyon worked as a teacher for 20 years. Then she began to raise money to open a college for women. She started Mount Holyoke Female Seminary in 1837, in Massachusetts.

Before the mid-1800s, women did not have many rights. Anything a woman owned belonged to her husband when they got married.

In the mid- to late 1800s, women got some rights. Some states recognized the right of a woman to own her own property even after she married. Some states passed laws that gave rights to divorced women. These laws had to do with who raised the children. Several states decided to allow a woman to get a divorce if her husband drank alcohol too often.

Many careers were closed to women, however. They had to struggle to work in some professions. Two examples were medicine and the ministry. In the 1800s, women began to break through these barriers.

networks

The Spirit of Reform

Lesson 3 The Women's Movement, *Continued*

Elizabeth Blackwell tried many times to get into medical school. Many schools said no. Finally, she was accepted to Geneva College in New York State. Blackwell graduated first in her class. She became a famous doctor.

Maria Mitchell also broke down walls for herself and for women after her. Maria Mitchell had been taught by her father.

- In 1847, she became the first person to discover a comet with a telescope.
- The next year, she was the first woman elected to the American Academy of Arts and Sciences.
- In 1865, Mitchell became a teacher at Vassar College.

Women had made many gains during the 1800s. There were many limits to what they could do, however. The struggle for equality continued.

Education for Women	Marriage and Family	Career
• better training for traditional roles • can be good teachers • Troy Female Seminary teaches math, history, science	• women gain right to own property • divorced women gain rights in raising children • women gain right to divorce husbands who abuse alcohol	• Elizabeth Blackwell breaks the barrier to women in medicine

/ / / / / / / / / / / Glue Foldable here / / / / / / / / / / /

Check for Understanding

List three demands made at the Seneca Falls Convention in 1848.

_____

_____

_____

List two gains that women made in the field of education.

_____

_____

_____

FOLDABLES®

7. Place a two-tab Foldable along the dotted line to cover Check for Understanding. Write the title *Seneca Falls 1848* on the anchor tab. Label the tabs *Cause* and *Effect*. Recall and record the reasons for the convention in 1848, and how it changed lives of women. Use the Foldable to help answer Check for Understanding.

Toward Civil War

Lesson 1 The Search for Compromise

ESSENTIAL QUESTION

Why does conflict develop?

GUIDING QUESTIONS

1. **What political compromises were made because of slavery?**
2. **What is the Kansas-Nebraska Act?**

Terms to Know

fugitive person who runs away from the law

secede leave

border ruffian armed pro-slavery supporter who crossed the border from Missouri to vote in Kansas

civil war fighting between citizens of the same country

Where in the world?

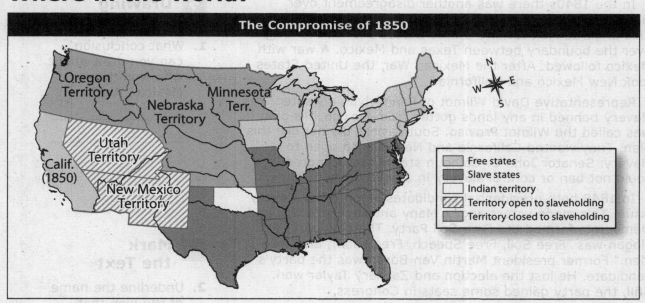

The Compromise of 1850

Free states
Slave states
Indian territory
Territory open to slaveholding
Territory closed to slaveholding

When did it happen?

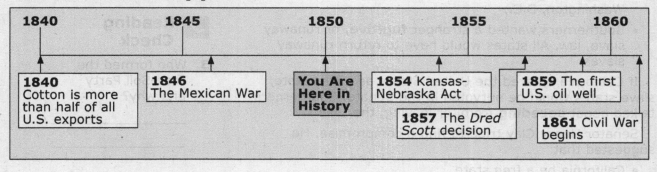

1840 — 1845 — 1850 — 1855 — 1860

1840 Cotton is more than half of all U.S. exports

1846 The Mexican War

You Are Here in History

1854 Kansas-Nebraska Act

1857 The *Dred Scott* decision

1859 The first U.S. oil well

1861 Civil War begins

Toward Civil War

Lesson 1 The Search for Compromise, *Continued*

Political Conflict Over Slavery

The question of slavery divided Americans. Many Northerners wanted to ban it. Most Southerners wanted Northerners to stay out of the South's business. Each time there was a debate over slavery, the nation's leaders came up with a compromise. For example, Congress passed the Missouri Compromise in 1820. This kept a balance of power in the Senate between slave states and free states. It also stopped the debate over slavery for a little while.

In the 1840s there was another disagreement over slavery in new territories. Texas became a state in 1845. This angered Mexico. The United States and Mexico fought over the boundary between Texas and Mexico. A war with Mexico followed. After the Mexican War, the United States took New Mexico and California.

Representative David Wilmot of Pennsylvania wanted slavery banned in any lands gotten from Mexico. His plan was called the Wilmot Proviso. Southerners did not like this plan. They wanted California and New Mexico open to slavery. Senator John C. Calhoun stated that Congress could not ban or control slavery in any territory.

In 1848 both presidential candidates ignored the slavery issue. This made voters angry. Many antislavery Whigs and Democrats formed the Free-Soil Party. The new party's slogan was "Free Soil, Free Speech, Free Labor, and Free Men." Former president Martin Van Buren was the party's candidate. He lost the election and Zachary Taylor won. Still, the party gained some seats in Congress.

The debate over slavery came up again in 1849 because:

• California wanted to become a state as a free state;

• antislavery groups wanted to ban slavery in Washington, D.C.;

• Southerners wanted a stronger **fugitive,** or runaway slave, law. All states would have to return runaway slaves.

If California entered the United States as a free state, slave states would be outvoted in the Senate. Southerners talked about **seceding** from, or leaving, the Union.

Senator Henry Clay tried to find a compromise. He suggested that:

• California be a free state.

• slavery would be allowed in new territories.

? Drawing Conclusions

1. What conclusion can you draw about who won the Mexican War?

_____

_____

Mark the Text

2. Underline the name of the plan that would ban slavery from any lands taken from Mexico.

✓ Reading Check

3. Who formed the Free-Soil Party and why?

_____

_____

210

Toward Civil War

Lesson 1 The Search for Compromise, *Continued*

? Critical Thinking

4. How do you think Clay's proposal for Washington, D.C., pleased both the North and the South?

_____

_____

A♭c Vocabulary

5. Who were the border ruffians?

_____

_____

- the slave trade would be illegal in Washington, D.C., but slavery itself would be allowed.
- there would be a stronger fugitive slave law.

Congress discussed the ideas and argued about them. Senator Stephen A. Douglas of Illinois solved the problem. He divided Clay's plan into parts. Congress voted on each part separately. In this way, Congress passed five laws. Together, they are called the Compromise of 1850.

Compromise of 1850	Major Ideas
Senator Henry Clay had the ideas.	1. Stronger Fugitive Slave Law
Senator Stephen A. Douglas made the plan.	2. California to be a free state
Five separate laws were passed.	3. Other new territories could have slavery
	4. Okay to have slaves in Washington, D.C.
	5. However, no slave trade in Washington, D.C.

The Kansas-Nebraska Act

In 1854 Senator Douglas suggested making the lands west of Missouri into two territories. They would be called Kansas and Nebraska. They were north of the line that limited slavery, so the two states would be free states. Douglas knew the South would object. He suggested that Congress repeal the Missouri Compromise. Instead, settlers in those areas would vote on whether to allow slavery. Douglas called this "popular sovereignty." That means the people are allowed to decide.

Many Northerners did not like Douglas' plan. It would allow slavery in places that had been free for years. Southerners liked the plan. They thought Kansas would be settled mostly by slaveholders from Missouri. Since slavery was legal in Missouri, those settlers would vote to make slavery legal in Kansas, too.

Pro-slavery and antislavery groups rushed to Kansas. Thousands of pro-slavery supporters crossed the border from Missouri just for the purpose of voting in Kansas. They traveled in armed groups. They were known as **border ruffians** (BOHR•duhr RUH•fee•uhns).

Toward Civil War

Lesson 1 The Search for Compromise, *Continued*

The Kansas-Nebraska Act passed in 1854. The pro-slavery group had won. Kansas passed laws in favor of slavery. People opposed to slavery refused to accept the laws. Instead, they held their own election. They adopted a constitution that banned slavery. By 1856, Kansas had two separate governments.

Both antislavery and pro-slavery groups had weapons. Soon fighting broke out. Pro-slavery supporters attacked a town where many antislavery supporters lived. Then John Brown, an abolitionist, led an attack on a pro-slavery group. Brown's group killed five slavery supporters. Newspapers called the conflict "Bleeding Kansas" and the "Civil War in Kansas." A **civil war** is a war between people of the same country.

/ / / / / / / / / / / / / Glue Foldable here / / / / / / / / / / / / /

Check for Understanding

Why did Senator Douglas suggest that Congress repeal the Missouri Compromise?

_____

_____

What two groups were involved in a "civil war" in Kansas?

_____

_____

☑ Reading Check

6. What events led to "Bleeding Kansas"?

_____

_____

_____

FOLDABLES®

7. Place a two-tab Foldable along the dotted line to cover Check for Understanding. Write the title *Slavery* on the anchor tab. Label the tabs *pro-slavery* and *antislavery*. Write two things you remember about each group. Use the Foldable to help answer Check for Understanding.

Toward Civil War

Lesson 2 Challenges to Slavery

ESSENTIAL QUESTION

Why does conflict develop?

GUIDING QUESTIONS

1. **How did a new political party affect the challenges to slavery?**
2. **Why was the Dred Scott case important?**
3. **How did Abraham Lincoln and Stephen A. Douglas play a role in the challenges to slavery?**

Where in the world?

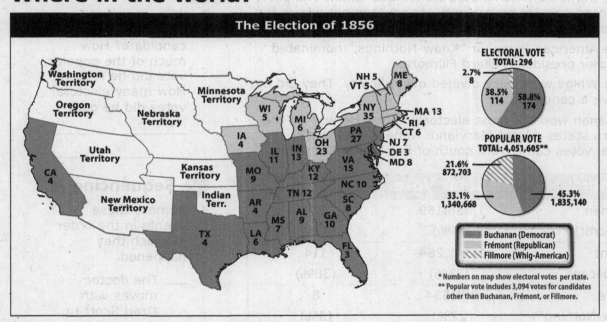

The Election of 1856

When did it happen?

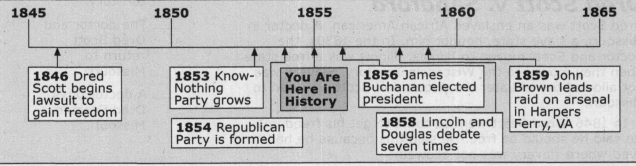

1846 Dred Scott begins lawsuit to gain freedom

1853 Know-Nothing Party grows

1854 Republican Party is formed

You Are Here in History

1856 James Buchanan elected president

1858 Lincoln and Douglas debate seven times

1859 John Brown leads raid on arsenal in Harpers Ferry, VA

Toward Civil War

Lesson 2 Challenges to Slavery, Continued

Birth of the Republican Party

The Kansas-Nebraska Act drove the North and South further apart. Many Northern Democrats left the party. In 1854, antislavery Whigs and Democrats joined with Free-Soilers. They started the Republican Party. They wanted to ban slavery in new territories. Northerners liked the Republican Party's message. The Republicans won seats in Congress. The Democratic Party became mostly a Southern party.

In the presidential election of 1856:

- the Republicans chose John C. Frémont as their candidate. The party called for free territories.

- the Democrats nominated James Buchanan. The party wanted popular sovereignty, or government where the people are the authority.

- the American Party, or "Know-Nothings," nominated former president Millard Fillmore.

- the Whigs were very divided over slavery. They did not have a candidate.

Buchanan won the most electoral votes. He won all the Southern states except Maryland. None of Frémont's electoral votes came from south of the Mason-Dixon line.

Candidate	Popular Vote	Electoral Vote
Buchanan (Democrat)	1,838,169 (45%)	174 (59%)
Frémont (Republican)	1,341,264 (33%)	114 (38%)
Fillmore ("Know-Nothing")	874,534 (22%)	8 (3%)

Dred Scott v. *Sandford*

Dred Scott was an enslaved African American. A doctor in Missouri, a slave state, bought him. In the 1830s, the doctor and Scott moved to Illinois. Illinois was a free state. Then they moved to the Wisconsin Territory. Slavery was not allowed there. Later the doctor and Scott returned to Missouri.

In 1846, Dred Scott went to court to get his freedom. He said he should be free. He said this because he had lived where slavery was not allowed.

✓ Reading Check

1. Who joined together to form the Republican Party? What was their goal?

_____

_____

👁 Visualize It

2. Who was the "Know-Nothing" Party's candidate? How much of the popular vote did he receive? How many electoral votes did he get?

_____

_____

📝 Sequencing

3. Number these events in the order in which they happened.

____ The doctor moves with Dred Scott to Illinois and then to the Wisconsin territory.

____ The doctor and Dred Scott return to Missouri.

____ A doctor buys Dred Scott in Missouri.

netw⊛rks

Lesson 2 Challenges to Slavery, *Continued*

Explaining

4. Why did Dred Scott think he should be free?

_____

_____

Reading Check

5. In the *Dred Scott* decision, why could voters or Congress *not* ban slavery?

_____

_____

Mark the Text

6. Underline the sentence(s) that tells what people liked about Lincoln.

The case finally came before the Supreme Court in 1857. The case gained a lot of attention. It gave the Court a chance to rule on the question of slavery itself. Justice Roger B. Taney was the head of the Supreme Court. He wrote the Court's decision.

This is what the Supreme Court decided:

- The fact that Scott had lived in areas where slavery was not allowed did not make Scott a free man.
- Dred Scott was not a citizen. Because of this he had no right to go to court.
- Enslaved people were property.
- The Missouri Compromise was not allowed, according to the United States Constitution.
- Popular sovereignty was not allowed, according to the United States Constitution.
- Neither Congress nor voters could ban slavery. That would be like taking away a person's property.

The Court's decision angered Northerners. Southerners believed that now nothing could stop the spread of slavery.

Lincoln and Douglas

In 1858 the Illinois Senate race was the center of attention throughout the country, because of the candidates. Senator Stephen A. Douglas, a Democrat, was running against Abraham Lincoln, a Republican.

Douglas was popular. People thought he might run for president in 1860. Lincoln was not as well known. He challenged Douglas to debate him. A debate is a kind of argument. There are rules for how to state your point.

Lincoln and Douglas debated seven times. Slavery was the main topic each time. All the debates were in Illinois. Thousands of people came to watch. Many newspapers wrote articles about the debates.

Douglas supported popular sovereignty. He believed people could vote to limit slavery. People in the South did not like him after that. Lincoln said that African Americans had rights. He said that slavery was wrong.

Douglas won the election. Even though he lost, Lincoln became popular around the nation. People thought of him as a clear thinker who could state his ideas well.

Southerners felt threatened by Republicans. In 1859 an act of violence added to their fears. Abolitionist John Brown

Toward Civil War

Lesson 2 Challenges to Slavery, *Continued*

led a raid on Harpers Ferry, Virginia. The target was an **arsenal** (AHRS•nuhl), a place where weapons are stored. Brown hoped to arm enslaved African Americans. He hoped they would revolt against slaveholders.

Local citizens and troops stopped the raid. Brown was convicted of treason and murder. He was hanged. His death divided the North. Some antislavery groups had never approved of Brown's violence. Others saw him as a **martyr**—a person who dies for a great cause.

/////////////// Glue Foldable here ////////////////

Check for Understanding

Name the three anti-slavery parties from which people came to start the Republican Party.

_____

_____

List two of the reasons the Supreme Court gave for its decision in the Dred Scott case.

_____

☑ **Reading Check**

7. Why did John Brown raid the arsenal at Harpers Ferry?

_____

_____

FOLDABLES®

8. Place a Venn diagram Foldable along the dotted line to cover Check for Understanding. Write the title *Opposed to Slavery* on the anchor tab. Label the three tabs *Republican Party*, *Both*, and *Dred Scott*. Write two things you remember about each and one thing they have in common. Use the Foldable to help answer Check for Understanding.

Toward Civil War

Lesson 3 Secession and War

ESSENTIAL QUESTION
Why does conflict develop?

GUIDING QUESTIONS
1. **What was the importance of the election of 1860?**
2. **What did the attack on Fort Sumter signify?**

Where in the world?

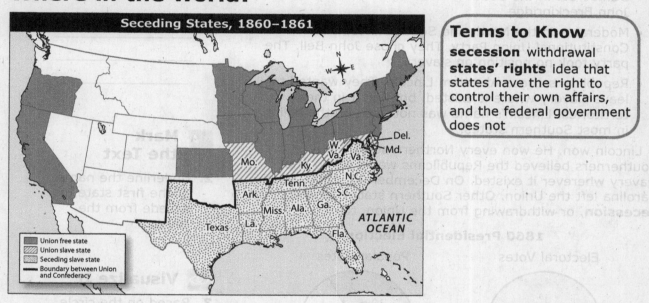

Seceding States, 1860–1861

Del.
W. Va.   Md.
Mo.   Va.
Ky.
N.C.
Tenn.
Ark.   S.C.
Miss.   Ala.   Ga.
Texas   La.   ATLANTIC
OCEAN
Fla.

- Union free state
- Union slave state
- Seceding slave state
- Boundary between Union and Confederacy

Terms to Know
secession withdrawal
states' rights idea that states have the right to control their own affairs, and the federal government does not

When did it happen?

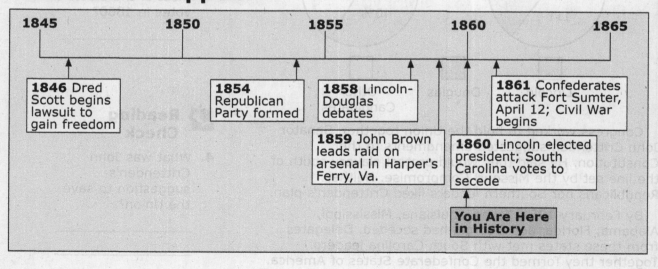

1845   1850   1855   1860   1865

1846 Dred Scott begins lawsuit to gain freedom

1854 Republican Party formed

1858 Lincoln-Douglas debates

1859 John Brown leads raid on arsenal in Harper's Ferry, Va.

1861 Confederates attack Fort Sumter, April 12; Civil War begins

1860 Lincoln elected president; South Carolina votes to secede

You Are Here in History

217

network̶s

Toward Civil War

Lesson 3 Secession and War, *Continued*

The 1860 Election

The issue of slavery split the Democratic Party in the presidential election of 1860.

- Democrats in the North supported popular sovereignty. They chose Stephen A. Douglas as their candidate.

- Democrats in the South favored slavery. They chose John Breckinridge.

- Moderates in the North and South started the Constitutional Union Party. They chose John Bell. The party took no position on slavery.

- Republicans chose Abraham Lincoln. They wanted to leave slavery where it existed, but ban it in the territories. Lincoln's name was not even on the ballot in most Southern states.

Lincoln won. He won every Northern state. Many Southerners believed the Republicans would try to end slavery wherever it existed. On December 20, 1860, South Carolina left the Union. Other Southern states debated **secession**, or withdrawing from the Union, too.

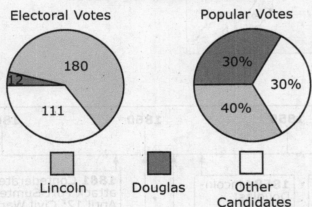

1860 Presidential Election

Electoral Votes

180
12
111

Popular Votes

30%
30%
40%

☐ Lincoln   ◼ Douglas   ☐ Other Candidates

Congress worked to hold the Union together. Senator John Crittenden suggested amendments to the Constitution. He said they would protect slavery south of the line set by the Missouri Compromise. Neither Republicans nor Southern leaders liked Crittenden's plan.

By February 1861, Texas, Louisiana, Mississippi, Alabama, Florida, and Georgia had seceded. Delegates from these states met with South Carolina leaders. Together they formed the Confederate States of America. They chose Jefferson Davis as their president.

🖉 Identifying

1. Name the 1860 political parties and their candidates for president.

_____

_____

_____

_____

🖉 Mark the Text

2. Underline the name of the first state to secede from the Union.

👁 Visualize It

3. Based on the circle graph, who won most of the electoral votes in 1860?

_____

✔ Reading Check

4. What was John Crittenden's suggestion to save the Union?

_____

_____

218

Toward Civil War

Lesson 3 Secession and War, *Continued*

FOLDABLES®

📝 Describing

5. Place a one-tab Foldable along the dotted line to cover "Southerners used the idea of states' rights ..." Write *Secession* on the anchor tab. Write *State's Rights* in the middle of the tab. Draw three arrows around the title and write three things about secession and states' rights.

📝 Summarizing

6. Describe in your own words the idea of states' rights.

_____

_____

✓ Reading Check

7. Why do you think Lincoln decided not to send armed troops to Fort Sumter?

_____

_____

/ / / / / / / / / / / / Glue Foldable here / / / / / / / / / /

Southerners used the idea of **states' rights** to explain their decision to secede. They argued that

- each state had joined the Union voluntarily.
- the Constitution was a contract between the federal government and the states.
- the government broke the contract because it did not give Southern states equal rights in the territories.
- therefore, a state had the right to leave the Union.

Not all Southerners believed in secession. Some Northerners were glad to see Southern states leave the Union. Most Northerners, however, thought secession would be bad for the country.

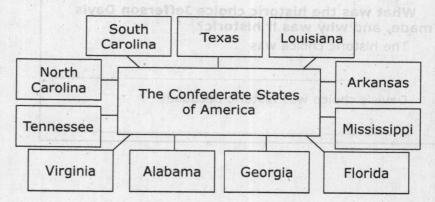

In March 1861, Abraham Lincoln took office as president. He asked the seceding states to rejoin the Union. He pleaded for peace. He also warned that he would enforce federal law in the South.

Fighting at Fort Sumter

The day after Lincoln took office, he received a message. It came from Fort Sumter, a U.S. fort on an island in Charlston Harbor, South Carolina. The fort's commander warned that supplies were low. He said the Confederates were demanding that he surrender. Lincoln sent an unarmed group with supplies. He ordered Union troops at the fort not to fire unless they were fired upon.

Jefferson Davis made a historic choice. He ordered Confederate troops to attack Fort Sumter before the supplies arrived. On April 12, 1861, the Confederates fired on Fort Sumter. Rough, high seas kept Union ships from

219

Toward Civil War

Lesson 3 Secession and War, *Continued*

coming to help. Two days later, Fort Sumter surrendered. The Civil War had begun.

Lincoln issued a call for troops. Volunteers quickly signed up. Meanwhile, Virginia, North Carolina, Tennessee, and Arkansas joined the Confederacy.

/ / / / / / / / / / / / Glue Foldable here / / / / / / / / / / /

Check for Understanding

Write the name of the new nation formed by the states that seceded and its president.

_____

_____

What was the historic choice Jefferson Davis made, and why was it historic?

The historic choice was

_____

Davis's choice was historic because

_____

FOLDABLES

8. Place a two-tab Foldable along the dotted line to cover Check for Understanding. Cut the tabs in half to form four tabs. Write *Jefferson Davis* on the anchor tab. Label the tabs *who*, *what*, *when*, and *where*. List what you remember about Jefferson Davis as you answer each question. Use the Foldable to help answer Check for Understanding.

networks

The Civil War

Lesson 1 The Two Sides

ESSENTIAL QUESTION
Why does conflict develop?

GUIDING QUESTIONS
1. **What were the goals and strategies of the North and South?**
2. **What was war like for the soldiers of the North and the South?**

Where in the world?

Union states
Union territories
Confederate states
Border states

CANADA

MEXICO

Gulf of Mexico

PACIFIC OCEAN

ATLANTIC OCEAN

When did it happen?

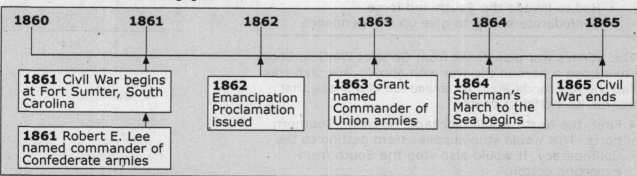

| 1860 | 1861 | 1862 | 1863 | 1864 | 1865 |

1861 Civil War begins at Fort Sumter, South Carolina

1861 Robert E. Lee named commander of Confederate armies

1862 Emancipation Proclamation issued

1863 Grant named Commander of Union armies

1864 Sherman's March to the Sea begins

1865 Civil War ends

The Civil War

Lesson 1 The Two Sides, *Continued*

Two Very Different Sides

For most states, choosing sides in the Civil War was easy. This was not true for Delaware, Maryland, Kentucky, and Missouri. They were **border states.** They had ties to both the North and the South.

The border states were important to the Union's plans. Missouri could control parts of the Mississippi River. It could control major routes to the West. Kentucky controlled the Ohio River. Delaware was close to Philadelphia. Maryland was close to Richmond, Virginia. Richmond was the Confederate capital. Washington, D.C., was within Maryland. It was the capital of the Union. If Maryland left the Union, the capital would be behind enemy lines. President Lincoln did many things to keep those states as part of the Union.

Each side had strengths and weaknesses. The North had more people than the South. The North had more resources, too. The South had great military leaders and a strong fighting spirit. Also, most of the war was fought in the South. This meant the army knew the land well. They were willing to fight hard to defend it.

Each side had different goals for fighting the Civil War.

The South (The Confederacy)

- Wanted to be an independent country
- Thought if they fought long and hard enough, the North would give up
- Hoped for support from Britain and France (Britain and France bought cotton from the South. Southerners hoped these countries might pressure the North to end the war.)

The North (The Union)

- Wanted to reunite North and South again
- Had to invade the South and force Confederate states to give up independence

---

The North's war plan came from General Winfield Scott. He had been a hero in the war with Mexico. His plan was called the Anaconda Plan. An anaconda is a snake that squeezes its victim to death.

- First, the North would blockade, or close, Southern ports. This would stop supplies from getting to the Confederacy. It would also stop the South from exporting cotton.

Mark the Text

1. Underline the four border states.

Explaining

2. Why did Lincoln need the support of the border states?

_____

_____

Reading Check

3. From what countries did the South hope to get help?

_____

_____

Critical Thinking

4. Why was the North's war plan called the Anaconda plan?

_____

_____

The Civil War

Lesson 1 The Two Sides, Continued

- Second, the North would aim to control the Mississippi River. This would split the Confederacy into two parts. It would cut Southern supply lines.
- The North wanted to capture Richmond, Virginia. Richmond was the capital of the Confederacy.

Americans Against Americans

In the Civil War, brother fought brother. Neighbor fought neighbor. Kentucky senator John Crittenden had two sons who became generals. One fought for the Confederacy. The other fought for the Union. Even President Lincoln's wife had relatives in the Confederate army.

Many men left their homes to **enlist** in, or join, the Union or Confederate armies. Each had his own reasons.

> **Some Reasons for Enlisting**
> - patriotism
> - to avoid being called a coward
> - to have an adventure

The average soldier was in his 20s. Many were younger. Some soldiers were younger than 18. Some were younger than 14. To get into the army, many teenagers ran away from home or lied about their age.

At first, the North refused to let free African Americans enlist. Later, they did allow it. The Confederacy did not want to give enslaved people guns. In the last days of the war, they did allow African Americans to fight.

When the war began, each side expected to win quickly. Both sides were mistaken. The war lasted a very long time, and many soldiers died before it ended.

Soldiers came from every part of the country. Most came from farms. Almost half of the Northern soldiers and almost two-thirds of the Southern soldiers had owned or worked on farms before becoming soldiers.

Total Soldiers in Civil War (1861–1865)

Northern Soldiers—2,100,000

Southern Soldiers—900,000

Listing

5. List the three main parts of the Anaconda Plan.

_____

_____

_____

Reading Check

6. Why weren't African Americans allowed to join the Confederate army until the end of the war?

_____

_____

Visualize It

7. Which side had more soldiers?

_____

_____

The Civil War

Lesson 1 The Two Sides, *Continued*

Confederate soldiers were sometimes called Rebels. Union soldiers were known as Yankees. Almost 200,000 African Americans served in the Union army. About 10,000 Mexican Americans served in the war.

On both sides, a soldier's life was hard. Soldiers wrote letters to family and friends describing what they saw. Many wrote about their boredom, discomfort, sickness, and fear.

Soldiers lived in army camps. There were some fun times. Often, however, a soldier's life was either dull or dangerous.

Both sides lost many soldiers during the war. There were thousands of wounded soldiers. They did not get good medical care. After the Battle of Shiloh, wounded soldiers lay in the rain for more than 24 hours. They were waiting to be treated. Around them lay dead and dying soldiers.

About 1 of every 11 Union soldiers and 1 of every 8 Confederate soldiers deserted. They left because they were afraid, sick, or hungry.

//////////// Glue Foldable here ////////////

Check for Understanding
What was the battle plan the South made, and why?

_____

_____

How would the Anaconda Plan harm the South?

_____

Drawing Conclusions

8. Why were Confederate soldiers called "Rebels"?

_____

_____

FOLDABLES®

9. Using a two-tab Foldable, cut the tabs in half to make four tabs. Place it along the dotted line to cover Check for Understanding. Write the title *Anaconda Plan* on the anchor tab. Label the tabs *Who*, *What*, *Where*, and *Why*. List the facts that you remember about the Anaconda Plan. Use both sides of the tabs. Use your Foldable to help answer Check for Understanding.

The Civil War

Lesson 2 Early Years of the War

ESSENTIAL QUESTION
Why does conflict develop?

GUIDING QUESTIONS
1. **What was the outcome of the first major battle of the war?**
2. **How did the Union respond to important defeats in the East in 1862?**
3. **What was the effect of the Emancipation Proclamation?**

Terms to Know
tributary stream or smaller river that flows into a larger river
ironclad a warship equipped with iron plating for protection
casualty a soldier who is killed, wounded, captured, or missing in battle
Emancipation Proclamation formal announcement from President Lincoln, dated January 1, 1863. It freed enslaved people in parts of the South that were in rebellion.

When did it happen?

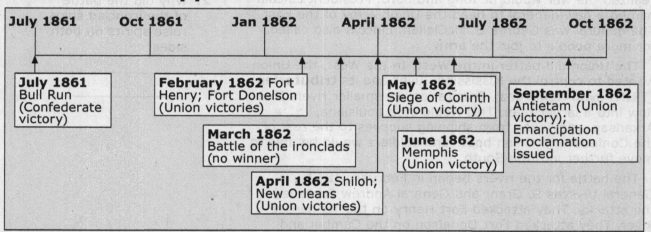

| July 1861 | Oct 1861 | Jan 1862 | April 1862 | July 1862 | Oct 1862 |

July 1861 Bull Run (Confederate victory)

February 1862 Fort Henry; Fort Donelson (Union victories)

March 1862 Battle of the ironclads (no winner)

April 1862 Shiloh; New Orleans (Union victories)

May 1862 Siege of Corinth (Union victory)

June 1862 Memphis (Union victory)

September 1862 Antietam (Union victory); Emancipation Proclamation issued

What do you know?

In the first column, answer the questions based on what you know before you study. After this lesson, complete the last column.

Now...		Later...
	What was important about April 25, 1862?	
	What happened at Antietam?	

225

Lesson 2 Early Years of the War, *Continued*

War on Land and at Sea

The first big battle of the Civil War took place on July 21, 1861. It happened in northern Virginia near a small river called Bull Run. About 30,000 Union soldiers attacked a smaller Confederate force. People came from nearby Washington, D.C., to watch the battle.

At first, the Yankees pushed the Confederates back. But General Thomas Jackson inspired the rebels to keep fighting. Jackson held his position "like a stone wall," so people called him "Stonewall" Jackson. The Confederates began fighting back hard. They forced Union troops to retreat. The crowd that was watching ran away.

The Battle of Bull Run shocked Northerners. They now realized the war would be long and hard. President Lincoln named a new general to head the Union army of the East. The general was George B. McClellan. Lincoln also called for more people to join the army.

The Union did better in the West. In the West, the Union wanted to control the Mississippi River and its **tributaries** (TRIH•byuh•tehr•eez). Tributaries are smaller rivers that flow into a larger river. This would stop Louisiana, Arkansas, and Texas from shipping supplies to the rest of the Confederacy. Union boats and soldiers would be able to move further into the South.

The battle for the rivers began in February 1862. General Ulysses S. Grant and General Andrew Foote led the attacks. They attacked Fort Henry on the Tennessee River. They attacked Fort Donelson on the Cumberland River. They captured both forts. Grant was now a hero in the North.

The Union had set up a blockade of Confederate ports. Southerners had a secret weapon. It was an old Union warship called the *Merrimack*. The Confederates rebuilt it and covered it with iron to protect it. The **ironclad** ship was renamed the *Virginia*.

On March 8, 1862, the *Virginia* attacked Union ships in Chesapeake Bay. The North fired shells at it, but they just bounced off. Northern leaders were afraid of the *Virginia*. Then, the North got an ironclad ship of its own. It was called the *Monitor*. On March 9, the two ships met in battle. The ships could not sink each other, so neither side won.

In early April 1862, General Grant led about 40,000 soldiers toward Corinth, Mississippi, an important railroad junction. The army stopped 20 miles (32 km) away, near Shiloh Church. More Union soldiers arrived.

226

🖐 Explaining

1. What was surprising about the battle at Bull Run?

❓ Critical Thinking

2. Why did the battle of the ironclad ships raise spirits on both sides?

_____

_____

Lesson 2 Early Years of the War, *Continued*

? Reading Check

3. How did the loss of New Orleans affect the Confederacy?

_____

_____

✓ Reading Check

4. What happened after the Battle of Antietam?

_____

_____

FOLDABLES®

✎ Explaining

5. Use a two-tab Foldable and cut the tabs in half to make four tabs. Place it along the dotted line to cover the heading "The Emancipation Proclamation." Write *Emancipation Proclamation* on the anchor tab. Label the four tabs *What*, *Where*, *When*, and *Why*. Use both sides of the tabs to write information about President Lincoln's proclamation.

The Confederates attacked first. The Battle of Shiloh lasted two days. Both sides lost many soldiers. There were more than 23,000 **casualties** (KA•zhuhl•teez)—people killed, wounded, or captured. In the end, the Union won.

Union soldiers moved on to Corinth. They surrounded it. No food or supplies could reach Corinth. The Confederates withdrew and Union troops entered on May 30. On June 6, they took Memphis, Tennessee. It seemed they would control the Mississippi River soon.

The Union navy also won an important battle. On April 25, the navy captured New Orleans, Louisiana. New Orleans was the largest city in the South. With Louisiana in Union control, the Confederacy could no longer use the Mississippi River to carry its goods to sea. The Union only had to capture Vicksburg, Mississippi, to have full control of the Mississippi River.

War in the Eastern States

In the East, the Union tried hard to capture Richmond, Virginia. That was the Confederate capital. Confederate soldiers fought hard to protect it. The South had good military leaders, such as General Robert E. Lee and General "Stonewall" Jackson. They knew the land well. They inspired their soldiers. They won important battles:

> the Seven Days' Battle (1862)
> the Second Battle of Bull Run (1862)
> Fredericksburg (1862)
> Chancellorsville (1863).

Lee moved his troops into Maryland. He had planned to continue into Pennsylvania. Lee split his army into four parts. He told each part to move in a different direction. He wanted to confuse General McClellan. Lee's plan did not work. A Confederate officer lost his copy of the plan, and it fell into McClellan's hands. On September 17, 1862, the two sides fought the Battle of Antietam near Sharpsburg, Maryland. The Union won this battle.

Antietam was the deadliest single day of fighting in the war. Lee went back to Virginia after the battle. His plan to invade the North had failed.

/ / / / / / / / / / / Glue Foldable here / / / / / / / / / / /

The Emancipation Proclamation

Abolitionists, including Frederick Douglass and Horace Greeley, wanted Lincoln to make the Civil War a fight to

227

The Civil War

Lesson 2 Early Years of the War, *Continued*

end slavery. They said slavery was wrong. They said it was the reason for the split between North and South. They believed Britain and France would be less willing to support the South if Lincoln said the Civil War was a war to end slavery. The South needed Britain's and France's support.

Lincoln believed that saving the Union was more important than ending slavery.

The Constitution did not give Lincoln power to end slavery. It did give him the power to take property from an enemy during a war, though. Enslaved people were considered to be property. On September 22, 1862, Lincoln said he would issue the **Emancipation Proclamation.** All enslaved people in Rebel-held territory would be freed on January 1, 1863.

The Emancipation Proclamation did not free any enslaved people right away. It was only for places held by the Confederacy. Lincoln had no power there. Also, the proclamation was not for the border states. Still, the proclamation was important. It said that slavery is wrong. If the Union won the war, slavery would end.

/ / / / / / / / / / / / / / / Glue Foldable here / / / / / / / / / / / / / /

Check for Understanding

Explain the Northern generals' plan to use the Mississippi River to defeat the South.

_____

_____

_____

How did the Emancipation Proclamation affect slaves in the South?

_____

_____

☑ **Reading Check**

6. How did the Emancipation Proclamation affect the reason for the war?

_____

_____

FOLDABLES

7. Glue a one-tab Foldable along the dotted line to cover Check for Understanding. Draw a large circle on the tab and label it *Civil War*. Draw two smaller circles inside it. Label the small circles *Mississippi River* and *Slavery*. Inside the circles, list facts that show why both were important to the war. Use the reverse side to write additional information. Use your Foldable to help answer Check for Understanding.

The Civil War

Lesson 3 Life During the Civil War

ESSENTIAL QUESTION

Why does conflict develop?

GUIDING QUESTIONS

1. **How did life change during the Civil War?**
2. **What were the new roles for women in the Civil War?**
3. **What were the conditions of hospitals and prison camps during the Civil War?**
4. **What political and economic changes occurred during the Civil War?**

Terms to Know

habeas corpus a legal order that guarantees a prisoner the right to be heard in court.

draft a system of selecting people for required military service

bounty a reward or payment

When did it happen?

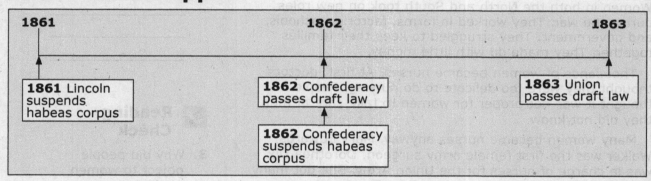

1861	1862	1863
1861 Lincoln suspends habeas corpus	**1862** Confederacy passes draft law	**1863** Union passes draft law
	1862 Confederacy suspends habeas corpus	

What do you know?

In the first column, answer the questions based on what you know before you study. After this lesson, complete the last column.

Now...		Later...
	How did the role of nurses change during the Civil War?	
	How did the Union blockade affect life in the South?	

229

The Civil War

Lesson 3 Life During the Civil War, *Continued*

A Different Way of Life

During the Civil War, life changed for young people. Many teenagers left home to serve in the army. About half of the school-age children did not go to school. Some had to stay home to help their families. Many schools were closed. Some were too close to battle sites. Some schools and churches were used as hospitals.

Most of the battles took place in the South, so people there suffered the most changes. Parts of the South that were in the paths of the armies were destroyed. Many people had to move away. They lost their homes and farms. Also, there was not enough food or other supplies. This made life hard for people everywhere in the South.

New Roles for Women

Women in both the North and South took on new roles during the war. They worked in farms, factories, schools, and government. They struggled to keep their families together. They made do with little money.

Thousands of women became nurses. At first, doctors thought they were too delicate to do nursing. People thought it was not proper for women to take care of men they did not know.

Many women became nurses anyway. Mary Edwards Walker was the first female army surgeon. Dorothea Dix was in charge of nurses for the Union Army. She got many other women to serve as nurses. Clara Barton was a famous nurse on the Union side. Captain Sally Tompkins was the only female officer in the Confederate army.

Some women were spies. Rose O'Neal Greenhow and Belle Boyd gathered information about Union plans and passed it to the Confederacy. Harriet Tubman also served as a spy and scout for the Union. A few women even dressed like men and became soldiers. Loreta Janeta Velázquez fought for the South and became a Confederate spy.

The Captured and the Wounded

Early in the war, the North and the South exchanged soldiers they had captured. Later, they set up prison camps. Prisoners had only a blanket and a cup. Many prisons were very dirty, and there was too little food.

At Andersonville prison in Georgia, prisoners slept on the ground. All they had to eat each day was a teaspoon of

230

☑ **Reading Check**

1. Why did many children not go to school during the war?

_____

☑ **Listing**

2. List three new roles for women during the Civil War.

_____

_____

_____

☑ **Reading Check**

3. Why did people object to women working as nurses during the war?

_____

_____

☑ **Reading Check**

4. What happened to soldiers who were captured by the enemy?

_____

_____

Lesson 3 Life During the Civil War, *Continued*

Mark the Text

5. Underline the meaning of *habeas corpus*.

Listing

6. List two ways in which a man could avoid the draft.

_____

_____

Explaining

7. Why did the New York City mobs attack African Americans?

_____

_____

salt, three tablespoons of beans, and a cup of cornmeal. They drank water from a stream that was also a sewer. Thousands of Union prisoners died from disease there.

At the Union prison in Elmira, New York, Confederate prisoners had no blankets or warm clothes, even in winter. They used a pond as a toilet and a garbage dump. A quarter of the prisoners held there died.

Wounded soldiers were treated in field hospitals near the battlefield. Volunteers gave out food to the wounded.

The camps were crowded places, and drinking water was dirty. As many as half the men got sick and died before they ever went into battle.

Political and Economic Change

Both the North and the South faced rebellions. People in the South did not have enough to eat. There were bread riots in Richmond, Virginia, and other cities.

In the North, the War Democrats did not like how Lincoln was running the war. Peace Democrats wanted the war to end right away. Many people thought Peace Democrats were dangerous traitors and called them Copperheads. Copperheads are poisonous snakes.

To deal with people who opposed the war, both President Lincoln (in the North) and President Davis (in the South) suspended **habeas corpus.** Habeas corpus helps protect people against unlawful imprisonment. Thousands who spoke out against the war were jailed without trial.

Soon both sides had trouble recruiting enough soldiers. The Confederate Congress passed a **draft** law in 1862. A draft orders people to serve in the military during a war. In the North, the Union paid a **bounty,** or a sum of money, to encourage volunteers. Then, in March 1863, the Union also passed a draft law. In both the North and the South, a man could avoid the draft by paying a fee or hiring a substitute.

The draft law made people angry. They said that rich people planned the war but only poor people had to fight. Riots occurred in several Northern cities. In July 1863, mobs rioted in New York City. The mobs attacked government and military buildings. They also attacked African Americans. Many workers had opposed the Emancipation Proclamation. They were afraid that freed African Americans would take their jobs. More than 100 people died in the riot.

231

The Civil War

Lesson 3 Life During the Civil War, *Continued*

The war was expensive for both sides. The two governments had three ways of paying for the war: They borrowed money, they took in more taxes, and they printed money.

The North's economy did better than the South's. Northern industries made money by producing war supplies. Farms also profited from the war. Still, prices grew faster than wages because goods were in high demand. This increase in prices is called inflation. Inflation made life harder for working people.

The South's economy suffered more. Much of the fighting took place in the South. It destroyed farms and railroad lines. The blockade stopped shipping. Important supplies could not reach the Confederacy. Hungry people rioted because there was not enough food. The riots were in Atlanta, Richmond, and other cities.

The South also suffered worse inflation than the North. After only one year of war, citizens begged Confederate leaders for help.

////////////////// Glue Foldable here ////////////////

Check for Understanding

List two ways that life changed during the Civil War.

_____

_____

How were prisoners mistreated during the Civil War?

_____

_____

_____

✓ Reading Check

8. How did the war affect the economy in the North and South?

_____

_____

FOLDABLES®

9. Place a three-tab Foldable along the dotted line to cover Check for Understanding. Write the title *War Brings Changes* on the anchor tab. Label the tabs *Women*, *Children*, and *Economy*. Recall how the Civil War affected people on both sides and list the ways that each changed during that time. Use both sides of the tabs. Use your Foldable to help answer Check for Understanding.

netw◉rks

The Civil War

Lesson 4 The Strain of War

ESSENTIAL QUESTION
Why does conflict develop?

GUIDING QUESTIONS

1. **What factors contributed to the early success of the Confederate forces?**
2. **What role did African Americans play in military efforts?**
3. **How was the battle of Gettysburg a turning point in the war?**

Terms to Know

entrench to place within a trench, or ditch, for defense; to place in a strong defensive position
flank the side or edge of a military formation

When did it happen?

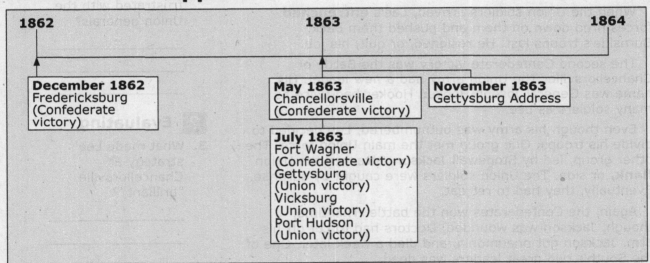

1862   1863   1864

December 1862
Fredericksburg
(Confederate victory)

May 1863
Chancellorsville
(Confederate victory)

July 1863
Fort Wagner
(Confederate victory)
Gettysburg
(Union victory)
Vicksburg
(Union victory)
Port Hudson
(Union victory)

November 1863
Gettysburg Address

What do you know?

Before reading the text, decide whether these statements are true or false. Write a T or an F in front of each. After reading, check your answers. Were they correct?

_____ 1. The Union had excellent generals throughout the war.

_____ 2. "Stonewall" Jackson was an important Confederate general.

_____ 3. African Americans enlisted in both the Union and the Confederate armies.

_____ 4. The battle at Gettysburg was an important win for the Confederacy.

_____ 5. President Lincoln's famous speech at Gettysburg was very short.

233

The Civil War

Lesson 4 The Strain of War, *Continued*

Southern Victories

After Antietam, the Confederacy won a number of battles in the East because Generals Robert E. Lee and Stonewall Jackson were so good at their jobs. They knew the land. They knew how to inspire the soldiers. They often defeated the Union armies in battle, even though they had fewer soldiers.

The first victory was the Battle of Fredericksburg. The Union leader, General Ambrose Burnside, began to march toward Richmond, Virginia. Richmond was the capital of the Confederacy. Lee moved his forces to Fredericksburg. They dug trenches in the hills and waited for the Union troops.

When the Union soldiers arrived, Lee's **entrenched** forces fired down on them and pushed them back. Burnside's troops lost. He resigned, or quit, his job.

The second Confederate victory was the Battle of Chancellorsville. The Union army had a new leader. His name was General Joseph Hooker. Hooker had twice as many soldiers as Lee.

Even though his army was outnumbered, Lee decided to divide his troops. One group met the main Union force. The other group, led by Stonewall Jackson, attacked the Union **flank,** or side. The Union soldiers were caught by surprise. Eventually, they had to retreat.

Again, the Confederates won the battle. This time, though, Jackson was wounded. Doctors had to cut off his arm. Jackson got pneumonia, and died a week later. One of the South's two great leaders was dead.

The army leaders in the East frustrated President Lincoln. In less than a year three different generals tried and failed to win the Civil War for the Union. The army's leadership was weak.

- **General McClellan** did not seem to want to do battle. He did not obey Lincoln's order to follow the Confederate troops after the Union's victory at Antietam.

- **General Burnside** lost at Fredericksburg. Lincoln replaced him with General Joseph Hooker.

- **General Hooker** lost at Chancellorsville. Within two months, Hooker resigned, too.

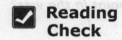

Explaining

1. What was Lee's strategy at Chancellorsville?

Reading Check

2. Why was Lincoln frustrated with the Union generals?

_____

_____

_____

Evaluating

3. What made Lee's strategy at Chancellorsville "brilliant"?

_____

_____

_____

Lesson 4 The Strain of War, *Continued*

? **Determining Cause**

4. Why would African Americans have been eager to enlist and fight for the Union?

_____

_____

Mark the Text

5. In one color, highlight adjectives and phrases that describe what African Americans faced in the military. In another color, highlight phrases that describe African American soldiers' conduct in war.

? **Identifying**

6 What was the result of Pickett's Charge?

_____

_____

African Americans in the Civil War

The Confederate army never accepted African American soldiers. Confederate officials believed that African Americans might attack their fellow troops or begin a revolt if they were armed.

Still many enslaved African Americans went to war with their white owners. They helped the Confederate army in many ways, like building fortifications.

At first, the Union army did not accept African American soldiers, either. Lincoln feared that allowing them to enlist would anger people in the border states.

By 1862, though, the North needed more soldiers. So Congress created all-black regiments. By the end of the war, about 10 percent of Union soldiers were African American. Some were freed people from the North. Others had run away from enslavement in the South.

It was not easy for African American soldiers in the Union army. Other Union soldiers resented them or thought they could not fight well. In battles, Southern troops, who hated them, fired at them the most.

Despite this, African Americans fought bravely and well. For example, in July 1863, the 54th Massachusetts Regiment served in the front lines of a battle to take Fort Wagner in South Carolina. The regiment suffered nearly 300 casualties. Their sacrifice made the 54th famous for its courage.

The Tide Turns

After the Confederate victory at Chancellorsville, Lee decided to invade the North. He hoped victories there would convince Britain and France to help the Confederacy.

On July 1, 1863, his forces went looking for supplies in Gettysburg, Pennsylvania. There, they encountered, or met, Union troops. Outnumbered, the Union troops fell back to higher ground on Cemetery Ridge.

On July 2, Southern troops tried and failed to force the Union troops from their positions on the hills.

On July 3, Lee ordered an all-out attack. Thousands of Confederate troops, led by General George Pickett, attacked Union forces on Cemetery Ridge. Half of those in Pickett's Charge were wounded or killed.

The Civil War

Lesson 4 The Strain of War, *Continued*

On July 4, Lee retreated. His army had suffered 25,000 casualties. Union troops had suffered almost as many.

Losing at Gettysburg ended Confederate hopes of getting help from Britain and France.

The Confederacy lost two other critical battles in July 1863:

- **Vicksburg** In April, Ulysses S. Grant laid siege to Vicksburg, Mississippi. A siege means surrounding a place to keep it from receiving food or supplies. The siege lasted 47 days. Many soldiers died—not only from wounds, but also from sickness and hunger. Vicksburg finally fell on the same day Lee retreated from Gettysburg.

- **Port Hudson** The Confederacy lost Port Hudson, its last stronghold on the Mississippi River. The Union had cut off Arkansas, Louisiana, and Texas from the rest of the Confederacy.

On November 19, 1863, the Soldiers' National Cemetery opened at Gettysburg, and people gathered there to dedicate it. First, the former governor of Massachusetts gave a two-hour speech. Then President Lincoln spoke for just two minutes. He finished by saying, "[T]hese dead shall not have died in vain. . . . [G]overnment of the people, by the people, for the people shall not perish from the earth." His powerful words became known as the Gettysburg Address.

/ / / / / / / / / / / Glue Foldable here / / / / / / / / / / / /

Check for Understanding

Why did Union leaders call for African Americans to be allowed to fight in the Civil War?

_____

_____

Why was the battle of Gettysburg a turning point in the war?

_____

_____

☑ **Reading Check**

7. How did the events at Vicksburg and Port Hudson help change the tide of the war?

_____

_____

FOLDABLES

8. Use a two-tab Foldable and cut the tabs in half to make four tabs. Place it along the dotted line to cover Check for Understanding. Write the title *Turning Points in 1863* on the anchor tab. Label the tabs *African Americans Enter the War, Battle of Vicksburg, Battle of Port Hudson,* and *Robert E. Lee Retreats.* Use both sides of the tabs to list facts about the people and events of 1863.

The Civil War

Lesson 5 The War's Final Stages

ESSENTIAL QUESTION
Why does conflict develop?

GUIDING QUESTIONS
1. **What events occurred at the end of the war?**
2. **What is total war?**

Where in the World?

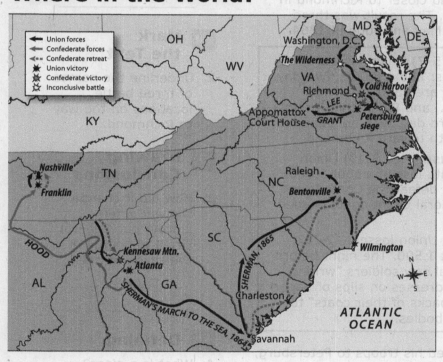

When did it happen?

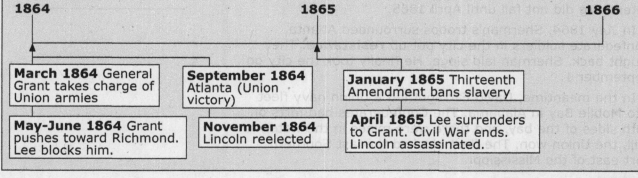

1864   1865   1866

March 1864 General Grant takes charge of Union armies

September 1864 Atlanta (Union victory)

January 1865 Thirteenth Amendment bans slavery

May-June 1864 Grant pushes toward Richmond. Lee blocks him.

November 1864 Lincoln reelected

April 1865 Lee surrenders to Grant. Civil War ends. Lincoln assassinated.

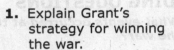

Lesson 5 The War's Final Stages, Continued

The Union Closes In

By 1864, Union forces had the South surrounded. Union ships blocked Southern ports. The Union controlled the Mississippi River. This cut off supplies to the South.

In March 1864, Lincoln put General Ulysses S. Grant in charge of all Union armies. Grant decided to attack from all sides. His armies would march to Richmond, Virginia, the Confederate capital. At the same time, Union General William Tecumseh Sherman would attack the Deep South.

Grant began moving closer and closer to Richmond in May 1864. Lee tried to stop him. The result was three major battles that took place in May and June of 1864:

- **"The Wilderness"** (May 5–7) Union losses: 17,666; Confederate losses: about 8,000. Two-day battle in a thickly wooded area about halfway between Washington, D.C., and Richmond, Virginia. On the morning of the third day, with no clear winner, Grant headed south toward Richmond.

- **Spotsylvania Court House** (May 8–19) Union losses: 18,399; Confederate losses: about 9,000. The Union army could not defeat the Confederate army. After ten days, General Grant again headed south toward Richmond.

- **Cold Harbor** (June 3–12) Union losses: 12,737; Confederate losses: about 1,500. The night before the battle, a Union general saw soldiers "writing their names and home addresses on slips of paper and pinning them to the backs of their coats" to help people identify their bodies.

After Cold Harbor, Grant moved his troops to Petersburg, Virginia. This city was a railroad center the Confederates needed for moving troops and supplies. Grant laid siege to the city, but Confederate troops held out for nine months. Petersburg did not fall until April 1865.

In July 1864, Sherman's troops surrounded Atlanta. Confederate soldiers in the city put up **resistance.** They fought back. Sherman laid siege. He finally took the city on September 1.

In the meantime, David Farragut led a Union navy fleet into Mobile Bay in Alabama. The Confederates had forts on both sides of the bay, and there were mines in the water. Still, the Union won. The fleet blocked the last Southern port east of the Mississippi.

238

✔ Reading Check

1. Explain Grant's strategy for winning the war.

_____

_____

✎ Mark the Text

2. Underline the names of three battle locations on the way to Richmond.

❓ Drawing Conclusions

3. How did it change the war when Lincoln put General Grant in charge of the Union armies?

_____

_____

Aᵇc Defining

4. What is a *siege*?

_____

_____

Lesson 5 The War's Final Stages, *Continued*

Mark the Text

5. Underline the sentence that tells why Sherman's and Farragut's victories were important to the Union.

Identifying

6. What finally ended slavery in the United States?

_____

_____

Defining

7. What is total war?

_____

_____

_____

So many soldiers were dying in 1864 that people in the North became more unhappy about the war. It looked like they were not going to vote for Lincoln in the November election. If Lincoln lost, the war would likely end. The Confederacy would be recognized as an independent country. This kept hope alive in the South.

Then the Union blocked Mobile Bay and took Atlanta. Northerners began to believe they could win. They reelected Lincoln after all. In the South, people were losing hope.

> Union fleet blocks Mobile Bay (August 1864)
>
> ↓
>
> Siege of Atlanta ends in Union victory (September 1864)
>
> ↓
>
> Lincoln is reelected (November 1864)

Many interpreted Lincoln's victory as a sign that voters wanted to end slavery. Congress passed the Thirteenth Amendment on January 31, 1865. It banned slavery in the United States.

The War Ends

After Sherman took Atlanta, his forces burned the city. Then they marched across Georgia to the Atlantic Coast. As they went, the troops tore up railroad lines. They burned cities and fields and killed livestock. This march across Georgia became known as Sherman's March to the Sea.

In his March to the Sea, Sherman used a strategy called **total war**. Total war is the systematic destruction of an entire land, not just its army. Sherman was not trying to punish the South. He wanted to convince Southerners to stop fighting and end the war.

After reaching the coast, Sherman's troops turned north through the Carolinas to join Grant's forces near Richmond. As they went, thousands of African Americans left their plantations to follow his army. They felt that the army protected them as they marched toward freedom.

On April 2, 1865, Petersburg finally fell to Grant's forces. When President Davis heard that Lee had retreated, he knew that Grant would come to Richmond next. Davis and other Confederate leaders prepared to leave the city. They

239

networks

The Civil War

Lesson 5 The War's Final Stages, *Continued*

ordered weapons and bridges in Richmond burned and then fled.

On April 4, President Lincoln walked around the city with his son, followed by grateful African Americans. When asked what to do with Confederate prisoners of war there, he said to "Let 'em up easy."

The Civil War finally ended on April 9, 1865. On that day, Lee's starving army found themselves surrounded at Appomattox Court House, Virginia. Lee knew it was over. He surrendered to Grant. The terms of the surrender were generous:

- Any soldier with a horse could keep it.
- Lee's officers could keep their small guns.

Grant gave food to the Confederate troops and let them go home.

The Civil War had been terrible. More than 600,000 soldiers died in it—more than in any other American war. Much of the South was destroyed, and it would take years to rebuild.

The North's victory saved the Union and freed millions of African Americans from slavery. Now the United States would have to figure out:

- a way to bring the Southern states back into the Union.
- the status of African Americans in the South.

These were two huge problems that the nation would face in the years following the war—the Reconstruction era.

////////// Glue Foldable here //////////

Check for Understanding

Name two important Union victories that helped ensure Lincoln's reelection.

_____

_____

Why did Sherman burn and destroy the South?

_____

_____

Copyright by The McGraw-Hill Companies.

☑ **Reading Check**

8. Why did General Lee finally surrender?

_____

_____

_____

❓ **Making Connections**

9. Why would the status of African Americans in the South be a problem after the war?

_____

_____

_____

FOLDABLES

10. Place a three-tab Foldable along the dotted line to cover Check for Understanding. Write *Final Stages of the Civil War* on the anchor tab. Label the tabs *Mobile Bay*, *Lincoln Reelected*, and *Sherman's March to the Sea*. Use both sides of the tabs to list two facts about each. Use your Foldable to help answer Check for Understanding.

netw⊙rks

The Reconstruction Era

Lesson 1 Planning Reconstruction

ESSENTIAL QUESTION
How do new ideas change the way people live?

GUIDING QUESTIONS
1. **Why did leaders disagree about the South rejoining the Union?**
2. **How did Lincoln's assassination change the plans for the South rejoining the Union?**

> **Terms to Know**
> **Reconstruction** the period of rebuilding the South and readmitting Southern states into the Union
> **amnesty** the granting of a pardon to a large number of persons

When did it happen?

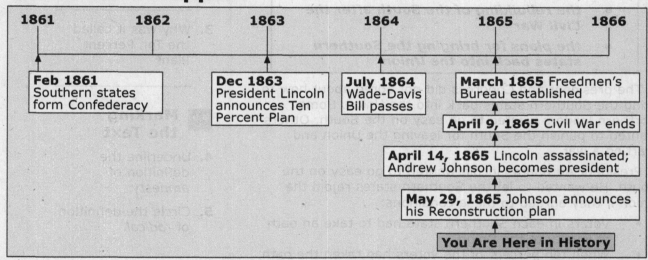

1861	1862	1863	1864	1865	1866

Feb 1861 Southern states form Confederacy

Dec 1863 President Lincoln announces Ten Percent Plan

July 1864 Wade-Davis Bill passes

March 1865 Freedmen's Bureau established

April 9, 1865 Civil War ends

April 14, 1865 Lincoln assassinated; Andrew Johnson becomes president

May 29, 1865 Johnson announces his Reconstruction plan

You Are Here in History

What do you know?

In the first column, answer the questions based on what you know before you study. After this lesson, complete the last column.

Now...		Later...
	When did the North begin planning on ways to bring Southern states back into the Union?	
	Who opposed Lincoln's plan?	
	Why was the Thirteenth Amendment to the Constitution important?	

241

The Reconstruction Era

Lesson 1 Planning Reconstruction, *Continued*

The Reconstruction Debate

The Civil War was fought from 1861 until 1865. The North, or Union, won the war. Now that the war was over, it was time for the country to become whole again. The states in the South needed to rejoin the states in the North. The nation needed to be rebuilt, or reconstructed.

The period of time that followed the Civil War is called **Reconstruction**. Reconstruction also refers to the plans for bringing the Southern states back into the Union. Northern leaders began forming these plans before the war even ended.

RECONSTRUCTION

- *the rebuilding of the South after the Civil War*
- *the plans for bringing the Southern states back into the Union*

The president and Congress did not agree about how to bring the Southern states back into the Union. Some Northern leaders wanted to go easy on the South. Others wanted to punish the South for leaving the Union and starting a war.

President Abraham Lincoln wanted to go easy on the South. He wanted to let the Southern states rejoin the Union if they agreed to these conditions:

- Voters in each Southern state had to take an oath of loyalty to the Union.
- When ten percent of the voters had taken the oath, the state could form a new government.
- The state would have to adopt a new constitution that banned slavery.

Lincoln's plan was called the Ten Percent Plan.

Lincoln went even further. He wanted to give **amnesty** to Southerners who would promise loyalty to the Union. Amnesty means a pardon, or forgiveness. Louisiana, Arkansas, and Tennessee agreed to Lincoln's requirements. However, Congress refused to accept the new states. They also did not allow their senators and representatives in Congress.

There were others who thought the South should be punished. They wanted a more radical, or extreme, approach. This group was called the Radical Republicans, or the Radicals. Thaddeus Stevens, a radical leader, said

---

[Abc] Defining

1. What are the two meanings of Reconstruction?

Explaining

2. Who proposed the Ten Percent Plan?

_____

3. Why was it called the Ten Percent Plan?

_____

[Abc] Marking the Text

4. Underline the definition of *amnesty*.

5. Circle the definition of *radical*.

242

Explaining

6. Why did the Wade-Davis Bill not become a law?

_____

Reading Check

7. What were the three requirements for rejoining the Union stated in the Wade-Davis Bill?

_____

_____

_____

FOLDABLES

Describing

8. Use a two-tab Foldable and cut each tab in half to make four tabs. Place it along the dotted line to cover the text beginning with "Meanwhile, Lincoln and Congress,..." Write the title *Freedman's Bureau* on the anchor tab. Label the four tabs *Who*, *What*, *Why*, and *How*. Use both sides of the tabs to write information about the Freedman's Bureau.

that Southern institutions "must be broken up or relaid, or all our blood and treasure will have been spent in vain."

Radical Republicans in Congress passed their plan for Reconstruction in 1864. The Plan was called the Wade-Davis Bill. The Wade-Davis Bill would make it difficult for Southern states to rejoin the Union.

The Wade-Davis Bill required the Southern states to do three things:

- A majority (more than 50 percent) of the state's white male adults had to promise loyalty to the Union.
- Only white males who swore they had not fought against the Union could vote for representatives to a convention to write a new constitution.
- All new states had to ban slavery.

The Wade-Davis Bill was harsher than Lincoln's Ten Percent Plan. The bill passed Congress, but President Lincoln refused to sign it. The bill did not become law. There were still no plans for Reconstruction.

///////////// Glue Foldable here ////////////

Meanwhile, Lincoln and Congress worked together to create a new government department called the Freedman's Bureau. The Freedmen's Bureau helped poor Southerners, especially freed African Americans, adjust to life after slavery. It provided food, clothing, and shelter. It set up schools. It helped people find work. It also helped some people get their own land to farm.

Johnson's Reconstruction Plan

President Lincoln was assassinated on April 14, 1865, as he was watching a play in Washington, D.C. During the play, John Wilkes Booth shot Lincoln in the head. Booth was an actor who sympathized with the South. African Americans and white Northerners mourned Lincoln's death.

Vice President Andrew Johnson became president. He had different ideas about Reconstruction than Lincoln did.

Johnson wanted to give amnesty to most Southerners. However, he would not give amnesty to Southern leaders unless they asked the president. Johnson wanted to humiliate these leaders. He thought they had tricked ordinary Southerners into the war. Johnson opposed equal rights for African Americans. He said, "White men alone must manage the South."

The Reconstruction Era

Lesson 1 Planning Reconstruction, *Continued*

Johnson's plan for Reconstruction required Southern states to write new constitutions that banned slavery. Johnson's plan also required Southern states to ratify, or approve, the Thirteenth Amendment to the Constitution. The Thirteenth Amendment banned slavery throughout the United States. By the end of 1865, all the former Confederate states except Texas had set up new governments under Johnson's plan. They were ready to rejoin the Union.

////////////////// Glue Foldable here /////////////////

Check for Understanding
How did Lincoln and the Radical Republicans disagree over Reconstruction?

_____

_____

List two ways that Lincoln's Ten Percent Plan and Johnson's Reconstruction plan were alike.

1. _____

2. _____

☑ **Reading Check**

9. What did the Thirteenth Amendment accomplish?

_____

_____

FOLDABLES

10. Place a three-tab Venn diagram Foldable along the dotted line to cover Check for Understanding. Write the title *Reconstruction* on the anchor tab. Label the tabs *Lincoln*, *Both*, and *Johnson*. Write information about each president's approach to Reconstruction. What did they have in common? Use the Foldable to help answer Check for Understanding.

The Reconstruction Era

Lesson 2 The Radicals Take Control

ESSENTIAL QUESTION
How do new ideas change the way people live?

GUIDING QUESTIONS
1. **How did the North attempt to assist African Americans in the South?**
2. **What elements were included in the Radical Republican idea of Reconstruction?**

Terms to Know
black codes laws passed in the South just after the Civil War aimed at controlling freed men and women, and allowing plantation owners to take advantage of African American workers

override to reject or defeat something that has already been decided

impeach to formally charge a public official with misconduct in office

When did it happen?

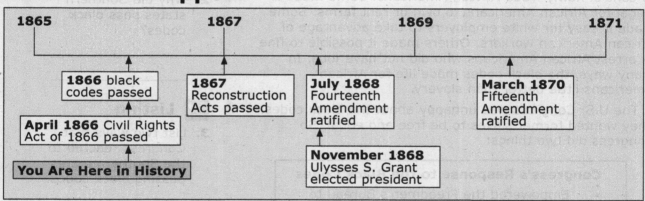

1865 — 1867 — 1869 — 1871

1866 black codes passed

1867 Reconstruction Acts passed

July 1868 Fourteenth Amendment ratified

March 1870 Fifteenth Amendment ratified

April 1866 Civil Rights Act of 1866 passed

You Are Here in History

November 1868 Ulysses S. Grant elected president

What do you know?

In the first column, answer the questions based on what you know before you study. After this lesson, complete the last column.

Now...		Later...
	How did Southern states try to control newly freed African Americans?	
	Why did Congress pass amendments to the Constitution during this period?	
	How did the United States govern the Southern states during Reconstruction?	

networks

The Reconstruction Era

Lesson 2 The Radicals Take Control, Continued

Protecting African Americans' Rights

In 1865, former Confederate states began creating new governments. They elected leaders to Congress, but the Radical Republicans would not seat them. They thought that Johnson's Reconstruction plan was too easy on the Southerners. Radicals wanted it to be difficult for Southerners to join the Union again.

White people in the South were unhappy that they had lost the war. They were angry that the slaves had been freed. To keep control of former slaves, Southern states passed laws called **black codes**. These laws were meant to control newly freed African Americans. Some made it illegal for African Americans to own or rent farms. Some made it easy for white employers to take advantage of African American workers. Others made it possible to fine or arrest African Americans who did not have jobs. In many ways, the black codes made life for African Americans little better than slavery.

The U.S. Congress was unhappy about the black codes. They wanted former slaves to be free and equal. So Congress did two things:

> ### Congress's Response to the Black Codes
> - Empowered the Freedmen's Bureau to set up courts to try people who violated African Americans' rights.
> - Passed the Civil Rights Act of 1866.

The Civil Rights Act gave citizenship to African Americans. It also gave the federal government the power to get involved in state affairs to protect African Americans' rights.

President Johnson vetoed both bills. He argued that they were unconstitutional because they were passed without Southern representatives. Radical Republicans in Congress were able to **override**, or overrule, each veto. Both bills became law.

Congress worried that the Civil Rights Act might be overturned in court, so it passed another amendment to the Constitution. The Thirteenth Amendment had ended slavery. The Fourteenth Amendment made African Americans citizens. It promised equal protection under the law. It also banned former Confederate leaders from

🖾 Explaining

1. Why would Radical Republicans not seat Southern senators and representatives in Congress?

🖾 Explaining

2. Why did Southern states pass black codes?

_____

_____

🖾 Listing

3. List two ways that Congress reacted to the Southern states passing black codes.

_____

_____

🅰️ᵇ꜀ Marking the Text

4. Underline the reason Congress passed the Fourteenth Amendment to the Constitution.

5. What did this amendment do?

_____

_____

_____

246

The Reconstruction Era

Lesson 2 The Radicals Take Control, *Continued*

Determining Cause and Effect

6. What allowed Radical Reconstruction to take place?

_____

_____

_____

Analyzing

7. How were the Southern states governed during Reconstruction?

_____

_____

_____

Identifying Central Issues

8. Why was Johnson able to control Reconstruction directly?

_____

_____

_____

holding office unless they had been pardoned. However, many Southern states would not ratify it. This made the Radical Republicans more determined than ever to treat the South harshly.

Radical Republicans in Charge

Radical Republicans were a powerful force in Congress. They became an even more powerful force in 1866. It was an election year, and they won many seats in Congress. There was no way Johnson could stop them. A period known as Radical Reconstruction began. The Radical Republicans passed the Reconstruction Acts.

Radical Reconstruction: The Reconstruction Acts	
Act	**What it did**
First Reconstruction Act	• said that states that had not ratified Fourteenth Amendment must form new governments • divided ten states into five military districts governed by generals • banned Confederate leaders from serving in new state governments
	• required new state constitutions • guaranteed African American men the right to vote
Second Reconstruction Act	• empowered army to register voters and help organize state constitutional conventions

The Southern states were now under the control of army generals. This angered Southerners. It also brought the differences between Radical Republicans in Congress and President Johnson to the boiling point.

The Radical Republicans in Congress had the majority. But as president, Johnson was in charge of the Army. He was in charge of the generals who governed the South. This meant that he could control Reconstruction directly. He could avoid Congress by giving orders to his generals.

The Reconstruction Era

Lesson 2 The Radicals Take Control, *Continued*

Congress knew this. So, to keep President Johnson from becoming too powerful, they passed laws to limit his power. One such law was the Tenure of Office Act. It said that the president could not fire any government officials without the Senate's approval. They were afraid Johnson would fire the Secretary of War, Edwin Stanton, because he supported Radical Reconstruction.

This did not stop Johnson. He suspended Stanton, or stopped him from working temporarily, without the Senate's approval. Radical Republicans in Congress believed that Johnson had violated the Tenure of Office Act.

The Radical Republicans reacted strongly. The House of Representatives voted to **impeach** Johnson—that is, formally charge him with wrongdoing. In 1868 the case went to the Senate for a trial. Not enough senators voted Johnson guilty, so he was able to remain president until Ulysses S. Grant was elected president in 1868.

In 1869, Congress took one more major step in Reconstruction. The Thirteenth Amendment had abolished slavery. The Fourteenth Amendment had granted citizenship to African Americans. This new Amendment—the Fifteenth—granted African American men the right to vote.

When the Fifteenth Amendment was ratified in 1870, many Americans thought Reconstruction was complete. However, there was still a long way to go.

/ / / / / / / / / / / / Glue Foldable here / / / / / / / / / / / /

Check for Understanding

List two ways that Congress tried to help African Americans before Radical Reconstruction began.

1. _____

2. _____

List three measures passed by Congress during Radical Reconstruction.

1. _____

2. _____

3. _____

Defining

9. Write a definition of *impeach*.

_____

_____

Identifying

10. What did the Fifteenth Amendment do?

_____

_____

FOLDABLES

11. Place a three-tab Foldable along the dotted line to cover Check for Understanding. Write the title *Amendments* on the anchor tab. Label the three tabs *13th*, *14th*, and *15th*. Write what you remember about the importance of each amendment. Use the Foldable to help answer Check for Understanding.

networks

The Reconstruction Era

Lesson 3 The South During Reconstruction

ESSENTIAL QUESTION
How do new ideas change the way people live?

GUIDING QUESTIONS
1. **How were African Americans discouraged from participating in civic life in the South?**
2. **What were some improvements and some limitations for African Americans?**

Terms to Know
scalawag name given by former Confederates to Southern whites who supported Republican Reconstruction of the South
corruption dishonest or illegal actions
integrate to unite, or blend into a united whole
sharecropping system of farming in which a farmer works land for an owner who provides equipment and seeds and receives a share of the crop

When did it happen?

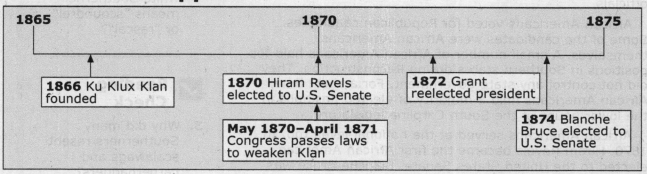

1865	1870	1875

1866 Ku Klux Klan founded

1870 Hiram Revels elected to U.S. Senate

May 1870–April 1871 Congress passes laws to weaken Klan

1872 Grant reelected president

1874 Blanche Bruce elected to U.S. Senate

What do you know?

In the first column, answer the questions based on what you know before you study. After this lesson, complete the last column.

Now...		Later...
	How did African Americans affect Southern politics and government during Reconstruction?	
	Who were "scalawags" and "carpetbaggers?"	
	What was life like for African Americans in the South during this period?	
	How many white and African American children attended school?	
	How does sharecropping work?	

networks

The Reconstruction Era

Lesson 3 The South During Reconstruction, *Continued*

Republicans in Charge

The Republicans were more powerful than the Democrats during Reconstruction. The groups in charge of state governments in the South supported Republicans. These included African Americans and some white Southerners. They also included whites from the North who moved to the South.

African Americans had fewer rights than white Southerners. But they supported the Republican Party and had a great effect on Southern politics. The Republican Party helped African Americans participate in government. Reconstruction marked the first time African Americans participated in government, both as voters and as elected officials.

African Americans voted for Republican candidates. Some of the candidates were African Americans themselves. A small number of African Americans held top positions in Southern states during Reconstruction. They did not control any state government. For a short time, African Americans held a majority of elected positions in the lower house of the South Carolina legislature.

African Americans served at the national level, too. In 1870, Hiram Revels became the first African American elected to the United States Senate. Blanche Bruce was elected to the Senate in 1874. He was the first African American senator to serve a full term. Eighteen African Americans served in the Senate and House of Representatives between 1869 and 1880.

Most Southern whites opposed the Republican Party, but some supported it. They were usually business people who had never owned slaves. These people were called **scalawags** by other whites. The word means "scoundrel" or "worthless rascal."

Some who supported the Republican Party were Northerners who moved South during Reconstruction. Many white Southerners did not trust their reasons for moving South. They suspected that the Northerners wanted to take advantage of the troubles in the South. Some of the Northerners were dishonest. Others were looking for opportunities. Many sincerely wanted to help rebuild the South. White Southerners called the Northerners "carpetbaggers."

Marking the Text

1. Underline the sentences that tell how many African Americans served in the national government.

Defining

2. What word for a white Southerner means "scoundrel" or "rascal"?

_____

Reading Check

3. Why did many Southerners resent scalawags and carpetbaggers?

The Reconstruction Era

Lesson 3 The South During Reconstruction, *Continued*

? **Critical Thinking**

4. How did the Klan's use of violence against African Americans help resist Republican rule?

_____

_____

_____

Aᵇc **Describing**

5. Who taught in African American schools in the South?

_____

_____

Aᵇc **Defining**

6. *Integrate* is the opposite of *segregate*. *Segregate* means "to separate." What does *integrate* mean?

_____

Why Were They Called Carpetbaggers?

Northerners who moved South were called carpetbaggers because they sometimes arrived with their belongings in cheap suitcases made of carpet fabric.

White Southerners said that Reconstruction governments suffered from **corruption**, or dishonest or illegal activities. Some officials did make money illegally. But there is no proof that corruption in the South was worse than in the North.

Life during reconstruction was hard for African Americans. Most Southern whites did not want African Americans to have more rights. White landowners often refused to rent land to them. Store owners refused to give them credit. Many employers would not hire them. Many of the jobs available were often jobs whites would not do.

Even worse, African Americans were victims of violence. Secret societies like the Ku Klux Klan used fear and violence to control them. Klan members disguised themselves in white sheets and hoods. They threatened, beat, and killed thousands of African Americans and their white friends. They burned African American homes, schools, and churches. Many Democrats, planters, and other white Southerners supported the Klan. They saw violence as a way to oppose Republican rule.

Education and Farming

African Americans started their own schools during Reconstruction. Many whites and African Americans from the North came to teach in these schools. In the 1870s, Reconstruction governments set up public schools for both races. Soon about 50 percent of white children and 40 percent of African American children in the South were attending school.

African American and white students usually went to different schools. A few states had laws requiring schools to be **integrated**. Schools that are integrated have both white and African American students. In most cases, integration laws were not enforced.

In addition to education, freed people wanted land. Having their own land to farm would allow them to feed and support their families. Some African Americans were able to buy land with the help of the Freedmen's Bank. But

251

netw🟊rks

The Reconstruction Era

Lesson 3 The South During Reconstruction, *Continued*

most failed in their efforts to get their own land. Many freed people had no other choice but to farm on land owned by whites.

In a system called **sharecropping** a landowner let a farmer farm some of the land. In return, the farmer gave a part, or share, of his crops to the landowner. The part demanded by landowners was often very large. This made the system unfair. After giving landowners their share, sharecroppers often had little left to sell. Sometimes there was not even enough to feed their families. For many, sharecropping was little better than slavery.

//////////// /Glue Foldable here/ ///////////

Check for Understanding

Name three ways that former slaves were discouraged from fully participating in Southern society.

1. _____

2. _____

3. _____

What improvements did Reconstruction bring for African Americans?

_____

_____

🖌 Explaining

7. What "rent" did the farmer pay the landowner under the sharecropping system?

_____

_____

✅ Reading Check

8. How would you describe the relationship between sharecroppers and landowners?

_____

_____

FOLDABLES®

9. Place a two-tab Foldable along the dotted line to cover Check for Understanding. Write the title *During Reconstruction* on the anchor tab. Label the tabs *Improvements* and *Limitations*. Write words or phrases that you remember about life for African Americans during Reconstruction in the South. Use the Foldable to help answer Check for Understanding.

The Reconstruction Era

Lesson 4 The Post-Reconstruction Era

ESSENTIAL QUESTION
How do new ideas change the way people live?

GUIDING QUESTIONS
1. How did Democrats regain control of Southern governments?
2. Why did freedom for African Americans become a distant dream after Reconstruction ended?

Terms to Know
poll tax a tax a person must pay in order to vote

literacy test a method used to prevent African Americans from voting by requiring prospective voters to read and write at a specified level

grandfather clause a device that allowed persons to vote if their fathers or grandfathers had voted before Reconstruction began

segregation the separation or isolation of a race, class, or group

lynching putting to death by the illegal action of a mob

Where in the world?

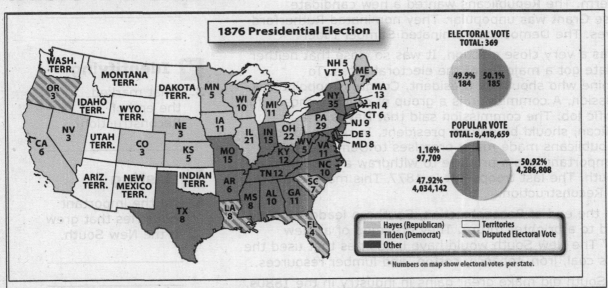

When did it happen?

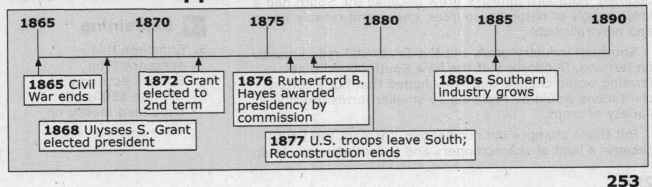

1865 Civil War ends

1868 Ulysses S. Grant elected president

1872 Grant elected to 2nd term

1876 Rutherford B. Hayes awarded presidency by commission

1877 U.S. troops leave South; Reconstruction ends

1880s Southern industry grows

253

Lesson 4 The Post-Reconstruction Era, Continued

Reconstruction Ends

As a general, Ulysses S. Grant had led the North to victory in the Civil War. He was elected president in 1868. He was reelected in 1872.

Grant's presidency had problems with corruption and dishonesty. Then, an economic depression struck: the Panic of 1873. The economy remained bad for years. These factors hurt the Republican Party. Democrats made gains in Congress.

Democrats also made gains at the state level. Southern democrats who came to power called themselves "redeemers." They wanted to redeem, or save, their states from "black Republican" rule.

The presidential election of 1876 was extremely important. President Grant thought about running for a third term. The Republicans wanted a new candidate because Grant was unpopular. They nominated Rutherford B. Hayes. The Democrats nominated Samuel Tilden.

It was a very close election. It was so close that neither candidate got a majority of the electoral votes. To determine who should be president, Congress appointed a commission. A commission is a group of officials chosen for a specific job. The commission said that Hayes, the Republican, should be named president. In return for this, the Republicans made many promises to Democrats. The most important was a promise to withdraw all troops from the South. The last troops left in 1877. This marked the end of Reconstruction.

With the end of Reconstruction, Southern leaders looked forward to a brighter future. They dreamed of a "New South." The New South would have industries that used the region's coal, iron, tobacco, cotton, and lumber resources.

The South did make great gains in industry in the 1880s. The tobacco, iron and steel, and lumber industries all boomed. Southern industry grew because the South had a large supply of natural resources, cheap and reliable labor, and new railroads.

Southern industry grew, but the South still relied mostly on farming. Supporters of the New South hoped that farming would change too. They hoped that huge cotton plantations would be replaced by smaller farms growing a variety of crops.

But those changes did not happen. Instead, the South became a land of sharecroppers and tenant farmers. Most

Explaining
1. Why did Grant become an unpopular president?
_____

Identifying
2. Why was a commission formed after the election of 1876?
_____
_____

Identifying
3. What marked the end of Reconstruction?
_____

Listing
4. List the important industries that grew in the New South.
_____
_____

Explaining
5. Complete this sentence: The South's economy in the late 1800s still depended mostly on
_____.

The Reconstruction Era

Lesson 4 The Post-Reconstruction Era, *Continued*

? Comparing

6. How was sharecropping similar to slavery?

_____

_____

✊ Explaining

7. Why did white Southerners pass new voting laws?

_____

_____

_____

ᴬᵇᶜ Marking the Text

8. Underline the definition of *segregation* in the text.

---

of the sharecroppers were former slaves. They ended up owing large amounts to white landowners. Laws made them stay on the land until their debt was paid—which could take years, or even a lifetime. This system made sharecropping little better than slavery.

A Divided Society

Reconstruction was over. The Union troops that had protected African Americans in the South left. The dream of freedom and justice for African Americans faded.

Southern government officials—the "redeemers"—passed laws that discriminated against African Americans. African Americans could do little about these government officials. The governments passed laws that made it nearly impossible for African Americans to vote. These laws enforced **poll taxes, literacy tests**, and **grandfather clauses**.

Restricting African Americans' Right to Vote in the South

Method	What it Was	How it Worked
poll tax	a fee people had to pay to vote	Many African Americans could not afford the tax, so they could not vote.
literacy test	a requirement that voters must be able to read and write at a certain level	Most Southern African Americans had little education, so literacy tests prevented many from voting.
grandfather clause	A law stating that a voter could vote if his father or grandfather had voted before Reconstruction.	African Americans could not vote until 1867, so they could not meet this requirement. This also allowed poor white Southerners who could not read to vote.

Other laws also discriminated against African Americans. In the late 1800s, **segregation** was common in the South. Segregation is the separation of races. Public places were

255

Lesson 4 The Post-Reconstruction Era, *Continued*

segregated by law. The laws that required segregation were called Jim Crow laws.

Even worse than segregation was the practice of lynching. **Lynching** happens when a mob kills a person, often by hanging. White mobs lynched many African Americans in the South.

Some African Americans managed to escape the South. Many fled to Kansas. They called themselves Exodusters after the biblical book of Exodus which describes the Jews' escape from slavery in Egypt.

Other African Americans escaped the South by joining the army. They fought in the Indian Wars of the late 1800s. The Apache and Cheyenne named these African Americans "Buffalo Soldiers."

//////////////////// Glue Foldable here ////////////////////

Check for Understanding

List three factors that aided the success of Southern industries in the late 1800s.

1. _____

2. _____

3. _____

List three ways that the redeemers prevented African Americans from voting.

1. _____

2. _____

3. _____

✓ Reading Check

9. What were Jim Crow laws?

_____

_____

A♭c Marking the Text

10. Underline the definition of lynching in the text.

FOLDABLES®

11. Place a two-tab Foldable along the dotted line to cover Check for Understanding. Write the title *Loss of Freedoms* on the anchor tab. Label the tabs *Cause* and *Effect*. Recall and list ways freedoms were lost after Reconstruction. Use the Foldable to help answer Check for Understanding.

Opening the West

Lesson 1 Mining and Railroads in the West

ESSENTIAL QUESTION

Why do people make economic choices?

GUIDING QUESTIONS

1. **How did mining lead to the creation of new states?**
2. **How did the railroads help the mining industry grow in the West?**

Terms to Know

subsidy money or goods given by a person or government to support a project that benefits the public

transcontinental going across a continent

time zone a geographic region in which the same standard time is used

Where in the world?

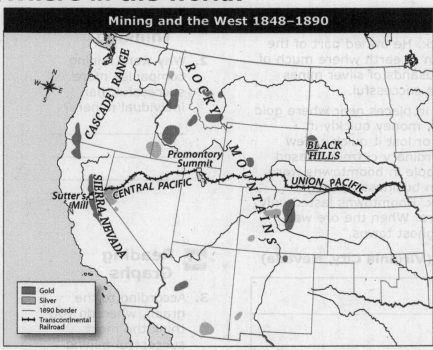

Mining and the West 1848–1890

When did it happen?

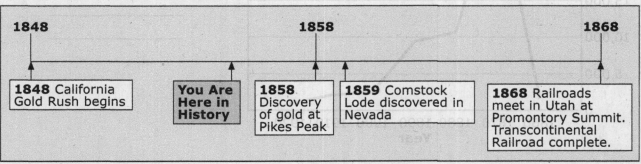

1848 California Gold Rush begins

You Are Here in History

1858 Discovery of gold at Pikes Peak

1859 Comstock Lode discovered in Nevada

1868 Railroads meet in Utah at Promontory Summit. Transcontinental Railroad complete.

257

Opening the West

Lesson 1 Mining and Railroads in the West, *Continued*

Gold, Silver, and Boomtowns

In 1849, people rushed to California to find gold. By the mid-1850s, the California Gold Rush was over. But miners still wanted to "strike it rich." They began looking for gold in other parts of the West. In 1858, they found it at Pikes Peak in the Colorado Rockies. By early 1859, about 50,000 miners had moved into Colorado's gold fields.

Some gold was found in streams, but most gold was deep underground. Mining companies came. They had machinery and many workers. They were more likely to find a lot of gold than a single miner was.

In 1859, miners found one of the world's richest deposits of silver ore in Nevada. It was called the Comstock Lode. It was named after Henry Comstock. He owned part of the land it was on. A lode is a section of earth where much of a precious mineral is found. Thousands of silver mines opened in the area, but few were successful.

Boomtowns grew up very fast in places near where gold and silver were found. People got money quickly in boomtowns, but they also spent or lost it quickly. Few boomtowns had police or jails. Ordinary citizens chased and punished criminals. Most people in boomtowns were men. Women who were there ran businesses, taught school, cooked, or did other work. Boomtowns lasted only as long as gold or silver was there. When the ore was gone, people left. This created "ghost towns."

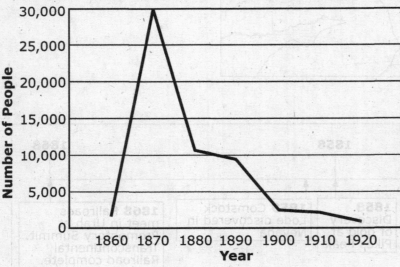

Population of a Boomtown (Virginia City, Nevada)

(Graph: Number of People vs. Year, 1860–1920. Population rises sharply to 30,000 around 1870, then declines steeply to near 1,000 by 1920.)

✓ Reading Check

1. Why did many boomtowns turn into ghost towns?

_____

_____

_____

? Critical Thinking

2. Why were mining companies more successful than individual miners?

_____

_____

_____

👁 Reading Graphs

3. According to the graph, when do you think the most successful mining took place in this boomtown?

_____

_____

_____

Lesson 1 Mining and Railroads in the West, *Continued*

[Ac] Defining

4. What are *subsidies*?

_____

_____

Identifying

5. At what place were the two sets of tracks joined to create the transcontinental railroad?

_____

_____

FOLDABLES®

Describing

6. Use a two-tab Foldable and cut the tabs in half to make four-tabs. Place it along the dotted line over the text that begins with "In time, people saw the need..." Write *Transcontinental Railroad* on the anchor tab. Label the tabs *What, When, Where,* and *Why.* As you read, respond to the questions about the railroad.

Soon there was less and less gold and silver, so miners dug for other metals. They dug for copper, lead, and zinc. People moved near the new mines. Thousands of settlers moved west. Besides mining, they farmed and started ranches. They opened businesses. By 1890, there were seven new states: Colorado, North Dakota, South Dakota, Washington, Montana, Wyoming, and Idaho.

Railroads Connect East and West

Mining communities needed transportation. Gold and silver had little value unless it could reach markets. People in boomtowns also needed supplies. Stagecoaches and wagons were not fast enough. To meet people's needs, many railroads were built between 1865 and 1890.

Railroads were so important to the nation that the federal government gave **subsidies,** or gifts of money or land, to the railroad companies. The government gave more than 130 million acres of land to railroad companies. The government got much of this land by buying it from or making treaties with Native Americans. States and towns also gave subsidies to have railroads built in their areas.

/ / / / / / / / / / / Glue Foldable here / / / / / / / / / / / /

In time, people saw the need for a **transcontinental** railroad. It would cross the country. It would connect the Atlantic coast and the Pacific coast. Southerners wanted the route of the transcontinental railroad to go through the South. Northerners wanted the route to go through the North. During the Civil War, the government chose a northern route.

The challenge of building a transcontinental railroad was to lay more than 1,700 miles of track. Tracks crossed plains, rivers, and mountains.

Two companies built the railroad. The Central Pacific Company worked eastward from California. The Union Pacific Company worked westward from Nebraska. (Railroad tracks already ran as far west as Nebraska.) Both companies worked as fast as they could. They hired thousands of workers. The Union Pacific Railroad hired Irish and African American workers. The Central Pacific Railroad hired Chinese immigrants.

On May 10, 1869, the two sets of tracks met at Promontory Summit in Utah Territory. Leland Stanford, California's governor, drove the final spike to finish the railroad. Then, the message was sent by telegraph:

259

Opening the West

Lesson 1 Mining and Railroads in the West, *Continued*

"The last rail is laid! The last spike driven! The Pacific Railroad is completed!"

Railroads had a big effect on the economy. They carried workers and goods to the West. Trains carried metals and other supplies to factories back East. Because train tracks are made of steel, the steel industry grew quickly. The new railroads helped many other industries grow as well. The coal industry, companies that made railroad cars, and construction companies got much business because of the railroads.

People built new towns along the railroads. Ranchers and farmers moved into the area. Trains had helped to build small towns into cities. Denver, Colorado, is one example.

Trains even changed how we measure time. Before the railroad, each area kept time based on where the sun was in the sky at noon. For example, clocks in Boston told time 11 minutes later than clocks in New York City. But differences in timekeeping made problems for trains. There could be mistakes in planning. There could even be train crashes.

The American Railway Association came up with a system. In 1883, they divided the country into four **time zones.** All towns in one time zone had the same time. The next zone was exactly an hour different. That made train travel safer and more reliable. Trains also helped to connect Americans in different regions. Trains were changing the way Americans lived.

////////////////// Glue Foldable here //////////////////

Check for Understanding
Name two places where gold and silver were discovered in the West.

_____

_____

How did railroads change life in America?

_____

_____

✔ Reading Check

7. How did railroads affect America's economy in the 1800s?

_____

_____

ᴬᵇ𝒸 Defining

8. What is a *time zone*?

_____

_____

FOLDABLES

9. Place a two-tab Foldable along the dotted line to cover Check for Understanding. Write the title *Changes in the West* on the anchor tab. Label the tabs *Mines* and *Trains*. On both, write two sentences telling what you found most interesting about how mines and railroads changed the West. Use your Foldable to help answer Check for Understanding.

Opening the West

Lesson 2 Ranchers and Farmers

ESSENTIAL QUESTION
How does geography influence the way people live?

GUIDING QUESTIONS
1. **How did ranchers get their cattle to market in the North and East?**
2. **What brought more settlers to the Great Plains?**

Terms to Know

long drive a trip of several hundred miles on which ranchers led their cattle to railroads and distant markets

vaquero a cowboy, particularly a Mexican cowboy

homestead to earn ownership of land by living on it

sodbuster name given to Great Plains farmers

dry farming a farming method that depends on plowing after every rain to trap moisture in the soil

Where in the world?

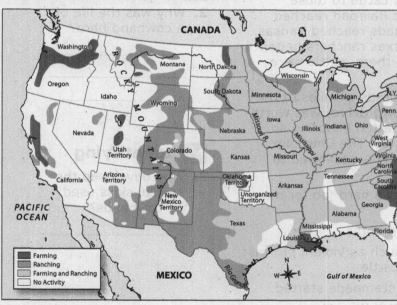

When did it happen?

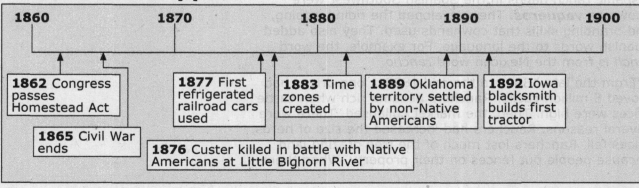

| 1860 | 1870 | 1880 | 1890 | 1900 |

1862 Congress passes Homestead Act

1865 Civil War ends

1877 First refrigerated railroad cars used

1876 Custer killed in battle with Native Americans at Little Bighorn River

1883 Time zones created

1889 Oklahoma territory settled by non-Native Americans

1892 Iowa blacksmith builds first tractor

261

Opening the West

Lesson 2 Ranchers and Farmers, Continued

Cattle on the Plains

In the 1500s, Spanish explorers first came to Texas. They brought cattle for food. Some of the cattle escaped. Over time, the cattle developed into a new breed called longhorns.

Much of Texas was open land. It was not fenced, so cattle roamed free. In the 1800s, there were thousands of cattle. Settlers in Texas rounded them up and started ranches.

There were fast-growing markets for beef in the North and the East. The value of cattle was about $3 to $4 each in Texas. In the North and East, cattle sold for $40 each.

Ranchers needed a way to get their cattle to those markets. By 1865, the Missouri Pacific Railroad reached Kansas City, Missouri. Later, the railroads reached Kansas, Nebraska, Colorado, and Wyoming. Texas ranchers began to herd cattle to railroad towns. From there, cattle were shipped to the North and East.

Sometimes cattle were herded hundreds of miles to the closest railroad. The trip, called the **long drive,** was worth the time and cost. The cattle drives started in spring so cattle would have food to eat on the way. The Chisholm Trail was one well-known path that ranchers followed to get to Kansas.

Herding cattle, or cattle driving, was a hard job for many reasons:

- The long drive took two or three months.
- Cowhands faced many dangers, such as violent storms and "rustlers" who tried to steal cattle.
- They had to control the herd if a stampede started.

Many cowhands had fought in the Civil War. Many were African Americans, Native Americans, and Hispanics. Hispanic ranch hands in the Spanish Southwest were known as *vaqueros.* They developed the riding, roping, and branding skills that cowhands used. They also added Spanish words to the language. For example, the word *ranch* is from the Mexican word *rancho.*

From the late 1860s to the mid-1880s, long drives had moved 5 million cattle. Ranchers became rich when cattle prices were high. Then, the market collapsed. There were several reasons. Ranchers had increased the size of herds. Prices fell. Ranchers lost much of the free grazing land because people put fences on their property. When there

Reading Check

1. How did railroads increase the value of Texas cattle?

_____

_____

Explaining

2. Why was the life of a cowhand hard?

_____

_____

_____

Identifying

3. Who developed the special skills used by cowhands?

_____

Explaining

4. Why did people who first saw the Plains think it was not good for farming?

_____

_____

Mark the Text

5. Underline the words that tell what a settler did to earn free land under the Homestead Act.

were too many cattle for sale, the price of beef went down. The cattle industry continued, but it was changed forever.

Farmers Settle the Plains

The people who first came to the Great Plains did not think it was good farmland. The Great Plains were known as the "Great American Desert." The land was dry and had few trees. Even so, farmers began to settle there in the late 1860s.

There were several reasons. Lots of rain, free land, and easy travel on the railroads encouraged people to move west to farm the land in the 1860s and 1870s.

Congress passed the Homestead Act in 1862. To **homestead** means to earn ownership of land by settling on it. The Homestead Act helped people to settle the Great Plains. The act gave free land to anyone who paid a $10 fee and lived on the land for five years. A settler could get up to 160 acres (65 hectares) of land.

Thousands of new settlers moved to the Great Plains. They included immigrants and African Americans who no longer felt safe in the South.

Some of the settlers were women. A married woman could not claim land. A single woman or a widow could claim land through the Homestead Act. In Colorado and Wyoming, 12 percent of the homesteaders were women.

Immigrants could file homestead claims. Thousands of people from a part of Europe called Scandinavia settled on the Great Plains.

Some settlers bought their land. The railroad companies advertised the Great Plains as a great place to live. So did steamship companies, land sellers, and western states and territories. People were eager to get cheap land, independence, and easy profits. They moved west.

However, life on the Great Plains was not easy at all. Farming in the Great Plains was hard. There were few trees, so farmers built houses of sod—packed soil held together by grass roots.

The climate was extreme. Some years there was too much rain. This brought floods to the Great Plains. Other years there was not enough rain. Then there would be droughts and brushfires.

Winter brought deep snow. This could trap people in their homes and bury the animals. Farm families planned ahead by storing food. The whole family worked on the

Opening the West

Lesson 2 Ranchers and Farmers, *Continued*

farm. Children often had so much farm work that they did not have time to go to school.

Farmers on the Great Plains were called **sodbusters.** They came up with new tools and new ways to farm the hard sod. One way was **dry farming.** With dry farming, farmers plowed the land every time it rained. This trapped water in the soil. Farmers also dug wells.

Sodbusters had to cut through tough layers of sod. They used steel plows to plow their fields. They planted a crop called winter wheat. This crop grows well in dry climates.

Even with these new methods, farmers often could not grow large enough crops. Many farmers lost their farms.

By the 1880s, only Indian Territory in present-day Oklahoma had not been settled. The law said only Native Americans could live there. There was one part of Indian Territory that was not assigned to any of the Indian groups. The government agreed to let non-Native American homesteaders settle there.

On April 22, 1889, more than 10,000 people lined up at the edge of these lands. A signal was given. Homesteaders rushed into the land to claim a piece for themselves. They found that some people had gone over the line early. These people were called "sooners," and they got the best land.

By 1890, all of America was settled. Life in America had changed, especially for Native Americans.

/ / / / / / / / / / / / / Glue Foldable here / / / / / / / / / /

Check for Understanding

How did Texans earn a living from wild herds of cattle?

_____

_____

What role did railroads play in getting people to settle the Great Plains?

_____

_____

✓ Reading Check

6. What new methods did farmers use on the Great Plains?

_____

_____

FOLDABLES®

7. Place a three-tab Foldable along the dotted line to cover Check for Understanding. Label the tabs *Cattle*, *Cowboys*, and *Sodbusters*. Use both sides of the tabs to write three or more facts that you remember about the roles of each. Use your Foldable to help answer Check for Understanding.

networks

Opening the West

Lesson 3 Native American Struggles

ESSENTIAL QUESTION
Why does conflict develop?

GUIDING QUESTIONS
1. **How did settlement on the Great Plains threaten Native Americans?**
2. **Why did conflict start between the Native Americans and the whites?**

Terms to Know
nomadic moving from place to place in a fixed pattern
reservation an area of land set aside for use by a group

Where in the world?

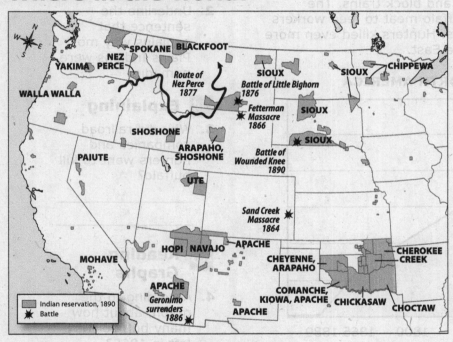

Route of Nez Perce 1877
Battle of Little Bighorn 1876
Fetterman Massacre 1866
Battle of Wounded Knee 1890
Sand Creek Massacre 1864
Geronimo surrenders 1886

SPOKANE BLACKFOOT
NEZ PERCE
YAKIMA
WALLA WALLA
SHOSHONE
PAIUTE
ARAPAHO, SHOSHONE
UTE
SIOUX
SIOUX
SIOUX
SIOUX
CHIPPEWA
MOHAVE
HOPI NAVAJO
APACHE
APACHE
APACHE
CHEYENNE, ARAPAHO
COMANCHE, KIOWA, APACHE
CHICKASAW
CHEROKEE
CREEK
CHOCTAW

Indian reservation, 1890
Battle

When did it happen?

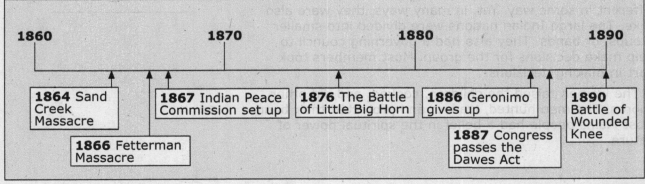

| 1860 | 1870 | 1880 | 1890 |

1864 Sand Creek Massacre
1866 Fetterman Massacre
1867 Indian Peace Commission set up
1876 The Battle of Little Big Horn
1886 Geronimo gives up
1887 Congress passes the Dawes Act
1890 Battle of Wounded Knee

265

Opening the West

Lesson 3 Native American Struggles, *Continued*

First People of the Plains

In the mid-1850s miners, ranchers, and farmers began to settle on the Great Plains. The region had been home to Native American nations for hundreds of years.

Some Plains Indians lived in communities as farmers and hunters. Most Plains Indians were **nomadic.** They traveled from place to place. They always followed their main food source, the buffalo.

After the Civil War, American hunters began to kill large numbers of buffalo. Railroad companies did not want the buffalo to stand on the tracks and block trains. The companies also wanted the buffalo meat to feed workers who were building the railroads. Hunters killed even more buffalo to sell their hides in the East.

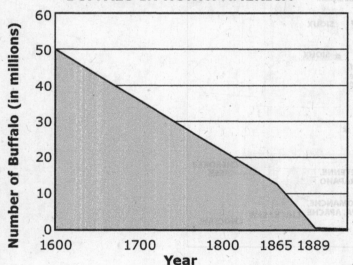

BUFFALO IN NORTH AMERICA

Groups of Native Americans living on the Plains were all different in some way. Yet, in many ways, they were also alike. The large Indian nations were divided into smaller groups, or bands. They also had a governing council to help make decisions for the group. Most members took part in making decisions.

The women raised the children, cooked, and did other chores. The men hunted, traded, and protected their band. Most Plains people had a belief in the spiritual power of nature.

☑ **Reading Check**

1. Describe the way of life of Plains Indians.

_____

_____

✎ **Mark the Text**

2. Underline the sentence that explains why most Plains Indians were nomadic.

✎ **Explaining**

3. Why did railroad companies and hunters want to kill buffalo?

_____

_____

👁 **Reading Graphs**

4. According to the graph, about how many buffalo were left in 1865?

_____

_____

Opening the West

Lesson 3 Native American Struggles, *Continued*

Mark the Text

5. Underline the sentence that tells what the Indian Peace Commission was set up to do.

Explaining

6. Why was the land on many reservations called "poor land"?

_____

_____

Explaining

7. Why did white settlers want the Native American land in the Black Hills?

_____

_____

Conflict on the Plains

As settlers took more and more land in the Plains, conflicts began. In 1867 the government set up the Indian Peace Commission. It would decide what to do about Native Americans who lived in the United States. The commission recommended that all Native Americans be moved to **reservations.** A reservation is land set aside for a group. The military had the power to move Native Americans by force. Congress set aside the largest reservations on the Great Plains. The Bureau of Indian Affairs was in charge of the reservations.

Often, Native Americans were tricked into moving to reservations. Native leaders wanted to be sure their people could farm and hunt. Many reservations were on poor land for farming or hunting. The government often did not deliver food or supplies. What they did send was of poor quality.

At first, many Native Americans agreed to move to reservations. When they saw the bad conditions, they wanted to leave. Some Native Americans refused to go.

There were fights. In 1862, Sioux fighters burned and looted the homes of white settlers. After that, the U.S. government forced most Sioux to move to reservations.

Miners were arriving in Colorado Territory to search for gold and silver. Cheyenne and Arapaho raided miners' and settlers' wagon trains. They killed 200 settlers. The governor told them to surrender. In November 1864, Cheyenne people went to make a peace treaty. The army attacked. This became known as the Sand Creek Massacre.

The Sioux continued to fight. They saw the U.S. Army building forts on a trail to Montana's gold mines. The trail led through Sioux lands. In December 1866, the Sioux trapped and killed 80 U.S. soldiers. This attack became known as the Fetterman Massacre.

A treaty in 1868 was supposed to bring peace with the Sioux. The Black Hills of the Dakotas had been set aside for Native Americans. White settlers moved in when they heard that the hills contained gold. Sitting Bull, a Lakota Sioux leader, refused to sell the land.

Lieutenant Colonel George Custer attacked the Sioux at Little Bighorn River. Custer and all his men were killed. News of the army's defeat shocked the nation. Before long, the army sent most Plains Indians to reservations.

Opening the West

Lesson 3 Native American Struggles, Continued

The Nez Perce lived in the Pacific Northwest. In the 1860s, gold was discovered on their land. The U.S. government ordered them to leave. Chief Joseph, their leader, left for Canada. The Nez Perce were caught by soldiers on the way. They were brought to a reservation. Chief Joseph spent the rest of his life trying to get better treatment for Native Americans.

The Chiricahua Apache were moved to a reservation in Arizona. Their leader, Geronimo, fled to Mexico. During the 1880s, he led raids in Arizona. In 1886 he surrendered.

Reservations, army attacks, and the killing of buffalo changed Native Americans' lives. Reformers also tried to change things. They wanted Native Americans to take on white culture. Congress passed the Dawes Act in 1887. It tried to break up reservations and tribal groups. Reformers hoped that Native Americans would become farmers. Some did, but many did not want to farm or to learn how.

In 1889, many Native Americans in the West began performing a ceremony called the Ghost Dance. It showed their hope that white settlers would go away, buffalo would return, and Native Americans would go back to their old way of life. In 1890 police killed Sitting Bull, whom the government thought had started the Ghost Dance. Hundreds of Lakota Sioux gathered at Wounded Knee, a creek in South Dakota. The army went there to take any Sioux weapons. A shot was fired. Then the army fired on the Sioux. More than 200 Sioux and 25 soldiers were killed. This event marked the end of armed conflict between the U.S. government and Native Americans.

/ / / / / / / / / / / / Glue Foldable here / / / / / / / / / / / /

Check for Understanding

What was the main source of conflict between Native Americans and whites?

_____

_____

How did Native Americans react to being forced to live on reservations?

_____

_____

☑ **Reading Check**

8. How effective was the Dawes Act?

_____

❓ **Sequencing**

9. Number these events in the order they happened.

____ Massacre at Wounded Knee

____ Geronimo escapes to Mexico

____ Sitting Bull is killed

____ The Dawes Act

FOLDABLES

10. Place a two-tab Foldable along the dotted line to cover Check for Understanding. Write the title *Conflicts on the Plains* on the anchor tab. Label the tabs *Causes* and *Effects*. List the facts that you remember about the conflicts between Native Americans and the settlers of the Plains. Use both sides of the tabs.

Opening the West

Lesson 4 Farmers—A New Political Force

ESSENTIAL QUESTION
How do governments change?

GUIDING QUESTIONS
1. **How did the National Grange and the Farmers' Alliances try to help farmers?**
2. **What were the ideas of the Populist Party?**

Terms to Know

National Grange network of local farmers' groups
cooperative cash-only store where farmers bought from each other
populism an appeal to the common people

Where in the world?

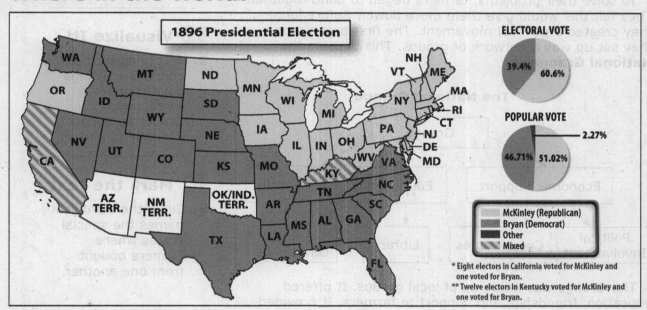

1896 Presidential Election

ELECTORAL VOTE
39.4%   60.6%

POPULAR VOTE
2.27%
46.71%   51.02%

McKinley (Republican)
Bryan (Democrat)
Other
Mixed

* Eight electors in California voted for McKinley and one voted for Bryan.
** Twelve electors in Kentucky voted for McKinley and one voted for Bryan.

When did it happen?

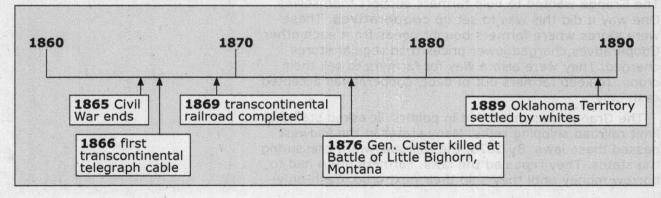

1860   1870   1880   1890

1865 Civil War ends

1866 first transcontinental telegraph cable

1869 transcontinental railroad completed

1876 Gen. Custer killed at Battle of Little Bighorn, Montana

1889 Oklahoma Territory settled by whites

269

Lesson 4 Farmers—A New Political Force, *Continued*

Farmers Unite

Farming expanded in the West and South after the Civil War. The supply of crops grew faster than the demand for them. Prices fell. However, farmers' expenses were still high.

Farmers blamed companies in the East that charged high prices. They blamed banks for charging high interest rates. Most of all they blamed the railroads for high shipping costs. Senator William A. Peffer of Kansas said that the railroad companies "took possession of the land" and the bankers "took possession of the farmer."

To solve their problems, farmers began to band together. They felt this would give them more power. Before long, they created a political movement. The first organization they set up was a network of groups. This became the **National Grange.**

The National Grange

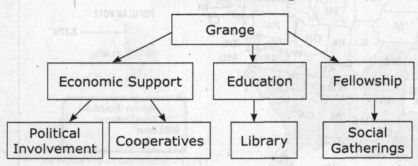

The Grange was made up of local groups. It offered education, friendship, and support to farmers. It provided books about planting crops and raising farm animals.

In the 1870s, the nation's economy took a downturn. The Grange wanted to help farmers support themselves. One way it did this was to set up **cooperatives.** These were stores where farmers bought goods from each other. Cooperatives charged lower prices than regular stores charged. They were also a way for farmers to sell their crops. To keep farmers out of debt, cooperatives accepted cash only.

The Grange became active in politics. It asked states to limit railroad shipping rates. Many states in the Midwest passed these laws. By 1878, the railroads were pressuring the states. They repealed the laws. Farmers often had to borrow money until they sold their next crop. Cash-only

270

✓ Reading Check

1. Why did farmers create organizations such as the Grange and the Farmers' Alliances?

_____

_____

👁 Visualize It!

2. According to the chart, the Grange gave support in three areas: Economic Support, Fellowship, and

_____

✏ Mark the Text

3. Circle the word that names the special stores where farmers bought from one another.

Opening the West

Lesson 4 Farmers—A New Political Force, *Continued*

? **Identifying Causes**

4. Why did the Grange's cooperatives fail?

_____

_____

✓ **Reading Check**

5. Why did people support the Populist Party?

_____

_____

▨ **Mark the Text**

6. Underline the sentence in the text that defines *free silver.*

_____

_____

? **Finding the Main Idea**

7. Why did the Populists believe free silver would help farmers and debtors?

_____

_____

_____

cooperatives could not survive when their customers had no cash.

The Farmers' Alliances were also set up to help farmers. This network was mostly in the West and the South. By 1890, the Southern Alliance had more than 3 million members.

There was a separate group called the Colored Farmers' National Alliance. This was a group of African American farmers. The group had one million members.

Like the Grange, the Farmers' Alliances supported cooperative buying and selling. They asked the government to store their crops in warehouses and lend them money. When prices rose the crops could be sold and the farmers would pay back the money. This would reduce the power that banks had over them. The alliances could have been a powerful force, but regional differences and personality differences got in the way of achieving this goal.

A Party of the People

In 1890 the Farmers' Alliances formed a political party. They called it the People's Party of the U.S.A. It was also known as the Populist Party. The candidates were elected governor in 6 states, won 3 seats in the U.S. Senate, and won 50 seats in the House of Representatives.

The party's goals were based on **populism**—an appeal to the common people. Populists wanted to replace the gold-based money system with one based on free silver. That does not mean that money is free. It just means there is an unlimited production of silver coins. Populists believed that with more silver coins in circulation, more farmers could pay their debts.

The Populist Party also:

- thought the government should own railroads and telegraph lines.
- wanted the president and vice president to serve only one term.
- wanted to elect senators directly.
- fought for shorter hours for workers.
- fought for a national income tax that would tax richer people at higher rates.

Farmers and people who owed money liked the idea of free silver. They hoped to pay their loans more cheaply. Silver-mining companies also liked the idea.

271

Opening the West

Lesson 4 Farmers—A New Political Force, *Continued*

In the 1896 election, Democrat William Jennings Bryan and Republican William McKinley ran for president. The Populist Party endorsed Bryan. He supported free silver and other Populist ideas. McKinley opposed free silver. By election time, the economy was improving and McKinley won by a landslide.

Still, the Populist Party made its mark. In the 1900s, the nation ended the gold standard. It also adopted an eight-hour workday, an income tax, and the direct election of senators.

/ / / / / / / / / / / / / / /Glue Foldable here/ / / / / / / / / / /

Check for Understanding

List two ways that the Grange and Farmers' Alliances helped farmers.

_____

_____

Which Populist Party ideas were eventually adopted by the government?

_____

_____

FOLDABLES

8. Place a three-tab Foldable along the dotted line to cover Check for Understanding. Write the title *Opening the West* on the anchor tab. Label the tabs *Grange, Farmers' Alliance*, and *Populist Party*. Write one or more sentences telling how each group affected farmers in the West and around the country. Use both sides of the tabs. Use your Foldable to help answer Check for Understanding.

The Industrial Age

Lesson 1 Railroads Lead the Way

ESSENTIAL QUESTION
How does technology change the way people live and work?

GUIDING QUESTIONS
1. **How did railroads pave the way for growth and expansion?**
2. **What industries benefited from the expansion of the railroad system?**

Terms to Know
consolidation combining companies
railroad baron powerful businessman who ran a large railroad
standard gauge the distance between the rails used by all American railroads
rebate discount
pool a group of businessmen who made secret agreements about prices and customers

When did it happen?

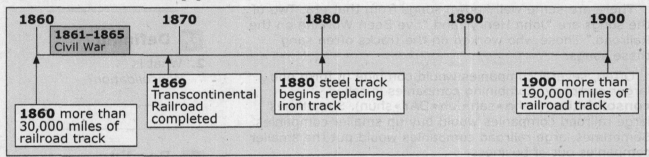

| 1860 | 1870 | 1880 | 1890 | 1900 |

1861–1865 Civil War

1860 more than 30,000 miles of railroad track

1869 Transcontinental Railroad completed

1880 steel track begins replacing iron track

1900 more than 190,000 miles of railroad track

What do you know?

In the first column, answer the questions based on what you know before you study. After this lesson, complete the last column.

Now...		Later...
	What industries benefited from railroads?	
	How did railroad companies expand?	

273

The Industrial Age

Lesson 1 Railroads Lead the Way, *Continued*

The Growth of Railroads

Many railroads were built between 1850 and 1900. More railroads helped the economy to grow.

Quick Facts About Railroad Tracks

- In 1860 there were 30,000 miles (48,280 km) of railroad track—almost as much as all the other countries in the world put together.

- By 1900, there were almost 193,000 miles (310,603 km) of railroad track.

- Between 1870 and 1916, workers put down about 11 miles (18 km) of track each day.

There are some well-known songs from that era. Two of the songs are "John Henry" and "I've Been Working on the Railroad." Those who worked on the tracks often sang these songs.

Often, several companies would combine to form one larger company. Combining companies is called **consolidation** (kuhn•sah•luh•DAY•shun). Sometimes large railroad companies would buy up smaller companies. Sometimes large railroad companies would put the smaller companies out of business.

Effects of Consolidation

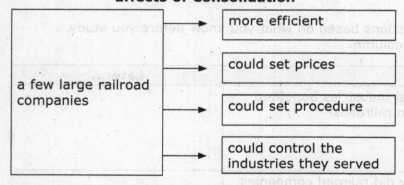

a few large railroad companies	→	more efficient
	→	could set prices
	→	could set procedure
	→	could control the industries they served

Powerful businessmen ran large railroads. These men were called **railroad barons** (BEHR • uhnz). One of the first railroad barons was Cornelius Vanderbilt. His railroad began in New York City and ended at the Great Lakes.

James J. Hill was a second railroad baron. His company built the Great Northern Line. This railroad line went from Minnesota west to Washington State.

Collis P. Huntington and Leland Stanford were two other railroad barons. They started a railroad line called the Central Pacific Railroad. The Central Pacific Railroad went

274

? Drawing Conclusions

1. Reread Quick Facts About Railroad Tracks. What can you conclude about the American economy in the late 1800s?

_____

_____

A♭c Defining

2. What is *consolidation*?

_____

_____

✓ Reading Check

3. Name one good thing and one bad thing about consolidation.

_____

_____

_____

_____

✎ Listing

4. List the names of three railroad barons.

_____

_____

_____

The Industrial Age

Lesson 1 Railroads Lead the Way, *Continued*

Mark the Text

5. Underline the meaning of *transcontinental* in the text.

Identifying

6. What was one advantage of large railroad companies? What was one disadvantage?

_____

_____

_____

_____

Explaining

7. How did railroads help the steel industry grow?

_____

_____

_____

Understanding Cause and Effect

8. Why did standard gauge track make shipping faster and less expensive?

_____

_____

_____

_____

from California to Utah. It made up part of the transcontinental railroad. Transcontinental means crossing the entire continent.

There were not many laws to control how the railroad barons ran their businesses. They competed fiercely with each other.

One advantage of large railroad companies was that they were efficient. A disadvantage was that they drove small companies out of business. This led to less competition.

Railroads Aid Economic Growth

The growth of railroads changed the United States. More railroads made it easier for factories to get raw materials, such as lumber or iron ore. Trains carried finished goods from factories to places where they were sold. Railroads carried crops from farms to cities.

Industries That Grew Because of Railroads	
iron	tracks and locomotive engines
steel	tracks
lumber	wood for railway ties (holds tracks together)
coal	powered the steam engines that pulled railroad cars

Many industries and jobs benefited from the growth of railroads. Railroad companies provided thousands of jobs.

The first railroads only went short distances. Each railroad company had its own kind of railroad tracks. Each company's tracks were of a different gauge (GAYJ). This means the tracks of different companies were different distances apart. The train cars that belonged to one railroad company could not use another company's tracks because they were too narrow or too wide.

This was a problem. If a manufacturer had to use more than one railroad line to ship goods, workers had to unload goods from one train and reload them on another. This slowed down rail travel and made it more expensive.

This problem was solved when companies consolidated. They all began to use tracks that were the same width. This was called **standard gauge** track. Goods no longer had to be unloaded from one train and loaded onto another. This reduced shipping time and shipping costs.

netw✷rks

The Industrial Age

Lesson 1 Railroads Lead the Way, *Continued*

New technology improved railway transportation.

- George Westinghouse designed air brakes. This made trains safer.

- Eli H. Janney made "car couplers." They made it easier for railroad workers to link cars together.

- Gustavus Swift developed refrigerated railroad cars. This made it possible to keep meat and crops cold. They could be shipped over long distances without spoiling.

- George Pullman developed a "sleeping car." The seats opened out into beds.

Railroad companies competed with each other for customers. Large railroad companies gave their big customers discounts on shipping charges. These discounts were called **rebates.** Smaller railroad companies could not afford to give such discounts. They lost customers to large railroads, and often went out of business.

Large railroads also made secret agreements with each other to form **pools.** Companies in a pool secretly set prices and divided up business. There were some laws to stop railroads from doing things like this, but they were not effective.

The growth of railroads changed the United States. They helped industry expand into the West. They also carried settlers west. They helped people move from rural areas to cities.

////////////////////Glue Foldable here///////////////////

Check for Understanding

List three industries that were helped by the growth of railroads.

_____

_____

What changes did railroads bring to the United States?

_____

_____

☑ Reading Check

9. What were some new technologies that improved railroad travel?

_____

_____

_____

ᴬᵇᶜ Defining

10. What is a *rebate*?

_____

_____

_____

FOLDABLES®

11. Place a one-tab Foldable over Check for Understanding. Label the anchor tab *Railroads* and draw a railroad track across the middle of the Foldable. Around the track, list words and phrases that you remember about the importance of railroads to the growth of America. Use your Foldable to help answer Check for Understanding.

The Industrial Age

Lesson 2 Inventions Change Society

ESSENTIAL QUESTION

How does technology change the way people live and work?

GUIDING QUESTIONS

1. **How did innovations in communications change society?**

2. **How did new inventions improve people's lives?**

3. **How did the inventions of the late 1800s change society?**

Terms to Know

Model T affordable car made by Ford
assembly line factory method in which work moved past workers who performed a single task
mass production factory production of goods in large quantities

When did it happen?

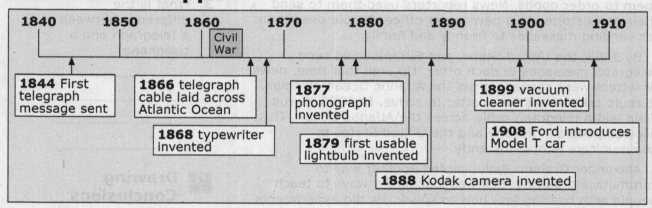

| 1840 | 1850 | 1860 | 1870 | 1880 | 1890 | 1900 | 1910 |

Civil War

1844 First telegraph message sent

1866 telegraph cable laid across Atlantic Ocean

1868 typewriter invented

1877 phonograph invented

1879 first usable lightbulb invented

1888 Kodak camera invented

1899 vacuum cleaner invented

1908 Ford introduces Model T car

What do you know?

In the first column, answer the questions based on what you know before you study. After this lesson, complete the last column.

Now ...		Later ...
	Who was the Wizard of Menlo Park?	
	How were telephones and telegraphs similar? How were they different?	

277

The Industrial Age

Lesson 2 Inventions Change Society, *Continued*

Technology Changes Communications

Samuel Morse developed the telegraph and built the first telegraph line. He sent the first telegraph message in 1844, from Baltimore to Washington, D.C. Within a few short years, there were thousands of miles of telegraph lines in the United States. The Western Union Telegraph Company had operators who were trained to transmit messages in Morse code.

Messages sent by telegraph are called telegrams. Telegrams could be sent almost instantly over long distances.

People used telegrams in many ways. Shopkeepers used them to order goods. News reporters used them to send their news stories to a newspaper office. People used them for sending messages to friends and family.

By 1866, the United States and Europe could send telegraph messages to each other. Up until that time, news or letters were carried across the Atlantic Ocean on ships. It could take weeks for a letter to arrive. In 1866, Cyrus Field laid a telegraph cable across the Atlantic Ocean. This allowed people in Europe and the United States to communicate almost instantly.

Alexander Graham Bell invented another way to communicate quickly. Bell was looking for ways to teach people with hearing loss how to speak. He did experiments with sending voice sounds over electric wires.

By 1876, Bell had invented a telephone. In 1877 Bell formed the Bell Telephone Company. By the 1890s, Bell had sold thousands of phones.

Telephones became part of everyday life. Businesses used phones. Then, people started using phones at home. By the early 1900s, even more people had this new technology. Like the telegraph, the telephone made communicating easier.

The Genius of Invention

Many important inventions came into being in the late 1800s. Between 1860 and 1890 the government processed patents for thousands of new inventions. A patent is a license that says only the inventor has permission to make or sell his or her invention, unless he gives permission to someone else.

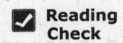

Identifying

1. Who developed the telegraph?

_____

2. Who invented the telephone?

_____

Reading Check

3. What is the difference between a telegraph and a telephone?

_____
_____
_____
_____

Drawing Conclusions

4. Why do you think patents are needed?

_____
_____
_____
_____
_____

278

Lesson 2 Inventions Change Society, *Continued*

☑ **Reading Check**

5. Which of Edison's inventions do you think is most important? Why?

_____

_____

_____

☑ **Reading Check**

6. Why did Henry Ford build the Model T?

_____

_____

FOLDABLES®

📝 **Describing**

7. Place a one-tab Foldable along the dotted line. Draw a large circle on the front of the tab and label it *Mass Production*. Draw a smaller circle within the large circle and label it *Assembly Line*. On the front and back of the tab, describe each. Explain their relationship.

Important Inventions of the Late 1800s	
Invention	**Inventor**
typewriter	Christopher Sholes
adding machine	William Burroughs
Kodak camera	George Eastman
vacuum cleaner	John Thurman

The greatest inventor of the time was Thomas Edison. Edison loved science and doing experiments. His mother let him set up a laboratory in the basement.

Edison soon set up a workshop in Menlo Park, New Jersey, in 1876. He invented so many amazing things that people called him "The Wizard of Menlo Park." Some of the things we use every day were invented by Edison. The phonograph (a way of playing recorded sound); the movie projector; and the light bulb were all his inventions.

All these things ran on electricity. In 1882, he built a power station. It made enough electricity to light 85 buildings. Soon, George Westinghouse invented a way to send electricity great distances. Electricity became the power source for homes and businesses.

Some inventors were African American. Lewis Howard Latimer made the light bulb better. Granville Woods invented an electric warmer and improved the braking system for trains. Elijah McCoy found a way to automatically oil machinery. Jan E. Matzeliger invented a machine that made shoes.

A Changing Society

In the early 1900s, most people did not have automobiles. The car was a new invention. Few people could afford to buy one. Henry Ford wanted to change that. He wanted to make a car that was cheap and easy to own. Ford and Charles Sorenson worked to create this car. They named it the **Model T**.

/ / / / / / / / / Glue Foldable here / / / / / / / / / /

Ford made the Model T on an **assembly line**. On Ford's assembly line, each worker did one job over and over again. As the Model T moved down the line, it was built a little at a time. The assembly line let Ford make a lot of cars quickly. The cars cost less to make because the assembly line was so efficient.

netw⊕rks

The Industrial Age

Lesson 2 Inventions Change Society, *Continued*

Because it cost less to make cars, Ford was able to lower the price of his cars. This allowed more people to afford them. Between 1908 and 1926, Ford sold 15 million Model Ts.

Other industries also began using assembly lines to make goods. They made large quantities of goods more quickly than ever before. Making large quantities of goods on an assembly line is called **mass production**.

In the early 1890s, inventors began to experiment with machines that could fly. Samuel Langley built a model airplane that was powered by a steam engine. It flew almost a mile before it ran out of fuel and crashed.

Wilbur and Orville Wright owned a bicycle shop. Between 1900 and 1902 they used their skills as mechanics to design a plane with a gas engine. In September 1903, they began to test their plane. Their test flights were at Kitty Hawk, North Carolina. On December 17, 1903, they made four flights. Their plane flew for just under one minute.

It would take some years for airplanes to be a common part of life, but the first steps had been taken.

//////////////////// Glue Foldable here ////////////////////

Check for Understanding

What effect did the telegraph have on American society?

_____

_____

Name two other inventions that made people's lives easier and explain how each did so.

_____

_____

📝 Identifying

8. Who built a steam-powered airplane?

_____

9. Who built a gas-powered airplane?

_____

FOLDABLES®

10. Glue two one-tab Foldables together at the anchor tabs. Place the two Foldables over Check for Understanding. Label the top anchor tab *Inventions Bring Change.* Label the top Foldable *Changes in Communication* and the bottom Foldable *Changes in Daily Life.* Make memory maps by drawing three arrows below each title. On the top tab, write three words and phrases about inventions that changed how we communicate. On the bottom tab write three things about inventions that changed daily life. Use your memory maps to help answer Check for Understanding.

280

netw⊕rks

The Industrial Age

Lesson 3 An Age of Big Business

ESSENTIAL QUESTION
How does technology change the way people live and work?

GUIDING QUESTIONS

1. **What is the role of the factors of production in making goods and services?**

2. **How did John D. Rockefeller and Andrew Carnegie build fortunes in the oil and steel industries?**

Terms to Know

factors of production land, labor, and capital

entrepreneur person who starts a business

corporation a business in which investors own shares

stock part ownership in a company

shareholder a person who buys stock in a corporation and is a partial owner

dividend a stockholder's share of a company's profits, usually as a payment

trust a group of companies run by a single board of trustees

monopoly total control of an industry by one person or one company

merger the combining of two or more businesses into one

When did it happen?

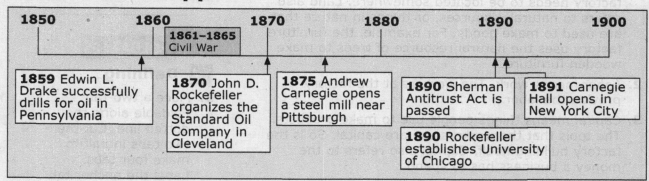

| 1850 | 1860 | 1870 | 1880 | 1890 | 1900 |

1861–1865 Civil War

1859 Edwin L. Drake successfully drills for oil in Pennsylvania

1870 John D. Rockefeller organizes the Standard Oil Company in Cleveland

1875 Andrew Carnegie opens a steel mill near Pittsburgh

1890 Sherman Antitrust Act is passed

1891 Carnegie Hall opens in New York City

1890 Rockefeller establishes University of Chicago

What do you know?

In the first column, answer the questions based on what you know before you study. After this lesson, complete the last column.

Now...		Later...
	What does capital have to do with the growth of business?	
	Who was Andrew Carnegie?	
	Why were "trusts" considered to be a problem?	

281

Lesson 3 An Age of Big Business, Continued

The Growth of Big Business

Oil, or petroleum, was first used as a kind of medicine. People collected it where it seeped out of the ground. No one drilled for oil like they do today. Later it was discovered that oil could be burned to make heat and light. It could also be used to lubricate machinery. In 1859 Edwin L. Drake drilled an oil well in Titusville, Pennsylvania. This was the beginning of the modern oil industry.

Industry developed rapidly in the late 1880s. The United States economy was changing from one based on farming to one based on industry.

Industry is based on the **factors of production.** The factors of production are the things needed to produce something. There are three factors of production: land, labor, and capital. Anyone who has a business is using the three factors of production.

1. *Land* refers to the land itself. For example, a furniture factory needs to be located somewhere. Land also refers to natural resources, or things in nature that are used to make goods. For example, the furniture factory uses the natural resource of trees to make wooden furniture.

2. *Labor* means work. The workers at the factory provide the labor.

3. *Capital* means things people use to make products. The tools that the workers use are capital. So is the factory building itself. Capital also refers to the money a business has to spend.

/ / / / / / / / / / / Glue Foldable here / / / / / / / / / / /

After the Civil War, many business owners wanted to raise capital so their businesses would grow. People who start businesses and run them are called **entrepreneurs** (ahn•truh•pruh•NURZ). To raise capital, many entrepreneurs formed corporations.

A **corporation** is a way to organize a company. It also allows many people to share ownership of one company.

The business owner sells small shares of the company to many investors. These shares of the company are called **stock.** The investors are called **shareholders.** By selling shares to shareholders, the business gets the money, or *capital*, it needs to operate or grow larger.

If the business does well and makes a profit, shareholders are given part of the profit. Payments to shareholders are called **dividends.**

Aᵇᶜ Listing

1. What are the three factors of production?
   1. _____
   2. _____
   3. _____

✔ Reading Check

2. Why is capital important for economic growth?
   _____

FOLDABLES

Defining

3. Place a two-tab Foldable along the dotted line. Cut the two tabs in half to make four tabs. Label the anchor tab *Corporations*. Label the four tabs *entrepreneurs*, *shareholders*, *stock*, and *dividends*. On the tabs, define each term as it relates to corporations.

Aᵇᶜ Identifying

4. Who buys stock?
   _____

The Industrial Age

Lesson 3 An Age of Big Business, *Continued*

👁 Visualize It

5. How is vertical integration different from horizontal integration?

_____

_____

_____

✓ Reading Check

6. How did Standard Oil become a monopoly?

_____

_____

📝 Identifying

7. Name two men who ran successful businesses in the late 1800s. What business was each one in?

_____

_____

_____

A𝑏𝑐 Defining

8. What is the Bessemer process?

_____

_____

The Growth of Oil and Steel

John D. Rockefeller was a very successful businessman. In 1870 he started an oil company called the Standard Oil Company. Rockefeller used a plan called "horizontal integration" to build his business. This means he combined companies that were competing with him into one company. Standard Oil grew powerful and wealthy.

Horizontal Integration

| competing company | ← takes over | Standard Oil Company | takes over → | competing company |

In 1882, Rockefeller formed an oil **trust.** A trust is a group of companies headed by one single board of trustees. Rockefeller's trust controlled many different oil companies. It controlled the entire oil industry. When one business or person has total control of an industry, that business or person is said to have a **monopoly.**

Andrew Carnegie was another very successful businessman of the late 1800s. Carnegie, however, made his fortune in steel.

A man named Henry Bessemer invented a new way to make large amounts of steel cheaply. It was called the Bessemer process. Carnegie learned about the Bessemer process. He then opened a steel plant near Pittsburgh, Pennsylvania.

Carnegie used "vertical integration" to build his business. This means that he bought companies that provided things he needed to make steel. For example, he bought iron and coal mines. He also bought railroads and ships to bring these raw materials to his factories. That way, he did not have to pay a lot for the things he needed to run his steel business. The Carnegie Steel Company was very successful. By 1900, this one company made one-third of the nation's steel.

Vertical Integration

Carnegie Steel Company
↑
iron and coal companies
↑
warehouses, ships, and railroads

The Industrial Age

Lesson 3 An Age of Big Business, *Continued*

Both Rockefeller and Carnegie earned hundreds of millions of dollars. They became philanthropists. A philanthropist is a person who gives money to good causes. Carnegie built the concert hall Carnegie Hall in New York City. He also paid to build many libraries across the United States and the world. Rockefeller established the University of Chicago and New York's Rockefeller Institute for Medical Research.

In the late 1800s, corporations grew larger. Many did so through **mergers.** A merger is when companies combine.

Many people thought that corporations had too much power. Because of this, Congress passed a law called the Sherman Antitrust Act. This law made trusts and monopolies illegal. At first, however, it had little effect.

Check for Understanding

List the factors of production and the role each plays in manufacturing.

_____

_____

_____

How did breakthroughs in technology lead to the rise of big business? Give one example.

_____

_____

_____

Mark the Text

9. Underline the definition of *philanthropist*.

Finding the Main Idea

10. Why did Congress pass the Sherman Antitrust Act?

_____

_____

_____

FOLDABLES®

11. Place a two-tab Foldable along the dotted line to cover Check for Understanding. Label the top tab *Industry*, and the bottom tab *Agriculture*. Draw an arrow from the bottom tab to the top tab to show the movement of the American economy from an agriculture-based economy to an industry-based economy. Write words and phrases to record what you remember about each. Use your Foldable to answer Check for Understanding.

284

The Industrial Age

Lesson 4 Workers in the Industrial Age

ESSENTIAL QUESTION

How does technology change the way people live and work?

GUIDING QUESTIONS

1. *How did working conditions change during the Industrial Age?*
2. *Why did workers form labor unions?*

Terms to Know

sweatshop a shop or factory where workers work long hours at low wages under unhealthy conditions

labor union organization of workers who seek better pay and working conditions

collective bargaining discussion between an employer and labor union representatives about wages, hours, and working conditions

strikebreaker person hired to replace a striking worker in order to break up a strike

injunction a court order to stop something from happening

When did it happen?

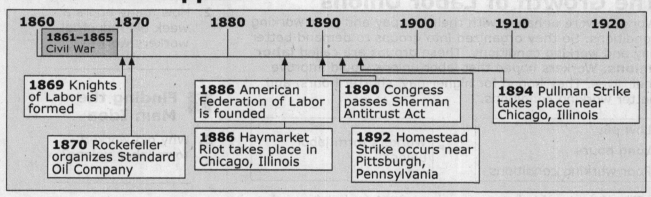

1860 — 1870 — 1880 — 1890 — 1900 — 1910 — 1920

1861–1865 Civil War

1869 Knights of Labor is formed

1870 Rockefeller organizes Standard Oil Company

1886 American Federation of Labor is founded

1886 Haymarket Riot takes place in Chicago, Illinois

1890 Congress passes Sherman Antitrust Act

1892 Homestead Strike occurs near Pittsburgh, Pennsylvania

1894 Pullman Strike takes place near Chicago, Illinois

What do you know?

In the first column, answer the questions based on what you know before you study. After this lesson, complete the last column.

Now...		Later...
	Who was Mother Jones and what was she known for?	
	Who would call in a strikebreaker?	

networks

The Industrial Age

Lesson 4 Workers in the Industrial Age, *Continued*

The Industrial Workforce

Industrial growth created many jobs, but the working conditions were terrible. Industrial workers labored six days a week for 10 to 12 hours a day. (Today, workers usually work five days a week, eight hours a day, for a total of 40 hours.) They worked in unsafe and unhealthy factories and mines. Garment workers worked in crowded and dangerous factories called **sweatshops.**

By 1900, more than one million women worked in industry. Women were paid about half of what men were paid for the same work. Hundreds of thousands of children under 16 also worked. Many children worked more than ten hours a day.

The Growth of Labor Unions

Workers were unhappy with their low pay and poor working conditions. So they organized into groups to demand better pay and working conditions. These groups are called **labor unions**. Workers hoped that labor unions would improve their lives. They hoped for higher pay, shorter hours, and better working conditions.

Low pay	
Long hours	→ Workers form labor unions
Poor working conditions	

The Knights of Labor was an important early labor union. It was founded in Philadelphia, Pennsylvania, in 1869. By the 1880s, the Knights of Labor had grown to be a national union. Unlike other unions, the Knights welcomed women, African Americans, immigrants, and unskilled laborers as members. Terrence V. Powderly led the Knights of Labor. The union had more than 700,000 members in the 1880s.

The American Federation of Labor (AFL) was another important labor organization. It was formed in 1886. The AFL represented skilled workers of many kinds. Its leader was Samuel Gompers. Gompers and the AFL worked for higher wages, shorter hours, and better working conditions. They fought for the right of collective bargaining. **Collective bargaining** is when unions discuss with business owners ways to improve wages and conditions for all the company's workers.

Many unions would not let women join. So some women formed their own unions. Some women became important labor leaders. One such leader was Mary Harris Jones.

Describing

1. Write three words that describe factory working conditions during the late 1800s.

   _____

   _____

   _____

✔ Reading Check

2. How many hours a week did industrial workers work?

   _____

❓ Finding the Main Idea

3. Why did workers form labor unions?

   _____

   _____

Mark the Text

4. Circle the name of the union that was founded in 1869. Who was its leader?

   _____

Identifying

5. What does AFL stand for?

   _____

286

The Industrial Age

Lesson 4 Workers in the Industrial Age, *Continued*

? Determining Cause and Effect

6. Why did so many people die in the Triangle Shirtwaist Company fire?

_____

_____

? Critical Thinking

7. Why is a strike not effective if strikebreakers are called in?

_____

_____

? Determining Cause and Effect

8. Name two effects of the Haymarket Riot.

_____

_____

✎ Sequencing

9. What happened at Andrew Carnegie's factory *just after* the governor sent soldiers to protect the strikebreakers?

_____

_____

Workers called her "Mother Jones" because she fought so hard for their rights. Mother Jones spent 50 years fighting for workers' rights.

In 1911 a terrible fire broke out at a women's clothing factory in New York City. The factory was owned by the Triangle Shirtwaist Company. (A shirtwaist is a type of woman's blouse.) The factory was a sweatshop. The workers were mostly young immigrant women. They could not escape the fire. Why? The company had locked the doors. Nearly 150 people died. This fire led to more demands for safer workplaces. A union called the International Ladies' Garment Workers Union (ILGWU) led these demands.

Economic depression hit working people hard in the 1870s and 1890s. In 1873, companies cut their costs by paying workers less. Some companies laid off workers.

Labor unions responded by having many workers go on strike. Sometimes strikes turned violent. One example was in 1877. Companies hired workers called **strikebreakers.** Strikebreakers took the place of the striking workers, and the work continued.

In 1886, striking workers gathered in Haymarket Square in Chicago. They were striking against the McCormick Harvester Company. The strikers wanted an eight-hour workday. Police broke up the rally and injured several strikers.

The next day, a large crowd gathered to protest what had happened to the workers. The police tried hard to break up the crowd.

Someone threw a bomb, which killed a policeman. A riot started, and more people were killed and injured. This event is known as the Haymarket Riot. It turned many people against labor unions. It made people think that labor unions caused violence.

Another important strike took place in 1892. Workers went on strike at Andrew Carnegie's steel plant in Homestead, Pennsylvania. The strikers were protesting cuts to their wages.

The managers of the plant hired strikebreakers. They were not members of the union. The managers hired guards to protect the strikebreakers. The guards and striking workers fought, and at least ten people died.

Pennsylvania's governor sent soldiers to protect the strikebreakers. The plant reopened with nonunion workers. Membership in the steelworkers union dropped.

The Industrial Age

Lesson 4 Workers in the Industrial Age, *Continued*

Two years later, in 1894, there was another dramatic, violent strike. It is called the Pullman Strike because it took place at George Pullman's railway-car factory near Chicago.

Pullman's workers went on strike when the company cut their wages. Members of a railroad workers' union helped the strikers. They refused to take care of trains that included Pullman cars.

Pullman and the railroad owners fought back. They convinced government leaders to get an **injunction**. This was a court order. It forced the union to handle the trains. The government said the union workers were blocking the railways "and holding up the mails." The strike went on, however. President Grover Cleveland sent in soldiers to end the strike.

The failure of the Pullman Strike was another blow to the union movement. Still, workers continued their efforts to get better pay and better working conditions.

Check for Understanding

Identify three things that labor unions tried to change.

_____

_____

_____

Why did unions become more popular during the Industrial Age?

_____

_____

📝 Explaining

10. Why did the government order railroad workers to take care of all trains?

_____

_____

✅ Reading Check

11. Why did many people turn against unions in the late 1800s?

_____

_____

FOLDABLES

12. Place a three-tab Foldable along the dotted line to cover Check for Understanding. Label the top tab *Employers*, the middle tab *Labor Unions* and the bottom tab *Employees*. On the the tabs, write words and phrases that you remember about each and explain how Labor Unions were in the middle of these two groups. Use your Foldable to help answer Check for Understanding.

An Urban Society

Lesson 1 The New Immigrants

ESSENTIAL QUESTION

Why do people move?

GUIDING QUESTIONS

1. *Why did many people immigrate to the United States during this period?*
2. *How did immigrants adjust to their new life in the United States?*

Terms to Know

assimilate blend in with the main, larger group of people

emigrate to leave the country where one was born

ethnic group people with the same culture or national background

nativist person who is against new immigrants coming to their country

recruit hire workers for jobs

steerage part of the ship where poor people traveled because tickets were cheaper

Where in the world?

When did it happen?

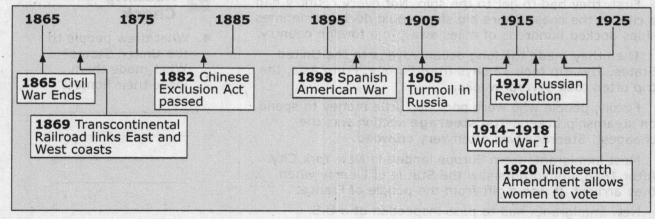

1865	1875	1885	1895	1905	1915	1925

1865 Civil War Ends

1869 Transcontinental Railroad links East and West coasts

1882 Chinese Exclusion Act passed

1898 Spanish American War

1905 Turmoil in Russia

1917 Russian Revolution

1914–1918 World War I

1920 Nineteenth Amendment allows women to vote

networks

An Urban Society

Lesson 1 The New Immigrants, *Continued*

A Flood of Immigrants

In the middle of the 1800s, immigrants to the United States were mostly from northern and western Europe. By the late 1800s, most immigrants were coming from southern and eastern Europe. They came from Italy, Russia, Poland, Hungary, Turkey, Greece, Serbia, and Croatia. Immigrants also came from China and Japan.

Many of the new immigrants were Catholic or Jewish. Most of the United States was Protestant. Also, most immigrants did not speak English. For these two reasons, they did not blend into U.S. society at first.

People decided to leave their home countries, or **emigrate,** because of problems there. The people heard that the United States offered many opportunities, so they moved there to have a better life.

Reasons to Leave Europe	Reasons to Go to the United States
poverty	jobs
overcrowding	land
crop failure	chance for a better life
lack of work	
unfair laws against certain ethnic groups	

Immigrants came to the United States even though the trip was often very hard to make.

First, they had to get to the ship. Not every country had a city on the coast where big ships could dock. Sometimes ships docked hundreds of miles away, in a foreign country.

Then they made the long ocean voyage to the United States. The trip took 12 days from Europe. From Asia, the trip often took several weeks.

Finally, people who were poor had little money to spend on steamship tickets. The **steerage** section was the cheapest. Steerage was often very crowded.

Most immigrants from Europe landed in New York City. After 1886, immigrants saw the Statue of Liberty when they arrived. It was a gift from the people of France.

New immigrants had to pass inspection at a U.S. government center before they could enter the country. Immigrants from Europe went to Ellis Island, near

? Contrasting

1. How were new immigrants different from immigrants who had come before?

_____

_____

_____

Mark the Text

2. Put checkmarks beside the three reasons why it was hard for immigrants to get to the United States.

? Drawing Conclusions

3. Where did most European immigrants land?

_____

✓ Reading Check

4. What drew people to the United States? What made them leave their homes?

_____

_____

_____

_____

290

An Urban Society

Lesson 1 The New Immigrants, *Continued*

? Critical Thinking

5. List the three problems immigrants had to solve in the order you think is most important.

_____

_____

_____

Explaining

6. Why did new immigrants from the same ethnic group often live in the same neighborhood?

_____

_____

_____

FOLDABLES®

? Analyzing

7. Use a one-tab Foldable and place it along the dotted line. Write the title *Cause and Effect of Nativist Attitudes*. On both sides, explain the reasons and results of opposition to immigration.

New York City. Most Asian immigrants sailed to California. They went through a government center on Angel Island, near San Francisco.

Government inspectors asked many questions and wrote down the name of each immigrant. Each immigrant had a health exam. Immigrants who did not pass this inspection could not enter the United States.

The Immigrant Experience

Immigrants to the United States faced important problems:

- Where would they work?
- Where would they live?
- How would they get used to life in their new country?

Finding a job was not easy. Sometimes immigrants were **recruited,** or hired, for a job even before they left their homeland. These were often unskilled jobs, such as unloading cargo or digging ditches. Some industries were growing fast and needed immigrant workers. For example, steel factories in Pittsburgh, Pennsylvania, hired immigrant men who worked 12 hours a day, seven days a week. Many immigrants worked long hours making clothing in factories called sweatshops.

Immigrants had to **assimilate,** or fit in with, life in the United States. They also wanted to keep their own culture alive. It was sometimes hard to do both. Parents spoke their native language, but their children learned English at school and with friends. Women in the United States often had more freedom than they did in their homelands.

Another problem immigrants faced was where to live. Many immigrants came from farms and small villages. In the United States, they could not afford farms, so they often lived in cities.

People from the same **ethnic group** often lived in the same neighborhood. There they tried to preserve their old way of life. Their houses of worship were like those in the old country. They published newspapers in their native languages. Their neighborhoods had theaters, stores, and social clubs that kept the old languages and customs alive.

Some Americans, called **nativists,** didn't want the new immigrants to come to the United States. They thought:

- New immigrants would take jobs from them.
- Employers would pay low wages to everyone, because immigrants were willing to work for low wages.

Glue Foldable here

An Urban Society

Lesson 1 The New Immigrants, *Continued*

Nativists wanted government to take action, so Congress passed laws to keep immigrants out.

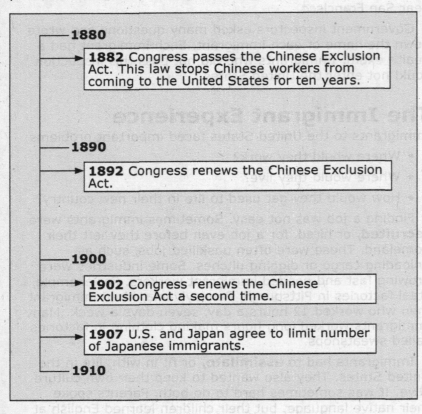

1880

1882 Congress passes the Chinese Exclusion Act. This law stops Chinese workers from coming to the United States for ten years.

1890

1892 Congress renews the Chinese Exclusion Act.

1900

1902 Congress renews the Chinese Exclusion Act a second time.

1907 U.S. and Japan agree to limit number of Japanese immigrants.

1910

///////////Glue Foldable here//////////////////

Check for Understanding

List two problems immigrants might have faced before leaving their home countries, and describe why they believed America would be different.

1. _____

2. _____

Why did factories hire immigrants?

_____

_____

_____

? **Making Connections**

8. What immigration problems are in the news today?

_____

_____

_____

✓ **Reading Check**

9. What were the main reasons some people opposed immigration?

_____

_____

_____

FOLDABLES®

10. Use a three-tab Foldable and place it along the dotted line to cover Check for Understanding. Write the title *New Immigrants* on the anchor tab. Label the three tabs *Before Sailing*, *During the Trip*, and *After Reaching America*. Use both sides to summarize what you remember about why people immigrated, their journey, and their new lives.

networks

An Urban Society

Lesson 2 Moving to the City

ESSENTIAL QUESTION

Why do people move?

GUIDING QUESTIONS

1. **What factors led to the growth of cities?**

2. **What problems faced the people who lived in urban areas?**

3. **What actions addressed the problems of cities?**

Terms to Know

middle class group of people who make a comfortable amount of money but are not rich

settlement house place in a city where poor people could get help

skyscraper very tall building in a city

slum run-down area where poor people live

suburb place outside the city center where people live

tenement run-down, crowded apartment buildings in cities

urban having to do with cities

Where in the world?

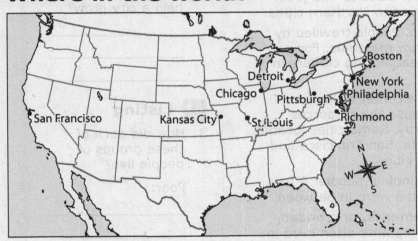

When did it happen?

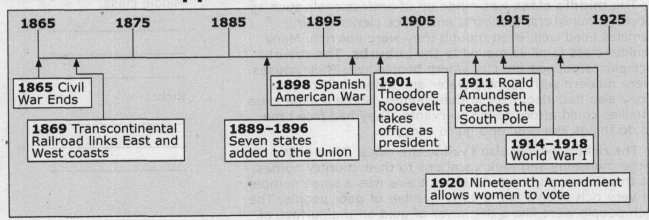

Lesson 2 Moving to the City, *Continued*

The Rise of Cities

After the Civil War, cities were growing fast. By 1910, almost half of all Americans lived in cities. The United States was becoming more **urban**—a nation of cities.

Immigration was one reason cities were growing. In 1890, 80 percent of the people who lived in big cities like New York, Detroit, and Chicago were immigrants.

At the same time, many Americans who had been born on farms were moving to cities. New farming machinery meant that fewer people were needed to work on the farm. These people still needed jobs, so they moved to cities to find work.

After the Civil War, African Americans began moving to cities. First, they moved to Southern cities to find jobs. Later, many African Americans moved to Northern cities.

Transportation was changing, too. People traveled by railroad. The railroad also moved raw materials. For example, it carried cattle to the meatpacking centers in Chicago and Kansas City.

The city of Pittsburgh grew into a center of iron and steel manufacturing. This was because the resources needed for that industry were nearby. Some cities located on the coasts developed as seaports. San Francisco and New York were two important port cities.

Cities became crowded with all kinds of people. A few were rich, many were poor, and some were in between.

The poorest people lived in **tenements,** or crowded, run-down apartment buildings. Immigrants often lived in tenements. Tenements were located in **slums,** or poor neighborhoods.

The **middle class** was made up of professionals such as doctors, ministers, teachers, and office clerks. Their families lived well, even though they were not rich. Many middle-class families moved to the **suburbs.** The suburbs are places outside the city where people live. Their houses were modern with running water and indoor bathrooms. They also had electricity in their homes. Some middle-class families could afford to hire servants. They had free time to do things like read and go to concerts.

The richest people also lived in the cities. They built large mansions and took vacations to their country homes. At this time in the United States, there was a small number of very rich people and a large number of poor people. The rich people were like a thin layer of gold on the surface of

Visualize It

1. Describe what you would find in an urban area.

_____

_____

_____

Reading Check

2. What kinds of things help a city grow?

_____

_____

_____

Listing

3. How did each of these groups of people live?

Poor:

_____

_____

_____

Middle class:

_____

_____

_____

Rich:

_____

_____

_____

netw⊕rks

Lesson 2 Moving to the City, *Continued*

✔ **Reading Check**

4. In what ways were cities unhealthy places to live?

_____

_____

_____

✏ **Identifying**

5. List three ways people tried to make life in the cities better.

_____

_____

_____

❓ **Critical Thinking**

6. What effects would a park have on a city with many tall buildings?

_____

_____

_____

_____

society. When something is covered in a thin layer of gold, but is not gold underneath, it is called *gilded*. That is why this period in U.S. history is known as the "Gilded Age."

Troubles in the Cities

The fast growth of cities caused problems. Cities were crowded and dirty. There was garbage in the city streets and animal waste from horses.

Because the cities were not kept clean, people often got sick. In 1900, in Chicago, many babies died before they were a year old. They died of diseases like measles, whooping cough, and diphtheria. New York City took steps to control the spread of disease. Children were checked in schools for disease. The city sent nurses to people's homes and set up health clinics.

Crime was another problem in cities. Poor people, especially homeless children, committed some **minor** crimes. There were neighborhood gangs, too.

Some individuals wanted to help with the problems of cities. They worked to help the poor and to improve their way of life. Some of those who helped were religious groups. They ran homes for orphans, and ran prisons, hospitals, and recreation centers. Other people started up **settlement houses** to help poor people.

The Changing City

As cities grew, they began to change. People built skyscrapers, improved transportation, and created parks.

In a city, space is very limited. Architects, who plan and build buildings, began to build upward. Two things made it possible to build taller buildings:

- The buildings were strengthened by iron supports.
- Elisha Otis invented the elevator in 1852.

In 1884, William LeBaron Jenney put up a 10-story office building in Chicago. It was the world's first **skyscraper.** More followed. In 1913, the Woolworth Building in New York was the tallest building in the world—55 stories.

A group called the "City Beautiful" movement wanted people in the city to be able to enjoy nature. They wanted to set aside parts of a city where people could not build, and put parks there instead.

An Urban Society

Lesson 2 Moving to the City, *Continued*

One such person was Frederick Law Olmsted. Olmsted designed New York City's Central Park and parks in other cities, too, such as Boston and Chicago.

New forms of transportation also helped to change cities. First, there were streetcars, which were pulled by horses. Then San Francisco built a system of cable cars. Richmond, Virginia, began to use trolley cars. A trolley is a small train with an electric motor. In 1897, the nation's first subway opened in Boston. In 1904, New York City opened the first section of its subway system. People used iron and steel in building these trains and the rails they traveled on.

Steel bridges also improved transportation in cities. Bridges connected parts of the cities that were separated by rivers. The Eads Bridge in St. Louis, Missouri, crossed the Mississippi River. The Brooklyn Bridge connected Manhattan and Brooklyn in New York City.

New forms of transportation connected parts of cities. They also helped people who lived in the suburbs. Suburbs grew up outside of cities, along the train or trolley lines.

////////////////////Glue Foldable here ////////////////////

Check for Understanding

List two ways that cities changed.

1. _____

2. _____

Name and describe three groups of people who lived in and around large cities.

1. _____

2. _____

3. _____

Mark the Text

7. Draw circles around the four new types of transportation that changed cities.

Reading Check

8. How did iron and steel change how cities looked and worked?

_____

_____

_____

FOLDABLES

9. Glue a three-tab Foldable under a one-tab Foldable. Place this Foldable booklet over Check for Understanding. Label the one-tab Foldable *Cities*. Label the three-tab Foldable *Rich*, *Middle Class*, and *Poor*. Use both sides of the top tab to list words and phrases you remember about growing cities. On the three-tab Foldable, list facts about the lifestyles of the different economic groups living in the city and suburbs.

netw✷rks

An Urban Society

Lesson 3 A Changing Culture

ESSENTIAL QUESTION
How do new ideas change the way people live?

GUIDING QUESTIONS
1. **What changes expanded opportunities for education?**
2. **How did the literature of this time period reflect the values of American society?**
3. **Why did new forms of recreation develop?**

Terms to Know
jazz form of music developed by African Americans

land-grant colleges colleges paid for by the sale of certain pieces of land

ragtime form of music related to jazz

spectator sport sport that fans enjoy watching

vaudeville live performance with singing, dancing, magic

yellow journalism a form of shocking news reporting that used many pictures and was not always accurate

Where in the world?

When did it happen?

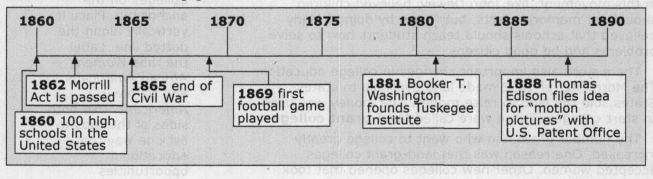

| 1860 | 1865 | 1870 | 1875 | 1880 | 1885 | 1890 |

1862 Morrill Act is passed

1860 100 high schools in the United States

1865 end of Civil War

1869 first football game played

1881 Booker T. Washington founds Tuskegee Institute

1888 Thomas Edison files idea for "motion pictures" with U.S. Patent Office

297

An Urban Society

Lesson 3 A Changing Culture, *Continued*

Expanding Education

As American cities and American industry grew, education became more and more important. By 1914, most states had laws saying children had to go to school. More than 80 percent of all children between the ages of 5 and 17 went to school.

This change in education is clear in the growing number of high schools in the country.

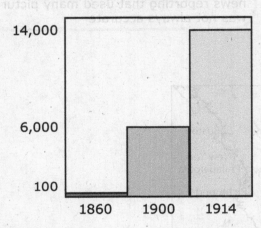

Number of U.S. High Schools

Many boys had to work instead of going to high school, so most high school students were girls.

These new educational chances were not for everyone. Often, African American children were not allowed to go to school with white children. In the South, many African American children received little or no schooling.

Around 1900, "progressive education" developed. People in this movement, like John Dewey, believed children should not memorize facts, but "learn by doing." Many believed that schools should teach students how to solve problems and be good citizens.

There were also important changes in college education. The Morrill Act of 1862 made land available to states. States sold the land to raise money. The money was used to start colleges. These were called **land-grant colleges**.

The number of women who went to college greatly increased. One reason was that land-grant colleges accepted women. Other new colleges opened that took only woman students. Fifty years later, almost 40 percent of college students were women.

Mark the Text

1. Underline the sentence that explains why education grew in the United States during this time.

_____

_____

Reading Check

2. Who benefited most from the new educational opportunities?

_____

_____

FOLDABLES

Identifying

3. Use a three-tab Foldable and write the title *Schools and Colleges* on the anchor tab. Place it vertically along the dotted line. Label the tabs *Women*, *African Americans*, and *Native Americans*. Use both sides of the tabs to list one way that educational opportunities changed for each.

Lesson 3 A Changing Culture, Continued

Copyright by The McGraw-Hill Companies.

Defining

4. List and define the two new styles of writing that developed during this time.

_____

_____

_____

Making Connnections

5. How are newspapers like the Internet?

_____

_____

_____

Reading Check

6. Why were there so many newspapers and magazines?

_____

_____

_____

_____

_____

Colleges like the Hampton Institute also began providing education for African American students. Booker T. Washington learned to be a teacher at Hampton Institute. In 1881, Washington founded a school in Alabama called the Tuskegee Institute. George Washington Carver joined its staff. Carver did scientific research. He found hundreds of uses for the peanut. He even found ways to make plastics and paper from peanuts.

Native Americans went to reservation schools and boarding schools. These schools provided useful training, but they also cut off Native Americans from their traditions and families.

A Nation of Readers

As education expanded, people began to read more. As a result, more new books, magazines, and newspapers were published. Also, more libraries opened during this period. Every state set up free public libraries.

Writers explored new subjects in new ways. One new style of writing was called *realism*. Realism tells stories about ordinary people. Another new style of writing was called *regionalism*. Stories in this style are set in one region of the country. The writer Mark Twain used both realism and regionalism in his stories. Other important writers from this time are Stephen Crane, Jack London, Edith Wharton, Paul Laurence Dunbar, and Horatio Alger.

There were new inventions for printing, making paper, and communication. Large cities, with many readers, often had many newspapers. Many ethnic groups published their own newspapers in different languages.

Joseph Pulitzer and William Randolph Hearst were two important newspaper publishers. They used pictures, dramatic stories, and large, shocking headlines. This is called **yellow journalism.**

The number of magazines also grew at this time. There were 700 magazines in 1865 and 5,000 in 1900. Today, you can still read some of these magazines, like the *Atlantic Monthly*, *Harper's Magazine*, and *Ladies' Home Journal*.

Leisure and the Arts

As fewer people worked in farming and more people worked in industry, many Americans had more free time. To fill that free time, new forms of recreation were offered to ordinary people.

An Urban Society

Lesson 3 A Changing Culture, *Continued*

There was a rise in **spectator sports.** In spectator sports, fans watch teams play a game. Three kinds of spectator sports are baseball, football, and basketball. In addition to spectator sports, people enjoyed playing games themselves. Wealthy people played tennis and golf. Many people enjoyed bicycle riding.

People went to the theater in their free time, too. Large cities had many theaters. Some shows were serious, and others were light and funny. In **vaudeville** shows, people sang, danced, told jokes, and did magic acts. Tickets were cheap, so vaudeville was popular. People also enjoyed going to the circus.

The first "moving pictures" were invented in the 1880s by Thomas Edison. People paid five cents to see a movie at a nickelodeon.

New forms of art and music developed after the Civil War as well. The new forms were clearly American. Two important American painters are Frederic Remington, who painted scenes of the American West, and Winslow Homer, who painted farmers, campers, and sea scenes.

The United States developed its own styles of music, too. One of these was marching music. African Americans in New Orleans developed **jazz**. Jazz mixed work songs, gospel music, and African rhythms. An important feature of jazz is its beat, called syncopation (SING•kuh•PAY•shuhn). **Ragtime** music was related to jazz. Scott Joplin was the leading composer of ragtime music.

Big cities like New York had fine symphony orchestras and opera houses.

/ / / / / / / / / / Glue Foldable here / / / / / / / / / / /

Check for Understanding

By 1914, most states had laws requiring children to go to school. How do you think this law changed the future of America?

_____

_____

Why do you think the culture of America changed so much in the years after the Civil War?

_____

_____

? **Critical Thinking**

7. Name other spectator sports people enjoy today.

_____

_____

_____

Mark the Text

8. Circle the name of the person who invented movies.

✓ Reading Check

9. What kinds of American music developed during this time?

_____

_____

FOLDABLES

10. Attach a three-tab Foldable along the dotted line to cover the Check for Understanding. Write *Important Changes* on the anchor tab. Label the three tabs *education*, *literature*, and *leisure*. Use both sides to list words and phrases you remember about each.

![networks logo]

The Progressive Era

Lesson 1 The Movement Begins

ESSENTIAL QUESTION

Why do societies change?

GUIDING QUESTIONS

1. **Which reforms addressed political and economic problems?**

2. **Why did reformers emerge during this era?**

Terms to Know

oligopoly a few large companies that took charge of prices for an entire industry

muckrakers reporters who told the public of corruption

initiative the right of voters to place an issue on the ballot in a state election

referendum the right of voters to accept or reject laws

recall the right of voters to remove elected officials who lacked ability for their jobs

When did it happen?

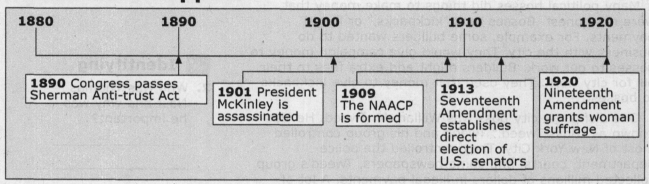

1880 — 1890 — 1900 — 1910 — 1920

1890 Congress passes Sherman Anti-trust Act

1901 President McKinley is assassinated

1909 The NAACP is formed

1913 Seventeenth Amendment establishes direct election of U.S. senators

1920 Nineteenth Amendment grants woman suffrage

What do you know?

In the first column, answer the questions based on what you know before you study. After this lesson, complete the last column.

Now ...		Later ...
	What kinds of problems did Progressives focus on?	
	Why was the Pendleton Act important?	
	What is the purpose of a recall election?	
	How did the Seventeenth Amendment change Congress?	

The Progressive Era

Lesson 1 The Movement Begins, *Continued*

Taking on Corruption

There were problems in American society in the late 1800s. Many Americans called for reform. Reformers are people who want to change society to make it better. Reformers during this time were called progressives. Progressives focused on problems affecting cities, government, and business.

"Political machines" were powerful groups linked to political parties. These powerful groups controlled local government in many cities. Cities were divided into political districts. A member of the political machine controlled jobs in each district. This person was called a political boss.

Many political bosses did things to make money that were not honest. Bosses took "kickbacks," or illegal payments. For example, some builders wanted to do business with the city. They would give campaign money to bosses to get work. Builders might add extra fees to their bill for city work. They used that money to give kickbacks to bosses.

One dishonest city boss was William M. Tweed. He was known as "Boss Tweed." Tweed and his group controlled most of New York City. They controlled the police department, courts, and some newspapers. Tweed's group collected millions of dollars in illegal payments. A lot of these payments came from companies that did business with the city. Thomas Nast was a political cartoonist. His political cartoons were printed in *Harper's Weekly.* The cartoons showed how Tweed's group did illegal things. Tweed later went to prison.

/ / / / / / / / / / / Glue Foldable here / / / / / / / / / / /

Reformers wanted to stop the power of political bosses. They worked to make city governments more honest and efficient.

Reformers wanted to end something called the spoils system. In the spoils system, elected officials rewarded their friends. They gave jobs to people who supported them. They did favors for them, too. Many people were not qualified to do the jobs given to them.

President Hayes and President Garfield both tried to change the spoils system. Neither of them succeeded. Congress passed the **Pendleton Act** in 1883. This act created the Civil Service Commission, which gave tests for people wanting federal jobs. If they passed the test, it would prove they had the skills to do the job. By 1900, the commission was in charge of hiring many federal workers.

302

 Mark the Text

1. Underline the definition of *kickbacks*.

 **Identifying**

2. Who was Thomas Nast and why was he important?

_____

_____

FOLDABLES®

Defining

3. Glue a one-tab Foldable over "Reformers wanted to stop the power of political bosses." Label the anchor tab *Common Practice.* Write *Spoils System* in the middle of the Foldable tab. Create a memory map by drawing arrows around the title and writing six words or phrases about the spoils system.

The Progressive Era

Lesson 1 The Movement Begins, *Continued*

✅ **Reading Check**

4. How did the Pendleton Act help to end the spoils system?

_____

_____

✏️ **Explaining**

5. What are tariffs? Why did American business owners like them?

_____

_____

_____

✅ **Reading Check**

6. What was one major difference between socialists and progressives?

_____

_____

Many Americans believed that trusts had too much control over the economy and the government. A trust is a powerful group of companies. Congress passed the **Sherman Antitrust Act.** The act was passed in 1890. It was the first federal law to control trusts.

Railroads were important to people and businesses. Large railroad companies wanted to make more money. The companies agreed to not compete against each other. Together, they set higher prices.

The railroads formed an **oligopoly.** An oligopoly is a group of large companies that set prices for a type of product or service. Reformers wanted to limit the rates that railroads charged. Congress passed the **Interstate Commerce Act** in 1887. It made railroads charge fair rates.

Tariffs are taxes charged on imported goods. Imported goods are made in other countries. Tariffs would make imported goods cost more. Congress passed a tariff bill in 1890. It increased tariffs on many imported goods. Many American business owners liked high tariffs. They thought it would make Americans buy more of their products.

The New Reformers

In the early 1900s, reformers wanted to make society better. Reformers believed that people were not treated fairly. They came up with new ideas to solve problems in society. These ideas included socialism and progressivism.

Socialists felt that it was unfair that a few people had most of the wealth and power in America. They believed more people should have wealth and power. Socialists wanted the government to own and operate businesses. Eugene V. Debs helped create the American Socialist Party in 1898. Debs ran for president five times. He never received more than 6 percent of the popular vote.

Progressives also believed that it was unfair for a few people to own most of the wealth and power. Progressives disagreed with socialists on how to solve this problem. They did not think the government should own businesses. Progressives wanted the government to regulate businesses. This meant that the government would make rules that businesses would have to follow.

Newspaper reporters helped the reformers. They investigated problems and wrote newspaper and magazine stories about them. These reporters were called

The Progressive Era

Lesson 1 The Movement Begins, *Continued*

muckrakers. Their stories told the people about the "muck," or dirt, in business.

One muckraker was Ida Tarbell. She wrote articles about the oil trust's unfair practices. People became upset after reading her articles. They asked the government to take charge of big business.

Another muckraker was Upton Sinclair. He wrote a book called *The Jungle* (1906). It described the dirty and unsafe conditions of the Chicago meatpacking industry. Americans were shocked. Congress passed the Meat Inspection Act and the Pure Food and Drug Act in 1906. It made businesses put labels on food and medicine. The labels told people what the businesses had put into food and medicine. Food that might cause harm could not be sold.

Oregon made important reforms. The **initiative** allowed citizens to put an issue up for voting. The **referendum** allowed people to vote for or against a law. The **recall** allowed voters to remove elected officials from office. These reforms were called the Oregon System. Many states began using these reforms.

The Constitution allowed state legislatures to choose senators. People felt there were problems doing it this way. Party bosses often controlled the process. Businesses also were too involved in the process. Progressives wanted people to be able to vote for their senators directly.

Congress passed the Seventeenth Amendment to the Constitution in 1912. It allowed people to vote for their senators in elections.

/ / / / / / / / / / / Glue Foldable here / / / / / / / / / / / / /

Check for Understanding

List two forms of media that helped Progressive reformers.

_____

_____

How did the Progressive reforms of this time make life better for Americans today?

_____

_____

Identifying

7. What is a *muckraker*?

_____

_____

_____

FOLDABLES

8. Cut a two-tab Foldable in half to make four tabs. Place it along the dotted line to cover Check for Understanding. Write *Progressives & Reforms* on the anchor tab. Label the tabs *Pendleton Act*, *Sherman Antitrust Act*, *Interstate Commerce Act*, and *17th Amendment*. On the front and back of the tabs, write words or phrases that outline what you remember about each Progressive reform.

The Progressive Era

Lesson 2 Women and Progressives

ESSENTIAL QUESTION
Why do societies change?

GUIDING QUESTIONS
1. **How did opportunities for women change during this era?**
2. **What was the goal of the suffrage movement?**
3. **What methods did women use to bring about social reform?**

Terms to Know
suffragists men and women who fought for woman suffrage, or women's right to vote

prohibition laws that banned making or selling liquor

When did it happen?

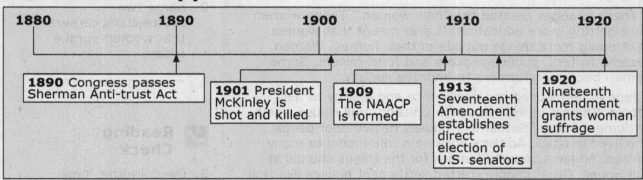

| 1880 | 1890 | 1900 | 1910 | 1920 |

1890 Congress passes Sherman Anti-trust Act

1901 President McKinley is shot and killed

1909 The NAACP is formed

1913 Seventeenth Amendment establishes direct election of U.S. senators

1920 Nineteenth Amendment grants woman suffrage

What do you know?

In the first column, answer the questions based on what you know before you study. After this lesson, complete the last column.

Now ...		Later ...
	What is "suffrage"?	
	What was the purpose of the Nineteenth Amendment?	

305

The Progressive Era

Lesson 2 Women and Progressives, *Continued*

New Roles for Women

Americans wanted urban reform in the late 1800s. This meant that people wanted to improve cities. Many leaders of urban reform were women. These women were often from the middle class. The lives of middle-class women changed during the late 1800s. They had more free time. Their lives were not based on taking care of a home.

People need to have special skills to do professional jobs. This usually means they have to go to college to learn new facts and skills. Many middle-class women began going to college. This helped them to get professional jobs. Many professional women were teachers. Some worked in nursing, medicine, and other fields.

These changes created the "new woman." These women were getting more education. It also meant that women were doing more things outside of their homes. Women became writers, public speakers and fund-raisers. Some women became reformers to improve society.

Jane Addams used her intelligence and energy to help people. She set up Hull House in Chicago. Hull House was a settlement house. Settlement houses helped poor people who lived in cities. Addams became a role model to many women. Addams became famous for the things she did at Hull House. Other people started settlement houses like Hull House.

Women found another way to use their skills and energy. Some women started women's clubs. The number of women's clubs grew. At first, women members were interested in things such as music and painting. Later, many clubs became more concerned about social problems.

Some clubs refused to allow African Americans. African American women began to set up their own clubs. In 1896 women from these clubs created the National Association of Colored Women. Mary Church Terrell was the founder of the association. She was also the association's first president. She worked hard to get more rights for women.

Women and Voting Rights

The Fifteenth Amendment had given voting rights to freed men. It did not give women the right to vote. Some men and women became **suffragists.** Suffragists believed that women should have the right to vote. Suffragists worked hard to try to win this right for women.

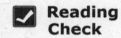 **Listing**

1. Name two ways the role of women changed in the late 1800s.

_____

_____

? Making Connections

2. Name two professional careers that women pursue today.

_____

_____

✓ Reading Check

3. Describe the "new woman" of the late 1800s.

_____

_____

Explaining

4. What did suffragists want to achieve?

_____

_____

The Progressive Era

Lesson 2 Women and Progressives, *Continued*

Identifying

5. Who formed the National Woman Suffrage Association?

_____

_____

Reading Check

6. What were some reasons that suffragists wanted the vote for women?

_____

_____

Describing

7. How did women put pressure on lawmakers?

_____

_____

Suffragists created groups. The purpose of these groups was to help women get the right to vote. Elizabeth Cady Stanton gave speeches about women. She talked about how women were not treated fairly. At a women's rights convention in 1848 she asked that women be given the right to vote. She and Susan B. Anthony worked together for years for suffrage. Stanton helped create the National Woman Suffrage Association in 1869. Stanton also became the association's president. This association and another suffrage group joined together in 1890. It became known as the National American Woman Suffrage Association. Stanton and then Anthony served as president.

Many working-class women wanted to have the right to vote. They hoped they could elect people who would help women and protect female workers.

More and more people began joining the suffrage movement. Suffragists put pressure on lawmakers. They organized marches. They also made speeches on street corners.

The suffragists won some early victories. Wyoming led the country by giving women the right to vote. Some other states began to let women vote. Suffragists continued to work hard. They wanted women to be able to vote in every state. Alice Paul founded the National Woman's Party in 1916. Paul wanted suffrage for women. She also wanted women to have equal rights.

Alice Paul met with President Woodrow Wilson in 1917 to talk about suffrage. Wilson did not support woman suffrage at that time. Paul organized a protest. They protested in front of the White House. Many of the protesters were arrested for blocking the sidewalk. Some people felt that the women did not do anything wrong. The arrested women started a hunger strike. This meant that they refused to eat.

More people began to support the woman suffrage movement. By 1917, the National American Woman Suffrage Association had more than two million members. President Wilson had changed his mind. He began supporting woman suffrage. By 1919, women could vote in some elections in most of the 48 states. This caused Congress to talk about the issue. The House of Representatives passed the Nineteenth Amendment in 1918. The Senate passed it in 1919. The amendment gave women the right to vote. It went into effect in 1920. Women could vote in that year's presidential election.

The Progressive Era

Lesson 2 Women and Progressives, *Continued*

Women and Social Reform

Women became involved in other reform movements. They supported and worked in libraries, schools, and settlement houses. They also raised money for charities.

Some women worked for other causes. They wanted the government to pass laws to help women and children who worked. They wanted the government to inspect factories. They put pressure on Congress. Congress created the Children's Bureau. The Children's Bureau became part of the Labor Department.

Working women also helped the reform movement. Many unions did not allow women to join. The Women's Trade Union League (WTUL) was created in 1903. The WTUL urged working women to start their own labor unions. The league also supported laws that protected the rights of women factory workers.

Women also led the fight against alcohol. The Woman's Christian Temperance Union (WCTU) and the Anti-Saloon League called for temperance. This meant that they supported **prohibition**—laws that would stop the making or selling alcohol.

Some Progressive reformers believed that alcohol caused many problems. They felt that drinking alcohol caused more crime. They also believed that it caused problems with families. Congress passed the Eighteenth Amendment in 1919. This amendment made it illegal to make, transport, or sell alcohol in the United States. The Eighteenth Amendment became known as the Prohibition Law. It was ratified in 1919.

////////////////// Glue Foldable here /////////////////

Check for Understanding

How did education change the lives of some women during the Progressive Era?

_____

_____

Why do you think it took so long for women to have the right to vote?

_____

_____

☑ **Reading Check**

8. What was the goal of the temperance movement?

_____

_____

FOLDABLES

9. Use a two-tab Foldable and cut the tabs in half to make four tabs. Place it along the dotted line to cover Check for Understanding. Write the *Women and Progressives* on the anchor tab. Label the four tabs *Women's Roles*, *Women's Clubs*, *Women's Right to Vote*, and *Women and Social Reform*. Use the front and back of the tabs to record what you remember about how progressives influenced each. Use your Foldable to help answer Check for Understanding.

The Progressive Era

Lesson 3 Presidents of the Progressive Era

ESSENTIAL QUESTION

Why do societies change?

GUIDING QUESTIONS

1. **How successful was Roosevelt in implementing his policies?**
2. **What were the similarities and differences between the policies of Roosevelt and Taft?**

Terms to Know

trustbuster a government official who breaks up business groups that limit competition

arbitration the process of settling disputes by accepting the decision of a neutral party

Square Deal fair and equal treatment for all, as promised by President Theodore Roosevelt

conservation protection of natural resources

When did it happen?

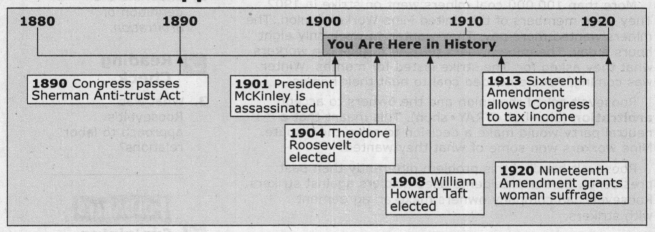

1880 — 1890 — 1900 — 1910 — 1920

You Are Here in History

1890 Congress passes Sherman Anti-trust Act

1901 President McKinley is assassinated

1904 Theodore Roosevelt elected

1908 William Howard Taft elected

1913 Sixteenth Amendment allows Congress to tax income

1920 Nineteenth Amendment grants woman suffrage

What do you know?

In the first column, answer the questions based on what you know before you study. After this lesson, complete the last column.

Now ...		Later ...
	Why was Roosevelt called a trustbuster?	
	What did Americans learn about conservation during the Progressive era?	
	Why did progressives support an income tax?	

netw⊕rks

The Progressive Era

Lesson 3 Presidents of the Progressive Era, *Continued*

Theodore Roosevelt

Theodore Roosevelt was vice president in 1900. He became president after President McKinley was killed in 1901. Only 42 years old, Roosevelt was the youngest president in the country's history. He agreed with progressive ideas.

President Roosevelt wanted to regulate trusts. Trusts were groups of businesses that set their own rules about prices and who could sell that product or service. Some trusts were not following the Sherman Antitrust Act. Roosevelt brought legal charges against many trusts. Roosevelt was called a **trustbuster.** He wanted to break up the trusts he thought were harmful.

More than 100,000 coal miners went on strike in 1902. They were members of the United Mine Workers union. The miners wanted more pay. They wanted to work only eight hours a day. The mine owners refused to give the workers what they asked for. The strike lasted for months. Winter was coming. People needed coal to heat their homes.

Roosevelt asked the union and the owners to accept **arbitration** (ahr•buh•TRAY•shun). This meant that a neutral party would make a decision to solve the dispute. Mine workers won some of what they wanted.

Roosevelt handled this problem differently than past presidents. Earlier presidents used soldiers against strikers. Roosevelt had company owners make an agreement with strikers.

/ / / / / / / / / / / Glue Foldable here / / / / / / / / / / /

Roosevelt ran for president in 1904. He promised the people a **Square Deal.** This meant fair and equal treatment for all. He easily won the election.

Roosevelt's Square Deal called for government regulation of business. This approach differed from that of some earlier presidents. They felt the government should leave businesses alone.

Roosevelt supported the Meat Inspection Act and the Pure Food and Drug Act. The acts gave the government power to visit businesses and **inspect,** or carefully examine, products.

Roosevelt has been called the first environmental president. He believed in the need for **conservation.** This meant that natural resources would be protected and saved. In 1905, Roosevelt suggested making the U.S. Forest Service. He asked Congress to set aside millions of acres of national forests. He also formed the National

✏️ **Explaining**

1. Tell how Roosevelt wanted to handle trusts.

_____

_____

🔤 **Mark the Text**

2. Underline the definition of *arbitration*.

✅ **Reading Check**

3. What was Roosevelt's approach to labor relations?

_____

_____

FOLDABLES

🔤 **Explaining**

4. Glue a one-tab Foldable over "Roosevelt ran for president ...". Label the anchor tab *Roosevelt: 1904.* Write *Square Deal* in the middle of the tab. Make a memory map by drawing arrows around the title and listing five or more words or phrases about Roosevelt's Square Deal promise.

310

Progressive Era

Lesson 3 Presidents of the Progressive Era, *Continued*

Reading Check

Identifying

5. What did the Sixteenth Amendment allow?

_____

_____

Analyzing

6. Why was the tax on individual incomes passed by Congress considered fairer than other kinds of taxes?

_____

_____

Conservation Commission. The commission took the first survey of the country's natural resources.

William Howard Taft

No U.S. president had ever served more than two terms. Roosevelt decided not to run again in 1908. He chose his friend and fellow Republican William Howard Taft to run for president. Roosevelt thought that Taft would carry on the progressive Republican ideas. Taft easily defeated the Democrat's candidate, William Jennings Bryan.

Taft did carry out many of Roosevelt's policies. The Taft administration won more antitrust cases than Roosevelt had won. Taft also favored safety standards for both mines and railroads.

Taft supported the Sixteenth Amendment. It allowed Congress to tax people's income. Progressives believed income taxes were fairer than other taxes. They hoped a new tax would allow the government to lower tariffs. This would lead to lower prices. This would help poor people. The Sixteenth Amendment was added to the Constitution in 1913. Congress also passed laws so that people who made more money had to pay more tax.

Roosevelt and other progressives were disappointed with Taft. They were unhappy that Taft did not fight for a lower tariff. Taft also changed some conservation policies.

By 1912, Roosevelt was unhappy with Taft. Roosevelt decided to run against him for the Republican presidential nomination. Roosevelt won every **primary.** Primaries are elections that help political parties choose candidates. Taft had the backing of party leaders. Taft also had the support of powerful businesses. Taft won the nomination.

Roosevelt and his supporters formed a new political party called the Progressive Party. The Progressives nominated Roosevelt for president. Roosevelt felt ready to fight, so he said, "I feel as fit as a bull moose!" People then called the party the Bull Moose Party. This split in the Republican Party lost votes for both Taft and Roosevelt. It allowed Democrat Woodrow Wilson to win the election.

President Wilson did not like big government or big business. His program was called the "New Freedom." He asked Congress to pass a lower tariff. This would help foreign companies compete with American companies. President Wilson believed this would force American companies to make better products and to lower prices.

The Progressive Era

Lesson 3 Presidents of the Progressive Era, *Continued*

Congress also passed the **Federal Reserve Act** to regulate banking. The act created 12 regional banks. It was supervised by a central board. Many banks had to join the Federal Reserve System and follow its rules.

Wilson wanted the government to have more control over business. In 1914, Congress set up the Federal Trade Commission (FTC). The FTC's job was to see that corporations traded fairly. Wilson also supported the **Clayton Antitrust Act** of 1914. The government could use this act to fight against trusts.

The government also tried to regulate child labor. Congress passed the Keating-Owen Act of 1916. Goods made by children in one state could not be sold in other states. This law was struck down two years later.

The public began to lose interest in progressive ideas. Americans were more concerned with world affairs. By 1914, war was beginning in Europe.

////////////////// Glue Foldable here ////////////////////

Check for Understanding

What part did the Progressive Party play in the presidential election of 1912?

_____

_____

Why do you think there was a shift in interest from progressive reform to world affairs at the end of Wilson's first term?

_____

_____

✓ Reading Check

7. How did Roosevelt's run for the presidency affect the election of 1912?

_____

_____

🖎 Explaining

8. Why did Wilson support lower tariffs?

_____

_____

FOLDABLES®

9. Place a three-tab Foldable along the dotted line to cover Check for Understanding. Write the title *Progressive Presidents* on the anchor tab. Label the tabs *Roosevelt*, *Taft*, and *Wilson*. On both sides of the tabs, list what you remember about the successes of each. Use your Foldable to help answer Check for Understanding.

The Progressive Era

Lesson 4 Excluded From Reform

ESSENTIAL QUESTION
What are the causes and consequences of prejudice and injustice?

GUIDING QUESTIONS
1. **What problems did members of ethnic and religious groups face?**
2. **How did minority groups react to discrimination?**

Terms to Know
discrimination unfair treatment of a person or group, usually because of prejudice about race, ethnic group, religion, age group, or gender
segregation separation of one group from another
mutualistas aid groups for Mexican Americans
barrios Mexican neighborhoods

When did it happen?

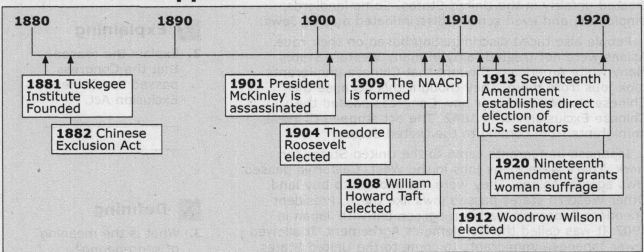

1880 — 1890 — 1900 — 1910 — 1920

1881 Tuskegee Institute Founded

1882 Chinese Exclusion Act

1901 President McKinley is assassinated

1904 Theodore Roosevelt elected

1908 William Howard Taft elected

1909 The NAACP is formed

1912 Woodrow Wilson elected

1913 Seventeenth Amendment establishes direct election of U.S. senators

1920 Nineteenth Amendment grants woman suffrage

What do you know?

In the first column, answer the questions based on what you know before you study. After this lesson, complete the last column.

Now ...		Later ...
	Who was "protected" by the American Protective Association?	
	What was the "Gentleman's Agreement"?	
	What were some of W.E.B. DuBois' accomplishments?	

313

The Progressive Era

Lesson 4 Excluded From Reform, *Continued*

Prejudice and Discrimination

Many Americans born in the United States were white and Protestant. People who were not white and Protestant often faced **discrimination.** *Discrimination* means they received unequal treatment. Immigrants faced discrimination. The government did little to stop discrimination in the 1800s.

Some Americans faced discrimination because of their religion. Some Protestant Americans felt that Catholic immigrants threatened the "American" way of life. The American Protective Association (APA) was created in 1887. Its members would not hire or vote for Catholics.

Many Jewish immigrants came to the United States to escape discrimination in their homelands. Many were treated unfairly in the United States. Some landlords, employers, and even schools discriminated against Jews.

People also faced discrimination based on their race. Asians were not treated fairly in many Western states. Many white Americans thought that Chinese immigrants took jobs from them. They thought this because the Chinese worked for lower pay. Congress passed the Chinese Exclusion Act in 1882. The act stopped Chinese immigrants from coming to the United States.

Japanese immigrants came to the United States for work. There were many jobs in the West. California passed laws against Asians. They were not allowed to buy land. Other Western states passed laws like these. President Theodore Roosevelt made an agreement with Japan in 1907. It was called the Gentlemen's Agreement. It allowed fewer Japanese immigrants to come to the United States. This did little to stop anti-Japanese feelings, however.

African Americans also faced discrimination in the North and the South. African Americans did not have the same rights as white citizens.

Most African Americans lived in the South. Some worked on farms. Others had low-paying jobs in cities. African Americans were separated from white people. They had their own neighborhoods, schools, parks, restaurants, and theaters. The Supreme Court made **segregation** legal in 1896. Segregation means that groups of people are separated. The case of *Plessy* v. *Ferguson* allowed "separate but equal" places for blacks and whites. Most places were not equal at all.

The Ku Klux Klan was a terror group. The Klan wanted America to be white and Protestant. They lashed out against African Americans. They also did not like

Mark the Text

1. Underline the definition of *discrimination*.

Explaining

2. Explain the reason that the Congress passed the Chinese Exclusion Act.

_____

_____

Defining

3. What is the meaning of *segregation*?

_____

_____

Reading Check

4. Which Supreme Court decision made segregation legal?

_____

_____

Lesson 4 Excluded From Reform, *Continued*

immigrants and other minorities. The number of Klan supporters grew. Many Klan members were from the North as well as the South.

The country had economic problems in 1893 and 1907. Many people lost their jobs. Whites often took out their anger on minorities. Whites lynched more than 2,600 African Americans between 1886 and 1916. Most lynchings happened in the South. Some Chinese immigrants were lynched in the West.

Seeking Equal Opportunity

Some reformers had biased, or prejudiced views. These reformers did not believe everyone was equal. Some reforms only helped certain groups of people.

Trade unions would not allow some people to become members. This included African Americans, women, and immigrants. The unions tried to get better working conditions for skilled workers. They did not help many unskilled workers.

Minorities were not allowed to join many progressive groups. African Americans, Native Americans, Mexican Americans, and Jewish Americans created their own groups. They had to fight to be treated fairly on their own.

African Americans rose to the challenge. Booker T. Washington was born into slavery. He taught himself to read. He created the Tuskegee Institute in Alabama in 1881. The school taught African Americans farming and business skills.

Washington felt that African Americans needed more economic power. He thought that it would help African Americans win civil rights. He created the National Negro Business League to help African American businesses.

W.E.B. Du Bois also worked for civil rights. He was the first African American to earn a doctoral degree from Harvard University. He believed the right to vote was important. Du Bois thought that it could end discrimination, stop lynching, and gain better schools.

Du Bois helped start the Niagara Movement in 1905. The movement wanted equal opportunity for African Americans. It wanted to stop discrimination. It also wanted to end legal segregation. The movement led to the creation of the National Association for the Advancement of Colored People (NAACP) in 1910. The NAACP fought for civil rights for African Americans throughout the twentieth century.

Listing

5. List five groups of people, besides women, who were targets of discrimination in the late 1800s and early 1900s.

_____

_____

_____

_____

_____

? Sequencing

6. Which group came before the NAACP?

_____

The Progressive Era

Lesson 4 Excluded From Reform, *Continued*

African American women also created groups. These groups also wanted to end discrimination. The National Association of Colored Women tried to stop violence against African Americans.

Ida B. Wells wrote a book called *A Red Record*. She explained that white people most often lynched successful African Americans. Other lynching victims had businesses that competed against white businesses. Congress did not pass an anti-lynching bill. Still, the number of lynchings dropped because of Wells and other activists.

Native Americans also faced discrimination. They created the Society of American Indians. It was created to make life better for Native Americans. They taught whites about native cultures. One leader was Dr. Carlos Montezuma. He showed people how the government treated Native Americans unfairly. Montezuma believed Native Americans needed to make their own way in white society.

The Mexican American population quickly grew in the early 1900s. Many Mexicans came to the United States. They were escaping fighting and economic problems in Mexico. Mexican Americans created **mutualistas,** or aid groups. They provided insurance and legal help. Some promoted Mexican American rights. Mutualistas tried to improve **barrios,** or Mexican neighborhoods. They helped the poor and tried to solve problems such as overcrowding.

Jewish Americans also faced prejudice. To stop discrimination they created groups such as the American Jewish Committee and the Anti-Defamation League. Many of these groups continue their work today.

/ / / / / / / / / / / / / / Glue Foldable here / / / / / / / / / / / / / /

Check for Understanding

Name two organizations that minorities created to protect their rights.

_____

_____

How did the organizations you named help minorities?

_____

_____

Mark the Text

7. Underline an action of Ida B. Wells to fight against lynching.

Defining

8. What were *mutualistas*?

FOLDABLES

9. Use a two-tab Foldable and cut the tabs in half to make four tabs. Place it to cover Check for Understanding. Write *Actions Against Prejudice* on the anchor tab. Label the tabs *Asian Americans, African Americans, Native Americans* and *Mexican Americans*. Use both sides of the tabs to list words and phrases about actions taken to counter prejudice. Use your Foldable to help answer Check for Understanding.

Rise to World Power

Lesson 1 Seeking New Frontiers

ESSENTIAL QUESTION
Why does conflict develop?

GUIDING QUESTIONS

1. **What did the United States do to open trade with Japan?**

2. **How did Alaska become a territory of the United States?**

Terms to Know

isolationism the belief that a nation should stay out of the affairs of other nations

expansionism the practice of spreading a nation's territorial or economic control beyond its borders

imperialism the policy of extending a nation's rule over other territories and countries

Where in the world?

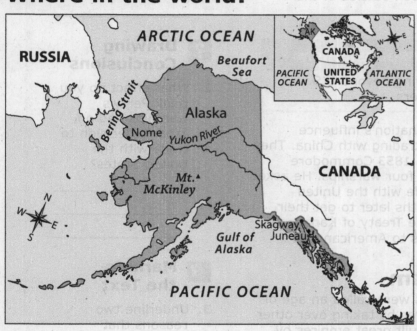

When did it happen?

1853 Commodore Perry visits Japan

1861–1865 Civil War

1867 United States purchases Alaska

1889 Pan-American Conference

1890s Gold discovered in Alaska

317

Lesson 1 Seeking New Frontiers, *Continued*

Changing Foreign Policy

When he left office, President George Washington warned America to stay away from "permanent alliances with ... the foreign world." Some people thought he supported a policy of **isolationism**. This means that the United States would not become involved in world affairs.

Others believed in **expansionism**. They wanted the United States to grow beyond its borders. By the mid-1800s, most of the land between the Atlantic Coast and the Pacific Coast was already settled. People who wanted the United States to expand began to look outside of the nation's borders.

isolationism	expansionism
not becoming involved in world affairs	growing beyond U.S. borders

Americans looked to expand the nation's influence overseas. Merchants were already trading with China. They wanted to trade with Japan also. In 1853 Commodore Matthew Perry sailed to Japan with four warships. He asked the Japanese to open ports for trade with the United States. Perry returned several months later to get their answer. Japanese leaders signed the Treaty of Kanagawa. In it, they agreed to open two ports to American ships.

An Age of Imperialism

The late 1800s and the early 1900s were called an age of **imperialism.** Countries built empires by taking over other lands. Powerful European nations built great empires by taking economic and political control of weaker nations. They were looking for raw materials for manufacturing. They also wanted to sell goods in new areas. They competed against each other for power in Asia and Africa. This competition helped lead to World War I.

After the Civil War, some Americans wanted the United States to build an empire. They wanted the United States to become one of the most powerful nations in the world. William H. Seward was Secretary of State after the Civil War. He supported the idea of an American empire which would control countries in the Caribbean Sea and Central America. He also hoped to control the Pacific Ocean.

His vision, or plan, was to link the Atlantic and Pacific Oceans with a canal through Central America. He also

Marking the Text

1. Underline the sentence that defines *expansionism*. Why did people want to expand beyond America's borders?

_____

_____

Drawing Conclusions

2. What effect do you think Perry's warships had on Japan's decision to trade with the United States?

_____

_____

_____

Marking the Text

3. Underline two reasons that European nations competed for power in Asia and Africa.

Lesson 1 Seeking New Frontiers, *Continued*

wanted to build a railroad system to transport people and goods. The third part of his plan was a telegraph system. It would provide fast communication, or exchange of information, across the new American empire.

Listing

4. List three parts of William Seward's plan for expanded American influence.

_____

_____

_____

Explaining

5. Why did some religious leaders support imperialism?

_____

_____

_____

Describing

6. What was the purpose of the Pan-American Union?

_____

_____

_____

Seward's Plan

- Connect the Atlantic and Pacific Oceans with a canal across Central America

- Build a railroad system serving the United States

- Build a telegraph system for fast communication across the American empire

Seward moved to make his vision come true. In 1867 he bought Alaska from Russia for $7.2 million. It was a low price for an area that is twice the size of Texas. Some people laughed at the purchase because they thought Alaska was worthless. Because Alaska was so cold, they called it "Seward's icebox" and "a polar bear garden." Then gold was discovered in Alaska in the 1890s. Buying Alaska now seemed like a good idea. Alaska later became a U.S. territory in 1912.

Some Americans supported imperialism for another reason. They thought that much of the world was "uncivilized." This included Africa, Asia, and Latin America. They believed that American Christianity and culture would help people in these areas. Some religious leaders thought an American empire would help "lift up" people in other countries and make their lives better.

Another reason for supporting American imperialism was the desire to increase trade. The United States and Latin America already traded a lot in the late 1800s. But American merchants wanted to trade even more. James G. Blaine ran for president in 1884. He declared the United States should expand its trade with Latin America. He did not win the election but later became Secretary of State. To improve relationships with Latin America, he invited Latin American leaders to a Pan-American Conference in Washington, D.C., in 1889. The conference led to the Pan-American Union. Members of the Pan-American Union hoped to work together for the good of all members.

As a country expanding its influence, the United States needed a strong navy. The president of the Naval War

319

Rise to World Power

Lesson 1 Seeking New Frontiers, *Continued*

College, Captain Alfred Thayer Mahan, said that sea power
was essential for a country to be strong. During the 1880s,
the U.S. Navy switched from ships with sails to ships using
steam power. The new ships also had steel hulls instead of
wooden ones. By the early 1900s, the United States had
built a powerful navy. The nation now needed new bases
around the world to refuel its ships.

> **Reasons for U.S. Imperialism**
> - Find raw materials for manufacturing
> - Sell products in new areas
> - Spread Christianity and American culture
> - Increase trade with Latin America

/////////////// Glue Foldable here ///////////////

Check for Understanding

**List two reasons some Americans wanted to
build an empire.**

1. _____

2. _____

**List two ways the Age of Imperialism affected
America.**

1. _____

2. _____

7. Use a three-tab
   Foldable and place it
   horizontally along
   the dotted line to
   cover the Check for
   Understanding.
   Write the title
   *Describe and
   Compare* on the
   anchor tab. Label
   the three tabs
   *Isolationism,
   Expansionism,* and
   Imperialism. Write
   one thing that you
   remember about
   each. Use the
   Foldable to help
   answer Check for
   Understanding.

netw⊙rks

Rise to World Power

Lesson 2 Imperialism in the Pacific

ESSENTIAL QUESTION
Why does conflict develop?

GUIDING QUESTIONS

1. **Why did the Hawaiians resist American influence in their country?**
2. **How did the United States expand its trading interests in China?**
3. **How did the United States help settle the Russo-Japanese War?**

Terms to Know
provisional government temporary government
sphere of influence section of a country in which a foreign nation enjoys special rights and powers

Where in the world?

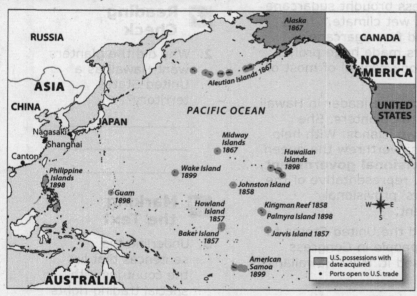

When did it happen?

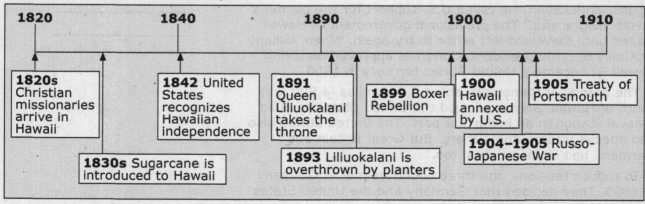

1820	1840	1890	1900	1910

1820s Christian missionaries arrive in Hawaii

1830s Sugarcane is introduced to Hawaii

1842 United States recognizes Hawaiian independence

1891 Queen Liliuokalani takes the throne

1893 Liliuokalani is overthrown by planters

1899 Boxer Rebellion

1900 Hawaii annexed by U.S.

1904–1905 Russo-Japanese War

1905 Treaty of Portsmouth

321

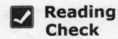

Lesson 2 Imperialism in the Pacific, *Continued*

Hawaii and the United States

Americans wanted to build a trading empire in the Pacific. In 1867, the United States claimed the Pacific islands of Midway under Secretary of State William H. Seward. They are 3,000 miles (4,800 km) west of California. Ships could stop there on their way to China. But the United States needed to control more areas to be a strong power.

The Hawaiian Islands are about 2,000 miles (3,200 km) west of California. Americans and Hawaiians had been trading since the 1790s. Later, Christian missionaries came to spread their religion. American merchants who worked in whaling also settled in Hawaii.

In the 1830s, an American business brought sugarcane to Hawaii. It grew well in the warm, wet climate. Missionaries and traders bought land for sugarcane plantations. Soon, American planters made huge profits from selling sugar. They gradually took control of most of the land and businesses in Hawaii.

In 1891, Queen Liliuokalani became the leader in Hawaii. She tried to take power away from the planters. She wanted Hawaiians to control their own islands. With help from the United States, the planters overthrew the queen in 1893. They set up their own **provisional government**, or temporary government. The U.S. representative of the federal government said the planters' provisional government was the true government.

The provisional government asked the United States to annex, or take over, Hawaii. Some people in Congress supported the idea and some opposed it. Most Hawaiians were against it.

President Benjamin Harrison signed an annexation treaty. But Congress did not approve it while Harrison was president. The next president, Grover Cleveland, was against annexation. He called U.S. support for the planter's revolt "disgraceful." The provisional government of Hawaii waited until Cleveland left office to try again. When William McKinley became president, Congress approved annexing Hawaii. It became a United States territory in 1900.

The islands of Samoa are about 3,000 miles (4,800 km) south of Hawaii. Samoa allowed the United States to build a naval station in an important port. The United States also had special trading rights there. But Great Britain and Germany had trading rights, too.

To reduce tensions, the three countries met in Germany in 1899. They decided that Germany and the United States

Examining Details

1. List three important years in Hawaii's history and what happened.

_____

_____

_____

Reading Check

2. Why did the planters want Hawaii as a United States territory?

_____

_____

_____

Marking the Text

3. Underline the sentences that list the countries with special trading rights in Samoa. What action did they take?

_____

_____

Lesson 2 Imperialism in the Pacific, *Continued*

? Comparing

4. Compared to the countries that controlled the spheres of influence in China, how strong was China's economy and military during this time?

_____

_____

_____

✓ Reading Check

5. Explain the purpose of the Open Door policy.

_____

_____

_____

✓ Describing

6. What role did the United States play in the end of the Russo-Japanese War?

_____

_____

_____

would control Samoa while Great Britain would control other Pacific islands. They did not discuss the idea with anyone in Samoa. The United States quickly annexed its part of Samoa.

An Open Door to China

Gaining control of Pacific islands would help the United States trade with China. Ships could stop there on the way to China. China was weak from wars and had little industry. It could not resist the countries that wanted to exploit, or make use of, its raw materials and markets.

By the late 1890s, Japan, Germany, Great Britain, France, and Russia each had special rights and powers in sections of China. These sections were called **spheres of influence**. They competed for economic power. This type of competition helped lead to World War I.

The United States wanted to trade in China. But it didn't have trading rights. Secretary of State John Hay came up with an Open Door policy. This meant that every foreign country would have equal trading rights. The trading countries did not accept this idea.

In 1899, a secret Chinese society called the Boxers rose up against foreigners in China. They did not like foreign attempts to control parts of their country. They called the traders "foreign devils."

Many foreigners died in the fighting. The next year, the Boxers were defeated by foreign troops. After the rebellion, the foreign powers in China worried about more problems in the future. They decided to go along with a second Open Door policy proposed by the United States. It allowed equal trading rights to the United States. It also stated that foreign powers would allow China to remain independent and respect its borders.

Relations with Japan

Japan wanted to expand its power in Asia. It ignored the Open Door policy. In 1904, Japan and Russia went to war. Both countries wanted to control the natural resources in Manchuria. Manchuria was an area controlled by China.

President Theodore Roosevelt wanted to end the war between Russia and Japan. He met with Russian and Japanese leaders in Portsmouth, New Hampshire, in 1905. Japan and Russia signed the Treaty of Portsmouth which ended the war. But the treaty did not end the tensions in

Rise to World Power

Lesson 2 Imperialism in the Pacific, *Continued*

Asia. Japan soon built the strongest navy in the Pacific. It challenged the United States for power in the region.

Many Japanese people had settled in California before the Russo-Japanese War. Many faced discrimination. In 1906, the San Francisco Board of Education ordered all Asian students to attend separate schools. They could not attend schools with white students.

President Roosevelt forced the school board to change its policy. In return, Japan agreed to limit the number of immigrants from Japan to the United States. But relations between Japan and the United States grew worse. To avoid war, President Roosevelt sent 16 white battleships on a cruise around the world. Japan was impressed by the power of the "Great White Fleet." By 1909, the United States and Japan had settled many of their differences.

//////////// Glue Foldable here /////////

Check for Understanding

List three American presidents involved in the annexation of Hawaii and describe their actions.

1. _____

2. _____

3. _____

List three examples that prove that American expansionism was more popular than isolationism.

1. _____

2. _____

3. _____

FOLDABLES

7. Place a three-tab Foldable along the dotted line to cover Check for Understanding. Write *American Influence* on the anchor tab. Label the three tabs *Hawaii*, *China*, and *Japan*. Use the space on both sides to write what you remember about the involvement of the United States in each of these countries. Use your Foldable to help answer Check for Understanding.

Rise to World Power

Lesson 3 War with Spain

ESSENTIAL QUESTION
Why does conflict develop?

GUIDING QUESTIONS
1. **Why did the United States go to war with Spain?**
2. **How were Cuba, Puerto Rico, and the Philippines ruled after the Spanish-American War?**

Terms to Know
armistice an agreement to end fighting
protectorate a country under the control of a different country
territory area completely controlled by a country

Where in the world?

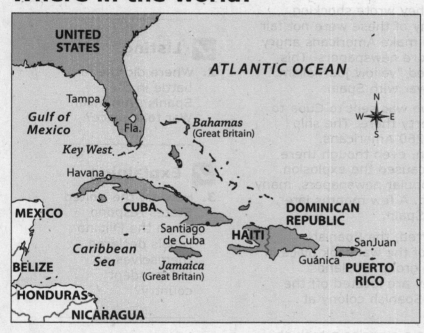

When did it happen?

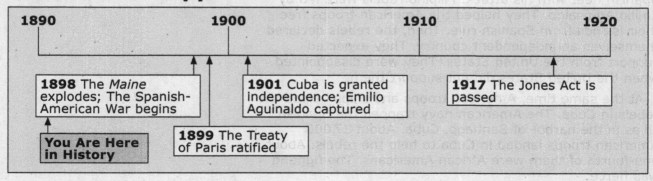

1890   **1900**   **1910**   **1920**

1898 The *Maine* explodes; The Spanish-American War begins

1901 Cuba is granted independence; Emilio Aguinaldo captured

1917 The Jones Act is passed

You Are Here in History

1899 The Treaty of Paris ratified

325

netw⦿rks

Lesson 3 War with Spain, *Continued*

"A Splendid Little War"

In the late 1800s, Cubans struggled to free their country from years of Spanish rule. Rebels destroyed Spanish property. Spain responded harshly. Thousands of Cubans died of starvation and disease.

Many Americans were concerned about the revolt in Cuba. Businesses did not want to lose property or economic trade in Cuba. The government worried about a revolution so close to the United States. Some people were shocked at how Spain treated the Cubans.

Some American newspapers wanted America to get involved in the Cuban revolution. They wrote shocking reports about Spanish actions. Many of these were not fair or true. The newspapers wanted to make Americans angry at Spain. The stories helped sell more newspapers. This kind of sensational writing was called "yellow journalism." It was meant to get support for a war with Spain.

In 1898, the battleship USS *Maine* was sent to Cuba to protect American people and property there. The ship exploded in Havana Harbor, killing 260 Americans. American newspapers blamed Spain, even though there was no clear evidence about what caused the explosion. Following the suggestions of the popular newspapers, many Americans wanted a war with Spain. A few months later, the United States declared war on Spain.

Events in Cuba triggered, or started, the Spanish-American War. But the first battle of the war took place in the Philippines. The Philippines is a group of islands thousands of miles from Cuba. They are located off the coast of China. The islands were a Spanish colony at the time.

Commodore George Dewey made a surprise attack at Manila Bay in the Philippines. He destroyed most of the Spanish fleet with his attack. Filipino rebels were led by Emilio Aguinaldo. They helped the American troops free their islands from Spanish rule. Then, the rebels declared themselves an independent country. They expected support from the United States. They were disappointed when the United States did not support them.

At the same time, American troops and ships helped the rebels in Cuba. The American navy trapped the Spanish ships in the harbor of Santiago, Cuba. About 17,000 American troops landed in Cuba to help the rebels. About one-fourth of them were African Americans. The fighting was fierce.

Marking the Text

1. Underline the text that describes the explosion of the USS *Maine*. How did Americans respond?

_____

_____

Listing

2. Where did the first battle in the Spanish-American War take place?

_____

Explaining

3. How did the United States respond when the Filipino rebels declared themselves an independent country?

_____

_____

networks

Rise to World Power

Lesson 3 War with Spain, *Continued*

☑ **Identifying**

4. Who were the Rough Riders?

_____

_____

? **Comparing and Contrasting**

5. How are a protectorate and a territory similar? How are they different?

_____

_____

_____

☑ **Describing**

6. What was the Platt Amendment?

_____

_____

Theodore Roosevelt organized a group of volunteers to join the fighting. They were called the Rough Riders. They fought along with African American soldiers in the Battle of San Juan Hill. The Americans captured San Juan Hill.

Two days later, Spanish warships tried to escape from Santiago Harbor. The U.S. warships destroyed the Spanish warships. United States troops also landed on the Spanish island of Puerto Rico and took control. Soon, Spain signed an **armistice**, or peace treaty, to end the fighting. Spain was forced to give up its control of Cuba and Puerto Rico.

Secretary of State John Hay called the Spanish-American War "a splendid little war." In about four months of battle, 400 Americans had died from wounds and about 2,000 had died from diseases. African Americans fought alongside Cuban and American troops, but suffered from discrimination. The United States was now recognized as a major power in the world.

Acquiring New Lands

The Treaty of Paris ended the war and broke up the Spanish empire. Cuba became an American **protectorate.** A protectorate is an independent country under the control of another country. Puerto Rico and the Pacific island of Guam became **territories** of the United States. Territories are areas completely controlled by another country. The Philippine islands were turned over to the United States for $20 million. The United States now controlled an empire. Not everyone in America liked the idea.

In 1901, the United States gave Cuba independence with certain limits. The Platt Amendment said that Cuba could not make treaties. It also had to allow an American naval base at Guantanamo Bay. The United States still has this base. The United States could also respond if it thought another country would try to take over Cuba.

The United States controlled Puerto Rico. It set up a new government in 1900. In 1917, Congress passed the Jones Act. All Puerto Ricans became American citizens. Still, many people in Puerto Rico wanted to be independent.

Americans argued about whether the nation should control the Philippines. Some thought it was against democratic principles to build an empire. Others did not want to send troops to control the Philippines. Some worried that Philippine workers would end up competing for American jobs.

networks

Rise to World Power

Lesson 3 War with Spain, *Continued*

Imperialists saw the Philippines as very useful. It could be a naval base for the military, a stop for ships on the way to China, and a place to sell American goods. Others thought America should help the Filipinos because they were less civilized. The imperialists won the debate.

Filipinos soon revolted against American rule. The Filipino leader Emilio Aguinaldo led the revolt. He had helped the Americans when the Americans fought the Spanish. More than 4,000 Americans and about 220,000 Filipinos died in a bloody rebellion against American rule. Aguinaldo was captured in 1901. Some Filipinos refused to surrender.

The United States set up a civilian government under William Howard Taft. It tried to prepare the islands for eventual, or later, self-rule. The Philippines finally gained independence in 1946.

/ / / / / / / / / / / / Glue Foldable here / / / / / / / / /

Check for Understanding

List two events that led up to the Spanish-American War.

1. _____

2. _____

List two events that occurred after the Spanish-American War.

1. _____

2. _____

Marking the Text

7. Underline the name of the man who led the rebellion against the United States in the Philippines. When was he captured?

_____

FOLDABLES

8. Use a two-tab Foldable and cut the tabs in half to make four tabs. Place it along the dotted line to cover Check for Understanding. Write the title *Spanish-American War* on the anchor tab. Label the four tabs *What*, *Where*, *When*, and *Why*. Use both sides of the tabs to write what you remember about the purpose, location, time frame, and reasons for the war. Use your Foldable to help answer Check for Understanding.

netw⊕rks

Rise to World Power

Lesson 4 Latin American Policies

ESSENTIAL QUESTION
Why does conflict develop?

GUIDING QUESTIONS
1.   **What steps did the United States take to build the Panama Canal?**
2.   **What was the United States' foreign policy in Latin America?**

Terms to Know
isthmus narrow strip of land connecting two larger bodies of land
anarchy disorder and lawlessness caused by lack of effective government
dollar diplomacy the policy of using economic investment to protect U.S. interests abroad

Where in the world?

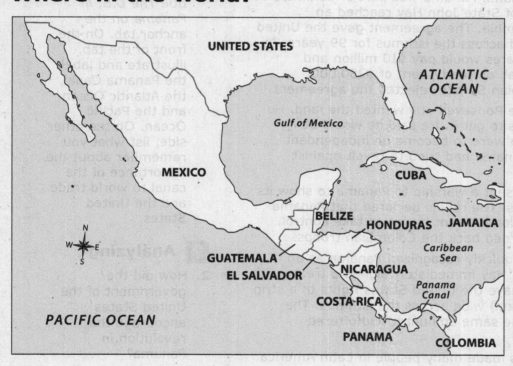

When did it happen?

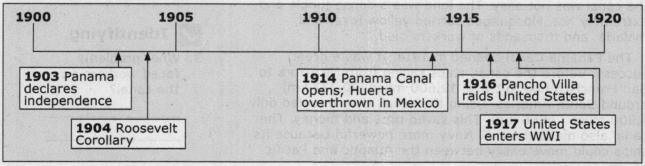

1903 Panama declares independence

1904 Roosevelt Corollary

1914 Panama Canal opens; Huerta overthrown in Mexico

1916 Pancho Villa raids United States

1917 United States enters WWI

329

Rise to World Power

Lesson 4 Latin American Policies, *Continued*

The United States in Panama

////////// *Glue Foldable here* ///////////

Americans and Europeans wanted to build a canal through Central America for many years. The canal would connect the Atlantic and Pacific oceans. Ships would not have to sail around South America to get from one ocean to the other. The French tried to build a canal across Panama in the 1880s. They did not succeed.

Panama was a perfect site for a canal because it is an isthmus. An **isthmus** is a narrow strip of land connecting two larger bodies of land. Panama was part of Columbia at the time. Secretary of State John Hay reached an agreement with Colombia. The agreement gave the United States control of land across the isthmus for 99 years. In return, the United States would pay $10 million and promise to pay annual, or yearly, rent of $250,000. However, the Colombian Senate rejected the agreement.

President Theodore Roosevelt still wanted the land. He looked for other ways to get it. He said he would be "delighted" if Panama were to become an independent country. People in Panama had tried to revolt against Colombia before.

The United States sent a warship to Panama to show its support for the rebels. The rebels declared that Panama was independent. Colombia sent troops to take control. American soldiers turned back the Colombian troops.

The United States quickly recognized Panama as an independent country. Hay immediately signed a treaty with the new country. It gave the United States rights to a strip of land 10 miles (16 km) wide across the isthmus. The United States paid the same amount it had offered Colombia before.

Roosevelt's actions made many people in Latin America angry. Roosevelt was proud of his actions because the United States was able to begin work on the canal. Building the canal was not easy. The land was a dense jungle and extremely hot. Mosquitoes carried yellow fever and malaria, and thousands of workers died.

The Panama Canal opened in 1914. It was a great success. Before the canal, ships sailing from New York to San Francisco had to travel 12,600 miles (20,277 km) around South America. Using the canal, they traveled only 4,900 miles (7,886 km). This saved time and money. The canal also made the U.S. Navy more powerful because its ships could move easily between the Atlantic and Pacific

FOLDABLES

🖌 Describing

1. Use a one-tab Foldable and place it horizontally under the heading *The United States in Panama*. Write the title *The U.S. in Panama* on the anchor tab. On the front of the tab, illustrate and label the Panama Canal, the Atlantic Ocean and the Pacific Ocean. On the other side, list what you remember about the importance of the canal to world trade and the United States.

❓ Analyzing

2. How did the government of the United States encourage the revolution in Panama?

_____

_____

✔ Identifying

3. What problems faced workers on the canal?

_____

_____

Rise to World Power

Lesson 4 Latin American Policies, *Continued*

☑ **Describing**

4. What were the good effects of dollar diplomacy? What were the bad effects?

_____

_____

_____

☑ **Describing**

5. How would you describe Mexico's situation before Francisco Madero took power?

_____

_____

oceans. It was valuable property that the United States would protect. This meant that the United States would stay very involved in Latin American affairs.

American actions involving the canal made many people in Latin America angry. That anger lasted for many years. It hurt relationships between Latin American countries and the United States. The United States finally turned the canal over to Panama at the end of 1999.

Policing the Western Hemisphere

President Theodore Roosevelt often quoted an African proverb: "Speak softly and carry a big stick." This meant that he believed the United States should not rely on threats to respond to foreign problems. Instead, it should use military force to prevent **anarchy** in the world. Anarchy is lawlessness caused by lack of effective government.

The United States had followed the Monroe Doctrine to keep European countries from gaining power in Latin America. Roosevelt added the Roosevelt Corollary to the Monroe Doctrine. He claimed the right to get involved in Latin American affairs if a nation seemed unstable. It gave the United States the right to act as a "policeman" in places in Latin America.

The United States used this power in 1905 in the Dominican Republic. It took control of the country's finances after a revolution overthrew the government. The United States also sent troops to Cuba in 1906 in order to prevent a revolution.

The next president, William Howard Taft, took a different view from Roosevelt. He wanted the United States to help countries build roads, railroads, and harbors, and to increase trade and profits. He suggested "substituting dollars for bullets." President Taft's idea was called **dollar diplomacy**. This policy was both good and bad. American dollars helped maintain U.S. power in Latin America. It also helped build roads and harbors and helped increase trade. But it also increased Latin American anger against the United States.

Mexico was a poor country in the early 1900s. A small group of rich landholders and U.S. investors controlled it. A reformer, Francisco Madero, led a successful revolution in 1911. Two years later, General Victoriano Huerta killed Madero. Huerta was a dictator who favored wealthy Mexican businessmen and foreign interests.

331

Rise to World Power

Lesson 4 Latin American Policies, *Continued*

The new American president, Woodrow Wilson, knew military power was important. But he wanted to base his foreign policy on moral principles, or ideas of right and wrong. He wanted to end U.S. imperialism. His ideas were called "moral diplomacy." President Wilson refused to recognize the Huerta government. He did not approve of their actions in taking control. He called them a "government of butchers."

When a civil war began in Mexico, Wilson hoped Huerta would lose. Huerta's opponents were led by Venustiano Carranza. Wilson helped by selling them weapons.

Huerta's troops arrested some American sailors in the Mexican port of Veracruz. Wilson sent troops to capture the port. This support helped Carranza take power in Mexico. The United States quickly backed him.

Rebel leader Pancho Villa turned against Carranza. Villa was angry at the United States. He shot 16 Americans. Then he and his followers crossed the border into New Mexico. They burned a town and killed 18 more Americans.

American forces, led by General John J. Pershing, chased Villa and his men into Mexico. Villa escaped. After about a year, the United States turned its attention to World War I. The American troops left Mexico soon afterwards.

The nations had come close to war. Many Mexicans remained angry at the United States. The United States showed that it was willing to use force to protect its interests.

////////////////////////////// Glue Foldable here ///////////////////////////

Check for Understanding

List three different American foreign policies between 1900 and 1920.

1. _____

2. _____

3. _____

List two areas where the United States used force to further its interests in Latin America.

1. _____

2. _____

☑ Explaining

6. Why did President Wilson support Huerta's opponents in the Mexican civil war?

_____

_____

FOLDABLES®

7. Use a three-tab Foldable and place it along the dotted line to cover Check for Understanding. Write the title *The Western Hemisphere* on the anchor tab. Label the tabs *Military Force*, *Investment and Economic Influence*, and *Moral Diplomacy*. Use the space on both sides to list facts you remember about American foreign policy. Use your Foldable to help answer Check for Understanding.

networks

World War I

Lesson 1 War in Europe

ESSENTIAL QUESTION
Why does conflict develop?

GUIDING QUESTIONS
1. **What factors led to the outbreak of war in Europe?**
2. **What changes made World War I become a long and deadly war?**

Terms to Know
nationalism a feeling of intense loyalty to a country or group

militarism celebration of military ideals, and a rapid buildup of military power

alliance system a system in which countries agree to defend each other

balance of power an equality of power among different countries that discourages any group from acting aggressively

stalemate a situation in a conflict in which neither side can make progress against the other

U-boat a German submarine

Where in the world?

When did it happen?

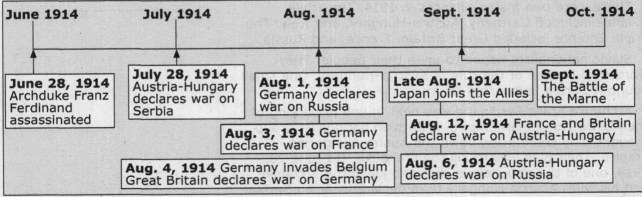

June 1914	July 1914	Aug. 1914	Sept. 1914	Oct. 1914

June 28, 1914 Archduke Franz Ferdinand assassinated

July 28, 1914 Austria-Hungary declares war on Serbia

Aug. 1, 1914 Germany declares war on Russia

Late Aug. 1914 Japan joins the Allies

Sept. 1914 The Battle of the Marne

Aug. 3, 1914 Germany declares war on France

Aug. 12, 1914 France and Britain declare war on Austria-Hungary

Aug. 4, 1914 Germany invades Belgium Great Britain declares war on Germany

Aug. 6, 1914 Austria-Hungary declares war on Russia

333

World War I

Lesson 1 War in Europe, *Continued*

Troubles in Europe

In the early 1900s, a great deal of tension developed in Europe. **Nationalism** caused much of this tension. Nationalists felt strong loyalty to their country or group. Some groups united into new nations such as Italy and Germany. Some ethnic groups broke away from the nations that controlled them. New nations wanted to show off their power. This made older nations fear them.

Countries grew more powerful by building great empires. France and Great Britain had large empires but wanted to expand. Germany, Italy, and Russia wanted new colonies in Asia and Africa, too. As these empires grew, some countries were brought into conflict with each other.

Each empire wanted to be stronger than the others, so they each built up their military forces. This buildup of military power is called **militarism**. This militarism only made European nations more nervous.

Militarism in Europe	
Countries	**What They Built Up**
France, Germany, Russia	Huge armies
Germany, Great Britain	Large navies

/ / / / / / / / / / / Glue Foldable here / / / / / / / / / /

The nations created an **alliance system**. Nations in an alliance promised to help others if they were attacked. The alliance system was meant to keep peace. It was supposed to stop one country from being more powerful than the others. This was called a **balance of power**. However, this system was also dangerous. When one nation attacked another, an entire alliance would help defend it. Many countries would be pulled into a war.

There were two major alliances in 1914. The Triple Alliance included Germany, Austria-Hungary, and Italy. The Triple Entente included Great Britain, France, and Russia.

Slavic nationalists hoped to unite their people. They wanted to be free of the rule of Austria-Hungary. One small country, Serbia, supported them.

Archduke Franz Ferdinand was next in line to be king of the Austro-Hungarian Empire. A Serbian nationalist group thought they could bring down the Austro-Hungarian Empire. Their plan was to kill the archduke. On June 28, 1914, one of the nationalists shot and killed the archduke and his wife. Austria-Hungary then declared war on Serbia.

FOLDABLES

? Cause and Effect

1. Use a two-tab Foldable and place it horizontally along the dotted line over the text beginning with "The nations created ..." Write the title *Alliance System* on the anchor tab. Label the first tab *Cause* and the second tab *Effect*. Use the space on both sides of the tabs to list the causes and effects of the alliances formed in 1914.

? Explaining

2. What did Serbian nationalists hope to accomplish by killing Archduke Franz Ferdinand?

_____

_____

334

World War I

Lesson 1 War in Europe, Continued

? Cause and Effect

3. What effect did the alliance system have on World War I?

_____

_____

? Explaining

4. How did Belgium help the Allies?

_____

_____

_____

? Identifying

5. What effect did trench warfare have on the progress of the war?

_____

_____

The alliance system brought many nations into the war. Russia had agreed to protect Serbia. As a result, the Triple Entente nations joined in, too. Austria-Hungary was in the Triple Alliance, so its allies were ready to help. The war spread quickly.

A World War Begins

The "Great War" had begun. At this point, the names and members of the alliances changed a bit.

The Allied Powers "The Allies"	The Central Powers
Great Britain France Russia Japan Italy	Germany Austria-Hungary The Ottoman (Turkish) Empire

Germany invaded Belgium on its way to attack France. It took the powerful German army nearly three weeks to defeat the Belgians. This delay gave France and Great Britain more time to prepare for war.

The French and the British met the Germans at the Marne River in September 1914. After a week, the Allies stopped the German advance. This battle made everyone realize that neither side would win easily.

Ground soldiers dug a system of trenches along the front lines. The trenches protected soldiers from flying bullets and shells. The war became a **stalemate** where neither side could make progress. To try to break the stalemate, both sides launched major attacks.

Germany attacked at Verdun. The battle lasted from February to December of 1916. About 750,000 soldiers were killed. Germany gained some ground but lost it again.

France attacked at the Battle of the Somme in July 1916. The Allies suffered very high casualties and eventually gained 7 miles (11.2 km).

During this war, new weapons caused more deaths and injuries than ever before. Better artillery fired larger shells farther. Better rifles shot more accurately. In April 1915, the Germans used poison gas against the Allied troops. Poison gas could injure or kill anyone who came into

Lesson 1 War in Europe, *Continued*

contact with it. Soldiers began to wear gas masks. The Allies began to use gas, too. In January 1916, the Allies started using armored tanks. Their tanks worked so well that the Germans began making tanks, too.

Airplanes changed the warfare for both sides. Pilots could report troop movements and bomb targets. Fighter planes had machine guns to shoot down enemy planes. Germany also used blimps to drop bombs on Allied cities.

The armies on land were not making progress against one another, so both sides tried a new tactic. Great Britain blocked ports used by the Germans. The blockade caused severe shortages of a variety of goods. Many Germans went without food and other supplies.

The Germans fought back with another weapon, the **U-boat**, or submarine. Submarines sank supply ships on their way to Great Britain. U-boat attacks on Americans at sea brought the United States into the war.

/ / / / / / / / / / / / Glue Foldable here / / / / / / / / / / / /

Check for Understanding

List four advancements in technology that made warfare in World War I so deadly.

1. _____

2. _____

3. _____

4. _____

How did the alliance system contribute to a war which involved nearly all the nations of Europe?

_____

_____

Marking the Text

6. Underline each new weapon that was used on land.

Reading Check

7. What was the result of German U-boat attacks on Americans at sea?

_____

_____

FOLDABLES

8. Use a three-tab Foldable and place it along the dotted line to cover Check for Understanding. Write the title *Technology & New Weapons* on the anchor tab. Label the three tabs *Land*, *Air*, and *Sea*. On the front and back of the tabs, write words and phrases that you remember about the advancements in warfare on land, air, and sea and the effects of each. Use your Foldable to help answer Check for Understanding.

networks

World War I

Lesson 2 America's Road to War

ESSENTIAL QUESTION
Why does conflict develop?

GUIDING QUESTIONS
1. **Why did the United States try to remain neutral during the war?**
2. **What made the United States decide to enter the war?**

Terms to Know
propaganda information used to influence opinion
autocracy a government in which one person with unlimited power rules

When did it happen?

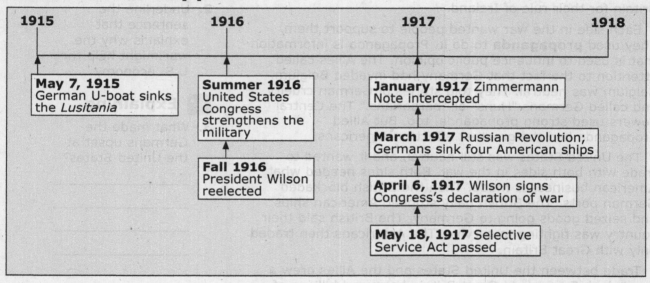

| 1915 | 1916 | 1917 | 1918 |

May 7, 1915
German U-boat sinks the *Lusitania*

Summer 1916
United States Congress strengthens the military

Fall 1916
President Wilson reelected

January 1917 Zimmermann Note intercepted

March 1917 Russian Revolution; Germans sink four American ships

April 6, 1917 Wilson signs Congress's declaration of war

May 18, 1917 Selective Service Act passed

What do you know?

In the first column, answer the questions based on what you know before you study. After this lesson, complete the last column.

Now ...		Later ...
	Which side did Americans favor early in the war?	
	How did the war in Europe affect the U.S. economy?	
	How did Americans feel about the Russian Revolution?	

337

World War I

Lesson 2 America's Road to War, *Continued*

American Neutrality

President Wilson declared that the United States would be neutral in the war in Europe. But more than 30 million Americans were either foreign-born or were children of immigrants. They felt strong ties to one side or the other in the war. Most Americans favored the Allies. Their language, customs, and traditions were like those in Great Britain.

About 8 million Americans had come from Germany or Austria and favored the Central Powers. Many of the 4.5 million Irish Americans did, too. They were angry at Great Britain for their rule of Ireland.

Each side in the war wanted people to support them. They used **propaganda** to do it. Propaganda is information that is used to influence public opinion. The Allies called attention to the fact that Germany had invaded Belgium. Belgium was neutral. They told stories of German cruelty and called Germans "Huns" or "barbarians." The Central Powers used strong propaganda, too. But Allied propaganda had the greatest effect on Americans.

The United States was still neutral, and it wanted to trade with both sides in the war. Both sides needed what American businesses made. Then the British blockaded German ports. The British navy stopped American ships and seized goods going to Germany. The British said their country was fighting to survive. The Americans then traded only with Great Britain.

Trade between the United States and the Allies grew a great deal. France and Great Britain borrowed billions of dollars from the United States to pay for their war efforts. This war spending caused an economic boom in the United States. It also made the Germans angry. They were angry because they did not believe that a neutral nation, such as the United States, should help the Allies.

The Germans could not stop the British blockade. Instead, they decided to stop ships trading with Britain. In 1915, Germany said they would sink all ships that were using British ports. President Wilson warned Germany that he would hold Germany responsible for any American lives that were lost in attacks.

On May 7, 1915, a U-boat fired on the *Lusitania*. It was a British passenger ship. As it sank, more than a thousand people died. Among them were 128 Americans. This made Americans very angry. Later, Americans learned that the *Lusitania* had also carried war supplies.

Explaining

1. What is the purpose of propaganda?

Marking the Text

2. Underline the sentence that explains why the war might help the U.S. economy.

Explaining

3. What made the Germans upset at the United States?

_____

_____

_____

_____

338

World War I

Lesson 2 America's Road to War, *Continued*

Copyright by The McGraw-Hill Companies.

📓 Explaining

4. What was the Sussex Pledge?

_____

_____

❓ Determining Cause and Effect

5. What actions did the United States take in response to German submarine attacks?

_____

_____

📓 Analyzing

6. Why did the Zimmermann Note upset Americans?

_____

_____

A few months later, another submarine attack injured some Americans. They were aboard the French passenger ship *Sussex*. This attack also made Americans angry. Germany offered money to the injured people to try to keep the United States from entering the war. It also promised to warn neutral ships before attacking them. This promise was the Sussex Pledge.

> **German Actions:**
> * Invaded Belgium
> * Sank the *Lusitania*
> * Attacked the *Sussex*
> * Made the Sussex Pledge

The End of Neutrality

The submarine attacks made Congress take action. In the summer of 1916, Congress passed laws to strengthen the military. They doubled the size of the army. They also provided money to build warships.

Still, President Wilson hoped to stay out of the war. Most Americans agreed. But some saw the military buildup as a step toward entering the war. One Democratic campaign slogan for Wilson that year was, "He Kept Us Out of War." Wilson won by only a small margin.

> **January 1917**
> **Germany warns they will sink on sight all ships using Allied ports.**

By 1917, Germany believed they could defeat the Allies. They wanted to do this before the United States became involved. In January, they warned that they would sink all ships using Allied ports.

A few weeks later, British agents seized an important message. Arthur Zimmermann was the German foreign minister. He sent a note to the government of Mexico. He offered to form an alliance with Mexico if the United States joined the war. The note made Americans even more angry at Germany.

> **March 1917**
> **Revolution begins in Russia**

World War I

Lesson 2 America's Road to War, *Continued*

In March 1917, a revolution began in Russia. It was an effort to overthrow the government. The Russian ruler had power with no limits. This type of government is an **autocracy**. The Russians defeated their ruler. Their new government would be more democratic. The new rulers said they would have free elections and promised to keep fighting Germany, too. Russia's new government raised the Allies' hopes. Wilson could now say that they were fighting a war for democracy.

In the same month, Germany sank four American trading ships. Thirty-six Americans died.

> April 1917
> **The United States declares war on Germany**

President Wilson decided the nation must enter the war. On April 2, 1917, he asked Congress to declare war against Germany. Congress debated the president's request. On April 6, they agreed that the United States must defend its rights as a world power. They passed the declaration of war. President Wilson signed it on April 6.

U.S. military forces would have to grow quickly. On May 18, Congress passed the Selective Service Act. This set up a military draft. A draft requires people to register and serve in the military if chosen. Millions of men from ages 21 to 30 registered. Three million were called to serve and two million more joined as volunteers. For the first time, women enlisted, but they did not serve in combat. They served as clerks, radio operators, and nurses.

More than 300,000 African Americans joined the armed forces. They were not treated fairly. Most of these men held low-level jobs at military bases. The military sent about half of them to Europe. Many served with honor. One regiment received medals from France.

Check for Understanding
List two actions that prove the United States was not totally neutral.

1. _____

2. _____

What do the *Lusitania* and the *Sussex* have in common?

_____

Marking the Text

7. Underline the statement that gives the reason Congress agreed to declare war.

Identifying

8. What was the purpose of the Selective Service Act?

_____

_____

FOLDABLES

9. Use a two-tab Foldable and place it along the dotted line to cover Check for Understanding. Write *Reasons for* ... on the anchor tab. Label the two tabs *U.S. Neutrality* and *U.S. Entering the War*. Use both sides of the tabs to list what you remember about why the United States tried to remain neutral and what made that change. Use your Foldable to help answer Check for Understanding.

netw⦿rks

World War I

Lesson 3 Americans Join the Allies

ESSENTIAL QUESTION
Why does conflict develop?

GUIDING QUESTIONS
1. **How did American troops help to turn the tide of the war toward the Allies?**
2. **What events occurred that led to the armistice being signed?**

Terms to Know
convoy a group of ships that escort and protect other ships
kaiser German emperor

When did it happen?

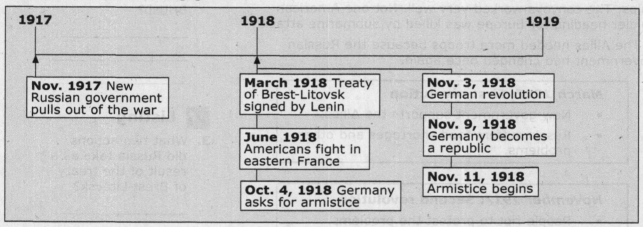

1917

Nov. 1917 New Russian government pulls out of the war

1918

March 1918 Treaty of Brest-Litovsk signed by Lenin

June 1918 Americans fight in eastern France

Oct. 4, 1918 Germany asks for armistice

1919

Nov. 3, 1918 German revolution

Nov. 9, 1918 Germany becomes a republic

Nov. 11, 1918 Armistice begins

What do you know?

In the first column, answer the questions based on what you know before you study. After this lesson, complete the last column.

Now...		Later...
	How did the U.S. Navy help the British when the United States entered the war?	
	What effect did the second Russian Revolution have on World War I?	
	What effect did the revolution in Austria-Hungary have on the Central Powers?	
	What role did President Wilson play at the end of World War I?	

341

networks

World War I

Lesson 3 Americans Join the Allies, *Continued*

Supplying the Allies

The Allies needed help from American soldiers. By 1917, the Allied armies were exhausted from fighting in the trenches. The British were running low on food and war supplies. Some of the French troops had stopped fighting. German submarines sank one of every four ships leaving British ports. Supplies could not move in or out.

The United States entered the war and had an immediate effect. The U.S. Navy helped the British destroy the German submarines that blocked British ports. Teams of navy ships called **convoys** helped supply ships cross the ocean. Convoys kept German submarines away from supply ships. The convoys worked very well. Not one American soldier heading for Europe was killed by submarine attack.

The Allies needed more troops because the Russian government had changed once again.

March 1917: First revolution

- New government supports the Allies.
- Russia suffers food shortages and other problems.

November 1917: Second revolution

- People riot to protest the problems.
- The Bolsheviks, led by Lenin, take over.
- The Russians pull out of the war.

In March 1918, Vladimir Lenin signed the treaty of Brest-Litovsk with Germany. This treaty took Russia out of the war. Russia also gave up a large amount of land to the Germans. As a result, the Germans were able to move thousands of their troops away from Russia. Those troops went to fight against the Allies on the Western Front. After the treaty was signed, the Germans attacked the Allied lines. They pushed the Allies back to within 40 miles (64 km) of Paris. It looked as if Germany might win the war.

In the spring of 1917, the AEF (American Expeditionary Force) arrived in Europe, led by General John Pershing. They were warmly welcomed in Paris. They were called "doughboys" because of the shape of the buttons on their uniforms. In June, 1918, they faced difficult fighting. They helped turn back an attack at Château-Thierry, on the Marne River east of Paris. The AEF then moved to Belleau

342

Marking the Text

1. Underline the reason the British had run so low on food and supplies.

Explaining

2. How did U.S. Navy convoys help the British?

_____

_____

_____

Listing

3. What two actions did Russia take as a result of the treaty of Brest-Litovsk?

_____

_____

Describing

4. How did the French react when the AEF arrived in Europe?

_____

_____

World War I

Lesson 3 Americans Join the Allies, *Continued*

? Paraphrasing

5. Explain what General Pershing meant by saying the battles "turned the tide of war."

_____

_____

_____

_____

✍ Explaining

6. Why was the Battle of the Argonne Forest important?

_____

_____

_____

✓ Reading Check

7. What troubles did the Austro-Hungarian empire face in 1918?

_____

_____

_____

Wood. Soldiers fought constantly for three weeks against a solid line of machine-gun fire.

American and French troops fought along the Marne and Somme rivers and stopped the Germans. General Pershing wrote that these battles "turned the tide of war."

Now the Allies could start their own military push. In the fall of 1918, the Americans helped fight at Saint-Mihiel. Half a million American troops fought off the Germans. Next, more than a million American troops joined the Allies to fight in the Argonne Forest. It was to be the largest attack in American history.

The Battle of the Argonne Forest lasted about seven weeks. It ended in early November. Allied troops struggled through the heavy forest in rain, mud, and barbed wire. They faced German machine guns. When this battle ended, the Allies had pushed the Germans back and broken their lines. Now the Germans faced an invasion of their own country.

Two brave Americans caught the nation's attention. These soldiers' actions earned each the Medal of Honor.

Corporal Alvin York	Captain Eddie Rickenbacker
fought at the Argonne Forest	captain of the 94th Aero Squadron
killed several enemy soldiers	fought 134 air battles
captured machine guns	shot down 26 aircraft
took 132 prisoners	

The End of the War

Fighting went on along the Western Front. In late 1918, Germany's allies had trouble, too. A revolution broke out in Austria-Hungary. Ethnic territories began to break away from the empire and Austria-Hungary surrendered. The Ottoman Empire was also breaking apart. It surrendered, too.

The American troops and supplies had made the Allies very strong. At home, Germans suffered because they had little food. Other supplies were also low. German leaders realized they had little chance of winning the war.

networks

World War I

Lesson 3 Americans Join the Allies, *Continued*

On October 4, 1918, German leaders spoke with President Wilson. They asked for an armistice. An armistice is an agreement to stop fighting. Wilson agreed, but wanted these things:

- Germany must accept his peace plan.
- Germany must promise not to start fighting again.
- All German troops must leave Belgium and France.
- President Wilson would work only with leaders who were not in the military.

While the Germans thought over the agreement, things changed in Germany.

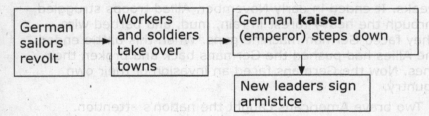

Two days after Germany became a republic, the armistice began. It began on November 11, 1918. It began at the 11th hour of the 11th day of the 11th month in 1918.

Germany withdrew its sea forces from the Baltic Sea. It pulled its land forces back across the Rhine River. Germany also gave up huge amounts of war equipment. The "Great War" was over. It was the most destructive war in history at that time.

////////////// Glue Foldable here ///////////////

Check for Understanding

List three ways in which American troops helped change the outcome of the war.

1. _____

2. _____

3. _____

How did the two Russian Revolutions affect the course of the war?

_____

_____

Marking the Text

8. Underline the definition of *armistice*.

_____

_____

_____

_____

FOLDABLES

9. Use a three-tab Foldable and place it along the dotted line to cover Check for Understanding. Write the title *Americans Join Allies* on the anchor tab. Label the left tab *Allied Forces Pushed Back*, the middle tab *Allied Forces Push Forward*, and the right tab *Armistice*. Use the space on both sides of the tabs to list facts you remember about each event. Use your Foldable to help answer Check for Understanding.

World War I

Lesson 4 The War at Home

ESSENTIAL QUESTION
Why does conflict develop?

GUIDING QUESTIONS
1. **How did the United States prepare to fight the war?**
2. **Why did the U.S. government approve legislation to control public opinion?**

Terms to Know
mobilization the gathering of resources and troops in preparation for war
ration to limit use
socialist a person who believes industries should be publicly owned
pacifist a person who is opposed to the use of violence
dissent disagreement or opposition

When did it happen?

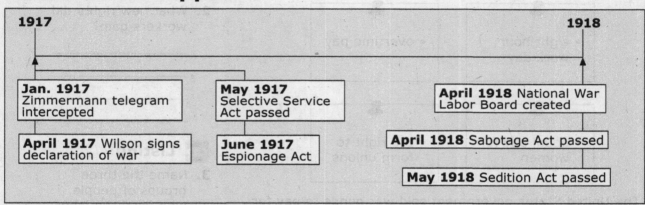

1917	**1918**

Jan. 1917 Zimmermann telegram intercepted

April 1917 Wilson signs declaration of war

May 1917 Selective Service Act passed

June 1917 Espionage Act

April 1918 National War Labor Board created

April 1918 Sabotage Act passed

May 1918 Sedition Act passed

What do you know?

In the first column, answer the questions based on what you know before you study. After this lesson, complete the last column.

Now ...		Later ...
	How did World War I affect workers' rights?	
	What groups gained jobs during this time?	
	What groups opposed the war?	
	How did the government react to criticism of the war?	

World War I

Lesson 4 The War at Home, *Continued*

Mobilizing the Nation

The United States declared war on Germany in 1917, so the nation had to get ready. **Mobilization** is preparing for war by gathering troops and resources. This process changed American life.

The government set up the National War Labor Board to make sure that war materials were produced. The board also made sure workers making war materials would keep working. The board urged businesses to agree to some worker demands. If the demands were met, the workers agreed not to strike. Workers won the following rights:

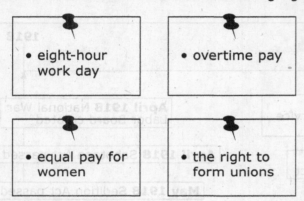

- eight-hour work day
- overtime pay
- equal pay for women
- the right to form unions

The United States government sold war bonds to pay for the war. The government also raised taxes.

To produce war materials, industries needed to grow. However, millions of men left their jobs to serve in the armed forces. Immigration had also slowed. There were few immigrants to take jobs. As a result, there were not enough workers for industry to expand.

Many women had never worked outside the home before the war. This was a new opportunity for them. Women filled jobs that men left.

From 1914 to 1920, between 300,000 and 500,000 African Americans moved to the North. They came from the South looking for jobs. This became known as the Great Migration. In addition, thousands of Mexicans moved north looking for work.

The United States had to produce food for its citizens. It also had to feed the Allies. A new agency called the Food Administration urged farmers to grow more. The agency also asked the public to eat less. They encouraged voluntary **rationing** of food and other goods. Rationing is when the use of something is limited. In this case,

Copyright by The McGraw-Hill Companies.

Identifying

1. What was the purpose of the National War Labor Board?

_____

_____

Identifying

2. What new rights did workers gain?

_____

_____

_____

Listing

3. Name the three groups of people who filled the labor shortage.

_____

_____

Summarizing

4. What did Americans have to do about food during the war?

_____

_____

World War I

Lesson 4 The War at Home, *Continued*

 Marking the Text

5. Underline the sentence that describes how the CPI wanted people to see the war.

? Comparing

6. How were the Food Administration and the Fuel Administration similar?

_____

_____

_____

? Evaluating

7. Do you think people who opposed the war were un-American? Explain.

_____

_____

Americans limited the amount of food they used. The Food Administration made sure there was enough food to send to the Allies.

Another agency, the War Industries Board, supervised the nation's industries. Many factories were needed to produce war-related goods. They had to stop making what they had been making before the war. The Board also set prices for certain products.

The government also created a Fuel Administration. It managed the nation's coal and oil. The Fuel Administration called for "Heatless Mondays" to save fuel. It also started daylight saving time.

Some Americans still did not think the United States should enter the war. President Wilson formed the Committee on Public Information or CPI. The CPI's job was to present the war as a fight for democracy and freedom. The Committee produced pamphlets, articles, and books in support of the war. Newspapers were given articles written by the government. The Committee also hired speakers, writers, artists, and actors who used their talents to build support for the war.

Public Opinion and the War

The war was good for the American economy, but it did have some harmful effects. The government tried to quiet people who were against the war. Some people began to reject those they saw as different.

Those Who Opposed the War	Why
Some German Americans and Irish Americans	They favored the Central Powers.
Socialists (people who believe industries should be owned by the public)	They thought the war would help rich business owners and hurt working people.
Pacifists (people who do not believe in the use of violence)	They were against the use of violence.

The CPI knew there was **dissent**, or opposition, to the war. They tried to silence this disagreement. The CPI made people seem un-American if they opposed the war.

World War I

Lesson 4 The War at Home, *Continued*

The Espionage Act of 1917 set up laws and punishments for spying. A person who helped the enemy or interfered with Army recruiting could also be punished.

In 1918, Congress passed the Sabotage Act. It punished anyone who damaged or destroyed war materials. Congress also passed the Sedition Act to silence dissent. If a person said, wrote, or published anything that criticized the government, they could be punished. Thousands of people were punished under these laws.

New Laws	Purpose
The Espionage Act of 1917	to prevent people from spying or helping the enemy
the Sabotage Act of 1918	to punish people who destroyed war materials
the Sedition Act of 1918	to silence opposition to the war

Americans were used to speaking freely. Many people spoke out against these new laws. However, most Americans felt that, during a war, no law could be too harsh for traitors and disloyal Americans.

/ / / / / / / / / / / / /Glue Foldable here/ / / / / / / / / / / / / /

Check for Understanding

Define mobilization and list four ways it changed life in America.

1. _____

2. _____

3. _____

4. _____

How did the U.S. government react to opposition to the war at home?

_____

_____

Copyright by The McGraw-Hill Companies.

✓ Reading Check

8. Why do you think Congress passed laws to punish people who criticized the government?

_____

_____

FOLDABLES®

9. Use a two-tab Foldable and cut the tabs in half to make four tabs. Place it along the dotted line to cover Check for Understanding. Write the title *Describe the Purpose of ...* on the anchor tab. Label the four tabs *National War Labor Board*, *Food Administration*, *War Industries Board*, and *Fuel Administration*. Use both sides of the tabs to list words and phrases you remember about each. Use your Foldable to help answer Check for Understanding.

World War I

Lesson 5 Searching for Peace

ESSENTIAL QUESTION

Why does conflict develop?

GUIDING QUESTIONS

1. **Why did the Allies oppose Wilson's plan for peace?**
2. **Why did the U.S. Senate reject the Treaty of Versailles and the League of Nations?**

Terms to Know

national self-determination the right of people to decide how they should be governed

reparation payment for damages caused during a war

When did it happen?

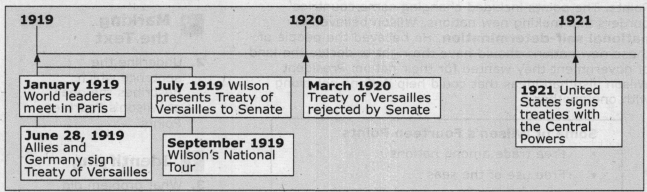

1919

January 1919 World leaders meet in Paris

June 28, 1919 Allies and Germany sign Treaty of Versailles

July 1919 Wilson presents Treaty of Versailles to Senate

September 1919 Wilson's National Tour

1920

March 1920 Treaty of Versailles rejected by Senate

1921

1921 United States signs treaties with the Central Powers

What do you know?

In the first column, answer the questions based on what you know before you study.
After this lesson, complete the last column.

Now ...		Later ...
	What was the purpose of President Wilson's Fourteen Points?	
	What was the goal of the League of Nations?	
	What countries were leaders in the Paris peace conference?	
	How did the U.S. Senate react to the Treaty of Versailles?	

World War I

Lesson 5 Searching for Peace, *Continued*

Making a Peace

In January 1919, world leaders from 27 nations came to Paris, France. They met for a peace conference after World War I. There were problems to solve. In Europe, France, Russia, Germany, and Austria-Hungary had each lost between 1 and 2 million dead. Millions more people were wounded. The war had destroyed towns and farms. Russia was having a civil war. Some European people were trying to form their own nations. At the same time, influenza, or the flu, killed millions of people around the world.

Woodrow Wilson wanted the world to have a fair and lasting peace. He described his peace plan in the Fourteen Points. The points included changing some countries' borders and making new nations. Wilson believed in **national self-determination**. He believed the people of these new nations should have the right to decide the kind of government they wanted for their nation. President Wilson also had ideas that could help nations get along with one another.

Some of Wilson's Fourteen Points

- Free trade among nations
- Free use of the seas
- No more secret treaties
- Limit weapons each nation may have
- Countries should peacefully settle conflicts over colonies
- Form League of Nations

Wilson's final, or last, idea was to create a League of Nations. Its purpose was to preserve peace and prevent future wars among member nations.

Many Europeans liked Wilson's ideas, but they worried that some of them were not complete. For example, in areas where several cultures were grouped together, there was no plan for how to make national self-determination work.

Neither Germany nor Russia sent leaders to the peace talks. They were not invited. Among those who attended were leaders from the United States, France, Great Britain, and Italy. They were called the Big Four.

? Contrasting

1. How was the European war experience different from that of the United States?

_____

_____

_____

✎ Marking the Text

2. Underline the sentence which describes the goal of Wilson's Fourteen Points.

? Identifying

3. What problem did some Europeans find with Wilson's ideas?

_____

_____

_____

? Listing

4. Which two nations did not send representatives to Paris? Why?

_____

_____

_____

World War I

Lesson 5 Searching for Peace, *Continued*

Lesson 5 Searching for Peace

✓ Reading Check

5. Why didn't Great Britain, France, and Italy support Wilson's Fourteen Points?

_____

_____

? Analyzing

6. Why do you think Great Britain and France wanted Germany to pay large reparations?

_____

_____

_____

✓ Reading Check

7. Why did Wilson bring the Treaty of Versailles to the U.S. Senate?

_____

_____

The Big Four	
President *Woodrow Wilson*	United States
Prime Minister *David Lloyd George*	Great Britain
Premier *Georges Clemenceau*	France
Prime Minister *Vittorio Orlando*	Italy

Wilson did not want to punish defeated nations. The Europeans wanted revenge. They did not support Wilson.

Clemenceau and Lloyd George wanted Germany to make large **reparations**. Reparations are payments for damages caused by war. Clemenceau wanted Germany to be broken up into smaller countries. Wilson believed in his own ideas, but he finally had to give in to the Allies' demands.

On June 28, 1919, The Allies and Germany signed the Treaty of Versailles. It was harsh, but the Germans had no choice but to sign.

According to the treaty, Germany had to:

- pay billions of dollars in reparations to the Allies
- completely disarm
- give up overseas colonies
- give up some land in Europe.

The treaty also broke up the Austro-Hungarian and Russian Empires. It made new nations and brought back old ones. These actions allowed the people in the new areas to have national self-determination, but there would be trouble later. Wilson's League of Nations remained in the treaty. He felt it would be able to correct any mistakes in the rest of the treaty.

Opposition at Home

In July 1919, Wilson brought the Treaty of Versailles to the U.S. Senate. They would have to approve it before Wilson could sign it. But some Americans had objections.

The main American objections:
• The Treaty was too hard on Germany.
• The League of Nations would keep America involved in the problems of other nations.

Lesson 5 Searching for Peace, *Continued*

Wilson was a Democrat, but the Republicans controlled the Senate. Some of the senators wanted to embarrass Wilson and his party by not approving the treaty. Other senators did not agree with parts of the treaty, especially the League of Nations. A few would not sign any treaty at all.

Henry Cabot Lodge was a powerful senator. He headed the Senate Foreign Relations Committee. Lodge was also an enemy of Wilson. He wanted the treaty to limit the United States' promises to other nations.

Senator Lodge did the following:

- He argued that if the United States joined the League of Nations, other nations might order the United States to go to war.

- He delayed a vote on the treaty to give time for other opponents to speak.

- He proposed changes to the treaty to limit obligations of the United States.

In September 1919, Wilson went on a national tour to gather support for the treaty. When he came back he was too ill to fight for it.

In March 1920, the Senate finally voted to reject the Treaty of Versailles. Over the next year, the United States signed a different treaty with each of the Central Powers. The United States never joined the League of Nations.

/ / / / / / / / / / / / Glue Foldable here / / / / / / / / / /

Check for Understanding

What did Wilson do to promote the Treaty of Versailles?

_____

_____

Why do you think his efforts failed?

_____

_____

☑ Reading Check

8. Why did Republicans oppose the Treaty of Versailles?

_____

_____

_____

_____

_____

FOLDABLES®

9. Use a two-tab Foldable and place it along the dotted line to cover Check for Understanding. Label the anchor tab *Treaty of Versailles.* On the left tab, write the question *Who signed it and why?* On the right tab, write the question *Who did not sign it and why?* Use both sides of the tabs to answer the questions about the Treaty of Versailles. Use your Foldable to help answer Check for Understanding.

networks

The Jazz Age

Lesson 1 Time of Turmoil

ESSENTIAL QUESTION

How do new ideas change the way people live?

GUIDING QUESTIONS

1. How did Americans respond to people who had new ideas about social change?

2. Why did social change lead to labor unrest and racial tension?

When did it happen?

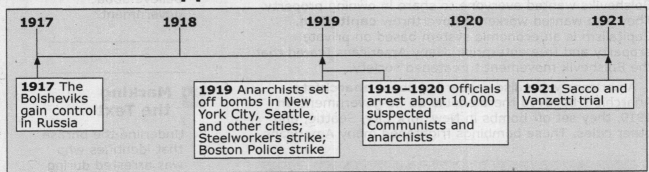

1917 The Bolsheviks gain control in Russia

1919 Anarchists set off bombs in New York City, Seattle, and other cities; Steelworkers strike; Boston Police strike

1919–1920 Officials arrest about 10,000 suspected Communists and anarchists

1921 Sacco and Vanzetti trial

What do you know?

In the first column, answer the questions based on what you know before you study. After this lesson, complete the last column.

Now...		Later...
	Who were the Bolsheviks?	
	What events happened during the Red Scare?	
	How effective were the strikes by steelworkers and Boston police officers?	
	What African American organization grew strong during this time?	

353

The Jazz Age

Lesson 1 Time of Turmoil, *Continued*

Fear of Radicalism

The years after World War I were hard for the American people. The war and America's responsibilities in the world had made them tired. They wanted to go back to a simpler life like they had before the war. They wanted things to get back to normal.

Americans became suspicious of some groups of people. People from other countries made them nervous. People with different ideas about society did, too. They were called radicals.

Americans worried about Bolsheviks. Bolsheviks were Communists. They had gained control of Russia in 1917. Bolsheviks wanted everyone to share in owning property. They also wanted workers to overthrow **capitalism**. Capitalism is an economic system based on private property and free enterprise. Many Americans feared that the Bolshevik movement threatened society.

Americans were also concerned about **anarchists**. Anarchists believed there should be no government. In 1919, they set off bombs in New York City, Seattle, and other cities. These bombings frightened many Americans.

Bolsheviks	Anarchists
Communists who wanted to end capitalism	People who believed there should be no government

Americans' fear of these ideas led to the Red Scare. Communists were also called "Reds." During the Red Scare, the government took action against Communists and others with radical views. The U.S. Attorney General, Mitchell Palmer, and his deputy, J. Edgar Hoover, ordered the arrest of about 10,000 people. The government thought they were anarchists and Communists. It also raided the headquarters of groups they thought were suspicious. But the government did not find large supplies of weapons like they expected.

Most people who were arrested were released. There was no evidence against them. A few hundred of the foreigners who were arrested were **deported**. This means they were forced to leave the United States.

Nicola Sacco and Bartolomeo Vanzetti were Italian immigrants. They admitted they were anarchists. They were accused of killing two men in a robbery. In 1921, they

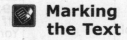

Reading Check

1. Why did Americans fear Bolsheviks?

_____

_____

Describing

2. What did anarchists believe about government?

_____

_____

Marking the Text

3. Underline the phrase that identifies who was arrested during the Red Scare. Why were they arrested?

_____

_____

354

The Jazz Age

Lesson 1 Time of Turmoil, *Continued*

? Critical Thinking

4. What events of the 1920s are examples of prejudice against immigrants?

_____

_____

📝 Finding the Main Idea

5. What was the main reason for labor strikes?

_____

_____

📝 Examining Details

6. Which two cities are mentioned as examples of labor conflict? Which of the conflicts was the most violent?

_____

_____

were convicted of the crime. Many Americans wanted Sacco and Vanzetti put to death. Some people thought they did not get a fair trial because of their beliefs. Both men said they were innocent. In 1927, a special committee said that the verdict was correct. They were executed soon afterwards. Their trial showed that Americans were afraid of foreigners and people with different ideas about society.

Labor and Racial Strife

After World War I, prices rose quickly. Workers' wages didn't keep up with these price increases. Some workers went on strike for higher wages. Many Americans thought that Bolsheviks and other radicals were causing the trouble. Many white Americans were angry with African Americans, too. They thought African Americans in the North were competing with them for factory jobs.

The Russian Revolution had put Communists in control of Russia. Strikes in America made people afraid that Communists were trying to start a revolution in the United States, too. The Attorney General, Mitchell Palmer, thought the strikes were a threat to American values. He thought they threatened the American values of religion, private property, and democracy. He said the idea of revolution was "eating its way into the homes of the American workingman."

In September 1919, about 350,000 steelworkers went on strike. They wanted higher wages and an eight-hour workday. The steel companies accused them of being "Reds." The strike turned violent, and 18 strikers died in Gary, Indiana. In the end, the strikers did not get what they wanted.

Other strikes failed, also. For example, in 1919, Boston police officers went on strike. They wanted to form a union. Many people did not think that public employees like police and firefighters should be able to go on strike. The governor called out the National Guard to keep order. When the strike ended, all the police officers were fired.

Many Americans believed that radicals were behind the unions and strikes. Businesses and the government also put pressure on people to not join unions. As a result, the number of Americans who were members of a union dropped sharply in the 1920s.

One exception was a union started by A. Philip Randolph. He organized a new union of African American railroad

The Jazz Age

Lesson 1 Time of Turmoil, *Continued*

workers. The union grew even more in the 1930s when the government began to encourage unions.

Tensions also increased between whites and African Americans. In the South, more than 70 African Americans were lynched in 1919. In the North, hundreds of thousands of African Americans had moved to northern cities during the Great Migration. This took place during World War I and after. Many white people were frightened by the change in their cities.

These tensions sometimes caused riots. For example, in Chicago a group of whites threw stones at an African American boy swimming in Lake Michigan. The boy drowned. African American and white gangs fought for two weeks. Fifteen whites and 23 African Americans died. More than 500 people were injured.

Marcus Garvey was an African American leader in New York's Harlem area. Many African Americans in New York and other cities liked his ideas. Garvey formed the Universal Negro Improvement Association (UNIA). UNIA promoted African American pride. It helped African Americans get stronger economically.

Garvey did not believe in **integration**. Integration is whites and African Americans living side-by-side. Garvey wanted African Americans to move back to Africa. He said they could establish their own country there.

Check for Understanding

List three groups of people that came under attack in the United States during the 1920s.

1. _____
2. _____
3. _____

What effect did the economy have on labor and racial tensions after World War I?

_____
_____
_____

✔ Explaining

7. What were Marcus Garvey's views on integration?

_____
_____
_____

Finding the Main Idea

Examining Details

FOLDABLES®

8. Use a three-tab Foldable and place it along the dotted line to cover Check for Understanding. Write the title *Fears After WWI* on the anchor tab. Label the three tabs *Radicalism*, *Labor Conflict* and *Racial Conflict*. Use both sides of the tabs to list facts that you remember about each. Use your notes to help answer Check for Understanding.

Glue Foldable here

The Jazz Age

Lesson 2 Desire for Normalcy

ESSENTIAL QUESTION
How do new ideas change the way people live?

GUIDING QUESTIONS
1. **How did Harding and Coolidge try to return America to quieter ways?**
2. **How did the United States try to avoid involvement in international disputes?**

Terms to Know
lease to rent
laissez-faire a belief that government should have as little involvement in private life as possible

When did it happen?

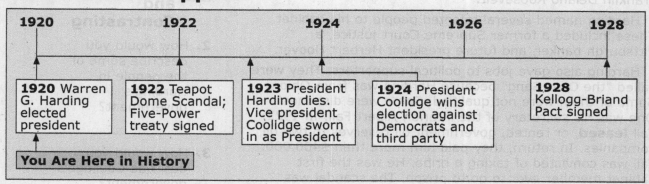

| 1920 | 1922 | 1924 | 1926 | 1928 |

1920 Warren G. Harding elected president

1922 Teapot Dome Scandal; Five-Power treaty signed

1923 President Harding dies. Vice president Coolidge sworn in as President

1924 President Coolidge wins election against Democrats and third party

1928 Kellogg-Briand Pact signed

You Are Here in History

What do you know?

In the first column, answer the questions based on what you know before you study. After this lesson, complete the last column.

Now...		Later...
	Why did Americans want to return to "normalcy?"	
	Who were "the Ohio Gang?"	
	How did Harding and Coolidge treat businesses?	
	What did Harding and Coolidge think about the League of Nations?	

The Jazz Age

Lesson 2 Desire for Normalcy, *Continued*

Harding and Coolidge

Warren G. Harding and Calvin Coolidge were the Republican candidates for president and vice president in 1920. Harding promised a return to "normalcy." It was not clear exactly what Harding meant, but the idea sounded good to Americans. They wanted to return to a time when things were simpler. They didn't want to worry about war and other problems. To many people, normalcy meant a return to life the way it used to be.

In 1920, Harding and Coolidge won the election easily. This was the first time women were allowed to vote. They defeated the Democratic candidates James Cox and Franklin Delano Roosevelt.

Harding named several talented people to his cabinet. These included a former Supreme Court justice, a Pittsburgh banker, and future president Herbert Hoover.

Harding also gave jobs to political supporters. They were called "the Ohio Gang" because Harding was from Ohio. Some of them were not qualified. Some were dishonest. One was his secretary of the interior, Albert Fall. In 1922, Fall **leased**, or rented, government oil reserves to two oil companies. In return, they paid him more than $400,000. Fall was convicted of taking a bribe. He was the first cabinet member ever to go to prison. The scandal was called "Teapot Dome" because that was the name of the location of one of the oil reserves. It became a symbol of dishonesty in Harding's government.

Harding was not personally involved in any of the scandals. But he was very troubled by the problems. In 1923, he took a trip west to get away from the problems. On the trip he had a heart attack and died.

Calvin Coolidge learned about Harding's death while on vacation in Vermont. His father gave him the oath of office to become president because his father was a justice of the peace.

Coolidge was the opposite of Harding in many ways. Harding loved to talk and meet people. Coolidge was called "Silent Cal." He had a reputation for being honest. He appointed honest people to government positions. He supported investigations into Teapot Dome. He quickly replaced dishonest members of the Ohio Gang.

Harding and Coolidge thought that government should be involved as little as possible in business and private lives. This is known as **laissez-faire**. He said that if the

---

✓ **Reading Check**

1. Why did Harding tell Americans he would focus on "normalcy"?

_____

_____

❓ **Comparing and Contrasting**

2. How would you describe some of the people in Harding's government?

_____

3. How would you describe Coolidge's government?

_____

🔤 **Defining**

4. Underline the sentence that explains the meaning of *laissez-faire*.

The Jazz Age

Lesson 2 Desire for Normalcy, *Continued*

? Critical Thinking

5. Why was Coolidge called "a friend to businesses"?

_____

_____

✎ Listing

6. Which countries signed the Five-Power treaty?

_____

_____

_____

✓ Reading Check

7. Why wasn't the Kellogg-Briand Pact successful?

_____

_____

✎ Explaining

8. Why had troops been in the Dominican Republic and Nicaragua?

_____

federal government disappeared, most people would not realize it for "a considerable length of time."

Coolidge helped businesses. While he was president, Congress passed several laws to support business. The government cut spending, cut tax rates for corporations and wealthy Americans, and raised tariffs. They also overturned laws that regulated child labor and women's wages. All of these changes helped businesses earn larger profits.

Coolidge was very popular. The Republicans nominated him to run for president in 1924. He easily won the 1924 presidential election. He got 54% of the popular vote. He defeated both a Democrat and a third party candidate. 1924 was also the first year that women were elected to be state governors. Nellie Tayloe Ross won in Wyoming and Miriam Ferguson won in Texas.

Foreign Policy

Harding and Coolidge believed that the United States should have a limited role in world affairs. This policy is called isolationism. Many Americans supported this policy. They did not want the United States to join the League of Nations or foreign alliances. Harding had promised he would not lead the nation into joining the League.

But both presidents also worked for world peace. In the years after World War I, the United States, Britain, and Japan had raced to build the strongest navy. In 1921 Harding sent Secretary of State Charles Evan Hughes to meet with officials from Japan and Britain. They discussed ways to prevent a buildup to war. In 1922, France and Italy joined the three nations in signing the Five-Power Treaty. They all agreed to limit the size of their naval forces. It was the first time in modern history that strong nations had agreed to disarm.

In 1928, the United States and 14 other nations signed the Kellogg-Briand Pact. This agreement outlawed war. In a few years, 48 other nations had signed it. But the agreement did not provide any way to force countries to follow the agreement.

American troops had been in Latin America since the early 1900s to protect American business interests. Relations with Mexico were tense. In the 1920s, the United States tried a more peaceful approach. Troops were withdrawn from the Dominican Republic and Nicaragua after those countries held elections.

The Jazz Age

Lesson 2 Desire for Normalcy, *Continued*

The Mexican government threatened to take over companies owned by foreigners. Businesses wanted President Coolidge to send troops to protect them. Instead, he negotiated with Mexico. He reached an agreement peacefully. He did not send in troops.

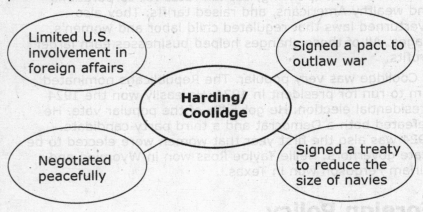

Limited U.S. involvement in foreign affairs

Signed a pact to outlaw war

Harding/ Coolidge

Negotiated peacefully

Signed a treaty to reduce the size of navies

/ / / / / / / / / / / / / / Glue Foldable here / / / / / / / / / / / /

Check for Understanding

Why were people searching for a return to normalcy?

_____

_____

How would you describe foreign policy under Harding and Coolidge?

_____

_____

FOLDABLES®

8. Use a three-tab Venn diagram Foldable and place it along the dotted line to cover Check for Understanding. Write the title *Compare and Contrast* on the anchor tab. Label the left tab *Harding*, the middle tab *Both*, and the right tab *Coolidge*. List facts you remember about each president and what they had in common. Use your Foldable to help answer Check for Understanding.

Lesson 3 A Booming Economy

ESSENTIAL QUESTION

How does technology change the way people live?

GUIDING QUESTIONS

1. **How did electricity improve the lives of people in the 1920s?**
2. **How did the automobile change America during the 1920s?**

Terms to Know

recession an economic downturn
gross national product the total value of all goods and services produced by a nation
productivity worker output, per given amount of time and resources
installment buying purchasing products by making small payments over a period of time

When did it happen?

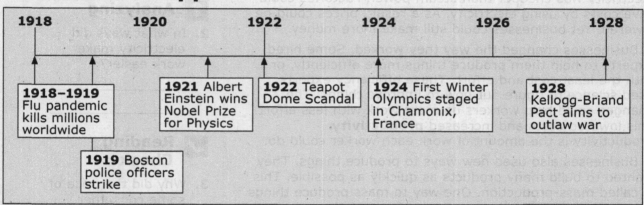

| 1918 | 1920 | 1922 | 1924 | 1926 | 1928 |

1918–1919 Flu pandemic kills millions worldwide

1919 Boston police officers strike

1921 Albert Einstein wins Nobel Prize for Physics

1922 Teapot Dome Scandal

1924 First Winter Olympics staged in Chamonix, France

1928 Kellogg-Briand Pact aims to outlaw war

What do you know?

In the first column, answer the questions based on what you know before you study. After this lesson, complete the last column.

Now...		Later...
	What happened to the U.S. economy after World War I?	
	How did companies treat their workers during this period?	
	What percentage of American homes had electricity by the 1920s?	
	How did the growth in the auto industry affect the rest of the economy?	

networks

Lesson 3 A Booming Economy, *Continued*

Growth in the 1920s

Immediately after World War I, the United States went through a **recession**. A recession is an economic downturn. In the early 1920s, however, the economy began to grow. The **gross national product** (GNP) increased. The GNP is the total value of all goods and services produced in a nation. In 1922, the GNP was $70 billion. By 1929, it was $100 billion.

Industries grew quickly. There were several reasons for this growth. Electrical power was more available. Before World War I, only about 30% of U.S. factories used electricity. By 1929, 70% were powered by electricity. Electricity was cheaper than steam power. Factories could save costs by using electricity. As a result, prices could be lowered. Yet businesses could still make more money.

Businesses changed the way they worked. Some hired experts to help them produce things more efficiently, or with the least cost and effort. These efficiency experts used science to figure out how to improve things. The changes could help workers do more work with less effort. This lowered costs and increased **productivity**. Productivity is the amount of work each worker could do.

Businesses also used new ways to produce things. They wanted to build many products as quickly as possible. This is called mass-production. One way to mass produce things is by using an assembly line. On an assembly line, the product moves from one worker to another. Each worker only does one task over and over. These changes lowered costs and increased productivity.

Another change in management involved how companies treated their workers. They wanted to build better relationships with their workers. They began safety programs which cut down on the number of deaths and injuries at work. Some companies offered health and accident insurance. Some encouraged workers to buy stock in the company. That way they would help the company do its best. This approach was called welfare capitalism. Companies hoped to make workers happier so they wouldn't join labor unions.

By the 1920s, more than 60% of American homes had electricity. Most farming areas did not have electricity, but many cities did. More and more homes would soon get electricity. Businesses made new products that used electricity. These new products included stoves, refrigerators, vacuum cleaners and radios. Electric

Marking the Text

1. Underline the sentence that defines gross national product. How did the GNP change during the period?

_____

Analyzing

2. In what ways did electricity make work easier?

_____

_____

Reading Check

3. Why did the price of some consumer goods become less expensive?

_____

_____

Reading Check

4. What was the goal of welfare capitalism?

_____

_____

The Jazz Age

Lesson 3 A Booming Economy, *Continued*

? Making Connections

5. How are increased advertising and installment buying related?

_____

_____

Abc Marking the Text

6. Underline the sentence that describes a Model T. What new production technique helped make it inexpensive?

_____

appliances made household work much easier. People had more free time.

To sell their new products, businesses spent more money on advertising. Newspapers and magazines had many ads. As radio became more common, businesses created a new way to advertise. It was called a commercial announcement, or just a commercial.

To buy new products, people tried a new way of paying for them. They used **installment buying**. Buyers, or consumers, promised to pay small, regular amounts over a period of time.

New American Management Idea	Goal
hiring efficiency experts	lower costs and increased productivity
mass-production techniques	increased productivity and lower production costs
welfare capitalism	less union participation
increased advertising	increased buying
installment buying plans	increased buying

The Automobile Age

The automobile became an important part of American life in the 1920s. It also became an important part of the economy. The auto industry boomed in the 1920s. Four million people worked making cars or in related jobs. Detroit, Michigan, was the most important city in the world for making cars.

Henry Ford was a pioneer in the automobile industry. His company made the Model T using an assembly line. It was a reliable and inexpensive car. He also paid workers well. Many of his workers could afford to buy their own Model T. Later, companies such as General Motors and others sold more cars, too. All the companies made improvements. The industry continued to grow.

The booming auto industry led to growth in other industries. The steel, rubber, and glass industries grew. They supplied materials used in cars.

363

The Jazz Age

Lesson 3 A Booming Economy, *Continued*

Thousands of people were hired to help build new highways. Businesses such as gas stations and restaurants were built along the new roads. Suburbs also grew. Because they had cars, workers could live farther from their jobs.

Not everyone shared in the growing economy of the 1920s. During World War I, the government bought many farm products for the troops. Prices were high. After the war, the demand fell. European farmers began to grow their own food instead of buying food from America. Because there was less demand, prices went down. Farmers made less money. Many lost their farms.

Other changes took place because of changing technology. New trucks took business away from railroads. Coal miners lost jobs because electricity replaced coal as a power source. Many textile factories also shut down because people were buying fewer cotton clothes. They bought clothes made from new, synthetic materials instead. By 1929, nearly three-fourths of all families had incomes below what was considered necessary for a comfortable life.

////////////// Glue Foldable here //////////////

Check for Understanding

List two reasons industries grew quickly during the 1920s.

1. _____

2. _____

How did new technology affect railroad workers and workers in the coal and textile industries?

_____

_____

? Determining Cause and Effect

7. How did automobiles affect where people lived?

_____

_____

☑ Reading Check

8. Which people and industries in the United States did not share in the nation's economic boom?

_____

_____

FOLDABLES

9. Use a two-tab Foldable and place it along the dotted line to cover Check for Understanding. Write the title *1920s Economic Boom* on the anchor tab. Label the left tab *Cheap Electricity*, and the right tab *Growth of Auto Industry*. Use both sides of the tabs to list what you remember about the effects of both.

Lesson 4 The Roaring Twenties

ESSENTIAL QUESTION

How do new ideas change the way people live?

GUIDING QUESTIONS

1. **Why did American art and society change during the 1920s?**
2. **Why did various groups clash over important issues?**
3. **Who were the presidential candidates of 1928, and what were the major issues of the campaign?**

Terms to Know

flapper a carefree young woman of the 1920s

mass media forms of communication that can reach millions of people

expatriate someone who chooses to live in another country

Prohibition a total ban on the manufacture, sale, and transportation of liquor throughout the United States, achieved through the Eighteenth Amendment

nativism belief that native-born Americans are superior to foreigners

quota system an arrangement setting the number of immigrants allowed from each country

evolution scientific theory that humans and other species changed and developed over long periods of time

When did it happen?

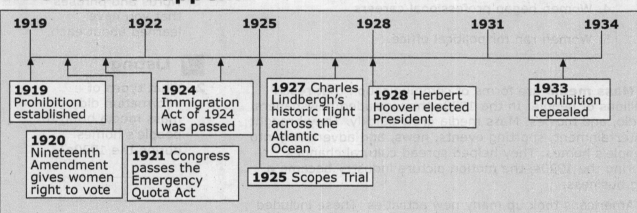

| 1919 | 1922 | 1925 | 1928 | 1931 | 1934 |

1919 Prohibition established

1920 Nineteenth Amendment gives women right to vote

1921 Congress passes the Emergency Quota Act

1924 Immigration Act of 1924 was passed

1927 Charles Lindbergh's historic flight across the Atlantic Ocean

1925 Scopes Trial

1928 Herbert Hoover elected President

1933 Prohibition repealed

What do you know?

In the first column, answer the questions based on what you know before you study. After this lesson, complete the last column.

Now...		Later...
	How did the young women of the 1920s called flappers look and dress?	
	In what areas was Prohibition most successful?	
	Who supported a ban on teaching evolution?	

365

The Jazz Age

Lesson 4 The Roaring Twenties, *Continued*

Social and Cultural Change

The 1920s were a time of great social change. Women won the right to vote in 1920 through the Nineteenth Amendment. More women began to work outside the home. Most became teachers or office workers. Some began professional careers. Others ran for political office. The symbol of the new woman of the 1920s was the **flapper**. Flappers were carefree young women. They wore short "bobbed" hair, heavy makeup, and short skirts.

Changes for Women in the 1920s

1. Women won the right to vote in 1920.

2. Women worked outside the home.

3. Flappers were a symbol for new women.

4. Women began professional careers.

5. Women ran for political office.

/ / / / / / / / / / / Glue Foldable here / / / / / / / / / / /

Mass media are forms of communication that reach millions of people. In the 1920s they included newspapers, radio, and movies. Mass media grew quickly. They brought entertainment, sporting events, news, and advertising into people's homes. They helped spread cultural changes. During the 1920s, the motion picture industry became a big business.

Americans took up many new activities. These included such things as board games, crossword puzzles, flagpole sitting, and dance marathons.

Jazz is a kind of music. Its roots are in African American culture. Jazz became popular during this period. Many people call the 1920s the Jazz Age.

Jazz helped inspire a cultural movement centered in Harlem in New York City. It was called the Harlem Renaissance. African American writers wrote about their experiences in novels, poems, and short stories.

During the 1920s, some writers questioned American ideals. Some of them moved to other countries. They became **expatriates**. Other writers stayed in the United States and wrote about American experiences.

FOLDABLES

📝 Summarizing

1. Place a three-tab Foldable over the text that begins with "Mass media are forms ..." Label the anchor tab *Social and Cultural Change*. Label the three tabs *Mass Media*, *Jazz*, and *American Writers*. On the front and back of the tabs, list words and phrases that you have learned about each.

📝 Listing

2. What types of information did mass media bring to people's homes during the 1920s?

_____

_____

📝 Defining

3. What was the Harlem Renaissance?

_____

_____

366

netw⊙rks

The Jazz Age

Lesson 4 The Roaring Twenties, *Continued*

 Describing

4. What did the Eighteenth Amendment do?

_____

_____

5. What did the Twenty-First Amendment do?

_____

_____

✓ **Reading Check**

6. What is a quota system?

_____

_____

Making Connections

7. Why did Prohibition lead to an increase in crime?

_____

_____

A Clash of Cultures

Prohibition: Alcohol was banned.

Nativism: Native-born Americans are superior to foreigners.

A Clash Between New and Traditional Culture

Religion: Evolution was illegal to teach in schools.

Some Americans feared social change. They thought it was a threat to the traditional American way of life. The Eighteenth Amendment to the Constitution established **Prohibition**. This was a total ban on the making, selling, and transporting of liquor.

Prohibition divided the country. Some people in the South and Midwest were for it. In other areas, the demand for alcohol led people to break the law. Illegal bars, called speakeasies, began to appear in cities.

Prohibition led to more crime. Gangsters made and sold illegal alcohol. They made millions of dollars. Americans came to realize that Prohibition had failed. Prohibition ended in 1933 with the passage of the Twenty-First Amendment.

During the 1920s, **nativism** increased. Nativism is the belief that native-born Americans are superior to foreigners. Nativism led to the rebirth of the Ku Klux Klan. It moved from the South into other areas of the country. The Klan used scare tactics and violence against African Americans, Catholics, Jews, and immigrants. Some people also feared that foreigners would take their jobs.

Nativism also led to a **quota system** that was established by the government. The quota system limited the number of immigrants to the United States from each country. The system favored people from northern and western Europe. But the quota system did not apply to Mexico or Canada. Immigration from these countries increased at that time.

Lesson 4 The Roaring Twenties, *Continued*

Disagreements between old and new values happened in religion, too. A Tennessee law made it illegal to teach **evolution**. Evolution is the scientific theory that humans evolved over vast periods of time. John Scopes ignored the law. He was brought to court for teaching evolution in his high school. Many Christians believed in strictly following the Bible. They were called fundamentalists. They were against the theory of evolution because it did not follow their religious beliefs. Two famous lawyers argued the case. The trial made it appear that some Christians were trying to force their religious beliefs on all Americans.

The Election of 1928

President Coolidge surprised people when he announced that that he would not run for another term. Herbert Hoover was nominated by the Republican Party. Hoover was a Quaker from the Midwest. He was known for his work in helping get food to Europe after World War I. He also tried to get government and business to work together. Hoover supported Prohibition.

The Democratic nominee was Alfred E. Smith. He was a son of immigrants and was governor of New York. Smith was the first Catholic candidate for president. He fought for workers and the poor. He opposed Prohibition.

The 1928 election showed the tensions in American society. Hoover was also helped by a strong economy. He easily won the election. He represented traditional values.

Marking the Text

8. Underline the definition of evolution. What group opposed teaching evolution?

_____

Reading Check

9. Describe Hoover's beliefs about business and government.

_____

_____

FOLDABLES®

10. Use a two-tab Foldable and cut the tabs in half to make four tabs. Place it along the dotted line to cover Check for Understanding. Write *1920s Changes & Conflicts* on the anchor tab. Label tabs for *Women*, *Alcohol*, *Immigration*, and *Religion*. On the front and back of the tabs, write what you remember about the conflicts and changes of each.

Check for Understanding

List three ways that women made progress during the 1920s.

1. _____

2. _____

3. _____

List three areas of cultural conflict during the 1920s and give a short description of the conflict.

1. _____

2. _____

3. _____

,Glue Foldable here

networks

networks

The Depression and the New Deal

Lesson 1 The Great Depression

ESSENTIAL QUESTION

Why do people make economic choices?

GUIDING QUESTIONS

1. *Why did the stock market crash?*
2. *How did the Great Depression bring hardship?*
3. *How did Hoover start to involve the government in the economic crisis?*

Terms to Know

invest spend money on something in the hopes of making more money in the future

stock exchange system in which shares, or part-ownership, of businesses are bought and sold

default fail to pay money that is owed

relief aid for the needy

public works projects such as highways, parks, and libraries built with public funds for public use

When did it happen?

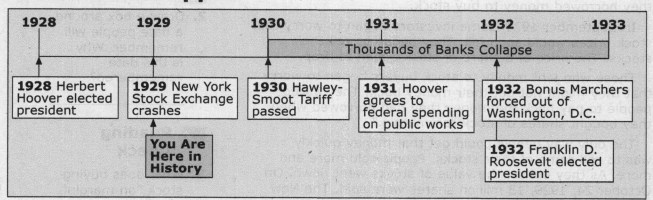

| 1928 | 1929 | 1930 | 1931 | 1932 | 1933 |

Thousands of Banks Collapse

1928 Herbert Hoover elected president

1929 New York Stock Exchange crashes

You Are Here in History

1930 Hawley-Smoot Tariff passed

1931 Hoover agrees to federal spending on public works

1932 Bonus Marchers forced out of Washington, D.C.

1932 Franklin D. Roosevelt elected president

What do you know?

In the first column, answer the questions based on what you know before you study. After this lesson, complete the last column.

Now...		Later...
	Why did people buy stock during the 1920s?	
	Why did some banks fail during the Great Depression?	
	What did President Hoover believe about how the economy should work?	

The Depression and the New Deal

Lesson 1 The Great Depression, *Continued*

The Stock Market Mania

In the 1920s the economy in the United States was strong. Many people had jobs. Leaders said everyone would prosper, or grow rich.

People thought one way to make a lot of money was to buy shares of stock. The **stock exchange** is a system of buying and selling shares of stock. Shares of stock are small parts of corporations. Buyers were **investing**. People bought stock at one price, for example, $1. They expected the price to go up. Then they would sell the shares and get more back than they spent. Some people got rich this way.

Throughout the 1920s, prices for shares of stock went up and up. People also bought shares "on margin." That is, they borrowed money to buy stock.

In September 1929, some investors began to worry that stock prices would soon fall. They began to sell their stocks. The price of a share of stock began to drop.

Those who lent money to stock buyers began to worry that they might not get their money back. They asked people to pay back the money they had borrowed when they bought shares of stock "on margin."

The only way people could get that money quickly was to sell some of their stocks. People sold more and more. As they did so, the value of stocks went down. On October 24, 1929, 13 million shares were sold. The New York Stock Exchange closed for a few days. This stopped people from selling for those few days. The stock market had "crashed."

The Great Depression Begins

In the next two years, the nation went into a deep economic crisis. Companies made less. People bought less. They lost their jobs. The Great Depression had begun.

The stock market crash was not the only cause of the Great Depression. Some experts had noticed problems in the economy all through the 1920s. Wealth was not evenly divided among Americans.

Some Americans made a lot of money, but most did not. As a result, many people borrowed money from banks for things that they needed. The borrowed money to buy land, farm equipment, cars, or homes.

After the stock market crash, many people **defaulted** on their loans. They could not pay back money they had borrowed from the bank. When people defaulted, some

370

Explaining

1. Why did people invest their money in stocks?

_____

_____

_____

Mark the Text

2. Draw a box around a date people will remember. Why is this date remembered?

Reading Check

3. What does buying stock "on margin" mean?

_____

_____

Understanding Cause and Effect

4. What happened when people defaulted on loans?

_____

_____

Lesson 1 The Great Depression, *Continued*

banks went out of business. Thousands of banks closed between 1930 and 1933. Millions of people lost money.

In 1930, Congress placed a tariff, or tax, on imported goods. It was called the Hawley-Smoot Tariff. It made imported goods cost more. People bought fewer imported goods. Foreign countries raised their tariffs, or taxes, on American goods. They bought fewer American goods.

Farmers and manufacturers already had trouble selling their products. Some factories produced too much but sold very little. They did not need to make more products. The factories cut wages and laid off workers. Both foreign and American businesses were hurt.

By 1932, one-fourth of all American workers had no jobs. Those who had jobs worked fewer hours for less pay. People who had no jobs felt worthless. Some tried to shine shoes or sell apples to raise money.

People did not have enough food. Cities often had soup kitchens. People waited in line for bread, coffee, or a bowl of soup. People lost their homes. They sometimes built shacks. Villages of shacks were built. People called these villages "Hoovervilles." They were named for the president, Herbert Hoover. People all over the country wondered why the president was not doing enough to help.

Hoover Reacts to the Depression

President Hoover did not believe the government should be involved in the economy. He thought the economy would recover on its own. He asked business leaders not to cut production or wages. He also asked charities to help the needy. The number of people who needed help went up. The need for **relief** was far too great for the charities to handle.

> **Hoover's ideas included:**
> * Get business leaders and charities to help.
> * Start a public works program.
> * Set up the Reconstruction Finance Corporation

In 1931, Hoover finally knew things had gotten too bad. The government had to do something. He agreed to spend money on **public works** projects. These projects involved building public spaces such as highways, parks, and

✓ Reading Check

5. Why did the Hawley-Smoot Tariff make the Depression worse?

_____

_____

Abc Mark the Text

6. Underline the sentence that tells what some people did for food and where they lived.

Abc Listing

7. Name two examples of public works.

_____

_____

371

The Depression and the New Deal

Lesson 1 The Great Depression, *Continued*

libraries. It seemed like a good idea, but state and local governments did not have money for these projects.

Hoover also asked Congress to create the Reconstruction Finance Corporation, or RFC. The RFC was unsuccessful. It would not loan money if there was too much risk involved.

The story of the Bonus Marchers turned many Americans against Hoover for good. Congress had promised veterans of World War I that they would get extra money in 1945. By 1932, thousands of veterans wanted to ask for the money sooner.

They called themselves the Bonus Army. They traveled to Washington, D.C., and camped near the city. They marched into Washington and demanded the bonus payment. Congress said no. Some veterans left, but about 2,000 stayed. President Hoover called in the Army to remove the veterans and their families. Many Americans were upset that the government had treated veterans so badly. They decided it was time to change the government.

//////////////////// Glue Foldable here ////////////////////

Check for Understanding

What was the difference between the 1920s and the 1930s?

_____

_____

What are two things Americans did to get money, food, and places to live in the 1930s?

_____

_____

Reading Check

8. How did Americans feel about the way Hoover treated the Bonus Army?

_____

_____

_____

FOLDABLES

9. Place a two-tab Foldable along the dotted line to cover Check for Understanding. Write *Compare and Contrast Decades* on the anchor tab. Label the left tab *1920s America* and the right tab *1930s America*. On the front and back of the tabs, list words and phrases about each decade. Use your notes to complete the Check for Understanding.

The Depression and the New Deal

Lesson 2 The New Deal

ESSENTIAL QUESTION

How do governments change?

GUIDING QUESTIONS

1. **What did Roosevelt do to improve the American economy?**
2. **How did the New Deal affect areas of American life?**

Terms to Know

subsidy government money paid to a person or company to do work that will benefit the public

work relief programs that give needy people jobs

When did it happen?

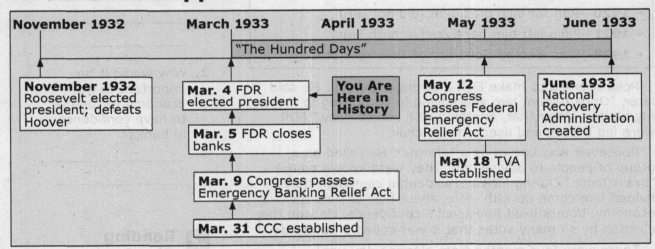

November 1932	March 1933	April 1933	May 1933	June 1933

"The Hundred Days"

November 1932
Roosevelt elected president; defeats Hoover

Mar. 4 FDR elected president

You Are Here in History

May 12 Congress passes Federal Emergency Relief Act

June 1933 National Recovery Administration created

Mar. 5 FDR closes banks

May 18 TVA established

Mar. 9 Congress passes Emergency Banking Relief Act

Mar. 31 CCC established

What do you know?

In the first column, answer the questions based on what you know before you study. After this lesson, complete the last column.

Now...		Later...
	What was Roosevelt's political position?	
	How did polio affect President Roosevelt?	
	How did Roosevelt use work relief?	

373

The Depression and the New Deal

Lesson 2 The New Deal, Continued

Roosevelt in the White House

In 1932 the economy of the United States was falling apart. President Hoover was running for reelection. He knew that not many people would vote for him, though.

The Democrats thought they would win the election. They asked Franklin Delano Roosevelt (FDR) to run for president. FDR was President Theodore Roosevelt's cousin.

Timeline of FDR's Early Life

- **1910**—Was elected to New York State Senate
- **1913**—Was appointed Assistant Secretary of the Navy
- **1920**—Ran for vice president (did not win)
- **1921**—Polio left him paralyzed in both legs.
- **1928**—Was elected Governor of New York State

Polio seemed to make FDR a stronger person. He said later, "Once I spent two years lying in bed trying to move my big toe. After that, anything else seems easy." FDR wore leg braces and used a wheelchair.

Roosevelt was known as a reformer. He relied on a group of people to advise him. They were known as the "Brain Trust." During FDR's presidential campaign they helped him come up with ideas about how to help the economy. Voters liked Roosevelt's confidence. He won the election by so many votes that it was called a "landslide."

There were four months from election day until Inauguration Day. The economy got worse and worse, but Roosevelt was not yet in office. The day he took office he made a speech to the American people. He said, "The only thing we have to fear is fear itself."

One big problem was the nation's banks. Many had gone out of business. Many people had lost their savings. When Roosevelt took office, he immediately closed all the banks for four days. This gave Congress time to pass the Emergency Banking Relief Act.

The president spoke on the radio to tell Americans about his plan to find out which banks had enough money to reopen. People began to trust him. As a result, the plan worked. Roosevelt continued to make these radio broadcasts. They were called his "fireside chats."

Roosevelt had many good ideas for helping the country. During his first hundred days in office, Congress passed many new laws based on his ideas. People felt hopeful again.

374

? Critical Thinking

1. Why did people like FDR?

_____

_____

2. Why would it be important to the economy for people to have confidence in banks?

_____

_____

✓ Reading Check

3. Why did Roosevelt broadcast his "fireside chats"?

_____

_____

The Depression and the New Deal

Lesson 2 The New Deal, *Continued*

FOLDABLES®

✏ Identifying

4. Place a two-tab Foldable under the heading *The New Deal Takes Shape*. Write *New Deal* on the anchor tab. Label the left tab *Subsidies* and the right tab *Work Relief*. Use both sides of the tabs to explain how each program helped individuals and the economy.

A♭c Mark the Text

5. Underline the purpose of work relief. Circle two public works programs.

✅ Reading Check

6. What did the TVA accomplish?

_____

_____

The New Deal Takes Shape

/ / / / / / / / / / Glue Foldable here / / / / / / / / / /

In the first 100 days Roosevelt was in office, he worked with Congress to start new programs and pass new laws. These programs and laws were called the "New Deal." The laws affected many parts of life. They had to do with banking, the stock market, industry, farming, public works, helping poor people, and conservation.

FDR knew that people wanted to work. He created programs to provide **work relief.** These programs put jobless people to work.

One such program was the Civilian Conservation Corps, or CCC. CCC laborers worked on projects that helped the public. They planted trees, improved national parks, and did other things to help the environment.

Roosevelt also asked Congress to pass the Federal Emergency Relief Act, or FERA. FERA gave federal money to the states. The states used the money to help the poor and needy.

One program, called the Agricultural Adjustment Act (AAA) helped farmers. This act gave payments called **subsidies** to farmers. Farmers needed money because they could not sell their products at a fair price. Subsidies gave them enough money to continue farming.

The AAA paid farmers not to use some of their land. It paid farmers to destroy some of their crops. People were shocked, but supporters of the New Deal claimed this was the only way to keep prices high enough for farmers to earn money.

One large public works program was the TVA—the Tennessee Valley Authority. This project helped many people. It gave people jobs. Workers built dams that controlled flooding. They also produced electricity. Thousands of people got electricity for the first time.

Effects of the Tennessee Valley Authority

1. Improved the region's economy

2. Produced electricity

3. Controlled flooding

Lesson 2 The New Deal, *Continued*

Some people argued against the TVA. They did not understand why one region should get so much help. In the end, most people agreed that the TVA was a good idea.

Another important New Deal law was the National Industrial Recovery Act (NIRA). The NIRA created the National Recovery Administration (NRA). The NRA worked with businesses to set up codes regulating prices, wages, and other business practices. It pushed businesses to pay workers a minimum wage.

The New Deal included several other programs to help the economy.

One was the Public Works Administration (PWA). PWA workers built roads, hospitals, and schools. The Federal Deposit Insurance Corporation (FDIC) and the Securities and Exchange Commission (SEC) helped the nation's financial system. The FDIC insured people's bank accounts in case their bank went out of business. This helped people have more trust in banks. The SEC had the power to regulate the stock market. It could also punish dishonest sellers of stocks and bonds.

Roosevelt was able to do a lot in a short time. The Depression continued, however, and recovery was slow. Still, many people were confident that better times were on the way.

//////////////////////Glue Foldable here ///////////////////

Check for Understanding

How did the New Deal and the Hundred Days help the country?

_____

_____

_____

Which New Deal agency helped put people back to work? How?

_____

_____

_____

Classifying

7. Match the word from the list that best fits each of the New Deal programs below.
   a. *stock market*
   b. *banks*
   c. *wages and prices*
   d. *public works*

NRA _____

PWA _____

FDIC _____

SEC _____

FOLDABLES®

8. Use a two-tab Foldable and cut the tabs in half to make four tabs. Place it along the dotted line to cover Check for Understanding. Write the title *Explain* on the anchor tab. Label the four tabs *TVA, NRA, PWA,* and *FDIC and SEC*. Use both sides of the tabs to record what you remember about each. Use your Foldable to help answer Check for Understanding.

The Depression and the New Deal

Lesson 3 Living Through the Depression

ESSENTIAL QUESTION

Why do people make economic choices?

GUIDING QUESTIONS

1. **Why was the Depression difficult for Americans?**

2. **How did minority groups adapt to hard times?**

3. **How did the 1930s become a golden age in entertainment and the arts?**

Copyright by The McGraw-Hill Companies.

Terms to Know

migrant worker a person who moves from place to place to find work

fascism a political philosophy that stresses the glory of the state over individual needs and that favors dictatorship

Where in the world?

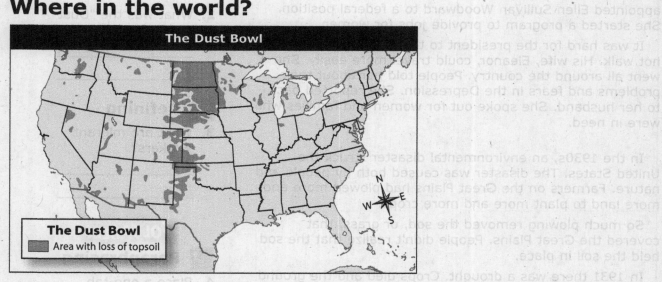

The Dust Bowl

The Dust Bowl
Area with loss of topsoil

When did it happen?

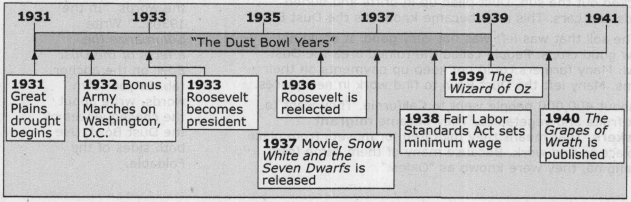

"The Dust Bowl Years"

1931 · 1933 · 1935 · 1937 · 1939 · 1941

1931 Great Plains drought begins

1932 Bonus Army Marches on Washington, D.C.

1933 Roosevelt becomes president

1936 Roosevelt is reelected

1937 Movie, *Snow White and the Seven Dwarfs* is released

1938 Fair Labor Standards Act sets minimum wage

1939 *The Wizard of Oz*

1940 *The Grapes of Wrath* is published

377

The Depression and the New Deal

Lesson 3 Living Through the Depression, *Continued*

Hard Times in America

The Depression was a very bad time for millions of Americans. People were without jobs. They could not afford medical care. Many lost their homes. Families broke apart.

Women took jobs outside the home. They usually were paid less than men. Women worked harder at home, too. To save money, they made their own clothes and baked their own bread. They canned vegetables. Some women started businesses at home.

Women began to work in government. FDR appointed more than 100 women to federal jobs. He named Frances Perkins as secretary of labor. Perkins was the first woman ever to work as part of a president's cabinet. FDR appointed Ellen Sullivan Woodward to a federal position. She started a program to provide jobs for women.

It was hard for the president to travel, because he could not walk. His wife, Eleanor, could travel more easily. She went all around the country. People told her about their problems and fears in the Depression. She reported back to her husband. She spoke out for women and families who were in need.

/ / / / / / / / / / Glue Foldable here / / / / / / / / / / /

In the 1930s, an environmental disaster struck the United States. The disaster was caused both by people and nature. Farmers on the Great Plains had plowed more and more land to plant more and more crops.

So much plowing removed the sod, or grass, that covered the Great Plains. People didn't realize that the sod held the soil in place.

In 1931 there was a drought. Crops died and the ground dried out. Windstorms blew the dried soil into huge dust clouds. The clouds were so big and full of dust that they blocked out the sun. Dust piled up in drifts and buried roads and cars. This area became known as the Dust Bowl.

The soil that was left was not very good. It could not grow good crops. People called the ruined area the Dust Bowl. Many farmers could not keep up payments on their farms. Many left the Dust Bowl to find work in new places.

About 400,000 people went to California. They went to pick fruits and vegetables. They became **migrant workers.** That means they migrated, or moved, from place to place to find work. Because many of them came from Oklahoma, they were known as "Okies."

Indentifying

1. List two ways that Eleanor Roosevelt helped the nation during the Depression.

_____

Reading Check

2. What was the "Dust Bowl"?

_____

_____

Defining

3. What are migrant workers?

_____

_____

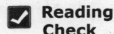

Paraphrasing

4. Place a one-tab Foldable along the dotted line above the words, "In the 1930s..." Write *Summarize the effects of the Dust Bowl* on the anchor tab. In your own words, write about the consequences of the Dust Bowl. Use both sides of the Foldable.

networks

The Depression and the New Deal

Lesson 3 Living Through the Depression, *Continued*

Summarizing

5. How did FDR and Eleanor Roosevelt show support for African Americans?

_____

_____

_____

_____

Listing

6. List four changes that helped Native Americans during the Depression.

_____

_____

_____

Minorities in the Depression

Minority groups had a very hard time during the Depression. Many members of minority groups had no jobs at all. Those who had jobs were not paid well. Many were not treated fairly in other ways.

About half of the African Americans who lived in the South had no jobs. Many who had jobs were fired so white workers could take their jobs. About 400,000 went north. The National Association for the Advancement of Colored People (NAACP) fought discrimination. Thanks to the NAACP, more than 500,000 African Americans joined labor unions. President Roosevelt appointed several African Americans to federal jobs. He had a group of African American advisers. They were called the "Black Cabinet."

FDR's Advisers in the "Black Cabinet"	
Robert Weaver	college professor
Ralph Bunche	became civil rights leader
Mary McLeod Bethune	founded Bethune-Cookman College in Florida

Eleanor Roosevelt also helped African Americans. In 1939, singer Marian Anderson was told she could not sing at a private hall. The First Lady arranged for Anderson to sing at the Lincoln Memorial instead.

Native Americans received some help during the Depression. John Collier was the head of the Bureau of Indian Affairs. He made some changes called the "Indian New Deal." These changes included:

- Reservation land could not be sold
- CCC hired about 77,000 Native Americans
- The Public Works Administration (PWA) gave money to build new schools on reservations
- Congress passed the Indian Reorganization Act of 1934. This paid for more land to make some reservations larger. It restored tribal governments.

About 2 million Latinos lived in the United States in the 1930s. Many had come from Mexico and lived in California. Some were farmers. Some were factory workers. Some were migrant workers.

The Depression and the New Deal

Lesson 3 Living Through the Depression, *Continued*

During the Depression, many Mexican American workers lost their jobs. Many Mexican Americans were sent to Mexico, even if they did not want to go. Those who stayed in the United States often faced discrimination.

The hard times caused some people to think in new ways. Some Americans joined political groups that wanted to make big changes. These radical ideas included communism and socialism.

Fascism was another radical idea. It put the glory of the nation above the needs of its people. Fascists also favored dictatorship. Fascists blamed Jews, Communists, and liberals for the troubles of the Depression. Few Americans were attracted to this type of thinking.

Depression-Era Entertainment

The 1930s was a golden age for entertainment and the arts. There were two main types of entertainment. There was the kind that helped people laugh and forget their troubles. Then there was the kind that showed the injustice and suffering of the Depression years.

Radio shows were very popular. There was drama, adventure, and comedy. Millions of people went to the movies. Movies were a way to escape from worry.

Painters, photographers, and writers used art to show how hard life was. The subject of their art was everyday people in everyday situations.

/ / / / / / / / / / / Glue Foldable here / / / / / / / / / /

Check for Understanding

Name two reasons the Depression was hard on minority groups.

_____

_____

How did the Depression change the lives of women in America?

_____

_____

📝 **Listing**

7. Name three radical political ideas.

_____

_____

_____

✔️ **Reading Check**

8. Why were movies and radio so popular during the Depression?

_____

_____

_____

FOLDABLES

9. Use a two-tab Foldable and cut the tabs in half to make four tabs. Place it along the dotted line to cover Check for Understanding. Write *Hard Times in America* on the anchor tab. Label the tabs *Women*, *African Americans*, *Native Americans*, and *Latino Americans*. On the tabs, write about each group's challenges. Use your Foldable to help answer Check for Understanding.

net works

The Depression and the New Deal

Lesson 4 Effects of the New Deal

ESSENTIAL QUESTION
How do new ideas change the way people live?

GUIDING QUESTIONS
1. **Why did Roosevelt's New Deal programs face growing opposition?**
2. **What did the Second New Deal introduce to America?**
3. **Why was the Second New Deal challenged by the Supreme Court?**

When did it happen?

1935	1936	1937	1938	1939
	Economy Recovering			

1935 Second New Deal begins

1936 Roosevelt reelected to second term

1937 FDR submits Supreme Court plan

1938 Fair Labor Standards Act passes

1935 WPA established

1937 Economic downturn

1935 Social Security Act passes

You Are Here in History

What do you know?

In the first column, answer the questions based on what you know before you study. After this lesson, complete the last column.

Now...		Later...
	Why did some people object to Roosevelt's New Deal?	
	What was the purpose of the Second New Deal?	
	Why did Roosevelt try to "pack" the Supreme Court?	

381

The Depression and the New Deal

Lesson 4 Effects of the New Deal, *Continued*

The New Deal Draws Fire

The New Deal had many critics. Business leaders felt FDR was spending too much money. Some people felt that government had too much power, which they thought was a threat to people's freedoms. However, other critics felt that Roosevelt's New Deal did not go far enough.

Important New Deal Critics

- **Father Charles Coughlin** was a priest from Detroit, Michigan. He wanted rich people to pay higher taxes. He wanted government to take over all banks. Coughlin had a radio program, during which he stated his ideas. His extreme views about minorities and other groups caused him to lose support.
- **Francis Townsend** wanted retired people to get a **pension.** A pension is a monthly payment. Congress did not support the idea, but Townsend made Americans think of older, poor people.
- Senator **Huey Long** of Louisiana was the biggest threat to FDR. He had been governor of Louisiana. His plan was called, "Share the Wealth." He wanted rich people to pay high taxes.

As a senator, Long had a lot of influence. Many people liked his ideas and he planned to run for president. Of course, people who would have to pay for this plan did not like it. Long was popular with many voters, but was killed by an assassin in 1935.

Roosevelt's Second New Deal

The economy was improving by 1935, but recovery was slow. To help speed it up, Roosevelt proposed several reforms that are known as the Second New Deal. It changed American life even more than the laws that were passed in his first Hundred Days.

One of every five workers still did not have a job in 1935. From 1935-1941, the Works Progress Administration (WPA) put 2 million people to work. Under the WPA, people built airports, public buildings, bridges, and roads. The WPA hired artists, writers, and musicians. Some WPA workers created paintings on the walls of buildings. Authors wrote books. Some books were about American folktales and songs. They preserved African American stories and Native American traditions.

Explaining

1. Why did many people oppose the New Deal?

Critical Thinking

2. Why was Father Coughlin able to influence so many people?

_____

_____

Reading Check

3. What group was Townsend's pension plan designed to help?

_____

_____

networks

The Depression and the New Deal

Lesson 4 Effects of the New Deal, *Continued*

? Identifying

4. Who might have objected to the Revenue Act?

_____

_____

_____

? Assessing

5. Why was the Social Security Act such an important piece of legislation?

_____

_____

_____

? Evaluating

6. Do you think President Hoover would have supported the Social Security Act? Why or why not?

_____

_____

_____

? Contrasting

7. How does a sit-down strike differ from other strikes?

_____

_____

_____

Important Programs of the Second New Deal
• **The Revenue Act** (1935) raised taxes on wealthy people and corporations.
• The **Works Progress Administration** (1935) provided government jobs to the unemployed.
• The **Social Security Act** (1935) provided government pensions for retired workers and payments to persons who were unemployed.
• The **National Labor Relations Act** (1935) gave workers the right to join labor unions.
• The **Fair Labor Standards Act** (1938) banned child labor and established a minimum hourly wage.

The Social Security Act created pensions. Tax money paid for the pensions. Both workers and employers paid the tax. The act also had employers pay tax that would go to **unemployment insurance.** Unemployment insurance made payments to people who had lost their jobs.

Social Security also helped people with disabilities. It helped the elderly poor and children whose parents could not support them, too. With this law the federal government took responsibility for the welfare of all citizens.

The National Labor Relations Act (NLRA) is also known as the Wagner Act. Its passage allowed labor unions to grow stronger. In 1936, autoworkers used a new technique, called a "sit-down strike," against General Motors in Flint, Michigan. Instead of going out on strike, they remained inside the plant and refused to leave. This kept the company from hiring workers to replace them. After 44 days, the company gave in to their main demand—the right to have the United Auto Workers union represent them.

The United Auto Workers was an industrial union. This means that all workers in the industry belonged to the same union, whatever their job. It was part of a new labor organization formed around that time called the Congress of Industrial Organizations (CIO).

Unlike the American Federation of Labor (AFL), which organized workers by their craft or skill, the CIO organized workers by industry. CIO members were both skilled and unskilled. Many women and African Americans joined the CIO. By 1938, the CIO represented 4 million workers.

383

The Depression and the New Deal

Lesson 4 Effects of the New Deal, *Continued*

Roosevelt and the Supreme Court

Starting in 1935, the Supreme Court began to declare parts of the New Deal unconstitutional. Roosevelt felt that the 1936 election for president would show if Americans were behind his New Deal. Roosevelt won. He had 61 percent of the vote.

After his reelection, Roosevelt tried to stop the Supreme Court's attack on the New Deal. He asked Congress to increase the number of justices on the Court from nine to fifteen. He hoped to add justices who supported his New Deal programs.

Many people accused the president of trying to "pack" the Court. Roosevelt's idea might have upset the system of checks and balances. Checks and balances between branches of government make sure no one branch is more powerful than the others.

The Court ruled in favor of the Wagner Act and the Social Security Act. Then the Court "packing" issue died. The Supreme Court stayed at nine members, but Roosevelt lost some of his support.

The economy improved for a few years. Then in 1937 it started to get worse again. Critics called this the Roosevelt recession. President Roosevelt tried to fix the problem by spending more on public works.

Even with all the New Deal programs, the economy did not fully recover from the Great Depression. The 1930s came to an end. However, something new began to catch the attention of concerned Americans. Dangerous things were going on in Asia and Europe.

/ / / / / / / / / / / / / / Glue Foldable here / / / / / / / / / / / / / /

Check for Understanding

Tell how the first New Deal and the Second New Deal were similar.

_____

_____

Tell how the first New Deal and the Second New Deal were different.

_____

_____

✓ **Reading Check**

8. Why was FDR's Supreme Court Plan criticized?

_____

_____

FOLDABLES

9. Use a two-tab Foldable and cut the tabs in half to make four tabs. Place it along the dotted line to cover Check for Understanding. Write *Second New Deal* on the anchor tab. Label the tabs *Revenue Act*, *WPA*, *Security Act of 1935*, and *Labor Laws*. On the front and back of the tabs, record what you remember about each. Use your Foldable to help complete Check for Understanding.

America and World War II

Lesson 1 War Clouds Gather

ESSENTIAL QUESTION

Why does conflict develop?

GUIDING QUESTIONS

1. **What events led to the rise of dictators in Europe?**
2. **Why did other nations allow Germany to expand its territory?**

Terms to Know

dictator leader who controls by force

anti-Semitism dislike of or discrimination against Jews

totalitarian seeking to control all aspects of life through dictatorship

appeasement giving in to demands of others in order to keep peace

Where in the world?

When did it happen?

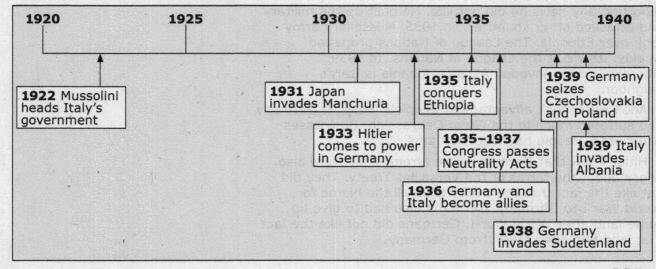

1922 Mussolini heads Italy's government

1931 Japan invades Manchuria

1933 Hitler comes to power in Germany

1935 Italy conquers Ethiopia

1935–1937 Congress passes Neutrality Acts

1936 Germany and Italy become allies

1938 Germany invades Sudetenland

1939 Germany seizes Czechoslovakia and Poland

1939 Italy invades Albania

385

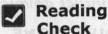
Lesson 1 War Clouds Gather, *Continued*

The Rise of Dictators

Several **dictators** came to power in the 1920s and 1930s.
A dictator is someone who rules by force. The dictators
came to power at a time when people were angry and
worried.

The Treaty of Versailles ended World War I. Many
Europeans did not like what the Treaty of Versailles had
done. Then, in the 1930s there was an economic
depression. Because of the depression, many people did
not have jobs. They did not know when they were going to
get jobs, either.

Leaders like Adolf Hitler made promises to the people.
They promised the people that they would have enough
money again. They promised that their nations would be
great again. Leaders made promises so people would want
them to be in power. After they were in power, the leaders
became dictators. They ruled by force.

Benito Mussolini came to power in Italy. He was the first
dictator in Europe after World War I. Italians were upset
that Italy did not get much from the Versailles Treaty. They
wanted order in their lives because things in Europe were
unsettled.

Mussolini was a fascist (FASH-ist). Fascism is a non-
democratic form of government that stresses the greatness
of a race or nation. By 1922, the Fascist Party forced Italy's
king to say Mussolini was the head of the government.

Mussolini was called *Il Duce* (DOO-chay). *Il Duce* means
"the leader." Mussolini outlawed all other political parties.
He took away people's rights. He stopped newspapers from
reporting any news he did not like. He built up the military
and attacked other countries. In 1935, Mussolini's army
took over Ethiopia. The League of Nations protested
weakly. Italy quit the League of Nations. In 1939,
Mussolini's army invaded Albania. Albania is Italy's
neighbor.

Adolf Hitler took advantage of people's feelings. Germany
had suffered much in the Great Depression. Businesses
had closed. People had lost their jobs.

Hitler knew that Germans were afraid. They were also
angry about the terms of the Versailles Treaty. They did
not like the fact that the treaty gave all the blame for
World War I to Germany. Germany also had to give up
some land after World War I. Germans did not like the fact
that land had been taken from Germany.

✓ Reading Check

1. What plans did
Mussolini and Hitler
share?

_____

_____

Mark the Text

2. Underline the names
of the dictators of
Italy, Germany, and
the Soviet Union.

Explaining

3. How did the Treaty
of Versailles hurt
Germany?

_____

_____

America and World War II

Lesson 1 War Clouds Gather, *Continued*

Reading Check

Paraphrasing

4. What reason did Hitler give for invading Austria?

_____

_____

_____

Critical Thinking

5. Why did Japan invade Manchuria?

_____

_____

Hitler was the head of the Nazi (NAH-tzee) Party (the National Socialist Party). The Nazis believed that Germans were better than other people. Hitler blamed the Jews for Germany's problems. Hitler's **anti-Semitism,** or hatred of Jews, had many terrible results.

Hitler came to power in 1933. He ended democracy in Germany. He set up a **totalitarian** government. A totalitarian leader gets rid of anyone who opposes him. A totalitarian government controls every part of life.

Hitler thought Germany had a right to take more territory. The Versailles treaty said Germany could not rebuild its army, but Hitler did it anyway. He formed a partnership with Italy in 1936.

The Soviet Union was a dictatorship too. In the 1920s, Joseph Stalin became the leader of the Communist Party in the Soviet Union. He killed his enemies and sent "disloyal" people to labor camps.

In Japan, people suffered during the Great Depression. Not enough people had jobs. There was not enough food. Military leaders like Hideki Tojo wanted more land and more resources. In 1931 Japan invaded northeastern China. This region is called Manchuria. There are many minerals in Manchuria.

The League of Nations criticized Japan for invading China, but they did nothing else.

In 1937 Japanese soldiers invaded China. Japan joined Italy and Germany in 1940 to form a group known as "the Axis."

Dictators rose to power, but the United States did not take sides. Congress passed Neutrality Acts. These laws said the United States could not lend money or sell weapons to nations that were at war.

Germany Pushes the Limits

In March 1936, Hitler ordered his soldiers into an area of Germany called the Rhineland. The Treaty of Versailles said that Germany could not have soldiers there, but Hitler sent them anyway.

Two years later, Hitler invaded Austria. He insisted that Austria should be part of Germany.

Next, Hitler focused on the Sudetenland (soo-DAY-tuhn-land). This was a part of Czechoslovakia (CHECK-oh-slo-VAH-kee-uh). Many people there spoke German. Hitler

387

America and World War II

Lesson 1 War Clouds Gather, *Continued*

claimed they were being mistreated. He used this excuse to claim the land for Germany.

Czechoslovakia was ready to fight to keep its land. Britain and France did not want to go to war to help Czechoslovakia. In September 1938, European leaders met in Munich, Germany. They told Czechoslovakia to give Germany the land or to fight Germany alone. They were using a policy called **appeasement** (uh-PEEZ-mihnt). Hitler promised not to expand German territory any more.

Hitler did not keep his promise for very long. In 1939, his army took the rest of Czechoslovakia. Next, he wanted to invade Poland. Poland was on the border of the Soviet Union, so he worried about what Stalin would do. In August 1939, Hitler and Stalin signed a treaty. It said that they would not fight each other. With this treaty, Hitler was able to attack Poland without worrying that the Soviets would attack Germany.

/ / / / / / / / / / / / Glue Foldable here / / / / / / / / /

Check for Understanding

What conditions led to the rise of dictators?

_____

_____

What message did the Neutrality Act send to dictators in Europe and Asia?

_____

_____

✔️ **Reading Check**

6. Why was Germany able to invade Poland?

_____

_____

_____

FOLDABLES®

7. Use a two-tab Foldable and place it along the dotted line to cover Check for Understanding. Write *1930s* on the anchor tab. Label the first tab *Rise of Dictators* and the second tab *Rise of Hitler and Germany*. On the front and back of the tabs, list what you remember about each. Use your Foldable to help answer Check for Understanding.

America and World War II

Lesson 2 World War II Begins

ESSENTIAL QUESTION

Why does conflict develop?

GUIDING QUESTIONS

1. **How did World War II begin?**
2. **Why did the United States gradually become involved on the side of the Allies?**
3. **What happened as the result of the attack on Pearl Harbor?**

Terms to Know
blitzkrieg "lightning war"
disarmament giving up military weapons

Where in the world?

When did it happen?

1935 Neutrality Act limits trade with warring nations

1938 Germany invades Austria and Czechoslovakia

You Are Here in History

1939 Hitler seizes Poland

1940 Selective Training and Service Act passes; German troops occupy Paris; Hitler orders bombing of Britain

1941 Lend-Lease Act passes; Germany attacks Soviet Union; Japan bombs Pearl Harbor, Hawaii; United States declares war

389

networks

America and World War II

Lesson 2 World War II Begins, *Continued*

War in Europe

On September 1, 1939, Hitler sent German soldiers into Poland. The attack was fast and fierce. The Germans called it a **blitzkrieg,** (BLIHTS-kreeg) or "lightning war." Poland was quickly defeated. Two days later, Britain and France declared war on Germany. There was little they could do to help Poland, however. The attack had happened too fast.

Hitler and Stalin divided Poland between them in late September 1939. Stalin also set up army bases in other countries. He set up bases in Latvia, Lithuania, and Estonia. He also tried to set up an army base in Finland, but the Finns fought back. They fought until March 1940. Then they had to surrender.

France and Britain were known as the Allies. They believed Germany would attack France after it attacked Poland. Allied soldiers waited at the border between Germany and France. That part of the border is called the Maginot (mah-zhuh-NOH) Line. The soldiers were there to defend France from a German attack.

Germany did not attack France then. Instead, Germany attacked Denmark, Norway, the Netherlands, and Belgium. After Belgium surrendered, the Allied soldiers pulled back. They went to a port in northern France, called Dunkirk. The soldiers were trapped between the Germans and the English Channel. The British sent 800 warships, ferries, and fishing boats back and forth across the English Channel. The ships rescued more than 300,000 French and British soldiers.

In June 1940, the Germans invaded France. Italy joined with Germany against France. On June 14, German soldiers marched into Paris, the capital city. France surrendered a week later.

By the summer of 1940, Hitler had captured almost all of Europe. England was the only country he did not have. England got ready to be attacked. First, Germany sent planes to bomb England. They bombed air bases, shipyards, factories, and cities. Many people were killed in the bombing raids. The attacks went on from August to October 1940. Britain never surrendered. The British Royal Air Force shot down many German planes. Finally, Hitler gave up his plan to invade Britain.

In 1941 Hitler broke his treaty with Stalin and attacked the Soviet Union. He wanted Soviet resources and land. At first, the Germans were successful. Then, Stalin ordered the Soviets to burn everything. They destroyed their own

Mark the Text

1. Underline in the text the meaning of *blitzkrieg*.

   _____

   _____

Visualize It

2. Describe how the Allied troops escaped from Dunkirk.

   _____

   _____

   _____

Reading Check

3. Why did Hitler end plans to invade Britain?

   _____

   _____

390

America and World War II

Lesson 2 World War II Begins, *Continued*

Mark the Text

4. Underline the sentence that tells what the word *neutral* means.

Reading Check

5. Why did isolationists oppose the Lend-Lease Act?

_____

_____

Critical Thinking

6. Why do you think Roosevelt helped Great Britain?

_____

_____

crops, cities, and dams. The Germans found it hard to supply their troops.

The United States and the War

Most Americans wanted the Allies to win. However, they did not want America to fight. A small group wanted America to stay completely out of Europe's problems.

Roosevelt promised to remain neutral. Neutral means not taking either side in an argument. Roosevelt kept on getting ready for war, just in case. In 1939, Congress passed a new Neutrality Act. It said that nations at war could buy U.S. goods. Roosevelt made a deal with Britain. He gave them 50 warships in exchange for leases on eight British army bases. Roosevelt then signed a new draft law. The law said that American men, ages 21 to 35, could be called to serve in the military.

In 1940, Roosevelt ran for a third term as president and won. He was the first president to go beyond two terms. He promised Americans, "Your boys are not going to be sent into any foreign wars."

In March 1941, Congress passed the Lend-Lease Act. This law allowed America to provide weapons to countries that were important to America's safety. Isolationists did not like the Lend-Lease Act. They said it brought America closer to war.

Roosevelt took other steps to help the Allies without fighting. He told the American Navy to protect British ships that were near America's shores. After German soldiers fired on American ships, Roosevelt said Americans could shoot at German and Italian ships in certain areas.

In August 1941, President Roosevelt and Britain's Winston Churchill signed the Atlantic Charter. It set goals for the world after the Nazis were defeated. The two leaders urged **disarmament**—giving up weapons.

The Japanese Threat

The Germans and Italians advanced in Europe. At the same time, Japan advanced in the Far East. After France fell to Germany, the Japanese captured French-ruled Indochina. They also planned to capture the Philippines, an American territory, the Dutch East Indies, and British Malaya.

Roosevelt responded to the threat. The Japanese could not get any of their money that they had in American

Lesson 2 World War II Begins, *Continued*

banks. He also stopped selling gasoline and other resources to Japan.

The Japanese prime minister wanted to hold talks with the United States. He did not believe that Japan could beat the United States in a war. General Hideki Tojo did think Japan could beat the United States. The prime minister resigned and Tojo began to plan his attack. On December 7, 1941, the Japanese made a surprise attack on Pearl Harbor, Hawaii. The attack destroyed many U.S. warships and planes. More than 2,300 Americans died in the attack.

President Roosevelt called December 7 "a date which will live in infamy." The next day, Congress declared war on Japan. On December 11, Germany and Italy declared war on the United States. The United States joined the Allies. Now the Allies were Great Britain, France, China, the Soviet Union, and the United States. The Axis was Germany, Italy and Japan. The Allies and the Axis were at war.

/////////////////// Glue Foldable here ///////////////////

Check for Understanding

List three events that occurred before the United States joined the war.

_____

_____

_____

How did Roosevelt balance neutrality and getting ready for war?

_____

_____

✓ **Reading Check**

7. Why did Japan attack Pearl Harbor?

_____

_____

🖊 **Identifying**

8. Which countries made up the Axis and Allied Powers?

_____

_____

FOLDABLES

9. Place a three-tab Foldable on the dotted line to cover Check for Understanding. Write *Explain the relationship between ...* on the anchor tab. Label the three tabs *Germany and Italy: Europe*; *Japan: Far East and Pearl Harbor*; and *America: Neutrality and War*. Use both sides of the tabs to write about the relationships between each. Use your Foldable to help you answer Check for Understanding.

netw⊙rks

America and World War II

Lesson 3 On the Home Front

ESSENTIAL QUESTION

Why does conflict develop?

GUIDING QUESTIONS

1. **How did the United States refocus its economy to provide supplies for the war effort?**

2. **How did Americans help the war efforts?**

Terms to Know

ration to limit the number of items that are available to people

civil defense protective measures taken in case of attack

internment camp place where Japanese Americans were sent during World War II

When did it happen?

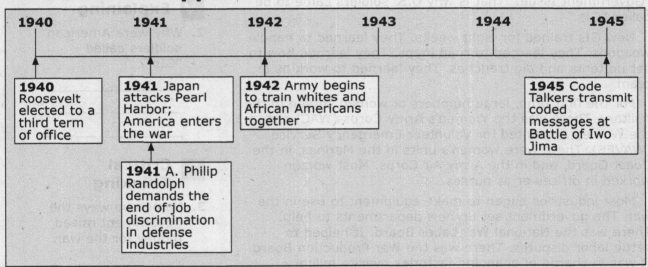

1940 Roosevelt elected to a third term of office

1941 Japan attacks Pearl Harbor; America enters the war

1941 A. Philip Randolph demands the end of job discrimination in defense industries

1942 Army begins to train whites and African Americans together

1945 Code Talkers transmit coded messages at Battle of Iwo Jima

What do you know?

In the first column, answer the questions based on what you know before you study. After this lesson, complete the last column.

Now...		Later...
	What kinds of goods were rationed?	
	How did industries change during wartime?	

393

networks

Lesson 3 On the Home Front, *Continued*

The United States Prepares

America had been preparing for war even before the Japanese attack on Pearl Harbor. The United States had added soldiers to the armed forces with the Selective Service Act.

Now that the country was at war, more than 15 million more Americans joined the armed forces. They volunteered or were drafted.

People who wanted to join the army had to pass a medical test first. Then they got their uniforms and equipment. Uniforms were labeled "G.I." That stood for "Government Issue." That is why U.S. soldiers came to be called "GIs."

New GIs trained for eight weeks. They learned to handle weapons. They learned to read maps. They learned how to set up tents and dig trenches. They learned to work as a team.

For the first time, large numbers of women served in the military. There was the Women's Army Corps (WAC) and the Women Appointed for Volunteer Emergency Service (WAVES). There were women's units in the Marines, in the Coast Guard, and in the Army Air Corps. Most women worked in offices or as nurses.

Most industries began to make equipment to use in the war. The government set up new departments to help. There was the National War Labor Board. It helped to settle labor disputes. There was the War Production Board. It was in charge of changing factories over to military products. For example, automakers made trucks, jeeps, and tanks instead of cars. By 1942, almost all major industries had changed to war production.

The United States spent more than $320 billion on the war. That is 10 times as much as the cost of World War I. To raise money for the war, the government raised taxes on businesses. They made most Americans pay income tax. Congress approved a system to take taxes directly out of people's paychecks.

The government also borrowed money from its citizens. As in World War I, the United States sold war bonds. These were like loans that the government would repay. Movie stars and other famous people urged Americans to buy bonds to support the war.

☑ **Reading Check**

1. How did the United States prepare for war?

_____

_____

_____

🖋 **Explaining**

2. Why were American soldiers called "GIs"?

_____

_____

_____

❓ **Critical Thinking**

3. Name two ways the government raised money for the war.

_____

_____

America and World War II

Lesson 3: On the Home Front, *Continued*

📝 Listing

4. Identify three items that people used ration stamps to buy.

_____

_____

_____

ᴬᵇᴄ Mark the Text

5. Underline the sentence that tells who the code talkers were.

The United States at War

Americans at home felt the effects of the war. Families worried about loved ones fighting overseas. Americans faced shortages of many goods. The government **rationed** products needed for war. When something is rationed, people can only buy it in limited amounts. People got ration stamps which allowed them to buy their share of certain items. There were ration stamps for gas, tires, sugar, coffee, shoes, meat, and other things.

People found many ways to help the war effort. Children collected scrap metal for industry. Adults worked in **civil defense**, or protective measures taken in case of attack. Volunteers watched for enemy planes. People in cities along the coasts had to keep windows covered or keep the lights off. If an enemy plane was flying overhead, it would not see the city. An Office of War Information urged people to get behind the war effort. It encouraged people to be patriotic.

Life changed for women. Millions of women filled the jobs of men who had gone to war. A famous ad campaign showed a woman called "Rosie the Riveter." She urged women to go to work. Many women had never worked outside of their homes.

The war helped people change their attitudes about minority groups. About 1 million African Americans served in the war. At first, they were in segregated units. They had unpleasant jobs.

In 1942, the army began to train whites and African Americans together. African Americans began to get combat assignments in 1944.

An African American fighter group known as the Tuskegee Airmen destroyed more than 250 enemy planes. Benjamin Davis, Jr. was a commander of one of the units of the Airmen. He went on to become the first African American general in the Air Force. His father had been the first African American general in the Army.

In 1941, a labor leader named A. Philip Randolph demanded that the government outlaw discrimination in certain industries. President Roosevelt signed an order that created the Fair Employment Practices Committee. The order said there could be no discrimination in the government or in defense industries.

Native Americans also worked in defense plants and joined the military. Ira Hayes of the Pima tribe became a hero in the battle for Iwo Jima. During the war, a group of

America and World War II

Lesson 3 On the Home Front, *Continued*

Navajo used a code based on their language. The coded messages were about battle plans. These Native Americans were called "code talkers." The Japanese were never able to figure out the code.

Hundreds of thousands of Latinos served in the armed forces. Thirteen Mexican Americans received the Medal of Honor. This is the nation's highest military honor. With the wartime need for labor, the U.S. started the bracero (brah-SEHR-oh) program. More than 200,000 Mexican workers came to help harvest crops and to build and maintain railroads. Still, they often faced discrimination.

Some Japanese Americans served as fighters. Two of these fighting units won the most medals of any in the history of the army.

However, after Japan bombed Pearl Harbor, some military leaders and political leaders were worried. They did not know what these Japanese Americans would do if Japan invaded the United States. As a result, President Roosevelt ordered the Army to send more than 100,000 Japanese Americans to **internment** (ihn-TUHRN-muhnt) **camps.** Many Japanese Americans lost their possessions when they were moved to the camps, which were crowded and uncomfortable. Many Japanese Americans were kept in camps for the next three years. In 1988, the U.S. government finally apologized for this action.

/ / / / / / / / / / / / / Glue Foldable here / / / / / / / / / / / / / /

Check for Understanding

Write how the war affected any two of these groups: families, women, African Americans, Hispanic Americans, and Japanese Americans.

_____

_____

_____

Why was it necessary to make changes at home while the United States was at war?

_____

_____

_____

Explaining

6. What happened to many Japanese Americans during the war?

_____

_____

FOLDABLES®

7. Place a three-tab Foldable on the dotted line to cover Check for Understanding. Cut each tab in half to make six tabs. Write *How did the war affect* on the anchor tab. Label the six tabs *families, women, African Americans, Native Americans, Hispanic Americans,* and *Japanese Americans.* On both sides of the tabs, describe what you remember about the effects war had on each. Use the information to help you complete the Check for Understanding.

netw⊛rks

America and World War II

Lesson 4 The European Theater of War

ESSENTIAL QUESTION

Why does conflict develop?

GUIDING QUESTIONS

1. **What strategies allowed for a successful campaign against the Axis powers in North Africa?**

2. **How did the two-front war fought by the Allies lead to the defeat of the Axis powers?**

3. **What is the Holocaust, and how did it begin?**

Terms to Know

siege military blockade

genocide killing an entire ethnic group

Holocaust the mass slaughter of Jews by Nazis during World War II

concentration camp large prison camp used to hold people for political reasons

When did it happen?

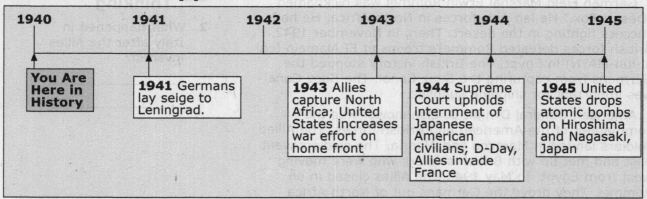

1940	**You Are Here in History**
1941	**1941** Germans lay seige to Leningrad.
1942	
1943	**1943** Allies capture North Africa; United States increases war effort on home front
1944	**1944** Supreme Court upholds internment of Japanese American civilians; D-Day, Allies invade France
1945	**1945** United States drops atomic bombs on Hiroshima and Nagasaki, Japan

What do you know?

In the first column, answer the questions based on what you know before you study. After this lesson, complete the last column.

Now...		Later...
	Why did the Allies invade North Africa first?	
	What was Operation Overlord?	

397

America and World War II

Lesson 4 The European Theater of War, *Continued*

Focusing on the Nazi Threat

When the United States joined the war, the Axis armies already controlled most of Europe. They also controlled much of North Africa. They were trying to control the Soviet Union. There was a possibility that Germany could win the war.

Stalin wanted the Allies to attack Europe. That would force Hitler to pull soldiers out of the Soviet Union. Churchill and Roosevelt wanted something else. They wanted to attack the edges of German-controlled lands. They decided to invade North Africa. This would give U.S. soldiers time to get used to fighting. It would also help the British, who were already fighting in Egypt against the Axis.

German Field Marshal Erwin Rommel was nicknamed "Desert Fox." He led Axis forces in North Africa. He had success fighting in the desert. Then, in November 1942, British forces defeated Rommel's troops at El Alamein (ehl al-luh-MAYN) in Egypt. The British victory stopped the Germans from capturing the Suez Canal. The Suez Canal was important for shipping supplies.

American General Dwight D. Eisenhower was the commander of the American and British forces. The Allied soldiers landed in Morocco and Algeria. The soldiers went east and met up with British soldiers who were moving west from Egypt. In May 1943, the Allies closed in on Rommel. They drove the Germans out of North Africa.

Allied soldiers then went to southern Europe. First they took the island of Sicily, which is part of Italy. In September 1943, they landed on the mainland of Italy. Eisenhower planned this invasion too. Under Eisenhower was U.S. General George Patton and British General Bernard Montgomery. These two generals led the troops.

The Allies moved forward. The Italians overthrew Mussolini. There was a new government, and it surrendered to the Allies. German soldiers who were in Italy kept fighting, but in the end, they lost. In June 1944, the Allies captured Rome, Italy's capital.

The Allies Take Control in Europe

The war was fought on two fronts. Allied soldiers fought German troops in North Africa. Germans were also fighting in the Soviet Union. In June 1941, the Germans began a **siege** (SEEJ) of Leningrad. During a siege, nothing can go in or out of a city.

398

Mark the Text

1. Underline the name of the general who led the German forces in North Africa. Circle the name of the general who led the Allies.

Critical Thinking

2. What happened in Italy after the Allies invaded?

_____

_____

Reading Check

3. Why did the Allies invade North Africa first instead of Europe?

_____

_____

America and World War II

Lesson 4 The European Theater of War, *Continued*

✓ Reading Check

4. Why was the Battle of the Bulge an important Allied victory?

_____

_____

_____

FOLDABLES®

📖 Describing

5. Place a one-tab Foldable under the heading *The Holocaust.* Write *Escalation of Violence Against Jews* on the anchor tab. In your own words, describe how the Jews were treated after Hitler became leader. Draw an arrow from the Bottom of the tab pointing up. Begin your list at the bottom of the Foldable and go up to show the escalation of violence.

The siege of Leningrad lasted almost 900 days. Food ran out, and hundreds of thousands of Soviets died. Even so, they did not surrender. In early 1944, Soviet soldiers were able to end the siege.

The Germans tried to take other cities in the Soviet Union. In 1941, they tried to take the capital city, Moscow. It was slow going. Many Germans died. When the Germans finally reached Moscow, the Soviets fought hard. The Germans had to leave. In 1942, the Germans attacked and captured Stalingrad. After they went into the city, Soviet soldiers surrounded it. The Soviets cut off German supplies. The soldiers inside Stalingrad began to starve. They finally surrendered in February 1943. This was a big turning point in the war. The Soviets started attacking. The German army pulled back.

The Allies planned an attack. The attack was called Operation Overlord. The Allies would invade Western Europe. On June 6, 1944, soldiers landed on the beaches of Normandy, France. Within a few weeks, a million Allied soldiers were there. June 6, 1944 is known as "D-Day."

The Germans could not stop the Allies. The Allies moved across France. They pushed the Germans back. On August 25, French and American soldiers freed the city of Paris.

In the fall of 1944, Germany was fighting to survive. Then they attacked in Belgium. They pushed the Allies back. The German line had a bulge in it. This became known as the Battle of the Bulge. After weeks of fighting, the Allies pushed back the Germans and headed into Germany. The Soviets reached Berlin in February 1945. On April 30, 1945, Hitler committed suicide. Germany surrendered on May 7. The next day became V-E Day which stands for "Victory in Europe."

President Roosevelt died on April 12, 1945. He did not live to see the end of the war. Harry S. Truman had been vice president. He became president.

The Holocaust

/ / / / / / / / / / Glue Foldable here / / / / / / / / / / /

As Allied troops freed German-held areas, they discovered proof of Nazi cruelty. After Hitler came to power, the Nazis began to carry out the "final solution," or **genocide** (JEH-nuh-syd). Genocide is to wipe out an entire group of people. Two-thirds of Europe's Jews were killed in the **Holocaust** (HAH-luh-kawst). The total number of Jews the Nazis killed was six million. The Nazis killed millions of

America and World War II

Lesson 4 The European Theater of War, *Continued*

others, too. They killed communists, Roma (Gypsies), disabled people, and others.

Beginning in 1942, the Nazis built death camps and sent the Jews there. It was a crime to be Jewish. Two such camps were Auschwitz (OWSH-vitz) and Treblinka. Jews were killed with poison gas. Many died of starvation. Many others were victims of cruel medical experiments.

Healthy prisoners were forced to do slave labor. Anyone who was sick or weak was sent to gas chambers and killed with poison gas. Then their bodies were burnt in furnaces.

Allied governments knew about death camps as early as 1942. Today, historians wonder how something so horrible could have happened and why so little was done to stop it.

The United States Holocaust Memorial in Washington, D.C., honors the victims. The World War II Memorial honors those who served in the military. It is dedicated to those who served their country in the military, those who died, and those who served on the home front.

> ### Check for Understanding
> **Explain why fighting a war on two fronts led to the defeat of the Axis Powers.**
>
> _____
>
> _____
>
> **Why was Operation Overlord a success?**
>
> _____
>
> _____

Glue Foldable here

☑ Reading Check

6. What groups did the Nazi government victimize?

_____

_____

❓ Critical Thinking

7. Why are the Holocaust Memorial and the World War II Memorial important?

_____

_____

FOLDABLES®

8. Place a two-tab Foldable along the dotted line to cover Check for Understanding. Write *Two-Front War* on the anchor tab. Label the top tab *West: Europe and North Africa* and the bottom tab *East: Russia*. On the front and back of each tab, list what you remember about the war on each front. Use your Foldable to help answer Check for Understanding.

America and World War II

Lesson 5 The War in the Pacific

ESSENTIAL QUESTION
Why does conflict develop?

GUIDING QUESTIONS
1. **What events occurred on the Pacific front?**
2. **How did the United States' use of the atomic bomb bring about Japan's surrender?**

Terms to Know
island hopping a strategy of capturing an island and using it to leapfrog to the next island
kamikaze a Japanese suicide pilot

Where in the world?

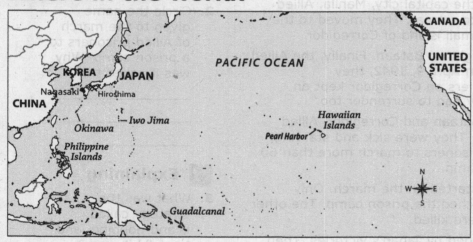

When did it happen?

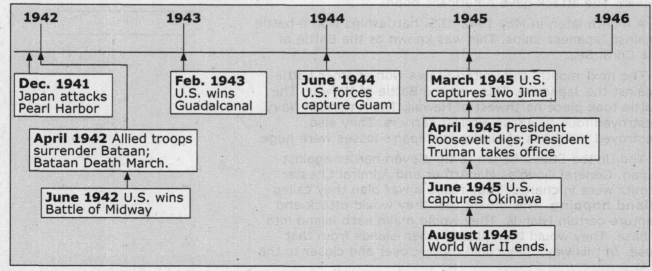

| 1942 | 1943 | 1944 | 1945 | 1946 |

Dec. 1941 Japan attacks Pearl Harbor

April 1942 Allied troops surrender Bataan; Bataan Death March.

June 1942 U.S. wins Battle of Midway

Feb. 1943 U.S. wins Guadalcanal

June 1944 U.S. forces capture Guam

March 1945 U.S. captures Iwo Jima

April 1945 President Roosevelt dies; President Truman takes office

June 1945 U.S. captures Okinawa

August 1945 World War II ends.

America and World War II

Lesson 5 The War in the Pacific, *Continued*

The Pacific Front

The war with Japan was not like the war in Europe. The war took place in the huge Pacific Ocean. There are hundreds of islands there of different sizes. Most of the war had to do with capturing islands.

On the day of the Pearl Harbor attack, Japan also bombed American airfields in the Philippines, Wake Island, and Guam. These were key American bases. Then Japanese troops invaded Thailand and Malaya. Japan captured Guam, Wake Island, and Hong Kong.

In December 1941, Japanese troops landed in the Philippines. They captured the capital city, Manila. Allied soldiers there were forced to retreat. They moved to the Bataan Peninsula and the small island of Corregidor.

For months the Allies fought on Bataan. Finally, the Allied soldiers were exhausted. On April 9, 1942, they surrendered. However, soldiers on Corregidor kept on fighting. A month later, they had to surrender too.

The Japanese captured Bataan and Corregidor. Allied troops were taken prisoner. They were sick and starving. The Japanese forced the prisoners to march more than 60 miles (97 km) to a prison camp.

About 76,000 prisoners started on the march. Only about 54,000 prisoners reached the prison camp. The other 20,000 prisoners died or were killed.

Americans were discouraged by Japan's victories. Then in April 1942, U.S. planes bombed Tokyo. The attack started from the deck of an aircraft carrier in the Pacific Ocean. The attack gave Americans hope.

A month later, in May 1942, U.S. battleships won a battle against Japanese ships. This was known as the Battle of the Coral Sea.

The next month, the United States won another battle against the Japanese. This was the Battle of Midway. The battle took place northwest of Hawaii. The American Navy destroyed four Japanese aircraft carriers. They also destroyed hundreds of airplanes. Japan's losses were huge.

The United States began to fight even harder against Japan. General Douglas MacArthur and Admiral Chester Nimitz were in charge. They made a war plan they called **island hopping.** This meant that they would attack and capture certain islands. They would make each island into a base. They would then attack other islands from that base. In this way, they could move closer and closer to the

☑ Reading Check

1. What is significant about the Battle of Midway?

_____

_____

🔤 Mark the Text

2. Circle the name given to the march of Allied prisoners to a prison camp. Why was it called that?

_____

_____

_____

🖌 Explaining

3. What was the strategy called island-hopping, and how did it work?

_____

_____

_____

America and World War II

Lesson 5 The War in the Pacific, Continued

☑ **Reading Check**

4. What was the goal of the Manhattan Project?

_____

_____

🔤 **Defining**

5. Why were kamikaze pilots called suicide bombers?

_____

_____

Philippines. More importantly, they could move closer and closer to Japan.

The plan worked.

- Between August 1942 and February 1943, U.S. forces captured Guadalcanal.
- In June 1944, U.S. forces captured Guam and other nearby islands.
- In October, U.S. ships destroyed many Japanese ships at the Battle of Leyte Gulf. This was in the Philipines.
- In March 1945, U.S. forces captured the island of Iwo Jima.
- In June 1945, U.S. forces captured the island of Okinawa.

Iwo Jima and Okinawa were close to Japan. The Japanese fought fiercely to keep them. Thousands of American soldiers died. Thousands more were wounded.

The Allies had destroyed most of Japan's air force and most of Japan's navy. U.S. planes bombed Tokyo and other Japanese cities.

In return, the Japanese sent pilots called **kamikazes** (kah-mih-KAH-zee). Kamikaze pilots were suicide bombers. They crashed their planes into American ships. In this way, they sank several ships. This happened during the battle for Okinawa.

The Atomic Bomb Ends the War

The battle of Iwo Jima and Okinawa showed that the Japanese would keep fighting no matter what. They refused to surrender. Therefore, the United States decided to use a powerful new weapon. That weapon was the atomic bomb.

Six years earlier, in 1939, the scientist Albert Einstein warned President Roosevelt that the Nazis were trying to build "extremely powerful bombs." These bombs used atomic energy. Roosevelt gathered a group of scientists. They told Roosevelt he should start building an atomic bomb for America. Roosevelt created a top secret program called the "Manhattan Project" to build the bomb. On July 16, 1945, the first atomic bomb was tested in the New Mexico desert.

U.S. officials discussed whether to use the atomic bomb. The final decision was up to President Truman. Truman had

America and World War II

Lesson 5 The War in the Pacific, *Continued*

been Vice President. When President Roosevelt died in April 1945, Truman took over.

President Truman decided to use the bomb. He believed it would end the war sooner and save American lives.

President Truman and the Allied leaders first sent a warning to Japan. Japan did not surrender. Truman gave the order to drop the bomb on Japan.

On August 6, 1945, a U.S. plane dropped an atomic bomb on the Japanese city of Hiroshima. It killed between 80,000 and 120,000 people. Three days later, the United States dropped a second bomb. This bomb was dropped on the Japanese city of Nagasaki. It killed between 35,000 and 74,000 people. Thousands more suffered from illness and burns caused by the bombs.

On August 15, 1945, the Japanese surrendered. This became known as "V-J Day." Japan signed a formal surrender on September 2.

World War II was finally over. It was the most destructive war in history. Millions of people had died. Millions more were left sick or wounded. The Soviet Union lost the most people. There, at least 18 million people died.

Survivors faced many challenges. Countries were faced with a huge job of rebuilding.

/ / / / / / / / / / / / / / Glue Foldable here / / / / / / / / / / / / / /

Check for Understanding

Which strategy changed the course of the war in favor of the Allies, and how?

_____

_____

What were two main actions that helped the Allies win against Japan?

_____

_____

Explaining

6. Describe what Truman did before giving the order to use the atomic bomb.

_____

_____

Identifying

7. On which two cities were atomic bombs dropped?

_____

_____

FOLDABLES®

8. Use a three-tab Foldable and place it along the dotted line to cover Check for Understanding. Write *The Pacific Front* on the anchor tab. Label the three tabs *Allied Troops Defensive*, *Allied Troops Offensive*, and *Allied Victory*. On the front and back of the tabs, write one thing you remember about each. Use your Foldable to help answer Check for Understanding.

networks

The Cold War Era

Lesson 1 Roots of the Cold War

ESSENTIAL QUESTION
What are the consequences when cultures interact?

GUIDING QUESTIONS

1. *What plans were created for the organization of the postwar world?*
2. *How did Western Allies resist Soviet attempts to halt the plans for uniting West Germany?*
3. *How did the United States and the Soviet Union become rivals and influence the world?*
4. *How did the Cold War heighten American fears of communism?*

Where in the world?

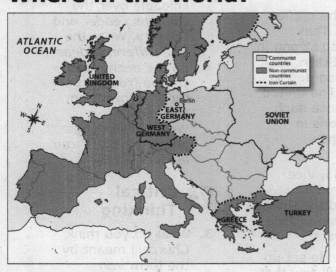

Terms to Know

iron curtain political divison in Europe between communist countries and democracies.
containment stopping communism
airlift deliver supplies by airplane
cold war conflict in which two enemies fight in other ways besides combat
perjury the crime of lying when you have promised to tell the truth
subversion attempt to overthrow a government
espionage spying
censure to criticize in an official way

When did it happen?

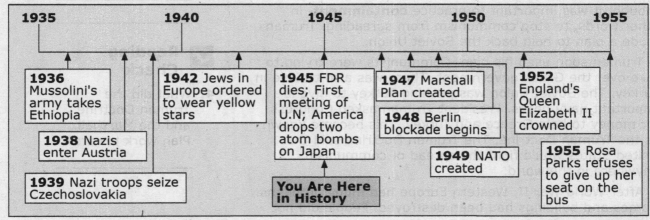

| 1935 | 1940 | 1945 | 1950 | 1955 |

1936 Mussolini's army takes Ethiopia

1938 Nazis enter Austria

1939 Nazi troops seize Czechoslovakia

1942 Jews in Europe ordered to wear yellow stars

1945 FDR dies; First meeting of U.N; America drops two atom bombs on Japan

You Are Here in History

1947 Marshall Plan created

1948 Berlin blockade begins

1949 NATO created

1952 England's Queen Elizabeth II crowned

1955 Rosa Parks refuses to give up her seat on the bus

405

networks

The Cold War Era

Lesson 1 Roots of the Cold War, *Continued*

Wartime Relationships

Before the end of World War II, leaders from major Allied countries met to talk about the future. They wanted to talk about what should happen to Europe after the war. The leaders had different ideas about what should happen.

Glue Foldable here

Leader	Country
Franklin D. Roosevelt	United States
Winston Churchill	Great Britain
Joseph Stalin	Soviet Union

The U.S. president was Franklin Roosevelt. The prime minister of Great Britain was Winston Churchill. They wanted to stop the Soviet Union from getting too strong in Eastern Europe. The Soviet leader was Joseph Stalin. He wanted to control Eastern Europe. The leaders agreed to split Germany up. They split it into four zones. The United States, Great Britain, the Soviet Union, and France each took one zone. Stalin agreed to hold free elections in Eastern Europe. He also offered to help plan a new international organization.

President Roosevelt died suddenly in April 1945. Vice President Harry S. Truman became president. Truman helped set up an international organization called the United Nations, or U.N. Fifty nations met for the first time in June 1945. They hoped the U.N. could help prevent wars.

Stalin kept Soviet soldiers in Eastern Europe. He set up communist governments there. Winston Churchill saw that Eastern Europe was cut off from Western Europe. Churchill called this division an **"iron curtain."** President Truman thought it was important to practice **containment,** in other words, to stop communism from spreading. Truman made a plan to hold back the Soviet Union.

Truman soon used his plan. Communists were trying to take over the Greek government. There was also trouble in Turkey. The Soviet Union was pushing Turkey to give it important navy bases. President Truman asked Congress for money to help Greece and Turkey. This became known as the Truman Doctrine. The Truman Doctrine said the United States would fight the spread of communism anywhere in the world.

After World War II, Western Europe had many problems. Homes and buildings had been destroyed. People did not

Mark the Text

1. Circle the countries that controlled the four zones in Germany.

Describing

2. Place a one-tab Foldable over the columns *Leader* and *Country.* Write the title *Different Ideas* on the anchor tab. On the front, draw three arrows from the anchor tab. Write three things about the Big Three leaders' ideas.

? Critical Thinking

3. What do you think Churchill meant by the term *iron curtain?*

_____

_____

☑ Reading Check

4. What did the Truman Doctrine and the Marshall Plan work toward?

_____

_____

The Cold War Era

Lesson 1 Roots of the Cold War, *Continued*

have jobs. They were hungry. People wanted anything that would make their lives better, even communism. The United States gave help. From 1948 to 1951, the U.S. sent $13 billion worth of food, supplies, machinery, and aid to Western Europe. This program was called the Marshall Plan. The United States hoped the aid would keep Western Europe from becoming communist.

Crisis in Berlin

Germany was divided into four zones. The three western zones were controlled by the United States, Great Britain, and France. The eastern zone was held by the Soviet Union. Berlin was Germany's capital. It, too, was divided into four zones. Berlin was deep within the Soviet zone.

Truman wanted to reunite the different parts of Germany. Stalin did not want to. He thought this would be a danger to the Soviet Union. The United States, Great Britain, and France said they would unite their three zones. This included their parts of the city of Berlin.

Stalin tried to block this. He put soldiers outside of West Berlin to stop supplies from coming into the city. He thought the Western countries would change their minds.

President Truman wanted to stick to his plan, yet he didn't want to risk war by taking military action. The United States and Great Britain organized an **airlift.** This means they used airplanes to drop in food, fuel, and other supplies. They bypassed the Soviet soldiers.

The Cold War Deepens

Berlin was an early problem in the Cold War. A **cold war** is a war in which the two sides try to frighten each other with their words and weapons, but they do not fight.

Democracies in the West worked together. In 1949, the United States, Canada, and 10 other countries formed the North Atlantic Treaty Organization, or NATO. Each country agreed to help another if it was attacked. In response, the Soviet Union created the Warsaw Pact. This included the communist governments in Eastern Europe.

Other parts of the world saw changes. Many countries that had been colonies won their freedom. These included the Philippines, India, Burma, and Pakistan. The U.N. also created the state of Israel. In China, communist forces took over the government. Their leader was Mao Zedong. The United States was afraid that communism was growing

☑ Reading Check

5. Why was the Soviet Union against reuniting Germany?

_____

_____

✐ Mark the Text

6. Underline the definition of the word *airlift*.

✐ Mark the Text

7. Underline four countries that became independent or won their freedom during the Cold War.

netw⊙rks

The Cold War Era

Lesson 1 Roots of the Cold War, *Continued*

even stronger. It seemed that Asia was a strong ally of the Soviet Union.

A New Red Scare

During the Cold War Americans feared communist **subversion.** Subversion is an effort to overthrow a government. Americans worried that communists were sneaking into the government.

There were stories in the news about **espionage,** or spying. In 1948 Whittaker Chambers said Alger Hiss had given him secret U.S. documents which Chambers had passed on to the Soviet Union. Hiss was sent to jail for **perjury,** or lying in court. Julius and Ethel Rosenberg were members of the Communist Party in America. They were accused of giving the Soviet Union secrets about America's atomic bomb. They were put to death.

Senator Joseph McCarthy from Wisconsin hunted for communists in American government. He accused many people of being communists. Often, he did not have any proof. People who were accused lost their jobs. At first, people believed McCarthy. Many people were afraid he could accuse them of being spies. McCarthy's hearings were on television. He accused respected Army officials of being spies. People began to see that McCarthy was wrong. They saw him as a bully. The word **McCarthyism** is used to describe a serious accusation without evidence. Congress **censured,** or publicly criticized, Senator McCarthy.

/////////////// Glue Foldable here ///////////

Check for Understanding
Explain the purpose of the United Nations.

_____

_____

What did the Truman Doctrine hope to accomplish?

_____

☑ **Reading Check**

8. What concerns did the West have about China?

_____

_____

☑ **Reading Check**

9. What claim did McCarthy make against the Army?

_____

_____

FOLDABLES

10. Cover Check for Understanding with a three-tab Venn diagram Foldable. Write *The Beginning of the Cold War* on the anchor tab. Label the first tab *Democratic Countries*, the middle tab *The Cold War*, and the last tab *Communist Countries*. List facts to show how countries were involved in the Cold War. Use the Foldable to help answer Check for Understanding.

The Cold War Era

Lesson 2 Early Cold War Politics

ESSENTIAL QUESTION
Why do people make economic choices?

GUIDING QUESTIONS
1. ***Why did the United States face rising prices and labor unrest during the late 1940s?***
2. ***Why did Truman and the Republicans disagree about how to solve the nation's economic problems?***
3. ***What civil rights reform did the Truman administration push for?***

Where in the world?

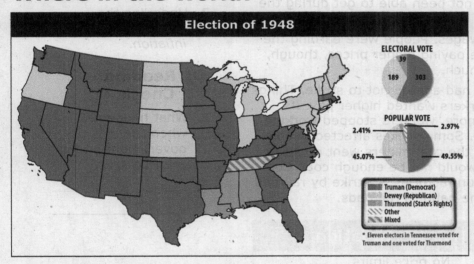

Election of 1948

ELECTORAL VOTE
39
189   303

POPULAR VOTE
2.41%   2.97%
45.07%   49.55%

■ Truman (Democrat)
▨ Dewey (Republican)
▧ Thurmond (State's Rights)
▨ Other
▨ Mixed

* Eleven electors in Tennessee voted for Truman and one voted for Thurmond

Terms to Know
inflation increase in prices
Fair Deal a program aimed at solving some of the nation's economic problems
closed shop business forced to hire only union members
desegregate end the separation of people according to race

When did it happen?

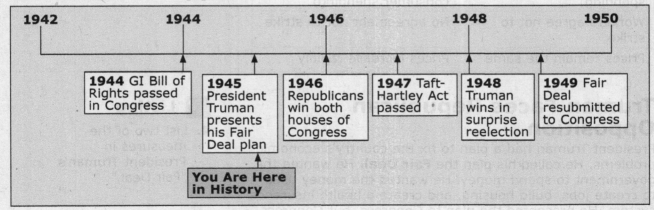

1942   1944   1946   1948   1950

1944 GI Bill of Rights passed in Congress

1945 President Truman presents his Fair Deal plan

1946 Republicans win both houses of Congress

1947 Taft-Hartley Act passed

1948 Truman wins in surprise reelection

1949 Fair Deal resubmitted to Congress

You Are Here in History

409

The Cold War Era

Lesson 2 Early Cold War Politics, Continued

The Peacetime Economy

The economy had to adjust after World War II. Industries had made supplies for the war. They had to switch back to making products for everyday use. People had to be retrained to do this. Soldiers were also returning. They needed jobs and training.

During the war, the government had set limits on prices. This kept prices low. After the war, the government ended the price limits. Prices began to rise. The rise in prices is called **inflation.** People began to spend more and more money on things they had not been able to get during the war. When people spend a lot of money, prices rise.

Prices rose faster than wages. People were earning the same as before. They were paying higher prices, though, so they could not buy as much.

During the war, workers had agreed not to strike. Things changed after the war. Workers wanted higher pay. If employers would not pay more, workers stopped working. This is called a labor strike. Some strikes affected people all over the country. When the coal miners went on strike, people worried that there would not be enough coal. Coal was used for heat and to run factories. A strike by railroad workers shut down all of the nation's railroads.

Stable economy	Inflation
Government limits prices	No price limits
Limited goods (stable spending)	Unlimited goods (high consumer spending)
Workers agree not to strike	No agreement not to strike
Prices remain the same	Prices increase rapidly

Truman Faces Republican Opposition

President Truman had a plan to fix the country's economic problems. He called his plan the **Fair Deal.** He wanted the government to spend money. He wanted the money used to create jobs, build housing, and create a health insurance system. He presented the plan to Congress, but Congress did not vote for Truman's plan.

Many people blamed the president and Congress for the economic problems. In the next election, they voted for

✍ Explaining

1. What did factories have to do after the war ended?

_____

_____

🔤 Mark the Text

2. Underline the definition of *inflation.*

✔ Reading Check

3. What happened when the government ended price controls?

_____

_____

✍ Listing

4. List two of the measures in President Truman's "Fair Deal."

_____

_____

Lesson 2 Early Cold War Politics, *Continued*

Explaining

5. What changes did the Republicans want?

_____

_____

_____

Identifying

6. Which Republican ran against Truman in 1948?

_____

Reading Check

7. Whose votes helped Truman win the election?

_____

_____

Republicans. Republicans were the majority in both houses of Congress. They wanted to control how much money the government was spending. They also wanted to limit the power of labor unions, which were organizations representing many workers.

In 1947, the Republicans introduced a law. It was called the Taft-Hartley Act. It put a limit on the power of labor unions. It said that unions could not force a business to hire only union workers. (Forcing businesses in this way was known as the **closed shop.**) The Taft-Hartley Act also gave the government power to stop any strike that could harm public safety. Thanks to this, there would not be any more coal miners' strikes or railroad workers' strikes.

Labor unions did not like the plan. They had fought hard since 1933 to protect workers' rights. The president vetoed, or refused to sign, the Taft-Hartley Act. Congress voted again. They canceled the president's veto. The Taft-Hartley Act became law.

Truman and Congress did agree on some things. In 1947, Congress passed the National Security Act (NSA). This act put all the military under control of the Department of Defense. The NSA created a new agency, the Central Intelligence Agency (CIA). The CIA would gather information about other countries and pass the information on to the president. Many Americans worried about the CIA. They worried that the CIA would spy on Americans. Truman promised that the CIA would not do this.

There was an election in 1948. Most people did not expect President Truman to win. The Democrats did not support him fully, and Truman was a Democrat. Southern Democrats did not like Truman's support of civil rights for African Americans.

Thomas Dewey was the Republican governor of New York, and he was very popular. He ran against Truman. Most people thought Dewey was sure to win.

Truman campaigned hard. He traveled all around the country and gave many campaign speeches. On Election Day, Truman was reelected by more than 2 million votes. Many of his votes came from workers, African Americans, and farmers.

Truman's Fair Deal

Truman believed his win meant that voters wanted things to change. He sent his Fair Deal back to Congress. Some reforms passed. Congress raised the minimum wage.

411

The Cold War Era

Lesson 2 Early Cold War Politics, *Continued*

It made the Social Security program larger. It provided housing programs for people with low incomes.

Truman spoke to Congress about ending discrimination. Discrimination is unfair treatment based on race, religion, or ethnic origin. He wanted Congress to protect African Americans better. Congress did not do this, so Truman used his own power. He ordered federal agencies to end job discrimination against African Americans. He ordered the armed forces to **desegregate,** or stop separating people based on race. He told the Justice Department to carry out any civil rights laws that were already in force.

In 1949, Truman asked Congress to pass laws about health insurance, minimum wage, and money for use in public schools.

Truman's Civil Rights Reform Efforts

1. Told Congress to end discrimination
2. Asked Congress to pass laws that better protected African Americans
3. Ordered federal agencies to end discrimination against African Americans
4. Ordered the desegregation of the armed services
5. Told the Justice Department to enforce civil rights laws that were already there

---

/////////////// Glue Foldable here ///////////////

Check for Understanding

Why did unions not want the Taft-Hartley Act? What happened to the bill?

_____

_____

List two reasons why you think workers, African Americans, and farmers helped Truman win reelection.

_____

_____

☑ **Reading Check**

8. What civil rights reforms did President Truman achieve?

_____

_____

FOLDABLES®

9. Use a two-tab Foldable and place it along the dotted line to cover Check for Understanding. Write the title *Truman's Fair Deal* on the anchor tab. Label the first tab *Before Reelection* and the last tab *After Reelection.* Use the front and back of the tabs to write words and phrases about each. Use the Foldable to help answer Check for Understanding.

The Cold War Era

Lesson 3 The Korean War

ESSENTIAL QUESTION
Why does conflict develop?

GUIDING QUESTIONS

1. **Why did Americans under the United Nations' flag fight the Korean War in the 1950s?**

2. **Why did Truman and MacArthur disagree over how to fight the Korean War?**

> **Terms to Know**
> **stalemate** neither side is winning, but the conflict goes on
> **Demilitarized Zone** area where military forces are not allowed

Where in the world?

SOVIET UNION

PEOPLE'S REPUBLIC OF CHINA

Yalu River

NORTH KOREA

P'yŏngyang

Seoul

UN landing Sept. 1950

SOUTH KOREA

JAPAN

▪▪▪▪ Farthest advance of North Koreans, Sept. 1950
▪▪▪▪ Farthest advance of UN forces, Nov. 1950
━━ Farthest advance of North Koreans and Chinese, Jan. 1951
━━ Truce line, July 1953

When did it happen?

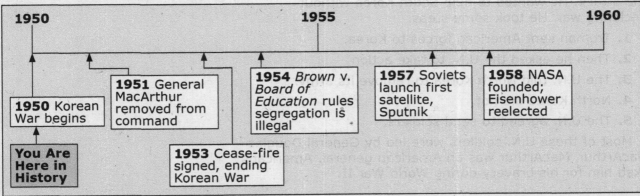

1950 — 1955 — 1960

1950 Korean War begins

You Are Here in History

1951 General MacArthur removed from command

1953 Cease-fire signed, ending Korean War

1954 *Brown* v. *Board of Education* rules segregation is illegal

1957 Soviets launch first satellite, Sputnik

1958 NASA founded; Eisenhower reelected

413

The Cold War Era

Lesson 3 The Korean War, Continued

Conflict in Korea

The Korean Peninsula is in Asia. After World War II, the United States and the Soviet Union both took control of the country of Korea. They split the country into North Korea and South Korea. They divided Korea along the 38th parallel. A *parallel* is a line of latitude.

North Korea had a communist government. South Korea's government was not communist. It was supported by the United States. North Korea and South Korea did not get along well.

Copyright by The McGraw-Hill Companies.

> ### What Are "Lines of Latitude"?
> - Lines of latitude are a way to show where something is on Earth.
> - Lines of latitude show how far north or south a place is from the equator.
> - Lines of latitude are measured in degrees.
> - Each degree is about 69 miles (about 111 km).
> - Another name for a line of latitude is a _"parallel."_
> - When you read that Korea was split at the 38th parallel, that means the country was divided at a distance 38 degrees away from the equator. (It was north of the equator.)
> - That is about 2,600 miles, or about 4,200 km.

North Korea wanted to unite the country again. In 1950, the North Korean army invaded and took control of most of South Korea. South Korea controlled only a small area around a port city, Pusan.

President Truman thought the Soviet Union had backed the attack. He wanted to help South Korea without declaring war. He took some steps.

1. Truman sent American forces to Korea.
2. Then he asked the U.N. to take action.
3. The U.N. told North Korea to remove its army.
4. North Korea did not.
5. The U.N. agreed to send soldiers.

Most of these U.N. soldiers were led by General Douglas MacArthur. MacArthur was an American general. Americans liked him for his bravery during World War II.

Identifying
1. Who invaded first? Whom did they invade?

_____

Reading Check
2. Why did President Truman and the U.N. send troops to Korea?

_____

_____

_____

networks

The Cold War Era

Lesson 3 The Korean War, Continued

Analyzing

3. Was MacArthur able to keep his promises to Truman? Explain.

_____

_____

_____

Reading Check

4. Why did President Truman fire General MacArthur?

_____

_____

_____

Analyzing

5. Do you think Truman was right to fire MacArthur? Explain.

_____

_____

_____

The U.N. and U.S. forces had a good start. They pushed the North Koreans back into their own country. Then MacArthur wanted to invade North Korea. He told President Truman that neither China nor the Soviet Union would enter the war. He told the president that the war would not take long. He promised that the soldiers would be "home by Christmas." This was in September.

When U.N. forces invaded North Korea, they got very far North. They got close to the Chinese border. The Chinese saw this as a threat to their own country. They sent hundreds of thousands of Chinese soldiers to fight in North Korea. China had indeed become involved in the war.

The Chinese soldiers pushed the U.N. forces back into South Korea. The Chinese soldiers captured South Korea's capital city, Seoul.

American Leadership Splits

U.N. soldiers captured Seoul again. They then managed to push communist forces back into North Korea. There was much fighting at the 38th parallel. For a long time, neither side advanced too far. This is known as a **stalemate.** The stalemate went on for almost two years.

President Truman and General MacArthur disagreed about what to do in this war. MacArthur wanted to drop atomic bombs on China. He thought bombing supply lines and bases would bring victory. Truman did not want to drop bombs. He thought this would make the war worse.

MacArthur criticized the president. He wrote a letter to a member of Congress. He said in the letter that he was being stopped from doing his job.

The president could not allow his general to disobey an order. Truman concluded, or decided, to fire General MacArthur because of his disobedience.

The American public protested Truman's decision. They liked MacArthur. After he was fired, MacArthur did not simply leave. He was greeted as a hero in the United States. He made a speech to Congress. "Old soldiers never die," he said. "They just fade away."

In July 1951, peace talks began that would end the Korean War. The fighting finally ended in 1953. Truman's term as president had ended. Dwight Eisenhower then became president.

415

The Cold War Era

Lesson 3 The Korean War, *Continued*

The agreement to end the war set up a **Demilitarized Zone** between North Korea and South Korea. This is a place where no military forces are allowed.

There was no clear winner in the war. The borders had hardly changed. More than 36,000 Americans had been killed. The total number of wounded was 103,000. Two million Koreans and Chinese had been killed.

The United States had shown the Soviet Union that it would use force to stop communism. That is the main purpose for which the Korean war was fought.

Check for Understanding

How did dividing Korea into two countries after World War II lead to conflict? Give two reasons.

_____

_____

How did the United States work with the U.N. to achieve its goals in Korea?

_____

_____

Mark the Text

6. Underline *Demilitarized Zone* and its definition.

FOLDABLES

7. Use a two-tab Foldable and place it along the dotted line to cover Check for Understanding. Write the title *Conflict in Korea* on the anchor tab. Label the top tab *North Korea*, and the bottom tab *South Korea*. Illustrate and label the *38th Parallel* along the middle edges of the tabs. Write words and phrases to describe what you remember about the governments of each and what led to the conflict. Use the Foldable to help answer Check for Understanding.

networks

The Cold War Era

Lesson 4 Life in the 1950s

ESSENTIAL QUESTION

How do new ideas change the way people live?

GUIDING QUESTIONS

1. **What policies did Eisenhower promote for prosperity at home and to compete against the Soviets?**

2. **How did a booming economy change the social and cultural life in America in the 1950s?**

3. **Why did many Americans not share in the prosperity of the 1950s?**

Terms to Know

surplus an amount left over

arms race countries compete to be the stronger military power

summit meeting of heads of government

standard of living measure of comfort based on quantity and quality of goods that people have

affluence wealth

materialism focus on collecting money and possessions

When did it happen?

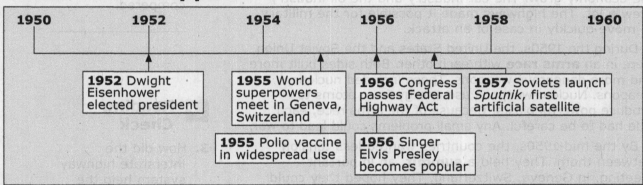

1950 — 1952 — 1954 — 1956 — 1958 — 1960

1952 Dwight Eisenhower elected president

1955 World superpowers meet in Geneva, Switzerland

1955 Polio vaccine in widespread use

1956 Congress passes Federal Highway Act

1956 Singer Elvis Presley becomes popular

1957 Soviets launch *Sputnik,* first artificial satellite

What do you know?

In the first column, answer the questions based on what you know before you study. After this lesson, complete the last column.

Now ...		Later ...
	What was the arms race?	
	What were some signs of affluence in the 1950s?	
	What were suburbs and why were they built?	

417

networks

The Cold War Era

Lesson 4 Life in the 1950s, *Continued*

Eisenhower in the White House

Republican Dwight D. Eisenhower was elected president in 1952. Eisenhower had been a United States Army general and a hero in World War II. People liked and trusted him. He served two terms in office.

Eisenhower wanted a smaller federal government. He supported free enterprise. Free enterprise is letting people and businesses make economic decisions, not the government. He cut the amount of money the government spent. After his second term, there was a large **surplus,** or amount left over. The surplus was over $300 million.

Congress passed the Federal Highway Act in 1956. It provided money to build over 40,000 miles (64,000 km) of highways throughout the United States. The highway system connected people and businesses. Highways helped the economy grow. The car industry and the oil industry grew a lot. The highways made it possible for the military to move quickly in case of an attack.

During the 1950s, the United States and the Soviet Union were in an **arms race** with each other. Both sides built more and more dangerous weapons. These included nuclear weapons. Nuclear weapons use energy from atoms to produce powerful blasts. Because of the arms race, each side had to be careful. Any small problems could lead to war.

By the mid-1950s, the countries wanted less tension between them. They held a **summit,** an important meeting, in Geneva, Switzerland. They hoped they could discuss peace.

In 1956, the two countries faced two big problems.

Problems in 1956	
Egypt	**Hungary**
Egypt took over the Suez Canal, which was controlled by Europe. Britain, France, and Israel sent soldiers. The Soviet Union threatened to send soldiers, but did not. All armies pulled out of Egypt.	A new government in Hungary told Soviet armies to leave. Soviet Leader Nikita Khrushchev refused, and had soldiers stop the revolt. Eisenhower criticized this, but did not do more.

The nations continued to compete. There was a "space race," a competition to explore space. The Soviets launched the first satellite, *Sputnik*, in 1957. The U.S. set up a space program. NASA was in charge of it.

418

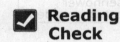

Mark the Text

1. Underline the sentence that tells what kind of government Eisenhower supported.

Identifying

2. Name two areas in which the United States and the Soviet Union competed.

_____

_____

Reading Check

3. How did the interstate highway system help the economy of the United States?

_____

_____

Lesson 4 Life in the 1950s, *Continued*

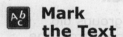 **Understanding Cause and Effect**

4. Why were more schools needed in the 1950s?

_____

_____

Mark the Text

5. Underline the definition of *standard of living*.

☑ **Reading Check**

6. The United States in the 1950s was called a consumer society. What does this mean?

_____

_____

_____

Prosperity and Change

In the 1950s, people were making more money and spending more money. Factories were busy. People had more children. This was called a *baby boom*. Many women stayed home to raise children. More schools were needed.

The **standard of living,** or level of economic comfort, increased for many Americans. They had more money, or **affluence.** There were more products to choose from. People paid with credit cards, charge accounts, and payment plans.

Consumers wanted the newest things, like dishwashers, washing machines, and television sets. People wanted fancier cars. Advertisements made people want to buy more things. People spent money on "fads," or fashions. Fads included Hula-hoops™—large plastic rings people twirled around their waists.

The television set became popular. The first sets had small screens. The black-and-white picture was not very clear, yet by the end of the 1950s, most families had one.

Television changed American life. It became the main form of entertainment. It was an important source of news. It shaped people's ideas about what life should be like.

Rock 'n' roll is a type of music that first became popular in the 1950s. This music gave teenagers something in common. It was one way that older and younger generations did not understand each other.

Other advances occurred during the 1950s. These included antibiotics and a vaccine for polio. Polio was a terrible disease that could leave people paralyzed.

More housing was needed. Homes were built in planned communities called suburbs, or areas outside of big cities. Houses were affordable and private. These houses had space for cars. The builders often would not sell to minorities, though.

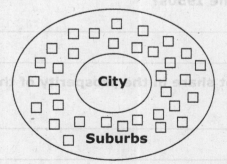

The Cold War Era

Lesson 4 Life in the 1950s, *Continued*

Technology changed Americans' way of life. It helped the economy grow by increasing production. Computers were created in the 1950s. They were very large at first.

Problems in a Time of Plenty

Not everyone was doing well in the 1950s. Some of the advances hurt certain groups. People with small farms could not keep up with large farms. Large farms used new technology to grow larger amounts of food.

The coal industry was not doing well. This affected coal miners and others who lived in Appalachia, where coal was mined. During the 1950s, 1.5 million people left Appalachia.

Many people moved out of the cities into the suburbs. This left poor people behind. Cities had a great deal of poverty, yet people still moved to cities to try to find work. Many African Americans and Latinos moved to the cities.

There were few good jobs for poor people in the cities. Factories moved to the suburbs and hired fewer people because of new technology. There was a lot of discrimination. Crime and violence were a problem.

Thinkers called social critics noticed these changes in American society. Some questioned the new American values. They felt people were all acting the same way. Social critics did not approve of **materialism.** Materialism is when people spend a lot of time and effort collecting money or things. Critics thought people were ignoring important problems, such as poverty.

Writers and poets called the "Beats" had much to say about the problems in American life.

/ / / / / / / / / / / / / / / (Glue Foldable here) / / / / / / / / / / / / / /

Check for Understanding

Who do you think benefited from the booming economy of the 1950s?

_____

_____

Who did not share in the prosperity of the time?

_____

_____

Analyzing

7. Why were small farmers not doing well?

_____

_____

Reading Check

8. Which groups did not benefit from the prosperity of the 1950s?

_____

_____

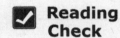

9. Use a two-tab Foldable to cover Check for Understanding. Write *1950s* on the anchor tab. Label the first tab *Progress* and the second tab *Problems.* Use both sides of the tabs to summarize and list examples of what you remember about the 1950s. Use the Foldable to help answer Check for Understanding.

The Civil Rights Era

Lesson 1 The Civil Rights Movement

ESSENTIAL QUESTION
Why does conflict develop?

GUIDING QUESTIONS

1. **How did supporters of civil rights challenge discrimination in public schools?**

2. **How did nonviolent protests help African Americans secure their rights?**

> **Terms to Know**
> **boycott** to refuse to use
> **civil disobedience** the refusal to obey laws that are considered unjust

Where in the world?

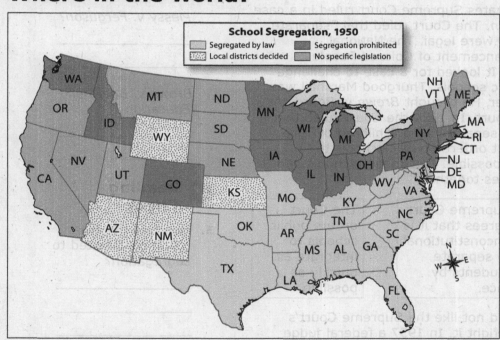

School Segregation, 1950
- Segregated by law
- Local districts decided
- Segregation prohibited
- No specific legislation

When did it happen?

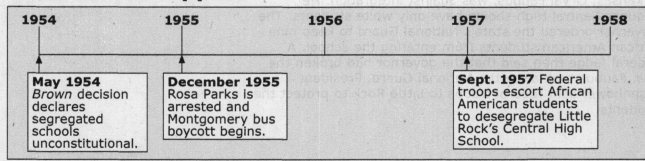

1954	1955	1956	1957	1958

May 1954 *Brown* decision declares segregated schools unconstitutional.

December 1955 Rosa Parks is arrested and Montgomery bus boycott begins.

Sept. 1957 Federal troops escort African American students to desegregate Little Rock's Central High School.

421

The Civil Rights Era

Lesson 1 The Civil Rights Movement, *Continued*

Ending Inequality in Education

In the mid-1900s, African Americans began to make progress against discrimination. They wanted equal rights in jobs, housing, and education. In 1942 the Congress of Racial Equality (CORE) was founded. Protests by CORE ended segregation in restaurants and other public places in many Northern cities. Segregation is the separation of people of different races.

During World War II, African Americans had greater opportunities in jobs and the military. After the war, they wanted more opportunities at home, too. Changes did not come quickly and the civil rights movement began.

In 1896 the United States Supreme Court ruled in a case called *Plessy* v. *Ferguson*. The Court ruled that "separate but equal" public places were legal. The National Association for the Advancement of Colored People (NAACP) did not agree. It looked for a case to challenge the segregation of public schools. Thurgood Marshall was the NAACP's chief lawyer. He brought *Brown* v. *Board of Education* before the Court. In 1954 the Court ruled that it was unconstitutional to separate schoolchildren by race. The next year, the Court ordered public schools to integrate as quickly as possible. This meant schools had to teach children of all races together.

Thurgood Marshall: "separate but equal" is not just.	→	Supreme Court agrees that it is unconstitutional to separate students by race.	→	The Court orders public schools to integrate as quickly as possible.

Some local leaders did not like the Supreme Court's ruling. They decided to fight it. In 1957 a federal judge ordered Central High School in Little Rock, Arkansas, to admit African American students. The governor of Arkansas, Orval Faubus, was against integration. He thought Central High should have only white students. The governor ordered the state's National Guard to keep nine African American students from entering the school. A federal judge then said that the governor had broken the law. Faubus took away the National Guard. President Eisenhower sent federal troops to Little Rock to protect the students.

Marking the Text

1. Circle the term that means the opposite of segregate.

? Contrasting

2. What did the Supreme Court rule in:

Plessy v. *Ferguson*?

_____

_____

Brown v. *Board of Education*

_____

_____

✓ Reading Check

3. How had the *Plessy* ruling contributed to segregation?

_____

_____

_____

422

The Civil Rights Era

Lesson 1 The Civil Rights Movement, *Continued*

✎ Explaining

4. Why did downtown businesses and the bus company lose money during the boycott?

_____

_____

? Critical Thinking

5. In the space below, list one cause and one effect of the Montgomery Bus Boycott.

Cause:

_____

_____

Effect:

_____

_____

✓ Reading Check

6. How did the Montgomery bus boycott lead to a change in policy?

_____

_____

_____

Challenges to Segregation
Protests by the Congress of Racial Equality (CORE)
Brown v. *Board of Education of Topeka, Kansas*
Supreme Court order to integrate schools
Integration of public high school in Little Rock, Arkansas

Moving Beyond the Schoolhouse

African Americans made other gains in the 1950s. On December 1, 1955, Rosa Parks got on a bus in Montgomery, Alabama. She found a seat in the section for whites. The driver told Parks to move to the back of the bus where African Americans were supposed to sit. Parks refused. Police came and arrested Parks and took her off the bus. She was fined.

African Americans in Montgomery organized a **boycott** of the city's buses. They refused to ride the buses until the law was changed. African Americans worked together to make the boycott a success. Normally, about 75% of bus riders were African American. The boycott lasted more than a year.

The bus company lost money from fares. Downtown businesses lost customers. The Supreme Court finally ruled that the bus segregation law was unconstitutional. In December 1956, the boycott ended.

Rosa Parks refuses to give up her seat to a white bus rider.

↓

Parks is arrested and fined.

↓

The bus boycott begins.

↓

Montgomery businesses and bus company lose money.

↓

The city changes its policies about segregated buses.

423

Lesson 1 The Civil Rights Movement, *Continued*

Dr. Martin Luther King, Jr., was a leader of the bus boycott. Dr. King was influenced by the ideas of two people. One was A. Philip Randolph, a well-known African American labor leader. The other was Mohandas Gandhi. Gandhi had used **civil disobedience** to help India gain independence from Britain. Civil disobedience happens when a person refuses to obey unjust laws. Dr. King believed that African Americans should do this too. He asked them to disobey unjust laws without using violence.

Dr. King and other important ministers in the South started a new organization. They called it the Southern Christian Leadership Conference (SCLC). This organization trained African Americans and others in civil disobedience. They were preparing for the civil rights struggle to come.

/ / / / / / / / / / / / / / Glue Foldable here / / / / / / / / / / / / / /

Check for Understanding

What role did the Supreme Court play in changing civil rights laws?

_____

_____

What was the purpose of the Southern Christian Leadership Conference (SCLC)?

_____

_____

FOLDABLES

7. Use a three-tab Foldable and place it along the dotted line to cover Check for Understanding. Write the title *Civil Rights Movement* on the anchor tab. Label the three tabs *Integration*, *Boycott*, and *Civil Disobedience*. On both sides of the tabs write two things you remember about each. Use your memory notes to help answer Check for Understanding.

The Civil Rights Era

Lesson 2 Kennedy and Johnson

ESSENTIAL QUESTION
How do new ideas change the way people live?

GUIDING QUESTIONS
1. **Why did John F. Kennedy's presidency appeal to many Americans?**
2. **How did the Johnson administration expand Kennedy's domestic plans?**

Terms to Know
poverty line income level deemed necessary to acquire the necessities of life
Medicare federal health insurance program mainly for older people
Medicaid federal-state health insurance program for low-income people

Where in the world?

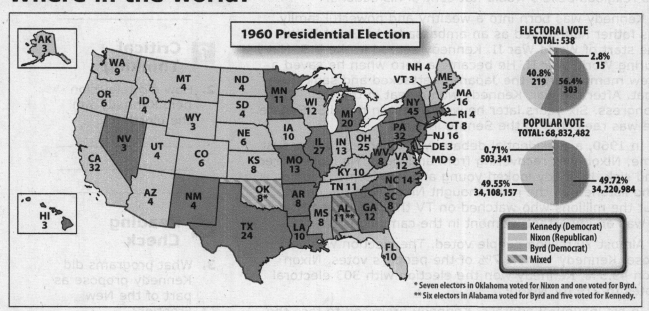

1960 Presidential Election

ELECTORAL VOTE TOTAL: 538

POPULAR VOTE TOTAL: 68,832,482

Kennedy (Democrat)
Nixon (Republican)
Byrd (Democrat)
Mixed

* Seven electors in Oklahoma voted for Nixon and one voted for Byrd.
** Six electors in Alabama voted for Byrd and five voted for Kennedy.

When did it happen?

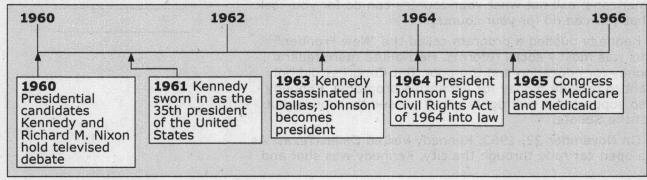

1960 Presidential candidates Kennedy and Richard M. Nixon hold televised debate

1961 Kennedy sworn in as the 35th president of the United States

1963 Kennedy assassinated in Dallas; Johnson becomes president

1964 President Johnson signs Civil Rights Act of 1964 into law

1965 Congress passes Medicare and Medicaid

425

The Civil Rights Era

Lesson 2 Kennedy and Johnson, *Continued*

Kennedy and the New Frontier

In 1960 there was a presidential election. The Republican candidate was Richard M. Nixon. He was serving as Vice President for President Eisenhower. Nixon promised to continue Eisenhower's policies. Democrat Senator John F. Kennedy ran against Nixon. Kennedy promised new programs which would "get the country moving again."

Polls showed that Nixon was ahead of Kennedy for much of the race. One reason was that Kennedy was Roman Catholic. Many Americans did not want a Catholic president. They were afraid Kennedy would be more loyal to his church than to the country. Kennedy promised that his religious beliefs would not control his actions.

Kennedy was born into a wealthy and powerful family. His father had served as an ambassador to Great Britain at the start of World War II. Kennedy served in the U.S. Navy during World War II. He became a hero when he saved a crew member after the Japanese attacked and sank their boat. After the war, Kennedy won a seat in the U.S. Congress. Six years later he won a seat in the U.S. Senate. He was reelected to the Senate in 1958.

In 1960, a presidential debate was televised for the first time. Nixon was recovering from an illness. He looked tired and sick. Kennedy looked young and handsome. People who listened on the radio thought Nixon won the debate. But the millions who watched on TV thought Kennedy won. It was an important moment in the campaign.

Almost 70 million people voted. The election was very close. Kennedy won 49.7% of the people's votes. Nixon won 49.5%. Kennedy won the election with 303 electoral votes to 219 for Nixon.

In his inaugural address, Kennedy promised to face the nation's challenges. He inspired many Americans to take action to help the country. He said, "And so my fellow Americans: ask not what your country can do for you—ask what you can do for your country."

Kennedy pushed a program called the "New Frontier." This was mostly social reforms. He wanted more federal money for education and the poor. But Congress did not want to provide money for expensive programs. Kennedy also supported a civil rights bill. It passed the House, but not the Senate.

On November 22, 1963, Kennedy visited Dallas Texas. As his open car rode through the city, Kennedy was shot and

Marking the Text

1. Underline sentences in the text that describe American reactions to the possibility of a Catholic president. How did Kennedy respond?

_____

_____

Critical Thinking

2. How did television help Kennedy win the election?

_____

_____

_____

Reading Check

3. What programs did Kennedy propose as part of the New Frontier?

_____

_____

_____

Lesson 2 Kennedy and Johnson, *Continued*

Defining

4. Define the terms below:

poverty line

_____

_____

Medicare

_____

_____

Medicaid

_____

_____

Identifying

5. Name three of Johnson's Great Society programs.

_____

_____

_____

Reading Check

6. What was the purpose of the Job Corps?

_____

_____

_____

killed. Vice President Lyndon B. Johnson immediately became president.

Americans were stunned and grief-stricken. Lee Harvey Oswald was charged with the murder. He was shot and killed on the way from one jail to another. Some people thought Kennedy's killing was planned by more than one person. The government appointed a commission to investigate. It ruled that Oswald acted alone.

Johnson's Great Society

Johnson shared many of Kennedy's goals. He wanted to reduce poverty, promote civil rights, and improve education. Johnson called for a "Great Society," which was made up of many programs. He was able to get many of them passed by Congress.

Johnson declared the War on Poverty. It involved programs to help people who lived below the **poverty line**. This is the minimum income needed to to get necessities such as food, clothing, and shelter. Head Start provided preschool education for poor children. The Job Corps trained young people.

In 1965, Congress passed two programs related to health care. **Medicare** provided health insurance for older Americans. **Medicaid** provided health insurance to poor people.

Great Society
• Head Start—preschool education for poor children
• Job Corps—job training for young people
• Medicare—health insurance program for older Americans
• Medicaid—health insurance program for poor Americans

Johnson also wanted to rebuild older cities and improve education. In 1966, Congress created the Department of Housing and Urban Development or HUD. It supported public housing for poor people. The Model Cities program helped rebuild cities. The Elementary and Secondary Education Act of 1965 helped schools.

Johnson supported civil rights for all Americans. He pushed Congress to pass the Civil Rights Act of 1964. It was the strongest civil rights act in history. It banned

The Civil Rights Era

Lesson 2 Kennedy and Johnson, *Continued*

discrimination in jobs, voting, and public places. It also banned discrimination based on race, gender, religion, and national origin.

Social Reforms	
Kennedy	**Johnson**
• "New Frontier"	• "Great Society"
• Federal aid to education	• War on Poverty
• Federal aid for poor people	• Health insurance for elderly and poor people
• Civil rights bill	• Support for public housing for poor people
• Most programs were not passed	• Civil Rights Act of 1964
	• Most programs were passed

//////////// Glue Foldable here ///////////

Check for Understanding

What happened to President Kennedy's social reforms?

_____

_____

List two of President Johnson's social reforms.

1. _____

2. _____

FOLDABLES®

7. Use a two-tab Foldable and place it along the dotted line to cover Check for Understanding. Write the title *Programs for Social Reform* on the anchor tab. Label the left tab *J. F. Kennedy's "New Frontier"*, and the right tab *L.B. Johnson's "Great Society."* On the front and back of the tabs, write two things you remember about each. Use your memory list to help answer Check for Understanding.

The Civil Rights Era

Lesson 3 Civil Rights in the 1960s

ESSENTIAL QUESTION
How do new ideas change the way people live?

GUIDING QUESTIONS
1. **What leaders and groups emerged during the civil rights movement?**
2. **Why did some African American leaders disagree with Dr. King's nonviolent protest?**

Terms to Know
sit-in the act of protesting by sitting down, commonly used as a method of nonviolent protest
interstate moving between two or more states

When did it happen?

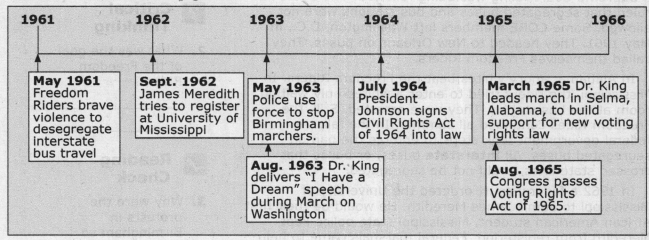

| 1961 | 1962 | 1963 | 1964 | 1965 | 1966 |

May 1961 Freedom Riders brave violence to desegregate interstate bus travel

Sept. 1962 James Meredith tries to register at University of Mississippi

May 1963 Police use force to stop Birmingham marchers.

Aug. 1963 Dr. King delivers "I Have a Dream" speech during March on Washington

July 1964 President Johnson signs Civil Rights Act of 1964 into law

March 1965 Dr. King leads march in Selma, Alabama, to build support for new voting rights law

Aug. 1965 Congress passes Voting Rights Act of 1965.

What do you know?

In the first column, answer the questions based on what you know before you study. After this lesson, complete the last column.

	Now...		Later...
	What type of discrimination did African Americans face in the North?		
	Who were the Freedom Riders?		
	What important groups worked for civil rights during this period?		
	What was Black Power?		

429

networks

The Civil Rights Era

Lesson 3 Civil Rights in the 1960s, *Continued*

The Growing Civil Rights Movement

Discrimination was common in the North, too. African Americans began to fight it there as well as in the South. Students staged sit-ins against stores that practiced segregation. At a **sit-in**, people protest by sitting down. The sit-ins made many stores decide to integrate. Ella Baker was a civil rights activist who helped students create their own civil rights group. The students started the Student Nonviolent Coordinating Committee (SNCC). It became an important civil rights organization.

The Congress of Racial Equality (CORE) wanted to see if a Supreme Court ruling was being followed. The Court had ruled that segregated buses and bus stations were not allowed. Some CORE members left Washington, D.C., in May 1961. They headed to New Orleans on buses. They called themselves Freedom Riders.

In Alabama, angry whites beat the Freedom Riders. In Mississippi, the riders tried to enter a whites-only waiting room at the bus station. They were arrested. Still, the Freedom Rides continued all summer. In the fall, the federal government took steps to enforce the ban on segregated buses. All **interstate** buses, or buses that crossed state lines, could not be segregated.

In 1962 a federal court ordered the University of Mississippi to admit James Meredith. He would be their first African American student. Mississippi state police kept Meredith from registering. Federal marshals came to help and protect Meredith. Riots broke out and two people were killed. In June 1963, Alabama governor George Wallace promised to block integration at the University of Alabama. President Kennedy sent the Alabama National Guard to make sure African Americans could register. Wallace backed down.

In the spring of 1963, protests were held in Birmingham, Alabama. The protests were against segregation. Dr. Martin Luther King, Jr., and hundreds of others were arrested. National television showed police attacking unarmed demonstrators. President Kennedy sent troops to restore peace. On June 11, 1963, Medgar Evers, an NAACP official, was murdered. Days later, the president introduced new civil rights legislation.

Dr. King and the Southern Christian Leadership Conference (SCLC) organized a march to support the civil rights bill. The march took place on August 28, 1963.

Marking the Text

1. Underline the sentence that describes the results of early sit-ins. Where were most sit-ins held?

_____

_____

Critical Thinking

2. What was the goal of the Freedom Riders?

Reading Check

3. Why were the protests in Birmingham so important to the progress of the civil rights movement?

_____

_____

The Civil Rights Era

Lesson 3 Civil Rights in the 1960s, *Continued*

FOLDABLES

Summarizing

4. Use a two-tab Foldable and place it vertically along the dotted line to cover the two paragraphs beginning "During the summer of 1964, ... " Write the title *Voting* on the anchor tab. Label the two tabs *Freedom Summer* and *Voting Rights Act 1965*. List facts that you learned about each on the front of the tabs and summarize the effects on the reverse sides.

Identifying

5. Who was Stokely Carmichael?

_____

_____

Marking the Text

6. Underline the sentences that tell why the Black Panther Party was formed.

Glue Foldable here

More than 200,000 people marched in Washington, D.C. The march was peaceful. At the march, Dr. King delivered his powerful "I Have a Dream" speech.

During the summer of 1964, thousands of civil rights workers went to the South. They helped African Americans register to vote. They called the campaign "Freedom Summer." The workers sometimes met with violence.

The next year demonstrators in Selma, Alabama, protested for the right to vote. Police attacked them. President Johnson stepped in. He urged the passage of the Voting Rights Act of 1965. The act gave the federal government more power. It would be able to force local officials to allow African Americans to register to vote. This led to dramatic political changes throughout the South. Many more African Americans voted and were elected to office.

> **SNCC**=Student Nonviolent Coordinating Committee: a civil rights organization created by students
>
> **CORE**=Congress of Racial Equality: tested United States Supreme Court ruling about segregated public bus stations
>
> **SCLC**=Southern Christian Leadership Conference: organized march to Washington in support of the civil rights bill

Different Views

Some African Americans wanted change to go more quickly. Malcolm X became an important voice for these African Americans. He first thought that African Americans should separate themselves from whites. Then he changed his ideas and called for "white-black brotherhood." Soon afterwards, he was murdered by rivals.

There were other, more radical leaders. Stokely Carmichael promoted Black Power. This idea said that African Americans should be proud of their race. They should create their own culture and change society. It became popular in poor city neighborhoods. The Black Panther Party was formed in California. They were angry about poverty and lack of jobs. They demanded reforms. Leaders were involved in several clashes with police.

The Civil Rights Era

Lesson 3 Civil Rights in the 1960s, *Continued*

Malcolm X	Black Power
• thought African Americans should separate from whites • changed his mind and spoke for brotherhood between blacks and whites	• promoted by Stokely Carmichael • said African Americans should be proud of their race • sometimes led to armed resistance against police

In the summer of 1965, people rioted in the Watts section of Los Angeles. It was the first of several race riots over the next few summers. Major riots happened in Newark, New Jersey, and Detroit, Michigan. Many people died and millions of dollars in property was destroyed.

On April 4, 1968, Dr. Martin Luther King, Jr., was murdered. He was in Memphis, Tennessee, to lead a march. His murder set off riots around the country. Millions mourned the death of this American hero.

/ / / / / / / / / / / Glue Foldable here / / / / / / / / / / / /

Check for Understanding

Name two African American leaders who promoted change using methods that differed from Dr. King's philosophy.

1. _____

2. _____

What do you think triggered race riots in the mid- to late 1960s?

Copyright by The McGraw-Hill Companies.

Describing

7. How did people react to the murder of Dr. Martin Luther King, Jr.?

_____

_____

_____

FOLDABLES

8. Use a three-tab Venn diagram Foldable and place it along the dotted line to cover the Check for Understanding. Write the title *Compare and Contrast* on the anchor tab. Label the left tab *Non-violent Protests*, the middle tab *Both*, and the right tab *Violent Protests*. On both sides, write what you remember about each as you compare and contrast the different approaches to civil rights. Use the Foldable to help answer Check for Understanding.

networks

The Civil Rights Era

Lesson 4 Other Groups Seek Rights

ESSENTIAL QUESTION
How do new ideas change the way people live?

GUIDING QUESTIONS
1. **How were American women influenced by the civil rights movement?**
2. **What other groups struggled for equality?**

Terms to Know
feminist activist for women's rights
Latino person with family background from Latin America or Spain

When did it happen?

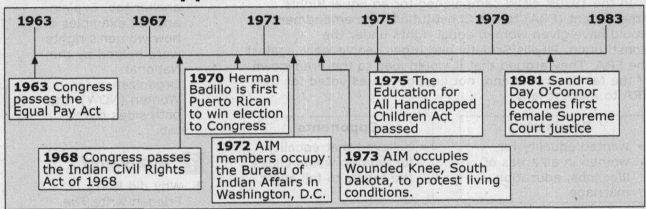

| 1963 | 1967 | 1971 | 1975 | 1979 | 1983 |

1963 Congress passes the Equal Pay Act

1968 Congress passes the Indian Civil Rights Act of 1968

1970 Herman Badillo is first Puerto Rican to win election to Congress

1972 AIM members occupy the Bureau of Indian Affairs in Washington, D.C.

1973 AIM occupies Wounded Knee, South Dakota, to protest living conditions.

1975 The Education for All Handicapped Children Act passed

1981 Sandra Day O'Connor becomes first female Supreme Court justice

What do you know?

In the first column, answer the questions based on what you know before you study. After this lesson, complete the last column.

Now...		Later...
	How did women's pay compare with men's pay for the same job before the 1960s?	
	Why were some women opposed to the Equal Rights Amendment?	
	From what countries have America's Latino population come?	
	What types of actions did Native Americans take to gain equal rights?	

433

Lesson 4 Other Groups Seek Rights, *Continued*

The Battle for Women's Rights

/ / / / / / / / / / / Glue Foldable here / / / / / / / / / /

The civil rights movement helped women and other groups. In 1963 Congress passed the Equal Pay Act. This act barred employers from paying women less than men for the same work. The same year, *The Feminine Mystique* was published. In this book, Betty Friedan described women's hopes for greater opportunities.

In 1966 **feminists** created the National Organization for Women (NOW). Feminists are activists for women's rights. NOW fought for equal rights for women in jobs, education, marriage, and other parts of life.

In the 1970s, NOW campaigned for an Equal Rights Amendment (ERA) to the Constitution. The amendment would have given women equal rights under the Constitution. Phyllis Schlafly and other people were against the ERA. They argued that it would lead to the breakdown of the family. In the end, not enough states voted for the ERA to make it law.

Feminists	Opponents
• wanted equality for women in all areas of life: jobs, education, marriage	• believed that equality for women would cause the family to fall apart

Still, the women's movement made progress. Women gained more job opportunities. More women rose to high-level jobs and became doctors and lawyers. They filled more political offices. In 1981 Sandra Day O'Connor became the first female justice of the U.S. Supreme Court.

Women's Rights Movement

- National Organization for Women (NOW) organized 1966
- Support for Equal Rights Amendment (ERA) not successful
- Gained more job opportunities
- More women rose to high-level jobs
- More women in government offices
- Sandra Day O'Connor became first female Supreme Court justice 1981

FOLDABLES

? Explaining

1. Use a one-tab Foldable and place it along the dotted line under the heading "The Battle for Women's Rights." Write *Civil Rights & Women* on the anchor tab. Explain and list examples of how women's rights were helped by the National Organization for Women (NOW). Use both sides of the tab.

? Analyzing

2. Why did Betty Friedan write *The Feminine Mystique*?

_____

_____

✓ Reading Check

3. What was the purpose of the Equal Pay Act?

_____

_____

The Civil Rights Era

Lesson 4 Other Groups Seek Rights, Continued

Analyzing

4. In what ways were the United Farm Workers successful?

_____

_____

Analyzing

5. Why did many Cubans come to the United States?

_____

_____

? Comparing

6. How were the lives of Latinos, Native Americans, and Americans with disabilities similar before the 1960s?

_____

_____

Expanding Opportunities

Latinos, or Hispanics, are people who have a family background from Latin America or Spain. The Latino population in the United States has grown quickly. It rose from 3 million in 1960 to about 50 million in 2010.

In the 1960s, the Latino population also sought equal rights. They fought against discrimination in schools, courts, and government.

The largest Latino group in the United States comes from Mexico. Americans of Mexican background have lived in the United States since before it was founded. Many Mexican Americans came in the early 1960s. By 2010, over 30 million Mexican Americans lived in the United States.

Mexican American migrant farm workers formed the United Farm Workers (UFW). This union fought for better wages and working conditions. Led by César Chávez, the UFW went on strike. To support the unions, people refused to buy certain food products. For example, in 1965, 17 million people refused to buy grapes. These boycotts helped the union win higher wages and shorter working hours.

Latinos have a wide variety of histories. People who live in Puerto Rico are U.S. citizens. But many have moved to American cities in search of jobs. Like African Americans, Puerto Ricans suffered from job discrimination. Puerto Ricans have also had a great influence on American history and culture. Herman Badillo was the first Puerto Rican to win a seat in Congress in 1970.

Fidel Castro set up a Communist government in Cuba in 1959. Many Cubans have come to the United States to escape his government. More than 200,000 Cubans fled to the United States in the 1960s. Thousands more came in the 1980s. The largest number of Cubans settled in southern Florida.

In the 1960s, Native Americans came together and demanded political power. Tribal government had been weakened since the end of World War II. Many Native Americans left reservations but could not find jobs in cities. More than one-third of Native Americans lived in poverty. In response, Congress passed the Indian Civil Rights Act of 1968. This act protected Native Americans' constitutional rights. It also recognized the right of Native American nations to make laws for their reservations.

In 1968 a group of young Native Americans set up the American Indian Movement (AIM) to work for equal rights

netw🟦rks

The Civil Rights Era

Lesson 4 Other Groups Seek Rights, *Continued*

and better living conditions. They organized several important protests. In 1969 members occupied Alcatraz Island, a former prison in San Francisco Bay. They took over the building to demand attention for Native American rights. They surrendered in 1971. They took over the Bureau of Indian Affairs in Washington, D.C., in 1972. In 1973, they occupied land on the Sioux reservation at Wounded Knee, South Dakota. This protest left several people dead. The Native American protests focused attention on the poor living conditions for many Native Americans.

Native American Goals

- more control over reservation lands and laws
- improvement of living conditions
- equal protection under the Constitution
- more job opportunities

People with disabilities also sought equal treatment. Congress responded by passing several laws. One law required that public buildings remove barriers that made it difficult for disabled people to use them. Other laws created more job opportunities for disabled people and ensured equal education for disabled children.

/////////////// Glue Foldable here ///////////////

Check for Understanding

List two ways you think the civil rights movement helped all groups struggling for equality.

1. _____

2. _____

List three organizations that worked for equal rights during this period and the groups they represented.

1. _____

2. _____

3. _____

☑ Reading Check

7. Why did the American Indian Movement form?

_____

_____

FOLDABLES®

8. Use a three-tab Foldable and place it along the dotted line to cover Check for Understanding. Write the title *Equal Rights Organizations* on the anchor tab. Label the three tabs *National Organization for Women*, *United Farm Workers*, and *American Indian Movement*. On both sides of the tabs, write what you remember about the goals of each organization. Use your Foldable to help answer Check for Understanding.

networks

The Vietnam Era

Lesson 1 Kennedy's Foreign Policy

ESSENTIAL QUESTION
What motivates people to act?

GUIDING QUESTIONS

1. **Why did President Kennedy seek new ways to deal with the challenges and fears of the Cold War?**

2. **How did the Kennedy administration respond to the Cold War crises in Cuba and Berlin?**

3. **Why did the United States force the Soviet Union to remove missiles placed in Cuba?**

Terms to Know
guerrilla warfare fighting by small groups using tactics such as the ambush
flexible response President Kennedy's plan to help nations fighting Communist movements by providing special military units trained to fight guerilla warfare
blockade to block or obstruct

Where in the world?

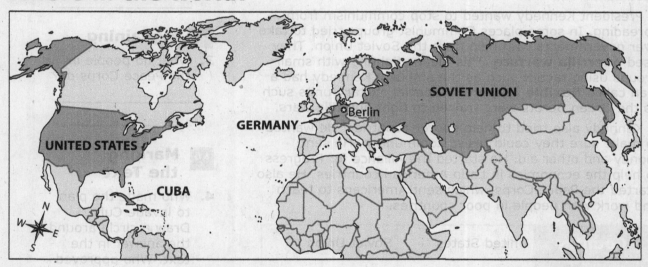

When did it happen?

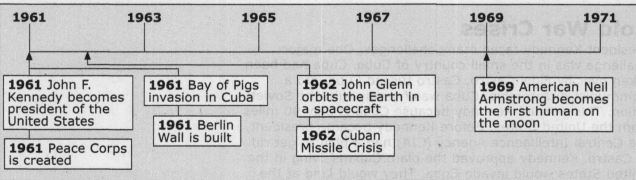

1961 John F. Kennedy becomes president of the United States

1961 Peace Corps is created

1961 Bay of Pigs invasion in Cuba

1961 Berlin Wall is built

1962 John Glenn orbits the Earth in a spacecraft

1962 Cuban Missile Crisis

1969 American Neil Armstrong becomes the first human on the moon

437

The Vietnam Era

Lesson 1 Kennedy's Foreign Policy, *Continued*

A New Leader

John F. Kennedy became the U.S. president in 1961. This was during the Cold War. A "Cold War" is a period when there is no active fighting, but both sides have weapons and troops ready in case a war begins.

During the Cold War, the United States and the Soviet Union were enemies. The Soviet Union was a powerful Communist nation. Communism is a system where the people are controlled by their government. The government makes choices for how people can live. People have few rights and freedoms. The leader of the Soviet Union was Nikita Khrushchev.

This was a dangerous time for the world. If the U.S. and the Soviet Union started a war, they might use nuclear weapons. Nuclear weapons could cause massive destruction on Earth.

President Kennedy wanted to stop communism from spreading. In some places Communist groups tried to take over governments with help from the Soviet Union. They used **guerrilla warfare**. This means fighting with small groups using tactics such as the ambush. Kennedy had a plan called **flexible response**. Special military units such as the Green Berets were trained to fight guerrilla wars.

Kennedy also tried to help poorer countries. He wanted to make sure they could resist Communism. He sent money and other aid. He started the Alliance for Progress to help the economies in Latin American countries. He also started the Peace Corps, which sent Americans to teach and work with people in poor countries.

Country	United States	Soviet Union
Leader	John F. Kennedy	Nikita Khrushchev

Cold War Crises

President Kennedy faced many challenges. One major challenge was in the small country of Cuba. Cuba had been taken over by Fidel Castro. Castro turned Cuba into a Communist dictatorship. Cuba was friendly with the Soviet Union. This worried Kennedy because Cuba is only 90 miles from the United States. Before Kennedy became president, the Central Intelligence Agency (CIA) had a plan to get rid of Castro. Kennedy approved the plan. Cubans living in the United States would invade Cuba. They would land at the

438

Marking the Text

1. Underline the definition of *guerrilla warfare*.

Reading Check

2. What was the purpose of the Alliance for Progress?

_____

_____

Explaining

3. What do people in the Peace Corps do?

_____

_____

Marking the Text

4. Who made the plan to invade Cuba? Draw a circle around the answer in the text. Who approved the plan?

_____

_____

The Vietnam Era

Lesson 1 Kennedy's Foreign Policy, *Continued*

Reading Check

5. What was the purpose of the Berlin Wall?

_____

_____

Marking the Text

6. Underline the names of the nations involved in the Cuban Missile Crisis.

Explaining

7. Why were people all over the world frightened by the Cuban Missile Crisis?

_____

_____

Reading Check

8. How did the Cuban Missile Crisis end?

_____

_____

Bay of Pigs. But the plan failed, partly because Kennedy chose not to give air support. As a result, Latin American countries lost trust in the United States. Also, the Soviet leader Khrushchev thought Kennedy was not a strong leader.

Another challenge was in Germany. After World War II, Germany had been divided into two parts. East Germany was ruled by Communists. West Germany was free. The capital of Berlin was also divided. It was located in East Germany. Many people in East Germany wanted to leave. They wanted to live free lives in West Germany. Many fled to West Berlin. So the Communist leaders of East Germany built a wall in Berlin to keep people in. The Berlin Wall cut the city of Berlin in two. It became a symbol of communism.

The Cuban Missile Crisis

In 1961, an American spy plane flying over Cuba found something serious. The Soviet Union was building missile launch sites in Cuba. Because Cuba is so close to Florida, these sites would let the Soviet Union attack the United States very quickly. Kennedy made a plan to **blockade** Cuba. This closed off Cuba from the rest of the world. He warned that the U.S. would destroy any Soviet ship that tried to go through the blockade. He also warned he would attack the Soviet Union with nuclear bombs if any missiles were fired from Cuba. Kennedy said he would end the blockade when the Soviets removed their missiles.

This was a very dangerous time. It seemed that a nuclear war might start at any moment. The entire world waited in fear to see what would happen. Finally the Soviet Union agreed to remove its weapons. There was no nuclear attack.

After the crisis, the leaders of the United States and the Soviet Union decided to make some changes. They set up a "hot line" so they could talk any time there was a problem. This would help stop problems before they got worse. Both sides also agreed to stop testing nuclear weapons.

The space race was a competition between the United States and the Soviet Union. Both nations wanted to be the first to explore space. The Soviet Union was first to have a pilot orbit the earth in 1961. American astronauts followed. Kennedy set a goal for the United States to land on the moon by the end of the 1960s. In 1969, American Neil Armstrong became the first person to walk on the moon.

439

The Vietnam Era

Lesson 1 Kennedy's Foreign Policy, *Continued*

Cause	Effect
Kennedy wanted to stop the spread of communism.	Troops trained to fight Communist forces; aid given to poor countries; Alliance for Progress created; Peace Corps created
Kennedy wanted to get Fidel Castro out of Cuba.	CIA made the Bay of Pigs plan to invade Cuba. The plan failed, and Castro stayed in power.
Communists wanted to keep people from leaving East Germany.	Berlin Wall built to close off East Berlin from the West
Americans found Soviet missile launch sites in Cuba.	The Cuban Missile Crisis brought the world close to nuclear war; the crisis ended when the Soviets agreed to remove their missiles from Cuba.

//////////////////// Glue Foldable here ////////////////////

Check for Understanding

What motivated Kennedy to set up plans to help poor countries?

_____

_____

Why did the United States force the Soviet Union to remove missiles placed in Cuba?

_____

_____

FOLDABLES®

9. Place a two-tab Foldable along the dotted line to cover the Check for Understanding. Write the title *The Kennedy Administration* on the anchor tab. Label the two tabs *Alliance for Progress and Peace Corps* and *Cuban Missile Crisis*. On both sides of the tabs, list what you remember about the cause and effect of each program. Use your Foldable to help answer Check for Understanding.

The Vietnam Era

Lesson 2 The Vietnam War

ESSENTIAL QUESTION
Why does conflict develop?

GUIDING QUESTIONS
1. **How did Vietnam become a divided country?**
2. **Why did the United States become involved in the war in Vietnam?**

Terms to Know

regime a form of government, government in power, or period of time

search-and-destroy mission mission by American forces to seek out and destroy North Vietnamese forces

napalm an intensely burning explosive used to destroy jungle growth

Agent Orange a chemical herbicide used to clear out forests and tall grasses

Where in the world?

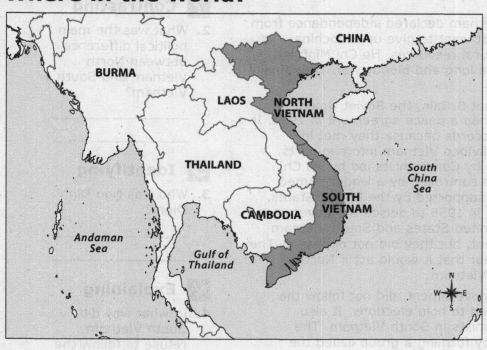

When did it happen?

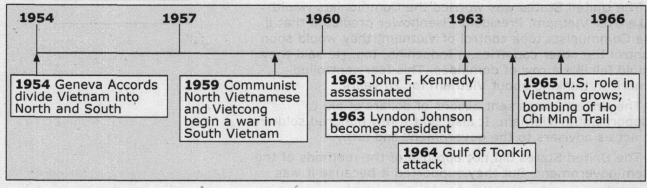

1954	1957	1960	1963	1966

1954 Geneva Accords divide Vietnam into North and South

1959 Communist North Vietnamese and Vietcong begin a war in South Vietnam

1963 John F. Kennedy assassinated

1963 Lyndon Johnson becomes president

1964 Gulf of Tonkin attack

1965 U.S. role in Vietnam grows; bombing of Ho Chi Minh Trail

networks

The Vietnam Era

Lesson 2 The Vietnam War, *Continued*

The Conflict Begins

In the early 1960s, the United States became more involved in a war in Vietnam. The United States wanted to prevent the spread of communism in the region. This conflict became know as the Vietnam War. It did not go as Americans hoped.

During World War II, the Japanese captured the French colony of Indochina. It included the modern nations of Cambodia, Laos, and Vietnam. Communist forces fought against the Japanese. Their leader was Ho Chi Minh (HOH • CHEE • MIHN).

After World War II, Vietnam declared independence from France. But France did not want to give up Indochina because it had many natural resources. Ho Chi Minh led troops against France in a long and bloody war. They finally defeated France in 1954.

The United States, Great Britain, the Soviet Union, China, and Vietnam reached a peace agreement in 1954. It was called the Geneva Accords because they met in Geneva, Switzerland. It divided Vietnam into two parts. North Vietnam was ruled by Communists led by Ho Chi Minh. South Vietnam was controlled by a leader named Ngo Dinh Diem who was supported by the United States. There would be elections in 1956 to decide the government for all of Vietnam. The United States and South Vietnam did not sign the agreement, but they did not oppose it. The United States made it clear that it would act if North Vietnam attacked South Vietnam.

The Diem **regime**, or government, did not follow the Geneva Accords. It refused to hold elections. It also cracked down on Communists in South Vietnam. The Communists responded by forming a group called the Vietcong. In 1959, the Vietcong began a war against the Diem regime on orders from Ho Chi Minh.

The United States was worried the Communists would take over Vietnam. President Eisenhower predicted that if the Communists took control of Vietnam, they would soon control the other countries in Indochina, too. He said they would fall like a row of dominoes. This fear controlled American thinking about Vietnam for 20 years.

The United States sent billions of dollars of aid to support South Vietnam. It also sent a few hundred soldiers to act as advisers to the government and army.

The United States did not approve of the methods of the Diem government. But they supported it because it was

Marking the Text

1. Underline the sentence that describes the main reason the United States got involved in Vietnam.

? Contrasting

2. What was the main political difference between North Vietnam and South Vietnam?

_____

_____

☑ Identifying

3. Who was Ngo Dinh Diem?

_____

_____

A b c Explaining

4. In what way did South Vietnam refuse to follow the Geneva Accords?

_____

_____

netw⊕rks

The Vietnam Era

Lesson 2 The Vietnam War, *Continued*

❓ Analyzing

5. Why did the United States support the Diem regime? Why did it later support its overthrow?

_____

_____

_____

❓ Summarizing

6. Why was the reported attack in the Gulf of Tonkin important?

_____

_____

_____

☑ Describing

7. How did the number of U.S. troops in Vietnam change from Kennedy's death in 1963 to 1968?

_____

_____

_____

not Communist. The Diem government took away some of the people's freedoms, especially those of Buddhists. Hundreds of Buddhists were jailed and some were killed. The Buddhists protested. Some burned themselves in protest.

President Kennedy sent aid and special forces troops to train and advise the South Vietnamese. Some Americans were angry that Kennedy was helping Diem. Kennedy tried to get Diem to give more rights to people in South Vietnam.

In 1963, South Vietnam's army overthrew Diem and killed him. The United States supported the revolution but did not support killing Diem. A few days later, President Kennedy was assassinated. The new president, Lyndon Johnson, had to decide how to handle the Vietnam War.

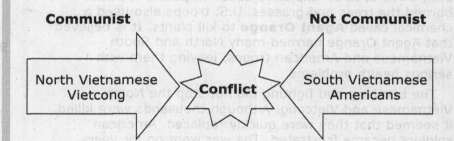

The Conflict Deepens

At the time of Kennedy's death, there were about 16,000 U.S. troops in Vietnam. The U.S. Secretary of Defense told President Johnson that the Vietcong would win if the United States did not increase its support for South Vietnam. Johnson had doubts about the war. Privately, he said, "I don't think it's worth fighting for, but I don't think we can get out."

Johnson needed support from Congress to increase U.S. support. In 1964, it was reported that North Vietnamese boats attacked American ships in the Gulf of Tonkin. Because of this attack, Congress gave President Johnson more power to fight the war.

Johnson decided to send more soldiers to Vietnam. The numbers rose quickly. About 180,000 American soldiers were in Vietnam by the end of 1965, almost 400,000, by the end of 1966, and more than 500,000 by 1968.

The U.S. also bombed more enemy targets in Vietnam. Operation Rolling Thunder was a major plan of attack. U.S.

443

networks

The Vietnam Era

Lesson 2 The Vietnam War, *Continued*

planes bombed bridges, docks, factories, and military bases in the North. It also targeted an enemy supply route called the Ho Chi Minh Trail. The goal was to destroy the trail. This would cut off the enemy's supply of food and weapons into South Vietnam. From 1965 through 1968, the United States dropped more bombs on Vietnam than they did in all of World War II.

Fighting in Vietnam was very hard for the military. They used **search-and-destroy missions** to hunt down the enemy. When ground troops found the enemy, they called in helicopters to help attack them.

The soldiers had to fight in wet, muddy fields and jungles. This was dangerous because the enemy could hide among the jungle plants and make surprise attacks. To clear out the jungles and make fighting easier, soldiers on both sides used an explosive called **napalm.** Napalm burned the trees and grasses. U.S. troops also used a chemical called **Agent Orange** to kill plants. It is believed that Agent Orange harmed many North and South Vietnamese and American troops, leaving them with serious health problems.

The bombing and fighting did not stop the North Vietnamese and Vietcong. Although thousands were killed, it seemed that they were quickly replaced. American soldiers became frustrated. The war went on for years.

Many Americans did not want the United States to fight in Vietnam. These people protested the war. As the Vietnam War went on, some U.S. leaders started to think that the war could not be won.

/ / / / / / / / / / / Glue Foldable here / / / / / / / / / /

Check for Understanding
How did Vietnam become a divided country?

_____

_____

Why did the United States get involved in Vietnam?

_____

_____

? Drawing Conclusions

8. Why might it be easier for U.S. soldiers to fight the enemy after they had cleared away all jungle plants?

_____

_____

_____

FOLDABLES®

9. Label a one-tab Foldable *The Vietnam War*. Glue a two-tab Foldable under the one-tab along the anchor tab. Label the two tabs *North Vietnam* and *South Vietnam*. Place the Foldable along the dotted line to cover the Check for Understanding. List what you remember about the causes and effects of the Vietnam War on the one-tab. Write about the similarities and the differences of each country on the two-tab. Use your Foldable to help answer Check for Understanding.

The Vietnam Era

Lesson 3 The Vietnam Years at Home

ESSENTIAL QUESTION
What motivates people to act?

GUIDING QUESTIONS
1. **How did the war in Vietnam lead to sharp divisions between Americans?**
2. **How was 1968 a turning point in the Vietnam War and the nation's political life?**

Terms to Know
counterculture a culture with values that differ from those of established society
deferment postponement of, or excuse from, military service
conscientious objector a person who refuses to serve in the armed forces or bear arms on moral or religious grounds
credibility gap the difference between what is said and what people believe or know to be true

Where in the world?

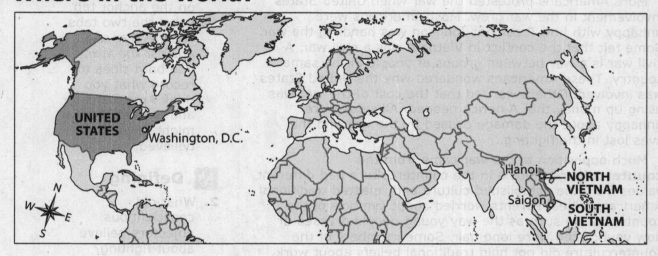

When did it happen?

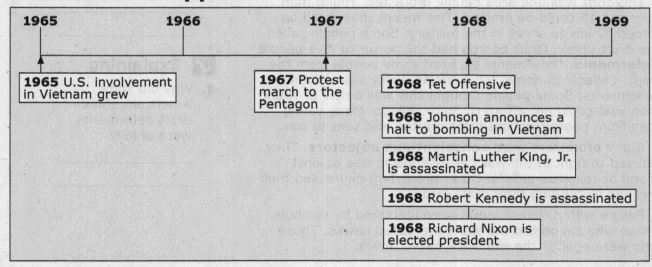

1965 U.S. involvement in Vietnam grew

1967 Protest march to the Pentagon

1968 Tet Offensive

1968 Johnson announces a halt to bombing in Vietnam

1968 Martin Luther King, Jr. is assassinated

1968 Robert Kennedy is assassinated

1968 Richard Nixon is elected president

445

networks

The Vietnam Era

Lesson 3 The Vietnam Years at Home, *Continued*

////////// Glue Foldable here ////////////

Young People Protest

As the war in Vietnam continued, the war seemed to split America. People for and against the war staged public demonstrations to express their views. They also became angry with each other. Some of those against the war called President Johnson and war supporters "killers." Some supporting the war called opponents "traitors." Some differences resulted from different views of age groups. Many younger people opposed the war and had different ideas than older people. This was called "the generation gap."

More Americans protested the war when United States involvement in the war grew. Most Americans were unhappy with how President Johnson was handling the war. Some felt that the conflict in Vietnam was a civil war. A civil war is a war between groups of people in the same country. These Americans wondered why the United States was involved. Others worried that the cost of the war was using up money that America needed. All sides were unhappy about the damage caused by the war and the lives lost in the fighting.

Much opposition to the war came from the **counterculture**. People in the counterculture had different values from the established culture and rejected traditional American values. Parents worried about symbols of the counterculture such as the way young people dressed or how young men wore long hair. Some members of the counterculture did not hold traditional beliefs about work, family, or personal success.

The draft was one area people protested. Young men over age 18 could be drafted. This meant they could be forced by law to serve in the military. Some people called the draft unfair. Draft boards had the power to give people **deferments**. Deferments excused some people from the draft. College students, for example, were often given deferments. Some people thought this was unfair to young men who could not afford to go to college. Many young men from poorer families were drafted and sent to war.

Some protestors were **conscientious objectors**. They refused to fight in the war because killing was against moral or religious beliefs. Other protesters expressed their feelings by burning their draft cards.

People with different views were identified by symbols. Those who supported the war were called hawks. Those who were against the war were called doves.

FOLDABLES

Describing

1. Place a two-tab Foldable along the dotted line to cover the heading "Young People Protest." Write the title *Americans Disagree* on the anchor tab. Label the two tabs *For the War* and *Against the War.* Use both sides to record what you think Americans for and against the war might have felt or believed.

Defining

2. What did conscientious objectors believe about fighting?

_____

_____

Explaining

3. Why did some Americans think draft deferments were unfair?

_____

_____

The Vietnam Era

Lesson 3 The Vietnam Years at Home, *Continued*

📝 Marking the text

4. What was the Tet Offensive? Underline the answer in the text. Why was it important?

_____

_____

❓ Critical Thinking

5. Why was McCarthy's strong showing in a Democratic primary so important?

_____

_____

_____

✔️ Reading Check

6. What actions did Johnson take to limit American involvement in the war?

_____

_____

_____

1968—Year of Crisis

In early 1968, North Vietnam began a series of major attacks on U.S. and South Vietnamese forces. They began on the Vietnamese New Year which is called Tet. The attacks were called the Tet Offensive. They were a turning point in the Vietnam War.

Communists attacked U.S. military bases and cities in South Vietnam. Vietcong troops raided the United States embassy in South Vietnam's capital of Saigon. They attacked the city of Hue (hyoo•AY) which is the ancient capital of Vietnam.

In the end, the Tet Offensive was a disaster for Communist forces. After a month of fighting, American and South Vietnamese forces had caused heavy enemy losses. But the Tet Offensive surprised and upset the American people. The Johnson administration had led them to believe that the North Vietnamese and Vietcong were close to defeat. This created a **credibility gap.** People did not trust what the administration said about the war.

After the Tet Offensive, more Americans protested the war, and more people were angry with President Johnson. They wanted him to pull American soldiers out of Vietnam. Johnson also faced opposition from his own party. Two Democratic candidates for president were against the war. One was Eugene McCarthy, a senator from Minnesota. Another was Robert Kennedy, President John F. Kennedy's brother. McCarthy surprised everyone by making a strong showing in an early primary.

Johnson had to think about what to do. He decided he would not send more troops to Vietnam, even though the commander there asked for them. Johnson went on TV and told America that he was ordering U.S. troops to stop bombing cities in North Vietnam. He hoped this would be a step towards peace. Then he surprised the country by saying he would not run for president in the next election.

Tragedy struck twice in 1968. In April, a gunman shot and killed Martin Luther King, Jr., the leader of the civil rights movement. People all over America were angry and upset by his death. Riots broke out in many cities. Army troops had to restore order in some areas.

The second tragedy happened on the day of the Democratic primary in California. Vice President Hubert Humphrey decided to run for president, too. But he did not enter primary elections. In California, the choice was between Eugene McCarthy and Robert Kennedy. The

447

The Vietnam Era

Lesson 3 The Vietnam Years at Home, *Continued*

winner was Kennedy. Right after Kennedy gave his victory speech, a gunman shot and killed him.

Many antiwar demonstrators came to protest outside of the Democratic convention in Chicago. They were angry that the Democrats were nominating Humphrey. Humphrey supported Johnson's Vietnam policy. The protesters clashed with police. Many were beaten and arrested. This violence was shown on television. Humphrey won the nomination, but the convention was a disaster for the Democrats.

Humphrey ran against two candidates in the 1968 election. George Wallace of Alabama represented a third party. He promised a return to law and order. He also opposed busing to integrate schools. The Republican candidate, Richard Nixon, said the he represented the "silent majority." They were the people who wanted law and order and did not protest or demonstrate. He also promised "peace with honor" in Vietnam, but did not say how that would happen. Nixon won but got only 43.4% of the popular vote. Combined with Wallace, 57% of the people had voted for candidates who had promised to restore law and order.

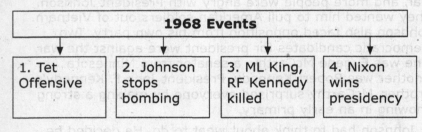

1968 Events

| 1. Tet Offensive | 2. Johnson stops bombing | 3. ML King, RF Kennedy killed | 4. Nixon wins presidency |

/ / / / / / / / / / / Glue Foldable here / / / / / / / / / / /

Check for Understanding

How did the war in Vietnam "split" America?

_____

_____

How was 1968 a turning point in the Vietnam War?

_____

_____

✓ Explaining

7. Why was the Democratic convention in Chicago a disaster for Democrats?

_____

_____

FOLDABLES

8. Use a two-tab Foldable and cut the tabs in half to make four tabs. Place it along the dotted line to cover the Check for Understanding. Write the title *1968* on the anchor tab. Label the four tabs *Tet Offensive*, *Assassinations*, *Bombing Stops*, and *"Peace with Honor."* On both sides of the tabs, write what you remember about the importance of each. Use the Foldable to help answer Check for Understanding.

networks

The Vietnam Era

Lesson 4 Vietnam in the Nixon Years

ESSENTIAL QUESTION
What motivates people to act?

GUIDING QUESTIONS
1. *What steps did Nixon take to bring American forces home and end Vietnam?*
2. *Why did new antiwar protests take place as Vietnamization moved forward?*
3. *How did the peace talks lead to a withdrawal of all American forces in Vietnam?*

Terms to Know
Vietnamization President Nixon's plan calling for the South Vietnamese to take a more active role in fighting and for Americans to become less involved
martial law emergency military rule
MIA American soldier classified as missing during a war or other military action

---

Where in the world?

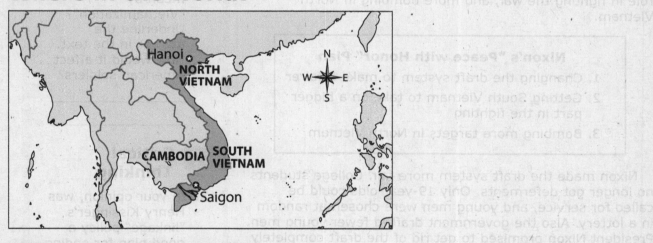

When did it happen?

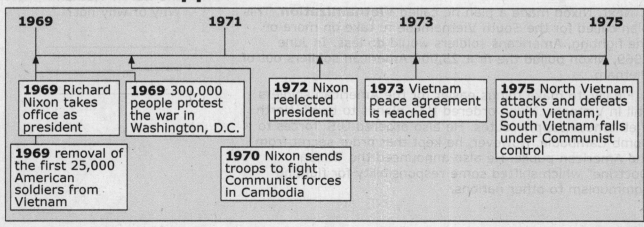

1969 Richard Nixon takes office as president

1969 300,000 people protest the war in Washington, D.C.

1972 Nixon reelected president

1973 Vietnam peace agreement is reached

1975 North Vietnam attacks and defeats South Vietnam; South Vietnam falls under Communist control

1969 removal of the first 25,000 American soldiers from Vietnam

1970 Nixon sends troops to fight Communist forces in Cambodia

449

The Vietnam Era

Lesson 4 Vietnam in the Nixon Years, *Continued*

Nixon Takes Office

Richard Nixon had run for president with the promise of "peace with honor" in Vietnam. As president, he began working to end the United States' role in the war.

Nixon named Henry Kissinger as his National Security Advisor. Kissinger had authority to help make peace in Vietnam. He had a plan he called "linkage." The goal of this plan was to build better relationships with the Soviet Union and China. These countries were important because they gave support and supplies to North Vietnam. Kissinger hoped to get the Soviet Union and China to reduce their aid to North Vietnam. He hoped this would help to end the war.

Nixon's plan for "peace with honor" had three parts: changing the draft system, giving South Vietnam a bigger role in fighting the war, and more bombing in North Vietnam.

Nixon's "Peace with Honor" Plan

1. Changing the draft system to make it fairer
2. Getting South Vietnam to take on a bigger part in the fighting
3. Bombing more targets in North Vietnam

Nixon made the draft system more fair. College students no longer got deferments. Only 19-year-olds could be called for service, and young men were chosen at random in a lottery. Also the government drafted fewer young men. President Nixon promised to get rid of the draft completely in the future. People liked these changes.

Next, Nixon made a plan he called **Vietnamization**. This plan called for the South Vietnamese to take on more of the fighting. Americans soldiers would do less. In June 1969, Nixon pulled the first 25,000 American soldiers out of Vietnam.

Finally, to make things easier for the American soldiers still in Vietnam, Nixon ordered U.S. planes to bomb North Vietnamese supply routes. He also ordered U.S. forces to bomb Cambodia. However, he kept that order secret from the American public. He also announced the "Nixon Doctrine" which shifted some responsibility for fighting communism to other nations.

✏️ Listing

1. What were the three ways Nixon changed the draft system to make it more fair?

_____

_____

✏️ Marking the Text

2. What did Nixon mean by "Vietnamization"? Underline the answer in the text. How would it affect American soldiers?

_____

_____

❓ Critical Thinking

3. In your opinion, was Henry Kissinger's "linkage" policy a good plan for ending the war in Vietnam? Why or why not?

_____

_____

The Vietnam Era

Lesson 4 Vietnam in the Nixon Years, *Continued*

? Comparing

4. How was the war in Cambodia similar to the war in Vietnam?

_____

_____

✔ Reading Check

5. Describe one effect of each of these events.

Another war started in Cambodia; Effect:

_____

Nixon sent troops into Cambodia; Effect:

_____

Violent protest at Kent State University; Effect:

_____

Pentagon papers released; Effect:

_____

? Analyzing

6. Why did North Vietnam agree to return to peace talks?

_____

_____

_____

The Protests Continue

Nixon and Kissinger tried to get the North Vietnamese to agree to a peace deal, but the war continued.

Then another war started in Cambodia between Communist and non-Communist forces. Nixon sent troops to Cambodia to attack Communist bases there. Americans were angry that Nixon had gotten involved in this new war.

At home, Americans continued to protest the Vietnam War. There were protests all over the nation. In October 1969, more than 300,000 people joined a huge protest in Washington, D.C.

Many protests were on college campuses. Most were peaceful. A protest at Kent State University in Ohio turned violent. Ohio's governor declared **martial law**. Martial law means emergency military rule. The National Guard told the protesters to leave. Instead of leaving, some students threw rocks. National Guard members fired their weapons. Four students were killed. There was another violent protest at Jackson State University in Mississippi. This time two students were shot and killed.

Nixon also lost support in Congress. Its members were angry that he had not told them about the invasion of Cambodia. Then Daniel Ellsberg gave some secret papers to the *New York Times*. These papers were called the Pentagon Papers. The papers gave details about past presidents and the war. They showed that some officials had misled Congress and the public. Many Americans saw that the government had not been honest with them.

Peace and the War's Effects

President Nixon was still working to end the war. In 1972 he ordered a major bombing attack. The heaviest bombing of the war fell on North Vietnam. Nixon hoped this would convince North Vietnam to return to peace talks. His plan succeeded.

Americans pressured South Vietnam to accept peace terms. On January 27, 1973, all sides made a peace deal. The North Vietnamese agreed to return all American prisoners of war. The United States agreed to pull its troops out of Vietnam.

American's part in the Vietnam War was over. But the conflict was not. North Vietnam still wanted to bring all of Vietnam under Communist rule. In 1975 the North began a major attack. On April 30, 1975, South Vietnam fell to the Communists.

451

netw⊕rks

The Vietnam Era

Lesson 4 Vietnam in the Nixon Years, *Continued*

More than one million Vietnamese people died in the war. Vietnam's cities and countryside were in ruins. Also, more than 58,000 Americans died in Vietnam. Another 300,000 were wounded. Thousands of U.S. soldiers were missing in action—**MIA**. No one knew if they were dead or alive. Families of the MIA tried to find their loved ones. As the years passed, it became clear that there was little chance of finding them alive.

The war was also expensive for the United States. The government spent more than $150 billion on the Vietnam War.

Check for Understanding

What steps did Nixon take to bring American forces home and end the Vietnam War?

_____

_____

_____

Why did Ohio's governor declare martial law during the Kent State protest?

_____

_____

Glue Foldable here

Defining

7. What does "MIA" stand for?

_____

_____

FOLDABLES®

8. Place a two-tab Foldable vertically along the dotted line to cover the Check for Understanding. Label the anchor tab *Progress and Protests*. On the top tab write the question *What progress was made to end the war?* On the bottom tab write *What protests made national news and why?* Use both sides of the tabs to record what you remember about each. Use your Foldable to help answer Check for Understanding.

A Troubled Nation

Lesson 1 Nixon's Foreign Policy

ESSENTIAL QUESTION

How do governments change?

GUIDING QUESTIONS

1. **What did President Nixon do to improve relations with China and the Soviet Union?**

2. **What was Nixon's foreign policy toward the Middle East?**

3. **How did the Nixon administration try to halt the spread of communism in Latin America?**

Terms to Know
détente an attempt to ease international tensions
embargo a ban on trade

Where in the world?

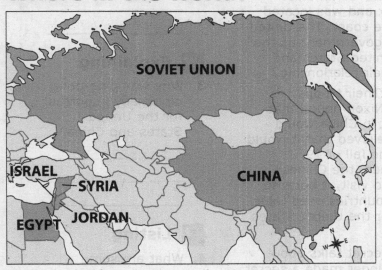

When did it happen?

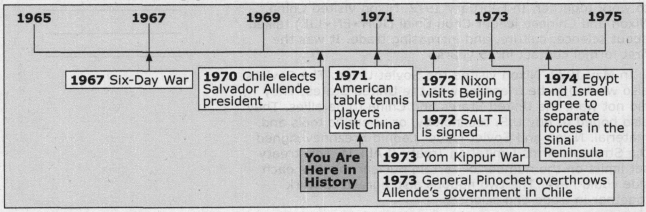

| 1965 | 1967 | 1969 | 1971 | 1973 | 1975 |

1967 Six-Day War

1970 Chile elects Salvador Allende president

1971 American table tennis players visit China

You Are Here in History

1972 Nixon visits Beijing

1972 SALT I is signed

1973 Yom Kippur War

1973 General Pinochet overthrows Allende's government in Chile

1974 Egypt and Israel agree to separate forces in the Sinai Peninsula

453

A Troubled Nation

Lesson 1 Nixon's Foreign Policy, *Continued*

A Thaw in the Cold War

President Nixon believed the world could be more peaceful if the United States had better relationships with the Soviet Union and China. National Security Advisor Henry Kissinger and Nixon felt that peace would come through talking rather than making threats or using force. They believed in a policy called **détente** in which countries would try to relax tensions when problems arose. Nixon felt that détente required a balance of power. This meant that all countries would have equal strength.

In 1949, a revolution in China led to Communist control of the Chinese government. The Communist government in China and a separate anti-Communist government claimed to be the rightful rulers of China. The anti-Communist government was led by Chiang Kai-shek and was located on the island of Taiwan near the Chinese coast. The United States refused to treat the Communist government as the rightful rulers. But by 1970, both the United States and Communist China wanted to improve their relationship.

China did not trust the Soviet Union. Their troops sometimes fought along their borders. Nixon hoped that recognizing the Communist government in China would help end the war in Vietnam. He also believed that it would divide the Soviet Union and China. In the fall of 1970, Nixon said he wanted to visit China. When, the Chinese invited an American table tennis team to visit, it became known as "ping-pong diplomacy." The countries used table tennis to become friendlier. A week later the United States said it would begin to trade with China.

American and Chinese officials held secret talks about building a closer relationship. After Kissinger made a secret trip to China in July 1971, Nixon said that he would visit China. He wanted to make it normal for the two countries to work together. In February 1972, Nixon visited China. Nixon and Chinese leader Chou Enlai (JOH•EN•LIE) talked about science, culture, and increasing trade. It was the first formal contact in 25 years.

In May 1972, Nixon visited the Soviet Union. The Soviets also wanted to be friendlier with the United States. They did not want the United States and China to be allies. They also hoped to buy U.S. technology, or scientific tools and material. Nixon and Soviet leader Leonid Brezhnev signed the Strategic Arms Limitation Treaty (SALT I). This treaty set limits on the number of certain nuclear missiles each side could have. The two nations also agreed to work together in trade and science.

Vocabulary

1. What is détente?

_____

Identifying

2. What were the two governments in China in 1949?

_____

_____

Explaining

3. Why was ping-pong diplomacy important for the United States and China?

_____

_____

_____

Listing

4. What are some examples of today's technology?

_____

_____

_____

Lesson 1 Nixon's Foreign Policy, *Continued*

🖊 Analyzing

5. Why did Egypt and Syria attack Israel in 1973?

_____
_____
_____

🖊 Explaining

6. Why did some Arab countries place an oil embargo on the United States?

_____
_____
_____

✅ Summarizing

7. What happened in the United States because of the oil embargo?

_____
_____
_____

🖊 Explaining

8. Why were Henry Kissinger's visits to the Middle East called "shuttle diplomacy"?

_____
_____
_____

Middle East Tensions

The Jewish state of Israel was founded in 1948. Many Arab nations opposed its creation. The United States supported Israel when it was attacked by its Arab neighbors.

Egypt and Israel had strong disagreements. On June 5, 1967, Israel bombed Egyptian airfields because it thought Egypt was making threats. Jordan and Syria joined Egypt in fighting Israel. In six days, Israel defeated the Arab states. It destroyed their air bases and captured areas held by Egypt and Jordan and an area which was part of Syria.

The conflict was called the "Six-Day War." After the war, the United Nations asked the Israelis to leave the areas they had captured. It also asked the Arab nations to accept Israel's right to exist as a country. The Arabs refused to talk, and Israel kept the areas it captured.

After the war, thousands of Palestinians lived in areas held by Israel. Thousands more fled to neighboring Arab states. They demanded their own country. This became another source of tension.

Arabs and Israelis continued to disagree. In 1973, Egypt and Syria attacked Israel. They wanted to recapture land lost in the Six-Day War. This attack took place on Yom Kippur, an important Jewish holy day. The conflict became known as the Yom Kippur War.

In early battles, many Israeli planes were shot down. Egypt and Syria took land they had previously lost. Israel struck back with American help. The United Nations convinced both sides to stop. Israel had recaptured the land lost in the Arab attack.

Arab states that produced oil were angry because the United States supported Israel. They placed an **embargo** on oil. They refused to sell oil to the United States. The embargo caused problems for the U.S. economy. It led to an oil shortage. Oil and gasoline prices went up. There were long lines at gas stations.

President Nixon sent Henry Kissinger to the Middle East to gain Arab trust, solve the oil crisis, and help Israel and its neighbors make an agreement. Kissinger traveled back and forth between Middle Eastern nations. This was called "shuttle diplomacy."

In 1974, the prime minister of Israel and the president of Egypt agreed to separate their forces in the Sinai Peninsula. In March of 1974, Kissinger convinced the Arab nations to end the oil embargo. He promised large amounts

455

A Troubled Nation

Lesson 1 Nixon's Foreign Policy, *Continued*

of foreign aid to Egypt. This improved U.S. relations with Egypt, the most powerful Arab state.

Latin America

President Nixon wanted to prevent countries in Latin America from becoming Communist. In 1970 Chile elected the Marxist Salvador Allende (uh•YEN•day) president. He believed that the country's wealth should be more equally divided among the people. His government took over large businesses, gave land to the poor, and raised workers' wages. The economy grew, although there were food shortages. Businesses also raised prices because they had to pay higher wages.

Allende's Marxist plans frightened wealthy Chileans. Many took their money out of the country. They then invested it in other countries. The United States was angry when Allende took over U.S. companies. The Nixon administration wanted to weaken Allende's government. It gave money to his political opponents and encouraged workers in Chile to strike. Nixon also convinced other countries and businesses to stop loaning money to Chile. By 1972, Chile's economy was in terrible shape.

In 1973 Chile's military took action. Military leaders under General Augusto Pinochet (peen•oh•SHAY) took control of the government. The Central Intelligence Agency (CIA) helped Pinochet take over the government. The United States quickly recognized the new government. It once again gave foreign aid to Chile.

////////////// Glue Foldable here /////////////

Check for Understanding

List one effect of Nixon's foreign policy on the Middle East and Latin America.

_____

_____

How effective were U.S. attempts at reducing tensions with China and the Soviet Union?

_____

_____

🖐 Identifying

9. List two positive and two negative effects of Allende's government on Chile.

_____

_____

_____

✓ Analyzing

10. Why did the United States oppose Salvador Allende?

_____

_____

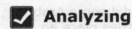

11. Use a two-tab Foldable and cut the tabs in half to make four tabs. Place it along the dotted line to cover Check for Understanding. Write *Nixon's Foreign Policy* on the anchor tab. Label the four tabs *China*, *Soviet Union*, *Middle East* and *Latin America*. Use both sides of the tabs to write words and phrases about the actions Nixon took to improve relations with each.

A Troubled Nation

Lesson 2 Nixon and Watergate

ESSENTIAL QUESTION
How do governments change?

GUIDING QUESTIONS

1. **How did the role of the federal government change under Nixon?**
2. **Why was Nixon forced to resign during his second term?**
3. **How did Ford attempt to unite the nation after the Watergate scandal?**

Where in the world?

Washington, D.C.

ATLANTIC OCEAN

Terms to Know

revenue sharing a policy in which the federal government gives states some of its revenue to be used at state and local levels

affirmative action an approach to hiring or promotion that favors disadvantaged groups.

deficit when government spending is greater than government revenue, or income

executive privilege the principle that White House conversations should remain secret to protect national security

impeach to officially charge someone with misconduct in office

amnesty protection from prosecution

When did it happen?

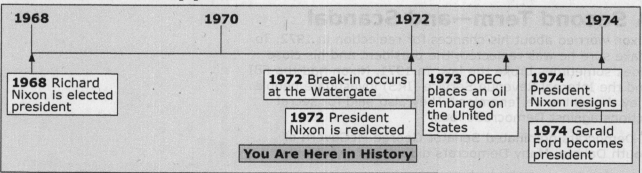

1968   1970   1972   1974

1968 Richard Nixon is elected president

1972 Break-in occurs at the Watergate

1972 President Nixon is reelected

1973 OPEC places an oil embargo on the United States

1974 President Nixon resigns

1974 Gerald Ford becomes president

You Are Here in History

457

Lesson 2 Nixon and Watergate, *Continued*

Domestic Policies under Nixon

One of Nixon's goals at home was to bring back "law and order" to the country. He wanted stronger punishments for lawbreakers. He used federal money to help state and city police forces. Nixon appointed four justices to the Supreme Court. He hoped they would make conservative decisions.

Another goal was to reduce federal involvement in people's lives and give more power to state and local governments. His plan was called New Federalism. One part was **revenue sharing**. It gave states some of the money collected in federal taxes to use or to help cities and towns. It began in 1972. Nixon closed the agency which led the War on Poverty, but created new agencies that protected workers' safety and the environment.

Nixon opposed creating racially mixed schools with forced busing—sending students from all-white or all–African American areas to schools in other areas. Nixon did work to integrate schools under federal court orders. He supported **affirmative action** which favors the hiring or promoting of people from disadvantaged groups.

/ / / / / / / / / / , Glue Foldable here / / / / / / / / / / / .

Economically, manufacturers faced strong competition from foreign countries. There was a rise in the prices of goods and services—called inflation—and increases in the price of oil. In addition, the United States faced slow economic growth and high unemployment.

When prices rise and business activity is slow, experts call the mixture "stagflation." First, Nixon tried cutting federal spending and raising interest rates, then a temporary freeze on wages and prices. Later, Nixon tried a third plan. He increased federal spending to help the economy grow. This plan helped the economy grow for a short time, but it created a budget **deficit**. This is when government spending is greater than government income.

A Second Term—and Scandal

Nixon worried about his chances for reelection in 1972. To make sure he was reelected, the president and his close aides sometimes broke the law. In 1971, Nixon had the FBI and the Internal Revenue Service (IRS) investigate people they thought were "enemies." They also paid for secret actions against Democratic foes.

Democrats nominated Senator George McGovern of South Dakota. Many Democrats did not agree with his

Marking the Text

1. Underline the sentence in the text that defines *stagflation*.

FOLDABLES®
Explaining

2. Use a one-tab Foldable along the dotted line. Glue it over the text that begins "Economically, manufacturers faced strong competition ..." Write the title *Economic Issues* on the anchor tab. Use the front of the Foldable to list Nixon's three plans for reducing inflation and helping the economy. On the back, explain if these efforts helped the economy.

networks

A Troubled Nation

Lesson 2 Nixon and Watergate, *Continued*

✎ Explaining

3. Why did the Democratic Party lose the 1972 election?

_____

_____

_____

_____

❓ Making Inferences

4. Why did the investigators want to hear Nixon's tapes?

_____

_____

_____

✎ Identifying

5. Who were President Nixon's vice presidents?

_____

_____

✔ Explaining

6. How did Gerald Ford become president?

_____

_____

views. When the economy improved and peace in Vietnam seemed possible, Nixon won a landslide victory.

During Nixon's second term, the economy got worse. This was mainly caused by the 1973 oil embargo. Many American companies laid off workers and raised prices. The president urged Americans to use less energy. He also supported drilling for oil in new places, such as Alaska.

In Nixon's second term, a small scandal turned into a disaster. In June 1972, Nixon's reelection committee sent a team of burglars to break into the Democratic Party's office in the Watergate office complex in Washington, D.C. The burglars tried to get information about the Democrats' campaign. They tried to plant bugs on the telephones.

A security guard caught the burglars. At the time, no one knew that the group was working for the Nixon campaign. In fact, few people paid any attention to the story. In November, voters gave Nixon a landslide victory.

Reporters at the *Washington Post* newspaper kept digging into the burglary. The Nixon administration denied knowing anything. In fact, the burglars were paid by the White House and were told to plead guilty and remain silent. "Watergate" had become a scandal.

In May 1973, the Senate held hearings on the scandal. They learned that a secret taping system recorded conversations in the president's office. They demanded the tapes. Nixon refused. He claimed **executive privilege**. This is the principle that a president's conversations should remain secret to protect national security.

A special prosecutor asked a court to force Nixon to hand over the tapes. Nixon ordered the prosecutor fired. Nixon's attorney general and a deputy attorney general quit in protest. The nation was shocked by Nixon's actions.

Another scandal also struck. Vice President Spiro Agnew was charged with taking bribes while he was governor of Maryland. In October 1973, Agnew resigned. Nixon named Congressman Gerald R. Ford of Michigan as vice president.

Nixon released some tapes, but they were not complete. The Supreme Court ruled that the president had to turn over all the tapes. Then, a House committee voted to **impeach** Nixon, or officially charge him with misconduct in office. Before the full House could vote, investigators found clear evidence against him. Impeachment seemed certain. On August 9, 1974, Nixon resigned his office in disgrace. Gerald Ford became president.

A Troubled Nation

Lesson 2 Nixon and Watergate, *Continued*

Healing the Nation

Because of Nixon's actions, the public lost faith in its political leaders. Gerald Ford hoped to heal the nation. But then he granted Nixon a pardon which meant he could not be prosecuted for his part in the cover-up. Many Americans were angry that Nixon escaped punishment.

Another controversy arose when Ford gave **amnesty**, or protection from prosecution, to men who illegally avoided military service during the Vietnam War. Some people thought these "draft dodgers" should be punished.

Like Nixon, Ford worked for détente with the Soviet Union and China. In 1975, he signed the Helsinki Accords with the Soviet Union and other nations. The countries promised to respect their citizens' human rights. Chinese leader Mao Zedong (MOW ZUH•DAWNG) died in 1976 and China's new leaders wanted to increase trade with the United States.

Ford faced a troubled economy. Inflation, unemployment, and oil prices remained high. Foreign countries challenged U.S. economic power. This caused factory closings, high unemployment, and a reduced standard of living.

To fight inflation, Ford asked Americans to save rather than spend money. He also tried to cut government spending. When this failed, the president asked Congress to pass a tax cut. But the cuts meant the government took in less money and faced a budget deficit. Ford could not solve the nation's economic problems.

/////////////// Glue Foldable here ///////////////

Check for Understanding

List two ways Nixon's reelection campaign broke the law.

1. _____

2. _____

What actions did Ford and Nixon take to address economic problems? How successful were they?

_____

_____

Identifying

7. Which countries did Ford work with to continue Nixon's foreign policies?

_____

Identifying

8. What economic problems occurred during Ford's presidency?

_____

_____

FOLDABLES

9. Use a two-tab Foldable and cut the tabs in half to make four tabs. Place it along the dotted line to cover Check for Understanding. Draw an arrow from the left edge of the anchor tab to the right to show a sequence of events. Label the four tabs *Re-election Campaign*, *Watergate*, *Resignation*, and *President Ford*. List one fact that you recall about each. Use your notes to help answer Check for Understanding.

networks

A Troubled Nation

Lesson 3 The Presidency of Jimmy Carter

ESSENTIAL QUESTION

How do governments change?

GUIDING QUESTIONS

1. **What problems did President Carter face?**

2. **What were some successes and challenges of President Carter's foreign policy?**

Terms to Know

trade deficit when the value of foreign imports is greater than the value of American exports

human rights the basic rights and freedoms that all people should have

apartheid racial separation and discrimination against nonwhites

fundamentalist someone who believes in strict obedience to religious laws

Where in the world?

UNITED STATES

AFGHANISTAN

ISRAEL

IRAN

EGYPT

When did it happen?

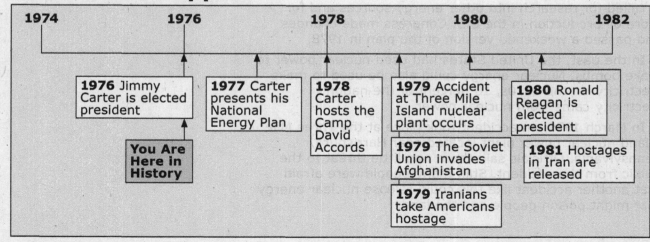

1974   1976   1978   1980   1982

1976 Jimmy Carter is elected president

1977 Carter presents his National Energy Plan

1978 Carter hosts the Camp David Accords

1979 Accident at Three Mile Island nuclear plant occurs

1980 Ronald Reagan is elected president

You Are Here in History

1979 The Soviet Union invades Afghanistan

1981 Hostages in Iran are released

1979 Iranians take Americans hostage

461

A Troubled Nation

Lesson 3 The Presidency of Jimmy Carter, *Continued*

An Informal Presidency

President Ford planned to seek election in 1976. Ronald Reagan also sought the nomination. Reagan was a former actor and governor of California. He had strong support from conservative voters. Ford still won the nomination.

Jimmy Carter was the Democratic candidate. During his campaign, he stressed his integrity, or moral character, and his religious faith. Carter was a former Georgia governor. He had never worked in Washington, D.C., and had no connection to the Watergate scandal.

Ford ran on his record as president. Carter ran against the memory of Nixon and government corruption. Carter won a close election. He got strong support from African American voters in the South. He set an informal tone. For example, at his inauguration, he wore an ordinary business suit rather than more formal clothing.

Carter cut taxes and increased spending to help the economy. Unemployment went down, but inflation went up. Carter then called for spending cuts and a tax cut. Carter's change of policy made him seem weak and uncertain. The president had trouble getting support in Congress because he came from outside Washington.

Carter also tried to solve the country's energy problems. The high cost of energy made inflation worse. The high price of imported oil also led to a growing **trade deficit**. This means that the value of foreign imports was greater than the value of U.S. exports.

In April 1977, Carter presented a National Energy Plan. He wanted to create a Department of Energy to oversee energy policy. The plan described ways to conserve energy. It called for research into other energy sources and for more oil production in the U.S. Congress made changes and passed a weakened version of the plan in 1978.

In the past, the United States had used nuclear power to make bombs. Nuclear energy could also be used to make electricity. In the 1970s, 10 percent of the nation's electricity came from nuclear power.

In March 1979, an accident took place at the Three Mile Island nuclear power plant located near Harrisburg, Pennsylvania. Officials said there was little threat to the public from the accident. Still, many people were afraid that another accident like this could release nuclear energy that might poison people and the land.

🖐 Identifying

1. What was the first step Carter took to improve the economy?

_____

_____

🖐 Listing

2. What was the second step Carter took to improve the economy?

_____

_____

❓ Making Connections

3. What are some alternative energy sources we use today?

_____

_____

Lesson 3 The Presidency of Jimmy Carter, *Continued*

Identifying

4. Which countries did Carter criticize for their human rights abuses?

_____

_____

Describing

5. How did the United States' reaction to the Cuban "boatlift" change over time?

_____

_____

_____

Explaining

6. Why were the Camp David Accords important for peace?

_____

_____

_____

Some people protested the use of nuclear power. Carter did not want to stop using it. Supporters of nuclear power argued that it was not harmful if used properly.

Carter's Foreign Policy

Carter based his foreign policy on **human rights**. Human rights are the basic rights and liberties all people should have. He said that the United States should not support any nation that did not respect human rights. For example, Carter said South Africa's policy of **apartheid** (uh•PAHR•TAYT) should be changed. Apartheid means racial separation and discrimination against nonwhites.

In 1980 Fidel Castro was the Communist leader of Cuba. He allowed thousands of Cubans to leave Cuba by boat for Florida. The U.S. accepted the Cubans at first because Carter had criticized the lack of human rights in Cuba. The United States had trouble helping such large numbers of people. By the time Cuba ended the "boatlift," about 125,000 people had entered the United States. A few were criminals. Public opinion turned against the Cubans.

U.S. control of the Panama Canal had caused friction between the United States and Panama. To improve things, Carter signed two treaties with Panama in 1977. The treaties turned the Panama Canal over to Panama by the year 2000. The canal would also remain a neutral waterway open to all shipping. Some Republicans in the Senate tried to block passage of the treaties. They said that Carter was giving away U.S. property. This effort failed. The Senate approved the treaties in 1978.

President Carter also wanted to bring peace to the Middle East. In 1978 talks between Israel and Egypt stalled. Carter invited Israeli prime minister Menachem Begin and Egyptian president Anwar el-Sadat to a meeting at Camp David in the United States. The three leaders reached an agreement known as the Camp David Accords.

The agreement led to a peace treaty between Egypt and Israel. The treaty was signed in March 1979. It was the first time that Israel and an Arab nation had made peace.

Carter spoke out against human rights abuses by the Soviets. He also tried to improve relations with them. In June 1979, Carter and Soviet leader Leonid Brezhnev signed a second Strategic Arms Limitation Treaty, or SALT II. However, Congress did not approve it right away.

Then in December 1979, any hope of Senate approval ended when the Soviet Union invaded Afghanistan, a

Lesson 3 The Presidency of Jimmy Carter, *Continued*

country in southwest Asia. Carter expressed Americans' anger. The United States and other nations refused to take part in the 1980 Olympic Games in Moscow.

In the 1970s, Iran was a major U.S. ally. Shah Mohammad Reza Pahlavi was Iran's ruler. He built a powerful military with U.S. aid. Many Iranians were angry with corruption in the shah's government. Others disliked Western influences in Iran. They felt these weakened traditional Muslim values.

In January 1979, Islamic **fundamentalists** forced the shah to flee Iran. Fundamentalists are people who believe in strict obedience to religious laws. The Ayatollah Khomeini took power. Khomeini opposed the United States because it had supported the shah.

In November 1979, Iranian students broke into the American embassy in Tehran, the capital of Iran. The group captured 52 Americans and held them hostage. The United States was outraged. Attempts to gain the release of the hostages failed. The American military then tried a daring desert rescue attempt, but it failed and eight American soldiers died. The hostage crisis dragged on. It became a major issue in the presidential election of 1980.

Many Americans blamed President Carter for the weak economy. They were also angry that the hostages had not been released. The Republicans nominated Ronald Reagan. He spoke of lower taxes, less spending, strong defense, and national pride. Reagan won the election easily. Republicans also gained control of the Senate.

During the last weeks of his presidency, Carter worked to free the hostages. He failed. The Iranians finally did release them—after Ronald Reagan took the oath of office. The hostages had been in captivity for 444 days.

Check for Understanding

List two things you consider successes of President Carter's administration.

1. _____

2. _____

Why did many voters in the 1980 election think of President Carter as weak or uncertain?

_____

_____

✓ Summarizing

7. Why did the United States boycott the 1980 Olympics?

_____

_____

? Making Inferences

8. Why did Iranian students capture Americans and hold them hostage?

_____

_____

_____

FOLDABLES®

9. Place a two-tab Foldable along the dotted line to cover Check for Understanding. Write the title *Challenges During the Carter Presidency* on the anchor tab. Label the first tab *Domestic* and the second tab *Foreign*. Use both sides of the tabs to list examples of each kind of challenge. Use the Foldable to help answer Check for Understanding.

Glue Foldable here

.Glue Foldable here.

New Challenges

Lesson 1 The Reagan Revolution

ESSENTIAL QUESTION

What are the consequences when cultures interact?

GUIDING QUESTIONS

1. **How did President Reagan bring a new conservative approach to government?**

2. **Why did the Reagan administration take strong action to resist Communist influence overseas?**

3. **What events occurred during Reagan's second term?**

Terms to Know
deregulation the removal of rules and regulations
federal debt the amount of money owed by the federal government

Where in the world?

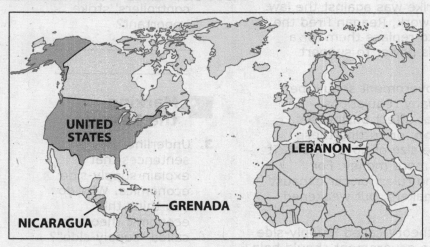

UNITED STATES

LEBANON—

—GRENADA

NICARAGUA

When did it happen?

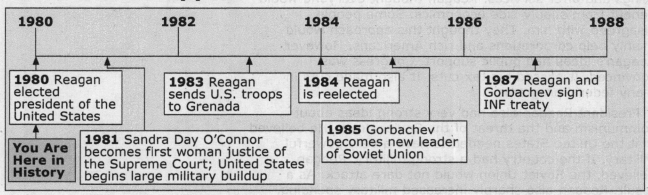

1980	1982	1984	1986	1988

1980 Reagan elected president of the United States

You Are Here in History

1981 Sandra Day O'Connor becomes first woman justice of the Supreme Court; United States begins large military buildup

1983 Reagan sends U.S. troops to Grenada

1984 Reagan is reelected

1985 Gorbachev becomes new leader of Soviet Union

1987 Reagan and Gorbachev sign INF treaty

465

New Challenges

Lesson 1 The Reagan Revolution, *Continued*

The Nation Changes Course

Conservative ideas gained strength in the 1970s. In general, conservatives in politics prefer a small government which has a limited effect on business and people's lives. President Reagan was elected because of his conservative ideas.

Reagan had strong ideas about government. He talked about traditional values. These included hard work, love of country, respect for law, and family life. Reagan followed presidents who had focused on different things. Therefore, people called his programs the "Reagan Revolution."

He thought that the government should cut taxes so people would have more money. The government would also cut spending on social programs.

A few months after taking office, the nation's air traffic controllers went on strike. The strike was against the law. When they refused to go back to work, Reagan fired the controllers. He used the military to replace them for a while. He showed he would use his power to support policies he believed in.

In his conservative view, the government should be smaller and should not have so many regulations. Regulations are laws and rules that affect businesses. Reagan believed that **deregulation**, or cutting these regulations, would help reduce the size of government. It would also help businesses make more money. For example, his government made the rules for car exhaust systems weaker. This helped carmakers, but weakened efforts to reduce pollution.

President Reagan supported a theory called "supply-side economics." This theory is that the government should help the suppliers. Suppliers are the businesses that make things and offer services. Reagan thought everyone would benefit from supply-side economics. Some people disagreed with him. They thought this approach would mainly help corporations and rich Americans. However, Reagan's ideas had public support. Congress was convinced. It passed big tax cuts. It also made cuts in many federal programs.

President Reagan also had very strong ideas about communism and the threat of the Soviet Union. He believed that the United States needed to have a very powerful military. If the country had a strong military, Reagan believed, the Soviet Union would not dare attack. As a result, Reagan also sharply increased military spending.

466

✓ Reading Check

1. What was the effect of deregulation on carmakers and the environment?

? Analyzing

2. Why were Reagan's actions in response to the air traffic controllers' strike important?

_____

_____

Marking the Text

3. Underline the sentences that explain supply-side economics. Why do you think this economic theory is called "supply-side"?

_____

_____

New Challenges

Lesson 1 The Reagan Revolution, *Continued*

☑ **Reading Check**

4. What caused the federal debt to grow in the 1980s?

_____

_____

✎ **Identifying**

5. What was the name of Reagan's program to protect the country against missiles?

_____

☑ **Reading Check**

6. Why did Reagan send troops to Grenada?

_____

_____

☑ **Explaining**

7. Why did Reagan withdraw troops from Lebanon?

_____

_____

Together, the big tax cuts and the large increase in military spending increased the **federal debt**. The federal debt is the amount of money owed by the federal government. While Reagan was president, the federal debt increased greatly. At first, unemployment rose. Later, the economy recovered and the economy grew.

Reagan favored judges who believed in strictly interpreting the Constitution. He appointed several new Supreme Court justices. Among them was Sandra Day O'Connor. She was the first woman to serve on the Supreme Court.

Foreign Policy under Reagan

President Reagan believed that communism was a dangerous force in the world. That was why he was willing to spend so much money on the military. Reagan's defense program included the Strategic Defense Initiative (SDI), or "Star Wars." SDI was a system to destroy missiles that might be launched against the United States. SDI was never finished.

Reagan also believed that pro-Communist governments in Latin America could be a threat to the United States. So he sent aid to a group called the Contras in Nicaragua. The Contras were fighting against Nicaragua's new pro-Communist government.

In 1983, Reagan sent the U.S. military to invade the island of Grenada in the Caribbean. A group of Marxist rebels had started an uprising against the government there. Reagan wanted to set up an anti-Communist government. In addition, American medical students were attending a university in Grenada. Reagan wanted to make sure the students were safe.

President Reagan also sent troops to Lebanon, a small country in the Middle East. They were sent to help remove outside fighters and keep the peace. A car bomb and other terror attacks killed over 300 Americans and French. Reagan decided that the cost was too high. He brought the American troops back home.

A Second Term

The U.S. economy was strong. Reagan remained a popular president. He easily won reelection in 1984, winning the electoral votes in 49 of 50 states. A year later, terrorists

networks

New Challenges

Lesson 1 The Reagan Revolution, *Continued*

kidnapped some Americans and would not let them go. These terrorists had ties to Iran.

Some of Reagan's officials decided to secretly try to free the hostages. The officials sold weapons to Iran. They thought that this would persuade Iran to help free the hostages. Then these officials gave the money from the weapons sale to the Contras in Nicaragua. They thought the money would help the Contras get rid of the Communist government there. These actions were against U.S. policy. They were also against the law. The secret deal became known as the Iran-Contra scandal. Congress held hearings to investigate. They did not find that Reagan was directly involved.

Reagan was more successful with the Soviet Union. The new Soviet leader, Mikhail Gorbachev, wanted to make changes in the government. He wanted to allow new ideas into Soviet society. This policy was called *glasnost*. He also reduced government control of the economy. He called this policy *perestroika*. In 1987, Reagan and Gorbachev signed an agreement called the Intermediate Range Nuclear Forces (INF) Treaty. In the treaty, they agreed to decrease the nuclear weapons of both countries. The treaty was a big step towards reducing the threat of a nuclear war.

Check for Understanding

Why do you think President Reagan easily won re-election in 1984?

_____

_____

What was the relationship between the United States and the Soviet Union during Reagan's time as president?

_____

_____

Naming

8. What was the name given to the secret deal made by Reagan's officials?

_____

Marking the Text

9. Circle the names of the two changes that took place in Soviet domestic policy in the 1980s. Underline the sentences that describe them.

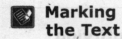 **FOLDABLES**®

10. Use a two-tab Foldable and place it vertically along the dotted line. Write the title *President Reagan* on the anchor tab. Label the top tab *Domestic Policy* and the bottom tab *Foreign Policy*. Describe the effects of President Reagan's leadership at home and abroad. Use both sides of the tabs.

New Challenges

Lesson 2 The First President Bush

ESSENTIAL QUESTION

What are the consequences when cultures interact?

GUIDING QUESTIONS

1. **What global events led to the end of the Cold War in the Bush presidency?**

2. **How did the Bush administration set out to develop a new foreign policy after the end of the Cold War?**

3. **What were the domestic challenges faced by the Bush administration?**

Terms to Know
coalition a group formed for a common purpose
downsize the practice of laying off workers to make a company smaller
bankrupt a condition in which a person or a business cannot pay its debts

Where in the world?

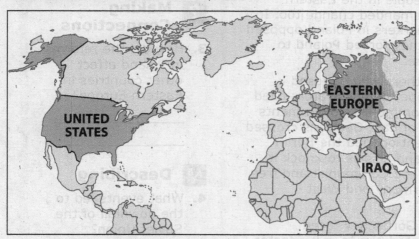

UNITED STATES

EASTERN EUROPE

IRAQ

When did it happen?

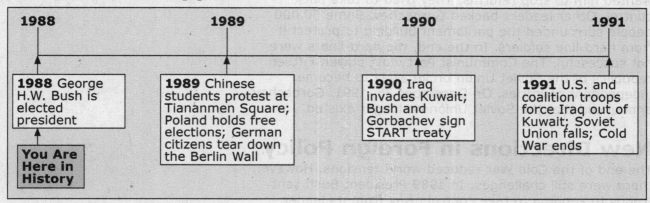

1988	1989	1990	1991
1988 George H.W. Bush is elected president	**1989** Chinese students protest at Tiananmen Square; Poland holds free elections; German citizens tear down the Berlin Wall	**1990** Iraq invades Kuwait; Bush and Gorbachev sign START treaty	**1991** U.S. and coalition troops force Iraq out of Kuwait; Soviet Union falls; Cold War ends

You Are Here in History

New Challenges

Lesson 2 The First President Bush, *Continued*

The Cold War Ends

Republican George H.W. Bush won the 1988 election easily. But the election did not change the power in Congress. The Democrats still controlled both the House and Senate.

The Cold War between the United States and the Soviet Union began after World War II. As George H.W. Bush became president, big changes were taking place in the Soviet Union. Gorbachev was the Soviet leader. He wanted to end the arms race with the United States so he could reform his country. He and President Bush signed a treaty called the Strategic Arms Reduction Treaty or START. The treaty marked the first time that nuclear powers agreed to destroy some of their nuclear weapons. But this did not get Gorbachev more support in the Soviet Union. The people there wanted to improve their economy.

As the Soviet Union changed, people in the Eastern European countries it controlled demanded change too. In 1980, a labor union for shipyard workers in Poland opposed Communist rule. Finally, in 1989, they forced Poland to hold free elections for the first time.

The victory in Poland inspired others who opposed communism. All over Eastern Europe, demonstrators filled the streets. Borders opened up. Communist governments collapsed. In Germany, thousands of East Germans crossed into West Germany. The government opened the Berlin Wall. People came with hammers and chisels to knock it down. The Berlin Wall had divided the Communist and free parts of the city. In 1990, East Germany and West Germany were united.

Meanwhile, in the Soviet Union, Gorbachev faced opposition on two sides. Some wanted him to move faster to make changes. Some hard-line Communist leaders wanted him to stop reforms. They tried to take back control. Other leaders backed Gorbachev. Some 50,000 people surrounded the parliament building to protect it from hard-line soldiers. In the end, the hard-liners were not successful. The Communist Party lost power. Fifteen republics of the Soviet Union broke away to become independent countries. On December 25, 1991, Gorbachev announced that the Soviet Union no longer existed.

New Directions in Foreign Policy

The end of the Cold War reduced world tensions. However, there were still challenges. In 1989 President Bush sent troops to Panama to take control away from its leader.

Identifying

1. What two countries were involved in the Cold War?

_____

Marking the Text

2. Underline the reason that Gorbachev signed START.

Making Connections

3. How did the reforms in Poland affect other countries in Eastern Europe?

_____

_____

Describing

4. What events led to the downfall of the Soviet Union?

_____

_____

470

New Challenges

Lesson 2 The First President Bush, *Continued*

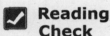

Listing

5. List two places where President Bush sent U.S. troops.

_____

_____

✔ Reading Check

6. Why did President Bush send U.S. troops to the Middle East?

_____

Marking the Text

7. Underline the sentences that define *downsizing* and *bankrupt*.

They arrested him for selling and shipping drugs. Panama held elections and formed a new government.

Communist China started to change. It slowly gave its people more freedom to buy, sell, and make things. But its people still had no political freedom. In 1989, many students and workers demanded freedom. They gathered in Tiananmen (tee•AHN•ahn•men) Square in the capital city of Beijing (BAY•ZHING). The government called in troops to stop the protest. Hundreds of protesters were killed. Bush spoke out strongly against the killings.

In 1990 Iraq's dictator Saddam Hussein sent troops to invade Kuwait. Kuwait is a small country near Iraq. It is rich in oil. President Bush demanded that Hussein's forces leave Kuwait. Hussein refused. Bush then called on other nations to form a **coalition** against Hussein. First they bombed Iraq. Then the coalition sent troops to drive Iraq out of Kuwait. The Persian Gulf War was over in just six weeks.

As the Soviet Union collapsed, Communist Yugoslavia fell apart too. It was made up of several republics. In the early 1990s, Slovenia, Croatia, and Bosnia-Herzegovina all declared their independence. Another part of Yugoslavia, called Serbia, claimed parts of Croatia and Bosnia for itself. A civil war broke out. Serbia helped Serbs in the other countries to fight against the new governments. Serbs were accused of mass killings of civilians in the war. Thousands of people died before NATO troops stopped the fighting. The opposing sides signed a peace plan called the Dayton Accords in 1995.

Bush and Domestic Policy

At home, the economy slid into a recession. The end of the Cold War was partly to blame. The government cut its military spending. This hurt defense-related industries. Many workers in these industries lost their jobs. Other businesses also **downsized** by laying off some of their workers. Some could not pay their debts and became **bankrupt**. Some people believed that more government spending would help the economy. President Bush disagreed He refused government involvement except to extend jobless benefits.

The nation's savings and loan associations (S&Ls) were hit very hard. S&Ls are like banks that make loans to homebuyers. President Reagan had reduced the regulations on S&Ls. This meant that S&Ls could make riskier loans.

netw⊙rks

New Challenges

Lesson 2 The First President Bush, *Continued*

When people could not pay back the loans, many S&Ls went out of business. The government paid about $160 billion so the S&Ls would not fail and so that people who had savings in these S&Ls would not lose their money.

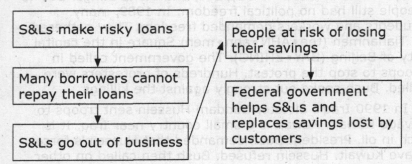

S&Ls make risky loans

Many borrowers cannot repay their loans

S&Ls go out of business

People at risk of losing their savings

Federal government helps S&Ls and replaces savings lost by customers

President Bush worked with Congress on several important measures. Congress passed an updated Clean Air Act to reduce air pollution. The Americans with Disabilities Act banned discrimination against people with disabilities. It also improved access to workplaces, transportation, and housing. Bush also created the Office of National Drug Control Policy to fight the war on illegal drugs.

Check for Understanding

When did the Cold War begin? Why did the Cold War end in 1991?

_____

_____

Name two actions that President Bush took to prevent Iraq from taking over Kuwait.

_____

_____

✓ Reading Check

8. Why did so many S&Ls fail?

_____

_____

FOLDABLES®

9. Place a two-tab Foldable along the dotted line to cover Check for Understanding. Write *Factors of the Bush Presidency* on the anchor tab. Label the top tab *Domestic Challenges* and the bottom tab *Foreign Events.* List the facts that you remember about the problems at home and abroad during the Bush presidency. Use your Foldable to help answer Check for Understanding.

Glue Foldable here

New Challenges

Lesson 3 Toward a New Century

ESSENTIAL QUESTION
How do governments change?

GUIDING QUESTIONS
1. **What positive and negative events occurred in the Clinton administration?**
2. **Why was the United States divided politically during a time of economic prosperity?**

Terms to Know
grassroots movement a movement made up of individuals and small groups in multiple locations around the nation who join together for a shared goal

deficit spending spending more money than is received and creating debt as a result

gross domestic product the value of all goods and services produced in a nation in one year

perjury the act of lying after swearing to tell the truth

Where in the world?

When did it happen?

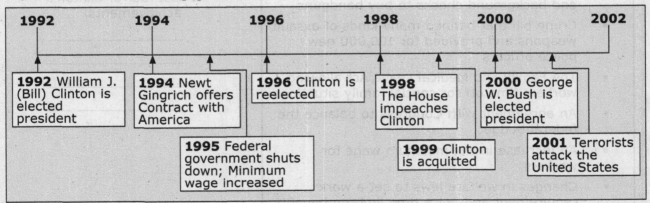

1992 — **1992** William J. (Bill) Clinton is elected president

1994 — **1994** Newt Gingrich offers Contract with America

1995 Federal government shuts down; Minimum wage increased

1996 — **1996** Clinton is reelected

1998 — **1998** The House impeaches Clinton

1999 Clinton is acquitted

2000 — **2000** George W. Bush is elected president

2001 Terrorists attack the United States

2002

New Challenges

Lesson 3 Toward a New Century, *Continued*

The Clinton Presidency

At the end of President George H.W. Bush's term, the economy was still a problem. In the election of 1992, the president faced Democratic candidate Bill Clinton. Another candidate also entered the race. Ross Perot, a wealthy businessman, was unhappy with both candidates. Perot was worried about the government's **deficit spending**. For a long time, the federal government had been spending more money than it was taking in.

People in local communities started a **grassroots movement**. They wanted to make Perot a third-party candidate for president. He received more votes in the election than third-party candidates usually do. But Clinton won the election, beating Bush and Perot.

President Clinton worried about the deficit, too. He proposed cutting spending and raising taxes for middle class and wealthy Americans. Poor people would pay less. Congress passed Clinton's plan by a very small amount.

Clinton wanted to change the nation's health care system so that more Americans could afford health care. Many members of Congress thought Clinton's plan cost too much money. They argued that it made the government too big. So they defeated it. However, Congress later passed laws to improve health care for children and the elderly. Clinton had other successes in getting his programs enacted into law.

Other Major Clinton Successes
• The Brady Bill, requiring a waiting period and background checks to buy handguns
• Crime bill that banned many kinds of assault weapons and provided for 100,000 new police officers
• The Family and Medical Leave Act allowing workers time off for special family situations
• An agreement with Congress to balance the federal budget
• An increase in the minimum wage for workers
• Changes in welfare laws to set a work requirement and put a time limit on benefits

Marking the Text

1. Underline the names of the candidates for president in 1992. Who won the election?

_____

Defining

2. What is deficit spending?

_____

_____

Applying

3. Check where leadership comes from in a grassroots movement.

☐ local communities

☐ party leaders

Listing

4. List four of Clinton's achievements.

_____

_____

_____

_____

networks

New Challenges

Lesson 3 Toward a New Century, *Continued*

Describing

5. How did the 1994 elections change Congress?

_____

_____

Defining

6. Perjury is a type of

_____ .

Identifying

7. How did NAFTA encourage trade?

_____

_____

Listing

8. Name two areas of the world where Clinton worked to achieve peace.

_____ .

Many Republicans in Congress opposed Clinton's plans. Led by Newt Gingrich, they came up with the Contract with America in 1994. It called for a smaller federal government, a balanced budget, and lower taxes. In the 1994 mid-term elections, Republicans won a majority in both houses of Congress for the first time in 40 years.

The new Congress and President Clinton soon clashed over the federal budget. Both sides refused to give in. Then the federal government ran out of money. It shut down for nearly a month. Many government services stopped. Government workers went without pay. Finally, Congress passed a bill that balanced the budget.

The nation's economy grew steadily. One way to measure the size of an economy is by the **gross domestic product**, or GDP. This is the value of all goods and services a nation produces in a year. As the GDP grew, the government collected more taxes. At the same time, the government cut spending. By 1998 the United States had the first budget surplus in 30 years.

Clinton was reelected to a second term in 1996. The strong economy helped keep him popular. However, personal scandals threatened his presidency. Clinton was accused of helping to set up illegal loans when he was governor of Arkansas. During that investigation, he was accused of an improper relationship with a White House worker. He was also accused of lying under oath when he was asked about it. This kind of lying is called **perjury**. It is against the law. The House voted to impeach the president for this crime, but the Senate did not convict him. He stayed in office.

Clinton also faced challenges in foreign policy. He believed the nation would benefit if trade with Mexico and Canada was easier. In 1993, Congress approved the North American Free Trade Agreement (NAFTA). This treaty ended tariffs on Canadian and Mexican goods sold in the United States and on U.S. goods sold in Canada and Mexico. Not everyone agreed with NAFTA. People who supported it thought (1) businesses could export more goods, and (2) prices would be lower for Americans. People who opposed it thought (1) U.S. workers would lose jobs, and (2) farmers would be hurt by cheaper farm imports.

Clinton worked for peace in the Middle East. In 1993 Israel agreed that the Palestine Liberation Organization (PLO) represented the Palestinians. The PLO said Israel had a right to exist. However, violence continued. Clinton worked for peace in the former Yugoslavia. He led peace

Lesson 3 Toward a New Century, *Continued*

talks to end civil war in Bosnia. Later, U.S. and NATO forces forced the Serbs to leave the region of Kosovo.

A New President for a New Century

When Clinton left office, the budget was balanced. The economy was strong. Democrats nominated Vice President Al Gore in 2000. Republicans chose George W. Bush, son of former president George H. W. Bush. They disagreed on most issues. Ralph Nader ran as a third-party candidate.

The election of 2000 was very close. Gore won more popular votes. However, neither candidate had a clear majority of electoral votes. There was a dispute over who won Florida's electoral votes. The winner of Florida's electoral votes would be president. It was so close, a recount began. Republicans and Democrats fought over how to recount Florida's votes properly. The dispute finally went to the Supreme Court to be decided. The Court stopped the recount, and Bush became president.

Power had shifted between Democrats and Republicans. In 2002, Republicans gained control of both the House and the Senate.

President Bush worked to carry out his campaign promises. Congress passed a law to lower taxes. It also passed education reforms that required yearly testing to measure student performance in grades three to eight.

Bush believed new military programs would make America stronger and safer. However, the nation suffered a terrorist attack on September 11, 2001. It showed that a new kind of war threatened the United States.

////////////////// Glue Foldable here ////////////////////

Check for Understanding
What happened when Congress could not agree on the federal budget in 1995?

_____

_____

List two issues that divided Americans during the Clinton administration.

_____

_____

Identifying
9. Which state determined the election of 2000?

_____

✔ Reading Check
10. What was George W. Bush's policy on education?

_____

_____

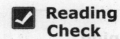

11. Use a three-tab Venn diagram Foldable and place it horizontally along the dotted line. Write the title *Federal Budget 1995* on the anchor tab. Label the left tab *Democrats*, the middle tab *Congress*, and the right tab *Republicans*. Write facts about each to compare and contrast opinions and consequences. Use your Foldable to help answer Check for Understanding.

New Challenges

Lesson 4 The Global War on Terror

ESSENTIAL QUESTION

Why does conflict develop?

GUIDING QUESTIONS

1. *What events occurred on September 11, 2001?*

2. *Why did Bush lose support during his second term?*

3. *Why did Americans choose Barack Obama as president in a historic election?*

Terms to Know

terrorism violence committed in order to frighten people or governments into granting demands

insurgent a person who revolts against a government or others in power

levee high walls or an embankment to prevent flooding in low-lying areas

bailout a rescue, such as from financial ruin

Where in the world?

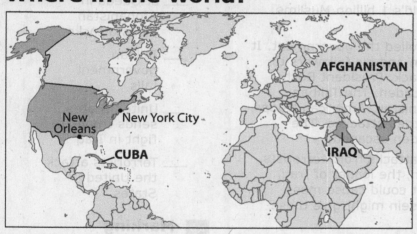

When did it happen?

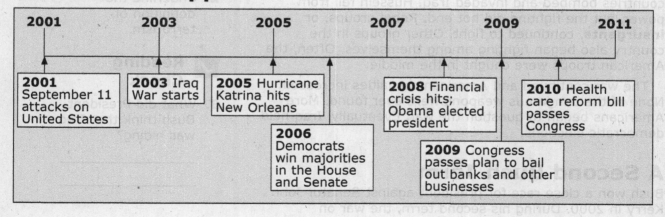

| 2001 | 2003 | 2005 | 2007 | 2009 | 2011 |

2001 September 11 attacks on United States

2003 Iraq War starts

2005 Hurricane Katrina hits New Orleans

2006 Democrats win majorities in the House and Senate

2008 Financial crisis hits; Obama elected president

2009 Congress passes plan to bail out banks and other businesses

2010 Health care reform bill passes Congress

New Challenges

Lesson 4 The Global War on Terror, Continued

The Day That Changed the Nation

On September 11, 2001, terrorists attacked the United States. Using airplanes as weapons, they killed nearly 3,000 people. Two planes crashed into New York City's World Trade Center. One crashed into the Pentagon in Washington, D.C. A fourth crashed in a field in Pennsylvania. Passengers had attacked the terrorists before the plane reached its target.

The events of September 11 were acts of **terrorism** that were planned by a group in the Middle East called al-Qaeda. Terrorism is violence meant to frighten people or governments into granting demands. Osama bin Laden was the leader of al-Qaeda. It is a small group of Muslims who believe terrorism should be used against those who do not share their beliefs. Most of the world's 1 billion Muslims reject this kind of thinking.

In Afghanistan, the Taliban controlled the government. It supported bin Laden. It allowed him and his followers to live in the country and plan the attack. President Bush asked the Taliban to turn over bin Laden. The Taliban refused. Bush sent troops to Afghanistan. American troops, and those from several other countries attacked. The Taliban government fell, but bin Laden escaped.

Americans worried about future attacks from terrorists. Bush believed that Saddam Hussein, the leader of Iraq, was hiding dangerous weapons that could cause mass destruction. Bush worried that Hussein might give these weapons to terrorist groups.

The president decided to send U.S. troops to Iraq. In 2003, troops from the United States and a few other countries bombed and invaded Iraq. Hussein fell from power, but the fighting did not end. Rebel groups, or **insurgents**, continued to fight. Other groups in the country also began fighting among themselves. Often, the American troops were caught in the middle.

The war continued and American casualties increased. None of the dangerous weapons were ever found. More Americans began to question the war. Eventually, Iraq held democratic elections.

A Second Bush Term

Bush won a close race for president against Senator John Kerry in 2000. During his second term, the war on terrorism raised questions about civil liberties. Civil

? **Sequencing**

1. Number these events in the order in which they happened.

   ____ United States attacks Afghanistan

   ____ Hussein is removed from office

   ____ al-Qaeda in Afghanistan plans attacks

   ____ Taliban government falls

   ____ United States sends troops to fight in Iraq

   ____ Terrorists attack the United States

A\|b\|c **Marking the Text**

2. Underline the definition of terrorism.

✓ **Reading Check**

3. What did President Bush think that Iraq was hiding?

   _____

   _____

New Challenges

Lesson 4 The Global War on Terror, *Continued*

✐ Explaining

4. What did President Bush believe about the prisoners at Guantanamo?

_____

✓ Reading Check

5. What did the Supreme Court rule about the prisoners at Guantanamo Bay?

_____

✐ Marking the Text

6. Underline the name of the storm that hit New Orleans.

❓ Determining Cause and Effect

7. Why did this storm do so much damage?

_____

✓ Reading Check

8. What made the election of 2008 historic?

_____

liberties are basic rights. Americans debated what to do with suspected terrorists and certain others captured in the fighting. Some of these prisoners were sent to the U.S. naval base in Guantanamo Bay, Cuba. In Cuba, they were given only limited rights. President Bush believed the prisoners were illegally fighting for the enemy. The prisoners wanted the right to be heard in court.

The prisoners' case made its way to the Supreme Court in 2004. The Supreme Court said the prisoners did have some legal rights. Later, the Supreme Court said the prisoners could not be tried in military courts. Bush also appointed two new conservative Supreme Court justices.

In the summer of 2005, a very strong hurricane hit New Orleans and the Gulf Coast of the United States. Along the Mississippi River, **levees** had been built to keep floodwater out of the city. These levees were not strong enough to stop damage from Hurricane Katrina. Much of the city of New Orleans was flooded. The floods left thousands of people homeless. At least 1,800 people died.

It took the local, state, and federal governments a long time to help the people who were trapped by the flood. President Bush said that federal funds would help rebuild the city. By this time, the president was losing support.

In 2006, the Democrats won the majority in both houses of Congress. The president said his plan was to send more troops to Iraq to win the war. Many Democrats called on the president to set a date for when the troops would leave Iraq. The war was dividing Americans.

A Historic Change

The 2008 elections made history. Barack Obama, a senator from Illinois, was the Democratic candidate. He was the first African American to be the presidential candidate of a major party. Sarah Palin, the governor of Alaska, was the Republican candidate for vice president. She was the first Republican woman to run on a presidential ticket.

The weak economy concerned many Americans. Then in the fall of 2008 a severe financial crisis hit the nation. Voters seemed to blame the Republicans for the crisis. Obama won the election easily and the Democrats won majorities in both the House and the Senate.

Obama faced the major economic crisis as soon as he took office. He proposed a spending bill that included benefits for the jobless, tax cuts for workers, and funding to create jobs. Congress passed the bill. Obama also

479

New Challenges

Lesson 4 The Global War on Terror, *Continued*

thought a **bailout** for some companies was needed. Critics said that the measures cost too much. They worried about the national debt, which was already very high.

Obama had promised to fight to change the health care system. He wanted to make health care less expensive. Also, millions of Americans had no health insurance. Obama wanted them to be able to get coverage. Finally, a bill was passed and became law in 2010.

Critics of Obama's reforms said they cost too much money. The national debt continued to grow. Some protested at "tea parties." These were named after the protesters who threw tea into Boston Harbor in 1773. In 2010, Republicans gained control of the House and won more seats in the Senate. They promised to overturn the health-care reform and make deep cuts in spending.

Obama had promised to end the war in Iraq. By August 2010, combat operations by American troops had ended. Some troops stayed to help the government keep order.

In Afghanistan, fighting continued. Obama sent more troops to help in the fighting. The Taliban and al-Qaeda remained a serious threat. However, Obama pledged to begin removing troops in mid-2011. In May 2011, U.S. forces finally located and killed Osama bin Laden in Pakistan.

In the Middle East, protesters succeeded in overthrowing dictatorships in Tunisia and Egypt. In Libya, a dictator used force to try to stop protestors. The United States joined with other countries to stop these attacks against his people. It was not clear how much or how long the United States would be involved.

/ / / / / / / / / / / / Glue Foldable here / / / / / / / / / / / /

Check for Understanding

Why did President Bush lose popular support?

_____

_____

List two foreign countries in which President Obama faced challenges.

_____

_____

Explaining

9. Why did critics argue against Obama's plan for the economic crisis?

_____

_____

Stating

10. When did U.S. combat operations end in Iraq?

_____

FOLDABLES

11. Use a three-tab Foldable and place it along the dotted line. Write the title *Challenges of G.W. Bush Presidency* on the anchor tab. Label the left tab *9-11-2001*, the middle tab *Guantanamo Bay*, and the right tab *Katrina*. Identify the president's response to each and summarize the effects of his decisions.

New Challenges

Lesson 5 Twenty-First Century Challenges

ESSENTIAL QUESTION
How do new ideas change the way people live?

GUIDING QUESTIONS
1. **How did the global economy benefit from technology but suffer during the financial crisis?**
2. **What are the key environmental and social issues facing the U.S.?**

Terms to Know
interdependent relying on each other
globalization the increasing economic interaction between people, companies, and governments of different nations
trade deficit what happens when the value of imports is greater than the value of exports
free trade the free flow of goods and services among countries through the removal of tariffs and other trade barriers
outsourcing the practice of moving production of goods or services to another location where the cost of labor is cheaper
acid rain rain containing high amounts of chemical pollutants from the burning of fossil fuels

When did it happen?

2008	2009	2010
2008 Financial crisis hits; Congress agrees to bailout; Obama elected president	**2009** Government bails out banks; More troops sent to Afghanistan	**2010** Gulf oil spill; Health care law passes Congress; Obama reduces troops in Iraq

What do you know?

In the first column, answer the questions based on what you know before you study. After this lesson, complete the last column.

Now...		Later...
	What invention triggered the technology revolution?	
	How did the changes in technology change businesses around the world?	

481

Lesson 5 Twenty-First Century Challenges, *Continued*

The Global Economy

Today, the countries of the world are **interdependent**. That means that the health of one country's economy depends on the health of other countries' economies. What happens in one place often affects what happens somewhere else in the world. Countries rely on each other for raw materials and markets to sell goods. Most nations take part in a global economy.

The most important growth in the new global economy is related to the development of computers and other technology. Scientists developed the integrated circuit in the 1960s and microprocessors in the 1970s. This made it possible to make small, fast computers that store a lot of information.

New technology helped the global economy grow. Then, in 2008, a major financial crisis hit the United States. It affected other countries, too. American banks had been making risky home loans. Many people could not pay back their loans. Some of them lost their homes. As the economy slowed, people stopped buying things. Businesses slowed down. People lost their jobs. Some banks did not have enough money to make new loans. These banks were at risk of going out of business. This became the worst economic crisis since the Great Depression of the 1930s.

By 2011, the economy was growing again. But unemployment was still high and many people were struggling to recover from economic problems.

Technology has helped lead to **globalization**, or the linking of the world's economies and societies. Businesses and people talk to one another and share information all over the globe. Technology has made trade between countries easier and much more common.

Marking the Text

1. Underline the words in the text that show the meaning of the word *interdependent*.

Determining Cause and Effect

2. What was the initial cause of the financial crisis?

_____

_____

Analyzing Visuals

3. Based on the diagram, which country is buying the goods? Which is collecting the money?

_____

_____

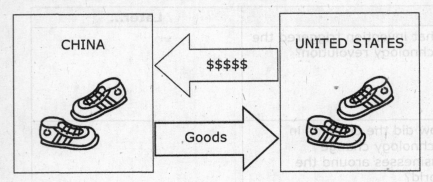

CHINA $$$$$ UNITED STATES   Goods

New Challenges

Lesson 5 Twenty-First Century Challenges, *Continued*

? Analyzing

4. Why might free trade agreements lead to outsourcing?

_____

_____

_____

Marking the Text

5. Underline the text that explains the possible effects of outsourcing.

Describing

6. What are some of the effects of acid rain?

_____

_____

Identifying

7. What area was affected by the oil spill in the Gulf of Mexico?

_____

_____

The United States is a leader in world trade. However, it buys many more goods from other countries than it sells. This causes a **trade deficit** because more money leaves the country than is taken in.

To help Americans sell products in other countries, many presidents have supported **free trade**. Free trade means removing barriers to trade, such as tariffs. NAFTA is a free trade agreement which got rid of tariffs on goods moving between the United States, Canada, and Mexico.

Some critics argue that these types of agreements lead to **outsourcing**. Outsourcing occurs when companies move the production of goods and services outside of the United States. Companies can pay lower wages to workers in foreign countries, which means the prices of the goods may go down. Some say outsourcing causes workers in the United States to lose their jobs. Others believe this process leads to economic growth which results in more and better American jobs.

Challenges for the Future

Globalization also affects the environment—the land, air, and water around us. Pollution in one place can affect the environment in other places. For example, the wind can carry air pollution far away. When oil or coal is burned, it pollutes the air. When this pollution mixes with water vapor in the air, it forms **acid rain**. Acid rain can damage trees and plants and spread pollution into lakes and rivers.

Oil is used to heat buildings, to make gasoline for cars and trucks, and to make many products. Americans use a lot of oil. The United States depends on other countries for most of its oil.

Oil is found deep below the surface of the earth. It is also found under the ocean floor. Because of advances in technology, oil drilling can take place in very deep water. In April 2010, workers in the Gulf of Mexico were drilling under the ocean floor. The rig they were working on exploded. Some workers died and many were hurt. The oil from under the ocean floor poured into the ocean. The oil polluted the waters for miles, traveling to the shores of Louisiana and along the Gulf Coast all the way to Florida. It took four months to stop the leak. The spilled oil killed many animals and damaged natural areas.

Many scientists think the Earth's climate is changing by getting warmer. If it continues to get warmer, many scientists predict there will be many floods in coastal

New Challenges

Lesson 5 Twenty-First Century Challenges, *Continued*

areas. Many scientists believe pollution is causing climate change, although some disagree.

In March 2011, a large earthquake struck Japan. It caused a tsunami—a large ocean wave which flooded many areas. It also damaged a nuclear power plant which released radioactive material. Some of it reached the United States. These problems started the debate over the safety of nuclear power again. Many people are not sure if nuclear power is safe enough to use.

The U.S. population has continued to change and grow. Because of better health care, there are many more older people. Part of the growth is because of immigrants. For example, the Latino population in the United States grew from under 15 million in 1980 to about 50 million in 2010. Many immigrants have followed the nation's laws to enter the country. However, there are currently about 11 million immigrants who are in the country illegally.

Americans disagree about how illegal immigrants should be treated. Some think they should be given amnesty and made citizens. Others think the United States should work harder to prevent illegal immigration. An Arizona law created conflict by giving the police more powers to identify illegal immigrants. Debates over immigration have been common in United States history. The United States continues to draw immigrants because it offers hope and freedom.

/ / / / / / / / / / / Glue Foldable here / / / / / / / / / / / /

Check for Understanding

List two things you think are positive effects of globalization.

_____

_____

How has technology helped the economy grow?

_____

_____

Copyright by The McGraw-Hill Companies.

✓ **Reading Check**

8. **Summarizing** How has the population of the United States changed?

_____

_____

_____

FOLDABLES

9. Place a one-tab Foldable along the dotted line to cover Check for Understanding. Write the title *Worldwide Economy* on the anchor tab. Write *Globalization* in the middle and draw five arrows around the title. List five words or phrases that you remember about globalization. Use your memory map to help complete Check for Understanding.

Instruction
and Templates

FOLDABLES®

Instruction and Templates

Table of Contents

For each kind of Foldable®, you will find an instruction page followed by several template pages.

Notebook Foldables®

Using Foldables® in the *Reading Essentials and Study Guide* will help you develop note-taking and critical-thinking skills.

One-Tab

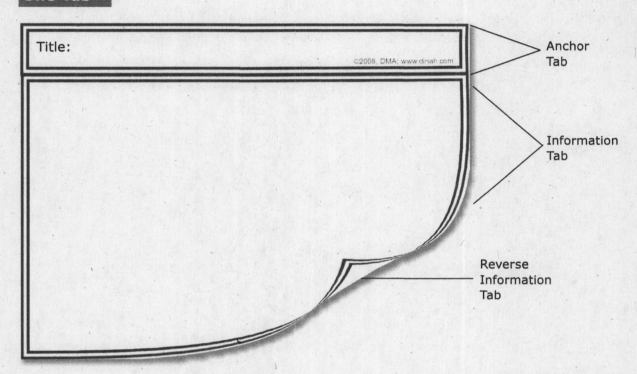

Title:

©2008, DMA; www.dinah.com

Anchor Tab

Information Tab

Reverse Information Tab

Folding Instructions

1. Cut out the One-Tab Foldable® template found on the following pages.

2. Fold the anchor tab over the information tab.

3. Glue the anchor tab to your workbook according to the instructions in the lesson.

Tip: Multiple Foldables® can be glued on top of each other by gluing anchor tabs on top of anchor tabs. This would make a small book on the page.

One-Tab Foldable® glued onto a Two-Tab Foldable® to make a study book.

FOLDABLES by Dinah Zike

Notebook Foldables

Using Foldables® in the Reading Essentials and Study Guide will help you develop note-taking and critical-thinking skills.

Title:

Anchor Tab

Information Tab

Reverse Information Tab

Folding Instructions

1. Cut out the One-Tab Foldable® template found on the following pages.

2. Fold the anchor tab over the information tab.

3. Glue the anchor tab to your workbook according to the instructions in the lesson.

Tip: Multiple Foldables® can be glued on top of each other by gluing anchor tabs on top of anchor tabs. This would make a small book on the page.

One-Tab Foldable® glued onto a Two-Tab Foldable to make a study book.

©2008, DMA; www.dinah.com

©2008, DMA; www.dinah.com

©2008, DMA; www.dinah.com

©2008, DMA; www.dinah.com

©2008, DMA; www.dinah.com

©2008, DMA; www.dinah.com

Cut out your
Foldable® along
the dotted line.

You can position a Foldable® three ways.

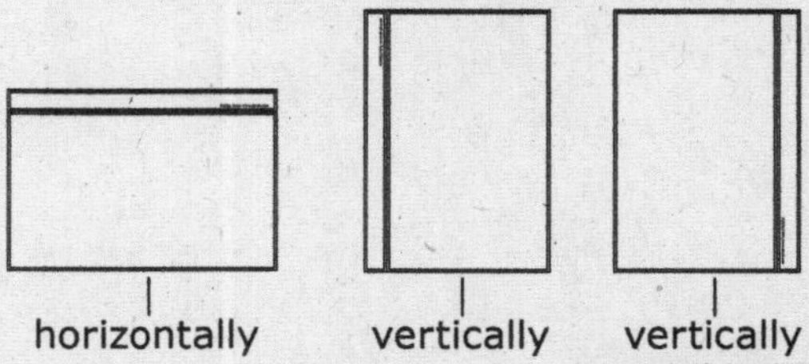

horizontally

vertically

vertically

Foldables 5

You can position a Foldable three ways.

Foldables 5   vertically   vertically   horizontal

Cut out your Foldable along the dotted line.

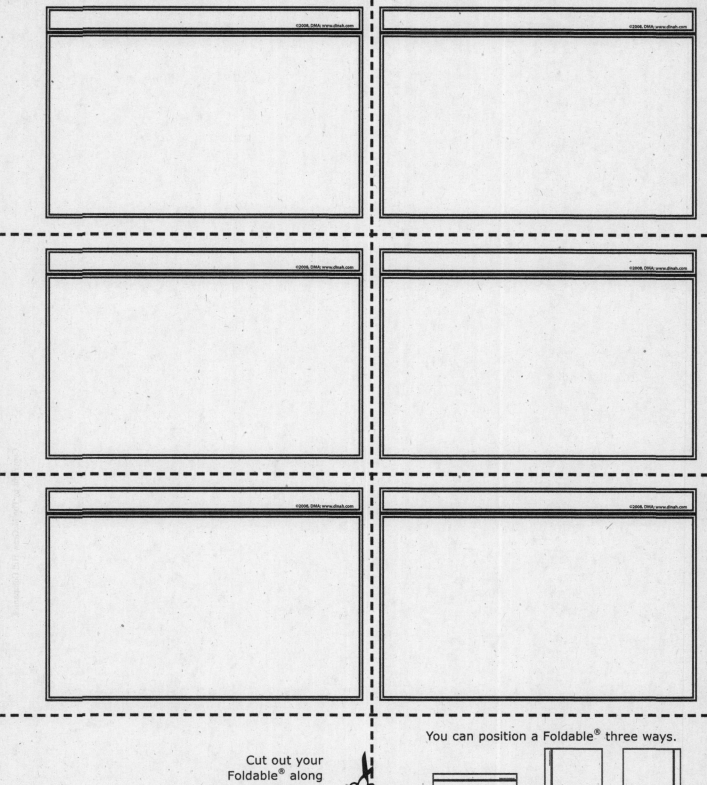

©2008, DMA; www.dinah.com

©2008, DMA; www.dinah.com

©2008, DMA; www.dinah.com

©2008, DMA; www.dinah.com

©2008, DMA; www.dinah.com

©2008, DMA; www.dinah.com

Cut out your
Foldable® along
the dotted line.

You can position a Foldable® three ways.

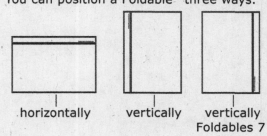

horizontally   vertically   vertically

Foldables 7

You can position a Foldable three ways.

Cut out your Foldable* along the dotted line.

horizontally

vertically

vertically

Foldables?

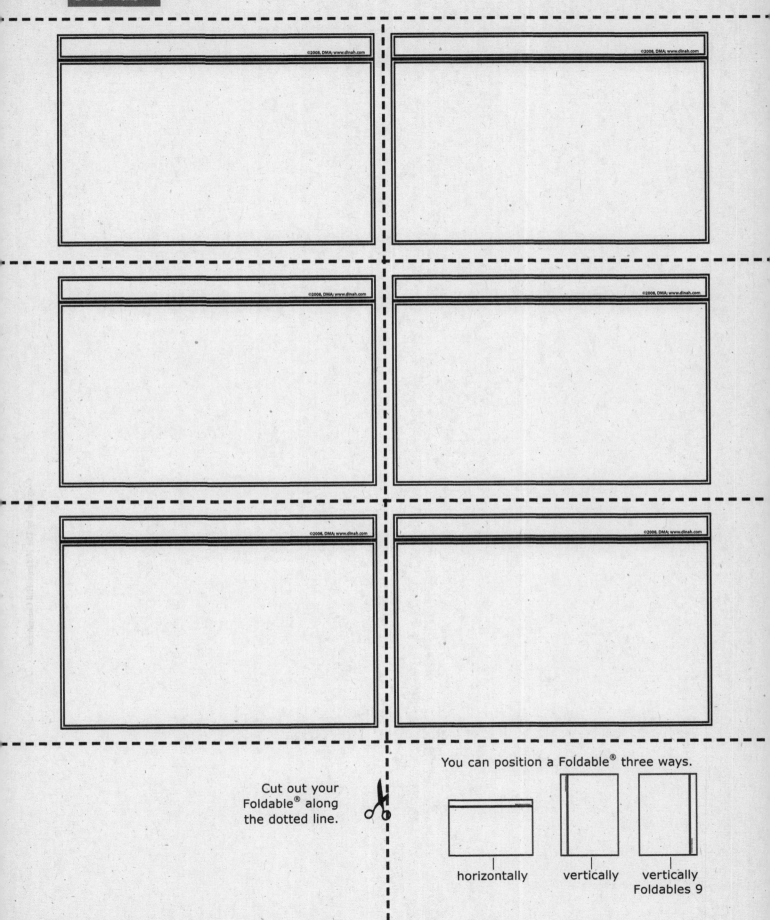

©2008, DMA; www.dinah.com

Cut out your
Foldable® along
the dotted line.

You can position a Foldable® three ways.

horizontally vertically vertically

You can position a Foldable® three ways.

Foldables 9 vertically   vertically   horizontally

Cut out your
Foldable® along
the dotted line.

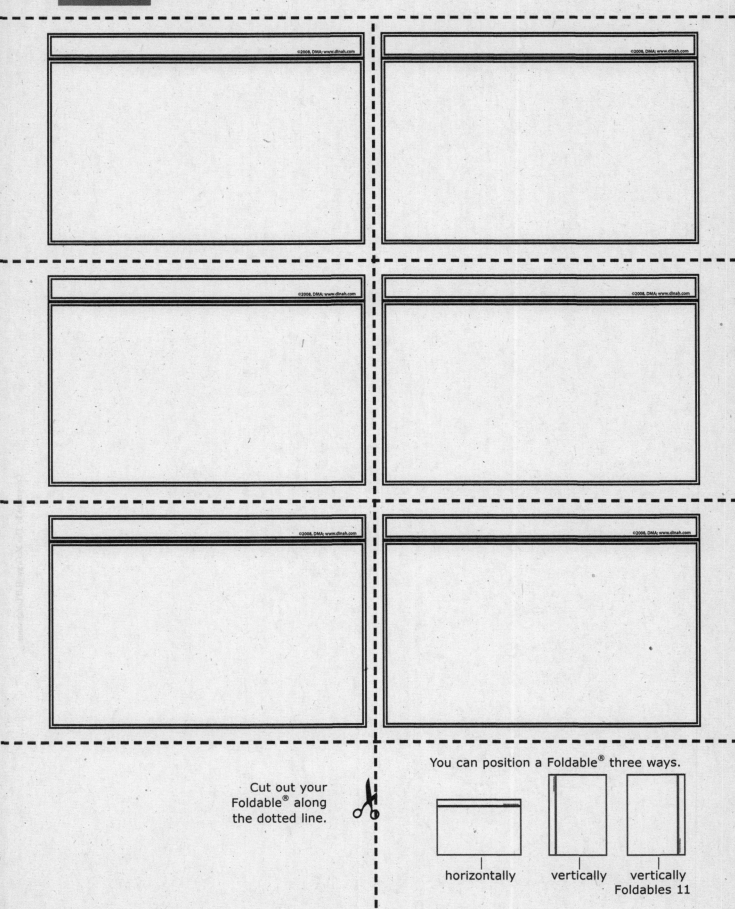

One-Tab

©2008, DMA; www.dinah.com

Cut out your
Foldable® along
the dotted line.

You can position a Foldable® three ways.

horizontally

vertically

vertically

Foldables 11

You can position a Foldable three ways.

vertically

vertically

horizontally

Cut out your
Foldable along
the dotted line.

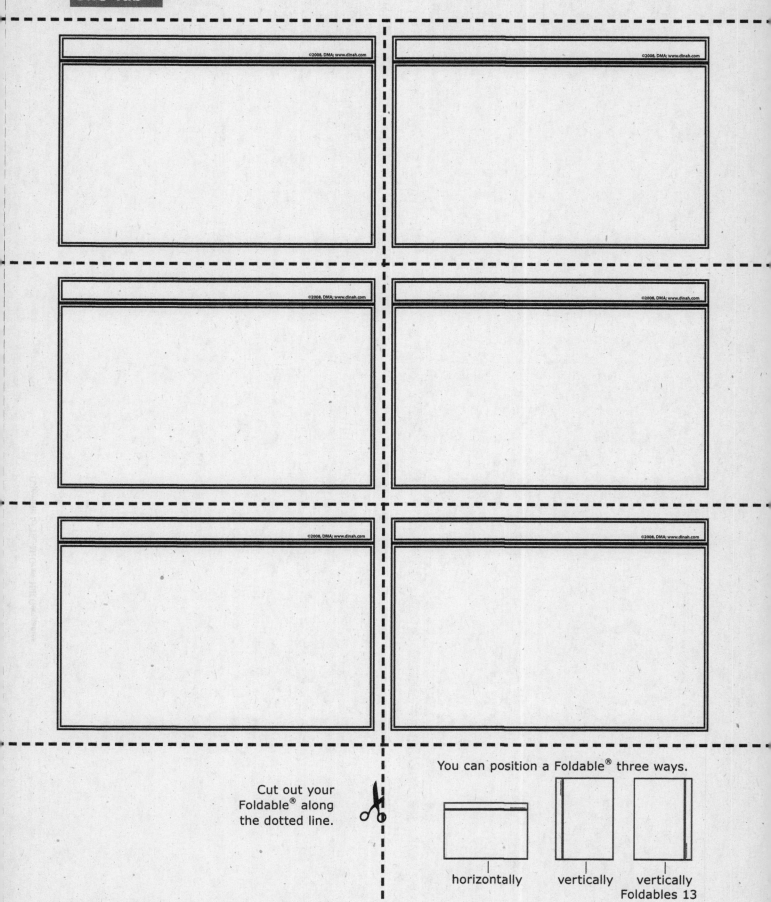

©2008, DMA; www.dinah.com

©2008, DMA; www.dinah.com

©2008, DMA; www.dinah.com

©2008, DMA; www.dinah.com

©2008, DMA; www.dinah.com

©2008, DMA; www.dinah.com

Cut out your
Foldable® along
the dotted line.

You can position a Foldable® three ways.

horizontally   vertically   vertically

You can position a foldable three ways.

Cut out your Foldable along the dotted line.

horizontally

vertically

vertically

Foldable 13

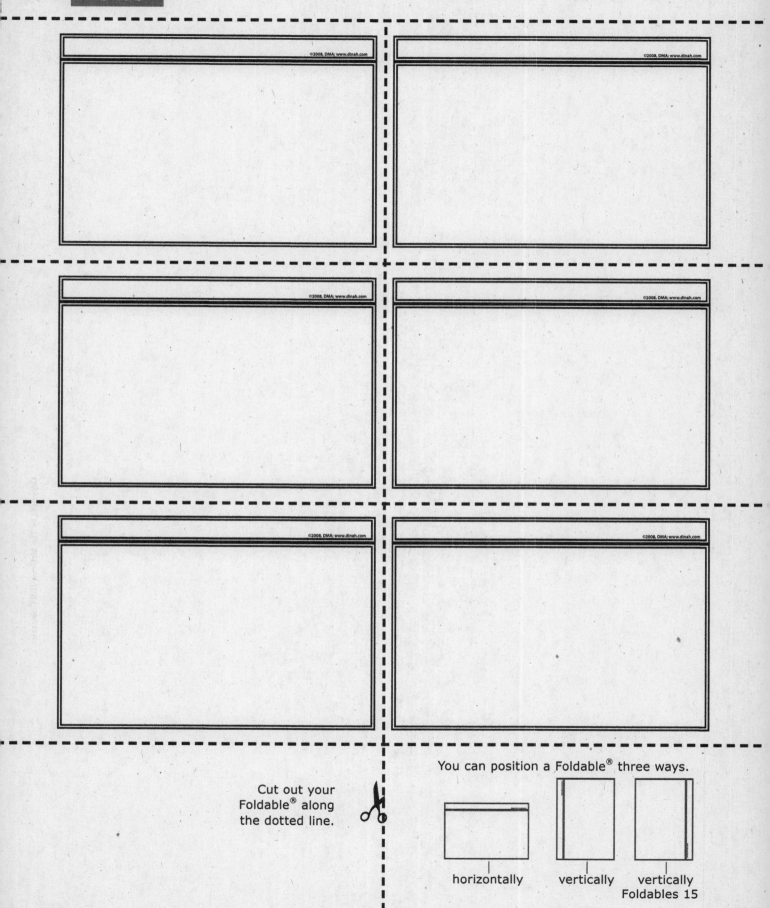

©2008, DMA; www.dinah.com

©2008, DMA; www.dinah.com

©2008, DMA; www.dinah.com

©2008, DMA; www.dinah.com

©2008, DMA; www.dinah.com

©2008, DMA; www.dinah.com

Cut out your
Foldable® along
the dotted line.

You can position a Foldable® three ways.

horizontally

vertically

vertically
Foldables 15

You can position a Foldable three ways.

Cut out your Foldable along the dotted line.

horizontally   vertically   vertically

Foldables 15

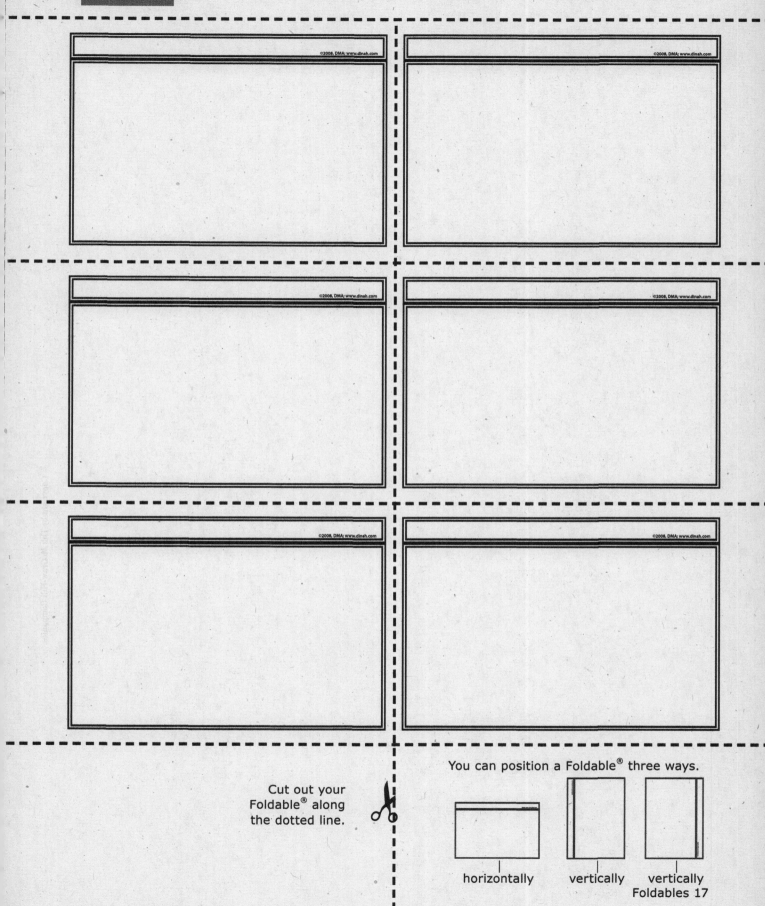

©2008, DMA; www.dinah.com

Cut out your
Foldable® along
the dotted line.

You can position a Foldable® three ways.

horizontally   vertically   vertically

Foldables 17

You can position a Foldable™ three ways.

Vertically
Foldables 17

vertically

horizontally

Cut out your
Foldable™ along
the dotted line.

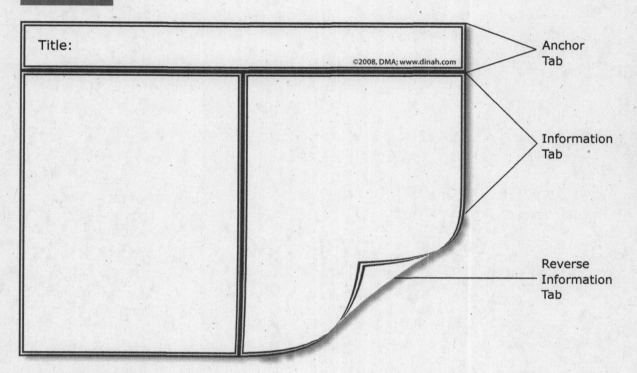

Notebook Foldables®

Using Foldables® in the *Reading Essentials and Study Guide* will help you develop note-taking and critical-thinking skills.

Two-Tab

Title:

©2008, DMA; www.dinah.com

Anchor Tab

Information Tab

Reverse Information Tab

Folding Instructions

1. Cut out the Two-Tab Foldable® template found on the following pages.

2. Fold the anchor tab over the information tab.

3. Glue the anchor tab to your workbook according to the instructions in the lesson.

4. Cut the information tab up to the anchor tab to create two tabs.

   Tip: Multiple Foldables® can be glued on top of each other by gluing anchor tabs on top of anchor tabs. This would make a small book on the page.

One-Tab Foldable® glued onto a Two-Tab Foldable® to make a study book.

Notebook Foldables

Using Foldables® in the Reading Essentials and Study Guide will help you develop note-taking and critical-thinking skills.

Title:

Anchor
Tab

Information
Tab

Reverse
Information
Tab

Folding Instructions

1. Cut out the Two-Tab Foldable® template found on the following pages.

2. Fold the anchor tab over the information tab.

3. Glue the anchor tab to your workbook according to the instructions in the lesson.

4. Cut the information tab up to the anchor tab to create two tabs.

Tip: Multiple Foldables® can be glued on top of each other by gluing anchor tabs on top of anchor tabs. This would make a small book on the page.

One-Tab Foldable® glued onto a Two-Tab Foldable to make a study book.

Foldables 19

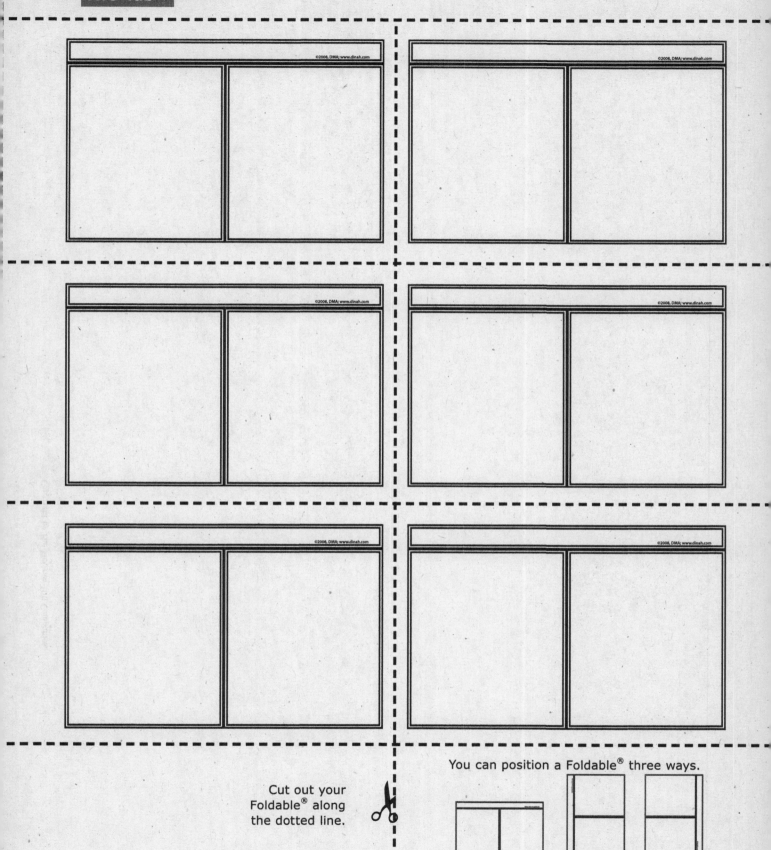

©2008, DMA; www.dinah.com

©2008, DMA; www.dinah.com

©2008, DMA; www.dinah.com

©2008, DMA; www.dinah.com

©2008, DMA; www.dinah.com

©2008, DMA; www.dinah.com

Cut out your
Foldable® along
the dotted line.

You can position a Foldable® three ways.

horizontally   vertically   vertically

Foldables 21

You can position a Foldable® three ways.

Cut out your
Foldable® along
the dotted line.

vertically   vertically   horizontally

Foldables 2!

©2008, DMA; www.dinah.com

Cut out your
Foldable® along
the dotted line.

You can position a Foldable® three ways.

horizontally   vertically   vertically

Foldables 23

You can position a Foldable three ways.

vertically   vertically   horizontally

Foldables 25

Cut out your
Foldable along
the dotted line.

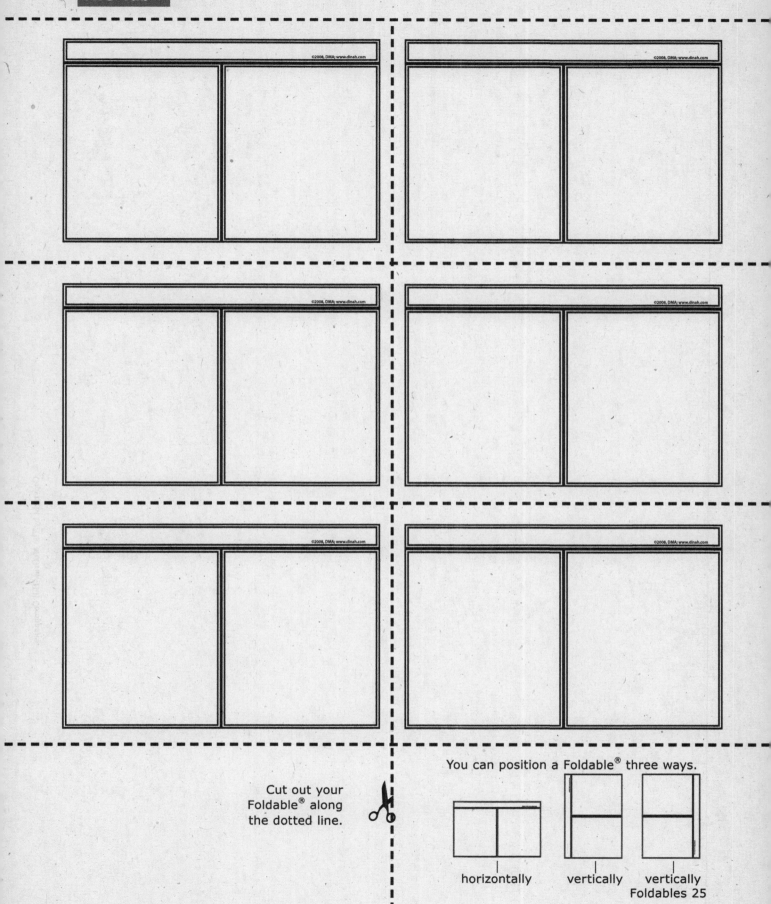

©2008, DMA; www.dinah.com

Cut out your
Foldable® along
the dotted line.

You can position a Foldable® three ways.

horizontally   vertically   vertically

You can position a Foldable three ways.

vertically

vertically

horizontally

Foldables 25

1. Cut out your Foldable along the dotted line.

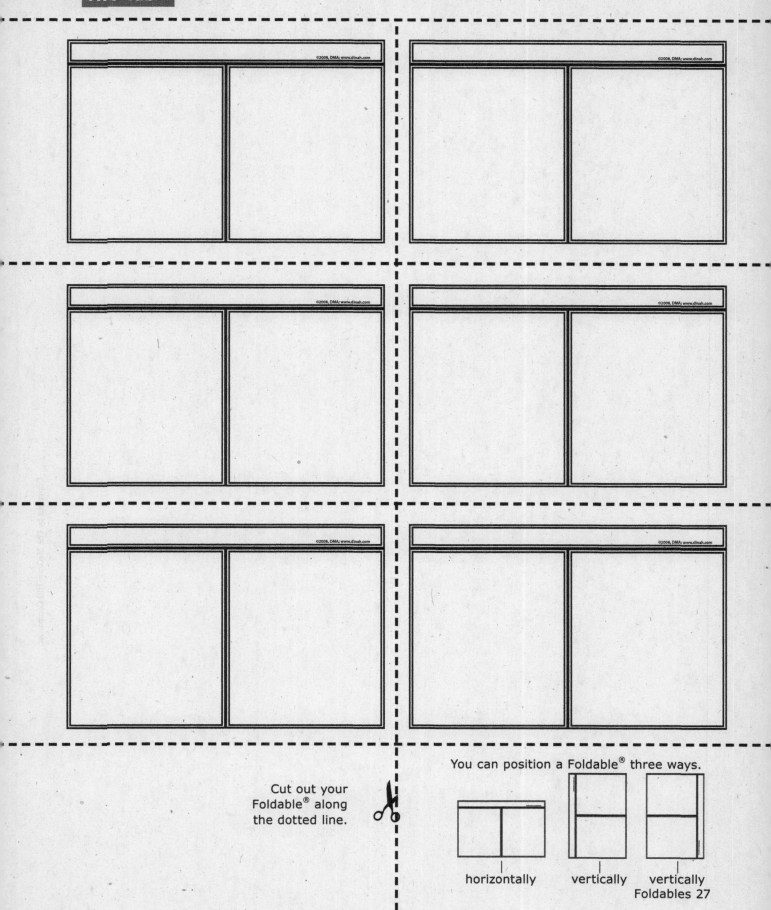

©2008, DMA; www.dinah.com

Cut out your
Foldable® along
the dotted line.

You can position a Foldable® three ways.

horizontally   vertically   vertically

You can position a Foldable three ways.

Cut out your Foldable along the dotted lines.

vertically   vertically   horizontally

Foldables 27

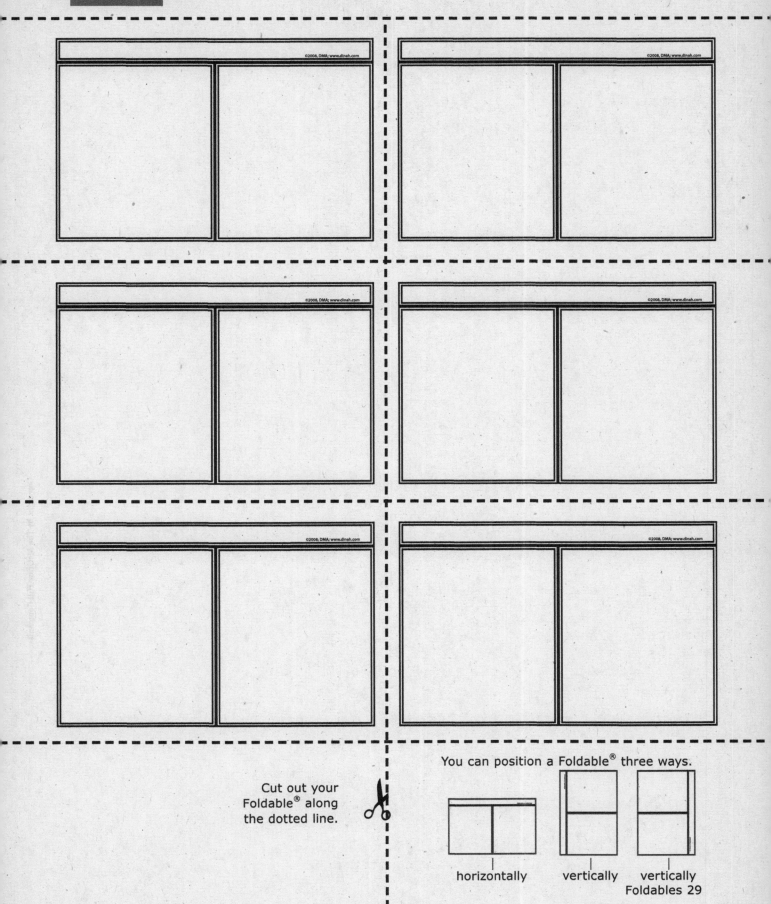

©2008, DMA; www.dinah.com

©2008, DMA; www.dinah.com

©2008, DMA; www.dinah.com

©2008, DMA; www.dinah.com

©2008, DMA; www.dinah.com

©2008, DMA; www.dinah.com

Cut out your
Foldable® along
the dotted line.

You can position a Foldable® three ways.

horizontally

vertically

vertically

Foldables 29

You can position a Foldable three ways.

Cut out your
Foldable along
the dotted line.

horizontally   vertically   vertically

Foldables 29

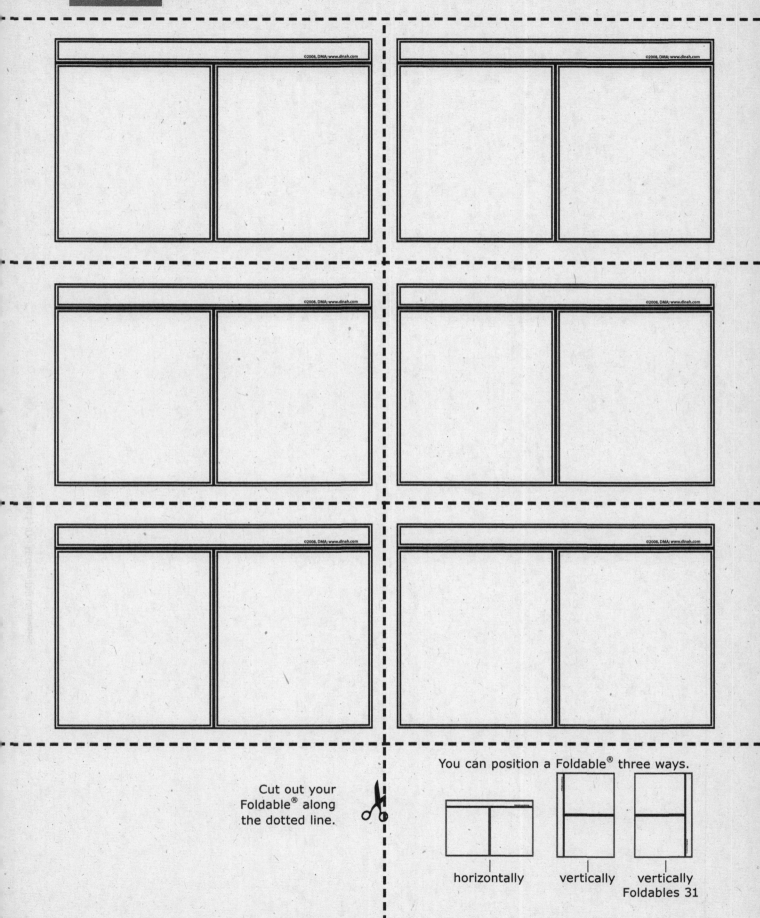

©2008, DMA; www.dinah.com

Cut out your Foldable® along the dotted line.

You can position a Foldable® three ways.

horizontally   vertically   vertically

You can position a Foldable three ways

vertically vertically horizontally

Foldables 21

Cut out your Foldable along the dotted line.

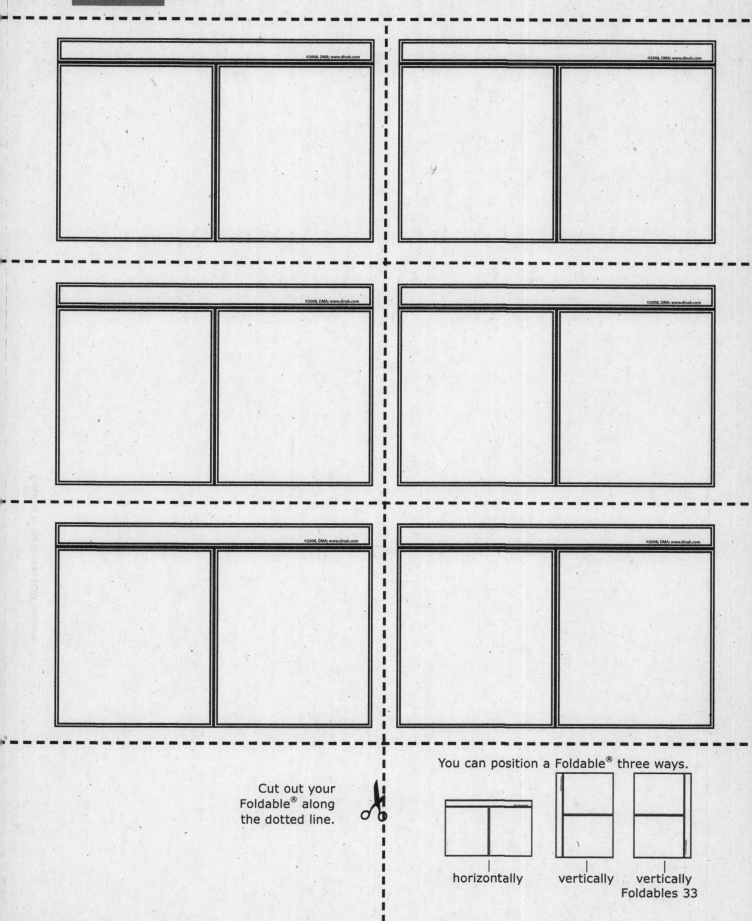

©2008, DMA; www.dinah.com

Cut out your
Foldable® along
the dotted line.

You can position a Foldable® three ways.

horizontally

vertically

vertically

You can position a foldable "three ways."

horizontally   vertically   vertically

Foldables 33

Cut out your foldable along the dotted line.

©2008, DMA; www.dinah.com

Cut out your
Foldable® along
the dotted line.

You can position a Foldable® three ways.

horizontally   vertically   vertically
Foldables 35

You can position a foldable three ways.

Cut out your
Foldable along
the dotted line.

horizontally

vertically

Foldables 35

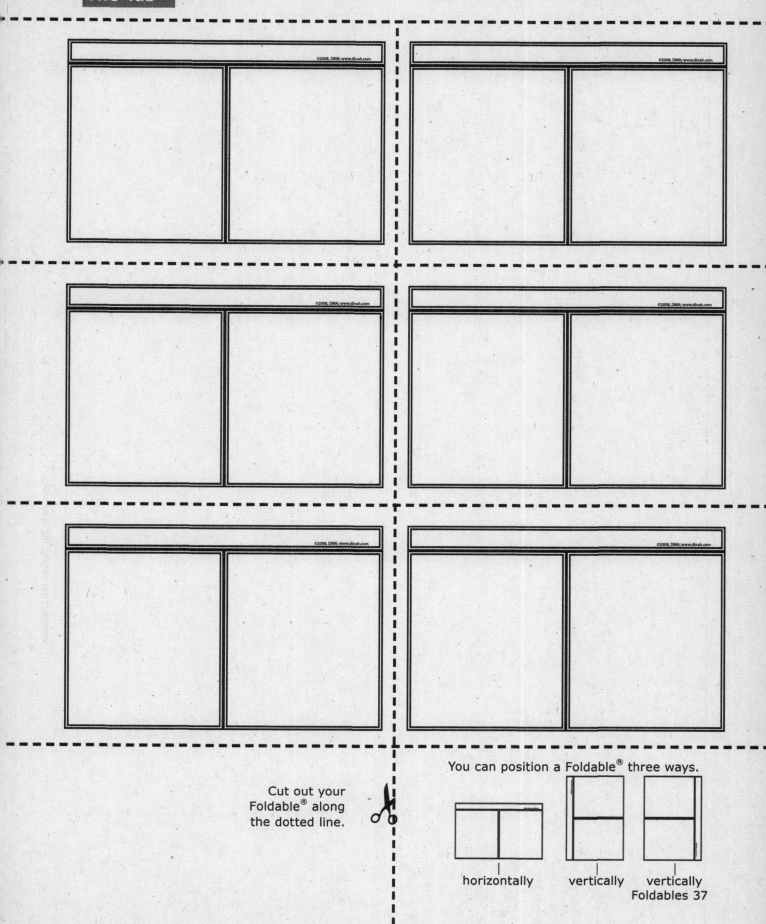

©2008, DMA; www.dinah.com

Cut out your
Foldable® along
the dotted line.

You can position a Foldable® three ways.

horizontally   vertically   vertically

©2008, DMA; www.dinah.com

Cut out your
Foldable® along
the dotted line.

You can position a Foldable® three ways.

horizontally   vertically   vertically

Foldables 39

You can position a foldable three ways

Cut out your
foldable along
the dotted line.

vertically horizontally
Foldables 39

vertically

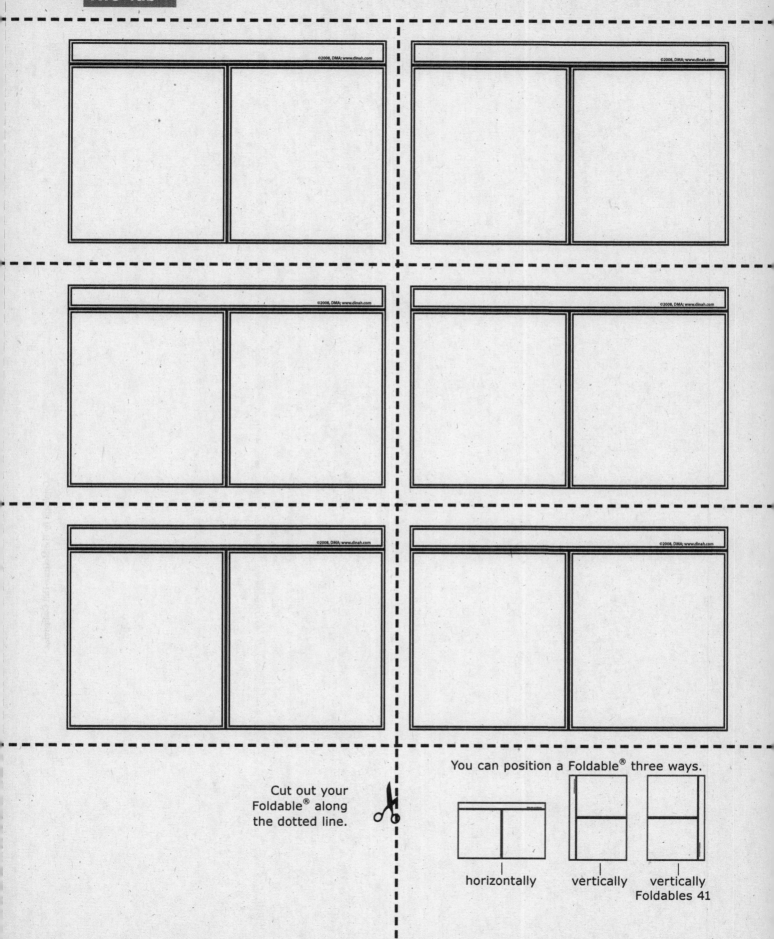

©2008, DMA; www.dinah.com

Cut out your Foldable® along the dotted line.

You can position a Foldable® three ways.

horizontally   vertically   vertically

You can position a Foldable three ways.

Cut out your foldable along the dotted line.

vertically   Vertically   horizontally

Foldables 4

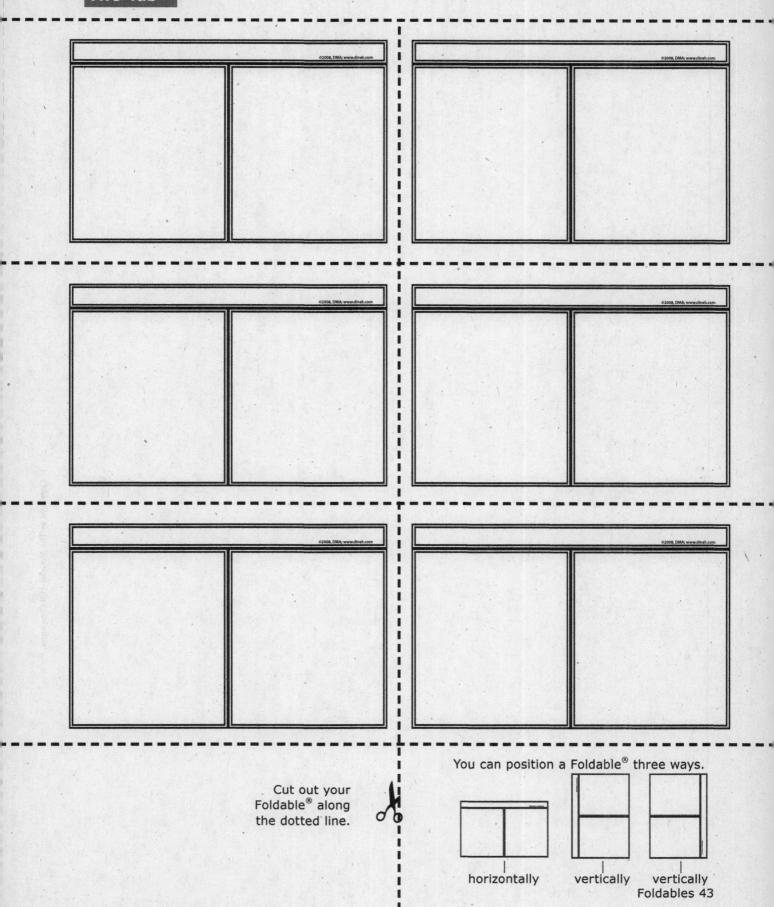

©2008, DMA; www.dinah.com

Cut out your
Foldable® along
the dotted line.

You can position a Foldable® three ways.

horizontally   vertically   vertically
Foldables 43

You can position a Foldable three ways.

Cut out your
Foldable* along
the dotted line.

Foldable 43   vertically   vertically   horizontally

Notebook Foldables®

Using Foldables® in the *Reading Essentials and Study Guide* will help you develop note-taking and critical-thinking skills.

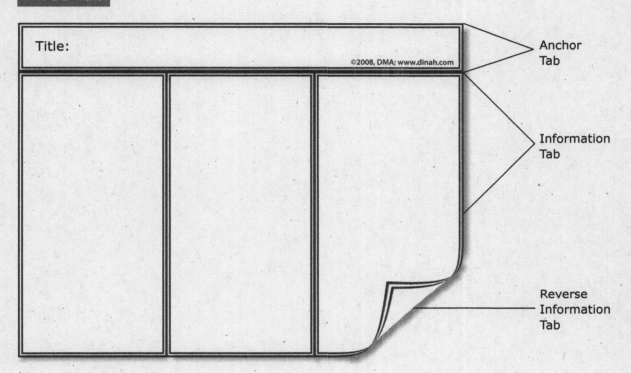

Title:

©2008, DMA; www.dinah.com

Anchor Tab

Information Tab

Reverse Information Tab

Three-Tab

Folding Instructions

1. Cut out the Three-Tab Foldable® template found on the following pages.

2. Fold the anchor tab over the information tab.

3. Glue the anchor tab to your workbook according to the instructions in the lesson.

4. Cut the information tabs up to the anchor tab to create three tabs.

Tip: Multiple Foldables® can be glued on top of each other by gluing anchor tabs on top of anchor tabs. This would make a small book on the page.

One-Tab Foldable® glued onto a Two-Tab Foldable® to make a study book.

Notebook Foldables®

Using Foldables® in the Reading Essentials and Study Guide will help you develop note-taking and critical-thinking skills.

Title:

Anchor Tab

Information Tab

Reverse Information Tab

Folding Instructions

1. Cut out the Three-Tab Foldable® template found on the following pages.

2. Fold the anchor tab over the information tab.

3. Glue the anchor tab to your workbook according to the instructions in the lesson.

4. Cut the information tabs up to the anchor tab to create three tabs.

Tip: Multiple Foldables® can be glued on top of each other by gluing anchor tabs on top of anchor tabs. This would make a small book on the page.

One-Tab Foldable® glued onto a Two-Tab Foldable to make a study book

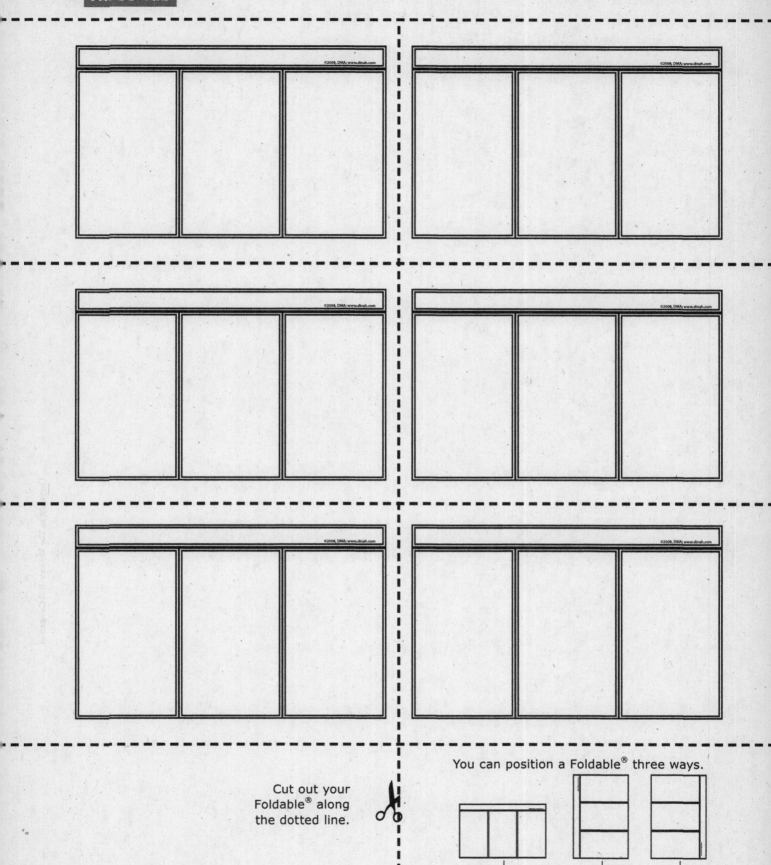

Cut out your
Foldable® along
the dotted line.

You can position a Foldable® three ways.

horizontally   vertically   vertically

Foldables 47

You can position a foldable three ways

Vertically   Vertically   Horizontally
Foldables 47

Cut out your
Foldable along
the dotted line.

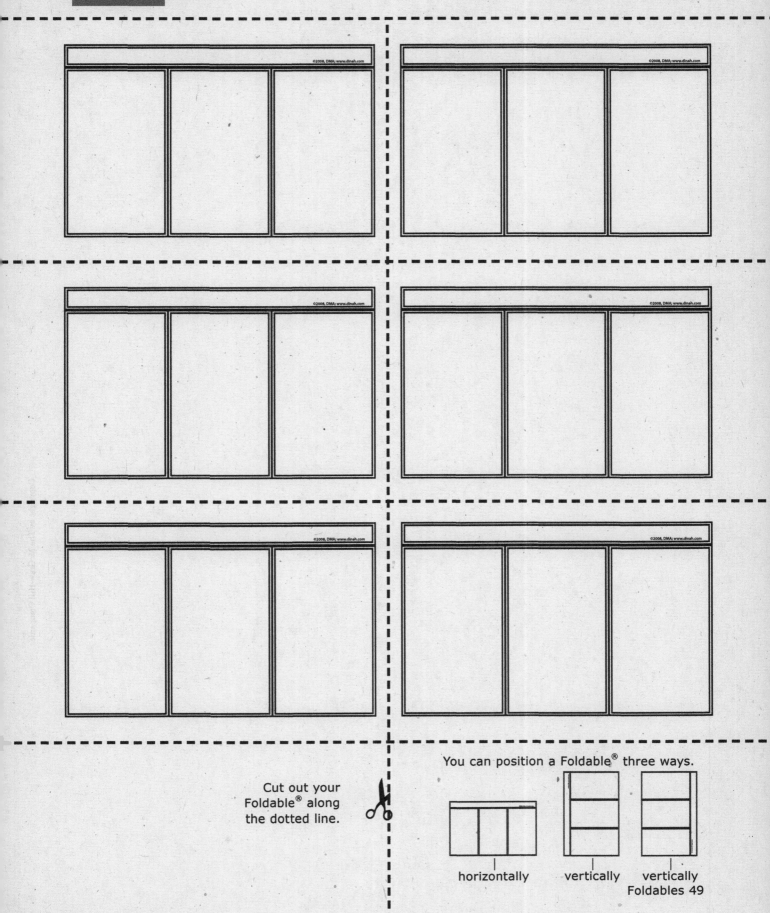

Three-Tab

©2008, DMA; www.dinah.com

Cut out your
Foldable® along
the dotted line.

You can position a Foldable® three ways.

horizontally   vertically   vertically

Foldables 49

You can position a Foldable three ways.

Cut out your
Foldable along
the dotted line.

Foldables 49
vertically   vertically   horizontally

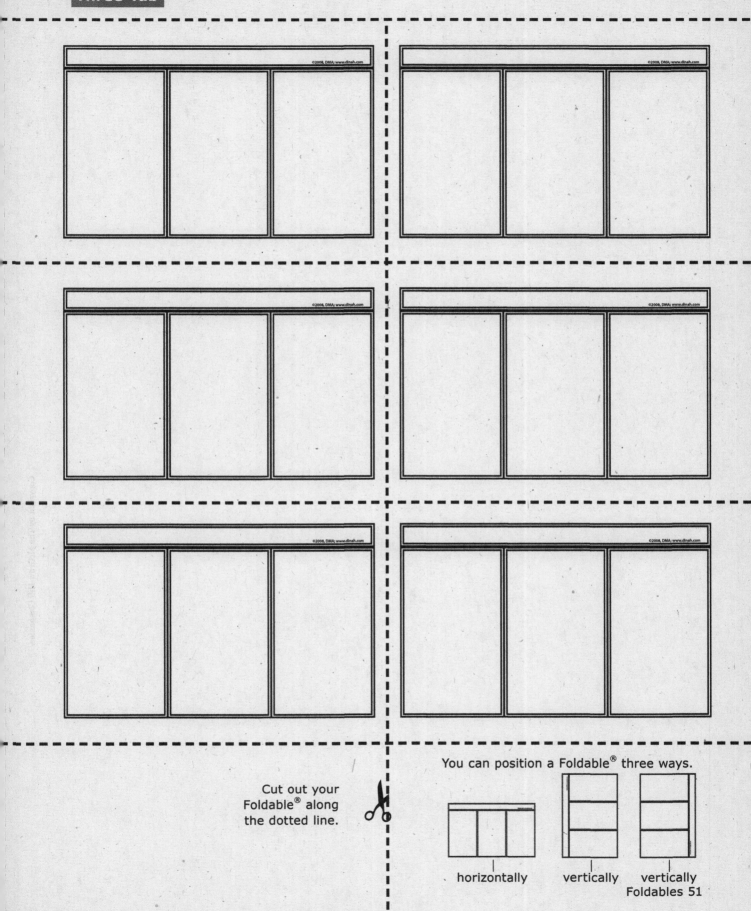

Three-Tab

Cut out your Foldable® along the dotted line.

You can position a Foldable® three ways.

horizontally   vertically   vertically

Foldables 51

You can position a Foldable™ three ways.

vertically   vertically   horizontally
Foldables 51

Cut out your Foldable™ along the dotted line.

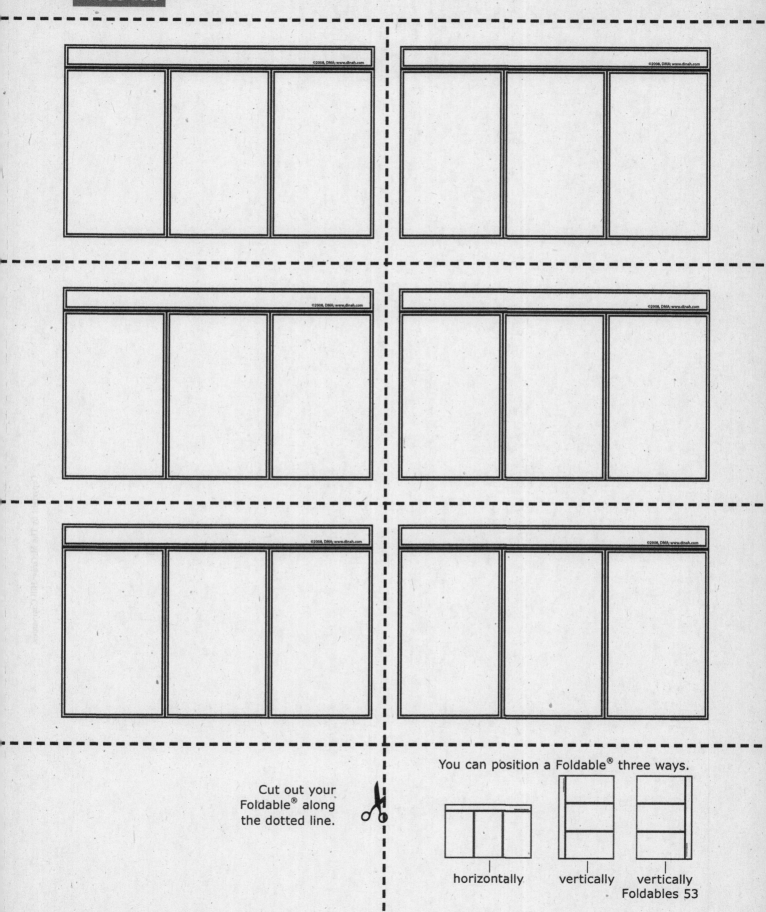

©2008, DMA; www.dinah.com

Cut out your
Foldable® along
the dotted line.

You can position a Foldable® three ways.

horizontally   vertically   vertically
Foldables 53

You can position a Foldable three ways.

Cut out your Foldable along the dotted line.

horizontally   vertically   vertically

Foldables 53

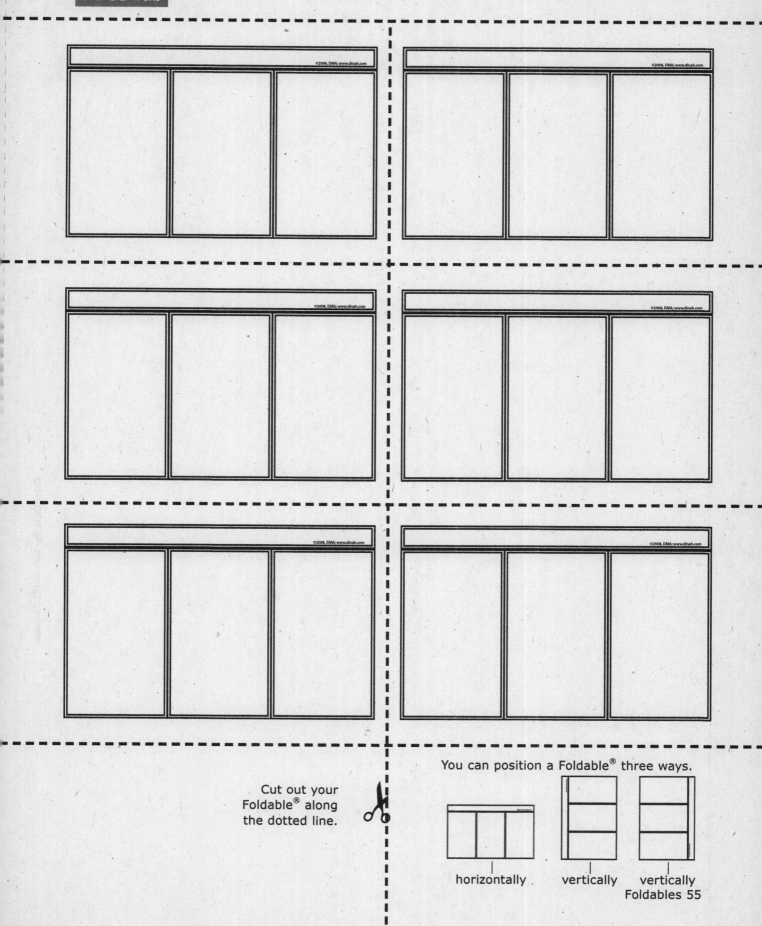

©2008, DMA; www.dinah.com

Cut out your
Foldable® along
the dotted line.

You can position a Foldable® three ways.

horizontally   vertically   vertically
Foldables 55

You can position a Foldable three ways:

Cut out your
Foldable along
the dotted line.

vertically   vertically   horizontally

Foldables 55

Three-Tab

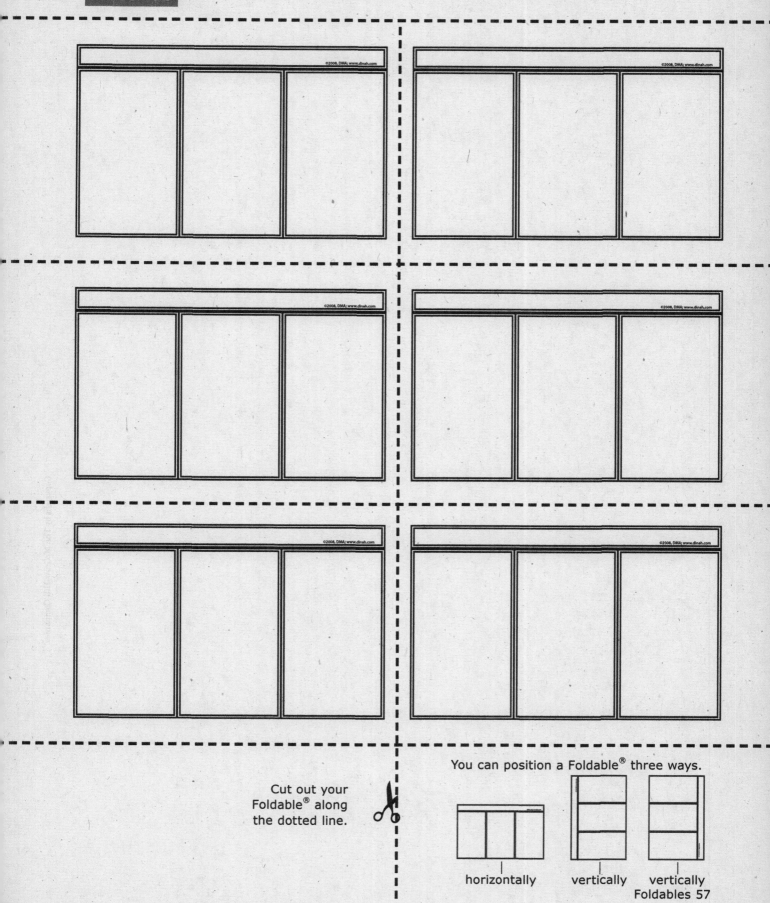

Cut out your
Foldable® along
the dotted line.

You can position a Foldable® three ways.

horizontally   vertically   vertically
Foldables 57

You can position a Foldable three ways.

Cut out your Foldable along the dotted line.

horizontally   vertically

Foldables 57

Notebook Foldables®

Using Foldables® in the *Reading Essentials and Study Guide* will help you develop note-taking and critical-thinking skills.

Venn Diagram

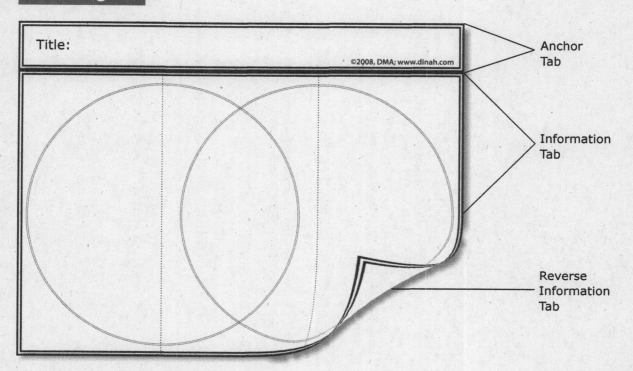

Title:

©2008, DMA; www.dinah.com

Anchor Tab

Information Tab

Reverse Information Tab

Folding Instructions

1. Cut out the Venn Diagram Foldable® template found on the following pages.

2. Fold the anchor tab over the information tab.

3. Glue the anchor tab to your workbook according to the instructions in the lesson.

4. If directed, cut the information tabs up to the anchor tab in the center of each circle to create three tabs.

Tip: Multiple Foldables® can be glued on top of each other by gluing anchor tabs on top of anchor tabs. This would make a small book on the page.

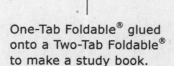

One-Tab Foldable® glued onto a Two-Tab Foldable® to make a study book.

Venn Diagram

Notebook Foldables

Using Foldables in the Reading Essentials and Study Guide will help you develop note-taking and critical-thinking skills.

Title

Anchor Tab

Information Tab

Reverse Information Tab

Folding Instructions

1. Cut out the Venn Diagram Foldable template found on the following pages.

2. Fold the anchor tab over the information tab.

3. Glue the anchor tab to your workbook according to the instructions in the lesson.

4. If directed, cut the information tabs up to the anchor tab in the center of each circle to create three tabs.

Tip: Multiple Foldables can be glued on top of each other by gluing anchor tabs on top of anchor tabs. This would make a small book on the page.

One Tab Foldable glued onto a Two-Tab Foldable to make a study book

Venn Diagram

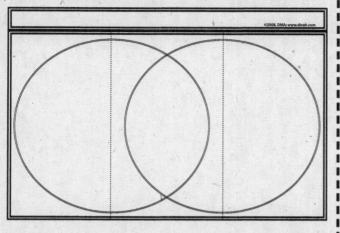
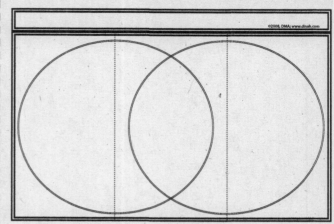
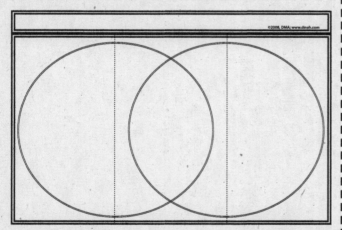
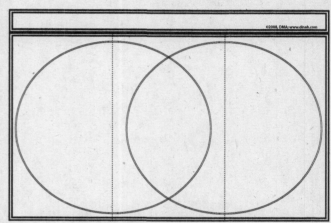
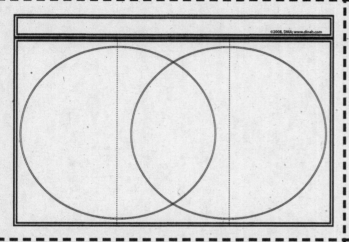
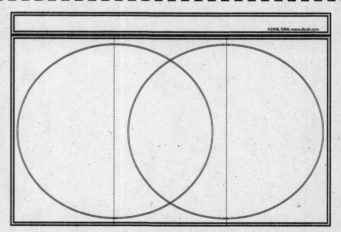

©2008, DMA; www.dinah.com

Cut out your Foldable® along the dotted line.

You can position a Foldable® three ways.

horizontally   vertically   vertically

Foldables 61

You can position a Foldable three ways.

Cut out your
Foldable along
the dotted line.

horizontally vertically vertically

Foldables 61

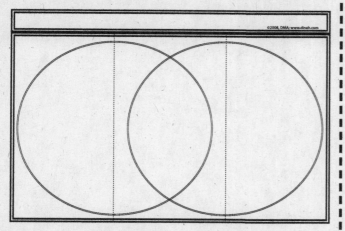

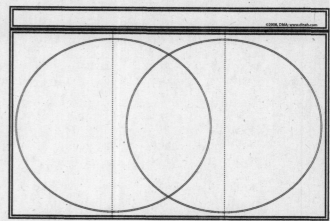

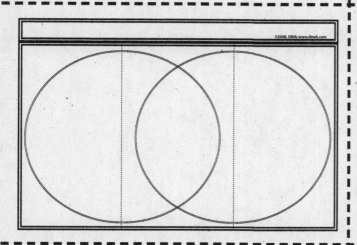

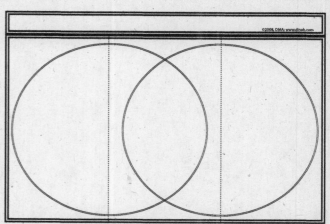

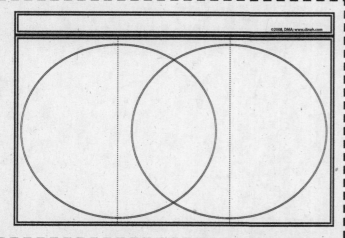

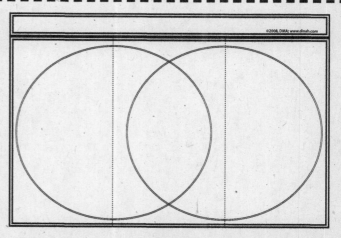

Cut out your Foldable® along the dotted line.

You can position a Foldable® three ways.

horizontally   vertically   vertically

Foldables 63

You can position a Foldable three ways.

vertically   vertically   horizontally
Foldables 3

Cut out your Foldable along the dotted line.